THE GLOBALIZATION OF I
SOCIETY

The Globalization of International Society re-examines the development of today's society of sovereign states, drawing on a wealth of new scholarship to challenge the landmark account presented in Bull and Watson's classic work, *The Expansion of International Society* (OUP, 1984). For Bull and Watson, international society originated in Europe, and expanded as successive waves of new states were integrated into a rule-governed order. International society, on their view, was thus a European cultural artefact—a claim that is at odds with recent scholarship in history, politics, and related fields of research.

Bringing together leading scholars from Asia, Australia, Europe, and the United States, this book provides an alternative account: it draws out the diversity of polities that existed at around *c.*1500; it shows how interacting identities, political orders, and economic forces were intensifying within and across regions; it details the tangled dynamics that helped to globalize the European conception of a pluralist international society, through patterns of warfare and between East and West.

The Globalization of International Society examines the institutional contours of contemporary international society, with its unique blend of universal sovereignty and global law, and its forms of hierarchy that coexist with commitments to international human rights. The book explores the multiple forms of contestation that challenge international society today: contests over the limits of sovereignty in relation to cosmopolitan conceptions of responsibility, disputes over global governance, concerns about persistent economic, racial, and gender-based patterns of disadvantage, and lastly the threat to the established order opened up by the disruptive power of digital communications.

The Globalization of International Society

Edited by
TIM DUNNE
and
CHRISTIAN REUS-SMIT

OXFORD
UNIVERSITY PRESS

OXFORD
UNIVERSITY PRESS

Great Clarendon Street, Oxford, OX2 6DP,
United Kingdom

Oxford University Press is a department of the University of Oxford.
It furthers the University's objective of excellence in research, scholarship,
and education by publishing worldwide. Oxford is a registered trade mark of
Oxford University Press in the UK and in certain other countries

Published in the United States of America by Oxford University Press
198 Madison Avenue, New York, NY 10016, United States of America

British Library Cataloguing in Publication Data
Data available

Library of Congress Control Number: 2016945405

ISBN 978-0-19-879342-7 (hbk.)
ISBN 978-0-19-879343-4 (pbk.)

Printed in Great Britain by
Clays Ltd, St Ives plc

Preface

The academic study of International Relations (IR) is prone to reflect on its self-identity. Is this because it is a relatively young and insecure discipline, or perhaps because it is a divided discipline? Or, more positively, because IR is a dynamic field of study in which previous ideas and concepts are critically engaged to advance current research? We do not want to imply that there is only one answer to the question of why IR reaches into its past with quite such regularity. It is clear to us as editors that *The Globalization of International Society* is intended to be a voice in a dynamic disciplinary conversation. It is at once a reflection on established ideas and concepts, and, more ambitiously, a contribution to a conversation about the future of IR; a future that will and must become more global than it has been in the first hundred years or so of the discipline's development.

The global has a history, although it is one that is almost impossible to tell as a single narrative—which is why world history was avoided until relatively recently. It is also why Hedley Bull and Adam Watson, when they conceived of an edited book on the making of modern international society, sought to restrict the focus to the evolving patterns of interactions among sovereign states as discrete entities; patterns that Bull and Watson believed had 'their own logic'.[1]

Thirty years after *The Expansion of International Society* was published, we thought it was time to revisit this claim of Bull and Watson's and many other themes in this classic work. Dominic Byatt, commissioning editor for politics and IR at Oxford University Press, was enthusiastic about the project from the moment we first mentioned it and has remained so ever since. The timing of our project coincided, fortuitously, with the publication of a new edition of *The Expansion* that includes a contextual introduction by Andrew Hurrell— who has continued to advise us during the compilation of this book. We hope the availability of these two new publications provides IR scholars and students with richer resources for understanding the element of society in the global order.

Edited books are greatly enhanced when they are the product of genuine collaboration. Just as *The Expansion* was workshopped in the context of the final phase of the British Committee on the Theory of International Politics, *The Globalization of International Society* benefited greatly from being workshopped at two critical junctures. The first of these was held at the University

---

[1] Bull and Watson 1984b: 9.

of Queensland (UQ) from 14 to 16 July 2014, where short summary documents were shared and discussed. This event was funded by the Academy of Social Sciences in Australia, the School of Political Science and International Studies, and the Faculty of Humanities and Social Sciences at UQ. We would like to acknowledge the considerable organizational support provided by Bronwyn Crook and Eglantine Staunton, as well as colleagues and PhD students in the School of Political Science and International Studies who chaired panels and acted as discussants.

We came away from this workshop knowing that there was work to be done in clarifying a number of fundamental questions about the scope of the project and the framing theories and concepts. From that point, the contributors—who had rightly pushed the editors to provide greater clarity—were asked to work more closely with a common set of concepts and propositions (which are defended in Part I). It was evident from the quality of the drafts at the second workshop, held at the International Studies Association (ISA) conference in New Orleans in February 2015, that far greater convergence had indeed been achieved. The workshop would not have happened without the support of ISA. We would also like to acknowledge the contribution of three colleagues who participated in one or other workshop: Janice Bially Mattern who was with us in Brisbane via Skype and New Orleans in person, and Beverley Loke, Dan Nexon, and Jason Sharman who attended the initial event in Brisbane.

The biggest debt of gratitude that we need to acknowledge is of course to the outstanding contributors. They were set a tall order: engage critically with Bull and Watson's classic work while drawing on a wealth of new scholarship which questions the historical and theoretical foundations of their conventional account. The upshot, we think, is that *The Globalization of International Society* is a deep and innovative book that aspires to make two important contributions to the renewal of a 'global IR'. First, it is a collection of revisionist arguments about a classic book in the field that was too narrow and ethnocentric in its reading of 'the expansion' process, and that conceived of the system/society boundary in ways that limited its sociological imagination. Second, becoming 'global IR' requires critical engagements with the disrupters that now challenge the society of states: the contests over the limits of sovereignty in relation to cosmopolitan conceptions of responsibility; disputes over procedural justice in a post-Western world; concerns about the failure to achieve racial and gender equality; and the disruptive power of digital communications, to name but a few.

Our collective efforts would appear far less polished, and the journey to publication would have been far more fraught, were it not for the legendary copy-editing skills of Mary-Louise Hickey. Her extraordinary eye for detail and commitment to harmonizing the work of twenty-three authors has taken the volume to another level. We thank her greatly for her patience, commitment, and unfailing good humour. We would also like to thank Constance Duncombe and Jocelyn Vaughn for their energetic and resourceful research assistance as the project evolved.

We would be remiss not to acknowledge the editors and contributors to the original 1984 book. Readers will encounter many criticisms of the book which need to be moderated by two factors: first, *The Expansion* reflects many cultural and historical misconceptions that were prevalent three to four decades ago; and second, relative to much of the IR published in the late 1970s and early 1980s, the editors and contributors to *The Expansion* asked many of the right questions. They understood the fact of political diversity and were motivated to know more about how devolved political orders established common approaches to reach their goals. As world order undergoes a further transition with the pivot to the economic powerhouses of India and China in particular, the question about the capacity of institutions to managing remains as prescient as it was at the time that *The Expansion* was written.

The life and work of Hedley Bull in particular has had a profound effect on the academic path that both of us have taken. Educated in both the Anglo-Australian and American academies, and intrigued by large-scale processes of global social change, Chris continues to wrestle with Bull's intellectual legacy, both as an inspiration and a site of critical engagement. Tim's path has been different. Through his then supervisor Andrew Hurrell, Tim was given access to many of Hedley Bull's unpublished papers, which featured prominently in his early works seeking to tell a different story about how a distinctive account of IR developed in Britain after 1945. Our paths have been distinct yet the two of us have a deeply shared interest in the history of IR and the productive possibilities that are immanent in classic works such as *The Expansion*. Once Chris joined UQ in 2013, the possibility of working together on a big project and collaborating with other outstanding colleagues at UQ was too good an opportunity to pass up. Our thinking has been so convergent throughout that we managed to arrive separately at the same preferred title in advance of a planned discussion about what to call the project. *The Globalization of International Society* thus reflects our shared view that the original book was largely a story about the Europeanization of international society and that this story needed to be retold from diverse standpoints. We like to think that Bull and Watson would have approved.

The cover of this book reproduces an image by the outstanding Brisbane-born Indigenous Australian photographer, Michael Cook. It is a wonderful and thought-provoking recreation of the first encounter between the British colonizers and Aborigines. The sequence of staged photographs is called *Civilised*; here, in *Civilised #13*, the Aboriginal man on horseback, wearing a naval uniform, is inverting the identity of colonizer and colonized. *Civilised #13* reminds us that *The Expansion* is not just a book but is at the same time a historical experience that must be remembered, acknowledged, and curated.

And Michael Cook shows us that this remembering can be beautiful and ironic too.

The conventional narrative about the 'expansion' of international society is a story of 'European' international society expanding outwards to encompass the globe, through processes of imperialism and then decolonization. It is a story of non-Europeans being integrated into an essentially Western order, socialized to accept European international norms and practices. The story we tell in the following chapters is one in which international society was, from the outset, profoundly influenced by encounters, engagements, and inter-actions between Europeans and non-European peoples, producing a global international order that is culturally and politically far more complex than the conventional narrative allows. Michael's photograph captures this com-plexity, and we thank him and his art dealer Andrew Baker for allowing us to showcase his extraordinary work.

Tim Dunne and Christian Reus-Smit
University of Queensland

Contents

List of Tables

List of Abbreviations

AAR	Alpena-Amberley Ridge
BRICS	Brazil, Russia, India, China, and South Africa
ECB	European Central Bank
ECOSOC	Economic and Social Council
EMU	Economic and Monetary Union
EU	European Union
G20	Group of Twenty
GDP	gross domestic product
ICC	International Criminal Court
ICISS	International Commission on Intervention and State Sovereignty
IMF	International Monetary Fund
IP	Internet Protocol
IR	international relations
IWSA	International Woman Suffrage Alliance
NGO	non-governmental organization
NPT	Nuclear Non-Proliferation Treaty
OAS	Organization of American States
OCA	optimum currency area
OCHA	Office for the Coordination of Humanitarian Affairs
PRC	People's Republic of China
R2P	responsibility to protect
UN	United Nations
UNGA	United Nations General Assembly
UNSC	United Nations Security Council
UPR	Universal Periodic Review

List of Contributors

Mark Beeson is Professor of International Politics at the University of Western Australia (UWA). Before joining UWA, he taught at Murdoch University, Griffith University, the University of Queensland, the University of York (UK), and the University of Birmingham, where he was also Head of Department. His work is centred on the politics, economics, and security of the broadly conceived Asia-Pacific region. He is the co-editor of *Contemporary Politics*, and the founding editor of *Critical Studies of the Asia Pacific*.

Stephen Bell is Professor and a former Head of the School of Political Science and International Studies at the University of Queensland, and an Honorary Professor at the University of Sheffield. He has held visiting appointments at the Australian National University and the Copenhagen Business School, and is a Fellow of the Academy of Social Sciences in Australia. He has published widely in leading Australian and international journals and is the author or editor of ten books. These include *Australia's Money Mandarins: The Reserve Bank of Australia and the Politics of Money* (2004), *Rethinking Governance: The Centrality of the State in Modern Society* (2009), *The Rise of the People's Bank of China: The Politics of Institutional Change* (2013), and *Masters of the Universe, Slaves of the Market* (2015). He is currently working on two projects funded by the Australian Research Council; one on China's banking reform, the other on international financial reform after the 2008 crisis.

Barry Buzan is Professor Emeritus at the London School of Economics (LSE), a Senior Fellow at IDEAS, and a Fellow of the British Academy. Previously, he was Montague Burton Professor of International Relations at the LSE. He has written, co-authored, or edited over twenty-five books, and written or co-authored more than 130 articles and chapters, mainly on IR theory and international security. His books relevant to this project include *International Systems in World History: Remaking the Study of International Relations* (co-authored with Richard Little, 2000), *From International to World Society? English School Theory and the Social Structure of Globalisation* (2004), *The United States and the Great Powers: World Politics in the Twenty-First Century* (2004), *An Introduction to the English School of International Relations: The Societal Approach* (2014), and *International Society and the Contest Over 'East Asia'* (co-edited with Yongjin Zhang, 2014).

Ian Clark is Professor of International Relations in the School of Political Science and International Studies, University of Queensland. He previously spent much of his career at Cambridge University, and then as E. H. Carr

Professor of International Politics at Aberystwyth University. He has held prestigious awards, such as a Leverhulme Major Research Fellowship and a UK ESRC Professorial Fellowship. He is the author of numerous books in the fields of international history and international theory, notably his trilogy on *Legitimacy in International Society* (2005), *International Legitimacy and World Society* (2007), and *Hegemony in International Society* (2011). These were followed by *The Vulnerable in International Society* (2013). His latest work is *Waging War: A New Philosophical Introduction* (2015), a rewritten second edition of his book first published in 1988. Professor Clark is a Fellow of the British Academy, a Fellow of the Learned Society of Wales, and an Honorary Fellow of Selwyn College, Cambridge.

Neta C. Crawford is Professor of Political Science at Boston University. Her research focuses on the causes of war and peace, change in world politics, and international ethics. She also co-directs the Costs of War Project at Brown University. She is the author of *Argument and Change in World Politics: Ethics, Decolonization and Humanitarian Intervention* (2002), *Accountability for Killing: Moral Responsibility for Collateral Damage in America's Post-9/11 Wars* (2013), and articles in scholarly books and journals, including *International Organization, International Security, Perspectives on Politics, Midwest Studies in Philosophy, International Theory, Ethics and International Affairs*, and *International Relations*. She has served on the editorial board of the *American Political Science Review* and on the advisory board of *International Relations*.

Richard Devetak is Associate Professor in International Relations and Head of the School of Political Science and International Studies at the University of Queensland. His research focuses on the history of international thought, the history of the states-system, and critical theories of international relations. He has published in *History of European Ideas, International Affairs, International Theory, Review of International Studies, Millennium*, and *Australian Journal of International Affairs*, and has held Visiting Fellowships at the Department of International Politics at the University of Wales (2003), the Department of Politics, Institutions and History at the University of Bologna (2008), and at the Department of Political and Social Sciences at the European University Institute (2012).

Tim Dunne is Executive Dean of the Faculty of Humanities and Social Sciences at the University of Queensland where he is also Professor of International Relations in the School of Political Science and International Studies. Previously he was Director of the Asia Pacific Centre for the Responsibility to Protect, where he continues to be a Senior Researcher. He is a Fellow of the Academy of Social Sciences in Australia. He has written and edited twelve books, including *Inventing International Society: A History of the English School* (1998), *Human Rights in Global Politics* (co-edited with Nicholas

J. Wheeler, 1999), *Worlds in Collision* (co-edited with Ken Booth, 2002), *Terror in our Time* (co-authored with Ken Booth, 2012), *International Relations Theories* (co-edited with Milja Kurki and Steve Smith, 2016), *Liberal World Orders* (co-edited with Trine Flockhart, 2013), and the *Handbook of the Responsibility to Protect* (co-edited with Alex J. Bellamy, 2016).

Ian Hall is Professor of International Relations in the School of Government and International Relations at Griffith University, and a member of both the Griffith Asia Institute and the Centre for Governance and Public Policy. His recent books include *Dilemmas of Decline: British Intellectuals and World Politics, 1945–1975* (2012) and *The Engagement of India: Strategies and Responses* (editor, 2014). His articles have appeared in various journals, including *Asian Survey, European Journal of International Relations, International Affairs*, and *Review of International Studies*. His research focuses on the intellectual history of international relations and Indian foreign policy. He is currently writing a book on India and the liberal international order.

Lene Hansen is Professor of International Relations in the Department of Political Science, University of Copenhagen. She has published on security theory, gender, the Bosnian War, Denmark's relationship with the European Union, cybersecurity, and images and international security in *International Studies Quarterly, European Journal of International Relations, Review of International Studies, Millennium, Journal of Peace Research*, and *Security Dialogue*, among other journals. She is the author of *Security as Practice: Discourse Analysis and the Bosnian War* (2006) and *The Evolution of International Security Studies* (co-authored with Barry Buzan, 2009). Professor Hansen is a former editor of *European Journal of International Relations* and a 2011 recipient of The Elite Research Prize of the Danish Ministry of Science, Technology and Innovation.

Paul Keal was formerly a Senior Fellow in the Department of International Relations, School of International, Political and Strategic Studies, College of Asia and the Pacific at the Australian National University. His previous appointments include the University of New South Wales at the Australian Defence Force Academy and La Trobe University, with visiting fellowships at Princeton University, Stanford University, the Russian Diplomatic Academy, Keele University, and the University of British Columbia. His publications include *European Conquest and the Rights of Indigenous Peoples: The Moral Backwardness of International Society* (2003), *Unspoken Rules and Superpower Dominance* (1983), and 'An "International Society"?' in Greg Fry and Jacinta O'Hagan (eds), *Contending Images of World Politics* (2000). His continuing research interests are indigenous peoples in world politics, concepts of indigenous sovereignty, and ethical and cultural factors in world order.

Hun Joon Kim is Associate Professor in the Department of Political Science and International Relations at Korea University. His research interests lie in international norms and institutions, international human rights and transitional justice, international ethics, and international relations theory. He has published in *International Organization, International Studies Quarterly, Journal of Peace Research, Chinese Journal of International Politics, Global Governance, Human Rights Quarterly, International Journal of Transitional Justice,* and *Annual Review of Law and Social Science.* His books include *The Massacres at Mt Halla: Sixty Years of Truth-Seeking in South Korea* (2014) and *Transitional Justice in the Asia Pacific* (co-edited with Renée Jeffery, 2014).

Audie Klotz is Professor of Political Science in the Maxwell School of Citizenship and Public Affairs at Syracuse University. Her interests span theories of international relations, qualitative methods, transnational activism, global migration, and identity politics, with a regional specialization in Southern Africa. Her first book, *Norms in International Relations: The Struggle against Apartheid* (1995), won the Furniss award in security studies. Her work also includes *Migration and National Identity in South Africa, 1860–2010* (2013), *Research Strategies for Constructivist International Relations* (co-authored with Cecelia Lynch, 2007), which has been translated into Korean (Kyung Hee University Press, 2011), *How Sanctions Work: Lessons from South Africa* (co-edited with Neta C. Crawford, 1999), and *Qualitative Methods in International Relations* (co-edited with Deepa Prakash, 2008). Her work has appeared in *International Organization, Review of International Studies, Third World Quarterly,* and *European Journal of International Relations,* among other journals and edited collections.

Jacinta O'Hagan is Associate Professor and Director of the Graduate Centre in International Affairs in the School of Political Science and International Studies at the University of Queensland. A former diplomat with the Irish Department of Foreign Affairs, she previously taught at the Australian National University and held visiting fellowships and affiliations at the University of Southern California, Massachusetts Institute of Technology, the University of Wales, Aberystwyth, and the European University Institute. She has published *Conceptions of the West in International Relations Thought: From Oswald Spengler to Edward Said* (2002), *Contending Images of World Politics* (co-edited with Greg Fry, 2000), and several articles and book chapters on the topics of civilization and culture in international relations and the politics of humanitarianism.

Andrew Phillips is Associate Professor in International Relations and Strategy in the School of Political Science and International Studies at the University of Queensland. His research focuses on the global state system's evolution from 1500 to the present, and on contemporary security challenges in East and

South Asia, with a particular focus on great power rivalry and counter-terrorism. He is the author of *War, Religion and Empire: The Transformation of International Orders* (2011) and *International Order in Diversity: War, Trade and Rule in the Indian Ocean* (co-authored with J. C. Sharman, 2015). He has articles published or forthcoming in *European Journal of International Relations, International Studies Review, International Studies Quarterly, Millennium, Review of International Studies, Pacific Review, Survival, Australian Journal of International Affairs, National Identities*, and *Security Challenges*.

Heather Rae is Senior Lecturer in the School of Political Science and International Studies, University of Queensland. She is the author of *State Identities and the Homogenisation of Peoples* (2002). She continues to take an interest in state violence and identity politics, both historical and contemporary. She is currently exploring the use of violence by liberal states, with a focus on how liberal states have engaged with non-liberal Others in ways which, while ostensibly aiming to protect and promote liberal values, often contradict, and indeed undermine, liberal principles.

Christian Reus-Smit is a Fellow of the Academy of the Social Sciences in Australia, and Professor of International Relations at the University of Queensland. He is author or editor of *Individual Rights and the Making of the International System* (2013), *American Power and World Order* (2004), *The Moral Purpose of the State* (1999), *Special Responsibilities: Global Problems and American Power* (co-authored with Mlada Bukovansky, Ian Clark, Robyn Eckersley, Richard Price, and Nicholas J. Wheeler, 2012), *The Politics of International Law* (editor, 2004), *The Oxford Handbook of International Relations* (co-edited with Duncan Snidal, 2008), 'Resolving International Crises of Legitimacy' (co-edited with Ian Clark, special issue, *International Politics* 2007), and *Between Sovereignty and Global Governance* (co-edited with Albert J. Paolini and Anthony P. Jarvis, 1998).

Gerry Simpson holds the Chair in Public International Law at the London School of Economics (LSE). He was previously the Sir Kenneth Bailey Professor of Law at University of Melbourne (2007–15), and has taught at the Australian National University (1995–8) and the LSE (2000–7). His work includes *Great Powers and Outlaw States* (2004), *Law, War and Crime: War Crimes Trials and the Reinvention of International Law* (2007), *Hidden Histories* (co-edited with Kevin Jon Heller, 2014), and *Who's Afraid of International Law?* (co-edited with Raimond Gaita, forthcoming). Professor Simpson's ongoing research projects include an Australian Research Council-funded project on 'Cold War International Law' with Matt Craven and Sundhya Pahuja, and a counter-history of International Criminal Justice. He is currently also writing about the literary life of international law.

Hendrik Spruyt is Norman Dwight Harris Professor of International Relations at Northwestern University. He previously served on the faculty of Columbia University and Arizona State University, and has been a visiting faculty member at the Institut d'Etudes Politiques. He served as chair of his department and as Director of the Buffett Center at Northwestern. He is the author, co-author, or co-editor of several books, among which are *The Sovereign State and Its Competitors* (1994), *Ending Empire: Contested Sovereignty and Territorial Partition* (2005), and *Contracting States: Sovereign Transfers in International Relations* (co-authored with Alexander Cooley, 2009). Some recent publications include 'Empires, Past and Present: The Relevance of Empire as an Analytic Concept', in *Empire and International Order* (edited by Noel Parker, 2013), 'Collective Imaginations and International Order: The Contemporary Context of the Chinese Tributary System', *Harvard Journal of Asiatic Studies* (forthcoming), and 'Unbundling Sovereign Rights through Incomplete Contracting' (forthcoming).

Emily Tannock is a Postdoctoral Research Fellow in the School of Political Science and International Studies at the University of Queensland. Her research interests include the relationship between international law and international relations, the politics of legitimacy, and the use of force. She is currently working on a monograph that examines the history of the complex, indeterminate arguments that surround war and the use of force. Her work has appeared in the *Lowy Interpreter*.

Sarah Teitt is Deputy Director and Researcher at the Asia Pacific Centre for the Responsibility to Protect (AP R2P), which is based at the University of Queensland. The AP R2P Centre is supported by the Australian Department of Foreign Affairs and Trade to deepen knowledge, advance policy, and build partnerships in the Asia-Pacific region in order to contribute to the prevention of genocide and other mass atrocities. Dr Teitt's research focuses on Chinese foreign policy and human security, the global politics of atrocity prevention, and gender, peace, and security in the Asia-Pacific. Her recent research has been published in *Global Governance, International Peacekeeping*, and *Australian Journal of International Affairs*, and she is presently completing a manuscript on Chinese foreign policy and the responsibility to protect.

Ann E. Towns is Associate Professor in Political Science at the University of Gothenburg and a Wallenberg Academy Fellow. Her research centres on questions of norms, hierarchy, and resistance in international politics, generally with a focus on gender. She is currently conducting a large research project on gender norms, gender practices, and hierarchies in diplomacy. Professor Towns is the author of *Women and States: Norms and Hierarchies in International Society* (2010). Her research has also appeared in *International Organization, European Journal of International Relations, Millennium, Party*

Politics, and other venues. She is associate editor of *International Studies Quarterly*, and a member of the editorial boards of *Cambridge Studies in Gender and Politics*, *Politics*, and *Internasjonal Politikk*.

Jennifer M. Welsh is Professor and Chair in International Relations at the European University Institute, and a Fellow of Somerville College, University of Oxford. She is the co-founder of the Oxford Institute for Ethics, Law and Armed Conflict, and currently directs a European Research Council Advanced Grant on 'The Individualization of War'. From 2013 to 2016, she served as the Special Adviser on the Responsibility to Protect to UN Secretary-General Ban Ki-moon. Professor Welsh is the author and editor of several books and articles on the responsibility to protect, humanitarian intervention, and the UN Security Council, as well as on theoretical issues related to sovereignty and norm evolution. She sits on the editorial board of *Global Responsibility to Protect*, *Ethics and International Affairs*, and *International Journal*, and on the Steering Committee of the American Academy of Arts and Sciences project on Ethics, Technology and War.

Yongjin Zhang is Professor of International Politics at the University of Bristol. He delivered the 39th Martin Wight Memorial Lecture at the London School of Economics in November 2013. His most recent publications include 'The Standard of "Civilisation" Redux: Towards the Expansion of International Society 3.0?' *Millennium* (2014), *Contesting International Society in East Asia* (co-edited with Barry Buzan, 2014), and *International Orders in the Early Modern World: Before the Rise of the West* (co-edited with Shogo Suzuki and Joel Quirk, 2014). He was awarded a Leverhulme Major Research Fellowship for 2015–17 to work on a book project: *International Relations in Ancient China: Ideas, Institutions and Law*.

Part I

Introduction

1

Introduction

Christian Reus-Smit and Tim Dunne

It is three decades now since Hedley Bull and Adam Watson published their classic work, *The Expansion of International Society*. Their purpose was 'to explore the expansion of the international society of European states across the rest of the globe, and its transformation from a society fashioned in Europe and dominated by Europeans into the global international society of today, with its nearly two hundred states, the great majority of which are not European'.[1] The book rapidly assumed canonical status within the English School,[2] joining Martin Wight's *Systems of States* as principal exemplars of the School's comparative and historical approach to the study of international society. The book's influence now extends well beyond its origins: in the last two decades, other International Relations (IR) scholars have rediscovered history and *The Expansion* has become a staple reference in works of diverse theoretical orientation.[3]

Bull and Watson's achievements were threefold. They recognized, first of all, the uniqueness of the global order of sovereign states produced by post-1945 decolonization. While most of their contemporaries in IR took this order as given, as a fundamental and enduring structural condition of international relations, Bull and Watson understood its novelty in world history. Never before had the sovereign state been the sole legitimate form of rule, and never before had the entirety of the globe been divided up into such states. Second, the editors of *The Expansion* gave this unique order a history, albeit now a widely contested one. Europe was where the society of states first developed, empires extended European rule across the globe, and as decolonization freed non-European peoples, more and more states were admitted to the norm-governed international society. Lastly, Bull and Watson posed far-reaching questions about the future of global international society: its stability in a culturally diverse world, how it was shaped by the broader dynamics of world

---

[1] Bull and Watson 1984b: 1.   [2] See Vigezzi 2005.
[3] Examples includes Krasner 1999; Philpott 2001; Hurrell 2007; and Nexon 2009.

society, and whether order could be preserved in the face of persistent economic and political injustice.

Yet despite these achievements, the book is a creature of its time. Its essays were prepared less than a decade after post-1945 decolonization had run its course, and published before the end of the Cold War, the tumultuous events of 11 September 2001, and the current wave of transnational terrorism and dramatic remaking of the Middle East. Moreover, the book was written before the intellectual renaissance that energized IR after the fall of the Berlin Wall— before the challenges of critical theory and poststructuralism, the rise of constructivism, the rejuvenation of the English School, the rediscovery of classic realism, the return to historical inquiry, and new waves of international political theory, political economy, and security studies. Like any work at any time, therefore, *The Expansion* was framed by the horizons of its present and informed by the repertoire of available ideas.

The last three decades have arguably been unkind to the book.[4] Many of its conceptual building blocks, analytical orientations, historiographical assumptions and methods, and normative perspectives have been called into question by more recent scholarship in IR, political theory, history, law, and sociology. The concept of 'international society' has itself been subjected to intense scrutiny.[5] Empire and sovereignty in the European order are now seen as much more deeply entwined.[6] The notion that sovereign equality means an absence of hierarchy has been contested.[7] Bull and Watson's understanding of how non-Western polities were socialized into the norms of international society has been called into question.[8] The Eurocentrism and linearity of their conception and narrative of 'the expansion' has been challenged by those who stress the influence of non-European peoples on the evolving global order.[9] The role of institutions such as international law in the evolution of international society has been critiqued.[10] And postcolonial scholars have rejected the entire practice of reading global history from the perspective of the metropole.[11]

Notwithstanding these challenges, however, the central question animating *The Expansion* remains critically important: how did today's global international society evolve? Not only is this order unique in world history, its development is a crucial background condition for many of the issues we struggle with in contemporary international relations. Only against the backdrop of a world organized into sovereign states can we make sense of debates over the rise of non-Western powers, humanitarian intervention and the responsibility to protect, the threat posed by violent transnational actors,

---

[4] This having been said, the revival of the English School after the end of the Cold War has also given *The Expansion* a new lease of life. See Epp 2010; Navari 2009.

[5] See, for example, Buzan 2004; Reus-Smit 2013a.   [6] See Keene 2002.

[7] See Dunne 2003; Lake 2009.   [8] See, for example, Suzuki 2009.

[9] See Hobson 2004.   [10] See Simpson 2004; Koskenniemi 2001.

[11] See, in particular, Chakrabarty 2008.

stalled multilateral trade talks, development and foreign aid, state governance of the Internet, and so much more. They all assume a particular sovereignty-based architecture of the globe. What is more, how we debate these issues is framed by the institutional norms and practices of global international society: sovereign equality, non-intervention, self-determination, territorial integrity, the laws of war, principles of multilateralism, and so on. And even when we lament the flaws and limitations of these institutions they remain our principal reference points.

It is timely, then, to reconsider Bull and Watson's central question from the vantage point of the early twenty-first century. This book reconsiders the question of how the global society of sovereign states has evolved over the course of five centuries drawing on a plurality of intellectual resources. Three decades after *The Expansion*, however, our engagement with this question differs from Bull and Watson's in four key ways.

First, we revise their conceptual apparatus. Concepts are the lenses through which we read the world: they make complexity intelligible by defining, categorizing, lending meaning, and relating. They are the underlying building blocks of any analysis: in the humanities, social sciences, as well as the natural sciences. *The Expansion* is built on a very distinctive set of conceptual foundations that led Bull and Watson to read the history of today's global international society in a very particular way. Most of these concepts receive little elaboration in *The Expansion* itself, and are drawn instead from key works in the English School corpus, particularly Bull's *The Anarchical Society*. In Chapter 2, we excavate and rethink several of these key concepts, most notably the definition of, and relationship between, an 'international society' and 'international system', the connection between international society and the 'world political system', the assumption that international society is a realm of settled norms, and lastly, the related conception of international society as rooted in a unitary culture.

Second, we understand the evolution of global international society as a process of 'globalization' instead of 'expansion'. In the wave of globalization literature published in the 1990s, the term was used to describe heightened global interconnections, the growing speed and density of transnational social, economic, and political relationships, and the corrosive impact of all of this on state sovereignty. While some of our authors do refer to these kinds of globalization processes, at least in the sense of heightened global interconnections (see Andrew Phillips, Chapter 3), this is not our principal use of the term. Rather, we use globalization to describe two things. The first is the global spread of the institution of the sovereign state, and of a set of distinctive social relationships among these states. Here we agree with David Armitage's observation that this is 'one of the most overlooked effects of globalization'.[12]

---

[12] Armitage 2007: 105.

'Globalization' also captures how the society of sovereign states transformed as it spread across the globe, and how it was shaped fundamentally by wider social formations and processes. The idea of 'expansion', by contrast, implies that European international society simply up-scaled, its rules and practices persisting over time while the size of the membership increased.

Third, we break with Bull and Watson's treatment of international society's globalization as a rational, even ordered, process. International society, as Bull famously argued, is a rational response by states to the imperatives of physical security, territorial integrity, and reliable commitments: to the need for order.[13] More than this, international society's expansion is presented as a rational process of incorporation. European states were faced with a practical problem: 'the challenge and difficulty of drawing in the non-European countries into their system of international relations in an orderly and humane way, as much as possible within the international legal guidelines they were themselves evolving to cope with the expanding domain of international law'.[14] To address this problem, they formulated rules to govern the membership of the club of recognized sovereign states, and over time, non-European polities accepted these rules as serving their best interests. As Bull put it, '[w]hile non-European communities in some cases were incorporated in the international system against their will, they have taken their places in international society because they themselves have sought the rights of membership of it, and the protection of its rules, both vis-à-vis the dominant European powers and in relation to one another'.[15] What this account neglects, wilfully or otherwise, is the domination and violence that often attended European international society's engagement with subjugated non-European peoples, and the waves of political struggle required to dismantle Europe's empires and force the expansion of international society.

Finally, we treat the globalization of international society as an ongoing process, not something realized in its final form at a particular moment in time. The latter view is never stated explicitly by Bull and Watson, but it is implied in Bull's writings on 'the revolt against the West', in which he assumed that a global international society was achieved by post-1945 decolonization but warned of its fragility under conditions of persistent injustice.[16] That a global society of sovereign states emerged fully after 1945 is clear in two developments: the geographical spread of sovereign states as Europe's empires collapsed, and the emergence of the sovereign state as the sole legitimate form of rule. Yet this global sovereign order is constantly changing. The meaning and implications of sovereignty, the terms of legitimate statehood, the balance between hierarchy and sovereign equality, which polities gain recognition and

---

[13] Bull 1977: 16–20.   [14] Gong 1984a: 171.
[15] Bull 1984b: 124.   [16] Bull 1983: 32–3.

which do not, the nature of challenges to the sovereign order, all are in flux or subject to continuous renegotiation.

When embarking on this project we enlisted contributors from a range of theoretical perspectives and intellectual persuasions. One of Bull and Watson's achievements was to stake out the development of a global society of sovereign states as a trademark concern of the English School, and notable representatives of this School are part of our team. But if the development of a global international society is as unique and significant as we claim, then understanding its evolution should command the attention of scholars with diverse affiliations. Furthermore, over the past three decades powerful new perspectives have emerged on both the social nature of international relations and the historical development of today's sovereign order, and it is crucial that a project such as this include scholars who have been at the forefront of these developments. By bringing together diverse authors, we hope that the book will engage a broad readership, including constructivists, critical theorists, historical institutionalists, postcolonial theorists, intellectual historians, and world historians.

The Globalization of International Society is divided into five parts. Part I introduces the volume, sets out our conceptual framework, and draws together key insights from subsequent chapters. The remaining parts address four broad issues: global context, dynamics of globalization, institutional contours, and contestation. This reflects our desire to capture, in turn, the global cultural, economic, and political universe in which a nascent international society first emerged in Europe between the fourteenth and seventeenth centuries, the multiple social forces that drove the globalization of this society, the diverse institutional structures and practices that have come to characterize it, and the varied forms of contestation now shaping the global order.

While there is an underlying diachronic logic to this organization of the volume, we are acutely aware that the diverse phenomena, processes, and practices examined by our contributors do not fit neatly into segregated periods or map on to a single chronology. Within this broad framework, therefore, we have given our authors considerable latitude in how they construct their historical accounts. For example, although Part II on global context focuses roughly on the period from the fourteenth to seventeenth centuries, Phillips's chapter on 'international systems' has a different periodization from Heather Rae's on 'identification' and Hendrik Spruyt's on 'economies'.

Part II examines the global context in which nascent sovereign states first emerged in Europe. In 1420, seven decades before early Spanish state builders, Ferdinand and Isabella, expelled the Jews from the Iberian Peninsula and licensed Columbus's conquest of the Indies, China's Ming dynasty completed construction of the magnificent Imperial Palace ('Forbidden City') in Beijing. This poses starkly a crucial yet frequently overlooked reality of the world in which European sovereign states first emerged. This was a world of multiple, often highly sophisticated, international orders, complex and competing forms of identification, and varied economic systems and practices. Furthermore, these 'worlds' were increasingly interconnected, shaping one another through engagement and example.

Bull and Watson acknowledge this reality, but only to emphasize the uniqueness of European developments. In the fifteenth century, they contend, the world comprised several regional international systems, each 'built upon elaborate civilizations, including complex religions, governments, law, commerce, written records, and financial accounts'.[17] With the exception of the European system, however, these were all hegemonial or imperial. 'At the centre of each was a suzerain Supreme Ruler . . . who exercised direct authority over the Heartland; and around this empire extended a periphery of locally autonomous realms that acknowledged the suzerain's overlordship and paid him tribute.'[18] In Europe alone, Bull and Watson claim, was this hegemonial principle slowly repudiated, and in the eighteenth century 'was the idea firmly implanted among European states that an attempt by any one of them to establish hegemony over the others was a violation of the rules of their international society'.[19] Whatever the merits of this claim, Bull and Watson acknowledge non-European orders only to highlight European distinctiveness, not to understand their richness, or to acknowledge, let alone comprehend, their mutual constitution.

Our goals in Part II are, first, to better locate the early development of the European order in a global context composed of diverse systems, identities, and economies, and second, to capture the dynamic interplay between these, showing, in particular, the constitutive effects of interaction on European developments. Our contributors focus on three key aspects of this global context: international systems, patterns of identification, and economies. Phillips examines the first of these, arguing, through an analysis of key 'Afro-Eurasian' civilizational complexes (the Indosphere, the Islamicate, the Sinosphere, Saharasia, and Latin Christendom), that prior to 1490, international systems became 'more internally diverse, externally differentiated, and mutually entangled'.[20] Rae focuses on evolving patterns of identification in the Aztec and Ottoman Empires, and how contrasting engagements with these empires transformed European self-understandings. While centuries of interaction between the Ottomans and Europeans produced mutually constituted 'relational identities' in both, Europeans encountered the Aztecs as a 'radical other'. Their 'discovery' had a profound effect on European identity, however: challenging established 'certainties about the unity of all humankind'

---

[17] Bull and Watson 1984b: 2.   [18] Bull and Watson 1984b: 3.
[19] Bull and Watson 1984b: 6.   [20] Chapter 3.

and 'contributing towards more relativist understandings of moral, social, religious, and political codes'.[21]

Spruyt addresses an issue that has been neglected by the English School: the nature and interaction of diverse economic systems, institutions, practices, and beliefs. Challenging conventional accounts that attribute European ascendancy to a unique conjunction of political decentralization and economic dynamism, and portray the expansion of international society as a one-way street, he highlights the economic dynamism of other, more hierarchical orders, and shows how high levels of interaction between different orders enabled 'an inter-ecumenical flow of cultural ideas and material practices well before the European maritime "breakout"'.[22] Neta C. Crawford's chapter engages the diversity of, and interaction between, varied international systems, the complex interplay between social and cultural identities, and the power politics structuring these relationships. Not only did complex indigenous international social orders exist well before European conquest, understanding the nature and sophistication of these orders challenges 'state of nature' accounts of the origins of cooperation, the assumption that the state is the highest form of political organization, and 'any notion that the norms of European international society were transferred peacefully and adopted voluntarily because it was a superior system'.[23]

Within the highly variegated cultural, economic, and political context described in Part II, the kernel of today's international society first emerged in Europe, and over the course of four to five centuries this distinctive political order globalized. Bull and Watson's account of this 'expansion' privileges processes endogenous to European international society. The development of sovereign states in Europe was the product of intra-European economic, political, and social processes. European imperialism drew large swathes of the non-European world under the rule of Europe's sovereigns. European powers defined the rules of the evolving international society, and it was they who managed the gradual incorporation of non-European polities into the expanding society of states. Bull and Watson acknowledge that the expansion was influenced by non-European practices, but they make no attempt to identify or explain these practices or their influence. Moreover, they insist that non-European polities were incorporated (largely voluntarily) into an essentially European social order. In Bull's words, 'The non-European or non-Western majority of states in the world today, which played little role in shaping the foundations of the international society to which they now belong, have sought naturally and properly to modify it so that it will reflect their own special interests. It should not be overlooked, however, that be seeking a

---

[21] Chapter 4.   [22] Chapter 5.
[23] Neta C. Crawford's chapter in this volume, p. 176.

place in this society they have given their consent to its basic rules and institutions.'[24]

Part III takes a critical and more complex view of the long-term processes that produced today's global international society; processes that transformed a small, regionally concentrated system of states, embedded within larger imperial complexes, into a sovereign order of global reach. Some of these processes were indeed largely endogenous to the European order: capitalism, war-fighting, particular ideational revolutions, the civilizational and extractive impulses of empire, anti-colonial movements in the metropole, and the membership practices of the evolving society of states. Yet privileging such processes is radically insufficient. Missing is the critical role of exogenous forces, as well as the blurred and problematic boundary between the very categories of endogenous and exogenous. For example, the globalization of international society resulted, in significant measure, from consecutive revolutions against imperial rule: revolutions driven by colonial peoples in the imperial periphery, revolutions that transformed the norms of international society as they forced its globalization.[25] From a conventional standpoint, these revolutions were exogenous: they were geographically remote from Europe, and until they gained sovereign recognition, colonial peoples were outside the evolving society of states. Yet not only were these 'exogenous' revolutions critically important in the globalization of international society, they were also 'endogenous' in crucial respects to the broader social and political processes of Europe's evolving sovereign-imperial complexes.

Our contributors explore different phenomena implicated in the globalization of international society. In Chapter 7, Richard Devetak and Emily Tannock enlist the methods and insights of contextual history to examine the changing norms and practices of the evolving European society of states, focusing in particular on the institutional impact of the Seven Years' War (1756–63). A clear link is established here between the normative/institutional development of international society and the politics of empire. This theme is pursued in the remaining four chapters of Part III. Jennifer M. Welsh challenges two of Bull and Watson's central themes: that the expansion process was 'rational and rule-governed', and that it was a 'one-way process of standardization', with 'European models' 'absorbed by peripheral societies'. In reality, she contends, Europe's imperial powers never achieved complete colonial mastery: their rule was often 'ill-defined', their jurisdiction 'uneven', and their 'legal authority was enmeshed with the law and customs of indigenous subjects'. This meant, she goes on to argue, that interaction between the European and non-European worlds produced not standardization but 'a diversity of political and legal forms'.[26]

---

[24] Bull 1984b: 124.   [25] Reus-Smit 2013a.   [26] Chapter 8.

War has long been seen as an engine of the sovereign order's development: in Charles Tilly's words, 'war makes states'.[27] Yet Paul Keal argues that Bull's unnecessarily narrow conception of war—'war in the strict sense'—obscures the very modes of warfare that were central to the globalization of international society: the frontier wars waged against indigenous peoples across the colonized world. Furthermore, Bull ignores the fact that Europe's imperial powers made a very similar conceptual move, defining war as a practice confined to 'civilized' states. By defining indigenous peoples as 'savage', Europeans simultaneously denied anti-colonial wars of resistance the status of 'war' and justified European wars of suppression.[28] This distinction between civilized and savage raises the broader issue of the role that ideas of civilization played in the globalization of international society, an issue taken up by Jacinta O'Hagan. Two contrasting yet interrelated discourses of civilization were implicated in the globalization of international society, she contends. The first treats civilization agents, 'loosely bounded but discrete social entities whose interaction is integral to the dynamics of the globalization of international society'. The second sees civilization as a 'generative force' that shapes the institutional and normative framework of international society and informs 'relations with those perceived as "outside" of that society'.[29]

The final chapter in Part III, by Yongjin Zhang, explores the constitutive impact on international society of non-European states that were not colonized or formally subjected to European rule, the key case being China. In contrast to conventional accounts of China's integration into expanding international society, which emphasize China's imperial decay, defeat in the Opium Wars, unequal treaties, and eventual admission to the club of states, Zhang stresses an earlier period of engagement, 1500–1800, in which 'European identity and Europe's understanding of its place in the world were manifestly informed by its precarious knowledge and contingent interpretations of the civilizational and imperial Other at the opposite end of Eurasia'. These encounters and understandings, Zhang argues, were 'indispensable for Europe to globalize its vision of the world in the nineteenth century when the project of European modernity became hegemonic and exhibited homogenizing effect'.[30]

In Part IV we move from the dynamics of globalization to the institutional contours of today's universal international society. International societies, and international orders more generally, are social institutions, the norms and practices of which sustain a system-wide configuration of political authority, characterized by recognized units of legitimate authority, and rules defining the bounds of legitimate political action.[31] We focus on three levels of institutions that together comprise the institutional architecture of modern

---

[27] Tilly 1985.   [28] Chapter 9.   [29] Chapter 10.
[30] Chapter 11.   [31] Reus-Smit 2013b: 169–70.

international society: constitutional, fundamental, and issue-specific institutions.[32] Constitutional norms and practices define the terms of 'legitimate statehood and rightful state action; fundamental institutions encapsulate the basic rules of practice that structure how states solve cooperation problems; and issue-specific regimes enable basic institutional practices in particular realms of interstate relations'.[33]

Barry Buzan examines the evolution of modern international society's core constitutional norm: universal state sovereignty.[34] He identifies three key phases in the universalization of sovereignty: prior to 1900, the long nineteenth century through to the end of the Second World War, and the post-1945 period. Building on an argument advanced in collaboration with George Lawson,[35] he emphasizes the latter two phases, casting the nineteenth century, in particular, as a crucial period of change. It was then that the 'revolutions of modernity' forged not only a critical link between sovereignty, territoriality, and nationalism, but also a global structure of combined but uneven development. This structure allowed a dramatic intensification of European imperial control, and produced a 'spectrum of divided sovereignty' in the non-European world.[36] Only after 1945 did decolonization dismantle Europe's empires and universalize sovereignty, a process Buzan attributes to 'a long working out within the core of the ideological features of the revolutions of modernity', and the use of these very same features by anti-colonial elites to justify independence.[37] Integral to the resulting global sovereign order is the principle of sovereign equality, but as Buzan acknowledges, hierarchy has long coexisted with such equality. Ian Clark's chapter probes this complex relationship between hierarchy and equality, showing how the tension between the two reached a 'symbolic' highpoint with post-1945 decolonization. From this point onward, more or less formal modes of hierarchy—from those famously institutionalized in the United Nations (UN) Charter to informally sanctioned hegemony—have been legitimized through a discourse of great power responsibility. Analysing three key cases—the UN Security Council, nuclear arms control, and US hegemony after the Cold War—Clark shows not only the centrality of ideas of responsibility, but the dynamic nature of these ideas.

Among the fundamental institutions of modern international society, two have been especially prominent: international law and the related institution of multilateralism. The multitude of issue-specific institutions negotiated by states over the past 150 years—in areas ranging from arms control and

---

[32] On this categorization, see Reus-Smit 1999: 12–15.   [33] Reus-Smit 1999: 14.

[34] Note that instead of the constitutional/fundamental/issue-specific categorization of institutions used here, Buzan uses the related categories of primary and secondary institutions advanced in his previous writings. See Buzan 2004: chapter 6.

[35] Buzan and Lawson 2015b.   [36] Chapter 12.   [37] Chapter 12.

economic governance to refugees and environmental protection—have, in large part, been instantiations of these two fundamental institutions: they have created new instruments of international law through the practice of multilateral diplomacy. We focus here on the first of these institutions, as multilateralism proliferates very much as a response to new, nineteenth-century conceptions of law, legal obligation, and law-making. Gerry Simpson stresses the 'constitutive force of law' as international society globalized. He challenges, however, the notion that European international public law simply expanded as European international society spread across the globe. He stresses instead the 'globalization of global law'. 'Globalization', he argues, 'suggests a less unilinear, more centrifugal process of law-making: not so much an expansion of legal forms outwards but more of a hybridization of parallel legal orders'. Similarly, '*global* law implies a more thoroughgoing saturation of law through, between, and beyond the sovereign state, a sort of heteropolar, or heterojurisdictional, legal order in which law is both a public international law between states as well as an assemblage of deformalized, private, interstitial norms reproduced in a number of different legal sites'.[38]

Classical English School writings are marked by their relative neglect of issue-specific institutions or 'regimes', a neglect Bull and Watson did little to rectify. Yet these institutions are not only the most numerous and tangible of the three levels of institutions, and the very sites in which international law and multilateralism are most clearly manifest, they have also been inextricably bound up with the changing nature and development of international society. To demonstrate this impact we focus on issue-specific institutions in two key areas: international finance, and human rights. The English School long assumed that constitutional and fundamental institutions conditioned issue-specific institutions, with lower-level regimes depending on the prior existence of norms of sovereignty and practices of law and multilateralism. Nothing we say here questions these constitutive dynamics. Our contributors show, how-ever, that the causal arrow can point the other way as well; that developments at the level of regimes can have a profound impact on constitutive and fundamental institutions.

Mark Beeson and Stephen Bell examine the effects of international financial institutions, stepping into the field of international political economy, a field famously ignored by Bull and Watson. Focusing on three key cases—the rise and decline of the Bretton Woods system, the 2008 international financial crisis, and the subsequent euro crisis—they show repeated cycles in which states constructed institutions to manage global finance, these generated unforeseen structural effects and attendant economic crises, and states responded with new institutional remedies, remedies that again had unintended

---

[38] Chapter 14.

structural effects. These cycles, they argue, 'have and are posing major challenges to state sovereignty, international cooperation, the efficacy of institutions, and the societal order underpinning international arrangements'.[39] Similar feedback effects are evident in the area of human rights, examined by Hun Joon Kim. The notion that international human rights threaten to undermine core constitutional norms such as state sovereignty has a long history: indeed, it was the position Bull himself took.[40] Yet in a wide-ranging survey of recent research, and his own examination of evolving patterns of standard setting, investigation, and accountability, Kim paints a more complex picture. It is the complex 'conjunction of sovereignty and human rights', he contends, 'that makes today's international society so unique',[41] a conjunction in which the urge to ground sovereignty in individual rights coincides with irreconcilable ideational tensions, together driving an historically novel process of mutual constitution.

Part V of *The Globalization of International Society* focuses on the nature and effects of different modes of contestation. Contestation was an important theme for Bull and Watson. They wrote in the immediate aftermath of post-1945 decolonization, and an abiding concern for Bull in particular was the potential for conflict over international society's basic norms in a global order populated by states of diverse cultural backgrounds, a potential accentuated by persistent inequalities and injustices. Yet this interest in contestation was circumscribed at best. Although Bull identified five phases in the 'revolt against Western dominance', all concentrated after the late nineteenth century, he was particularly concerned with post-1945 decolonization, and with the counter-hegemonic diplomacy of postcolonial states. This focus was a direct product of two assumptions characteristic of the English School's approach to the expansion of international society: that international society was a Western (originally European) cultural artefact, and that expansion occurred primarily through processes of integration and incorporation. From such a perspective, contestation was not envisaged as a long-term engine of international societal development, and only loomed as an issue once the assumed cultural unity of Western international society was replaced after decolonization by an inherently diverse global society of states. Part V seeks to move beyond this circumscribed understanding of contestation. This is partly because struggles over the norms and institutions of international society loom so large today; and more fundamentally, because we see contestation as a crucial and long-term driver of international societal development. Studying contestation, we contend, can reveal as much, if not more, about the nature of international society than focusing solely on settled norms and practices.

---

[39] Chapter 15.   [40] Bull 1977: 83.   [41] Chapter 16.

Sovereignty has long been considered the cardinal norm of international society, and until recently it was understood in highly categorical and invariant terms. In the 1986 edition of his classic work on the topic, F. H. Hinsley evinced precisely this tendency, defining sovereignty as 'the idea that there is a final and absolute political authority in the political community... *and no final and absolute authority exists elsewhere*'.[42] A wave of subsequent scholarship, by realists and constructivists alike, has shown, however, that sovereignty is in fact a variable institution, its meaning and behavioural implications shifting with broader political and ideational transformations. As the nineteenth-century shift from absolutist to popular sovereignty attests, such changes have always been the product of contestation, domestic and international. In Chapter 17, Sarah Teitt explores this connection between contestation and sovereignty, focusing on the political struggles that have attended the growing institutionalization of the principle of the 'responsibility to protect' (R2P).

Ian Hall revisits the 'revolt against the West', critically locating and engaging Bull's understanding, and exploring echoes and legacies of the 'revolt' in contemporary challenges to Western hegemony. The idea of the revolt, Hall shows, was not Bull's innovation, but was an idea that was well entrenched in British anxieties about the end of Empire. What is more, Bull invoked the idea as the high tide of Third World challenges to the Western order was receding, with the end of the Cold War, the 'triumph' of liberalism, and the unipolar moment little more than five years away. Of the five dimensions of the revolt emphasized by Bull, Hall argues that by the 1980s, the postcolonial world had achieved three: the struggle for equal sovereignty, the end of European rule, and the struggle for racial equality. Two dimensions have remained, however (the struggle for cultural liberation and the struggle for economic justice), intensified by continued Western material power and 'the reassertion of Western leadership over the normative agenda of international relations'.[43] The first of these is manifest most clearly in the rise of militant Islam; the second in the Brazil, Russia, India, China, and South Africa (BRICS) campaign for a greater role in global economic governance. While the BRICS challenge is essentially conservative, Hall argues, militant Islam poses a more radical challenge, contesting core constitutional and fundamental institutions.

The issue of racial equality is explored in greater depth by Audie Klotz, who finds 'many reasons to resist a teleological storyline', arguing instead that racial inequality has been an enduring axis of global inequality and contestation.[44] While finding much to recommend in R. J. Vincent's chapter on racial equality in *The Expansion*, Klotz paints a more complex picture of the global

---

[42] Hinsley 1986: 25–6, emphasis in original.   [43] Chapter 18.   [44] Chapter 19.

politics of race. Three moves are central to this story: an insistence that racism can endure even when explicit discourses of racial inequality and hierarchy have receded; an emphasis on the deep interconnection between developments at the level of international society and discriminatory practices domestically; and seeing change as driven less by enlightened hegemony than by actors traditionally on the margins of international society. Klotz draws out each of these by reconsidering the global politics of abolition, excavating the highly racialized transnational control of migration, and highlighting the parallels between the activist politics of abolition and post-1945 politics of the anti-apartheid movement, decolonization, and international human rights, throughout demonstrating the enduring tensions between liberal egalitarianism and racial equality.

A central theme of Klotz's analysis is the inextricable link between the international and the domestic; in particular, the link between the nature and constitution of hierarchies both within and between states. Ann E. Towns further advances this theme, examining the crucial issue of gender, power, and the globalization of international society. This is one of the most notable blind spots in Bull and Watson's account. Towns advances a powerful corrective, drawing a tight connection between the exclusion of women from formal positions of political rule within states, the standard of civilization and the legitimation of empire internationally, and the importance of transnational struggles in reversing both. Prior to the late eighteenth century, Towns argues, the world was populated by diverse polities with varied relationships between gender and formal political power. This changed dramatically over the course of the next century and a half, as women were systematically excluded from political office across the Western world, and then, as European imperialism accelerated, 'matrilineal kinship systems and female political authority were severely challenged and declined significantly across Africa, South East Asia, and Native America'.[45] This shift was sanctioned by the notorious standard of civilization, which identified a civilized polity with male rule. This has been gradually reversed over the past century, with women now formally enfranchised in most states, and excluded from political office in only a few. This reversal in the organization of political power globally is the result of successive waves of transnational activism, often only tenuously linked to Western liberal models.

It would be difficult today to conclude a discussion of contestation without a chapter on communication. Not only is contestation difficult (even impossible) without communication, contemporary axes of contestation are so clearly dependent on shifting modes, dynamics, and technologies of communication that its centrality is hard to ignore. Thirty years ago, however, Bull

---

[45] Chapter 20.

and Watson saw no such need, despite the fact that their scant references to communication point to its critical importance: for example, Bull attributed rising Third World consciousness to a 'revolution in communications'.[46] Yet as Lene Hansen points out in Chapter 21, communication is central to Bull and Watson's account (if not directly acknowledged as such). In an innovative theoretical move, Hansen distinguishes between four meanings of 'communication': communication as dialogue, as a mode of engagement (written, spoken, or bodily), as an institutional practice, such as diplomacy, and as a technology. She then rereads the chapters of *The Expansion* highlighting just how important communication, in its diverse modes, was to the globalization of international society. More than this, while arguing against technological determinism, Hansen takes two key communications technologies—the printing press and the Internet—and shows how these have structured other aspects of communication in the globalization of international society.

We suggested at the outset that revisiting the global development of today's international society was warranted for two reasons: first, that the issue itself remains critically important to understanding contemporary world politics, and second, that over the past thirty years a wealth of new scholarship has enabled a comprehensive rethinking of the nature and development of international society. The preceding overview of our contributors' chapters is testimony to the richness and implications of this new scholarship. The importance at this historical juncture of enlisting these insights cannot be understated. The future of the contemporary international order is a central issue of current debate, driven primarily by the rise of non-Western great powers, and the diffusion of power to transnational actors, most notably religiously inspired extremists. Yet much of this debate rests on a set of assumptions about the nature and origins of modern international society, assumptions often strikingly similar to those informing Bull and Watson's account—the Western cultural foundations of this distinctive order, the forms of agency that drove its development, the sources of its institutional architecture, and the importance of incorporation over contestation in its expansion. These assumptions constitute the starting point of many contemporary commentaries. But if much of this is no longer sustainable historically, as our contributors demonstrate in multiple contexts, then contemporary debates need to be reframed, to be given new foundations. *The Globalization of International Society* is a contribution to such reframing.

---

[46] Bull 1984c: 222.

2

The Globalization of International Society

Christian Reus-Smit and Tim Dunne

Over the past two centuries, international society has globalized. It has gone from a restive club of European monarchies to a worldwide, if highly diverse, society of sovereign states. As successive waves of imperial fragmentation brought new states into this emerging society, geographic globalization was matched by institutional globalization, as the norms and practices of the evolving sovereign order both spread and transformed. These globalizing processes transformed the architecture of world politics, replacing a long-standing hybrid order that bound sovereignty in the European core to empire in the non-European periphery with a universal order of sovereign states. This world is the product of a monumental transformation, very recent in its final phases. And so many of today's critical political issues, from the legitimacy of intervention to territorial disputes in the South China Sea, assume the global political architecture wrought by this transformation.

Understanding the globalization of international society is thus more than an historical curiosity. Not only were the parameters of many contemporary issues laid down by such globalization, its processes have only barely run their course, if indeed they have. The universal society of sovereign states is very young; less than fifty years old if we date it from the final phases of post-1945 decolonization. This means that the institutions of global international society, dense and functionally diverse as they might be, are innovations by historical standards. Furthermore, many of the contests and struggles now challenging international society—from the political activism of the BRICS (Brazil, Russia, India, China, and South Africa) to the rise of transnational religious insurgencies—are rooted in the recent transition from a sovereign/imperial order to universal sovereignty. The shadow of international society's globalization thus looms large over contemporary world politics.

Hedley Bull and Adam Watson's *The Expansion of International Society* is the most well-known account of the development of the global sovereign order, but many of its central claims, along with its distinctive historiography, have been challenged by more recent scholarship. As explained in Chapter 1, this book returns to Bull and Watson's project of understanding the development of our present global society of states, but drawing on a wealth of new scholarship, from the theoretical resources of constructivism, the revitalized English School, and postcolonialism, to new histories of diverse international orders and their interaction, the imperial origins of international law and multilateralism, and the transformative dynamics of struggle and contestation.

This chapter serves two tasks. First, it examines four accounts of the globalization of international society. This discussion is not meant to be exhaustive, as many literatures touch on aspects of the rise and global spread of the sovereign state. Rather, the accounts chosen are sufficiently distinctive, and sufficiently focused on the phenomenon in question, that comparing them helps clarify what is distinctive about Bull and Watson's account, as well as its relative strengths and weaknesses. The first two accounts are materialist, emphasizing geopolitics and material incapacity in one case, and structural change in the world economy in the other. As we shall see, both rest on unsustainable correlations, and tell us little about international society as an evolving social order. The second two are social: the Stanford School's argument about socialization into a world polity, and Bull and Watson's thesis about international societal incorporation. While both appreciate the social nature of international society, they are limited conceptually and inadequately equipped to grasp the dynamics of international societal change. The chapter's second task is to move beyond these conceptual limitations by rethinking key concepts and attendant theoretical propositions, so as to better accommodate the rich accounts advanced by our contributors in the following chapters.

FOUR ACCOUNTS OF THE GLOBALIZATION OF INTERNATIONAL SOCIETY

As noted in Chapter 1, International Relations (IR) scholars have recently rediscovered history, and *The Expansion* has become a standard reference, cited by realists, liberals, constructivists, and the English School alike. Outside the narrow confines of the English School, however, there has been little direct engagement with the book's overall argument and narrative, other than to cite the work as a classic account of the expansion. At the same time, within the English School, where the intricacies of the book have been thoroughly excavated, critically and otherwise, the tendency has been to examine the argument in isolation, seldom comparing it with other accounts of the globalization of international society.[1] Our approach is different. Before examining Bull and Watson's account, we consider three contrasting accounts. Again, this is a heuristic exercise, not intended to be exhaustive. Nor are we suggesting that the three alternative accounts were chronologically prior to *The Expansion*, or that Bull and Watson crafted their argument in response. The three accounts have been chosen as exemplars of prominent but contrasting theses on the expansion, against which the distinctiveness of Bull and Watson's account is usefully highlighted.

Geopolitics and Imperial Incapacity

The most prominent of materialist accounts attribute the globalization of international society to competition among great powers and imperial overstretch. There is almost no mention in such accounts, however, of 'international society' or its 'expansion' or 'globalization'. Rather, their focus is on the transfer of formal power and authority from the metropole to the 'periphery' through decolonization, the mechanism by which a world of empires transformed into a world of states.

Two propositions are common in such accounts. First, it is claimed that decolonization has frequently been spurred on by the meddling of rival great powers. Robert Hager and David Lake argue, for example, that great powers engage in practices of 'competitive decolonization' in an effort to shift the balance of power in their favour.[2] Watson himself advanced this kind of argument when discussing decolonization in the Americas:

> [A]fter the Napoleonic Wars Britain actively supported the independence of Latin America both for economic reasons, in order to open doors of that continent to what was then the world's most expansive economy, and for strategic reasons, in order to establish new and supposedly democratic states there to balance what were considered in London the reactionary tendencies of the Holy Alliance.[3]

Second, and this is the default explanation for decolonization, it is frequently held that metropolitan material weakness, combined with anti-colonial insurgencies, propelled the breakup of Europe's empires. In the words of L. H. Gann and Peter Duignan, by the end of the First World War 'Britain

---

[1] As an example of this tendency, see Vigezzi 2005; Watson 1992. In their otherwise brilliant essay on 'The Historical Expansion of International Society', Barry Buzan and Richard Little provide a detailed account of the story and its limits without giving any consideration to the character of the history that was being written and what made it distinctive from other accounts. See Buzan and Little 2014.

[2] Hager Jr and Lake 2000.   [3] Watson 1992: 266.

and France stood at the zenith of their imperial might, but at the very moment of success, real power was slipping from their grasp. They were exhausted'.[4]

Common as these arguments are, they suffer from two principal weaknesses. The first is correlational. One can certainly find examples of great powers fermenting anti-colonialism in rival empires, but this has hardly been a consistent factor in processes of decolonization. In fact, on notable occasions, rival powers have stayed their hands, refraining from aiding anti-colonial forces. Contrary to Watson's claim, the British withheld diplomatic and material support from independence movements in the Americas, waiting until they had gained *de facto* sovereignty. And despite its anti-colonial rhetoric, after the Second World War, the United States sided with imperial powers to oppose any 'right' to self-determination.[5] Similarly, evidence regarding imperial weakness, and/or insurgent strength, is mixed at best. Fragmentary dynamics have emerged in empires at moments of material strength (the Holy Roman Empire at the beginning of the sixteenth century), and been absent at moments of great imperial weakness (the Spanish Empire in the late eighteenth century). Even after the Second World War, when Europe's imperial powers were greatly weakened, this often strengthened their grasp on empire, seeing it as an engine for metropolitan recovery. And while powerful anti-colonial movements emerged in some colonies, this was not the case universally. The vast majority of states that gained independence in post-1945 decolonization—such as Gabon, Burkina Faso, Samoa, Malawi, Guinea, Madagascar, Gambia, Lesotho, Barbados, and so on—did not have the material or organizational capacities to wage successful insurgencies.[6]

The second problem is that these explanations at best contribute to a numerical or geographical account of the globalization of international society: they tell us how sovereign states proliferated, and how they spread into new regions as empires collapsed. But while great power rivalry and imperial incapacity might (or might not) explain the fragmentation of empires, they tell us little about the development of the distinctive international social order of which such fragmentation was a part. Empires did not fragment into nothing; nor did they fragment into a bare Waltzian system devoid of social structures, processes, and practices.

Structure of the World Economy

A second materialist explanation holds that decolonization is more likely, first, under conditions of economic hegemony, and second, during periods of global economic expansion. Economic hegemony, which exists when a state has

---

[4] Gann and Duignan 1967: 72.   [5] See Reus-Smit 2013a: 26, 160–1.
[6] Reus-Smit 2013a: 157.

'*simultaneously* productive, commercial, and financial superiority *over all other core powers*',[7] reduces great power competition and promotes free trade, encouraging imperial powers to loosen control over their colonies, and the hegemon to lower imperial economic barriers by supporting decolonization. Conversely, 'multicentric' systems, where power is distributed across several metropolitan states, are said to increase geopolitical competition, and heighten imperial control.[8] Global economic expansion is also said to encourage decolonization. As Christopher Chase-Dunn and Richard Rubinson argue, 'when average economic production in the system is expanding, the structure of control is less direct and political domination by core states over peripheral areas is relaxed'.[9]

Like the previous arguments about geopolitics and imperial weakness, these economic arguments are bedevilled by correlational problems. Superficially, the argument about economic hegemony seems supported by post-1945 history, when US hegemony coincided with rapid decolonization. In reality, though, as the Cold War escalated, Washington failed to match its wartime anti-colonial rhetoric with practical support for decolonization, and as Hendrik Spruyt demonstrates, imperial elites often tightened control over their empires.[10] The connection is no stronger if we turn to earlier periods of decolonization. As noted earlier, the British provided little in the way of serious support for decolonization in the Americas, and the Spanish showed no interest in relinquishing their empire, eventually fighting savage counter-insurgency wars to retain it. Arguments that link decolonization to periods of global economic expansion are equally problematic. After a detailed quantitative survey of decolonization trends since 1520, David Strang found no correlation, let alone a causal link. 'Periods of economic expansion (upswings in Kondratieff waves) are inconsistently related to decolonization across the model specifications', he concluded.[11]

Even if strong connections could be established between economic hegemony and expansion, on the one hand, and decolonization, on the other, this would tell us little about the international social order that gradually emerged out of successive waves of imperial collapse. The globalization of international society occurred over the *longue durée*, as the sovereign-imperial complexes constructed from the late fifteenth century onward were displaced by an expanding order of sovereign states. Not only did this lengthy process span patterns of hegemonic rise and decline, as well as periods of expansion and contraction in the world economy, the evolving institutional architecture of international society could only crudely be reduced to such factors. It is now

---

[7] Wallerstein, 1980: 39, emphasis in original.
[8] Chase-Dunn and Rubinson 1979.
[9] Chase-Dunn and Rubinson 1979: 462–3.
[10] Spruyt 2005.   [11] Strang 1991b: 441.

axiomatic that constitutional norms such as sovereignty, along with evolving norms of legitimate statehood, have complex social and political histories.[12] Similarly, John Gerard Ruggie demonstrated some time ago that hegemony itself cannot explain more functional institutions, such as post-1945 multilateralism. The US was hegemon, and the US played a key role in constructing the multilateral order, but it was the peculiar nature of *American* hegemony, and the embedded liberal bargain struck with European powers, that were critical.[13]

Socialization into the World Culture

If the social is marginalized in the previous two accounts it is front and centre in the explanation advanced by sociological institutionalists of the Stanford School. Furthermore, where the other accounts connect discrete periods of decolonization to discrete periods of hegemony, geopolitical rivalry, imperial incapacity, or economic expansion, the Stanford School seeks to explain decolonization as a linear process, accelerating over several centuries.

Their starting point is world society's modernist culture, a culture grounded in early modern Christianity and capitalism, and characterized by rational bureaucratic values; values that license the construction of rational bureaucratic states. As this culture has globalized, and its core values spread, it has encouraged the spread of modern nation-states. In this respect, 'nation-states are more or less exogenously constructed entities—the many individuals both inside and outside the state who engage in state formation and policy formulation are enactors of scripts rather more than they are self-directed actors'.[14] The Stanford School posits two mechanisms that connect modernist world culture to the proliferation of states. The first is the 'transmission of the nation-state model from Western powers to their dependencies'; the second is imitation, where early decolonization is copied by later anti-colonial movements.[15] Either way, the emphasis is on the diffusion of a nation-state norm, first vertically, from the metropole to the periphery, then horizontally, across the colonial and postcolonial worlds. Together, these mechanisms of socialization are said to explain not only the globalization of the sovereign state system, but also the acceleration of this process, especially after 1945.

There are numerous problems with this explanation, many of which are exposed in the following chapters. The idea that the rational bureaucratic state is a Western invention contradicts everything we know about the classical Chinese state. The image of state builders—Western or postcolonial—as

---

[12] This complexity is evident in Christopher Hobson's fine account of the rise of democracy as the dominant conception of legitimate political rule. See Hobson 2015.
[13] Ruggie 1993a: 31.   [14] Meyer et al. 1997: 150.   [15] Strang 1990: 847.

nothing more than enactors of scripts not only denies them any real agency, it is challenged by more recent literatures on norm localization.[16] And the notion that the norm of the nation-state diffused through simple, highly passive, processes of socialization washes out the contestation that surrounded any such processes, as well as how the norms themselves were transformed through struggle.[17]

What interests us here, however, is the thinness of this sociological account. In contrast to the previous two accounts, decolonization is understood here as a social process. This is a very thin social process, though, comprising little more than the diffusion of highly simplified norms of the nation-state, blind to the radical changes in conceptions of legitimate statehood that occurred in the eighteenth and nineteenth centuries. More than this, the understanding of the emergent international social order is equally thin. Over the years the Stanford School has produced numerous, often quantitative, studies of global isomorphism, showing striking patterns of policy convergence and regularities in practice across the member states of international society. Yet they are silent on the institutional structures and practices of international society itself. Its complex politics of membership and political legitimacy, its architecture of basic institutional practices, its dense network of functional regimes, and its shifting patterns of political, economic, and cultural resistance—all of these are occluded.

Incorporation into International Society

Against this background we can now detail the distinctive features of Bull and Watson's account. Three caveats are needed before proceeding, however. First, although we and our contributors identify a particular argument and approach with *The Expansion*, and we label this, by way of shorthand, the 'Bull and Watson' argument or account, we are mindful that theirs was a collaborative project, and that this argument was only loosely carried through *The Expansion*'s chapters. Some of their contributors only faintly echoed the thesis Bull and Watson set out in their framing chapters, while others amplify key elements. Second, *The Expansion* is located within a broader corpus of English School scholarship, and identifying and interpreting its central themes requires drawing connections with salient themes and propositions within that corpus. We readily acknowledge that others might draw these connections in different ways. Lastly, Bull and Watson did not necessarily see eye to eye on all aspects of what we will now call 'their' argument or account. Richard Little calls *The Expansion* the 'dominant' English School account, but notes

---

[16] See, for example, Acharya 2004, 2009.   [17] See Reus-Smit 2013a.

that eight years after its publication, and seven after Bull's untimely death, Watson published a quite different, less Eurocentric account of his own.[18] Elsewhere, others continue to unravel fine distinctions among classic English School writings on *The Expansion*,[19] but our purpose here is simply to draw out the central features of the 'Bull and Watson' account.

The Expansion was written in the shadow of Bull's classic work *The Anarchical Society*. There Bull argued that states could form not merely international systems—quasi-physical realms of bare interaction—but also international societies. Such societies 'exist when a group of states, conscious of certain common interests and common values, form a society in the sense that they conceive themselves to be bound by a common set of rules in their relations with one another, and share in the workings of common institutions'.[20] Historically, Bull held that a Christian version of such a society first emerged in sixteenth- and seventeenth-century Europe. This order secularized during the nineteenth century, and then spread to encompass the globe during the twentieth.[21] *The Expansion* takes up this history, exploring 'the expansion of the international society of European states across the rest of the globe, and its transformation from a society fashioned in Europe and dominated by Europeans into the global international society of today'.[22]

As noted in Chapter 1, Bull and Watson present the 'expansion' of international society as a process of rational incorporation. International society was a rule-governed order, and it expanded by admitting new rule-observant members. But like any club, how one admitted new members, and on what criteria, was a crucial issue that became especially difficult in the nineteenth century, when the aspiring members were increasingly non-European. In his chapter on China's entry into international society, Gerrit Gong posed this issue succinctly: 'the European powers faced the challenge and difficulty of drawing the non-European countries into their system of international relations in an orderly and humane way, as much as possible within the international legal guidelines which were themselves evolving to cope with the expanding domain of international law'.[23]

To deal with this problem, the European powers codified into international law a 'standard of civilization' that specified the legal criteria aspiring polities had to meet if they were to gain sovereign recognition.[24] This was a notorious instrument of European domination, which divided the world's peoples into civilized, barbarian, and savage categories, and justified European imperialism over the non-civilized world. *The Expansion* dwells little on this, though,

---

[18] Little 2005: 45; Watson 1992.

[19] For several detailed and nuanced accounts of the writing of *The Expansion* see Vigezzi 2005; Dunne 1998; and essays by Buzan and Little 2014; Dunne and Little 2014; Epp 2014; Suganami 2014; Vigezzi 2014.

[20] Bull 1977: 13. [21] Bull 1977: 27–40.

[22] Bull and Watson 1984b: 1. [23] Gong 1984a: 171. [24] See Gong 1984b.

focusing instead on how non-European polities—the Americas, the Ottoman Empire, China, and Japan—eventually[met the criteria and gained admission to international society. After 1945 the standard of civilization was abandoned, and colonial peoples gained a categorical right to self-determination.[25] Protracted struggle surrounded all of this, but *The Expansion* focuses on processes of voluntary incorporation. As Bull explains:

[handwritten margin note: Voluntary incorp.]

> The non-European or non-Western majority of states in the world today, which played little role in shaping the foundations of the international society to which they now belong, have sought naturally and properly to modify it so that it will reflect their own special interests. It should not be overlooked, however, that by seeking a place in this society they have given their consent to its basic rules and institutions.[26]

The Expansion is not just an exploration of a history Bull sketched in *The Anarchical Society*. It further expresses, and seeks to reason through, an abiding anxiety he had about the viability of a global international society. Undergirding both *The Anarchical Society* and *The Expansion* is an assumption that international societies grow out of unitary cultural foundations. This had been clearly articulated by Martin Wight, who argued that 'a states system will not come into being without a degree of cultural unity among its members'.[27] Bull echoed this in *The Anarchical Society*, claiming that past international societies 'were all founded upon a common culture or civilization', and that this aids 'the definition of common rules and the evolution of common institutions' and 'reinforce[s] the sense of common interests that impels states to accept common rules and institutions with a sense of common values'.[28] Wight feared that as decolonization brought more and more non-European states into the system, international society had 'outrun cultural and moral community'.[29] Bull stressed the pragmatic reasons states had to observe the rules and practices of international society, but he too worried about its dissolving cultural foundations. Not only does global international society lack a common civilizational base, 'diplomatic culture' is an elite affair, and 'international political culture'—the 'intellectual and moral culture that determines the attitudes toward the states system of the societies that compose it'—is largely absent.[30]

[handwritten margin note: The theory of IS]

After considering the 'challenge to Western dominance' that brought about the dissolution of Europe's empires, the final section of *The Expansion* examines the viability of international society in a culturally diverse global system. Bull and Watson took it as given that 'the cultural heterogeneity of the global international society of today is evidently a factor making against consensus

---

[25] See Jackson 1990.   [26] Bull 1984b: 124.   [27] Wight 1977: 22.
[28] Bull 1977: 16.   [29] Wight 1977: 33.   [30] Bull 1977: 316–17.

about its underlying rules and institutions'.[31] For some of their contributors, most notably Adda Bozeman, this gravely weakened international society.[32] Bull and Watson were more sanguine, though, stressing the pragmatic imperatives holding international society together, and speculating about the binding potential of the cosmopolitan culture of modernity. They argue that 'perceived common interest will often lead to the improvisation of the rules even in the absence of a common culture', and that '[i]nternational legal, diplomatic, and administrative institutions...clearly do rest upon a cosmopolitan culture of modernity, to which the leading elements of all contemporary societies belong even if the masses of the people often do not'.[33] This latter point echoed Bull's thoughts in *The Anarchical Society*, where he suggested that the 'future of international society is likely to be determined...by the preservation and extension of cosmopolitan culture...that can provide the world international society of today with the kind of underpinning enjoyed by geographically smaller and culturally more heterogeneous international societies of the past'.[34]

Of the four accounts of the globalization of international society considered here, only Bull and Watson's has a robust conception of the social order that became global. The two materialist accounts focus solely on the geopolitical and economic forces driving imperial fragmentation, telling us how successor sovereign states proliferated but nothing about the international social order they entered or constituted. The Stanford School highlights social processes of diffusion and socialization, attributing the global spread of nation-states to the culture of modernity, its attendant model of the rational bureaucratic state, and mechanisms of transmission and imitation. Yet beyond shared norms of the nation-state, this account says little more about the emergent international social order: its institutional architecture, constitutive practices, and inherent frailties. By comparison, Bull and Watson have a thicker conception of international society, imagining it as a society of mutual recognition, grounded in common interests and values, and sustained by common rules and institutions. Of course, this is a result of where they started. Unlike the other accounts, they began with a conception of international society, complete with foundational norms and basic institutional practices, and then asked how such a society expanded from Europe to encompass the globe.

But if this is a virtue at one level, it is a vice at another. *The Expansion* contains no explicit theory of international social change, even if several

No account of Change

---

[31] Bull and Watson 1984a: 432.

[32] She argued that 'an international system is as solid as the concepts that combine to compose it. Such concepts are solid if they are equally meaningful in the different local orders that are encompassed by the international system. We do not have such a globally meaningful system because world society consists today as it did before the nineteenth century of a plurality of diverse political systems, each an outgrowth of culture-specific concepts.' Bozeman 1984: 404.

[33] Bull and Watson 1984a: 435.   [34] Bull 1977: 317.

conceptions of change are at work at various points in its narrative.[35] Theories of international social change identify prevailing social structural conditions, as well as their potential for change, and specify 'what kinds of choices made by agents, and what kinds of adjacent processes, are likely to activate those transformative dispositions and generate new structural arrangements'.[36] No such theory exists in *The Expansion*. Instead, it consists of a series of inter-linked empirical narratives, structured and informed by an *a priori* conception of international society, one drawn largely from Bull's earlier writings. As noted earlier, this approach gives Bull and Watson's account a robust con-ception of the globalizing social order, but it has the perverse effect of limiting how *The Expansion* understands the processes of globalization. Because Bull and Watson and their contributors have no independent theory of inter-national social change, it is the concept of international society that structures their narratives of expansion, highlighting some dynamics while occluding others. This is accentuated by Bull's dichotomous mode of conceptualization, in which concepts are articulated within dyadic, or at times triadic, distinctions: society/system, international/world society, order/justice, and so on. The empirical narratives advanced in *The Expansion* are thus not only structured by the concept of international society, but by this broader architecture of conceptual distinctions.

[Handwritten margin note: Can't account for globalization]

CONCEPTUAL INNOVATIONS

Like *The Expansion*, this book provides no theory of international social change. We have pursued this in other work but chose here neither to impose our individual commitments on our fellow contributors nor squeeze out of them any new theoretical position. Instead, we have taken the more modest path of conceptual revision. Like Bull and Watson, we see the emergence of a global society of states as a landmark development in world politics worthy of sustained analysis. But thirty years of new scholarship, both within IR and other fields, has exposed the limits of their conceptual apparatus, as well as the blinkering effects it had on their historical account. This is reflected in our contributors' chapters, where their analyses not only sit uncomfortably within Bull and Watson's conceptual framework, but where they often challenge the

---

[35] The approach of scholars such as Herbert Butterfield and Wight—reflected also in Bull's work—was to uncover the reasons for institutional resilience rather than change. This led the English School to examine, primarily, the patterns of prevailing norms as embodied in the words and deeds of practitioners. For example, how the idea of the balance of power was given concrete historical expression in legal treaties and diplomatic language.

[36] Nexon 2009: 23.

veracity of its key definitions and distinctions. So as to better accommodate these analyses, we now propose a series of conceptual revisions.

Globalization not Expansion

Bull and Watson describe the transformation of international society from a European affair to a global political order as a process of 'expansion'. Elsewhere we too have used this language, employing it to describe, first, 'the increase over three to four centuries in the number and geographical spread of the system's constituent states', and second, 'the evolution and transmission of the legitimating institutions that sustain sovereignty'.[37] We are now persuaded, however, of the limitations of this terminology.

To begin with, saying that something 'expands' implies that it simply gets bigger; that as an entity it remains essentially the same but grows in size. When a balloon expands, for example, nothing changes in its basic makeup (beyond, of course, some molecular attenuation that eventually reaches a breaking point). This is essentially how Bull and Watson think about the transformation of international society. While their narratives note developments such as the nineteenth-century secularization of international society and the rise and decline of the standard of civilization, they state repeatedly that the expanding society of states was 'European' in character, and that new members, most of whom were non-European, 'embraced such basic elements of European international society as the sovereign state, the rules of international law, the procedures and conventions of diplomacy and international organization'.[38] Yet in reality, as international society became global it transformed in far-reaching ways. Underlying conceptions of the moral purpose of the state changed from Absolutism to popular sovereignty, the hybrid world of sovereignty in the core and empire abroad collapsed, and as Audie Klotz and Ann E. Towns demonstrate in Chapters 19 and 20, the racial and gender hierarchies that undergirded social and political power were reconstituted. The process of becoming global was precisely that, therefore: a process of 'becoming'.

Second, the notion of expansion, at least as used by Bull and Watson, privileges endogenous generative dynamics. International society emerged through processes internal to European society, it extended its global reach via European imperialism, these empires collapsed because of European weakness, and new members were drawn to international society by the magnetic pull of its constituent institutions. As the following chapters demonstrate, however, exogenous cultural, social, economic, and political forces were deeply implicated in all of these developments. European international

---

[37] Reus-Smit 2013a: 19, 22.   [38] Bull and Watson 1984a: 433.

society, like European society more broadly, was shaped by diverse civilizational engagements and encounters. The institutional architecture of evolving international society—its diplomatic practices and legal regime, in particular —were profoundly affected by the imperial project. The wholesale dissolution of Europe's empires after 1945 was driven, in significant measure, by actors in the imperial periphery, who in Bull and Watson's schema were yet to be admitted to the society of states. These examples point not only to the salience of exogenous forces in the global development of international society, but to the unstable, even untenable, boundary between the endogenous and exogenous. Were those anti-colonial movements fighting for self-determination, for example, internal or external to international society? Both and neither, we would suggest.

For these reasons this book uses the term 'globalization' rather than 'expansion'. In an earlier section we bracketed the distinction between the two, suggesting, for our purposes then, that both refer to 'becoming global'. Nothing we say now contradicts this. In a minimal sense, both do refer to the numerical increase in recognized sovereign states, the geographical spread of such states, and the development of a global institutional architecture to sustain a universal sovereign order. Yet the term globalization captures more than this. It captures not just the numerical, geographical, and institutional extension of international society, but its transformation in the process—its 'becoming' a qualitatively different international society than its European progenitor. More than this, it captures the global constitution of this society, the fact that its development was the product of global social forces. Globalization thus refers not just to international society becoming global, in both minimal and more expansive senses, but also to its global production.

It should be clear by now that we are not using 'globalization' in the conventional way. Since the 1990s the term has referred to heightened transnational interconnections and interdependencies, propelled by intensified global trade, production, and finance, new information and communication technologies, and looming crises of the global commons. Globalization, in this sense of the word, is often seen as inimical to a world organized into sovereign states, eroding the state's capacity to exercise supreme authority within its exclusive territorial jurisdiction.[39] Not only do we define globalization differently from this conventional usage, we see it as a process that led to, and institutionalized, this world of states. Note, though, that historically these two

---

[39] Within the extensive literature on globalization, scholars are divided on the implications for the sovereign state, with 'hyperglobalists' most confident in heralding its demise. An early mapping of this debate can be found in Held et al. 1999. More recently, the globalization debate is seen as having moved through three phases, with more recent work offering a more complex assessment of the impact of globalization on the sovereign state. A good overview of these developments is Martell 2007. For a recent discussion of the impact of globalization on political authority, see Held 2013.

forms of globalization have been related. As several of our contributors explain, early forms of globalization (in the conventional sense) played a key role in international society's initial phases of globalization (in our sense).[40]

Social All the Way Down

Throughout this book we refer to the globalization of international *society*, the same terminology used by Bull and Watson. Our understanding of the term is somewhat different to theirs, however. Like them, we use it to describe a distinctive configuration of political authority, one comprising multiple centres of independent, territorially bounded authority, grounded in mutual recognition, and sustained by institutional rules and practices. Where we differ, however, is on the distinction Bull drew between an international society and an international *system*,[41] a distinction that reappears in *The Expansion* as a way of talking about different degrees of international sociability. Bull and Watson feared, for example, that in the wake of decolonization, and at the height of the second Cold War, social bonds between states were eroding: international relations were becoming more systemic. The distinction sits uncomfortably, however, with a key insight of the wave of constructivist scholarship that came after the publication of *The Expansion*: that there is no such thing as a pre- or non-social international system.

Bull's primary concern in *The Anarchical Society* was determining the conditions of order among sovereign states, and his distinction between international society and system is best understood in this context. In his schema, international order and international society stand in a relationship of mutual dependence. International order, he argues, is 'a pattern of activity that sustains the elementary or primary goals of the society of states, or international society'.[42] The definition of the former thus presupposes the existence of the latter. And while international order is meant to serve the goals of international society, in Bull's account it is the rules and institutions of that society that generate order. 'Within international society ... order is the consequence ... of common interests in the elementary goals of social life; rules prescribing behavior that sustains these goals; and institutions that help make these rules effective'.[43]

International order, for Bull, is far from given: it is a desirable but allusive good. But if this is the case, he needs a way of conceptualizing relations among states when order is non-existent. 'International society' won't serve this

[40] See, for example, Chapter 3.
[41] For a detailed discussion of this distinction, including the different positions taken by classical English School scholars on the matter, see Dunne and Little 2014.
[42] Bull 1977: 8.   [43] Bull 1977: 65.

purpose, because it has forged such a close connection between order and society. A breakdown of international order is not merely a failure to realize the primary goals of the society of states; it is a failure of the rules and institutions that constitute that society. The concept of 'international system' is Bull's way of describing relations among states in the absence of society and order, the latter understood as a pattern of activity that sustains the elementary goals of the former. 'A *system of states* (or international system) is formed', he writes, 'when two or more states have sufficient contact between them, and have sufficient impact on one another's decisions, to cause them to behave—at least in some measure—as parts of a whole.'[44] As Barry Buzan explains, from this perspective, international systems are realms of physical/mechanical interaction, lacking any social content.[45]

While distinguishing between society and system flowed from Bull's concern with international order, the distinction has been widely criticized, principally on the grounds that international systems are always social. Alexander Wendt provided the most celebrated theoretical elaboration of this position, nicely encapsulated in his oft-quoted phrase 'anarchy is what states make of it'.[46] International systems have intersubjective as well as material structures, Wendt contended. Not only are these constituted through social practices, they shape the identities (and hence interests) of states, and affect how they understand (and respond) to the material conditions of anarchy.

If this is the case, Buzan contends, Bull's distinction between society and system breaks down.[47] If an international system—Hobbesian, Lockeian, or Kantian—always has social content, on what grounds can it constitute a separate form of inter-state interaction, one categorically distinct from an international society. Social interaction among states is impossible without physical interaction, but if such interaction is always embedded in social meanings then the concept of an international system, defined as a realm of physical interaction, has declining analytical utility. This is more than a theoretical nicety. As Buzan and others have pointed out, it is hard to find empirical examples of international systems as Bull understood them. For instance, it is often argued that mutual recognition is a key marker of society among states. As Wight puts it, 'not only must each claim independence of any political authority for itself, but each must recognize the validity of the same claim by all others'.[48] Yet as Christian Reus-Smit explains, the politics of

---

[44] Bull 1977: 10, emphasis in original.

[45] Buzan 2004: 98–108. Compare with Buzan 1993. Note that Buzan's earlier article viewed the system as a signifier of material capabilities and how these are distributed. The point here is not which of his readings is 'right' so much as noting that the system can be invoked as an analytical category that signifies structural characteristics which are basic determinants of international order at any historical moment. Bull (1977: 181) refers to war 'as a basic determinant of the shape of the system at any one time'.

[46] Wendt 1992.   [47] Buzan 2004: 106.   [48] Wight 1977: 23.

recognition attends all forms of inter-state interaction.[49] Bull admitted that an international system might display a wide spectrum of interactions: they 'may take the form of co-operation, but also conflict, or even neutrality or indifference with regard to one another's objectives'.[50] How such interactions are possible without recognition is decidedly unclear.

Given all of this, we and our contributors draw no distinction between international society and system, theoretically or historically.[51] As a consequence, nowhere will you find in the following chapters claims that an international system temporally or geographically preceded international society, or that as sociability declined among states relations became more systemic: all claims found in *The Expansion*. Rather, as the following section explains, we treat international society as a particular kind of social structural formation, preceded by, and embedded within, wider networks of global social and political interaction. And rather than seeing declining sociability as a marker of systemic politics, we see conflict and contestation as integral to any international social order.

International Society and the World Political System

In *The Anarchical Society*, Bull distinguished between international society, on the one hand, and the world political system, on the other. His definition of the former needs no repeating here. He defined the latter, however, as 'the worldwide network of interaction that embraces not only states but also other political actors, both "above" and "below" it'.[52] He denied that this system constituted in any way a 'world society', but insisted that international society had always existed within a broader world of political actors and relations: 'The states system has always been part of a wider system of interaction in which groups other than states are related to each other, to foreign states and to international and supranational bodies, as well as to the states in which they are located.'[53]

Curiously, his discussion of the world political system appears towards the end of *The Anarchical Society*, as he turned his attention to the possible decline of the states system.[54] He considers it only as a possible challenge or alternative to a world organized into sovereign states, a site in which to evaluate the impact of non-governmental and transnational actors. Nowhere does he consider the long-term constitutive effects of the world political system on the development of international society. While insisting that states have

---

[49] Reus-Smit 2013a: 17–18.   [50] Bull 1977: 10.

[51] Indeed, we could easily speak of the globalization of the international *system*, stressing, of course, the inherently social nature of such a system. This is the move Reus-Smit (2013a: 18–19) made elsewhere.

[52] Bull 1977: 276.   [53] Bull 1977: 278.   [54] Bull 1977: chapter 11.

always been embedded within a broader framework of political interaction, he showed little interest in how the latter conditioned the former. Not surprisingly, *The Expansion* largely ignores the constitutive role of the world political system. To the extent that it considers European international society's interactions with 'African political communities', the Ottoman Empire, Russia, China, and Japan, the focus is on European impact, not the reverse.

In contrast, we and our contributors takes seriously the idea that international society emerged and globalized within a broader world political system, and see its evolution as profoundly affected by social interactions within that system. This is usefully described in the language of relational sociology. We understand international society as a governance assemblage: one in which the principal political units are sovereign states, there is a distinctive institutional architecture that licenses these units and shapes their interactions, and where there are powerful endogenous processes and practices that help reproduce and reconstitute the assemblage over time. Furthermore, we see international society as a particularly important, and historically unique, assemblage, the globalization of which has had a profound effect on the contours and dynamics of world politics.

In describing international society as a governance assemblage, we are attributing to it a particular structural form, even if this form is in constant change. It is more than a set of interactions, therefore: it is an association constituted and sustained by institutional meanings and practices, as well as diverse material phenomena. Because of this structural form, our project is to understand something that is, at any given point in time, 'already assembled', to use Bruno Latour's terminology.[55] Yet because we are centrally concerned with the globalization of international society, we are primarily interested in what Latour describes as 'the tracing of new associations and the designing of their assemblages', with 'accounting for how society [in this case international society] is held together'.[56]

If global international society is a distinctive governance assemblage, it has evolved over the course of the past five centuries within a context of, and through interaction with, a shifting panoply of individual and institutional actors, coalescing around diverse social and political assemblages, each of which has constituted a distinct locus of social and political power—a world political system. In the following chapters, our contributors explore the constitutive effects of the broader system prior to the initial emergence of sovereign states in Europe, show how engagement with non-Western peoples and polities shape the evolving European order, and examine the diverse forms of contestation currently emanating from the contemporary world political system, as well as from within the society of states itself.

[55] Latour 2005: 12.   [56] Latour 2005: 13.

Power and Contestation

When Bull argued that international society exists when states share common values and interests, accept rules governing their interactions, and build and maintain institutions to uphold these rules, he encouraged a view of international society as a realm of settled norms. By showing the historical reality of such a society, and providing a theoretical reason for its existence, he moved us well beyond the realist insistence that society was impossible without a central authority. One consequence of this conception of international society, however, was that it muted the analysis of power and contestation. We have already seen this in Bull and Watson's understanding of expansion as a rational process of incorporation, where faced with the problem of admitting non-European peoples, Europe's imperial powers set legal standards of civilizational achievement, and when non-European polities met these standards they were admitted to the club of states. Missing from this account is the violence of imperialism and the revolutionary struggles required to dismantle it.

Power and contestation do, of course, appear in *The Expansion*, but in ways consistent with the overarching conception of international society as a realm of settled norms. The expanding society of states was a club of legally equal sovereigns, but it also had important dimensions of institutionalized hierarchy. Within the club, great powers were given special responsibilities for the maintenance of international order; responsibilities that carried with them a host of concomitant rights. Similarly, relations between international society and the world beyond were hierarchically ordered, with the standard of civilization ranking peoples, licensing gradations of European control and tutelage, and ordaining European states with the power of recognition.

The discussion of contestation in *The Expansion* takes a similar form, evident most clearly in the two versions of Bull's essay on 'the revolt against the West', one of which appeared in *The Expansion*, the other in his Hagey Lectures. Although no hard line can be drawn between these versions, the first is concerned primarily with what might be termed 'incorporative contestation'—contestation by non-European peoples aimed at admission to, and equality within, the club of states. In *The Expansion*, Bull identifies five phases in the revolt against the West: the struggle for equal sovereignty by formally independent states, such as China and Japan; the anti-colonial struggle by formally subjected peoples in Asia, Africa, the Caribbean, and the Pacific; the struggle for racial equality within white-dominated states; the struggle for economic justice; and the struggle for cultural liberation.[57] Each of these forms of struggle is compatible with Bull and Watson's view of the expansion of international society as a process of incorporation, as none are seen as

---

[57] Bull 1984c: 220–3.

challenging the core norms of European international society. In the Hagey Lectures, Bull's understanding of contestation is different. There he is concerned with 'corrosive contestation' that threatened to undermine international society itself. The focus is no longer on the revolt that attended the expansion of international society, but on revolt within the resulting global society of states. Reversing his earlier argument in *The Anarchical Society* about the priority of order over justice, he claimed that unless the West met Third World demands of international economic justice, developing states would have no stake in the order, no reason to observe its basic rules and practices.[58]

This book seeks to move beyond the structural treatment of power found in *The Expansion*, and to see contestation not just as incorporative or corrosive, but as an engine of international social development. The principal good international society distributes is membership. Recognized sovereign states have a bundle of basic rights: rights that constitute them as particular kinds of polities, and rights that give them legitimate social and political powers. Polities denied recognition lack these rights, depriving them of the ontological status of sovereign statehood, and circumscribing their realm of legitimate political action. International society is not only an assemblage of institutionalized power, therefore the unequal distribution of rights and status upon which it rests invites contestation. Furthermore, because such contestation is about recognition and rights—agency and legitimate action—it is always, and necessarily, a struggle for power. The globalization of international society was a product of such struggle, and contestation was one of the principal mechanisms through which international society transformed as it globalized.

This perspective on power and contestation raises again the question of endogenous and exogenous social forces in the globalization of international society. Bull's notion of international society as a realm of settled norms, and the associated assumption that colonial peoples lay outside international society until the moment of admission, suggests that their struggles were exogenous. We are suggesting here, however, that when international society distributes status and rights to some while denying them to others, it is structuring social relations beyond the narrow confines of the club of states. Furthermore, this structuring of wider social and political relations generates contestation, which has in turn had transformative effects on international society. The distinction between exogenous and endogenous social forces is of declining utility in such a context. As explained earlier, our solution is to treat international society as a particular kind of governance assemblage, characterized by distinctive norms and practices, but embedded within, and constituted by, the broader social universe of the world political system. So long as

[58] Bull 1983: 32.

Late-Bull reverses his stance on order over justice

"The principle good IS distributes is membership."

power is understood primarily in structural terms, and the focus is on incorporative contestation, grasping this embedded relationship will prove elusive.

The Ubiquity of Cultural Diversity

As we saw earlier, *The Expansion* echoes a long-standing assumption within the English School that international societies emerge out of unitary cultural contexts, that a common culture is essential if states are to have the common values and interests that sustain society under anarchy. Wight was insistent about this, and even though Bull stressed the pragmatic reasons states sought the protections of society, he too saw a common cultural background as a necessary, if not sufficient, condition for international social order. Only by recognizing this background assumption can we explain the persistent anxiety, fully expressed in *The Expansion*, about the viability of a global society of states; a society inherently, and inextricably, culturally diverse. And only by understanding this does Bull's less than confident hope in the binding effects of world cosmopolitan culture make any sense.

A very different perspective on culture and international society emerges from the following chapters, one that emphasizes the ubiquity of diversity and the crucial role cultural interaction and hybridity played in the development of international society.[59] Whether we are talking about the initial cultural context in which the European society of states first emerged or the cultural dynamics of its globalization, diversity, exchange, and fusion appear the norm, not monocultural constitution, a picture consistent with work in other disciplines. It is axiomatic now in anthropology, cultural studies, and sociology that there is no such thing as a unitary culture: all cultural formations are highly variegated, profoundly contradictory, loosely bounded, and deeply interpenetrated. As Anne Swidler explained some time ago, 'all real cultures contain diverse, often conflicting symbols, rituals, stories, and guides to action'.[60] This finding is so significant that some anthropologists argue that we should no longer study culture per se, but focus instead on the organization of diversity.[61] Unlike IR scholars, political theorists of multiculturalism were quick to emphasize the ubiquity of cultural diversity. For James Tully, culture is a 'strange multiplicity',

---

[59] See, for example, Phillips's account of early modern, cross-civilizational globalization (Chapter 3), Heather Rae's discussion of how European self-identity was shaped by early encounters with the Ottomans and Aztecs (Chapter 4), Spruyt's exploration of how the effects of economic interaction between different regional orders facilitated 'an inter-ecumenical flow of cultural ideas and material practices' (Chapter 5), Yongjin Zhang's argument that European self-understandings were profoundly affected by contingent knowledge of China (Chapter 11), and Gerry Simpson's account of the development of global law, which is less a story of the expansion of European forms of law than one of the 'hybridization of parallel legal orders' (Chapter 14).

[60] Swidler 1986: 277.   [61] Hannerz 2010.

a 'tangled labyrinth of intertwining cultural differences *and* similarities'.[62] Alan Patten holds that '[i]n groups of any size, beliefs and practices are heterogeneous and contested. They change and fluctuate over time. And they are formed interactively and dialogically with members of other groups, often taking on a recognizably hybrid character as a result.'[63]

If this is true of culture in general, then the idea that international societies emerge out of unitary cultural contexts is a nonsense, betraying long outdated understandings of culture. Not surprisingly, a wave of new histories now show that most, if not all, historical international orders emerged in hetero-geneous, not homogeneous, cultural contexts. The early modern European order developed out of the cultural ferment of the Protestant Reformation (1520–1750),[64] the Qing Chinese order (1644–1911) was characterized by 'intertwined cultural diversity',[65] and the Ottoman order (1299–1908) 'was not just Ottoman, Turkish, or Islamic. It was all of these combined with Roman and Byzantine, Balkan, and Turco-Mongol institutions and practices'.[66] What is more, these histories show that the management, or governance, of diversity was a key imperative of order-building, and institutions emerged in all of these orders to define and discipline cultural difference. As many scholars have noted, the institution of sovereignty was itself a solution to Europe's religious wars of the sixteenth and seventeenth centuries. Qing China developed the Lifanyuan system for governing ethnic minorities, and in the Ottoman Empire, the Janissary and Millet systems evolved to govern relations between Muslims, Christians, and Jews.[67]

The development of such institutions fits with a further insight from anthro-pology, cultural studies, and sociology. If culture is inherently diverse, what gives it form? One highly suggestive answer is that diversity is structured by social institutions. Such institutions are, of course, cultural artefacts themselves. But once constituted, and once instantiated in routinized social practices, institutions condition the 'flow' of culture. In Ulf Hannerz's words, '[i]n the continuous interdependence of "the social" and "the cultural"...the social structure of persons and relationships channels the cultural flow at the same time as it is being, in part, culturally produced'.[68] Recent research on multicul-turalism and racial justice has highlighted this structuring role of institutions. Kenan Malik explains how complex heterogeneity is structured by the institu-tions of multiculturalism, producing authorized forms of diversity, 'putting people into ethnic and cultural boxes...and defining their needs and rights accordingly'.[69] Similarly, Ellen Berrey shows how institutionalized 'diversity' policies have reconfigured the racial order of the United States.[70]

---

[62] Tully 1995: 11.   [63] Patten 2014: 40.   [64] Cameron 2012.
[65] Hao 2012: 91.   [66] Barkey 2008: 8.
[67] See Chia 2012; Barkey 2008; Goodwin 2006.
[68] Hannerz 1992: 14.   [69] Malik 2015: 21-2.   [70] Berrey 2015: 15.

Exploring systematically this relationship between institutional development and the management of cultural diversity in the globalization of international society is beyond the scope of this book.[71] As noted earlier, though, our contributors shed considerable light on the generative effects of cultural diversity, on how complex cultural interactions shaped the evolving global order. This itself is a significant departure from Bull and Watson's account, where diversity is considered, first, as a characteristic of global international society—a departure from the norm—and second, as a corrosive not generative phenomenon. Several of our contributors also touch on the development of international institutions for the management of diversity, including sovereignty (Chapter 12), standards of civilization (Chapter 10), the global racial order (Chapter 19), and the construction of global gender hierarchies (Chapter 20). Although far from comprehensive, this work challenges Bull and Watson's understanding of the cultural problematic of global international society. For them, the issue was how international society would survive in a culturally diverse world. From the perspective advanced here, by contrast, the issue is how a global society of states, already profoundly shaped by complex cultural interactions, and with a history of shifting institutional practices for the management of diversity, will accommodate new articulations of cultural difference, especially in the context of shifting global power relations.

CONCLUSION

Bull and Watson were clear that they addressed the development of global international society from a particular standpoint. They took it as given 'that international political life, including its normative and institutional dimension, has its own logic and is not to be understood simply as the reflection of economic interests or productive processes'.[72] They stressed the importance of cultural differences, and declared an interest in the moral issues raised by their subject. Most importantly, they held that their 'subject can be understood only in historical perspective, and that without an awareness of the past that generated it, the universal international society of the present can have no meaning'.[73] There is little in this book that challenges any of these commitments: indeed, it is animated by very similar sensibilities.

It will be clear from the preceding discussion, however, that *The Expansion* furthered Bull and Watson's commitments in a very particular way. This chapter has sought to locate their approach in relation to other accounts of international society's globalization—a comparison not undertaken

---

[71] This is part of a larger project, however, currently led by Reus-Smit.
[72] Bull and Watson 1984b: 9.   [73] Bull and Watson 1984b.

elsewhere—and to clarify the perspective advanced here. We have proposed a series of significant conceptual revisions to Bull and Watson's schema, revisions essential to accommodate the complex processes and dynamics associated with the globalization of international society. Of the existing accounts, Bull and Watson's is the only one with a robust conception of the international social order that emerged through imperial fragmentation and the proliferation of sovereign states. But this strength is compromised by problematic distinctions between society and system, insufficient attention to constitutive forces within the world political system, unnecessarily confined conceptions of power and contestation, and unsustainable understandings of culture. We have sought here to correct these conceptual limitations, opening space for a richer account of international society's globalization, an account brought to life in the following chapters.

Part II

Global Context

3

International Systems

Andrew Phillips

Influential English School works have historically cast the world in 1490 as comprising a constellation of self-contained and culturally unified regional international systems. For scholars such as Martin Wight, Hedley Bull, and Adam Watson, the globalization of international society entailed the relentless worldwide expansion from the late fifteenth century of one of these systems— the Western European one—until its institutions became universally dominant.[1] Against this interpretation, I advance an alternative perspective, which differs from the conventional account in three ways. First, it privileges themes of hybridity, rather than cultural and institutional uniformity, as being most deeply constitutive of international systems. Second, it foregrounds the dense webs of connectivity—manifest in Afro-Eurasian 'hemispheric integration'[2]—that were already reshaping the world before the sixteenth-century 'ages of discovery'. Third, it situates Latin Christendom as one of several expanding Afro-Eurasian civilizational complexes, which had become more internally diverse, externally differentiated, and mutually entangled in the centuries leading up to 1490.

This chapter endorses and expands on Bull's observation that 'the states system has always been part of a wider system of interaction'.[3] My central argument is that well before European international society's emergence, Latin Christendom had already been shaped through its entanglement with other Afro-Eurasian international systems. From the late fifteenth century, Western Europeans undeniably spearheaded a qualitatively higher increase in global interaction. But they did so off a foundation of pre-existing hemispheric interconnections. Before European international society spearheaded early modern globalization, it had itself first been constituted through an earlier wave of Afro-Eurasian hemispheric integration.[4] Late medieval hemispheric integration helped make European international society possible, before

---

[1] Bull and Watson 1984c; Wight 1977.   [2] Bentley 1998.
[3] Bull 1977: 268.   [4] Bentley 1998: 237.

European international society in turn coercively remade globalization in the centuries after 1490.

This chapter proceeds in three sections. Section one establishes my conceptual framework. This includes definitions of key terms, and a taxonomy of Afro-Eurasia's two main types of international systems prevailing in 1490. Section two then surveys these international systems in detail. I begin with the world's primary international economic systems: the Eurasian steppe (Saharasia)[5] and maritime Afro-Asia (the Indosphere). I then proceed to the Sinosphere, the Islamicate, and Latin Christendom. These civilizational complexes rested on hybrid syntheses of the local high cultures brought together through earlier waves of imperial consolidation. All three were also expanding rapidly in the late medieval period, as well as increasing in their internal diversity and external differentiation during this expansion. The chapter concludes by recapitulating my findings, before exploring the implications of my revisionism for our theoretical and historical understanding of international society's globalization in succeeding centuries.

No account of international systems can be completely comprehensive, and I have restricted my analysis to Afro-Eurasian international systems. I defend this move on two grounds. First, in 1490, the 'Afro-Eurasian ecumene'[6] encompassed most of the world's people, as well as most of the webs of inter-polity connection on which early modern globalization was later built. An Afro-Eurasian lens captures a far broader swathe of global interaction than a more traditional Eurocentric lens, without being so broad as to lose all conceptual focus. Second, in examining the world in 1490, we confront the reality that it was Afro-Eurasian civilizational complexes that expanded into the Americas, Oceania, and elsewhere, rather than vice versa. As Heather Rae's chapter in this volume demonstrates with respect to the Aztecs, New World international systems were far more sophisticated than first-generation English School scholars generally acknowledged. But these systems were less populous, smaller, and far less connected to one another than their Afro-Eurasian counterparts. Globalization and modern international society both originated out of late medieval entanglements among Afro-Eurasia's international systems. As this volume's primary focus is understanding international society's globalization, then, my geographic focus is restricted to the macro-region from which both modern international society and globalization first emerged.

---

[5] I take the term 'Saharasia' from Gommans 2007: 11.

[6] I take the idea of an Afro-Eurasian ecumene from Hodgson 1993: 17. The term encompasses the broad swathe of substantially urbanized agro-literate societies, interconnected by dense webs of commercial, cultural, military, and political exchange, which stretched from northern Africa, through the Mediterranean littoral, parts of northern Europe, the Asiatic steppe, and South and East Asia, from antiquity onwards. Hodgson 1963 develops the concept at length.

Last, a note on the intellectual resources from which I draw in the following account. This chapter draws inspiration from the 'Chicago school' of world history, and more generally from the subdiscipline of global history that it helped launch. Despite its ready availability, the contributors to *The Expansion of International Society* largely ignored the less Eurocentric world history that Marshall Hodgson and others had earlier pioneered at the University of Chicago.[7] In the thirty years since *The Expansion of International Society* was published, global history has blossomed as a distinct field of inquiry, and global historians have transformed our understanding of the centuries of inter-civilizational exchanges and encounters predating 1490.[8] International Relations scholars have drawn fruitfully from this literature to recast our understanding of the modern international system's polycentric foundations.[9] This chapter draws liberally from this scholarship, to provide a more genuinely global view of the fifteenth-century world from which international society eventually evolved.

CONCEPTUAL FRAMEWORK

Before outlining my approach to international systems, I must first define key terms. I begin with polities, international systems' constituent entities. I follow Yale Ferguson and Richard Mansbach's definition of polities, as bundles of authority ties possessing 'a distinct identity, a capacity to mobilize persons and resources for political ends, and a measure of institutionalization and hierarchy'.[10] This minimalist definition aims to capture the immense diversity of polity types that can comprise international systems. Beyond the states and empires that typically preoccupy IR scholars, the fifteenth-century world contained many other polity forms, including city-states, city-leagues, armed trading diasporas, and tribal confederacies.[11] Acknowledging this diversity is key to understanding the early modern world, before the globalization of European international society.

Just as heterogeneity defined fifteenth-century polities, so too did it also characterize Afro-Eurasia's international systems, which is why the chapter contests 'vanguardist' English School accounts of international society's expansion.[12] These accounts cast the fifteenth-century world as composed of neatly bounded and culturally coherent regional international societies. For

---

[7] See, for example, Hodgson 2009; McNeill 2009.

[8] For an overview of the field of global history, see generally Berg 2013.

[9] See, for example, Buzan and Lawson 2015b; Hobson 2004.

[10] Ferguson and Mansbach 1996: 262.   [11] Ferguson and Mansbach 1996.

[12] On the distinction between 'vanguardist' and 'syncretist' accounts of international society's expansion, see Buzan 2010: 3.

Wight, Bull, and Watson, international order arose in these societies out of cultural consensus, and the expanded possibilities for institutional construction this consensus enabled.[13] After 1490, European imperialism drew Europeans into contact with regions possessing radically different order-building traditions. Thus emerged a tension between culture and Columbus—between 'organic' regional orders grounded in local ideational consensus, and the imperatives of global order construction that European expansion brought into being. This tension supposedly resolved through the universal export of European international society, and the corresponding obliteration of non-European international societies.

This 'expansion' narrative is flawed on many levels, not least in its reliance on a clear distinction between international societies and international systems. Consistent with this volume's theoretical architecture, I reject hard distinctions between normatively 'thick' international societies versus international systems, composed of physical forms of interaction supposedly devoid of social content. As Tim Dunne and Christian Reus-Smit note, even in the absence of shared institutions, international systems are routinely constituted through social practices that shape actors' identities and interests.[14] Rather than positing a contrast between normatively 'thick' international societies and quasi-mechanical international systems, then, we are better served developing more fine-grained theoretical tools for unpacking the different types of international systems that constituted the fifteenth-century Afro-Eurasian ecumene. To do so, I draw from Barry Buzan and Richard Little's pioneering taxonomy of international systems, which distinguished different systems depending on their levels of integration at the cultural, military, diplomatic, and economic sectoral domains.[15]

Buzan and Little distinguished three distinct types of international system on the basis of the extent of sector-specific interactions that bound their units together. Two of these system types, what Buzan and Little called 'full international systems' and 'economic international systems'—are relevant to this discussion.[16] 'Full international systems' refers to systems exhibiting the whole gamut of interactions—military, political, economic, and socio-cultural—between their units.[17] 'Economic international systems' conversely encompass international systems that lack sustained military-political interaction, while nevertheless possessing high levels of economic and socio-cultural interaction.[18]

I draw inspiration from Buzan and Little's taxonomy, but adapt it to reflect the historical reality of the world in 1490. Corresponding closest to Buzan and Little's 'full' international systems, I argue, were Eurasia's primary civilizational complexes—the Sinosphere, the Islamicate, and Latin Christendom.

---

[13] Bull and Watson 1984c; Wight 1977.   [14] Chapters 1, 2, and 22 in this volume.
[15] Buzan and Little 2000: 94.   [16] Buzan and Little 2000: 96.
[17] Buzan and Little 2000: 96.   [18] Buzan and Little 2000.

Each of these civilizational complexes cohered around dense multi-ordinate interaction networks (military, political, economic, and socio-cultural) forged through earlier waves of imperial consolidation. Each possessed their own ordering institutions. Each also bore the hallmarks of extensive cultural hybridization. The high cultures integrating literate elites in these different international systems were irreducibly composite, permitting some communication and cross-pollination between these systems, despite their ostensible estrangement.

The term 'civilizational complex' has an august lineage among sociologists.[19] My use of it here may nevertheless provoke raised eyebrows, given my criticism of approaches conceiving international societies as resting on coherent and bounded 'civilization islands'. I defend my use of civilizational complexes here, because it acknowledges the importance of regionally dominant high cultures in shaping international societies' ordering institutions, without relying on Huntingtonian notions of culture as monolithic and closed to external influence. On the contrary, the notion of 'civilizational complex' is intended to get beyond the notion of civilizations as closed monads. Consistent with Jacinta O'Hagan's stress in Chapter 10 on the porous, politically constructed, and mutable character of civilizational identities, I stress here civilizational complexes' internal plurality, and their permeability to '"external" inputs from other civilizational complexes'.[20] The Sinosphere, the Islamicate, and Latin Christendom were sufficiently coherent, and possessed sufficiently distinctive ordering institutions and recognition practices, to warrant their comparability as civilizational complexes. Nevertheless, each grew more internally diverse and externally differentiated from one another in the late medieval period—precisely at the same time they were being drawn into greater contact with one another through hemispheric integration, via the super-circuits of Saharasia and the Indosphere.

Afro-Eurasia's civilizational complexes were entwined within two vast commercial interaction networks, traversing Eurasia's steppe and maritime frontiers. These super-circuits roughly conform to Buzan and Little's definition of economic international systems, characterized primarily by high economic and socio-cultural interaction, but only low to moderate military–diplomatic interaction.[21] IR scholars have unfairly neglected Saharasia and the Indosphere, despite their importance as the primary conveyor belts for cultural, commercial, and even microbial exchange between Afro-Eurasia's civilizational complexes. Their chief system-like characteristics and global significance are traced in this chapter.

---

[19] For an instructive discussion of the concept's genealogy in sociology, see generally Inglis 2010.

[20] Inglis 2010: 146.

[21] Although as we will see, Saharasia's growing violence interdependence in the late medieval period qualifies a purely economic characterization of it.

One of my central claims is that hemispheric integration, a form of 'proto-globalization',[22] drew Afro-Eurasia's civilizational complexes together in thickening webs of interdependence throughout the late medieval period. Throughout my analysis, I refer interchangeably to hemispheric integration and proto-globalization, which I understand in the traditional sense as a thickening of ties of connectivity across long distances, and especially across political frontiers and cultural boundaries. My approach thus draws heavily from global historians, who have sought to historicize globalization beyond the confines of the post-Columbian epoch.[23] This use of globalization contrasts with that of Dunne and Reus-Smit, who use the term in a very specific sense to refer to the concurrent spatial extension and substantive transformation of international society, as it spread globally through processes of struggle and contestation.[24] Although the two usages of globalization are distinct, I maintain they are commensurable, and indeed complementary. This is because Latin Christendom—the fountainhead of what became first European and then global international society—was itself first constituted in part through the radically expanded inter-civilizational contacts that attended late medieval 'proto-globalization'. 'The crystallization of Latin Christendom as a separate civilization was inseparable from its interaction with its "significant others"'.[25] The globalization of international society in the centuries after 1490 involved sustained contestation between European and non-European agents, as international society's institutional forms were made and remade through processes of colonization and decolonization. But European international society itself emerged from the chrysalis of Latin Christendom, a civilizational complex that formed alongside others through the proto-globalization that attended the late medieval period. It is now to an overview of both Latin Christendom and Afro-Eurasia's other international systems in 1490 that I turn.

THE WORLD IN 1490

The steppe and the sea: Commercial super-circuits in the Afro-Eurasian ecumene

The Eurasian steppe (Saharasia) and maritime Afro-Asia (the Indosphere) formed the primary connectors linking Afro-Eurasia's civilizational complexes in 1490. In Buzan and Little's taxonomy, they most closely approximate

---

[22] Inglis 2010: 146.   [23] See, for example, Hopkins 2002.
[24] Chapters 1, 2, and 22 in this volume.   [25] Arnason 2004: 37.

international economic systems. But for Saharasia especially, this characterization is imperfect. Long-distance trade undeniably constituted the most important force holding Saharasia together. Lacking anything like a system-wide diplomatic infrastructure, Saharasia was connected from Constantinople to Xi'an (north China) via an extensive *caravanserai* network.[26] *Caravanserais* provided lodgings for caravan traders plying the Silk Road, and formed the nuclei of the cosmopolitan oasis cities that dotted Afro-Eurasia's foremost land arterial.[27] These oasis cities fulfilled a function comparable to the Indosphere's port entrepôts, hosting self-governing merchant diasporas that collectively coordinated Saharasia's extensive long-distance trade.[28]

Nevertheless, Saharasia cannot be reduced purely to the Silk Road, for it also encompassed a vast Arid Zone from which pastoralist empire-builders periodically burst forth, massively disrupting neighbouring societies.[29] This territory included 'all the arid and semi-arid zones of Eurasia, in the north spanning from the eastern outskirts of Vienna to the Chinese Wall, in the south stretching from the Atlantic coast of the Maghreb to the south-eastern extremes of the Indian sub-continent'.[30] More than any other world region, Saharasia—with its vast grasslands and insulation from the tropical diseases of Monsoon Asia—has historically provided a highly conducive environment for horse-breeding.[31] Saharasia's grasslands consequently served as late medieval Eurasia's primary warhorse production centres, from which Indian and Chinese dynasties imported most of their cavalry mounts.[32] This economic and ecological niche provided the region's nomadic pastoralists with a potentially potent source of military and economic power, which they increasingly exploited from 1000.

Nomadic pastoralists from Saharasia had menaced neighbouring sedentary societies from antiquity. But from the eleventh century, Saharasian pastoralists integrated earlier technological developments—stirrups, deeper saddles, and other horse tack (for example, bridles and reins)—into their techniques of cavalry warfare.[33] These innovations improved the rider's stability and the horse's manoeuvrability. This made warhorses the main battle tanks of their day.[34] Simultaneously, a Eurasia-wide commercial expansion increased sedentary societies' demand for Central Asian warhorses, while also raising rulers' capacity to pay for these commodities.[35] The resulting expansion of the horse trade injected wealth into steppe-pastoralist societies. This consolidated tribal rulers' power, while whetting their appetite for expansion into sedentary polities.

---

[26] Foltz 2010: 10.   [27] Foltz 2010.   [28] Foltz 2010: 98.
[29] Gommans 1998a: 127.   [30] Gommans 1998a: 128.
[31] Gommans 2007: 5.   [32] Gommans 2007.   [33] Gommans 2007: 4.
[34] Gommans 2007.   [35] Gommans 2007: 5.

The resulting 'horse warrior revolution'[36] sparked a dramatic increase in Eurasia's 'violence interdependence'.[37] In particular, it spurred a rise in the regularity, severity, and geographic scope of pastoralist conquests of sedentary societies in the late medieval period. The most notorious of these—Genghis Khan's conquest of most of Eurasia—carved out history's biggest territorial empire. It also turbocharged hemispheric integration across all sectors of social life. Under the *Pax Mongolica*, Eurasia's long-distance trade surged.[38] This commerce accelerated the circulation of ideas and belief systems, as well as facilitating microbial exchange throughout the Old World.[39] Most spectacularly, the transfer of disease from Central Asia culminated in the Black Death in Latin Christendom, and equally catastrophic plagues in many Islamicate societies, with profound economic, cultural, and demographic consequences for each.[40]

Saharasia does not conventionally feature in accounts of international systems' evolution. But it should, for its significance for late medieval Eurasia was profound. From the eleventh century, Saharasia constituted 'a huge continental *mediterranée*, a vibrant interstitial region that widened the horizon of all its adjoining societies and opened new channels for pastoralists, warriors, merchants, pilgrims, and other restless wanderers'.[41] Throughout the early modern era, Saharasia would remain the 'political womb' out of which mighty conquest dynasties such as the Mughals emerged.[42] Well into the eighteenth century, invaders from Saharasia remained the most potent military threat to sedentary Eurasian societies. The relative exposure of the Sinosphere, the Islamicate, and Latin Christendom to this threat proved decisive to each region's evolution, and to the modern international system's development as a whole. Saharasia was pre-eminent as the epicentre of military threats to sedentary civilizations, and so was critical as a conduit for hemispheric integration. But as a commercial super-circuit, Saharasia was rivalled in importance by one other system—the Indosphere.

The Indosphere encompassed the vast rim of coastal territory stretching from Southern Africa, through the Persian Gulf and South Asia, deep into South East Asia as far as the South China Sea. Centred on the Indian Ocean, the Indosphere served from antiquity as a maritime trading supercircuit connecting Afro-Eurasian societies.[43] As with Saharasia, geography and climate were decisive in shaping Indosphere interactions. The Indian Ocean's near continuous littoral favoured trade, allowing 'short-legged' ships to shuttle between the Indosphere's entrepôts without having to brave forbidding

---

[36] Gommans 1998b: 11.
[37] I take the concept of violence interdependence from Deudney 2007: 4.
[38] Abu-Lughod 1989.   [39] Abu-Lughod 1989; see also generally Bentley 1993.
[40] McNeill 1976.   [41] Gommans 1998a: 130.   [42] Gellner 1995: 164.
[43] Bentley 1999: 219.

expanses on the scale of the Pacific or the Atlantic Oceans.[44] The region's great size and corresponding ecological diversity provided a further impetus to trade, as did the regularity of the monsoon winds.[45] The seasonal oscillation in the monsoon winds' direction helped merchants circulate throughout the Indosphere on both their outward and return journeys.[46] While they waited for the monsoon's direction to change, these merchants meanwhile settled in one of the Indosphere's port cities, enjoying rights of residence and self-rule under local rulers' protection.[47]

India formed the Indosphere's dynamic core. A 'metallurgical black hole', Indian markets sucked in precious metals from Africa and Central Asia, exporting textiles and spices in return.[48] Like China, India was economically self-sufficient except for precious metals and horses, the latter sourced mainly from Saharasia.[49] But unlike China, the Indian subcontinent remained politically divided, between terrestrial empires in the interior, and autonomous port cities along the coast.[50] The Indosphere therefore lacked a regional hegemon comparable to China in East Asia. Unlike China, Indian polities did not sponsor a regional suzerain state system. Instead, Indian power over neighbouring polities remained diffuse and indirect. This was evidenced in the 'Indianization' of many South East Asian polities in the early centuries of the second millennium CE, when local rulers selectively localized Indian religious and political ideas to consolidate their power.[51] Although India was central to it, both culturally as well as economically, subcontinental polities remained too divided and diverse to dominate the Indosphere.

The absence of local traditions of blue water naval warfare compounded the Indosphere's commercial and cultural, rather than political–military, nature. In Saharasia, the late medieval 'horse warrior revolution' had spurred a system-wide growth in violence interdependence. By contrast, before the Europeans' arrival in 1497, no maritime equivalent to Saharasia's steppe-conquest dynasties existed. Indosphere littoral societies generally conceived the high seas as an 'asocial' medium of commercial exchange, over which it would be futile to try to assert political control.[52] This disparagement of high seas naval warfare reinforced the Indosphere's commercial character, as a multicultural maritime superhighway devoid of system-wide military exchanges.

Much more than Saharasia, then, the Indosphere closely matched Buzan and Little's ideal type of an economic international system. This was reflected in its institutions, especially commercial extra-territoriality. Merchant diasporas provided the main conduit funnelling the Indosphere's trade. They did so by capitalizing on the trust inherent in extended kinship networks, placing

---

[44] Bentley 1999. [45] Prange 2008: 1382. [46] Prange 2008.
[47] Roy 2012: 9. [48] Dale 2010: 288–9. [49] Dale 2010.
[50] Reid 2010: 431. [51] Shaffer 1995: 24. [52] Steinberg 2001: 46.

agents at critical nodes in the Indosphere's main port cities to gather market intelligence and coordinate transactions with local merchants.[53] Because their trade generated customs revenue, local rulers welcomed these merchant diasporas.[54] This commercial hospitality sustained a necklace of cosmopolitan-trading entrepôts, which formed the primary connective tissue binding the Indosphere together. Unlike Saharasia, then, which encompassed the steppe hinterland as well as the Silk Road, the Indosphere remained overwhelmingly urban, a thin strip of cosmopolitan port cities clinging to the Indian Ocean littoral. A civilizational 'turn-table',[55] the Indosphere formed the circuit through which Indian mathematics had circulated to the Arab world and Indian Buddhism to South East Asia, and through which Islam in turn spread from its Arabian cradle to littoral societies in Africa, India, and beyond.

Following the end of the *Pax Mongolica* in the fourteenth century, the Indosphere eclipsed Saharasia as the Old World's primary 'great connector'. This was partially because in the pre-industrial era, it was nearly always cheaper to transport goods and people over water instead of land.[56] But it was also due to the lower protection costs merchants faced in the Indosphere versus Saharasia. Brigandage thrived on the steppe, just as piracy plagued the Indian Ocean. But from the fourteenth century, successive Turco-Mongol dynasties tried to replicate Genghis Khan's dream of universal conquest, fuelling instability throughout Saharasia.[57] Contrarily, the Indosphere up to 1490 remained free of Great Power maritime competition. Following China's withdrawal from the Indian Ocean in the 1430s, the Indosphere was a naval power vacuum. Eventually, the Indosphere's vast wealth would lure Western Europeans, and the ensuing struggle to control this wealth would define relations between hosts and European intruders for centuries thereafter. But in 1490 this lay in the future, and commercial and cultural connectivity continued to predominate over military and political interaction.

In beginning this account of Saharasia and the Indosphere, I stress two key points. First, Afro-Eurasia's civilizational complexes were already linked in dense webs of commercial and cultural exchange by the late fifteenth century. This hemispheric integration emerged with the rise of Saharasian pastoralist empires following the horse warrior revolution, and from a parallel surge in Indosphere commerce from the eleventh century. Undeniably, the authors of *The Expansion of International Society* were right to acknowledge that the challenges of cross-cultural diplomacy proved especially acute in the post-Columbian epoch, as Europe began to expand globally. My point here in recovering late medieval proto-globalization is to highlight that challenges of this kind were already present well prior to 1490, as hemispheric integration drew Afro-Eurasian civilizational complexes into closer and more regular contact.

---

[53] Tilly 2005: 65–6.   [54] Tilly 2005.   [55] Katzenstein 2010: 35.
[56] Buzan and Little 2000: 193.   [57] Darwin 2008a: 3–4.

Second, taking Saharasia and the Indosphere as our point of departure is essential because the relations of Afro-Eurasia's civilizational complexes to these frontiers affected decisively their own distinct patterns of expansion after 1490. Directly exposed to Saharasia, economically self-sufficient, and occupying the Indosphere's eastern terminus, China remained fixated on repelling 'barbarian' invaders. By 1490, Beijing had renounced maritime expansion as a redundant luxury, and the challenge of crushing, conciliating, or otherwise containing 'barbarian' incursions on 'civilization' stood thereafter as China's defining order-building challenge.[58]

Spanning territory from the Maghreb to the Malaysian Peninsula, the Islamicate partially overlapped with the Indosphere, and enjoyed the expansion opportunities that came with this proximity.[59] In particular, the experience of ruling large non-Muslim populations, combined with immersion in the Indosphere's cosmopolitan milieu, spurred practices of communal segregation and incorporation that would define Islamic statecraft for centuries after 1490. At the same time, the Mongol sacking of Baghdad in 1258 highlighted the Islamicate's vulnerability to assault from Saharasia. This offset Islamic cosmopolitanism with a Manichean division between the *Darul Islam* (House of Islam) and the *Darul Harb* (House of War) that would prove equally influential in conditioning the Islamicate's post-1490 evolution.[60]

Occupying Eurasia's north-western extremity, only Latin Christendom remained sheltered from Saharasia, but still capable of accessing the Indosphere's riches through long-distance maritime expansion. Paradoxically, remoteness from Eurasia's main commercial supercircuits proved decisive in placing Latin Christendom in pole position for global expansion after 1490. It is to a consideration of how Latin Christendom compared to its richer and more populous East Asian and Islamicate counterparts that I now turn.

The Behemoth, the Bridge, and the Backwater: Afro-Eurasia's Civilizational Complexes in 1490

The Sinosphere, comprising Ming China and its tributaries, was early modern Afro-Eurasia's most impressive power concentration. The Chinese behemoth not only dominated its immediate neighbours. Its immense wealth attracted adventurers from across the world, while Western appetite for Chinese luxury goods had fed persistent trade deficits with China from Roman times.[61] If one could identify a proverbial centre of the universe in 1490, the 'Middle Kingdom' was the obvious candidate.

---

[58] Finlay 1991: 4.   [59] Bentley 1993: 129.
[60] Armstrong 2014: 221.   [61] Liu 2001: 155.

The Sinosphere was organized as an *imperial hierarchy*, centred on the Ming emperor—the ruler of *tianxia* (all under heaven).[62] The emperor claimed supremacy over his neighbours, embracing a Confucian political cosmology that invested him with supreme religious as well as temporal authority. Claiming the 'Mandate of Heaven', the emperor ruled through ritually enacted moral virtue, as well as through traditional material induce-ments and coercion. In particular, the emperor was expected to perform the sacred rites (*li*) necessary to maintain a state of harmony (*ping*) within a universe where socio-political and cosmic order were inextricably intertwined.[63]

The Sinosphere's main international ordering institution was tributary diplomacy. The emperor organized his foreign relations in a 'hub and spokes' fashion, attempting to monopolize relations with vassals, and keep contact between them to a minimum.[64] Periodically, the emperor granted vassals' embassies the right to visit the imperial capital and genuflect before the emperor. Tributary diplomacy's ritual forms affirmed the bonds of asymmet-ric benevolence and obedience linking suzerains and vassals.[65] Terms of trade that Beijing engineered in its vassals' favour, meanwhile, gave vassals material incentives to submit to the emperor. Investiture missions—in which the emperor granted his imprimatur to local rulers and occasionally arbitrated succession disputes—constituted a further means through which the emperor reproduced regional hierarchy.[66]

Despite its Confucian underpinnings, however, the Sinosphere was hardly a cultural monolith. On the contrary, it was a decidedly hybrid civilizational complex. Even within China, Confucianism co-mingled with other cultural influences originating from beyond the 'Middle Kingdom'. Historically, Chinese rulers had drawn liberally from Buddhist ideas of the *cakravartin* (or universal ruler) to fortify their authority.[67] This reflected an early indebtedness to Indian religious and political ideas. But it was also a savvy adaptation of Chinese legitimating practices to attempt to incorporate eastern Saharasian pastoralists, who were typically Tibetan Buddhists.[68] Similarly, the Mandate of Heaven—a concept central to Chinese sacral kingship—spread to China from pre-Islamic Iran via Altaic (Mongolian) 'barbarian' kingdoms of the steppe.[69] Further afield, China's most loyal vassal, Korea, localized Confucianism to better conform to indigenous beliefs and practices.[70]

By the end of the fifteenth century, finally, Ming China had already dem-onstrated significant propensities for expansion. At sea, this was clear in Zheng He's seven long-range maritime expeditions from 1405 to 1433. Ming treasure fleets dwarfed the size of later European armadas, and travelled into

---

[62] Fairbank and Goldman 2006: 19.   [63] See generally Jiang 2011.
[64] Kim 1980: 7.   [65] Kim 1980.   [66] Lam 1968: 179.
[67] Crossley 1999: 235–6.   [68] Crossley 1999: 236.
[69] See generally Chen 2002.   [70] See generally Oliver 1959.

the Indian Ocean and as far away as East Africa.[71] But following Zheng He's last voyage, the Ming Dynasty abandoned maritime ambitions, returning its attention to the threat of 'barbarian' invasion from Saharasia.[72] Being economically self-sufficient except for precious metals and warhorses, China faced no compelling need to pursue high seas exploration or long-distance colonization. By 1490, then, China had turned its back on the high seas, leaving open the opportunity for other Afro-Eurasian power centres to expand.

Saharasia's proximity conversely demanded eternal vigilance. This was clearest in the Ming Dynasty's commissioning of the hugely expensive—and hugely ineffective—Great Wall of China.[73] Besides fortifying its frontiers, however, Ming China interacted with its northern neighbours in many other ways. Punitive expeditions, trade, cultural exchanges, and even marital alliances of course featured as prominent 'barbarian management' strategies for Beijing throughout Chinese history.[74] But by the late fifteenth century—following the late medieval neo-Confucian revival and the trauma of repeated northern invasions—the division between the 'civilized' and the 'barbarians' had undeniably emerged as the defining faultline demarcating collective identities within the Sinosphere. This pattern of collective identity formation would persist into the early modern era, eventually profoundly conditioning China's later encounter with European international society.

In contrast to the China-centric Sinosphere, the Islamicate had no equivalent centre of gravity. Instead, stretched out over diverse polities extending from the Maghreb and coastal West Africa, to the Middle East, North India, and South East Asia, the Islamicate was a vast 'bridge' civilizational complex between East and West.[75] It was also an extremely loose international system, organized around the principle of *heteronomous anarchy*. The system was heteronomous in that its units varied in their individual forms, and often territorially overlapped. But it was also anarchic, in that these Islamicate polities acknowledged no common suzerain, and were frequently at war.[76] Dense webs of cultural and commercial exchange nevertheless bound Islamicate polities together, with the requirement that Muslims undertake the *hajj* at least once in their lifetime providing a particularly strong spur for interaction. Epistemic communities of Islamic scholars, jurists, and intellectuals meanwhile further strengthened the Islamicate's interconnectedness, their reach extending 'across the "court societies" of Istanbul, Isfahan, Herat, Delhi and Cairo'.[77]

Of the civilizational complexes considered here, common ordering institutions were least developed in the Islamicate. Lacking a solar centre akin to China, the Islamicate possessed nothing like East Asia's system of tributary

---

[71] See again generally Finlay 1991.   [72] Finlay 1991: 4.
[73] See generally Waldron 1990.   [74] Waldron 1990: 33.
[75] Lawrence 2010: 157.   [76] Lawrence 2010: 169.
[77] Lawrence 2010: 163.

diplomacy. Nor did it possess anything comparable to the canon law of the medieval Church, which helped order conflict within Latin Christendom. Instead, throughout the Islamicate, Islamic jurisprudence provided a common epistemic (rather than ritual or legal) framework for thinking about morally and politically ordering relations among the Islamicate's constituent polities.[78]

In the absence of a system-wide hegemon or robust institutions of international order, then, religious identity formed the common bond uniting the Islamicate. Despite their differences, Muslims retained a sense of communal solidarity to the *ummah*, the universal community of faith uniting all Muslims. Following the late medieval assaults of the Crusades and the Mongol invasion of the Abbasid caliphate, the distinction between the *Darul Islam* and the *Darul Harb* moreover acquired ever greater salience, echoing the parallel hardening of the civilized/barbarian distinction in the late medieval Sinosphere.[79]

Nevertheless, Islamicate societies cannot be reduced to their Islamic character alone. Even more so than the Sinosphere, the Islamicate exemplified civilizational hybridity. Throughout the Islamicate, rulers undeniably justified their power through appeals to divine authority, and incorporated rich traditions of Islamic jurisprudence into their techniques of rule.[80] But this incorporation did not entail a collapse of the sacred/temporal distinction.[81] Nor did it signify an attempt to obliterate the immense cultural diversity that increasingly marked the Islamicate's expansive empires by the fifteenth century. Rather, in most Muslim-ruled societies, rulers wove Islamic norms of political legitimacy into more local idioms of power. In the Middle East and South Asia, the most influential of these was the Persian ideal of the ruler as *padshah*—a 'king of kings' who reconciled otherwise irredeemably diverse communities though the force of his own charisma.[82] Common too was a system of political ethics known as *siyasat* (discipline).[83] The *siyasat* tradition saw the ruler's function as upholding justice by maintaining a strict system of repression and punishment, and rested on the understanding that kingship had evolved 'to exercise a restraining influence on the animal nature of man'.[84] This idea had its roots in Medieval Islamic interpretations of the ideas of Plato and Epicurus—further reminding us of the hybrid foundations of Afro-Eurasia's civilizational complexes, and the high degree of cultural cross-pollination between them that existed by the late fifteenth century.

The Islamicate's immense heterogeneity finally both reflected and reinforced its geographic centrality within Afro-Eurasia. Islamicate societies

---

[78] Lawrence 2010; see also more generally Sood 2011.

[79] On the impact of the Mongol invasions in particular for the Islamicate, see Armstrong 2000: 34.

[80] Arjomand 2001: 463.   [81] Arjomand 2001: 464.

[82] For a discussion of the *padshah* conception of rulership, see for example Khan 2009: 50.

[83] Arjomand 2008: 11–12.   [84] Khan 2009: 46.

abutted both the Indosphere and Saharasia, and were deeply enmeshed in the commercial and cultural flows composing both systems. This centrality within Afro-Eurasia profoundly impacted the patterns and practice of the Islamicate's expansion, both before and after 1490. 'Through its presence in the Indian Ocean, Islam became a pan-Asian cultural agent',[85] especially as peripatetic Muslim traders spread their religion in the course of long-distance trade. Although the Europeans would eventually militarize and monopolize the Indian Ocean from the sixteenth century, for a time Muslim powers (especially the Ottomans) would seriously contest European dominance. Islam's early spread throughout the Indosphere meanwhile made the Indian Ocean a 'Muslim lake'[86] from the late medieval period, and indeed well into early modernity. In particular, it built a thick skein of commonality across the Indosphere, based as much on shared Islamic commercial practices as it was on religious beliefs.[87] By the fifteenth century, then, Islam was already well established in port cities from Gujarat to Malacca, priming many locals for conflict once Portuguese Crusaders began to encroach from 1497.

The Islamicate's connection to Saharasia was a less unambiguous good than its enmeshment within the Indosphere. Mongol invaders destroyed the Abbasid caliphate and unleashed plague throughout the Middle East in the thirteenth century. Nevertheless, Islam's spread into the Saharasian steppe throughout the late medieval period also seeded the growth of Turkic and Timurid conquest dynasties. These dynasties would lead the Islamicate's most powerful empires, including the Ottoman and Mughal Empires, by combining the military prowess of Saharasian cavalrymen with the commercial wealth and sophisticated statecraft of sedentary Islamicate societies.[88] Proximity to Saharasia thus left the Islamicate terribly exposed to danger. But it also offered the possibility of nourishing immensely powerful hybrid empires, which married the military strengths of Saharasia, with the cosmopolitanism and wealth of established Muslim polities. Of the three Afro-Asian civilizational complexes considered, then, the Islamicate would remain the most amphibious in its patterns of expansion well beyond 1490.

Beyond the Chinese behemoth and the Islamicate bridge, we come to Latin Christendom, which in 1490 remained Eurasia's backwater, at least when compared to the Sinosphere and the Islamicate.[89] Christendom in 1490 lacked Ming China's size, wealth, and political unity. It also lacked the Islamicate's geographic spread and centrality within Afro-Eurasia, as well as its cosmopolitan reach. But Latin Christendom was more insulated from Saharasian pastoralist invaders than either the Sinosphere or the Islamicate. Its rulers and merchants were also more tenaciously committed to maritime conquest than elsewhere.

---

[85] Lawrence 2010: 169.   [86] Vink 2007: 55.   [87] Sood 2011: 154.
[88] See generally Dale 2009.   [89] Fernández-Armesto 2013: 26.

This combination of insulation from the steppe and exposure to the sea favourably positioned Latin Christendom for global expansion after 1490.

Late medieval Latin Christendom was a *heteronomous diarchy*, albeit one evolving gradually towards sovereign anarchy. Whereas the Sinosphere and the Islamicate had seen a reconstitution of large-scale empires in late antiquity, the collapse of the Carolingian Empire in the ninth century left room for the Church subsequently to cement its status as Christendom's pre-eminent supra-local power.[90] Consequently, by 1490, the Church and the Holy Roman Empire still stood at the apex of a papal–imperial diarchy, where they respectively embodied the pre-eminent repositories of sacred and temporal authority. From the eleventh century, Church and Empire had fought a mutually enfeebling struggle for supremacy. This struggle—which coincided with the late medieval commercial revolution—opened up space for new power centres to emerge, of which the most notable were city-states, city-leagues, and sovereign states.[91] The last of these would eventually defeat all its opponents, including Church and Empire.[92] But in 1490, this triumph lay in the future, and Latin Christendom remained a web of overlapping ecclesiastical, imperial, sovereign, and seigneurial claims.

Canon law and feudal law comprised Latin Christendom's most important ordering institutions. From the mid-fifteenth century especially, monarchs had begun to consolidate power in states including England, France, and Spain.[93] But even with this consolidation, rulers depended on canon law to provide a medium for negotiating and guaranteeing agreements between one another.[94] Although the Church's authority was increasingly contested by 1490, Latin Christendom remained nominally religiously united. This provided a cultural consensus through which such pacts could be concluded and enforced. Canon law coexisted uneasily alongside a parallel tradition of feudal law.[95] Feudal law granted Europe's aristocracy the right to seek redress in conflicts by resorting to armed self-help, and was paradoxically also critical to maintaining order throughout Latin Christendom.[96]

Religious unity and the solidarity of a transnational aristocratic diaspora committed to preserving a feudal social order helped hold Latin Christendom together. As with the Sinosphere and the Islamicate, however, we would be wrong to attribute Latin Christendom's coherence to supposedly monolithic cultural conformity. On the contrary, Latin Christendom was a pre-eminently

---

[90] For the late medieval growth of Church power from the eleventh century, see generally Berman 1983.

[91] See generally Spruyt 1994.   [92] Spruyt 1994.

[93] Strayer 1970: 35.   [94] See generally Ullman 1976.

[95] On feudal law's development as a pan-European legal institution in the Middle Ages, see Berman 1983: chapter 9.

[96] Berman 1983.

hybrid civilizational complex. Its high culture rested on a Greco-Roman-Germanic synthesis forged in antiquity. Its dominant religion, meanwhile, originated as a breakaway Jewish cult in first-century Palestine, whose greatest ancient interpreter—Augustine of Hippo—was North African. And as it expanded further in the Middle Ages, through Crusades in Eastern Europe and the Levant, and the Iberian *Reconquista*, Latin Christendom's internal heterogeneity increased further still.[97] This late medieval wave of imperial expansion in particular clarified Christendom's identity boundaries. Crusades against Muslim 'infidels' and pagans infused Latin Christendom's civilizational identity with a religious intolerance, which would shape European international society's expansion long after the Reformation had destroyed Christendom's spiritual unity.[98] And the *Reconquista* brought with it a new obsession with 'purity of blood' (*limpieza de sangre*) that would later profoundly influence Europeans' racialized practices of colonial rule, especially in the New World.[99]

As with the Sinosphere and the Islamicate, then, late medieval expansion increased Latin Christendom's internal diversity, while simultaneously sharpening its identity boundaries relative to 'outsiders'. Latin Christendom in 1490 remained poorer and less populous than either the Sinosphere or the Islamicate. Its ordering institutions were also decomposing in the face of growing religious division and destabilizing military innovation. Against these disadvantages, and for all of its relative backwardness, Latin Christendom was nevertheless more insulated from Saharasia than either the Sinosphere or the Islamicate, and so less vulnerable to the pastoralist predation this proximity brought with it. Latin Christendom also possessed longstanding precedents for maritime expansion, and was predisposed by its relative poverty to look abroad for wealth. A trifecta of position, precedent, and poverty thus primed Latin Christendom as the likely vanguard of Afro-Eurasian expansion from 1490. The scale of this expansion—entailing extermination and territorial conquest on a continental level—far exceeded Christendom's more modest spread in the medieval era. But the violent mode of this expansion faithfully reflected medieval antecedents, underscoring the critical importance this earlier epoch had in shaping Europe's later expansion in the early modern era.

CONCLUSION

This chapter has stressed two core themes defining the world in 1490—hemispheric integration, and the growing internal diversification and external differentiation of Afro-Eurasian civilizational complexes as they expanded in

---

[97] See generally Moore 1997.   [98] Bartlett 1994: 313–14.   [99] Bartlett 1994: 242.

the late medieval era. From the eleventh century, 'the horse warrior revolution' and surging commerce along its steppe and maritime frontiers pulled Afro-Eurasia's civilizational complexes into far greater contact than before. Concurrent with this hemispheric integration, the era also saw an expansion in the geographical scope and internal diversity of Afro-Eurasia's civilizational complexes. The late medieval period saw China pulled into a tighter and more permanent antagonism with pastoralist empire-builders from eastern Saharasia. This culminated in 'barbarian' dynasties' repeated conquests of China, offset by periodic Chinese attempts to 'civilize' their northern neighbours. The Islamicate meanwhile also expanded enormously, with Muslim conquerors confronting the challenges of governing large numbers of non-Muslim subjects, either Hindus (as in South Asia) or Christians and Jews (in the eastern Mediterranean and the Balkans). Driven by the land-hunger of its 'aristocratic diaspora'[100] and the papacy's religious zeal, Latin Christendom also grew dramatically, permanently annexing swathes of northern and eastern Europe, as well as carving out more tenuous footholds in the Crusader kingdoms of the Levant.

The picture I have presented here contrasts starkly with the conventional story of international society's expansion. This story typically begins with the late fifteenth-century voyages of discovery that introduced Europe to the Americas, and won Europeans direct entry into the trading circuits of the Indosphere. Without denying the significance of this European breakout into the Americas and Asia, my goal here has been to enrich our understanding of international society's globalization, by widening the geographic scope of our analysis while increasing its temporal depth. Harnessing insights from global history, I have shown that the challenge of maintaining order within culturally diverse international systems did not begin with Columbus and Vasco da Gama. Nor was it a problem that can be understood within the framework of exclusively European political expansion. On the contrary, the late medieval period saw each of Afro-Eurasia's civilizational complexes expand considerably. This polycentric pattern of expansion would continue well until the late eighteenth century, with Europe definitively eclipsing the Sinosphere and the Islamicate only from 1800 CE onwards.

In the Sinosphere, the Islamicate, and Latin Christendom, late medieval hemispheric integration and civilizational expansion brought new challenges, the foremost being the challenge of mediating inter-polity relations across significant cultural divides. Elites in each civilizational complex imagined new boundaries of collective identification in response to this challenge, together with accompanying recognition practices that survived well into the early modern era.

---

[100] Bartlett 1994: 24.

Within the Sinosphere, the civilized/barbarian divide had long framed China's relations with outsiders. But it is only from the medieval period, with renewed barbarian invasions spurring the rise of neo-Confucianism and heightened efforts to civilize barbarians through *cultural assimilation*, that this polarity crystallized as the organizing principle that would govern Chinese elite identities, governance, and diplomacy down to the nineteenth century.[101]

In the Islamicate, Muslim conquests of large Christian, Jewish, and Hindu populations raised similar challenges, even before the growth of massive Islamic 'gunpowder empires' from the sixteenth century.[102] As Rae powerfully illustrates in Chapter 4, with particular reference to the Ottoman Empire, these generally resolved in strategies of *incorporation* and *segregation*, with non-Muslim communities granted religious tolerance and local self-rule in exchange for political subordination to Muslim rulers.[103] As we have seen, the double-headed assault of the Crusades and the thirteenth-century Mongol destruction of the Abbasid caliphate nevertheless sharpened and inflamed the divide between *Darul Islam* and *Darul Harb*, anticipating the renewed antagonism between Islamic rulers and 'infidels' in the early modern period.

Latin Christendom's annexation of northern and eastern Europe, its temporary encroachments in the Levant, and its reconquest of the Iberian Peninsula meanwhile finally forged a more coherent Western civilizational identity. This civilizational consolidation entailed recognition practices increasingly grounded in an insistence on religious conformity as a foundation for social order, accompanied by rulers' extensive recourse to strategies of *expulsion* and *extermination* directed towards 'heretics' and 'infidels' that refused to conform. The 'pathological homogenization' that attended both Absolutist state formation and the conquest of the New World was certainly of greater intensity than its medieval precedents.[104] But Europe's violent expansion after 1490—which laid the foundations of modern international society— was powerfully shaped by late medieval inter-civilizational encounters and the self-understandings that these encounters first forged.

My argument's larger significance is both theoretical and empirical. Theoretically, my goal here has been to overturn a tenacious but misleading 'vanguardist' conception of international society's expansion. This conventional conception is monocentric, rather than polycentric; Eurocentric, rather than Afro-Eurasian-centric; and unidirectional, rather than multi-directional, in its conception of the dynamics of international systems' expansion in the late

---

[101] On the relationship between 'barbarian' invasions and the rise and consolidation of Neo-Confucian orthodoxy, see Smith 2004: 304–5.

[102] Dale 2009: 7. The term 'gunpowder empires' is used advisedly, in light of Dale's reservations regarding its uneven applicability to the Ottoman, Safavid, and Mughal empires.

[103] In the Ottoman context, see generally Barkey 2008: chapter 4.

[104] Rae 2002: 57.

medieval and early modern periods. The vision I have presented here conversely affirms an alternative, 'syncretist' conception of the expansion story.[105] The syncretist account of international society's expansion foregrounds 'the two-way formative interaction between European and non-Western international societies',[106] rather than reducing international society's globalization to the story of one-way European expansion. In recovering the history of late medieval hemispheric integration and civilizational expansion, diversification, and differentiation, my argument further refutes the 'vanguardist' orthodoxy evident in *The Expansion of International Society*, while providing historical depth to ascendant revisionist 'syncretist' accounts of the globalization of international society.

Historically, my argument corroborates Hendrik Spruyt's insight in Chapter 5 that the world was already thickly interconnected through dense webs of commercial and cultural exchange in the centuries before 1490. Beyond reinforcing this claim, I have also sought to tease out the transformations in collective identities that emerged in the late medieval period, as civilizational complexes expanded in geographic reach, and became more mutually entangled. It would be wrong to presume an unbroken line of continuity between these late medieval encounters and the later tensions that accompanied European international society's expansion. But equally, our understanding of the dynamics of international society's globalization is obscured to the extent that we ignore the formative influence of these encounters in profoundly shaping the inter-civilizational contours of confrontation that later defined Europe's global ascendancy.

The contributors to this volume collectively demonstrate the radical transformations of international society over the course of its post-fifteenth-century globalization. But it is imperative that we recall that globalization was already radically reshaping Latin Christendom—the eventual cradle of international society—long before 1490. European international society undeniably formed the primary institutional prism within which globalization as we now know it took form. But this prism was itself forged in an earlier and forgotten period of proto-globalization, which I have sought to recover here.

---

[105] On syncretic accounts of international society's expansion, see Buzan 2010.
[106] Buzan 2014a: 71.

4

Patterns of Identification on the Cusp of Globalization

Heather Rae

In 1492, Christopher Columbus's landing in the Americas inaugurated 'a spatial and temporal implosion of the globe: the integration of separate and coexisting world systems, each enjoying a relatively autonomous social facticity and expressing its own laws of historicity, into a singular post-Columbian world system'.[1] While Hedley Bull and Adam Watson's volume looked to the processes of international political integration that were part of this implosion, they had little to say about questions of identity either within the European society of states or in societies outside of Europe.

As John Gerard Ruggie pointed out, some 'world systems' had long histories of coexistence, albeit coexistence in which cultural and economic exchange sat uneasily alongside military competition and religious differences. Other world systems were indeed separate unto themselves, containing complex regional systems of social, material, and spiritual exchange as well as alliances and relations of enmity or domination.[2] I use this difference as the axis on which to identify two sites of investigation of late fifteenth-century practices of identification. In the case of the Ottoman Empire and Western Europe, collective identities can clearly be seen as relationally constituted across mutually recognized civilizational and religious boundaries, although these boundaries may have been much more fluid, particularly in the fourteenth and fifteenth centuries, than was acknowledged until recently (as Andrew Phillips also shows more broadly in Chapter 3).

Contrasted with this are peoples that were not known to Europeans before Columbus's journey that had, as Ruggie put it, their own 'social facticity'.[3]

---

[1] Ruggie 1993b: 168.
[2] For examples, see Crawford 1994, on the Iroquois; Salisbury 1996; on the Aztecs, see later in this chapter.
[3] Ruggie 1993b: 168.

These diverse societies and cultures were involved in intergroup relations which, in turn, reflected and reinforced social differentiation within broader, shared civilizational complexes. Here I focus on the Aztec Empire as an exemplar, of an empire, a society, and a people which was radically 'Other' to the Europeans at the time of conquest. However, relational identities between Europe and the Aztecs (as with other peoples of the 'New World') came into play very quickly post-conquest. The 'discovery' by the Europeans of societies based on such profoundly different cosmologies to their own and with practices that Europeans found both incomprehensible and repulsive (most notably human sacrifice and the cannibalism that accompanied it in the case of the Aztecs) not only had a devastating transformational impact on those societies, but also called into question long-held European certainties about the unity of all humankind. As I discuss in more detail in what follows, this was to have far-reaching implications for Europe and, indeed, in contributing towards more relativist understandings of moral, social, religious, and political codes, and played a part in the development of the Renaissance and the momentous changes that were to follow.[4] These two cases are also of interest to consider together, as 1492, the year of Columbus's voyage, was also the year that the Catholic monarchs completed the *Reconquest* of Granada, finally expelling the Moors from the Iberian Peninsula while also expelling Jews from what would become Spain. Spanish hostility towards Islam would also influence 'the methods and manner of its conquest and colonization of America',[5] not least in the rejection of diversity.

Before investigating these two very different cases, I first turn to consideration of the concept of identity and outline how it may best be understood in terms of a broader conception of culture which is then used to look more closely, to the extent that this is possible with historically remote societies, at the practices and performances of identification that were in play in both the early Ottoman Empire and the late Aztec Empire. I conclude with some remarks on the politics of recognition (or non-recognition) and the impact of both these empires on European conceptions of self and Other.

THE CONCEPT OF IDENTITY

Discussing identity in the historically remote period of the late fifteenth century means using a concept that may be anachronistic and is, arguably, culturally specific rather than universal. The concept of identity that is used in the social sciences today is of relatively recent provenance with an original

---

[4] Pagden 1993.   [5] Elliott 2015: 59.

emphasis on individual identity and identity in crisis.[6] It is only since the late 1980s and early 1990s that identity came to be seen as salient to the study of international relations, with scholars building on earlier work in the social sciences.[7] In terms of collective identities, authors looked to Western history, drawing a long line back to the ancient Greeks or Romans.[8] Even when the important role of the relationship between the West and its Others in identity formation is investigated, the emphasis was on understanding Western identity/ies. Much of this work has been illuminating and at the time it broke new ground in the study of International Relations (IR).

What is meant by 'identity' is multidimensional and contested. Identity can be understood in 'personal, relational, or collective' terms and when looking at identity on a global scale, how personal, relational, and collective forms of identity may be interconnected (or not) needs to be articulated. Is identity a quality or a process, or something else? Should it be thought of as something that is fluid or stable? And what is the best way to trace such identities? These issues are amplified when considering how to trace collective forms of identification that were meaningful to myriad groups half a millennium ago and to do this on a global scale.

There is also debate over whether we should even bother with the concept of identity. For some, identity is a chimera. Richard Ned Lebow sees a coherent personal identity as an illusion.[9] Others, such as Rogers Brubaker and Frederick Cooper, argue that the term identity is so broad and, in their view, so overused that it has come to mean everything and therefore nothing.[10] An alternative view is that although the study of identities is indeed broad and disparate as it is pursued in such a wide range of fields, often with little communication between those fields, nonetheless there is a coherent set of 'theoretical ideas and empirical phenomena underlying the various uses of identity'.[11] Here the central issue is how humans, both as individuals and as collectivities, understand themselves and how they do so in relation to others, and what sort of practices arise from and contribute to these understandings. As Vivian Vignoles, Seth J. Schwartz, and Koen Luyckx note, we can think of identity as the answer that is given to the question of 'who am I?' or, in collective terms, 'who are we?' but 'identity comprises not only "who you think you are" (individually or collectively), but also "who you act as being" in interpersonal and intergroup interactions—and the social recognition or otherwise that these actions receive from other individuals or groups'.[12] Even if groups in the past did not think in terms of 'identity' as we might

---

[6] For overviews, see Vignoles et al. 2011; Neumann 1996.

[7] Neumann and Welsh 1991; Neumann 1996; Campbell 1992; Wendt 1992, 1994.

[8] For the Greeks, see Lebow 2012; for the Romans see Neumann 1996; see also Taylor 1989; and Connolly 1991.

[9] Lebow 2012.   [10] Brubaker and Cooper 2000.

[11] Vignoles et al. 2011: 13.   [12] Vignoles et al. 2011: 2.

understand it today, it is clear that they did *act* on the basis of conceptions of collectively shared forms of identification, with the boundaries between self and Other socially constructed and more or less open or closed, and relations more or less amicable or hostile in different contexts.

The reification of identities is the outcome of what may be a self-conscious project or a less self-conscious process, either way having political ramifications that need to be explored. We also need to take account of just how powerful such reifications can be so that although socially constructed, they come to have their own lived reality through shared meanings and practices. Thus the examination of the construction, maintenance of, and changes to the boundaries of collective identities is centrally important. In tracing identities we are looking at those processes—social, cultural, political, religious, and ethical—through which groups come to understand themselves and act as though they have certain commonalities and in which they generate socially shared conceptions of the boundaries between themselves and other collectivities. This can be done in different ways and using different criteria of identification, but we know that it is done. We also know that boundaries can be negotiated in very different ways, as consideration of the Ottoman and Aztec Empires of the late fifteenth century demonstrates. As Iver B. Neumann notes, 'what is at issue in delineation is not "objective" cultural differences, but the way symbols are activated to become part of the capital of the identity of a given human collective…Any difference, no matter how miniscule, may be inscribed by political importance and serve to delineate identities'.[13] It is through practices or performance, to use Jeffrey Alexander's term, that such symbols are activated.[14]

Criteria of Identity or Identification

Cultural formations impact on the development of all collective identities. Here, I follow Clifford Geertz in my understanding of culture as, 'not cults and customs but the structures of meaning through which people give shape to their experience'. As he argues, this is not a realm of human activity separate from the political: 'Politics is not coups and constitutions but one of the principal arenas in which such structures unfold'.[15] Therefore tracing the relationships between structures of meaning and how they play out in political life through the acts of agents is illuminating, although not necessarily easy, as Geertz acknowledged.[16]

Collective identity can be seen as a way of giving form to, and in many cases reifying, particular instantiations of the interaction of socially competent

---

[13] Neumann 1996: 166.   [14] Alexander 2004.
[15] Geertz 1973: 312.   [16] Geertz 1973: 312.

actors with shared structures of meaning. Through such interactions, political authority may be legitimated or it may be challenged, and over time those structures of meaning may change as a result, for they are not static. In this context, as Alexander argues, '[c]ulture is less toolkit than storybook'.[17] Thus, social action can be understood as 'cultural performance'. As he notes, it is 'the need for walking and talking—and seeing and listening to the walking and talking—that makes the practical pragmatics of performance different to the cultural logic of texts'.[18] It is through the performance of certain practices that conceptions of a collective self are constituted, reinforced, contested, and reinterpreted.

At the broadest level we can identify civilizational identities, which are generally heterogeneous and highly porous. As Peter Katzenstein notes, civilizations, 'nesting or nested in other cultural entities and processes' may be '[d]eeply meaningful to many members of the cultural elite [but] as self-conscious and lived identities, civilizations do not rank at the top for most people and typically do not manifest themselves in an everyday sense of belonging'.[19] To make identities at this level have a deeper reach is a political project.

Systems of religious belief can reach across, and provide criteria of identification for, broad civilizational complexes, as was the case with Western Christendom. It is those religious belief systems that are universalizing that are more likely to provide the means for intra-civilizational communication, mediation, and identification, as they provide resources for agents to reconcile the wider civilizational identity with local identities and practices. I take the role of religious identification in political legitimation and organization as being of central importance in both the Ottoman and Aztec Empires, albeit in very different ways, as it was also increasingly for Western European states and empires from the fifteenth century.

In their questioning of the utility of the concept of identity, Brubaker and Cooper ask if the concept is even necessary to narrative accounts.[20] But this overlooks the idea that narrative accounts are so often about telling, arguing over, enacting, and reinventing collectively shared conceptions of 'who we are'. Thus narrative is part of the practice or performance that, drawing on wider cultural structures, both enacts and gives form to the meanings that are ascribed to group identities. Narratives are 'stories of us' as well as stories of who is 'not us', who is 'Other', and in what—more or less exclusive—ways they are 'not us'. Thus in tracing stories of identification in the late fifteenth century, we must look to the different ways in which the collective self was 'performed'. In the non-European cases investigated here, these included written texts (in the Ottoman Empire), pictorial histories (in the case of the

---

[17] Alexander 2004: 568. For culture as toolkit, see Swidler 1986.
[18] Alexander 2004: 530.   [19] Katzenstein 2010: 13.
[20] Brubaker and Cooper 2000: 12.

Aztecs),[21] oral performances (sometimes based on texts), the performance of ritual, the design of cities and palaces, a range of visual images, diplomacy, and war. While not all of these forms can be covered in detail here, I aim to give a brief overview of the Ottoman and Aztec Empires.

COLLECTIVE IDENTITIES IN 1490:
THE OTTOMAN EMPIRE

In *The Expansion of International Society*, we are given what was then a standard account of the rise and decline of the Ottoman Empire, a decline that accompanied the gradual integration of an increasingly weak empire into the European society of states in the nineteenth century with the Sublime Porte only gradually, and through coercion, coming to accept European norms such as equal sovereignty.[22] However, recent work on the Ottoman Empire questions the simple story of rise and long decline, instead looking at the 'longevity and resilience' of an empire that lasted from the fourteenth to the twentieth centuries asking, instead, what made it strong for so long?[23] While expansionary war obviously played an important role in the development of the empire (just as it played an important role in European state- and empire-making, although critics of the Ottoman Empire often seemed to overlook that),[24] the long history of interaction between the empire (through trade, cultural exchange, or diplomatic interaction) and Europeans (whether individuals, cities, states, and empires) is highlighted.

There are two important aspects to Ottoman identity building explored here. In practices that were helping to create what we now call 'the international', following their mid-fifteenth-century conquest of Constantinople (1453), as well as asserting their military power, the Ottomans asserted their standing as the cultured inheritors of the legacy of the Greek and Roman Empires via Byzantium. At the same time, there was a process of internal consolidation of authority, which in this period most often eschewed the drive towards homogenization that was to be implemented in Western European proto-states.[25] The early Ottomans consolidated and extended their authority through the creative management of diversity rather than by attempting to wipe it out.[26]

---

[21] Boone 1994.

[22] Naff 1984. At around the same time, Michael Doyle 1986: 104–8 gave a similar, brief account. For a more recent reflection see Finkel 2005b.

[23] Barkey 2008.   [24] Goffman 2002.

[25] Barkey 2014a compares the Ottoman and Habsburg Empires as on opposite trajectories when it came to toleration.

[26] On diversity within the empires of Afro-Eurasia, see Chapter 3 in this volume by Andrew Phillips.

This was to change in the following centuries so that by the late eighteenth century, and particularly into the nineteenth century, the rise of nationalist claims against the empire met with growing religious intolerance.[27] However, as the fifteenth century drew to a close, the creative harnessing of diversity and the *relative* institutional and cultural flexibility of an empire that was internally heterogeneous, yet was also in the process of extending and consolidating as a unified political entity, stands out. This happened within the context of a gradual move towards a more unified conception of Islam and the development of the *millet* system under which recognized religious minorities, loyal to the empire, retained significant autonomy.

Constructing an Empire

Karen Barkey describes as 'institutional bricolage'[28] the strategies of the early Ottomans of the fourteenth and fifteenth centuries as they drew on a wide range of resources to make 'a uniquely hybrid civilization'.[29] The 'brokering of political deals'[30] was something in which the early Ottomans were adept, successfully bringing on board many would-be challengers, both Muslim and non-Muslim, while sidelining others. This extended to common people as well as to drawing elites into networks of power and patronage. For example, Sultan Mehmet II's policy in the wake of the conquest of Constantinople was one of absorption—of non-Muslims as well as a heterogeneous range of Muslims—and development, rather than wholesale pillage and destruction. As Barkey notes:

> Early Ottomans were not boundary-conscious and in fact they exhibited a strong syncretic religious understanding favored by a heterodox form of Islam. They also strategized that conquerors should practise a policy of *istimalet* [accommodation] that is, an attempt to make the indigenous [often non-Muslim] population look upon them favorably by offering incentives, promising generosity and concessions such as permissions to retain lands and resources.[31]

It was Mehmet II who instigated the *millet* system of religious pluralism after the fall of Constantinople. Under this system, religious communities were granted a great deal of internal autonomy under their own religious authorities who, in turn, answered to the imperial authorities. Although not an Ottoman invention, the Ottomans practised 'the most institutionalised version' of the system in which the state supported a form of religious pluralism, albeit one in

---

[27] Culminating in the genocide of 1915–16. See Rae 2002: 124–64.
[28] Barkey 2008: 13.   [29] Barkey 2008: 7.   [30] Barkey 2008: 29.
[31] Barkey 2014b: 473. Note that there were internal critics of Mehmet II's engagement with the traditions of Byzantium and his (relative) magnanimity towards those who were conquered. Krstić 2011: 66.

which Islam took precedence.[32] Non-Muslim communities were to operate according to specific rules, including the payment of poll taxes, specific codes of conduct, and the display of deference to Muslims. The Greek Orthodox *millet* was recognized in 1454 and the Armenian *millet* in 1461. The Jewish *millet* was less definite, although it was 'unofficially recognized around the same time as the other two'.[33] At this time, there was no single, unified Islam practised in the empire and some accommodation of this was needed. It was really only from the reign of Sultan Selim I (1512–20) that self-conscious attempts by imperial authorities to construct the empire as a Sunni Islamic realm were put into practice.[34]

Nonetheless, from the beginning of the fifteenth century, a number of texts were produced which were aimed at educating converts to Islam as well as putting the 'ignorant' common folk on the path of what the authors took to be correct belief and behaviour. These texts were produced in the vernacular, as for many, access to the Qur'an in Arabic was not possible. Tijana Krstić outlines how these texts worked in a largely non-literate society with, for example, one very influential work in verse by the brothers Yazicizade, *The Muhammediye*,[35] being memorized and recited by many across socio-economic boundaries, with it still today being 'the favourite religious literature of women'.[36] Thus, as Krstić observes, Ottoman Islam had a history of its own, one that accompanied the development of the empire.[37] In this, multiple 'interpretive communities' were brought together through the creation of common 'texts', which were not restricted to literary texts, with group experiences, individual life stories, and so on playing roles. Written texts were brought alive for many through private or public performance, in preaching, story-telling, or the recitation of works learnt by heart as acts of religious piety.[38]

There was at work a combination of both universalizing and localizing, or as Krstić calls it, indigenizing of Islam, bringing together heterogeneous peoples under a single religious code through Islamization. Krstić notes that 'popular preaching and storytelling had a distinct political dimension that appealed equally to those who ruled and those who resisted rule'.[39] Despite contestation, these narratives were, over time, helping to build a more unified identity for Muslim subjects of the empire. Even allowing for localization of the Islamization process, this meant that by the later fifteenth century, although it was still relatively fluid, boundaries were starting to be more strongly defined. As Barkey observes, in the fifteenth century '"new loci" of Muslim/non-Muslim boundaries were emerging and settling among populations' so a process of clearer differentiation was occurring over time.[40]

---

[32] Sahin 2012.   [33] Barkey 2005: 16.   [34] Barkey 2005: 11.
[35] Krstić 2011: 32.   [36] Krstić 2011: 34.   [37] Krstić 2011: 27.
[38] Krstić 2011: 38.   [39] Krstić 2011: 39.   [40] Barkey 2008: 62.

International Identity Construction

Much work has been done in IR to investigate the enmity between the Ottoman Empire and Western Europe, and a number of scholars have noted the important role of the Ottoman Empire as the threatening Other in the articulation of European self-identity.[41] In 1453, the fall of Constantinople to the Ottomans, followed by the fall of the Greek Byzantine successor state of Trebizond in 1461, marked the retreat of the Eastern Church. In 1492, Grenada fell to the forces of Ferdinand and Isabella, pushing Islam out of what would become Spain. That same year, the 'Catholic monarchs' authorized the expulsion of Jews from Spain marking the end of the centuries-long tradition of *convivencia*, in which Christian, Muslim, and Jewish communities had enjoyed a period of (relatively) peaceful coexistence. This was a harbinger of a growing demand for religious homogeneity in which state-builders began to consolidate their authority in centralizing dynamics within state boundaries that would spread across Western Europe.[42]

Yet at the same time there was also the circulation of goods and, often overlooked, of scholars and ideas, artists and images, and artisans and their products, between the Ottoman Empire and Europe. In the words of Lisa Jardine and Jerry Brotton, although not publicly sanctioned, the Ottomans along with the Portuguese and Italians were happy to turn a 'discursive blind eye or rather, deaf ear, to the cultural transactions that structured the economic ones with the Ottomans'.[43] The Ottoman Empire was, they argue, a 'politically sensitive, problematic point of mediation between Europe and the markets to the East rather than the shadowing at the bounds of Europe'.[44] The boundaries were permeable and 'even in situations of conflict, mutual recognition of icons and images could be used adversarially with creative verve'.[45] Moreover, even in times of conflict, trade and other exchanges continued unabated.[46] For example, the Genoese assisted both sides during the siege of Constantinople, and 'the siege and change of ruler did not damage relations between the Ottomans and the Christian West. Commercial and diplomatic treaties were renewed: an alliance was even agreed with the Venetians a year after the capture of Constantinople, despite their previously professed support for the Byzantine Emperor'.[47]

This period marked an acceleration of cultural production in the Ottoman Empire that was inherently tied to its relations with Western Europe. Gerald MacLean notes that:

> From the time of Fatih [conqueror] Mehmed [reigned 1451–83], the Ottoman court in Istanbul was joined with the great courts of Europe in a competitive

---

[41] Neumann and Welsh 1991.   [42] Rae 2002.
[43] Jardine and Brotton 2000: 60.   [44] Jardine and Brotton 2000: 60.
[45] Jardine and Brotton 2000: 8.
[46] On similar exchanges that linked Afro-Eurasia, see Chapter 3.   [47] Norton 2013: 5–6.

cultural dialogue that intimately linked artistic patronage and display with trading agreements and political maneuverings. Renowned throughout Europe,
Suleyman I [reigned 1520–66] earned himself the title of the 'the Magnificent'
in the West for the sheer opulence of his court and the enormous concentration
of wealth and military power it represented.[48]

Here, beginning with Mehmet II, we see the performance of sovereign legitimacy on the emergent European international stage. As Alexander argues,
'[l]ike any other text…collective representations, whether background or foreground, can be evaluated for their dramatic effectiveness'.[49] Thus we see in the
acknowledgement of the grandeur and standing of the Ottomans in Europe
that assertions of Ottoman sovereignty and legitimacy were certainly taking
effect. This could only happen within a wider shared symbolic context. Rulers
across Europe understood the meaning of the performance of Mehmet II in
the mid-fifteenth century, as he patronized European artists or bought ancient
manuscripts, demonstrating 'shared reverence for the same ancient sources'[50]
or as Suleyman displayed his wealth and taste as well as his military might in
the sixteenth century.

Thus, as Claire Norton notes, post-1453, the Ottomans were engaged in 'a
conscious self-fashioning that strove to present the Ottoman dynasty and state
as the heirs and the successors of the Byzantine Empire'. Here they were very
much performing sovereign legitimacy, taking part in 'the protocols and
performances of sovereignty'.[51] Like a number of authors, Norton looks to
the manufacture and distribution of medals as one very important example of
such performance. As Norton argues, the 'use of shared imperial iconography
and vocabularies of sovereignty is perhaps most potently exemplified in the
Renaissance practice of casting and exchanging medals: a custom that tran-
scended religious and geographical divides'.[52] As Tim Dunne and Christian
Reus-Smit note in Chapters 1, 2, and 22, as a corrective to Bull's conception of
an international system as asocial, a politics of recognition is implicit within an
international system of states as much as a society of states. Here, from the
earliest beginnings of what would come to be seen as a European system,
Mehmet II and his successors not only worked to consolidate a flexible yet
increasingly unified identity within the empire, but they also projected the
Ottoman Empire as legitimately sovereign in terms that were recognized by
friend and foe alike.

---

[48] MacLean 2005: 9.   [49] Alexander 2004: 530.
[50] Norton 2013: 15.   [51] Norton 2013: 18.
[52] Norton 2013: 18. The artist Constanzo da Ferrara, resident at the court of Mehmet II, drew
on a long European artistic tradition to craft a portrait medal of the Sultan around 1481. This was
extensively circulated in Europe and it became the representation of Ottoman sultans for
generations. The medal is reproduced in Jardine and Brotton 2000: 32; and in Raby 1982.

It is important to note that the Europeans were not always the most pressing concern for the Ottomans. In the late fifteenth century Mehmet II's successor Bayezid was at war with the Egyptian Mamluk dynasty until 1491, and it was only when he assisted them against the Portuguese in 1495 that the Mamluks recognized the ascendancy of the Ottomans.[53] This coincided with a rising threat from the Shi'a Safavids looming in Persia. Under conditions where centrifugal forces were still strong, as Caroline Finkel notes, '[t]he disenfranchised tribal populations of the Ottoman-Iranian borderlands were a liability for the Ottomans who, while they did not want them participating in the running of their state, did not want to lose them to the Safavids who would use them to promote their own military and political interests'.[54] It is clear that in the late fifteenth century the boundaries of the empire were still being articulated. A pragmatic and flexible response to large numbers of non-Muslims within the empire was combined with strategies to deal with threats posed by other Muslim powers, either through conquest or cooperation, and, increasingly, as would become more apparent in the sixteenth century, policies aimed at the pacification of internal differences among Muslims.[55]

Thus the year 1490 saw the Ottoman Empire on the cusp of a turn towards greater religious uniformity within the empire. While the Ottomans were consolidating their authority within the empire, they were also setting out to attain recognition as sovereign and as both culturally and militarily equal in Europe. The skilful management of diversity within the empire was combined with performances of sovereign legitimacy that crossed political, religious, and geographical boundaries. The Ottomans came to power by harnessing diversity to their advantage and innovated to consolidate their authority. They built a relatively 'inclusive polity and society' even if, by the turn of the fifteenth century, the push towards Islamic religious uniformity was becoming stronger. Nonetheless, the *millet* system meant that there were places for peoples of the book, Christians, and Jews, albeit in a subordinate status, at a time when religious minorities were being persecuted and expelled from states across Europe. This was a very different way to 'manage diversity' to that pursued by most Western European powers.

I turn next to consideration of collective identity construction in a context that was completely alien and shocking to Europeans of the late fifteenth and early sixteenth centuries, the case of the Aztecs. Here practices of subjection, war, tribute, and trade took place within the context of a rich and complex cosmology. Drawing on this, through institutional innovation, a lowly group

---

[53] Finkel 2005a: 90–4. Bayezid's son Selim conquered Egypt and Syria in the sixteenth century.

[54] Finkel 2005a: 96.

[55] As Phillips notes in Chapter 3, strategies of segregation and incorporation were predominant in the recognition practices of many Islamicate polities before and after 1490.

attained the status of an imperial power in a relatively short time. However, following this period of innovation, they became less flexible, and as we will see, by the time the Spanish conquistadores arrived in 1519, this inflexibility was already causing internal strain, while their practices of sharply defining boundaries between self and enemies would have negative consequences for the Aztecs when it came to resisting the Spanish.

COLLECTIVE IDENTITIES IN 1490: THE AZTECS

In *The Expansion of International Society*, Michael Donelan gestures towards questions of identity when he points to the importance of religion for the Aztecs, Incas, and the Spanish alike. However, the main concern of his chapter is to canvass later Spanish debates over the treatment of 'Indians' and whether or not the Spanish were justified in imposing their rule, so there is little said about the pre-conquest world.[56] Here I aim to give a brief outline of the cosmological context of Aztec identity construction and the practices that played such an important role in this. This in turn allows us to better understand the shock of contact—for both Europeans and Aztecs. It must be noted, though, that few direct sources exist, and most accounts of the Aztec's city of Tenochtitlan and of Aztec life and beliefs are either from accounts given by conquistadors, or from later accounts by Spaniards drawing on the memories of Mexica who survived the destruction of Tenochtitlan in 1521.[57]

In the Aztec Empire up to European contact, the construction of collective identities developed through sharp boundaries being drawn between self and Other within regional war systems that were at the same time based on a wider shared symbolic and religious framework.[58] In the case of the Aztecs, we see the interaction of institutional entrepreneurs with this shared framework who were able to raise a minor god in the pantheon into their own central god of war. What would have happened in the absence of the arrival of the Spanish cannot be known, but by the end of the fifteenth century, the Aztec Empire (like the Incan Empire)[59] was facing problems of institutional stasis that were, in part, caused by what had earlier worked as an innovation, namely the way in which practices of war and ritual sacrifice were both legitimated and accelerated by localized readings of Mesoamerican cosmology, in particular the myth of the god of war, Huitzilopochtli.[60]

---

[56] Donelan 1984.

[57] As with the Americas in general, accounts of pre-conquest life are often supplemented by archaeological findings.

[58] López Austin 2004.   [59] Conrad and Demarest 1984.   [60] Boone 1989.

From humble beginnings the Aztecs, or Mexica, had quickly risen to the status of imperial power. When they arrived in the basin of Mexico, this group 'encountered a long-standing urbanized way of life'[61] and proceeded to develop their own complex city on Lake Texcoco. By the late thirteenth century, the Aztecs shared the gods of other Mesoamerican societies, although these were not really gods in the Western sense, but rather 'divine complexes that could unfold into myriad aspects, depending on specific temporal and spatial associations'.[62] As, so the Mexica believed, the gods had sacrificed themselves to create the sun and set it on its daily path, their sacrifice must be repeatedly repaid with the sacrifice of both human blood and lives.[63] As David Carrasco notes, the word closest in meaning to 'sacrifice' in the Mexica's language, Nahuatl, was *nextlaoalli*, which meant 'paying of the debt'.[64] In the development of what was in effect a state religion,[65] particular gods in the pantheon took on greater significance for the Mexica, with the god of war Huitzilopochtli playing a central role in the story of their wandering, the foundation of their city, and their rise to power.

By the end of the fifteenth century, the Aztecs were the dominant power in a Triple Alliance of Texcoco, Tacuba, and Mexica, formed when the city of Azcapotzalco was overthrown around 1426–8. The Mexica's story of themselves stressed their 200 years of wandering before they founded their city, Tenochtitlan, which would become the core of their empire (and on whose ruins modern-day Mexico City would be built).

The city overawed the first conquistadors who arrived in 1519 with its impressive buildings, the craftsmanship and beauty of many of the goods on display, and the size of its population.[66] The empire, loosely connected, was held together with Tenochtitlan as the centre of extensive networks of trade and tribute supplying not only foodstuffs and labour, but also the important 'ritual consumables'[67] such as feathers, jewels, gold, and fine cotton fabric, necessary for the regalia of nobles, priests, warriors, and sacrificial victims. As the population had vastly outstripped what could be produced in the environs of the city, and as the demand for the goods needed in ritual display was immense, tribute and trade were, in a very real sense, its lifeblood.

Underpinning this, the ritual spilling of human blood and the sacrifice of human lives was, as noted, considered to be essential for the continuation of

---

[61] Carrasco 2011: 32. [62] Conrad and Demarest 1984: 26. [63] Smith 2013: 197.
[64] Carrasco 2011: 69. [65] Conrad and Demarest 1984: 30.
[66] At this time, Tenochtitlan had a population of around 200,000 people. Seville had around 60,000, and Paris and Constantinople about 300,000 each. Numerous authors cite not only the letters of Hernán Cortés, who tended to underplay what he saw and overplay his own achievements, especially in the first difficult (for the Spanish) years before the destruction of Tenochtitlan, but also in the memoir of the soldier Diaz (de Rojas 2012: 55). Cortés's second letter of 30 October 1520 is the only account of the city of Tenochtitlan before the Spanish conquest.
[67] Clendinnen 1991a: 28.

the rising of the sun and therefore of all life. Thus, Mexica collective identification took form through the performance of ritual according to a complex
calendar,[68] in which war-making and human sacrifice played central roles, but
which affected all aspects of life. The war system of the Aztecs was not new in
itself as there was a long history of violent struggle between city-states in
Mesoamerica as well as human sacrifice that long predated the rise of the
Aztecs,[69] but after the transformation of the 1420s when the Triple Alliance
rose to power, and with the rise of the cult of Huitzilopochtli, the war/sacrifice
cycle accelerated. On coming to power, from the 1420s, Mexica elites had
inaugurated 'sweeping reforms', including the burning of historical and religious texts, in effect redesigning their own history in an effort to connect their
victories and eventual domination with a lineage to the ancient and revered
Toltecs.[70] This was part of a restructuring of institutions, 'economic political,
social and ideological',[71] aimed at building Aztec legitimacy and increasing
their power. It also increased the power of the priesthood and contributed
towards greater hierarchy and inequality in a society whose population was
already vulnerable to famine when crops failed.

Inga Clendinnen describes Aztec politics as 'contest politics' in which the
role of the 'Other' was central to the 'theatre of power', so by definition strong
conceptions of self-other identification were in play. Other groups were
mocked and their characteristics (or caricatures) incorporated into performances.[72] The Tlaxcalan of Tlaxcala, 'the resolutely independent province
beyond the mountains' (strongly anti-Mexica and who later became Hernán
Cortés's staunchest allies), were the Mexica's 'exemplary enemy'.[73] At the
same time, the Mexica were ever watchful for threats from within their empire
and within the city itself, with a wary eye on the many outsiders who came to
trade or do other business in the imperial centre. Clendinnen asks, '[h]ow was
the terrifying, essential, casual permeability of the city boundaries to be
borne?' Her answer: '[i]n part, by insistence on difference',[74] which was
defined, she argues, both through violence and art,[75] respectively highly
ritualized or stylized, and bound together in enacting the Aztecs' cosmological
beliefs or what Alfredo López Austin called their 'cosmovision, of which myth
is most privileged expression'.[76]

Tenochtitlan was a material expression of this cosmovision.[77] The Grand
Temple, the Templo Mayor on the axis of the four quarters of the city, was the

---

[68] For the Aztecs, as for all Mesoamericans at this time, there were a number of 'intermeshing
time counts'. Of these, the two most important were the solar calendar, *xiuitl*, which had eighteen
months of twenty days each, 'ending with five days of ill-omen', and the complex 'ritual or sacred
calendar', *tonalpoalli*. Combined they made up a fifty-two-year cycle. Clendinnen 1991a: 35.
[69] Conrad and Demarest 1984: 18–30.   [70] Clendinnen 1991a: 28.
[71] Conrad and Demarest 1984: 32.   [72] Clendinnen 1991a: 32–4.
[73] Clendinnen 1991a: 33.   [74] Clendinnen 1991a: 34.
[75] Clendinnen 1991a: 34.   [76] López Austin 2004: 602.   [77] Moctezuma 1991.

architectural embodiment of Serpent Mountain, the mythical birthplace of the god Huitzilopochtli. One of the two main temples at Templo Mayor was dedicated to Huitzilopochtli, the other dedicated to the rain god Tlaloc. Huitzilopochtli was born at war. According to the myth, when his sister Coyolxauhqui found that their mother was pregnant, she called on her 399 siblings to help her kill the mother before Huitzilopochtli could be born. However, he emerged in full war regalia, and killed Coyolxauhqui, decapitating her, with her body breaking into pieces as it rolled down Serpent Mountain. Huitzilopochtli then hunted down the 399 siblings and destroyed them. Huitzilopochtli was also an incarnation of the Sun God, who triumphed over Coyolxauhqui, the moon goddess, and his 399 siblings, the stars.

This sequence of events was replayed in many sacrifices at Huitzilopochtli's temple when victims' hearts were ripped out, they were decapitated, and once they had been thrown down the steps of the temple where a massive stone tablet of Coyolxauhqui was situated,[78] their arms and feet would be removed before the bodies were flayed, to be worn by priests or those warriors who had captured the victims. Through the performance of sacrifice, the one to be sacrificed was, rather than 'representing' the relevant god as we might understand it today, understood to embody that god, being a 'receptacle for the divine being'.[79] As Carrasco notes, 'the myth is a model, not for a single sacrifice but for the escalation of sacrifice or ritual debt payment of many individuals'.[80] This is what Clendinnen describes as 'the elaboration and extension of the traditional reward system of a warrior society',[81] that is, the status that came from capturing other warriors for sacrifice.

What we call Aztec 'art', was for the Aztecs an aspect of giving form to the supernatural world which was in a sense more real than the ephemeral human world. As we have seen, the design of Tenochtitlan and its architecture were an expression of this, as was the stone of Coyolxauhqui on to which the bodies of sacrificial victims were thrown.[82] Tenochtitlan was the centre where 'Aztec culture, authority, and domination were expressed in buildings, stone, sound, myth, public spectacles and sacrifices'.[83] Although the Aztecs did not have a written script, they used painted manuscripts to record (and rewrite) their history and prescribe the rituals that marked different aspects of life according to the calendar.[84] The 'manuscript painters' or 'scribes' were highly honoured, while 'the poet-singers and musicians who called the painted book to life were only slightly less honoured'.[85] Such performances brought the Aztec narrative

---

[78] The 3.25-metre stone disc was discovered in 1978. It is illustrated in Moctezuma 1991: 215.
[79] Carrasco 2011: 69.   [80] Carrasco 2011: 75.   [81] Clendinnen 1991a: 39.
[82] This was, of course, only one, major, centre of sacrifice. Many others occurred in different locations according to the calendar and the ritual requirements of the event and Huitzilopochtli, although pre-eminent for the Aztecs, was but one of numerous 'gods' to whom sacrifices were made.
[83] Carrasco 2011: 15.   [84] Boone 1994.   [85] Clendinnen 1991a: 215.

of who they were as a 'corporate body' alive in the interpretation and elaboration of texts.[86] Clendinnen notes not only the beauty of the 'flower songs', but also their role in mediating between the human world and the sacred.[87]

Although seemingly 'unchallengeable masters'[88] of a huge empire that ruled over more than 400 towns and cities, by the late fifteenth century the Aztec Empire was in fact under internal pressure. Their imperial authority was reaching its territorial limits, and it is unlikely that they could have pushed much further. At the same time, existing tributary states were quick to push back if they saw any weakness. As the empire reached its territorial limits, what had once been institutional innovations that had allowed expansion were now entrenched and causing problems. With the raising of Huitzilopochtli to such a high status, this 'bricolage' had accelerated the dynamic of war and sacrifice. Although estimates vary and the exaggeration of conquistadors who took exception to the sacrificial culture (while setting out to conquer, possess, and in the process pillage this empire) must be taken into account, it seems that the growing rate of sacrifices demanded ever-expanding war and conquest, and in the medium to longer term this may not have been sustainable.

Slowing conquest and stalled expansion met 'hold out groups', who fought wars of attrition at the boundaries of the empire. The Aztecs did not always win in these, and such losses ran counter to the increasing demand for sacrificial victims, many of whom were specifically required to be warriors caught in battle.[89] Combined with this, continual war made the extraction of tribute increasingly difficult. If the source is repeatedly at war there can be no tribute. Thus, while earlier in the century the need for tribute and for sacrificial victims had once been 'coinciding objectives', by the late fifteenth century they had instead become 'conflicting', and by the beginning of the sixteenth century internal crisis was looming.[90] By the late fifteenth century, it was not innovation that the elites had in mind. The changes made earlier in the century had benefited those elites, including the priesthood, bringing about an increasingly hierarchical and unequal society, with the last ruler Moctezuma II revoking the practice of merit-based rise to office for non-nobles.

Geoffrey W. Conrad and Arthur A. Demarest note that the Aztecs may also have been trying to challenge their neighbours' less than flattering views of them as low-life upstarts.[91] While the accelerated militarism and sacrifice of the fifteenth century, tied as it was to a recently reconfigured 'cosmovision' which compelled the need for constant renewal through sacrifice, most likely played a legitimating role for rulers within the city, this was more problematic in the wider reaches of the empire. At this level they had achieved what can

---

[86] Boone 1994: 71.   [87] Clendinnen 1991a: 219–23.   [88] Clendinnen 1991a: 24.
[89] Conrad and Demarest 1984: 59.   [90] Conrad and Demarest 1984: 59–60.
[91] Conrad and Demarest 1984: 38.

best be described as 'conquest without consolidation'.[92] While the Ottomans of the fifteenth century sought to incorporate groups within the empire as it expanded and to demonstrate their sovereign standing in Europe, the Aztecs sought captives and new sources of tribute and through the acquisition of these, continued domination and, importantly, recognition of their standing. However, at the wider level, this did not fully convince. Their cosmovision did not allow for assimilation or inclusion of the conquered and there was no 'managing of diversity' as was the case with the Ottomans, no way of bringing those inclined to resist on board except through subjugation. Instead, there was the constant demand for tribute and sacrifices of those defeated in battle, and an overriding 'insistence on difference', played out repeatedly in the violent ritual that was so integral to this war culture.

Whatever its internal weaknesses, it was external forces, in the form of Cortés and his conquistadors, which brought about the end of this rich, complex, and contradictory empire. Arriving in 1519, Cortés met many setbacks and his undertaking could easily have failed. However in 1521, he and his men destroyed Tenochtitlan and the Aztecs' power. The Tlaxcalan, the Mexica's Other among all others, were Cortés's allies in this.[93]

There was no basis for mutual understanding or recognition between the Aztecs and the Spanish. When Cortés first arrived, Moctezuma II ordered a display by the Aztecs meant to show his lordly status and the general super-iority of Mexicans but Cortés, with no cultural understanding and with his own conception of European superiority, took it as an act of submission.[94] Over the course of two years, the Aztecs with their highly ritualized ways of battle were puzzled by the strange and, in their terms, uncivilized way that the Spanish fought,[95] a way that was to prove fatally effective. The catastrophic impact of the Spanish conquest on the Aztecs is a well-known story of conquest, disease, and devastation, a story that was repeated across the Americas. The Spanish set out to destroy temples, obliterating material rep-resentations of the cosmovision that underpinned the Aztec Empire, and in doing so sought to smash that world and bring surviving Mexica under the dominion of both the Christian church and the Spanish monarchy. Thus the Aztec Empire fell.

Post-conquest Europeans tried to make sense of the Aztec Empire in terms of the classical and Christian traditions, and this was how they tried to understand the Aztec's god Huitzilopochtli, either as a kind of 'Graeco-Roman deity' or as 'an incarnation of the devil'.[96] Elizabeth Boone argues that these two views can be aligned with the two sides of the later sixteenth-century debate over the

---

[92] Conrad and Demarest 1984: 53.   [93] Clendinnen 1991a: 33.
[94] Clendinnen 1991b: 91.   [95] Clendinnen 1991b.   [96] Boone 1989: 57.

Aztecs, either as equal to or surpassing the Greeks and Romans in culture, or as slaves by nature.[97]

The debates of the sixteenth century highlight the shock of the discovery of this new world. Previously unknown to the Europeans, the peoples of the Americas were considered to have existed outside history; it was only their 'discovery' by Europeans that brought them into history and it was only in terms of pre-existing European categories that Europeans could try to understand them. This contributed, for Europeans, to an 'unravelling world'[98] in which the previously taken-for-granted unity of humankind and the laws that had been understood to govern this unified humanity, the laws of nature, were called into question. Thus confidence in the oneness of the European, and more specifically the Christian, tradition were undermined.[99]

As the radically different conceptions of cosmology and society of the Americans 'contradicted the traditional Christian view that there could really only exist one type of person and one kind of society',[100] this created another path through which relativism was to enter into Western political and religious thought,[101] with the struggles around the Reformation and Counter-Reformation giving practical—and world-changing—form to these changes.

CONCLUSION

In this chapter I have sought to understand the ways in which practices and performances of identification and differentiation helped to shape conceptions of collective identity in the Ottoman and Aztec Empires of the late fifteenth century. The ways in which collective identities were shaped in these empires impacted on European conceptions of collective identity, albeit in very different ways, and in both of these we can examine the politics of recognition, which was a lack of recognition in the case of the Aztecs. In both cases, relatively obscure groups had risen to the status of imperial power in a short period of time. In the Ottoman Empire we see a process of conquest and, over time, consolidation initiated in the fifteenth century through the skilled management of diversity. In the case of the Aztecs we observe, to the extent that we can see this empire that the Spanish destroyed in the early sixteenth century clearly at all, a politics of difference that was entrenched in a culture based on war and human sacrifice.

---

[97] Boone 1989: 57; Todorov 1984; for a critique of Todorov that argues that he replays European conceptions of moral superiority, see Clendinnen 1991b.

[98] Pagden 2011: 459.   [99] Pagden 1993: 1–15.   [100] Pagden 2011: 460.

[101] For example, on the rediscovery of Lucretius's *The Nature of Things* and its impact, see Greenblatt 2011.

In the first case we see interaction with Europe from the beginning of the empire, although to state it thus does not do justice to the constitutive effects of the cross-fertilization of ideas and practices that can be seen between the Ottoman Empire and its European neighbours. As outlined here, from the time of the fall of Constantinople in 1453, Sultan Mehmet II engaged not only in strategies of internal consolidation through the management of diversity, but also in an explicit performance of sovereign—and cultural—legitimacy aimed at, and understood by, his European contemporaries. This continued into the sixteenth century and accompanied the shifting alliance politics of the empire in Europe, exemplified in the reign of Suleyman, called 'the Magnificent' with good reason. We should note here that much of the rediscovery of the ancients, so important to the development of the Renaissance in Western Europe, was mediated through the Islamic world, and Mehmet with his quest for recognition also played a role in this. More than this, though, the valuing of this learning and exchange between scholars from both East and West was vital.[102] Renaissance conceptions of the capacity of humans to be 'self-fashioning' would not have been possible without these exchanges.

In the case of the Americas, and specifically here, the Aztecs, the shock of the new was experienced by both Mesoamericans and Europeans, although in very different ways. It was world-destroying for the Aztecs, and for the Europeans it played a role in a major historical transformation. The Ottomans were Other but at the same time at least partially known to Europeans and, as I have argued, their practices of identification were bound up with Europe. In contrast, the Aztecs, like other peoples of the 'New World', were without precedent in European experience and posed a challenge to their conceptions of a unified humanity.

Thirty years on from the publication of *The Evolution of International Society*, I have sought to understand the practice and performance of identification in two fifteenth-century empires and the interaction of each with Europe, in a way that, I hope, illuminates, in a non-teleological manner, the world in the period around 1490, a world on the cusp of great change. Consideration of not only who the Ottomans, the Aztecs, and the Europeans thought they were, but also of how these conceptions arose and how they put into practice their ways of being, always in a cultural performance that brought into being self and others, provides insight into ways of understanding identity and difference in longer historical perspective.

---

[102] This is not to underplay the hostility towards the Ottoman Empire felt by many Europeans at this time. Akasoy 2013. Also see Hobson 2004: 173–86; MacLean 2005.

5

Economies and Economic Interaction across Eurasia in the Early Modern Period

Hendrik Spruyt

In *The Anarchical Society*, Hedley Bull recalled how 'the encounters between Europe and non-European states from the sixteenth century until the late nineteenth' were largely about matters of trade, war, peace, and alliances. These encounters, he argued, 'did not in themselves demonstrate there is an international society'.[1]

A considerable body of scholarship has sought to explain how the European state system emerged and transformed into an international society between the late Middle Ages and the early twentieth century. This system then gradually expanded to create a global state system, an international state system with the 'rules of the game' dictated by Western principles.[2]

No doubt the emergence of a system of juridically equivalent units, ordered along the principle of internal sovereignty without higher external authority (unless authorized by the state itself), remains an important feature of international relations today. But in emphasizing the European system and society (and the early English School was certainly not alone in this regard), this scholarship neglected significant patterns of social order beyond the European region.

At the moment of the European 'break-out' of the maritime empires, c.1500, the world in fact evinced a staggering multiplicity of highly diverse forms of polities. The emphasis on how the European system emerged needs to be augmented by analysis of how these diverse regional systems operated. How is it that the European system displaced other forms of regional and international order?

One prevalent theoretical narrative has emphasized the uniqueness in the European configuration of political rule and economic interaction. By

---

[1] Bull 1977: 15.
[2] In methodological terms this creates the problem of lack of variation on the dependent variable. Since the end result is clear, any number of possible accounts might appear plausible.

that account, the European order was distinct, and indeed unique, in that the relevant sphere of trade and economic interaction expanded beyond and across distinct political hierarchies. Given the failure of the imperial ambitions of the Carolingians; of the German emperors of the Middle Ages; of the later Habsburg dynasty; and of other would-be universalist rulers; and given the failure of imperial theocracy, Europe emerged as a pluralistic set of dynastic states that gradually established mutually recognized territorial parameters. Imperial aspirations were checked by the multiple autonomous entities that objected to imperial overrule either by emperor or pope. Commerce and merchants had to navigate across political frontiers and, later, mutually agreed borders.

By contrast, non-European regions were dominated by hegemonic political systems that contained and incorporated the geographic extent of most economic activities. Hierarchy and market concurred. Where economic activities stretched beyond the frontiers, imperial ambitions soon sought to bring these activities within the empire.

Consequently, so the narrative goes, empires stifled development. With few exit options, merchants lacked the means to resist forceful taxation and exploitation. In Europe absolutist monarchs were constrained in their means of exploitation given that entrepreneurs could relocate and take their business elsewhere. Thus Europe, and Europe alone, gave rise to capitalism. Competition among the dynastic states also gave impetus to mercantilist practices. Success in warfare and success in economic development went hand in hand. The first state-led, semi-capitalist enterprises were thus often in industries related to military technology (such as the Arsenale in Venice).[3] To this day, this remains a powerful and widely shared perspective of European success and an explanation of Asian stagnation.[4]

In this account then, European political diversity—the distinct polities that made up the nascent state system—created a unique constellation of how economic exchange related to political order. In the European system, political decentralization correlated with dense economic exchange against a shared background of rules and norms. The European system was an international society given that states were conscious of 'common interests and common values'.[5]

This common perspective makes a second critically important claim. It argues that universal imperial systems constituted self-contained regions. Although there was some economic interaction across empires, in the nature of trade in luxury goods, they did not interact to any great measure in terms of politics or cultural cross-fertilization. Indeed, in these areas, polities might

---

[3] McNeill 1974.   [4] Mokyr 2014.   [5] Bull 1977: 13–14.

form a system, in that they took account of each other's actions, but they did not form an international society.

This induces a particular conception of global economic expansion. If one accepts the success of the European model as the most efficient solution of how to configure political order with economic activity, this view lends itself to interpreting globalization as unidirectional 'expansion' rather than as mutual incorporation or bi-directional influence.

I contend that such accounts miss important features of how Europe interacted with other regions, and fails to recognize the dyadic nature of the processes that led to globalization. More specifically, I will develop the following claims in this chapter.

First, the alleged bifurcation of the European state system with systems outside of Europe misconstrues and misunderstands the logic of political and economic order in universalist empires. Hence, such a view overemphasizes the deleterious consequences of hierarchy. No doubt there are instances of stifled economic development, but the reverse also occurred. For example, Mongol, Safavid, Ottoman, and other rulers were often directly involved in disseminating and fostering 'best practices' and economic developments. Thus, globalization was not an inevitable process of superior European political and economic organization simply displacing other forms.

Moreover, we must recognize the high level of material and cultural interactions across the Eurasian sphere well before the European 'breakout'. While the military incursions of Islamic and Central Asian powers into Europe have been analysed in great detail, there has been little focus on how economic actions influenced and simultaneously implicated cultural and political practices across the Eurasian space. Far from simply moving material goods across boundaries, the transnational networks of actors created conduits of knowledge and cultural exchange. As Iver Neumann has suggested, 'most instrumental action is still imbued with meaning, and the most symbolic action also has some instrumentality'.[6] Thus, even though one might speak of economic conduits of trade, one cannot bracket such material practices from the cultural exchanges that simultaneously took place.

Furthermore, and following from the two previous points, one cannot see the non-European world as destined to 'receive' European superior political and economic models. Of course European imperial rule expanded over the centuries following the Iberian breakout to the Atlantic and the globe at large, but European customs layered on to extant practices, sometimes fully adapting to what they found, rather than replacing local practices with European ones. And indeed in some instances the conduits of knowledge flowed rather to, not from, Europe. The visual imagery invoked by nineteenth-century map-makers,

---

[6] Neumann 2011: 466.

the image of Europe 'filling in' the blank canvas of undeveloped regions, must be laid aside. The various non-European systems often constituted vibrant international societies in their own right.

In addition, I contend that the early English School has tended to favour a thick understanding of international society.[7] Christian Europe constituted a society given shared values and interests, and common recognition of such interests. Indeed, for Hedley Bull, such society was based on 'a common language, a common epistemology...a common religion, a common ethical code, a common aesthetic or artistic tradition'.[8] Given that perspective, one might readily dismiss the presence of international society in other regions. But, as I will suggest, a 'thinner' definition of society allows one to extend the notion of a shared society to non-European systems. These showed remarkable consistency in shared epistemologies and patterns of behaviour. This was equally true in hegemonic systems, such as the Chinese tributary system, as well as in systems that lacked a clear political centre, such as the South East Asian region.

Before proceeding we should acknowledge the major contributions of the early English School by locating it within the developments of the discipline at large. The English sociological approach stood in marked contrast to both the behavioural tenets of American political science as it emerged from the 1950s, as well as to the realist view of international relations that held sway after the Second World War. As opposed to the material, empiricist approach of behaviouralism, the sociological approach emphasized intent, collective beliefs, and shared understanding. As opposed to realism, and particularly structural realism, the sociological approach objected to imputing state interests and the emphasis on balances of power.

The methodological positioning vis-à-vis behaviouralism and structural realist views thus emphasized the study of norms, values, and collective deliberation and understanding as opposed to the atomistic individualism that informed the study of international relations, particularly in the United States. The analytic concentration on European international society and its subsequent expansion by early English School scholars as Herbert Butterfield, Martin Wight, Bull, and Adam Watson, thus sufficed to counter the atomistic, ahistorical perspective.

However, in focusing particularly on Europe, this methodological positioning came at the price of occluding the nature of international orders beyond Europe. Thus, some re-examination of the earlier literature is warranted, as I hope to demonstrate in this chapter. By continuing the comparison of world-historical

---

[7] As a consequence, scholars such as Hedley Bull questioned whether the contemporary system could sustain an international society if common values and interests were questioned by challengers, such as the developing states and communist countries.

[8] Bull 1977: 16.

systems we might refine some previous conceptualizations of system and society. In addition, recent historical work suggests that early modern systems interacted to significantly higher degrees than previously thought. Thus, some historians have argued for the presence of an inter-ecumenical flow of cultural ideas and material practices well before the European maritime 'breakout'.

Combined, these points cumulate to several key conclusions. First, international society was not the sole prerogative of the European state system. Second, as Andrew Phillips argues as well, various systems across the Eurasian space interacted both materially and culturally to a far greater extent than previously imagined.[9] Globalization did not commence with the European moment in history, when the first Iberian empires spread to the corners of the globe.

THE CONTRAST OF THE EUROPEAN STATE SYSTEM WITH SELF-CONTAINED UNIVERSALIST EMPIRES

The historical contours of European political and economic development are well known. With the fall of the Carolingian Empire, economic flows across West and Central Europe diminished. The Carolingians, in their efforts to forge a unified political empire that stretched from Spain to the Elbe River, had fostered economic development and trade across the region. Indeed, during the reigns of Charlemagne and Louis the Pious, they even managed to introduce a standardized system of coinage.

However, as the empire fragmented and incursions from Norsemen, Maygars, and various Islamic dynasties increased, trade flows diminished precipitously. Only Britain managed to maintain a relatively centralized political and economic system, although even there the multitude of weights, measures, and coinage was bewildering.[10]

The later Middle Ages, starting from the twelfth century on, marked a renewal of economic activity that centred on two core areas.[11] The north-western European region saw the rapid development of urban centres and mercantile pursuits with bulk goods as their main staple. The Mediterranean region, with the Italian cities as the key actors, made substantial wealth by linking to the cross-Eurasian trade networks that connected Europe through the Middle East to the economies as far as the Orient.[12] With limited maritime means to move such goods, this remained long-distance trade in luxury goods.

---

[9] See Chapter 3.   [10] Kula 1986.
[11] Bernard 1972; Blockmans 1988: 169, 1989: 733; Pirenne 1956.
[12] Scammel 1981.

The European system, however, differed from these other regions due to the absence of empire. Following the Carolingian imperial ambitions, the German emperors had embarked on a similar quest by the late tenth century and continued to pursue this strategy well into the fourteenth century. Confronted by royal dynasties and papal resistance, the latter with European-wide ambitions of its own, neither empire nor a hierarchical theocracy emerged. Europe would remain politically decentralized with European economic flows traversing political frontiers and later formal borders.

The purpose of this chapter, however, is not to shed new light on the emergence of this state system, but rather to highlight how the narrative of European development has tended to juxtapose it to the non-European world. Scholars such as Janet L. Abu-Lughod and Immanuel Wallerstein thus argue that the European region constituted a world-economic system that only tangentially linked with other geographic areas.[13] Whereas Europe constituted a region that was politically decentralized with cross-border economic interaction, the other regions of the world typically demonstrated a hierarchical imperial order which contained within it the primary spheres of economic interaction.

For Wallerstein, 'world-systems' constituted self-contained economic systems that displayed a division of labour and that incorporated a diversity of cultures:

> There have only existed two varieties of such world-systems: world-empires, in which there is a single political system over most of the area...and those systems in which such a single political system does not exist over all, or virtually all, of the space...we are using the term world-economy to describe the latter.[14]

Wallerstein is also quite clear that he views the development of the European system as the only world-economy. It was unique. 'There were world-economies before. But they were always transformed into empires: China, Persia, Rome.'[15]

Roberto Unger, similarly, argues that the relation of political authority to trade took two basic forms. 'One solution is the quasi-autarkic empire. Its most tangible feature is the overall coincidence of economic and political boundaries: most trade takes place within the borders of a territory that a single government and its officialdom claim to rule.'[16] The other solution, the overlord–peddler deal, occurs where trade was carried out in territories with diverse independent authorities. The European state system adopted a variation on this model, and thus constituted 'the acceptance of the incongruence between political and economic boundaries'.[17]

---

[13] Abu-Lughod 1989; Wallerstein 1974.   [14] Wallerstein 1974: 348.
[15] Wallerstein 1974: 16.   [16] Unger 1987: 113.
[17] Unger 1987: 115. He further notes that although there were periodic attempts to establish such autarkic empires in Europe, for example by the Habsburgs, these attempts ended in failure.

This is not to say that these perspectives were oblivious to the historical patterns of long-distance networks of private actors that had for millennia travelled and interacted throughout the Eurasian realm.[18] The famous Silk Road was only one of various routes across this space. But this pattern of trade remained resolutely driven by private actors, who intermittently, through indirect contacts, purchased and sold luxury items across Eurasia. At times political elites were enablers. The protection enjoyed by the Polo family as they traversed the Mongol empire is well documented. At other times political elites acted predatorially, bringing trade to a standstill. Ethnic and family ties formed the core of these private trading networks. Clan and family ties were the logical solution to facilitate sharing of information, foster credible commitments, and deal with principal–agent oversight issues.[19]

These trading networks flowed from nodes in the Mediterranean, of which the Genovese and Venetian trading companies constitute the best examples, and through Middle Eastern bases at the eastern rim of the Mediterranean. From there some networks connected through land routes to East Asia, while the maritime, southern routes connected to India and South East Asia. These relations constituted the overlord–peddler arrangements mentioned by Unger.

Bull and Watson shared this perspective. Recognizing the variation of non-European systems, they nevertheless argued that:

> They had one feature in common: they were all, at least in the theory that underlay them, hegemonial or imperial…Contacts among these regional international systems (and with the different world of medieval Latin Christendom) were much more limited than contacts within them. There was some diplomatic communication and military conflict…But not even the three Islamic systems (Arab-Islamic, Mongol-Tartar, and Indian) may be said to have formed among themselves a single international system or international society.[20]

Even when some scholars, such as Abu-Lughod, have acknowledged the various subsystems that shared significant degrees of interaction, they fall short of extending such analysis to the moment of European maritime expansion. Abu-Lughod's narrative stops at 1350 and she suggests a decline of this system thereafter.[21] It is only with the European 'expansion' that a global world system emerged.

Such accounts overemphasize the European maritime breakout as an integrative mechanism.[22] Of course maritime exploration brought the Americas,

---

[18] For detailed accounts in the historical literature, see Curtin 1984; Tracy 1990, 1991.
[19] Greif 1992: 128; Landa 1981: 349.   [20] Cited in Watson 1992: 215–16.
[21] Abu-Lughod 1989: 356.
[22] Arguably, world-systems and related perspectives privilege economic interaction and material factors above social and ideational dimensions of globalization. Nevertheless, the latter are inevitably implicated in this process. For a fuller discussion of this point see Chapter 10.

sub-Saharan Africa, and Asia increasingly into the European sphere of inter-action. But we should not reduce globalization to a single event or view it only as material exchange. Viewed as a process, Eurasian globalization occurred well before the Columbian moment that heralded the European arrival in the Americas and the Orient. Indeed, the process of globalization had been in play, with periodic swings, well before the late fifteenth century.

These views have also profoundly affected how scholarship has explained European economic 'take off' and Oriental and Islamic (alleged) stagnation, as well as the perceived lack of significant interaction among the various systems. The view that only Europe constituted a world-economy and only Europe formed an international society implies that the rise of European pre-eminence resulted in a unidirectional expansion of Western political influence and social practices to the rest of the globe, culminating in the extension of the sovereign territorial states system. The success of the European world-economy gradually incorporated the non-European subsystems into the advancing capitalist world-system that came to encompass the entire globe.[23] Most tellingly, such a perspective disavows the presence of shared norms and practices across the Eurasian space by focusing only on the degree of economic interactions. There was no 'international society' beyond Europe.

Instead, as I will demonstrate, while it might be too strong to argue that the Eurasian sphere constituted a 'thick' society with deliberately crafted and mutually agreed principles and norms, the level of shared economic and cultural exchanges was significant. Moreover, these exchanges were made possible against the background of widely diverse regional systems, some of which had hegemonic centres, such as the Chinese tributary system, while others, such as the regional systems of South East Asia, functioned largely on shared cultural principles, but lacked any dominant material or cultural centre. Shared practices and norms permeated the Eurasian space, even if they were not the creation of deliberate inter-state agreements.

BROADENING OUR UNDERSTANDING OF NON-EUROPEAN SYSTEMS AND SOCIETIES

The claim that the imperial hierarchies beyond Europe retarded economic growth and led to stagnation even in once technologically advanced empires continues to hold sway. Most recently economic historian Joel Mokyr reiter-ates the claim that political decentralization in Europe led to its surpassing of

---

[23] Eric Hobsbawn (1990: 25) too seems to accept the world-systems notion that 'capitalism was bred as a global system in one continent and not elsewhere, precisely because of the political pluralism of Europe, which neither constituted nor formed part of a single "world empire"'.

the Chinese economy.[24] In the latter, the lack of competition limited the demand for innovation. On the 'production' side, innovators and entrepreneurs had no exit options to avoid ruler predation.

In the European system, by contrast, predatory behaviour by rulers was tempered by the threat that mercantile interests might relocate to less authoritarian and exploitive systems.[25] Competition over time favoured efficient systems, such as the financial systems of Britain and the Dutch Republic, over those of absolutist monarchies that could not credibly commit to sound economic policy.[26]

However, this claim warrants further scrutiny. Hierarchy was not deleterious to economic activity on all occasions. Mongol hierarchy led to an expansion of economic activity over a wide area. Similarly, Asian imperial rulers, such as the Chinese Tang and Sung emperors, stimulated vibrant economic growth and guaranteed the security of transborder trade routes. While it is true that some imperial systems were detrimental to trade flows across the region, arguably the Ottomans were less disposed to trans-Eurasian trade routes across their empire, this cannot be held as a universal phenomenon.

Moreover, if imperial hierarchy is in all cases detrimental to innovation, economic development, and trade, then it is not clear why various non-European empires were well ahead of the European dynasties till the early modern age, or even beyond. For example, it has been argued that even in military technology, the European advantage did not fully manifest itself until the late eighteenth century.[27]

The idea that Europe rose to pre-eminence due to its competitive state system while, beyond Europe, universalist empires declined due to their formal hierarchical structures, thus needs further analysis. Were universalist claims to empire indeed as hierarchical as imagined? Did these universalist empires operate as self-contained economic political and economic systems or did they allow for significant cross-border exchange of goods and ideas?

To answer these questions I turn to recent historical scholarship that challenges the view that different regions in the Eurasian sphere developed in relative isolation from one another. This historical research sheds new light on existing perspectives in both history and political science. It suggests instead the presence of a considerable degree of inter-ecumenical contacts, exchanges, and even relative tolerance of diverse religions and ethnicities across vast imperial spaces.

Methodologically, I highlight two cases to interrogate the prevalent narrative that European uniqueness drove its development and positioned it to expand at the expense of the non-European systems. The Chinese tributary system at face value would seem to constitute a primary example of a universalist empire—a

---

[24] Mokyr 2014.   [25] Unger 1987; Badie and Birnbaum 1983.
[26] North 1981; North and Weingast 1989: 803.   [27] Cipolla 1965.

political hierarchy encapsulating the entire sphere of main economic interaction (save the luxury trade routes beyond the empire). Thus one might conclude that such a universal empire operated in isolation from other systems. This would be to misunderstand the logic of rule in the Chinese system, as well as the relations of China to its neighbours.

Focusing on the Chinese tributary system also serves to highlight other issues in the early scholarship of the English School. As Xiaoming Zhang points out, this scholarship tended to emphasize parallels between the European state system and the Warring States period.[28] The tributary system, that by his account lasted for two millennia, received far less attention. While he attributes this to Eurocentrism, one could also surmise that, since the intent of the English School focused on the study of international society, the apparent hierarchy of the Chinese tribute system logically precluded it from being labelled as an international society. The concept of international society after all was premised on the presence of independent polities in a given system.

By creating a bifurcated typology of state systems versus suzerain state systems, scholars such as Bull, Watson, and Wight, essentially separated the European Westphalian system from virtually all other systems given that the latter were conceived as universalist empires. Moreover, as a logical corollary, any notion of an international society was thus limited to the European experience.

A closer examination of the Chinese tributary system, as the archetypical case of a universalist empire, reveals that the system was less hierarchical than imagined and less insular than alleged. Instead the Chinese tributary system showed considerable fluidity in the multilayered patterns of hierarchy, as well as considerable degrees of economic and cultural interaction with polities beyond those commonly perceived as within the Chinese tribute system.

The artificial bifurcation between the European state system with its international society on one side, and the suzerain state systems without such international society on the other side, is further maintained by a strict definition of what constitutes a society. The European international society, which arguably only came to full fruition in the nineteenth century, was premised on shared values, common interests, and shared religion. These in turn informed common institutions. By these criteria, only a limited set of systems, the Greek city-states, the Hellenistic kingdoms, the Warring States period in China, and the state system of ancient India, constituted international societies.[29]

In that perspective, common rules and common institutions are key. But this is decidedly an agentic perspective of culture and civilization. Actors create shared rules and norms, rather than culture and civilization facilitating

---

[28] Zhang 2011b: 763.   [29] Bull 1977: 16.

and informing individual behaviours, preferences, and beliefs. The structural component is missing.

For these reasons I focus on a second example of how international society and system can operate in a different manner than the European configuration. First, South East Asia constituted a system of interacting polities but, contrary to the bifurcation of a European state system and suzerain systems beyond Europe, it was not organized around any hegemonic centre. Its political decentralization resembled European state anarchy.

Second, the South East Asian region provides an example of a system that evinced a high degree of cultural and material interaction. For Bull and Watson such a system, however, would likely be deemed to lack an international society. There were no agreed rules or institutions to facilitate interaction and exchange.

However, when viewed with a different understanding and a more structural view of shared perspectives and beliefs, the polities in this region certainly operated within a thinner view of international society. Even if they did not meet all the endowments that Bull saw as critical for societies, such as 'a common language, a common epistemology…a common religion, a common ethical code, a common aesthetic or artistic tradition', they certainly shared some of these elements. These commonalities laid the basis for systematic interaction. Their polities shared fundamental features of how political and social life should be organized.[30]

Finally, by focusing on these two cases one must inevitably question any strict temporal demarcation of when globalization began as well as how this process unfolded. Temporally the process of globalization commenced well before the advent of the powerful European maritime empires. Substantively, globalization encapsulated much more than European economic and political expansion and instead suggests the cross-fertilization of ideas and material practices.

THE CHINESE TRIBUTARY SYSTEM IN PRACTICE

I argue, first, that the claims to universal empire should not be mistaken for formal imperial hierarchy. Throughout the Eurasian region, rulers invoked the legacy of universalist kingship and empire. Even in Europe imperial rule was justified by rituals, symbols, and historical narratives that suggested a cosmological homology between divine order and political rule. The very invocation

---

[30] Andrew Phillips's usage of the term civilizational assemblage would likely come close to this understanding. I have in mind the shared civilizational ideas and practices that can be identified among various polities of a given region. For further discussions, see Chapters 3 and 10.

of adjectives to empire as 'Holy' and 'Roman' suggested this parallelism. The orb, held in the hand of the emperor, represented the globe, within it containing soil from all quadrants of the world. Beyond Europe, rulers similarly invoked cosmological order, demonstrated by rituals, architecture, and dress. Palaces and temples represented the *axis mundi*, the centre of the world, connecting the political and profane to the realm of the sacred.[31]

But as in Europe, these universalist claims should not be understood as actual representations of political hierarchy. Formal imperial hierarchy, although it might have existed in aspirations and ambitions, rarely covered the extensive networks of trade and commercial activity that flowed well beyond those polities. Across the Middle East and South Asia, one witnessed thus a multitude of rulers (at one time as many as twenty rulers all claimed to be the legitimate universalist world conquerors, heirs to Alexander the Great, Genghis Khan, and Timur (Tamerlane), the three recognized world conquerors).[32] Universalist claims thus justified and legitimated their rule, even if formal control seldom corresponded with such claims.

The Chinese imperial system, perhaps one of the most extensive and long-lasting, legitimated the emperor's rule by the mandate of heaven, by means of which all would be gathered (*tianxia*). However, the Chinese tributary system did not bring all of its relevant economic sphere under a single political hierarchy. Moreover, its central position, within this extensive trade network to the West and particularly to East Asia, was characterized by its cultural position rather than formal material control.

This tributary system of trade, which gained significant scholarly attention more than half a century ago, has attracted renewed attention.[33] The tributary system constituted a pattern of economic exchange well beyond the Chinese imperial frontiers, but it did not constitute hierarchy in the traditional sense in that it did not form a single polity or world empire. Instead, it was based on a shared cultural sphere of interaction, specifically Confucian norms and principles. Within this sphere operated Korea, arguably the one most tightly incorporated in this system, Japan, and to a lesser extent some of the South East Asian polities, most notably Vietnam.

The rationale, contours, and boundaries of this system are being re-examined.[34] Some recent scholarship has contested the idea that China stood at the apex of a cultural hierarchy. Other polities with whom China interacted operated tributary systems and trade networks of their own, which did not necessarily include China. Thus, rather than a 'hub and spoke' pattern

---

[31] Eliade 1959.   [32] Chann 2013.

[33] John Fairbank wrote the *locus classicus* in 1942. Fairbank 1942: 129. For recent scholarship, see Kang 2010.

[34] For a theoretical and empirical evaluation of the Chinese tributary system in recent scholarship, see Zhang 2009: 545.

of imperial relations between core and periphery, there were multiple over-lapping and cross-cutting trade networks that resembled tributary systems in their own right.

Moreover, some states that are not usually regarded as being part of this tributary sphere of interaction nevertheless traded quite substantially with China. For example, there is evidence that kingdoms with only limited expos-ure to Confucian principles of rule and administration nevertheless sent envoys and paid tribute, even if infrequently. Should they be regarded as part of this tributary trading network? Even the status of Vietnam as part of the tributary system is contested. Thus, the boundaries of this system were fluid and depended on the dynamism of the Chinese centre and the dynamism of rival trade networks throughout East, South, and South East Asia.

Furthermore, there is little doubt that there were substantial trade flows beyond the formal Chinese imperial system. As John Fairbank noted, even the Portuguese and Dutch joined in the ritualistic practice of paying tribute. This was not simply an inward-looking, isolated empire.

The Japanese position in this tributary system is also open to question, particularly since the emperor also claimed a divine mandate, thus logically precluding recognition of another ruler as superior. Previous scholarship has also suggested that the divine status of Japanese imperial rule prohibited expansive interactions beyond the Japanese islands.[35] The closure of Japan until the Meiji restoration is thus cited as perpetuating a system of internal hierarchy (after the civil wars of the sixteenth century) and closure from external polities. This argument is no longer widely accepted. 'The model proposed here…is one of active, autonomous Japanese relations with the world abroad, one that places Japan at the *center* of the world as Japanese conceived it, rather than at the margins of a China centered world or beyond the periphery of a Eurocentric one.'[36]

Well before the European expansion that started by the late fifteenth century, private trading networks and interstitial actors braided spheres of interaction across a vast Eurasian space. Although one might still distinguish various zones of economic density, what Abu Lughod termed economic subsystems in her study, these zones were not as segmented as once thought.

Moreover, actors who at one time might have been deemed parasitical to the core regions of these subsystems played an important part not only in disseminating practices across the Eurasian region, but were themselves dynamically involved with innovating practices. The frontier peoples of the Chinese civilization—those deemed outside the traditional tributary system—were not merely parasitical, passively adopting and absorbing Chinese prac-tices, but they actively developed advanced economic routines, once perceived

---

[35] Bendix 1978.   [36] Toby 1991: xvi.

to be the unique attributes of European emergent capitalism or Islamic business acumen and administrative knowledge. The Mongol rulers of Central Asia thus utilized tax farming in a very similar fashion to their European and Islamic counterparts and brought these ideas to the Chinese imperial court. With the Middle East and Ottoman rulers, they shared mercantile exchanges, such as the Ortuq business practices, that incorporated tax farming, government–business partnerships, and monetization. As Christopher Atwood remarks: 'This survey has demonstrated a remarkable parallel between the financial instruments used by the Mongols in their empire in East Asia and the Middle East, and by the Qing in their empire in Mongolia.'[37]

Such a view of relatively advanced economic and cultural practices contrasts with perspectives from earlier research. In comparing the shared rules of the European state system with non-European regions that lacked the element of society altogether, Bull argued that 'the relations of Chingis Khan's Mongol invaders, and the Asian and European peoples whom they subjugated, were not moderated by a belief on each side in common rules binding on both in their dealings with one another'.[38] Such a perspective no longer seems tenable.

In sum, despite the invocation of a common narrative to justify rule—the invocation that rulers constituted world conquerors and world emperors—patterns of economic and cultural interaction crossed vast geographical space and across distinct polities. World-empire was not the equivalent of a relatively self-contained economic subsystem. Moreover, claims to cultural hierarchy, as with China, did not correspond with claims to rule in any formal sense over the entire geographic sphere of interaction. And finally, the role of interstitial polities and private trade networks suggest a far more dyadic set of flows, even before the late fifteenth century.

ECONOMIC INTERACTION AND TRADE WITHOUT HEGEMONY: SOUTH ASIA, SOUTH EAST ASIA, AND THE ISLAMIC WORLD

South and South East Asia provides other evidence that the geographic sphere of economic interaction did not necessarily correlate with political empire. Indeed, studying these regions demonstrates even more so than the Chinese case that some significant trade networks outside Europe emerged without imperial imposition. They lacked both a political centre and a core civilizational polity.

South East Asia thus shared with Europe the absence of imperial hierarchy — either in formal or cultural, tributary terms. 'Southeast Asia was a region united

---

[37] Atwood 2013.   [38] Bull 1977: 43.

by environment, commerce, diplomacy, and war but diverse in its fragmented polities and cultures. In this it had more in common with Europe than with the great landmasses of Asia.'[39] But in Europe, the division of legal spheres between domestic sovereigns, and inter-state agreements to deal with the lack of hierarchy, came to typify the regulation of interactions across borders over the course of several centuries. The mutual respect of domestic hierarchy (sovereignty) and agreed borders arguably formed key constitutive rules of order in this system.

The patterns of trade throughout South East Asia, however, occurred against a different background. This region evinced considerable fluidity of rule which lacked any notion of fixed territorial boundaries. Political decentralization, however, did not entail diminished commerce; quite the contrary. 'Fragmented power meant that traders could move freely often with the encouragement of rulers who hoped to profit from their presence.'[40]

Instead, the interconnectedness of these polities occurred against shared ontological views of political order, and specifically the parallelism between cosmological perspective and political order. The South East Asian sphere, prior to its incorporation into the Eurocentric world order, demonstrated a fundamentally different social structure based on Brahmanic and Buddhist conceptions and shared notions of what constituted authority, who might lay claim to such authority, and how such authority might be exercised. Rule was made manifest by architecture, by ritual performances, through the invocation of specific titles, and the claim to specific lineages. These in turn influenced how polities interacted with each other across a vast geographic region.

Despite lacking any form of political hierarchy at any time in history, there were common traits among the multiple polities of the region. Motivating political and social organization was the desire to order the material world in such a way that it corresponded with religious and cosmological understandings:

> The primary notion with which we shall have to deal is the belief in the parallelism between Macrocosmos and Microcosmos, between the universe and the world of men ... Harmony between the empire and the universe is achieved by organizing the former as an image of the latter, as a universe on a smaller scale.[41]

These shared foundational elements spread by means of the Indianization of South East Asia—with the exception of Vietnam which remained heavily influenced by Chinese Confucianism and legalism. Thus, we find broad similarities in the political organization and the various means by which authority ruled in Thailand, Cambodia, Burma, and the Indonesian islands.[42]

---

[39] Reid 1993: 19.   [40] Curtin 1984: 124.

[41] Heine-Geldern 1942: 15. For a similar argument, see Wheatley 1967.

[42] On Thailand, see Tambiah 2013: 503; on Burma, see Lieberman 1987: 162. The Indonesian islands are discussed by Andaya 1993; and also in van Fraassen 1992.

These cosmological perspectives had a significant effect on material practices. For example, in many of these polities, the view held that the ideal polity should be organized along four quadrants. Vassals and alliances would be brought in line to duplicate the sacred numbers four or five (counting the centre as one with its four main vassals), or nine (the core five with another four sub vassals), or multiples thereof. We find, for example, the five and nine unions, or alliances, playing a key role in the dynamics of the Moluccan Spice Islands.[43] The newly arrived Portuguese, Spanish, and Dutch did not upset this collective imagination, but were interjected into these existing frameworks.

In sum, this shared collective consciousness of social and political order facilitated economic and political interaction without hegemonic imposition. No doubt individual rulers, such as the Srivijaya kings of medieval Sumatra, at times tried to monopolize trade routes, but the failure to do so provided the opportunities for a multiplicity of actors, private and public, to engage in commerce, partially aided by shared cultural perspectives.[44]

Cemil Aydin makes a similar observation regarding interactions across the Islamic world. Although by the late Middle Ages and early modern era there were arguably more than twenty distinct polities, trade flowed consistently across these different entities. A shared set of cultural practices, such as a widely held view that Sharia law should guide economic transactions, facilitated interactions regardless of the formal political arrangements:

> Even in times of military conflict and battles among various Muslim rulers, there were laws and principles that all had to abide by with regard to conduct of war, prisoners, civilians and cultural relations. This Muslim cultural system facilitated not only an intense level of mobility among scholars, students, pilgrims, traders, adventurers, and migrants, it also linked different regions of the world with each other, from Europe to Africa, from Central Asia to Southeast Asia and Anatolia.[45]

John Voll also notes these shared practices across the Islamic world. Rather than focusing on the exchange of material goods, the focus of Wallerstein's definition of 'world-system', he argues that despite the lack of imperial hierarchy, the Islamic world provided a shared discourse that made continuous interaction possible:

> This pattern of communication in the Islamic world is not primarily based upon exchange of goods, coordination of means of production, or a large network of economic activities. Instead, it is built on the shared sources of the Islamic

---

[43] Van Fraassen 1992.

[44] Philip Curtin (1984: 127) similarly talks about a vast region of ecumenical trade. However, he notes this was not based on shared culture. Keep in mind, however, that the region of his interest ranged from the Middle East, across South Asia to South East Asia.

[45] Aydin 2013: 8.

experience, which provide the basis for mutually intelligible discourse among all who identify themselves as Muslims within the Dar al-Islam.[46]

Thus, contrary to some of the early scholarship in the English School, we must recognize the vibrancy of international societies beyond Europe.

EURASIAN INTERCONNECTEDNESS
BEFORE THE EUROPEAN MOMENT

In view of these observations, the perspective that globalization constituted a more or less unidirectional flow, conceptualized as an *expansion* of the European political and economic system, must be revisited. Technological breakthroughs, particularly in maritime technology, no doubt played a role in allowing for a geographical expansion of European ambitions. Developments in lateen rigging styles and the emergence of the ocean-going carrack gave the Europeans the ability to expand beyond the Mediterranean and north European coastal waters.[47] Military technological developments also played their role, although the European lead in such technology arguably came after the European maritime 'breakout'.

The gradual intensification of European contacts with other parts of the globe became possible with a more efficient form of long-distance maritime trade and communication rather than land-based commerce. However, European forays into these new regions largely took place on the terms of extant polities. Trade occurred along coastal entrepôts, where Europeans mingled with well-established, long-standing trade networks. Within these entrepôts, the typical arrangement left the foreign merchants to self-rule. Rather than displacing extant systems or challenging political rule, the Europeans occupied one more niche among the diverse tapestry of nationalities and mercantile networks.[48] The familiar *millet* system of the Ottoman Empire had its parallel in many ports of the world.

This process of dyadic interaction and adjustment rather than displacement, or unidirectional expansion, also occurred in the Chinese tributary system. Both Portuguese and Dutch merchants accepted the constitutive rules of the system and paid tribute, engaging in the required ritual performances that legitimated the cultural supremacy of the Chinese rulers.[49] Only by the mid-nineteenth century did the European position change to the extent that English officials refused to acknowledge the need for tribute and ritualistic submission. This refusal was not based on economic calculation. Indeed, the tributary system in

---

[46] Voll 1994: 219.   [47] Parry 1981; Scammel 1981; Lewis and Runyan 1985.
[48] Chauduri 1991: 437.   [49] Fairbank 1942: 129.

economic terms constituted a net loss to the Chinese empire, due to the fact that reciprocity to those engaging in submission required imperial concessions and counter-gifts. The issue at heart in the nineteenth century was the refusal to submit to Chinese suzerainty, even if ritualistic in nature.

The monetary flows of gold and silver to the Orient provide more evidence of the decidedly secondary status of European powers. There is little doubt in contemporary scholarship that European trade with the Orient decidedly favoured the latter. Demand for Oriental products led to a massive outflow of silver which the Europeans could only finance by their holdings in the Americas. The trade balance ran against European mercantile interests.[50]

As Yongjin Zhang notes, the English School has tended to emphasize the expansion of Europe into China and East Asia in the nineteenth century, omitting the complex and dyadic nature of interaction before then.[51] As I have argued here, Eurasia was enmeshed in a much wider circulation of material and cultural practices, well before the European position had evolved to the point that it could seek to dominate Asia and other regions in a more unilateral fashion.

And even when European military and economic potential increased, both political administrators and mercantile interests had to graft their practices on previously existing business repertoires and had to use local knowledge. For example, in India the Brahmin scribes, the Kyasthas, became a critical part of both British political administration as well as economic organization.[52] Whatever its military prowess, Britain could not hope to control the vast populations of South Asia without adapting to and accepting the presence of long historical, indigenous practices.

Nor can one argue that the Asians were simply bystanders when European political domination started to come to full fruition. Indeed, at times they could invert the rules and laws imposed by the Western powers against the latter. Thus the Hong merchants, the Canton traders who had the authorized monopoly on trade with foreigners, in the mid-nineteenth century brought a suit against the British Jardine Fleming house, took them to court in the United States, and won their case.[53] In short, at times Asian trading networks inverted the European practices to limit the latter's influence.

CONCLUSION

This chapter has sought to interrogate common narratives of European development, its subsequent expansion to other regions, and ultimately the

---

[50] Barrett 1990.   [51] See Chapter 11.   [52] Bellenoit 2013.   [53] Wong 2013.

transposition of the European state system to the rest of the globe. One key feature of such narratives juxtaposes a decentralized European system to the hierarchical imperial systems in other regions of Eurasia. In Europe, economic interaction across borders occurred against the backdrop of political decentralization, whereas in other regions political hierarchy overlapped with the geographic sphere of interaction. Political hierarchy encapsulated the market.

At a minimum, this simple dichotomy is too impoverished and neglects a much wider array of political-economic arrangements beyond Europe. The distinction of state-system versus hegemonic-imperial orders misses the complexity of multiple systems throughout the Eurasian sphere. Many regional economic systems existed beyond Europe which were not politically integrated in universal empires.

But even with regards to universal imperial systems, extant narratives misconstrue the logic of rule and the actual conduct of economic relations. First, the universal imperial claim must be seen as a legitimating device. Rulers were keenly aware that their claims to rule as world conqueror were often unmatched by their material control over distant areas. Second, imperial hierarchy was not per definition a recipe for stagnation. Whatever the causes for European development and later industrialization, universalist empires were not antithetical to development and innovation, as the late Tang and Song dynasties proved in China. The synergy between political rulers and merchants went well beyond benign despotism. Often rulers were directly involved in encouraging and fostering trade as well as favouring foreign entrepreneurs to bring new business practices to their realms. Universalist empires were not relative backwaters which would in time simply be absorbed by the more efficient and successful European polities.

Third, and perhaps most importantly, this chapter challenges the notion that such universalist imperial systems, by containing the relevant sphere of interaction within the empire, constituted insular political entities. Eurasia consisted of a network of translocal interactions in material and cultural terms.

Even describing these interactions as economic systems does not quite get to the heart of the matter.[54] While no doubt economic interactions were often conduits of such exchanges, material practices were not, and could not be, isolated from the exchanges of beliefs, administrative practices, sources of political legitimation, and cosmological understandings. As Jacinta O'Hagan notes, the exchange, interplay, and mutual contestation of ideational and

---

[54] Barry Buzan and Richard Little (2000) distinguish international systems based on economic exchange from systems which have a more fully articulated pattern of interaction along military, political, economic, and cultural dimensions. While I concur with this distinction, I wish to avoid the perception that economic interaction would be entirely material in nature.

social meanings and practices are inevitably part of any material interaction that takes place on a regular basis.[55]

The juxtaposition of a non-hierarchical European system, endowed with an international society, against universalist empires, which logically (given the lack of autonomous polities) would not constitute an international society, also neglects that other regions without a dominant hegemonic polity constituted dense networks of interaction. Thus, although the South East Asian region lacked a clear hegemonic centre, it contained dense flows of trade and interaction. Shared cultural practices and common understandings of political order, norms, and corresponding views of legitimate authority all facilitated such exchanges. Similarly, the Islamic world, that lacked any unified empire following the fall of the Abbasids, evinced significant cross-border trade based on shared cultural understandings rather than the exercise of hierarchical authority. International society was not a European prerogative, contrary to the assertion by Bull and Watson.

To conclude, paying attention to the economic interactions across this vast region leads to a different interpretation of Europe's relations with the non-European world.[56] Rather than a unilateral set of flows of ideas and practices from Europe to other regions, material and cultural practices operated dyadically. It is worth quoting Aydin at length on this matter:

> However, these three zones should not be seen as a sharply demarcated civilizational system. They shared as much interaction and commonality as they had differences. In fact, there were no closed off and isolated regional Islamicate, Christian, or Chinese tribute system [sic] with hard boundaries. Some empires belonged to multiple traditions of imperial legitimacy, and regional order, such as the Ottoman, Russian or Mughal Empires. All of these regions had overlapping and connected structures in relation to other regions as well as to supra-regional global networks.[57]

We must thus recast our notions of European 'expansion'. No doubt European powers started to assert themselves more after 1500, but this new role occurred against an already existing system that demonstrated significant cross-border exchanges of economic goods, and the cross-fertilization of political ideas and cultural expressions.

---

[55] See Chapter 10.

[56] Similarly, Neumann suggests that Adam Watson and the early English School largely focused on the expansion of the European system as a metropolitan process, that is, from the centre out, thereby occluding the role of non-European actors. Neumann 2011: 469.

[57] Aydin 2013.

6

Native Americans and the Making of International Society

Neta C. Crawford

The contributors to *The Expansion of International Society* scarcely mention Native North and South Americans apart from sentences describing their conquest. While they discuss first contacts between Europeans, Americans, Africans, and Asians, Hedley Bull and Adam Watson were largely blind to the ways that Indigenous people *were* living in international societies and their frameworks *continue* to blind us to indigenous politics and movements. But the absence of Native Americans should not be surprising.[1]

Why are Native Americans largely absent from disciplinary International Relations (IR) theory? There are four basic reasons. First, we tend to see Native American, and Indigenous politics more generally, as of mainly historical interest (although the politics are quite alive in North, Central, and South America). While there are important exceptions, the history referred to in IR is generally of a stylized sort and found in recapitulations of the verities of Thomas Hobbes, Hans Morgenthau, and Kenneth Waltz. We act sometimes as if theory, or rudimentary game theory, can substitute for history and evidence.

Second, and related to the first reason, Indigenous politics are taken for granted as irrelevant or marginal to world politics because indigenous people don't count as agents in our disciplinary scheme of agents and structures. As Beier notes, 'the simple fact of our neglect of Indigenous peoples reflects an enduring deference to one of the most fundamental notions of settler state colonialism: the idea that Indigenous peoples do not constitute authentic political communities'.[2] An early exception was international historian

---

[1] We also don't know much about pre-colonial African, Australian Aboriginal, and Pacific Island relations. Indeed, as J. Marshall Beier (2005: 1) notes, there has been 'near complete neglect of Indigenous peoples by International Relations scholars'.

[2] Beier 2005: 15.

Dorothy V. Jones' *License for Empire* which examined treaties North American colonists made with Native American nations.[3]

Many IR scholars take the 'who' of international relations (states, alliances of states, or international organizations of states) and the 'where' (inside and outside states) as obvious. Waltz defines the who and the where as states (the units) operating in an anarchic international system structure. The units are determined by the structure: 'To say that "the structure selects" means simply that those who conform to accepted and successful practices more often rise to the top and are likely to stay there'.[4] Waltz acknowledges that states 'are not and never have been the only international actors'.[5] But states, he says, are the dominant units, whose most important attribute is their capabilities and they will 'long remain so'.[6] Further, the discipline tends to assume that anarchy is a situation that is characterized by distrust. In his interpretation of Jean-Jacques Rousseau's stag hunt, Waltz characterizes anarchy not simply as a context of uncertainty, but of distrust. He says, '[i]n cooperative action, even where all agree on the goal and have equal interest in the project, one cannot rely on others'.[7]

The third reason for the neglect of Native American history and contemporary relations, is that doing so would perhaps cause us to rethink the very agents and structures that discount Native American politics. Not only were Native American practices a challenge to the ideas that constituted the international order after 1500, Native Americans are *today* acting in ways that challenge the legitimacy of the international order. IR as a discipline 'needs' states to be the legitimate unit of analysis just as much as contemporary governments do; world politics has taken for granted the belief in and perception of the sovereignty and legitimacy of states. Examining IR with attention to the ontological challenges posed by Native Americans is profoundly destabilizing, disorienting, and denormalizing of our discipline's understanding of the world and itself—from its *assumptions* about human nature, sovereignty, units of analysis, property, and rights to the *actual* legal and de facto legitimacy of states. What is a state? What is 'international relations'? What is war? What is sovereignty? What is power? What is security? Constructivists and feminists have already taken us through the asking of these questions quite recently. How could we ask them again, and so soon? We need to ask these questions because to not ask them is to live in wilful and dangerous ignorance of both our discipline and of the working of power in our contemporary world.

And fourth, it is not clear how to do this work of integrating Indigenous history and perspectives without reproducing categories and paradigms that ought to be challenged or cause offence. Beier argues, 'even explicitly emancipatory projects give ready sustenance to the hegemonologue'.[8] Beier cautions

---

[3] Jones 1982.   [4] Waltz 1979: 92.   [5] Waltz 1979: 93.
[6] Waltz 1979: 95.   [7] Waltz 1959: 168.   [8] Beier 2005: 16.

that '[i]t is also important that there be sustained introspection on the manner of this opening inasmuch as even the most benignly conceived designs and emancipatory hopes are not immune to working unintended violences of their own'.[9] Nearly everyone who does this work is challenged by questions of epistemology and ontology, not to mention authority. Many who do this work also make one or more apologies about who they are or what they are doing.[10] In a way, attention to Native Americans' role in the constitution of IR theory, international law, and of the world of global politics offers a possibility for us to go to the end and the beginning of IR, reconceptualizing both at once.

Contributors to *The Expansion of International Society* sought to explain the rise of Europe, the expansion of what they understood as European 'international society' over the world, and the meaning and consequences of decolonization, or what was described as the 'Revolt against the West'. The aim of the work was, in other words, to say how the world got to be the way it was in the early 1980s. For the most part, *The Expansion* reads as if the ascendancy of Europe was natural and inevitable, and the authors implied that present international society had reached a kind of culmination. The key proposition, as articulated by Bull and Watson, was that contemporary international society is a legacy of European international society:

> The present international political structure of the world—founded upon the division of mankind and of the earth into separate states, their acceptance of one another's sovereignty, of principles of law regulating their coexistence and co-operation, and of diplomatic conventions facilitating their intercourse—is, at least in its most basic features, the legacy of Europe's now vanished ascendancy.[11]

An exception is Michael Howard's contribution where he clearly describes one of the processes that made European political, economic, and cultural domination possible, specifically the role of military force in enabling European domination.[12]

Bull and Watson, and those who thought and think very much like them, were not simply describing a world they found; their analysis shaped the world through their normalization of an idealized European international society. While no perspective could capture every essential feature of world politics, incompleteness is a problem if exclusions are distorting or marginalizing; excluding the perspective of Native American politics, and Indigenous perspectives more generally, is no minor omission.

---

[9] Beier 2009b: 3.

[10] I too apologize—I write about Native American international relations (almost) as if there were such a thing. In doing so, I am of course eliding and almost completely ignoring the diversity of configurations, relations, and practices of the different indigenous North and South Americans over many centuries, including our current one, so that it is possible to consider Native American diplomacies, conflict, and cooperation. David MacDonald (2014) makes a concerted effort to identify the people and the locations of theories of 'red power'.

[11] Bull and Watson 1984b: 2.   [12] Howard 1984.

The inclusion of Native American history and contemporary politics challenges IR theory in three important respects: narratives about the state of nature and human nature and related beliefs about the potential for cooperation; the idea that the state is the end of history and the most significant agent in world politics; and any notion that the norms of European international society were transferred peacefully and adopted voluntarily because it was a superior system.

Indeed, research on pre-Columbian Native American IR suggests that the founding narratives of IR, and particularly those that have structured the assumptions of the discipline, especially realist IR theory, overemphasize the potential for and actual violent conflict. While not denying high levels of violence in *parts* of Asia, Africa, and the Americas, Europe may have been more violent than other regions and Europeans may have thus shaped their institutions to assume that violence and distrust were the norm. Assuming that this high level of distrust and violence were natural and inevitable may have led us to create institutions that do not protect us from ourselves so much as they promote or at least replicate distrust and violence. To the extent that IR theory is rooted in understandings of human nature, political theory, and history that are at least incomplete and in some cases deeply mistaken, there is a possibility that our theories of world politics are incomplete and deeply mistaken. Research on Native American nations before and after contact with Europeans suggests diversity in the structures and processes of relations among Native American Nations—ranging from frequent warfare to cooperation in what could be described as security regimes and security communities.[13] By adding the perspective of Native America we have the potential to enrich and enlarge our understanding of human nature, political theory, history, and perhaps most importantly, our view of the potential for international society.

STAG HUNT NARRATIVES AND IR THEORY

We understand our world in part through received narratives that academics call—depending on their discipline—history, theory, or science—and in part through our own experiences, which are themselves filtered and shaped by these pre-existing narratives.[14] The present world of states and the flow of

---

[13] Crawford 1994, 2013, 2014.

[14] Critical IR theorists argue that important features of our present world are not so much *described* by theory as made real by our assumptions and practices. So, Jim George (1994: 3, 13, emphasis in the original) argues, realism is 'world-making'; 'power politics *promotes* certain kinds of behavior and often leads to self-fulfilling prophesies'.

goods and money across space have been constructed by our beliefs about what is possible and what is legitimate. But, of course, it is not just realism that is world-making; all belief systems are world-making. What happens if we see the world from inside other belief systems? And how is it that we came to have this particular world system if it is not necessarily 'natural' or the best?

Bull and Watson nicely historicize world politics and international society, reminding us that it was once organized differently. Among Europe's great powers 500 years ago, Christianity was the sign of cultural and political competence and the Pope was authorized to make decisions such as the boundary in the New World between Spanish and Portuguese colonies. As Tim Dunne and Christian Reus-Smit suggest, Bull and Watson gave this global order of sovereign states produced by post-1945 decolonization 'a history, albeit now a widely contested one. Europe was where the society of states first developed, empires extended European rule across the globe, and as decolonization freed non-European peoples, more and more states were admitted to the norm-governed international society'.[15]

Assumptions about human nature and life in the 'state of nature' abound in disciplinary IR theory.[16] Most of the authors in the Bull and Watson volume steer clear of pre-history and claims about human development. Nevertheless, there is a natural 'progressive development' arc to the narrative of *The Expansion*.[17] Bull says:

> An actual international society worldwide in its dimensions, as opposed to the merely theoretical one … emerged only as European states and the various independent political communities with which they were involved in a common international system came to perceive common interests in a structure of coexistence and co-operation, and tacitly or explicitly to consent to common rules and institutions.[18]

The Bull and Watson narrative did not differ substantially from the narratives of Francisco de Vitoria, Hobbes, Rousseau, Immanuel Kant, Georg Hegel, and Karl Marx, who all supposed they knew early human history. Native Americans were understood to be incompetent in deciding their fate. Hegel's views on Native Americans—'the inferiority of these individuals in all respects, even in regard to size'—and Africa, which he called the 'land of childhood', were the received wisdom.[19] Similarly, for Bull, in 'parts of Africa, Australia, and Oceana before European intervention, there were independent political communities that had no institutions of government [and accordingly] such entities fall outside the purview of "international relations"'.[20] Indeed, each of those progenitors of IR theory used their considerable intelligence to narrate a

---

[15] See Chapter 1.   [16] Neta C. Crawford 2011, 2012.
[17] Bull 1984b: 125.   [18] Bull 1984b: 120.   [19] Hegel 1956: 81, 91.
[20] Bull 1977: 9, quoted in Hobson 2012: 232.

plausible chain of events and reasons that humans moved from a state of nature to form political communities and sovereign states.

Perhaps the most influential of these narratives for IR theory is Hobbes's description of life in the state of nature as nasty, brutish, and short. As Karena Shaw argued, Hobbes is attentive to Native Americans as the exemplar of the 'state of nature'.[21] Rousseau's outline of the development of human sociality in his *Discourses on Inequality* is also fundamental to the received wisdom of IR theory. In a passage widely recalled in our discipline but rarely quoted, Rousseau describes a hunt among pre-literate humans:

> Taught by experience that the love of well-being is the sole motive of human actions, he [earliest man] was able to distinguish the rare occasions, when mutual interest ought to make him to rely on the assistance of his fellow men, and the still rarer occasions, when competition ought to make him wary of them. In the first case, he joined them in a herd, or at most some sort of free association that obliged no one, and lasted only as long as the temporary need that had formed it. In the second case, everyone sought his own advantage, either by open force, if he believed himself capable of it, or by adroitness and cunning if he thought himself too weak to do otherwise.
>
> That is how men may have gradually acquired a crude idea of their mutual commitments and the advantage of fulfilling them, but only insofar as their present and obvious interest required it, because they knew nothing of foresight, and far from concerning themselves with the distant future, they did not even think of the next day. If a group of them set out to take a deer, they were fully aware that they would all have to remain faithfully at their posts in order to succeed; but if a hare happened to pass near one of them, there can be no doubt that he pursued it without a qualm, and that once he had caught his prey, he cared very little whether or not he had made his companions miss theirs.[22]

Game theorists have made what they call an assurance or threshold public goods game out of the 'stag hunt' that resembles the prisoners' dilemma. IR theorists, most notably Waltz, have taken the stag hunt as a metaphor for international politics:

> Assume that five men who have acquired a rudimentary ability to speak and to understand each other happen to come together at a time when all of them suffer from hunger. The hunger of each will be satisfied by the fifth part of a stag, so they 'agree' to cooperate in a project to trap one. But also the hunger of any one of them will be satisfied by a hare, so, as a hare comes within reach, one of them grabs it. The defector obtains the means of satisfying his hunger but in so doing permits the stag to escape. His immediate interest prevails over consideration for his fellows.

---

[21] Shaw 2008.
[22] Jean-Jacques Rousseau, *Discourse on the Origin and Basis of Inequality Among Men*, in Rousseau 1974: 175.

The story is simple; the implications are tremendous. In cooperative action, even where all agree on the goal and have equal interest in the project, one cannot rely on others.[23]

Narratives of the stag hunt scenario, and other claims about human perfidy, do not comport with the little we know about how people close to the 'state of nature' posited in early IR theory related in hunter-gathering societies in both pre-history and in eras closer to our present. Yet, despite the fact that IR scholars could have read more widely in history and anthropology (the work of Margaret Mead and Ashley Montague, for example, was available as were more inclusive histories), *The Expansion of International Society* took for granted and tacitly reproduced a history of the world that was, in part, a fiction.

Today there is even more evidence available from archaeology which suggests that the 'stag hunt' metaphor is only one possible way humans could have acted in the state of nature. Specifically, prehistoric humans had sophisticated methods requiring long-term cooperation for hunting large animals. In 2008, archaeologists identified more than sixty stone structures (Drop 45) in the Alpena-Amberley Ridge (AAR), beneath what is now Lake Huron in North America. Preserved by flooding 8,000 years ago, the site is approximately 9,000 years old. The stone structures, constructed along an ancient caribou run, range from simple hunting blinds to more complex drive lanes with multiple blinds:

> Complex multielement structures such as Drop 45 [V-shaped hunting blinds] not only provide unambiguous evidence for intentional human construction, they also provide important insight into the social and economic organization of the ancient hunters that used the AAR. The larger size and multiple parts of the complex drive lanes would have necessitated a larger cooperating group of individuals involved in the hunt. Although the smaller V-shaped hunting blinds could be operated by very small family groups relying on the natural shape of the landform to channel caribou toward them, complex structures like Drop 45 that contain multiple blinds and auxiliary structures to channel the animals into the kill zone necessitated larger groups of hunters and their families cooperating...
>
> The Drop 45 discovery and other hunting features beneath Lake Huron provide a testable model of seasonal organization of prehistoric hunters. If increased hunting group size is coupled with the season of use, the AAR structures can be seen to represent distinctive spring and autumn hunting strategies. In the autumn, animals in prime condition were taken sequentially along the AAR by small groups of hunters before moving into winter camps. In contrast, spring hunting sees larger aggregations of individuals cooperating in what are presumably larger kills.[24]

---

[23] Waltz 1959: 167–8.   [24] O'Shea et al. 2014: 6914.

The legitimacy of the international system—in both its historical and contemporary construction—is also challenged by Native American IR. Indeed, as Paul Keal argues, 'the expansion of the European society of states to an international society global in scope entailed progressive dispossession and subordination of non-European peoples'.[25] Keal goes on to argue that respect for indigenous human rights is a measure of the legitimacy of states. 'The moral legitimacy of states with unresolved indigenous claims, like those that abuse human rights, is in question, and that it follows from this that the legitimacy of international society as a defender of such states is also questionable.'[26]

There are further normative implications to this revised and enlarged view of international relations from a Native American perspective. In *The Philosophy of History*, Hegel says: '[t]he real world is as it ought to be'.[27] I am not so sure. Indeed, as Keal and others show, the international legal order was designed for dispossession of Native lands, and then to defend the sovereignty of those who were successfully occupying those lands. It is no accident that the language of the Berlin West Africa Conference recognizes sovereignty in Africa as demonstrated by 'effective occupation'.

The foundations of contemporary international law are rooted in Native American difference as a justification for conquest, while the felt need to justify conquest makes international law look the way it does. As Shaw argues:

> The extent to which Indigenous peoples have not been incidental frills at the edges of but have always been central to international relations—both as a discipline and as practices of politics among nations—should not be erased. In particular, at the very least, we need to understand how the active marginalization of Indigenous peoples has been necessary for international relations to appear and function.[28]

In the sixteenth century, as international law and the laws of war in particular were being shaped, the preoccupations of many of the early humanist and scholasticist publicists of IR and international law were focused on explaining, justifying, or opposing the practices of colonial conquest in the Americas and war against other 'infidels'.[29] Narratives about and practices of the conquest of Native Americans, and of indigenous people more generally, are an essential context and constitutive feature of IR and international law.

For example, while the Pope asserted the right to order the conquest of the Americas between the Spanish and Portuguese in 1493, other Catholics disputed the right of conquest. Dominicans Bartolomé de Las Casas and Domingo de Soto write the strongest defence of Indians. Another Dominican, Vitoria, agrees with De Soto's argument against the assertion of Papal dominion over all the

[25] Keal 2003: 1.   [26] Keal 2003: 2.
[27] Hegel 1956: 36.   [28] Shaw 2008: 65.
[29] Outstanding discussions of this process include Keal 2003; Anghie 2005.

world, including the Americas.[30] Vitoria engages and criticizes Spanish war and conquest of the Indians in *The First Reflectio of the Indians Lately Discovered*. He argued specifically that Europeans had no right to Indian land or to the violent conversion of Indians. Moreover, Vitoria said, it was just for native peoples to fight aggressive acquisition of their land or forceful conversion. However, Vitoria does allow for making war to prevent cannibalism and other grave wrongs. And here we find the justification for colonization.[31]

Taking a stronger view of a right to conquest than Vitoria, Alberico Gentili, in *De Iure Belli*, later says: 'Therefore, I approve the more decidedly of the opinion of those who say that the cause of the Spaniards is just when they make war upon the Indians, who practiced abominable lewdness even with beasts, and who ate human flesh, slaying men for that purpose.'[32] On the other hand, Gentili argued for the occupation of vacant land, arguing that 'under the rule of Spain, is not almost all of the New World unoccupied?'[33] In *De Iure Belli ac Pacis* (1625), Hugo Grotius picks up and expands on the argument that 'War is lawful against those who offend against Nature'.[34] And Grotius also echoes Gentili's argument about the use or taking of land which is underused or unoccupied.[35] John Locke affirms and expands on Grotius's idea that it is lawful to take land that is underutilized, and argues explicitly that Europeans have the right to settle the 'vacant places of America'.[36]

In sum, the question of 'what to do with the Indians' and their lands was at the heart of medieval and renaissance IR theory and early international law. European international law was codified with the relationship with Native Americans and conquest in mind. The centrality of these practical concerns with colonialism is often lost to history and contributes to the sense that the arguments and laws that derive from these scholars were both disinterested and natural. The arguments for conquest and the justification for it are translated into the colonization *processes* in North and South America. As Keal shows, these concerns are deeply entwined with the development of the European law of nations, which eventually evolves into international law.

But not only is the constitution of the state system, international law, and international society a legacy of the dispossession of Native Americans (and of Indigenous people in Africa and Asia), the act of dispossession—and the mobilization of the means necessary for it—bolstered the power of particular state actors. As the encounter with the Americas 'propelled Europe's territorial expansion, it also energized the construction of a certain kind of Europe'.[37]

---

[30] See Tuck 1999: 72–3.   [31] See Tuck 1999: 73–4.

[32] Alberico Gentili, quoted in Tuck 1999: 34.   [33] Gentili, quoted in Tuck 1999: 48.

[34] Hugo Grotius, quoted in Tuck 1999: 103.   [35] Tuck 1999: 103–4, 105.

[36] John Locke, quoted in Tuck 1999: 175. Richard Tuck argues that Grotius takes this view because the Dutch had begun to move away from an emphasis on trade to annexing territory in North America in the early 1620s.

[37] Soguk 2009: 32.

Consider the continuity of thought between Gentili, Grotius, and Locke, in the views of Thomas Jefferson. First, in some of Jefferson's writings, the Native American is the Other who is used by the dominant power against the nascent United States. The US Declaration of Independence charges that, among the English King George's provocations, '[h]e has excited domestic insurrections amongst us, and has endeavoured to bring on the inhabitants of our frontiers, the merciless Indian Savages whose known rule of warfare, is an undistinguished destruction of all ages, sexes and conditions'. The author of the Declaration, Jefferson, is of course deeply engaged as the Governor of Virginia in colonial expansion against Indians during the Revolutionary War, and then after the war as the third President of the United States. As President, Jefferson continued westward expansion and the policy of extermination or removal of Native Americans throughout his presidency. From the beginning, Jeffersonian and later expansion narratives included elements of a hearts and minds strategy that combined cultural, economic, and spiritual elements. In a confidential letter to Congress in January 1803, Jefferson outlined his analysis and his plan for expansion into Indian lands:

> The Indian tribes residing within the limits of the U.S. have for a considerable time been growing more & more uneasy at the constant diminution of the territory they occupy, altho' effected by their own voluntary sales; and the policy has long been gaining strength with them of refusing absolutely all further sale on any conditions, insomuch that, at this time, it hazards their friendship, and excites dangerous jealousies & perturbations in their minds to make any overture for the purchase of the smallest portions of their land. A very few tribes only are not yet obstinately in these dispositions. In order peaceably to counteract this policy of theirs, and to provide an extension of territory which the rapid increase of our numbers will call for, two measures are deemed expedient.[38]

Familiar narratives of the emergence of the United States as a response to the tyranny of the English and its monarch are unsettled by attention to Native Americans and the reality of their treatment by the founders and later American expansionists. The colonial wars, the American War of Independence, the War of 1812, as well as the westward expansion of the US were intimately related to European–Native American contact. The constitution of the United States, and the development of America's physical infrastructure and its institutionalization, were as much about its relationships with Native peoples as its relations with a European 'other'. The state and federal institutions of the United States were implicated in and developed to respond to the felt needs of conquest and subordination of Native Americans.[39] This is not news to historians who pay attention to these things. But not only would IR need to be rethought, the diplomatic history of the US, narratives of American

---

[38] Jefferson 1803.   [39] See Rockwell 2010.

political development, and the history of US war-making would have to be rethought if Native America were fully included in our narratives of American origins and power.

One of the bridges between then (the pre-Columbian and settler colonial era) and now is the fact that contact with Native nations in North and South America was integral to state-making in the Western hemisphere and to European state-making. Like the transatlantic slave trade and African slavery, and the colonization of Africa and Asia, the dispossession of Native America is a latent and explicit challenge to the legitimacy and authority of states in the Western hemisphere. It is not enough for states to grant self-determination to Native Americans or other Indigenous peoples, or for international organizations to promote Native rights, although that would be, and is, desirable. The fact of indigenous dispossession and challenges to that legacy suggest that the world ought to be otherwise than it is and there ought to be an openness to acknowledge and challenge structures and processes that are illegitimate. It may be that the foundational elements of the state system itself are challenged by Native and indigenous peoples' challenges to territorial borders and to a conception of the earth as something to be exploited.

The myopia of *The Expansion* was not because the authors were too close *in time* to events. They were too close to other elements of their perspective—too close to Europe, too close to power, and too close to the views of authors (namely Hobbes, Rousseau, Kant, Hegel, and, yes, even Marx) who had shaped their understanding of the world. As John Hobson argues, in a word, their perspective was Eurocentric.[40] Bull and Watson are clear about their Eurocentrism and they think it is appropriate. 'Because it was in fact Europe and not America, Asia, or Africa that first dominated ... the world, it is not our perspective but the historical record itself that can be called Eurocentric.'[41]

ARGUING ABOUT THE MEANING OF THE IROQUOIS FOR IR

If we take Native American and indigenous conceptions of politics seriously, attending to their interactions, we may see a different world of possibility altogether. In 1994, in an article about Native American IR, I argued that the Haudenosaunee, known as the League of the Iroquois, among the Onondaga, Cayuga, Seneca, Mohawk, and Oneida, functioned as a security regime, keeping the peace among its members.[42] The League formed in about 1450 (the Tuscarora joined in about 1720) and lasted until 1777; its long duration

---

[40] Hobson 2012.   [41] Bull and Watson 1984b: 2.   [42] Crawford 1994.

and strength were due to its shared belief in the value of avoiding war, the institutionalization of conflict resolution through regular meetings where disagreements could be peacefully settled, the fact that its members were relatively democratic, and the development of shared identity over the course of the period of association:

> Both norms (namely, the peace-oriented belief system of the Iroquois League) and the fact that the League was composed of democracies may well be significant. Institutional factors are also important: the Iroquois League appears to have been better institutionalized than the Concert of Europe. The General Council of the League met at least annually; if the League lasted from 1450 to 1777, and members adhered to the practice of raising the question of renewal every five years, then Iroquois League members reaffirmed their regime over sixty times. Again, contrary to some suggestions, greater institutionalization (e.g., regular meetings, agreed-upon decision-making procedures, and a periodic discussion about whether to renew the regime) appears to help maintain security regimes. As one Oneida spokesperson explained to a European: 'You may say that Love & Affection may be strong in Absence as when present but we say not … Nothing more revives and enlivens affection than frequent Conferences'.[43]

I was moved to add Native American IR into our field because I was particularly disturbed by the reading of world politics dominant in both the English School and the American realist school of IR. The American school seemed profoundly ahistorical (it was deliberately so) while the English School's history seems profoundly Eurocentric (and deliberately so).

In my 1994 article, I was asking the following question: what happens when we open up the conception of the state to include non-Western forms of governance? Would I or anyone else find it possible to think differently about world politics after examining Native American IR at the time when modern IR was coming into being? Emphasizing the violence that Europeans used to overthrow and crush Native American peoples so that they could occupy the lands leads to a reaffirmation of the realist view of the primacy of power. It also exposes the cracks in the legitimacy of current borders, boundaries, and distributions of land power. Examining Native American relations with each other does that and more.

I compared the League to the nineteenth-century Concert of Europe, which has also been described as a security regime, and suggested that the League was more robust and better able to keep the peace among its members. Although I suggested that the League was worthy of study on its own terms, I suggested that a study of the Haudenosaunee might overturn the dominance of realist theorizing—especially the claim to cross-cultural and timeless validity.

---

[43] Crawford 1994: 379.

In part, I was throwing out a challenge to my field. I was, in effect, saying we have missed so much. And what we have excluded is not insignificant. It is not only possible for other kinds of relations to obtain between groups, based on different principles than realism supposes; international politics has worked differently in the past, quite successfully, and for long periods of time. As Shaw argues, 'Bull quietly excludes all those who have not achieved the Western state form from the constitution of international relations'.[44] I was not supposing the Iroquois or any other Native American Confederation were utopias. These confederacies were something *other* that the Europeans had to interact with and which they eventually dominated. I thought Kant had likely heard of the Iroquois League and may well have been influenced by them when he conceived of the role of a League to keep the peace.[45]

But before I could begin the analysis of the League and compare it to the Concert of Europe I had to answer the questions about whether it was appropriate to compare the League and the Concert. 'First, how can the international relations of Iroquois nations be compared with those of European states? Are not the political units so dissimilar as to make reasonable comparisons impossible?'[46] I rephrased the first issue in the following way: 'Native American nations are not the same as, or even analogous to, modern (post-1648) European states. Since we are not talking about states as they are commonly understood in international politics, the units are not comparable and the effort is irrelevant to international relations theory'. In an important sense, this question goes to the crux of the article and there are two layers of response. In another way, the question shows the Eurocentrism of IR scholarship and a fixation on ideas of nations, states, inter-national relations, sovereignty, and tribes that are fixed on some European-derived ideal type.[47]

I argued that it was useful and valid to compare the origins, operations, and dissolution of the League with similar phenomena in IR, including the Concert of Europe, because although the European and Native American 'units' were not the same in form, they were comparable in their function in the sense that Bull had described:

> The forms of Native American and European states certainly were different from each other, but their governments performed similar functions—functions that normally are associated with states: there were within Iroquois nations decision-making structures and ways to provide collective goods; there were elected and appointed representatives as well as hereditary leadership. Further similarities exist in the area of international relations: the nations of North America used diplomatic envoys, recognized the 'sovereignty' of other nations, and negotiated

---

[44] Shaw 2008: 61.

[45] The Iroquois were well known in the eighteenth century and Kant mentions an Iroquois sachem's experiences in Paris. See Kant 2007.

[46] Crawford 1994: 349.   [47] Crawford 1994: 349.

binding treaties. Finally, Iroquois governments had a monopoly on the use of force, although the egalitarian structure of the state meant that force could only be deployed after consensus was reached by all adult members of the nation. The Iroquois League nations of, for example, 1500 were different from European nations in that they were in general smaller, less urban, less industrialized, and more democratic than European states of the same period. But, just as the ideal of the 'state' does not quite correspond to the Iroquois nations, it also does not correspond to all European-type states. In fact, there is wide variation among the states that comprised the European international system (for example in terms of provision of collective goods, the criteria for political leadership, and the degree of democracy), both in comparison with one another and over time. So, although the units of analysis are not identical, if one understands states as institutional arrangements—performing certain 'governing' functions—that vary along several dimensions and change over time, then one can compare the international relations of Native North America with international relations in Europe.

More fundamentally, are different cultures/civilizations comparable? In one important sense, the answer is no, and we need to stop talking about different societies as if social science described one world. Multiple 'worlds' existed in sixteenth-, seventeenth-, and eighteenth-century North America, and their inhabitants had radically different views of the rights of citizens, the origin of species, and the afterlife. Thus, any comparisons between European and Native American states should be viewed with caution bordering on suspicion. On the other hand, the very differences highlighted by comparison may allow for a critical reappraisal of the modern European state and war systems. An examination of the Iroquois and of the similarities and differences between the two societies may tell us something new about international relations among European-type states. But even if the Iroquois did not tell us, by contrast, much about modern international relations, the Iroquois League is by itself worth knowing about.[48]

I had to deal with another problem, how to get and treat the evidence of the League since they were primarily an oral society: Wampum beads were a visual record of events and agreements, and the Iroquois used songs and stories to memorialize events and agreements. But, I argued, it was important not to 'privilege written text' as these are no more omniscient and accurate than oral histories. I then described what we know of the origins of the League, its' functioning through League councils, diplomacy with Native and European nations, and war by individual members of the League. The Concert of Europe, I argued, was much less robust in keeping the peace among its members than the Haudenosaunee. I described the peaceful dissolution of the League, by agreement of its members, and the attempt during the Revolutionary War by George Washington's Army to destroy the Iroquois.

[48] Crawford 1994: 350.

My argument about Native American IR was mostly greeted by silence in the mainstream. Yet there were some reactions which are instructive of how the discipline deals with challenges to dominant paradigms. Mainstream IR theorists found the argument wanting from the perspective of realism and Kantian IR, and at least some scholars of Native American IR found it essentialist and reinforcing of the dominant IR perspective.

For example, David Rousseau and Karl Mueller argued that the peace among members of the League was due to other factors, specifically '(1) the danger of the mourning war; (2) a matrilineal and matrilocal culture; (3) cross-cutting clan ties; and (4) societal norms emphasizing community and conformity'.[49] Rousseau and Mueller argue that 'the longevity of the League of the Iroquois was due more than anything to its flexibility and minimalism'. In their words:

> For all its impressive success, at its core the League of the Iroquois had only one, limited purpose, albeit a toweringly important one: to keep the peace among the previously fratricidal Five Nations. This stands in stark contrast to the objectives of less successful security regimes such as the Concert of Europe and the League of Nations, which sought to manage entire international systems. Unlike these entities, which were intended to do many things but did few of them very well or for very long, the Iroquois League accomplished its more modest ends effectively for three centuries. The fact that the League was limited in its objectives and placed few other constraints on its members' behavior gave it great durability because it depended upon no external conditions except that the members, encouraged by the institution they had established, continued to value not fighting with each other. Therefore, as the security environment of eastern North America changed and changed again, the League was able to continue its basic function while it adapted and evolved, for example from the loose association of the seventeenth century to the more alliance-like Iroquois Confederation of the eighteenth.[50]

While I argued that Iroquois League members were democratic, and that the League itself functioned democratically, which bolstered the security regime, Rousseau and Mueller, using Robert Dahl's criteria of democracy, argued that they were not fully democratic. Specifically, Rousseau and Mueller said that 'many of the elements essential for democratic institutions could be found in the Iroquois political system: freedom to form and join organizations; freedom of expression; right of political leaders to compete for support; access to alternative sources of information; and widespread eligibility for public office'.[51] Yet, they argued, Iroquois Sachems (spokespersons) were hereditary—a misunderstanding of the sachem position—and further, they lacked the hallmark of Western democracy. 'Perhaps the most important requirement on [Robert]

---

[49] Rousseau and Mueller 1995: 23.
[51] Rousseau and Mueller 1995: 22.
[50] Rousseau and Mueller 1995: 35.

Dahl's list missing from the Iroquois political systems was the practice of voting... Given that the western notion of democracy implies voting and majority rule, we find that the term "democracy" obscures rather than clarifies the nature of the Iroquois political system'.[52]

The Iroquois were realists according to Rousseau and Mueller and any explanation stressing Iroquois democracy was not realist enough: 'Iroquois behavior was for the most part consistent with the basic tenets of realism... Throughout the history of the League, the Five Nations sought to maximize their sovereignty and security in an increasingly hostile environment'.[53]

More recently, in a book focused on Kant's contributions to IR theory, Dora Ion takes issue with my analysis of the Iroquois as a possible realization of Kant's notion of a League of Peace. Ion also argues that 'seen from [Karl] Deutsch's perspective', the Iroquois League 'failed as a plural security community due to its lack of responsiveness to increasing external threat'.[54] Leaving aside the fact that Ion does not seem to grasp the differences and distinctions between the roles and functions of security regimes, pluralistic security communities, and collective security, it is more significant that she fails to take the Iroquois League's decision-making procedures as they were, on their own terms. Ion suggests that:

> The relationship between the Iroquois' internal democracy and the consensual character of the league is also to some extent exaggerated: while the nations' cultural tendency towards consultation cannot be denied, their role in decision-making was clearly 'differential', with the Onondaga lords having the final judgment, the Tuscaroras being denied a voice in the Great Council.[55]

In other words, like Rousseau and Mueller, Ion set the Iroquois against a Western idea of democracy, and found it wanting. I described the decision-making procedure of the League as a different form of representative government. Fifty sachems, representing the original five nations and the Tuscarora (who spoke through the Oneida), functioned as *representatives* of their respective nations at the League's annual Great Council:

> The Onondaga were designated the keepers of the 'fire' (meeting place) and the wampum bead records of the League. The Mohawk and the Seneca nations were known as the older brothers, and the Cayuga and Oneida were younger brothers. Decisions were reached by a series of caucuses: each 'brotherhood' talked separately about an issue and came to consensus before consulting the other side: 'First the question shall be passed to the Mohawk and Seneca Lords, then it shall be discussed and passed by the Oneida and Cayuga Lords. Their decisions shall then be referred to the Onondaga Lords, (Fire Keepers) for final judgment'. Elisabeth Tooker reports that if the Onondaga received the opinions of the other four

---

[52] Rousseau and Mueller 1995: 22–3.   [53] Rousseau and Mueller 1995: 31.
[54] Ion 2012: 135.   [55] Ion 2012: 132–3.

nations and disagreed, 'they referred it back for further discussion; but in so doing, they had to show that the opinion of the other tribes was in conflict with established custom or with public policy'. The decisions of the Great Council, even in times of great threat, were then to be confirmed by going back to the people of each nation.[56]

The nineteenth-century observer, Asher Wright, further corroborates this view:

> If any individual desired to bring any proposition before the general council, he must first gain the consent of his family, then his clan, next of the four related clans in his end of the council house, then of his nation, and thus in due course...the business would be brought up before the representatives of the confederacy. In the reverse order, the measures of the general council were sent down to the people for their approval. It was a standing rule that all action should be unanimous. Hence, the discussions were continued until all opposition was reasoned down, or the proposed measure was abandoned.[57]

In sum, while there were defined roles for participants, the League's decision-making procedures embodied the key characteristics of representative and participatory democracy, understood as decision-making practices that are inclusive, transparent, characterized by persuasion through the force of the better argument (as opposed to brute force), and accountable. On this understanding, I argue, decision-making in the League was more democratic than that among the European and settler colonial societies of the same period and more democratic than many contemporary 'democracies'.

Coming from the opposite perspective, David Bedford and Thom Workman explored the founding narrative of the Iroquois League, the 'Great Law of Peace'. Bedford and Workman were disappointed in scholarship that did not take the Great Law on its own terms and, using my 1994 article as an example, they asserted that my argument was a 'forced application of Realist-derived terms upon the Iroquoian document':[58]

> The Great Law is considerably more than a 'well-functioning security regime', as Crawford's recent analysis of the Iroquois Confederacy concludes. It is not the case that the great binding law merely facilitates the cultivation of life within nations; rather, it is a sphere in which the highest human values of love and charity receive complete expression. As discussed above, rational conduct between nations among the Iroquois is more than the instrumental safe-guarding of each nation's security interests. The Great Law is more than an agreement between autonomous states; rather, it is the affirmation that the principles that govern life within and between nations are the same. These principles of living well between the nations of the Iroquoian Confederacy extended to all nations outside the confederacy.[59]

---

[56] Crawford 1994: 358.   [57] Cited in Crawford 1994: 358.
[58] Bedford and Workman 1997: 90.   [59] Bedford and Workman 1997: 105.

Rather, they argue, '[i]n effect, The Great Law of Peace is a formal articulation of understandings and practices between nations that is fundamentally inconsistent with Realist understanding. In a more contemporary manner of speaking, the text codifies a non-Realist practice of international relations. One must struggle, therefore, to find an analytical conversation that does not do violence to The Great Law of Peace through the unselfconscious imposition of Western concepts and paradigms, but success in this struggle is both possible and fruitful'.[60]

More fundamental criticisms of work on Native American IR points to an important set of questions about the appropriate referent object. In 2008, Shaw suggested that I and several other scholars—including Bedford and Workman, and Franke Wilmer—had frozen Indigenous people into a role that is 'at best marginal contributors' to international relations.[61] As Beier argues, much of the work on Native American IR 'is still fundamentally about International Relations more so than about Indigenous peoples and global politics'.[62] Thus, Beier worries that, in common with mainstream theories, 'critical approaches enact violences of their own and are likewise complicit in the inaudibility of Indigenous voices in International Relations'.[63] Beier takes this up in relation to my work on the Iroquois League. Beier recalls my question:

> If international relations theory were based on a reading of [Haudenosaunee] history rather than primarily Western European history, would Kantian or Grotian perspectives of international relations have become dominant instead of the Hobbesian 'war of all against all' paradigm?' This is undoubtedly an important question *for International Relations*, perhaps for Western traditions of political philosophy more generally, but if our questioning ends there it also reduces Indigenous peoples and their diplomacies to a resource in aid of better theory. Why Kantian or Grotian? Why not Haudenosaunee? Why disciplinary international relations for that matter? Crawford's questions must be asked, but if we do not also ask these others then we do not break entirely with the idea of the 'timeless and cross-cultural validity' of European political-philosophical traditions ...
>
> To approach Indigenous peoples as repositories of knowledge whose ideas, perspectives, and experiences can *inform*—or subvert—theory is to reproduce both the function and the form of colonial knowledge production and thereby to deny them autonomous voice.[64]

Beier argues that my work 'treads very close to an evolutionist conjectural historicizing that teleologically imputes superiority to Euro-derived concepts and forms of socio-political organization by making an appeal to them as evidence of advanced society'.[65] More damning, Beier argues, 'forcing knowledges

---

[60] Bedford and Workman 1997: 90.   [61] Shaw 2008: 68.
[62] Beier 2009b: 3.   [63] Beier 2009b: 15.
[64] Beier 2009a: 25.   [65] Beier 2009a: 23.

and practices "constituted otherwise than modernity" into the straightjacket of a modernist framework begets assimilative violence where they exceed the ontological and epistemological possibilities delineated by the dominating knowledge system and its operant cosmology'.[66] Of course the challenge is how to discuss Native American IR in a way that does not, in the words of Beier, contribute to 'rendering [indigenous peoples] as spectacle'.[67]

CONCLUSION

The denial of subjectivity, and later the marginalization and erasure of indigenous people which has been constitutive of IR theory and international law, has served to reify the European-derived categories of sovereign states, with the double consequence that we often forget that the sovereign state is a recent construction and that Native American sovereignty is then seen through that lens and hence dismissed.

But, as the reaction to an attempt to understand the Iroquois League as IR theory shows, it is not easy to be more inclusive. David MacDonald suggests one way ahead, where he offers both a critique of IR's concepts and a reading of specific North American Indigenous beliefs, 'red power', as an alternative to dominant IR 'linear versus cyclical conceptions of time; natural over social power; change/flux versus stasis; and indigenous interconnectedness and dependence versus western conceptions of dominion'.[68] As he argues, 'some indigenous conceptions of power—which fuse the natural and the social into an interdependent inseparable vision of the world and how it operates', offer an alternative conception of power, our dominating concept.[69]

If we attend to the actual practices of Native American nations, we find that international relations were in North and South America before 'the Expansion' and for centuries afterward—sometimes organized along different principles than are now dominant. Indeed, attention to Native American practices, subjectivity, and the West's historical and contemporary treatment of Native Americans is profoundly denormalizing, defamiliarizing, and potentially destabilizing of IR theory and contemporary practices.

Contemporary Native nations are engaged in diverse politics—from militant resistance such as the Zapatistas in Chiapas Mexico, to non-recognition of, and cooperation across, state boundaries. Movements challenging land tenure, militarism, industrial farming, and deforestation related to and emanating from indigenous peoples are found across the globe.[70] These are not the old social movements of union organizers and peace activists, but new

---

[66] Beier 2009a: 23–4.   [67] Beier 2005: 8.   [68] MacDonald 2014: 1.
[69] MacDonald 2014: 14–15.   [70] See Mertes 2004.

social movements, oriented around biopolitics, the creation of alternative communities, and containing links to sacred/ancient traditions.[71] Native Americans have worked against the Keystone XL pipeline to transport oil from Canada through the US by lobbying the US and worked in favour of climate change mitigation at the United Nations and in the Arctic Council.[72] Like the politics of refugees and displaced peoples, the politics of Indigenous peoples who attempt to and actually constitute political communities within and across the borders recognized by the United Nations are in a permanent liminal condition on the one hand, and on the other hand, privileged by and with the state system with rights that are different and in some cases more than others. The inside/outside nature of indigenous peoples and practices, their 'transversality', troubles the international order. The multiple layers and overlapping forms of identity and governance structures—tribe, band, and Treaty Nation—form alternative locations for discourse and political argument within and across 'sovereign' political borders.

As the American novelist of the West and traditional Westerns, Louis L'Amour, said: '[t]here will come a time when you believe everything is finished; that will be the beginning'.[73] To attend to international history is to destabilize present institutions. To attend to Native American politics is to see how Native Americans challenge the origins and dominant structures and processes of world politics. If the historical narrative is amended, our sense of what is possible in the present and future might also be altered. The real world could be otherwise. In fact, it already is. World politics is already being reshaped by Native American, and other Indigenous, politics. When Native Americans and other Indigenous people participate in organic farming movements by providing heritage seeds, they not only diversify the food chain, they subvert big agricultural conglomerates and resist the patenting of seed. When Native people occupy land in Latin America and reclaim it they resist both deforestation and the system of property rights that excludes them and interferes with their self-determination. If it is possible to rethink the making of 'international society' from a different perspective, it is possible to reshape international society.

---

[71] Hawken 2007.   [72] See Cama and Wilson 2015; Smith and Wilson 2009.
[73] L'Amour 1980.

Part III

Dynamics of Globalization

7

Imperial Rivalry and the First Global War

Richard Devetak and Emily Tannock

INTRODUCTION: HISTORIOGRAPHICAL CONTEXT

In Hedley Bull and Adam Watson's classic account, European international society underwent expansion from the late fifteenth century, eventually to become a *global* society of states. The story told is one of progressive outward adoption and adaptation of a more-or-less coherent set of rules, norms, and institutions originating in Europe. From a planetary context comprising multiple regional systems there gradually emerged a single integrated global formation largely under the ascending power of Europe. In the words of Bull and Watson, '[t]he global international society of today is in large part the consequence of Europe's impact on the rest of the world over the last five centuries'.[1]

Bull and Watson's story made Europe the principal protagonist in the emergence and globalization of modern international society. Sensitive to charges of Eurocentrism, Bull and Watson claimed that while 'the historical record itself can be called Eurocentric', that is not their perspective.[2] Critics of Bull and Watson remain unconvinced by their exculpatory claim, alleging that their narrative represents an 'orthodox subliminal Eurocentrism'.[3] Still too focused on Europe as the principal actor in the story of expansion, it is argued that Bull and Watson ascribed too little agency to non-European actors, or failed either to register fully the harms inflicted by an essentially violent European 'expansion', or to recognize earlier non-Western ages of expansion and discovery.[4] Additionally, Bull and Watson were silent on the way that European international society legitimized one set of rules for governing

---

[1] Bull and Watson 1984b: 1.   [2] Bull and Watson 1984b: 2.
[3] Hobson 2012: chapter 8.
[4] For a sample see Hobson 2007, 2009: 680; Suzuki et al. 2014.

conduct inside Europe (coexistence among equal, independent states), but a very different set of rules for governing the conduct of European actors when interacting with outsiders (civilization and colonization through hierarchical relations).[5]

For these and other critics, the problem lies not just in Bull and Watson's story but in the history of international society itself; as a set of rules, norms, and institutions, international society has legitimized European conquest, colonization, and dispossession of non-European peoples.[6] Bull and Watson's failure to highlight this story is deemed to be evidence of their moral complicity with and apology for a history in which Europe possessed the agency to conquer, colonize, and dispossess a passive extra-European world.

Historiographically, both Bull and Watson and their critics operate with a 'presentist' or Whig philosophy of history that seeks either to legitimize or delegitimize international society and/or Europe for the underlying principle or logic expressed in history.[7] One historical approach treats international society as the global expression of a set of European-originated rules, norms, and institutions oriented to the principle of order, while the other, from an enlightened postcolonial position, treats it as the symptomatic expression of an underlying dynamic of Eurocentric colonization and exclusion. In both cases the point of the narrative is to account for the degree to which history realizes or completes international society's underlying principle or dynamic. For Bull and Watson the historical narrative reveals the universal realization of international society by outward expansion, and the challenge it faces by virtue of the twentieth century's decolonization processes.[8] For critics, a superior historical narrative should be more explicitly normative; it should reveal and condemn international society's underlying dynamic of exclusion and discrimination by measuring it against transcendent principles of justice revealed by postcolonial normativities, and ensuring that the non-European world becomes more than a passive bystander to global history. Indeed, if John Hobson is right, a more accurate historical narrative should recognize that the modern world of international relations in general and the West in particular are historical products of the East and what he calls 'Oriental globalization'.[9] By constructing an interpretation where the East's dynamism acts as the driver of change, and the rise of an imperializing West is but a momentary interruption of 'Eastern normalcy', such revisionist narratives present a mirror image of Eurocentric Whig tendencies.[10]

---

[5] Keene 2002.   [6] Keal 2003.
[7] For the classical statement on the Whig interpretation of history, see Butterfield 1973.
[8] On this see Wight 1992a: 85–90; Bull 1984c; Hall 2011.
[9] Hobson 2007, 2012.   [10] Hobson 2007: 421–3.

HISTORIOGRAPHICAL METHOD

Our approach attempts to gain some distance from the Whig tendencies and normative concerns of such presentist histories in order to grasp better what actually happened. In this section we briefly outline some of the features of our historiographical method which aims to contribute to a better understanding of the historical context in which the globalization of international society took place.

Our approach aims to take a more agnostic view of history by eschewing the Whig compulsion to identify one actor or civilization as more dynamic and progressive than another in narrating the history of international society.[11] Such judgements can be safely left to moral and political philosophers intent on using history to advertise their own moral preferences or theoretical positions. Insofar as it seeks to narrate the globalization of international society, our approach relinquishes historiographies 'suffused with moral judgment'.[12] Its primary purpose is not to legitimize or delegitimize international society as it has been historically constituted, but to offer a broad historical account of the context in which the globalization of international society should be understood.

The story that emerges is not one where international society is always only the partial or flawed manifestation of an underlying principle or dynamic; but one where global international society emerges epigenetically as the complex of rules, norms, and institutions improvised in the context of ongoing interactions among its principal actors—states—and in their engagement with other peoples and actors. Nor is it the story of a neat transition from the medieval to the modern wherein a heterogeneous system composed of different state forms is replaced by a homogeneous system of sovereign states.[13] No such neat transition ever occurred. The heterogeneity of state forms survived deep into what is regarded as modernity. So what is generally, and with good reason, referred to as a 'society of *states*' is at any given moment actually a society of different historical state forms—nation-states, empires, kingdoms, republics, principalities, cities, and so on.[14]

Finally, neither is it a story of the Europeanization of the world. There is no reason to assume that the twentieth-century post-imperial global society of

---

[11] Butterfield 1973: 42.   [12] Bayly 2006.   [13] Ruggie 1983.

[14] The historiographical opposition between state and empire is now being questioned by historians of early modernity. As David Armitage (2000: 15) points out, empires and states are rarely distinguishable during this period: 'Empires gave birth to states, and states stood at the heart of empires'. On this point see also Armitage 2013: 49; Mancke 2009; Fitzmaurice 2014; Burbank and Cooper 2010. The key historiographical distinction is between empire and the modern sovereign state. We use the concept 'state' to refer to the full historical range of coercive political associations claiming authority over others, whatever their degree of autonomy or heteronomy.

states, if that is an apt description of today's system, was the organic product of an embryonic European society that expanded and imposed itself unchanged on a supine globe. Instead, it emerged historically through unanticipated adaptations and integrations driven by a multitude of encounters, interactions, and transactions among originally separate regional international societies and their states. So, in keeping with genealogy, no attempt is made in this chapter to identify an origin or to recount an unbroken story of teleological development that can be measured against an ideal-type or judged against a transcendent principle of justice.[15] There are only the historically contingent complexes of rules, norms, and institutions that form the society of states at any given moment in time. These rules, norms, and institutions are both constitutive, in determining membership of international society, and regulative, in governing conduct.

Equally important if parochialism and Eurocentrism are to be avoided are the revived historiographical tradition of global history and the recent rise of oceanic histories. Both these bodies of writing prioritize 'connections and synchronic contexts in space over long intellectual continuities in time'.[16] These global and oceanic histories emphasize connections, encounters, exchanges, and networks as media through which international society globalized. The writings of Christopher Bayly, Sanjay Subrahmanyam, and David Armitage are exemplary here in accounting for the historical development of early modern connections, encounters, and exchanges.[17] Bayly, for example, provides a global history around the thematics of interconnectedness and interdependence, showing that the modern world is the product of a series of transformations occurring in multiple connected locales, not the consequence of an outward diffusion of European ideas, technologies, and practices of modernity.[18] The conclusion of these writings is that the forces of globalization and modernity did not emanate from a single site, but emerged through complex connections and interactions that led to conflictual and convergent patterns of political and economic activity as local and global forces fed off each other. By decentring the global history of international society these literatures serve to 'provincialize' Western historiography, to use Dipesh Chakrabarty's influential notion, showing that neither Europe nor any other civilization or actor holds a monopoly on cultural, moral, political, or intellectual developments.[19]

As we shall see, prior to the formation of a global society of states, there existed a plurality of 'international' societies or civilizations, largely anchored in geographical regions. Each had its own distinctive and often variegated forms of state and modes of governance, usually dominated by one or a few

---

[15] Foucault 1977.   [16] Sebastian Conrad 2012: 1005.

[17] Bayly 2004; Subrahmanyam 1997, 2007; Armitage 2000, 2007, 2013.

[18] Bayly 2004.   [19] Chakrabarty 2008. See also Sebastian Conrad 2012: 1007.

contending dynastic powers.[20] In many cases, although not all, these regional international societies conformed to what Martin Wight called 'suzerain state-systems', where a single state claims the 'sole source of legitimate authority, conferring status on the rest and exacting tribute or other marks of deference'.[21] In the sixteenth century, the Qing (or Manchu) of East Asia, the Mughal of South Asia, the Ottoman and Safavid empires of Asia Minor, the Duchy of Muscovy, and the Holy Roman Empire all claimed and achieved overlordship, albeit to different degrees and for different lengths of time, in their regions through war and colonial expansion. Contrary to the presumption of conventional international relations theories, hierarchy rather than anarchy was therefore central to these regional international societies as a hegemonic power asserted de facto authority and political primacy over others.[22]

Although there was interaction between actors of the different regional international societies—especially in the large Eurasian landmass—there is little evidence of an overarching complex of rules, norms, or institutions capable of integrating them into a single international society. The growth of such an overarching, and eventually global, assemblage required tighter interconnection among a number of the regional international societies and civilizations, such that as interaction intensified, the need for shared understanding of the rules also outgrew the localized and ad hoc arrangements.

The joining of various regional international societies into a single global one was primarily driven in its initial phase by imperial expansion, especially by actors on the Eurasian landmass. It was this imperial drive during the 'long sixteenth century', whether underpinned by universalist or commercial ideology, that created an interconnected political context of almost global extent. As we shall see, the very same inter-imperial rivalry that created an interconnected global context was also the catalyst, in the late eighteenth century, for political developments that would begin to dismantle *ancien régime* empires and give rise to an emergent global international society with its own constitutive and regulative rules. Our argument thus concurs with Bayly's, John Darwin's, and Armitage and Subrahmanyam's accounts of the worldwide crisis of *anciens régimes* triggered by war and revolution in the Americas, Asia, and Europe from the mid-eighteenth to the mid-nineteenth

---

[20] We are aware that the term 'international' is anachronistic in a pre-modern setting if taken literally to mean 'between or among nations'. We use it here as a convenient historiographical term to describe external relations among more-or-less independent political units, whether they be nation-states, kingdoms, empires, republics, principalities, and so on. This also allows for relations between distinct actors inside loose imperial formations to be described as 'international' also. See Wight 1977: 26–7.

[21] Wight 1977: 23.

[22] For the leading research on hierarchy in international society inter alia see Clark 2009b; Dunne 2003; Phillips 2014a; Phillips and Sharman 2015; Reus-Smit 2013a: 38–59.

century.[23] Although empires (and other forms of state) would persist deep into the twentieth century, forceful anti-imperial and anti-colonial movements beginning in the eighteenth century would yield new principles of legitimacy and give rise to an international society able to accommodate newly independent nation-states.[24] The shift in what Wight calls principles of international legitimacy from dynastic to popular sovereignty was a long, complex, and uneven historical process to which we cannot do justice here.[25] We do, however, wish to identify the global crisis triggered by the Seven Years' War that formed the context in which the principle of popular sovereignty was declared and given concrete expression.

THE 'LONG SIXTEENTH CENTURY': IMPERIAL RIVALRY AND REGIONAL INTERNATIONAL SOCIETIES

Historiographies of the expansion of international society, as we have seen, are generally divided between those that focus on the West as the origin and progressive agent of history, and those that attribute progressive agency to the East. Our aim in this section is not to extol the virtues of one or other actor in history, so much as to account for the way that imperial dynamics served to connect different regions during the 'long sixteenth century', from the middle of the fifteenth century to the early seventeenth century.

European Expansion

It has been a commonplace of Western historiography since the sixteenth century to note that the 'expansion' or 'globalization' of international society began in 1492 with the discovery of the 'New World'.[26] According to this historiography, discovery of the New World dramatically widened humanity's horizons, bringing the rest of the world into Europe's expanding social and political imaginaries as well as transforming 'the geopolitical relationship between the Occident and the rest of the Old World'.[27] Empirical evidence

---

[23] Bayly 2004: chapter 3; Darwin 2008b: chapter 4; Armitage and Subrahmanyam 2010.

[24] Bayly 2004: 106–8; Reus-Smit 2013a: chapters 2 and 4.

[25] Wight 1977: chapter 6.

[26] Bull and Watson 1984b: 1; Pagden 1995: 2. It should be noted that the Spanish 'discovery' of the Americas even featured in sixteenth-century Ottoman 'world histories'. See Subrahmanyam (2005: 44) for a detailed historiographical study of non-Western 'world histories' written in the sixteenth century.

[27] Elliott 1992b: 7; Darwin 2008b: 50.

brought back to Europe by travellers and explorers revealed the limits of the medieval cosmographies and authoritative classical texts, from Aristotle and Strabo to Ptolemy and *mappaemundi*, that Europeans used to understand the world and their place in it.[28] At the end of the sixteenth century, in an emerging new literary genre combining geography and travelogue with analysis of the interests and affairs of states, the Piedmontese Jesuit, Giovanni Botero, opened his *Relationi Universali* by declaring that 'Time and the Warres have altered much since Aristotle and Ptolomies dayes; whose Rules and Observations have since growne partly out of use, and beene partly bettered'.[29] These new literary genres could readily be put into the service of expanding imperial and maritime powers.

To be sure, renovation of the West's ways of thinking progressed slowly, especially with regard to the treatment of non-European peoples whose supposed cultural and political inferiority were thought to be grounds for dispossession and violent subjugation.[30] But discovery of the New World, or what is more accurately called the non-European Old World, helped Europe emerge from what Giancarlo Casale calls the 'state of otherworldliness'.[31] It was the gradual erosion of this other-worldly or metaphysical architecture of medieval Christianity, with its peculiar mix of Christian theology and ancient thought, and its replacement by a more outward-looking and this-worldly politics that the 'discovery' precipitated. In combination with intellectual advances of Renaissance humanism, and at the behest of rulers focused on practical matters of civic administration, reason of state, and commercial expansion, empirical geography's displacement of metaphysical cosmography opened fresh horizons for new political ideas and practices to take shape, including colonial and mercantile projects.[32]

The discovery had transformative effects on both Europe and the world beyond. In addition to affording Europeans opportunities to impose their interests and power on newly discovered lands and peoples, it also generated significant geopolitical and economic changes internal to Europe.[33] Outward expansion and the European struggle for supremacy were thus intimately connected, the one fuelling the other.[34] Resources and prestige accrued by conquest and exploitation of the New World were deployed by European powers (initially the Spanish and Portuguese, later the English, Dutch, and French) in the struggle for continental supremacy and survival, just as the European struggle for supremacy drove outward programmes of imperial conquest and colonization. As J. H. Elliott observed, the sources of power

---

[28] Brotton 2012: 156–75.   [29] Botero 1630 [1591]: 1.
[30] Abulafia 2008; Bowden 2005; Elliott 1992b: 14; Grafton, with Shelford and Siraisi 1992: 5–7; Keal 2003; Ryan 1981; Wight 1992a: chapter 4.
[31] Casale 2010: 15.   [32] Fitzmaurice 2007.
[33] Elliott 1992b: 7.   [34] Simms 2014: 33–6.

and prestige were no longer confined to Europe but, to borrow a phrase from Francis Bacon, extended well beyond the 'pillars of Hercules'.[35]

It is important to note that despite a shared Christianity, Latin Europe was far from being a uniform or unified international society. The European *respublica christiana* was in fact a heteronomous order, a region of 'composite monarchies' coexisting with 'a myriad of smaller territorial and jurisdictional units jealously guarding their independent status'.[36] More decisively, Europe was divided into rival confessions that cut across geopolitical interests and subregions and exploded into violent conflict in the sixteenth century.[37] During this period Europe's rival states engaged in continuing and shifting strategic alliances and balances of power to prevent 'universal monarchy'.[38] None of this should be taken to imply that Europe was the primogenitor of modern international society. The following provides a historiographical re-evaluation of Europe's role.

Provincializing Europe

European expansion and the discovery of the Americas, or Indies as they were initially known by contemporary Europeans, are only part of a larger and older story about empires, encounters, exchanges, and interactions between peoples, cultures, civilizations, and regional international societies. This larger story is global in scope, involving encounters and exchanges among a range of actors and regions, far beyond the 'pillars of Hercules'; and it is in this context that international society's globalization takes place, as imperial expansion linked and gradually integrated separate international societies, thereby transforming the space in which political ideas and practices governing the conduct of international relations arose, circulated, and were embedded.[39]

It is important to note that despite long-established trade routes such as the Silk Road, the early modern world was characterized by multiple regional international societies rather than a single integrated society. Centred on large landmasses and seas, these regional international societies developed their own identities and local practices, including norms and protocols within a suzerain state system. But they were far from hermetically sealed. Interactions across and between them occurred on a regular basis, giving rise to what Subrahmanyam described as 'a patchwork of competing and intertwined empires'.[40] In the

---

[35] Elliott 1992b: 79.   [36] Elliott 1992a: 51.

[37] For important accounts of the impact of Europe's confessional conflict on international relations during this period, see inter alia, Greengrass 2014; Reus-Smit 2013a: 77–97; Saunders 1997; Schilling 2008.

[38] Devetak 2013; Simms 2014: chapter 1; Wight 1977: chapters 4–5.

[39] Burbank and Cooper 2010: 19; Phillips 2014a.

[40] Subrahmanyam 2007: 1359.

sixteenth century, this patchwork spanned the globe from the Ming and Mughal empires of the east to the Ottoman and Iberian empires of the west. While there was little scope for the development of rules or protocols capable of shared agreement across all regions, local protocols and practices existed, both formal and informal.[41]

Non-European empires, cast as passive subjects in Eurocentric historiographies, played a vital role in sustaining and expanding the long-distance routes on land and sea that connected peoples and brought empires and their agents into contact, oftentimes violently. For example, by the sixteenth century, Andrew Phillips and Jason Sharman argue, the Indian Ocean had become a distinctive regional international society with extensive networks of social, economic, and political interaction, but one which increasingly functioned as 'the world's flywheel'.[42] It formed connections that not only integrated its constituent subregions, but also linked more distant regional international societies, 'most notably Latin Christendom, the Central Asian steppe and East Asia'.[43] The Pacific Ocean was another context, or assemblage of 'multiple sites of *trans-localism*', in which voyages of navigation, migration, and trade linked distant islands, peoples, empires, and landmasses.[44] The same can be said of the Malacca Strait—a dynamic entrepôt on the south-eastern tip of Eurasia joining the Indian Ocean to the South China Sea and Pacific, and a site of imperial rivalry between the Portuguese Empire, the Sultan of Malacca, the Chinese Ming dynasty, and the Siamese Empire.[45]

The Islamic world also experienced an 'age of expansion' and 'exploration' during this period.[46] Indeed, as a date to mark the advent of new imperializing or globalizing dynamics, 1453 is just as significant as 1492.[47] The Ottoman Empire under Sultan Mehmet II's rule embarked on a series of imperial campaigns that, for Europeans at least, caused great fear, after the spectacular capture in 1453 of the 'Golden Apple', Constantinople, the Byzantine capital of the eastern Roman Empire. It also prompted Pope Pius II's unrequited calls for a crusade to drive out the Ottoman infidel. Conquests by subsequent sultans expanded the empire southward into northern Africa and Persia, and further north into southern and eastern Europe, proving they could rival European empire-building projects by extending theirs deep into Europe.[48] By the middle of the sixteenth century, the Ottoman Empire had secured an empire to rival Rome in scale and established itself as 'a major international

---

[41] For a remarkable account of the array of diplomatic protocols and other political and economic relations between Europe and the Ottoman Empire, see Malcolm 2015.

[42] Phillips and Sharman 2015: 50–1.   [43] Phillips and Sharman 2015: 58.

[44] Matsuda 2012: 5, emphasis in original.   [45] Matsuda 2012: chapters 7 and 8.

[46] Darwin 2008b: 73; Casale 2010.

[47] Brendan Simms (2014: 7) begins his magisterial history of Europe's struggle for supremacy in the year 1453, saying the Fall of Constantinople marks 'the start of modern European geopolitics'.

[48] Casale 2010: 9.

power'.[49] Just as significantly, it achieved 'control at the vital junction of trade routes connecting Europe, the Indian Ocean, and the Eurasian landmass'.[50] It had become a vast land and sea empire built on Asiatic and Islamic identity.

Despite their different cultural and religious roots, there were notable 'family resemblances' among the old regime empires.[51] The Ottomans, for example, emulated and reinforced European patterns of politics with their own imperial projections and adoption of European cultural accoutrements to symbolize the universality of their empire and to legitimize their 'world-embracing ambitions'.[52] Sultan Suleiman I, no less than Charles V, aspired to 'universal monarchy'.[53] Mehmet II, for example, modelled himself on Alexander the Great and ordained himself 'Sultan of the Two Continents and the Emperor of the Two Seas, the Shadow of God in this world and the next, the favourite of God on the Two Horizons, the Monarch of the Terraqueous Orb'.[54] To their enemies, the universalist aspirations of the Spanish and Ottoman empires represented nothing short of menacing tyranny and terror.[55] The same could be said of the Chinese suzerain system where, from the late sixteenth century, the Manchu or Qing dynasty dictated the terms of engagement with others in East Asia as well as with European interlopers; and the Mughal Empire which used the notion of 'universal lordship' as a currency of power.[56]

An Early Modern Global International Society?

The key point of this discussion is that the early modern world was divided into dynamic regional civilizations or state systems. While these regional international societies may have developed rules, norms, and institutions of their own, there is little evidence that these were shared across civilizations or regions in any significant way. As Bull noted, actors were largely unable 'to appeal to established universal international institutions—diplomatic conventions, forms of international law, principles of hierarchy, or customs of war—such as did facilitate exchanges within the various regional international systems'.[57] In his study of the history of international law in inter-civilizational perspective, Yasuaki Onuma concurred, observing 'there scarcely existed a

---

[49] Imber 2012: 205.   [50] Burbank and Cooper 2010: 18; Darwin 2008b: 73–87.
[51] Bayly 2004: 30.   [52] Goffman 2002; Subrahmanyam 2006: 72.
[53] Simms 2014: 9. On the imperial ideology of Charles V and the Habsburg dynasty, see Pagden 1995: 40–6; Lesaffer 2003; Simms 2014: 7–17.
[54] Goffman 2002: 58; see also Pagden 2009: 270.
[55] Pagden 1995: 43–4, 2009: 275–6.
[56] On the Qing dynasty see Darwin 2008b: 125–32; Purdue 2005: chapter 3, 2009; Zhang 2014a. On the Mughal Empire see Bang 2011: 175.
[57] Bull 1984b: 118.

common norm (the equivalent with today's international law) among such regional worlds or civilizations'.[58] But there were, it appears, localized and ad hoc diplomatic relations across civilizations and regions.[59] As Randall Lesaffer states, individual regional international societies generally developed their own practices and laws of peacemaking and peace treaties. But in cases of regular and close interaction, for example between European powers and the Ottoman and Mughal empires, local practices evolved that 'built on the practices and laws of the two civilizations involved, forming a kind of supra-regional system particular to their mutual relations'.[60]

In this chapter we argue that it was only after regional international societies became more fully interconnected that it became possible or necessary for transregional or global rules, norms, or institutions to develop. The Seven Years' War provides an interesting case for understanding how the inter-imperial rivalry that created a globally interconnected international society was also the context for dramatic changes in the constitutive and regulative principles of the emergent global international society. 'It was the very success of these big regimes', argues Bayly, 'that caused their decline'.[61] In other words, the global reach of imperial rivalry and the global wars it occasioned, also created the conditions in which successive waves of rights struggles and independence movements began to break up imperial formations, thus creating the context in which Bull's 'universal international society' of formally equal sovereign nation-states would eventually take shape.[62]

THE SEVEN YEARS' WAR: GLOBAL WAR AND DECLARATIONS OF INDEPENDENCE

The Seven Years' War (1756–63) left a lasting legacy on international society by beginning the longer-term dissolution of empire and the transformation of international society's principles of legitimacy. If international society during early modern times was predominantly a society of imperial and monarchical states waging wars primarily for local dynastic reasons, the global and multi-faceted nature of the Seven Years' War created conditions where anti-colonial independence struggles outside Europe in the so-called New World could achieve statehood for a people and thus gain entry into an emergent global

---

[58] Onuma 2000: 11.
[59] See Halikowski-Smith 2006, who outlines a number of quasi-diplomatic relations and protocols developed by the Portuguese in Africa and Asia. For an account of the difficulties that the English faced in their diplomatic dealings with the Mughal Empire, see Barbour 1998.
[60] Lesaffer 2012: 90.   [61] Bayly 2004: 89.
[62] Bull 1984b; Bayly 2004: 107–14; Reus-Smit 2013a.

international society. As Hamish Scott observes of the Seven Years' War, although it may not have 'caused' the transformation of international society, 'it put pressure upon existing administrative structures and political practices, and set in motion developments of lasting importance for later European and world history'.[63] One indication of the war's importance is that, according to Scott, it 'may have been the first European conflict with its own immediate historiography'.[64] Right from the outset, historians recognized the war for its decisive and enduring consequences.[65] Indeed, if a vantage point outside Europe is taken to assess the war's significance, such as Montreal, St Augustine, or Calcutta, the Seven Years' War takes on a greater significance than the American Revolution.[66] Before explaining the impact and legacy of the Seven Years' War in more detail, we provide a brief description of the war and the contexts in which it broke out.

The 'First Global War' in Context

The Seven Years' War has been variously described by historians as a 'major turning point in European and Atlantic history', 'an indispensable precursor' to the American Revolution, and as having 'transformed the eighteenth-century states system'.[67] According to Matt Schumann and Karl Schweizer it was 'a struggle for survival and hegemony that strained the resources of the greatest European powers in every corner of the globe'.[68] Despite these assessments, historians of international relations, including Bull and Watson, have generally neglected this war that is now widely recognized by historians as the first global war.[69]

Like many wars, the Seven Years' War was what Jeremy Black has called an 'umbrella war'; a war made up of multiple, related campaigns on different continents without necessarily being joined up temporally.[70] Fought principally in Europe and North America, the war produced a decisive victory for the British and a humiliating defeat for the French. The outcome of the Seven Years' War had significant ramifications for the balance of power. Not only had the French empire in North America been effectively destroyed, France

---

[63] Hamish Scott 2011: 425.   [64] Hamish Scott 2011: 428.
[65] Hamish Scott 2011: 428.   [66] Anderson 2000: xviii.
[67] Schumann and Schweizer 2008: 1; Anderson 2000: 745; Scott 2001: 31.
[68] Schumann and Schweizer 2008: 2.
[69] Daniel Baugh 2011: 1 also notes that in Sir Winston Churchill's (1957) history of Britain, he named a chapter 'The First World War' which was devoted to the Seven Years' War. See also Danley 2012 for a useful overview of the war and recent research.
[70] Black 1992: 167. The war was also known by colonists in America as the 'French and Indian War' (1754–63). More recently historians have also referred to it as 'the Great War for Empire'. For comprehensive studies of the war see Anderson 2000; Schumann and Schweizer 2008.

conceded European primacy to Britain, whose ascendancy had been driven by unmatched transoceanic commercial and military capabilities.

The war is conventionally seen as comprising two distinct but connected theatres joined by the long-standing and escalating Anglo-French rivalry: one theatre in continental Europe between British-supported Prussia and their enemies, the 'triple alliance' of Habsburg Austria, Bourbon France, and Russia; the other in colonial territories outside Europe—in North America, the Caribbean, India, and West Africa—primarily between Britain and France, and later, Spain.[71] In Europe, war was precipitated by Frederick the Great's invasion of Saxony in August 1756; a pre-emptive war of survival calculated to catch off guard the circling anti-Prussian forces who were intent on partitioning the Hohenzollern monarchy.[72] The extra-European war's origins lay in continuing skirmishes in the Ohio Valley region between British and French colonists, and that, with the decisive participation of the local native peoples, led to open warfare by 1754.[73]

The larger historical backdrop to the war is one of great power rivalry, diplomatic upheaval, commercial conflict, and the role of native American peoples. By mid-century the long-standing Anglo-French great power rivalry reached across the Atlantic from Europe to the North American continent. Indeed, Britain and France had fought three inconclusive wars in North America between 1689 and 1748.[74] These wars—fuelled by what Istvan Hont, following David Hume, calls 'jealousy of trade'—fused both geopolitical and commercial interests as trade and war increasingly became conjoined instruments of state power.[75] The geopolitical balance in Europe had become inextricable from imperial and commercial fortunes in America.[76] Brendan Simms argues that both the French and British 'framed colonial issues in primarily European terms', with the value of the colonies thought to lie in their capacity to supply 'wealth, raw materials and manpower' for their European exploits. In other words, the American colonies were a means to continental ends.[77] The 'Diplomatic Revolution' of 1756, which overturned a centuries-old enmity, turning Bourbon France and Habsburg Austria into allies, led to a new balance of power in Europe with alliances based more on state interest and security than religious or dynastic affiliation.[78] The Austrians, still smarting

---

[71] Black 2007: 93–9; Scott 2001: 33; Shennan 1995: 56.
[72] Christopher Clark 2007: 197.   [73] Anderson 2000: 5–21; Ward 2012: 64.
[74] Purvis 2003.
[75] Hume's phrase 'jealousy of trade' was an adaptation of Thomas Hobbes's 'jealousy of state'. See Hont 2005: 2. Smith 1993: book IV, chapter 3, also emphasized the close connection between 'mercantile jealousy' and state interest.
[76] Simms 2007: 455.   [77] Simms 2007: 443, 449.
[78] The French instructions towards an armistice with Austria at the end of the War of Spanish Succession were called 'Interests of the Catholic Religion'. Burkhardt 2012: 109. On the Diplomatic Revolution, see Christopher Clark 2007: 197; Shennan 1995: chapter 8; Simms 2014: 107–10.

after the loss of Silesia to Frederick's Prussia in 1740, sought a rapprochement with France and an alliance with them, Russia, Sweden, and Saxony.[79] France, meanwhile, concerned at erstwhile ally Prussia's closer ties with archenemy and rival colonial power Britain, hesitatingly entered into alliance with its old enemy. The end result was an upheaval of the established order and alliances in European international society.

Unlike the wars of succession that dominated diplomacy and international relations of the eighteenth century, the Seven Years' War was comparatively bereft of religious and dynastic interests.[80] Instead, colonial and commercial interests and the ever-present concern with the balance of power were uppermost in the minds of Europe's rulers. These dimensions played into one another in fuelling the 'jealousy of trade' that political economists of the period despised.[81] For instance, the surge in seaborne trade that began around the last quarter of the seventeenth century was due to events outside Europe— the 'upturn' in the Iberian Pacific and a simultaneous expansion of population and demand in China.[82] This spurred Dutch and British merchants and trading companies into action. Their efforts to obtain gold and silver helped to stabilize European currencies, while the renewed attraction of colonial expansion in North America, the Caribbean, and the Far East fuelled further economic growth.[83]

The statistics of growth that characterize the period surrounding the Seven Years' War are telling; 'between 1740 and 1780 the value of world trade increased by between a quarter and a third ... In France the volume of foreign trade doubled between the 1710s and the late 1780s, but its value increased five times'.[84] This shaped the international order in two ways. On the one hand it increased the autonomy and power of colonial trading companies who had the right to wage war, providing a new sense of authority and heterogeneity in international society. On the other, it augmented perceptions of the importance of the world outside Europe. British policymakers began to stress the importance of colonial and maritime issues from the 1720s, owing to the success of their colonies and other factors including the effective neutralization of Dutch territory after the Diplomatic Revolution.[85] After 1750 France came to view Britain as its greatest rival largely because Britain's maritime commercial activities furnished the financial resources for enhancing its military power both in Europe and beyond.[86] The connection between commerce, colonialism, and power was not lost on the French foreign minister, duc de Choiseul, who asserted in 1758 that '[t]he true balance of power now

---

[79] Blanning 2007: 576.
[80] Burkhardt 2012: 126. On the eighteenth-century wars of succession, see Shennan 1995.
[81] Hont 2005: 30–7.   [82] Blanning 2002: 119.   [83] Blanning 2002: 119.
[84] Blanning 2002: 119.   [85] Baugh 1998: 3–5.
[86] Baugh 1998: 5, 11. See also Simms 2007: 455.

resides in commerce and America'.[87] Greater appreciation of the benefits of commercial and colonial enterprises and naval power therefore helped to mark a fundamental shift 'in the configuration of European power and the way it was assessed', which in turn increased the likelihood that war would be fought on a global stage.[88]

The Legacy

The immediate impact of the Seven Years' War was transformative in two respects. First, it transformed the European geopolitical landscape by integrating the different European subregions, particularly Eastern Europe, into a consolidated regional system, and confirmed a pentarchy of great powers including the emergent great powers Prussia and Russia.[89] The most dramatic transformations concerned the rise of Russia and the decline of France. At the beginning of the war, few would have considered Russia as part of Europe. Even less conceivable was the idea that Russia could decisively influence European geopolitical relations; and yet Russia was victorious in two important battles against Frederick II in the war, played a key role in the destruction of Sweden, and later triumphed against the Ottoman Empire (1768–74). At the war's end, Russia had not only earned recognition as 'a full member of the family of great powers', but had also 'become the arbiter of eastern Europe'.[90] Sir George Macartney, British minister in St Petersburg in the mid-1760s, wrote how Russia was 'no longer to be gazed at as a distant glimmering star, but as a great planet that had obtruded itself into our system, whose place was yet undetermined, but whose motions must powerfully affect those of every other orb'.[91] France, by contrast, experienced a corresponding and very dramatic decline. Its defeat to Britain in the colonies had been catastrophic, humiliatingly ceding control of its former colonial territories in America, the Caribbean, and West Africa, and leaving France's military capability and reputation in tatters.[92]

The severe losses in Europe and abroad saw the formerly superior military power reduced to third or fourth position.[93] Conversely, Britain's naval capability boosted its position as the supreme colonial power.[94] The war rewrote the script of European rivalry to include new characters, new neighbours, and new power relationships.

---

[87] Quoted in Simms 2007: 455. In 1760 the duc de Choiseul again emphasized this decisive connection when he said: 'Colonies, commerce, and the maritime power which accrues from them will decide the balance of power upon the continent'. Quoted in Scott 2001: 10.

[88] Baugh 1998: 3.   [89] Scott 2001: chapter 1; Simms 2014: 116.

[90] Scott 2001: 152, 44.   [91] Scott 2001: 50.   [92] Scott 2001: 55–6.

[93] Scott 2001: 57.   [94] Simms 2014; Dull 2005: 36–7.

The second way in which the Seven Years' War was transformative was by globalizing the dynamics of imperial rivalry. The war stretched across four continents (North America, the Caribbean, India, and of course Europe itself) and three oceans, and saw non-Europeans, especially American Native Indians, involved in a conflict largely driven by Anglo-French rivalry.[95] The global reach of this imperial rivalry and its pathologies were understood by actors of the time. Although Prussia's King Frederick II had initiated the war in Europe by invading Saxony, he recognized the connection between the continental European and colonial American theatres of war:

> Everyone knows that the turmoil that is agitating Europe has its beginnings in America, that the struggle that has broken out between the English and the French about the cod fishery and unknown areas of Canada has given impetus to the bloody war that sends our part of the world into sorrow. This war was so far removed from the possessions of the German princes that it is difficult to see how the conflagration can reach from one part of the world to another that seemingly has no connections to it. Thanks to the statecraft of our century there is no current conflict in the world, be it ever so small, that cannot reach into and divide all of Christendom in a short time.[96]

Frederick's insight was that the character of war was changing. Not only were the causes of war changing as commerce ('cod fishery') and colonialism ('unknown areas of Canada') intertwined with war, but the interests of the state increasingly expanded to a global scope, such that 'no current conflict in the world' might not reverberate to Europe. Modern historians have affirmed Frederick's point, arguing that the Seven Years' War 'created a seismic shift in Europe's alliance system and balance of power', even if 'its first shots were fired not on a European, but an American, frontier'.[97] These changing circumstances prompted recognition among European powers that the rules, norms, and institutions that had previously governed their regional international society were subject to change.

The war also changed the balance between 'the military needs of states and their financial capacity', a process that contributed significantly to the 'world crisis' between 1780 and 1820.[98] Relentless pressure was put on state finances to sustain the *ancien régime* war machine needed to wage military campaigns both in Europe and in far away colonial territories.[99] After the Seven Years' War, the British and French were both left with massive state debt. By the late 1760s, France's debt repayment consumed 60 per cent of the annual budget, and the measures it had introduced to service its war debt fell well short of what was required. Instead of reforming the system of fiscal privileges of the Bourbon court to service these new debts and avoid bankruptcy, further land

---

[95] Danley 2012: xliii–xlix; Armitage 2007: 8–9.   [96] Quoted in Luh 2012: 1.
[97] Anderson 2000: 11.   [98] Bayly 2004: 100.   [99] Anderson 1988: 135–56.

taxes and a stamp tax were proposed.[100] These were aimed at a broad spectrum of society—the privileged, underprivileged, and the church—and radicalized opposition to Louis XVI's rule.[101] Ultimately, the inability of the French state to command the esteem of its people in the decades after the Seven Years' War exacerbated by the strain of war debts, hastened the demise of the erstwhile hegemon, and delivered the *ancien régime* into financial and political crises conducive to republican revolution.

Britain may have been conclusive victors in the Seven Years' War, but it too had accumulated significant state debt to finance the war.[102] Moreover, Britain now had to find the human and financial resources to govern the vast territories captured from the French and Spanish, and to manage relations with Native Americans.[103] Parliament's proposal to impose on the colonies new taxes and trade regulations, however fiscally necessary, merely galvanized American resistance.[104] Colonists increasingly denied the legitimate authority of the British Crown or Parliament over America. In this context, questions of public power, political representation, and liberty exerted great pressure upon the royal and imperial structures of government, disrupting 'the prevailing equilibrium' between 'mother country and colonies'.[105] American colonists may have identified as British subjects before the war, but in its aftermath, and, as discontent with the British Crown's 'long Train of Abuses and Usurpations' grew stronger, the 'Political Bands' that once connected them were dissolved, to use the language of the American Declaration of Independence.[106] When war eventually broke out between Britain and its dependent colonies in April 1775, it was 'less a moment in which the birth of a nation [could] be glimpsed than the traumatic dissolution of a once affectionate relationship between Britain and its colonies'.[107] To the extent that the Seven Years' War created the conditions for imperial implosion, it may justly be seen as an 'indispensable precursor' to the American Revolution.[108] In other words, despite Britain's victory, the Seven Years' War created propitious conditions in the colonies for republican revolution, but unlike the French case, the American Revolution was also a War of Independence.

Here we arrive at perhaps the most significant and enduring legacy of the Seven Years' War: the creation of political conditions in which the constitutive rules of international society could be contested. The aftermath of the global imperial rivalry led to revolutionary movements predicated on alternative bases of authority to those underpinning the *anciens régimes*. Domestically

---

[100] Scott 2001: 69.   [101] Bossenga 2010: 57.
[102] Blanning 2007: 301; Wood 2002.   [103] Wood 2002: 16–17.
[104] Blanning 2007: 301–3; Wood 2002: 25–6.   [105] Hamish Scott 2011: 433.
[106] 'In Congress, July 4, 1776. A Declaration By the Representatives of the United States of America, in General Congress Assembled' 2007: 165–6.
[107] Anderson 2000: xxi.   [108] Anderson 2000: 745.

they challenged the legitimacy of dynastic or royal authority on the basis of republican political principles and popular sovereignty; internationally they challenged the legitimacy of imperial hierarchy or suzerainty and the colonial dependence it produced, contributing to the concept of sovereign statehood as independence. The longer-term consequence of the American colonies' renunciation of colonial dependence, therefore, was to reshape membership of international society both within and beyond Europe. The novelty lay not just in the emergence of popular sovereignty as a legitimate rival to dynastic sovereignty, but in the equally significant idea that sovereign states are free, independent, and equal. Often called 'external sovereignty' by international relations theorists, this is what the American Declaration of Independence meant when it claimed the right 'to assume among the Powers of the Earth, the separate and equal Station'.[109] In other words, the Seven Years' War provoked a 'transformative crisis' that, according to Armitage, comprised:

> repeated claims to local autonomy, a crisis of monarchy, rebellion, civil war, the redistribution of sovereignty, assertions of independence and the emergence of a new civil society and political economy in the context of emergent statehood amid a restructured international society within the Atlantic world.[110]

Of greatest significance for the globalization of international society is the fact that this 'transformative crisis' was not restricted to the territories of the British Empire alone. It may have originated in the British Empire's dissolution, starting with the Seven Years' War, but its example and effects quickly ramified across the globe, redefining the constitutive rules of modern international society.[111]

The theoretical rationale for the new principle of popular sovereignty and the correlative notion of sovereign independence was given emphatic expression in the early years of the Seven Years' War by Emer de Vattel. Published in 1758, Vattel's *Law of Nations* argued that just as men could not be deprived of their natural liberty without their consent, so a nation 'remains absolutely free and independent with respect to all other men, all other nations, as long as it has not voluntarily submitted to them'.[112] The natural liberty of nations would be undermined, Vattel argued, if 'others were to arrogate to themselves the right of inspecting and regulating her actions;—an assumption on their part, that would be contrary to the law of nature, which declares every nation free and independent of all the others'.[113] Written with a view to protecting the independence of small states in Europe, Vattel's natural law defence of 'freedom, independence and interdependence' was conveniently applied in the

---

[109] On 'external sovereignty', see Bull 1977: 8. For the words from the American Declaration of Independence, see 'In Congress, July 4, 1776' 2007: 165.

[110] Armitage 2007: 192.   [111] An argument set out in full in Armitage 2007.

[112] De Vattel 2008: 68.   [113] De Vattel 2008: 71.

American context where it influenced the American 'founding fathers' and was embodied in the Declaration of Independence.[114]

It was this act, of declaring to 'a candid World' America's right to independent statehood, which triggered a global phenomenon that reshaped international society's rules and norms relating to membership, as former colonies asserted their independence in line with new principles of popular sovereignty. The American Declaration of Independence was the start of 'an epidemic' or 'a contagion of sovereignty', the first wave of which lasted until 1848, beginning in the Low Countries in Europe, the Caribbean, Spanish America, the Balkans, West Africa, and Central Europe.[115] Armitage argues that it 'marked a major transition in world history: in this era a world of states emerged from a world of empires'.[116] It was in creating the conditions for an anti-colonial independence movement in America that the Seven Years' War takes on significance as an important conjuncture in the globalization of international society.

The Seven Years' War is thus a useful case study of the way in which international society was globalized, as it contains both the imperial rivalry that drove commercial and colonial expansion (in this instance, Anglo-French rivalry across a number of continents), and the forces of imperial breakdown that yielded independence movements built on popular sovereignty as post-imperial principles of legitimacy (American independence). The Seven Years' War was something of a 'tipping point', after which the political momentum driving the conception of sovereign or independent statehood gathered pace. This conception circulated widely and inspired contestation and adaptation of international society's rules, norms, and institutions to accommodate the new principles of legitimacy and sovereign statehood they concretely shaped.

The most significant configurative transformation epitomized by the war was the conjoining of regional international societies under conditions of imperial rivalry and the subsequent imperial implosion generated by anti-colonial independence movements. The war confirmed the extent to which what were once regional international societies were now connected to one another. Thenceforth it became possible, and indeed necessary, to develop transregional or global rules, norms, or institutions to govern an emerging global international society made up of states deriving their legitimacy from clashing conceptions of sovereignty and demanding recognition as free, independent, and equal. The independence movements that proliferated after 1776 enabled a number of new states to emerge out of the shadow of empire, thus expanding international society by growth of number. Although the high point of this development might not have been reached until the

---

[114] See Armitage 2007: 38–42; Hunter 2012: 178–81.
[115] Armitage 2007: 103.　　　[116] Armitage 2007: 104.

mid-twentieth century, the case demonstrates just how transformative the conditions were during the 'revolutionary age'.

CONCLUSION

Conventional historiography tends to be built on presentist or Whig philosophies of history where an underlying principle or logic is tracked across time with the intention of identifying the extent to which international society realizes a principle or logic on which normative judgement is also passed. For Bull and Watson, the gradual expansion of an original European international society to encompass the non-European world is presented as a positive historical development. For critics, this view both downplays the violent Eurocentric dynamics of exclusion and ignores the active role of non-Western peoples in the making of modern international society. Eschewing the compulsion to identify one actor or civilization as the driving force in history—evident in the critics as much as Bull and Watson—our approach has contextualized the globalization of international society in early modern imperial rivalry and war within and between different regional international societies.

It was during the 'long sixteenth century' that imperial expansion and war began bringing separate regional international societies and their principal actors into contact. By the middle of the eighteenth century the leading empires of the day battled over commercial and colonial territories in distant lands and on high seas. It was only once these regions were connected that the need for common rules, norms, and institutions emerged. Of particular importance in creating the conditions for this to occur was the Seven Years' War—a global war that marked the beginning of the end of the *ancien régime* at the very moment when imperial rivalry seemed to reach a global limit. As the 'first global war', the conflict confirmed Europe's embeddedness in a larger international society of global scale, but also inaugurated a new context in which anti-dynastic and anti-colonial principles of legitimacy arose. The American Revolution furnished the first republican government outside Europe; but of greater significance for the globalization of international society, it also declared and enacted a conception of sovereignty as free, independent, and equal statehood. It was this conception of external sovereignty or independent statehood, announced in the American Declaration of Independence and then emulated in waves of anti-colonial struggles across the nineteenth and twentieth centuries, that transformed the constitutive rules of international society and distinguished modern international society.

8

Empire and Fragmentation

Jennifer M. Welsh

This chapter engages with the subject matter that has most often been identified as the central weakness or empirical 'blind spot' of Hedley Bull and Adam Watson's book, *The Expansion of International Society*: the assumption of a coherent European international society that expands, through the vehicle of imperialism, to 'unite the whole world into a single economic, strategic, and political system'.[1] This process is conceived as both rational and rule-governed, downplaying or overlooking the reality of the contestation, violence, and dispossession that it engendered. It is also depicted as a one-way process of standardization, whereby European models—of political organization and of relations among political units—are transmitted and absorbed by peripheral societies that had previously been excluded due to deficits in civilizational attributes.

Already in the early 1990s, International Relations (IR) scholars were beginning to suspect that the story of the expansion of European international society was much more complex, involving an interaction between core and periphery that profoundly affected the contours and nature of the society which European states *themselves* were forging.[2] In short, European international society, complete with its rules and norms, made little sense without the non-European 'other'. In reality, the Eurocentric system was neither stable nor mature, but in a constant state of development as a consequence of its encounters with the non-European world. A similar kind of argument has been put forward by international legal scholars, such as Antony Anghie, who maintains that international law—the body of rules that supposedly came to colonies 'fully formed and ready for application'—was itself profoundly shaped by the practice of imperialism and interactions with the non-European world.[3] International law in the modern period was thus less about fostering

---

[1] Bull and Watson 1984c: 7.   [2] Neumann and Welsh 1991.
[3] Anghie 2005.

order among equal units, as is commonly assumed, and more about managing and overcoming difference.

In what follows, I venture beyond these initial amendments to the expansion thesis, both conceptually and empirically. More specifically, I challenge how IR scholars to date have depicted not only the nature of the interaction that took place between the European and non-European worlds, but also the by-product of that process. In so doing, following the editors of this volume, I adjust the frame of reference from the narrower notion of European expansion, which misrepresents the relations between West and non-West, to the global interplay between states, regions, and civilizations. C. A. Bayly's highly influential analysis of globalization and modernity takes these connections and interactions as its starting point, contesting the notion that Europe's ideas and material resources were in the driver's seat during the era typically characterized as European expansion.[4]

By focusing on both empire and fragmentation, this chapter forwards two main claims. The first is that we should not exaggerate the ability of European imperial powers to master completely the colonial spaces that they encountered. As contemporary historians of imperialism have demonstrated, European empire was a fabric 'full of holes',[5] whose boundaries were often ill-defined, whose territorial jurisdiction was uneven, and whose legal authority was enmeshed with the law and customs of indigenous subjects. This remained the case even during imperialism's high-water mark, the nineteenth century, when the international system moved definitively away from a polycentric world to an order delineated more clearly into core and periphery.[6] Consequently, the tendency of many IR scholars to conceive of empire as a blunt manifestation of power, which 'acts' upon less developed or less powerful spaces, must be revised to take account of local agency and processes of localization. As Bayly insists, non-European peoples were not 'passive recipients of Western bounty, or, alternatively, simply the West's supine victims'.[7] Even though territories became dominated physically by outside powers, the degree of ideational subservience varied. European ideas were often remoulded or localized, in some cases limiting the extent of domination by colonial powers.

Second, given the nature and limits of imperial power, the outcome of interaction between Europe and non-Europe was not standardization, or the wholesale adoption of the European model of governance, but rather a diversity of political and legal forms. The historians' depiction of overlapping authority structures in the early modern period—what Andrew Phillips and J. C. Sharman refer to as 'heteronomy'[8]—suggests that territorial sovereignty was not the only model populating the political imagination of Europeans or

---

[4] Bayly 2004.   [5] Benton 2010: 2.   [6] Pomeranz 2000: 4.
[7] Bayly 2004: 3.   [8] Phillips and Sharman 2015: 139.

non-Europeans. In some instances, territories enjoyed quasi-sovereignty, while in other cases of established colonies there was (almost) full territorial rule by the metropole. Moreover, the legal systems that prevailed varied greatly from one colonial context to the next, frequently sustaining multiple and even conflicting jurisdictions.[9] The core question is thus less 'who became part of international society and when', and more how various entities fit within a global order at different points in time—an order which contained elements of *both* system *and* society. Rather than employing the binary notions of inclusion or exclusion, which represent only one way of engaging in social theorizing about international relations, the analysis here thus draws on social theories that emphasize patterns of association and interaction.[10]

In formulating these arguments, I do not contest the thesis that there was a relatively closed group of states—or 'family of nations'—that coalesced in Europe by the early nineteenth century around certain institutions, rules, and values. However, interactions with the non-European world played a significant part in consolidating European states and elevating European international society into its pre-eminent position.[11] As a vivid illustration of this point, consider that it was in India where the modern, professional civil service was born, and then exported back to Britain.[12] Furthermore, we need to conceive of this European 'core' as one part of a larger social order, in which there were multiple centres of political organization and various kinds of interaction among them.[13] This is not to downplay the increasingly asymmetrical structure of this order, particularly in the latter stages of imperialism, or the long-lasting effects of the 'civilizational' narratives and practices that both contributed to and flowed from that structure[14] (a theme I will return to later). But the adoption of an interactional approach does emphasize the degree to which the development and evolution of states in the colonial world emerged through political processes that engaged both the colonizers and the colonized.[15] Thinking in these terms will in turn help us to understand why the structures and processes of contemporary international society—despite the formal structure of anarchy and homogeneity of political form—have continued to feature elements of hierarchy and heterogeneity.

Before proceeding with my central arguments, a brief word about sources. If Bull and Watson were the first to give international society a 'real' history (despite its shortcomings), their account should be viewed in its particular intellectual context. IR today benefits from not only a range of recent works of

---

[9] Burbank and Cooper 2013. [10] John Scott 2011.

[11] See Buzan and Lawson 2015b: 7. This is why these authors choose to speak of 'global modernity' rather than European or Western modernity.

[12] Metcalf 2007: chapter 1. [13] Keene 2014.

[14] For a more definitive analysis of international order outside of the confines of European international society, see Keene 2002.

[15] Benton 2002: 255.

historical sociology,[16] but also significant turns in the discipline of history itself. I refer here both to postcolonial literature, which warns against the tendency to adopt the perspective of the powerful metropole when analysing modern history,[17] and to the efforts of the new global historians to 'decentre' national histories and integrate large historical trends and sequences of events which were previously analysed separately in regional or national contexts.[18] This wider perspective encourages the discipline of IR to move beyond the rich analysis of Europe's interaction with societies that were *not* formerly colonized (for example, China and Japan),[19] to examine interaction with those many entities in Africa and Asia that were.[20] Late eighteenth-century international order was multi-centred, with significant parts of the world remaining outside the direct territorial control of Europe and later the United States, despite the clear disparities of power between 'locals' and 'outsiders' in these territories. And while the world did become dominated by the West, through the juggernaut of the nineteenth century's 'high imperialism', it was once again challenged in the twentieth century with the rise of Japan and different varieties of nationalism in the non-European world.

INTERACTION VERSUS EXPANSION

By adopting the assumption of interaction between the European and non-European world, three particular features of international order in the age of empire become more apparent.

Resistance and Local Agency

While European states, and in particular their significant material capabilities, were key motors in the process of empire-building, a more expansive conception of agency is required to understand why fragmentation, rather than standardization, was so often the product of Europe's relations with the non-European world. There are two main kinds of agents that tempered the homogenizing effect of imperialism.

The first is the array of private actors, including colonial administrators, settlers, and merchants, who in claiming power and economic goods often drew instrumentally upon the legal and political resources of the European

---

[16] See Hobson 2004; Spruyt 1994; Nexon 2009; Phillips 2011; Buzan and Lawson 2015b; Phillips and Sharman 2015.

[17] Chakrabarty 2008.   [18] Bayly 2004; Benton 2010; Belich 2009.

[19] See, for example, Suzuki 2009; Hui 2005.   [20] Buzan and Little 2014.

state to order and justify their interactions with indigenous populations.[21] These practices challenge the image conveyed by the expansion thesis, of a European empire-state acting upon colonial spaces. As historians of colonialism demonstrate, sovereignty in the core was multi-form, and in some cases not fully formed; thus, its exercise was extended to these spaces by dividing and decentralizing it.[22] This was particularly true for one of the key agents of imperialism, the chartered company. In spite of the role of European sovereigns in formally creating and supervising these corporations, each entity effectively 'took on a life of its own…They created courts, regulated property, collected taxes, and hired armies…and in so doing, offered a competing locus of loyalty'.[23] Even during the most intense periods of what Barry Buzan and George Lawson describe as 'rational state-building' in the nineteenth century,[24] the tools and mechanisms used to govern imperial spaces were not wholly state-sponsored or 'caged within' national territories.

In addition, the structural context—both material and ideational—in which these agents operated was not uniformly determining. With respect to the material elements of power, it is important to underscore that when the Europeans began their incursion into the Indian Ocean in the sixteenth century, they were thrust forward by their niche maritime capability, and not by their overall military or commercial advantage over land-based Asian powers.[25] It is also worth remembering that the French embrace of imperial expansion in the early-to-mid-nineteenth century was as much a means of addressing its own post-revolutionary instability and the perception of weakness vis-à-vis old rivals, as it was an expression of great power superiority.[26]

Turning to the ideational context of empire, we encounter the second form of agency that chipped away at the homogenizing effect of imperialism: those who contested and resisted the logic of expansion. Contestation of the imperial project can be observed at a very early stage, even in the writings of Francisco de Vitoria, regarded by some as the ideological forefather of modern imperialism.[27] In asking by what right the 'barbarians' were subjected to Spanish rule, Vitoria was also questioning the general legitimacy of empire.[28] Moreover, although he did not advocate extending sovereignty to the American Indians (those who were barbaric could not enjoy this privileged status), he did claim that non-Christian infidels had a right to political independence and thus countered prominent theological arguments that were used to justify the Spanish conquest of South America.[29]

---

[21] Benton 2010. [22] Benton and Ross 2013. [23] Halliday 2013: 269.
[24] Buzan and Lawson 2015b: 99–101. [25] Phillips and Sharman 2015.
[26] Pitts 2005. [27] Anghie 2005: chapter 1. [28] Pagden 2012.
[29] At the same time, of course, Vitoria's thought is underpinned by the notion of a rationally ordered *Christian* universe. He argued that the Spaniards had a right to 'save the innocents' from egregious harms, such as cannibalism and human sacrifice. See Bain 2013.

A significant degree of anti-imperialist sentiment also surfaced in the late eighteenth century, informed either by (in the case of Denis Diderot, Immanuel Kant, and Johann Gottfried Herder) a pluralist objection to attempts to judge or 'civilize' non-Europeans in accordance with European ideas of morality,[30] or by (in the case of David Hume, Adam Smith, and Edmund Burke)[31] concern about the effects of empire on the prosperity and freedom of both the colonized and the colonizers. The latter set of thinkers was largely supportive of the American Revolution, and in the case of Hume and Smith, actively questioned whether the establishment of colonies would increase overall 'utility'. Burke's attack on imperial rule focused less on the foundational issue of its legitimacy (indeed, he did not call for its dismantling), and more on the potential for injustice and oppression, the importance of respecting the culture and spirit of colonized peoples, and the effect of imprudent imperial conduct on British liberties and political culture.[32]

The ideologies of progress that came to dominate in the mid-nineteenth century, most notably liberalism and scientific racism, did serve to legitimize both the continuation of empire-building and the exclusionary practices associated with the 'standard of civilization'.[33] But although liberalism in this period always carried within it the potential for intolerance and triumphalism,[34] the civilizational self-confidence of Europeans was not wholly uncontested and in many respects contained the seeds of its own destruction.[35]

As a final point, it is crucial to note that the dominance and spread of the nation-state in the nineteenth century was not only a European phenomenon. The doctrine of popular sovereignty, born in the age of Europe's revolutions, did of course give ruling groups new resources to justify political authority and thus contributed to the 'moral rearmament' of the state in a post-dynastic era.[36] But this doctrine was also globalized, providing a tool for both legitimation and resistance everywhere—including within the new empire states of Europe. Thus, once 'high imperialism' took hold in the nineteenth century, national identity was sharpened both within European states that had been conquered by the French (think, for example, of the writings of Giuseppe Mazzini), and among indigenous political leaders and intellectuals in the non-European world—evidenced most vividly by the 1857 mutiny in India. Resistance movements in a variety of colonial spaces led to uprisings and revolts that undermined the exercise of authority by imperial powers and fostered transnational movements of solidarity against the hegemony of the West.[37]

---

[30] Muthu 2003.　　[31] Van de Harr 2013; Pitts 2005.　　[32] Mehta 1999; Welsh 2013a.
[33] Buzan and Lawson 2015b: chapter 4.　　[34] Mehta 1999.
[35] Buzan and Lawson 2015b: 123.　　[36] Bayly 2004: 106.
[37] Shilliam 2011; Mazower 2012.

Hybridity and Heterogeneity

Bull and Watson's core thesis is that between the sixteenth and late nineteenth centuries, European states consolidated their sovereignty, while the imperial zones (lagging behind) gradually moved towards the same political model. The interactional approach adopted here, however, casts doubt on the degree to which the expansion of the sovereign state was a foregone conclusion. As Phillips and Sharman suggest, the ubiquity of this model today makes it 'easy to misread the early history of European encounters with non-Western societies as a mere prologue to the later worldwide triumph of Western institutional forms'.[38]

Instead, the imperial confrontation between European and non-European societies defined both the extent and nature of this core 'institution' of international society. As Anghie notes, 'sovereignty was improvised out of the colonial encounter, and adopted unique forms which differed from and destabilized given notions of European sovereignty'.[39] The evidence provided by historians demonstrates that empires experimented with different legal and geographic variations with respect to their rule, ranging from loosely aligned jurisdictions, to treaty ports, to protectorates, to settlement and penal colonies, to—at the far end of the spectrum—direct-rule colonies. They also oversaw complex forms of partial sovereignty, as, for example, in the Princely States of India or the 'native states' of Dutch East Asia.

The heterogeneity of international order was most marked in the early modern era (*circa* the early sixteenth century to the late eighteenth century), when diverse political forms coexisted in colonial spaces and established stable relations among one another, even in the absence of the shared values or norms that theorists of international society have frequently assumed to be prerequisites for 'order under anarchy'. Nor was this period marked by an alternative source of order—namely, a hegemonic or imperial power. Instead of imposing stability, agents of Western imperialism are more accurately characterized, in Phillips and Sharman's terms, as 'ingratiating' and 'insinuating' themselves into the wealthy and populous societies they met, leaving key traditions and institutions intact.[40] As a consequence, at various points in global history, 'functionally dissimilar polities co-existed without the stabilizing ballast of either the conventions of a sovereign state system or the commands of an imperial international order'.[41] In the case of the Indian Ocean, three different but complementary polities—the Portuguese Estado da India, the Mughal Empire, and the so-called company sovereigns that exercised state-like prerogatives (the Dutch East India Company and the English

---

[38] Phillips and Sharman 2015: 219.   [39] Anghie 2005: 6.
[40] Phillips and Sharman 2015: 7.   [41] Phillips and Sharman 2015: 3.

East India Company)—came to constitute a highly diverse, yet stable, international system.

Two elements were particularly important in fostering and sustaining heterogeneity. The first were the concordant beliefs between Europeans and non-Europeans (the latter, primarily in Asia, Latin America, and Africa) that sovereignty was divisible and could be shared, rather than contained within territorially defined units.[42] Systems of extra-territorial rights for traders and merchants, so often viewed as *the* symbol of the power of European imperialists, was one manifestation of this congruence. While in the Ottoman Empire and China extraterritoriality became a Western privilege that was imposed, sometimes through violence, in other non-European spaces, particularly in Latin America, it actually contributed to state-making and the consolidation of political authority, as local agents employed it instrumentally to shape state institutions. In these contexts, foreign merchants—in the process of carving out exceptions to state control—inadvertently contributed to discourses about sovereignty that reinforced the authority of those with whom they negotiated.[43] Another illustration of congruence is the phenomenon of 'legal pluralism', which as Lauren Benton shows was the norm, rather than the exception, in colonial territories. Empires confronted the task of managing political communities with divergent constitutional traditions and a variety of forms and sources of law, and in many contexts both relied on and legitimized 'layered legal arrangements'.[44] Law was therefore often closely connected to local practices, and could be mobilized by multiple actors, including imperial subjects, to suit their own purposes. In the words of two recent historians of legal pluralism, although 'law was a tool of empire', it is not always straightforwardly clear 'who actually wielded this tool and for which goals and with which results'.[45]

The second element contributing to heterogeneity was the mechanism of localization. Continuous and complex negotiations between Europeans and indigenous actors, which sometimes morphed into concrete alliances in which Europeans provided financial or military support, served to legitimize the multiple and overlapping authority structures that developed in the non-European world. This dynamic of localization carried over into the nineteenth century, through the frequent sharing of authority between imperial agents and local interlocutors. Even when the previous balance of power between European and non-Europeans gave way to an era of Western ascendance, heterogeneity did not give way to homogenization of political units in the periphery according to Western standards. This was so for two main reasons.

First, as demonstrated by Phillips and Sharman, the intensification of Western imperialism was facilitated by collaborative relationships between

---

[42] Phillips and Sharman 2015: especially chapter 4.   [43] Benton 2002: 244–52.
[44] Benton and Ross 2013: 1.   [45] Burbank and Cooper 2013: 285.

local agents and agents of European expansion that had been established in the age of heterogeneity.[46] Hence, for example, a key source of success in the East India Company's advance in the nineteenth century was its utilization of Indian soldiers and intelligence networks, and its strategy of creating alliances with Indian polities in return for military protection. And second, when Europeans did attempt more coercive and direct methods of control, based on liberal ideologies that sought to elevate local societies out of their traditional backwardness, their strategies were challenged by resistance on the part of local interlocutors who were vital to the continuation of the imperial project. The Indian rebellion in 1857 against the British Raj, for example, forced the colonial masterminds in London to rethink their standardizing mission and to revert to modes of rule that acknowledged local autonomy and embodied notions of suzerainty rather than full sovereign control.[47]

Consequently, in many parts of the non-European world, imperialists continued to favour forms of indirect or differentiated rule that—even if more intrusive than in previous centuries—acknowledged and in some cases leveraged the exercise of quasi-sovereignty by sub-polities. This provides further evidence that sovereignty was not necessarily 'an indivisible quality that a state either possessed or failed to retain', but rather could 'be held by degrees, with full sovereignty reserved from the imperial power'.[48] Although local elites retained a degree of authority over the internal affairs of these political entities, they were not permitted or deemed capable of entering into international relations. One example of this kind of arrangement were the truces (and later protectorate agreements) that Britain formed with sheikhdoms in the Persian Gulf, which allied these entities permanently to Britain while recognizing local authority in internal matters. Another more familiar example are the princely states of India, which frequently threw up legal challenges concerning the extent and content of imperial rule. International lawyers and colonial officials, in grappling with the status of these quasi-sovereign entities, frequently made reference to a distinctive kind of 'imperial law', nested somewhere between foreign and domestic law, which both specified the *type* of sovereign power these sub-polities possessed and the *conditions* under which the dominant imperial power could intervene in their political affairs and suspend or subvert the 'normal' law regulating relations among independent political units.[49] In practice, this meant that some colonial

---

[46] Phillips and Sharman 2015: 175–81.

[47] For an overview of the rebellions that marked the British Empire, including the 1857 mutiny, see Darwin 2012: 223–64.

[48] Benton 2008: 603.

[49] Benton 2008: 599. It was only at the end of the nineteenth century that international lawyers, such as John Westlake, simplified the picture by claiming that empires amounted to a kind of municipal law, and that the inhabitants of the Indian princely states were effectively British subjects.

entities, by effectively asserting their jurisdiction over their internal affairs, forced imperial powers to justify intervention as a political act, thereby stretching what was legally permissible. As Benton provocatively suggests, rather than international law making empire obsolete, it was the colonial approach to managing degrees of sovereignty that raised questions about the relevance of international law for managing global order.[50]

Quasi-sovereign entities were thus situated along a spectrum of jurisdictions that were, to a greater or lesser extent, encompassed with the legal jurisdiction of the imperial power (often depending on their level of 'backwardness' or degree of 'remoteness'). But the blunt application of civilizational categories notwithstanding, the point to underscore here is the variety of relationships that colonial territories formed with the law. Buzan and Lawson conclude that '[a]lthough some aspects of the encounter between core and peripheral powers were consistent, not least the huge power gap that existed between them, this did not lead to the development of homogeneous political entities'.[51] This assessment invites scepticism about IR theory's general proclivity to assume that greater interaction between political communities will necessarily bring about a convergence in political form, or that fragmentation and diversity are symptoms of a weak international order.[52] In particular, it calls into question some of the existing sociological accounts of the expansion of the state system. According to theorists such as Bull and Watson, and more recently David Strang,[53] the European state system expanded globally through processes of socialization and 'selection': political entities sought legitimacy through the acquisition of sovereign statehood, which enhanced their prospects for survival, thereby contributing to greater convergence in political form. But as historians of the globalization of international society reveal, heterogeneity remained a prominent feature of international systems from the sixteenth to late nineteenth centuries, for a host of reasons: because dominant conceptions of political legitimacy did not so clearly dictate a common political institutional form; because the non-European world was not so infinitely malleable that it automatically conformed to European models; and because ideologies of civilizational categories continued to argue for differential treatment between political units.[54]

The Persistence of Hierarchy

This brings us to the final implication of drawing upon social theories of interaction: the persistence of hierarchy underneath formal equality.[55] As far

---

[50] Benton 2008: 618–19.   [51] Buzan and Lawson 2015b: 138.
[52] A critique of this dominant tendency is the main thesis of Phillips and Sharman 2015.
[53] Strang 1991a.   [54] Phillips and Sharman 2015: 30.
[55] This theme is taken up at greater length by Barry Buzan in Chapter 12.

back as the late eighteenth century, international lawyers had provided the intellectual building blocks for a truly global international society, based on the principle of sovereign equality. Bull and Watson's central claim was that this Vattelian principle, of equal and independent political communities, expanded beyond the European core to encompass all regions of the globe. Sovereign equality came to imply three further principles. The first is a principle of inclusion: all states, as holders of international legal personality, are entitled to participate in the formation of international law and in a variety of cooperative practices. This gives sovereign equality a fundamentally relational character, marking states out as peers in the making of international rules and institutions.[56] The second, which flows from the first, is the principle of reciprocity: all states—at least formally—are entitled to the same general rights and subject to the same general obligations. This means, in effect, that any state claiming a right under international law has to accord all others the same right. The final principle is one of jurisdiction: states have the authority to make and enforce rules within a particular territory, therefore limiting the reach of foreign laws or external authorities. This third principle, as Jean Cohen writes, 'is the sine qua non for international law' as it delimits legal systems from one another and enshrines plurality.[57]

Yet, during the age of empire (and arguably beyond), Emer de Vattel's conception of a system of equal and independent states has been primarily a normative ideal or aspiration than a reflection of a horizontally organized international order.[58] In reality, international order was largely bifurcated into civilized and uncivilized zones, and international law reinforced these distinctions by codifying principles to humanize relations among the states of Europe, while simultaneously loosening the restraints that earlier legal theorists had asserted should govern relations between Europe and the non-European world. This was evident, for example, in the development of the laws of war and especially the Hague Conventions, which, as Mark Mazower shows, aspired to regulate warfare only between civilized powers and thus enabled massacres, bombings, and systematic detentions in conflicts in the non-European lands 'deemed to be beyond law's sway'.[59]

Several IR scholars have demonstrated how *de facto* hierarchy continued to underpin the formal infrastructure of global international society well into the contemporary period.[60] The drastic redistribution of power that occurred over the nineteenth century, fuelled by the material forces of industrialization and the consolidation of Western states through more professional bureaucracies and new ideational sources of legitimacy, substantially compromised the formal institutions and rules of the formal inter-state order that developed.

---

[56] Cohen 2012: 156.   [57] Cohen 2012: 200.
[58] Pitts 2013.   [59] Mazower 2012: 78.
[60] Keene 2002; Bowden 2009; Zarakol 2011; Buzan and Lawson 2015b.

While international law continued to enunciate, and embody, the ideal of sovereign equality, it either denied that it was applicable everywhere, or consistently interpreted it restrictively.[61] It was thus sovereign equality for the few, and not for the many.

It was not merely, however, that sovereign equality was imperfectly practiced. There was also a shift in how the principle was understood. Vattel's substantively rich understanding of sovereign equality—as equality both in the law and before the law—was soon eroded by the rise of positivism and the emphasis on state consent. As Nico Krisch explains:

> rules were no longer regarded as per se applicable to all but as emanating from the consent of every single State. On this background, it seemed sufficient that States had the equal *capacity* to enter into new rules while the rules themselves could embody a high level of inequality, especially when created by way of treaty.[62]

Despite the ambitious aspiration of sovereignty equality, its concrete content actually offered new states very little protection against continuing factual inequalities, and in some cases—such as the United Nations Charter or the Nuclear Non-Proliferation Treaty—the international law *consented to by states* enshrined inequality. In sum, the spectre of an international society enlarging in a progressive and linear fashion, extending sovereign equality to new entities, masks not only the significant degree of hierarchy that existed outside the legal realm—in political institutions such as the Concert of Europe, for example—or between the 'civilized' and 'uncivilized' worlds, but also the way in which the developing international legal order continued to facilitate or entrench inequality.

In fact, as Buzan and Lawson point out, the hierarchical structure created during the height of imperialism divided international society into (at least) three tiers: a core of Western states that engaged in mutual recognition of sovereign equality, albeit with special roles and responsibilities for the great powers, and that slowly welcomed into their ranks mature entities such as Japan and the Ottoman Empire; a 'semi-periphery' of states, including China, Siam, Argentina, Egypt, and Iran, which on the one hand had sovereign independence, but on the other were not deemed fully 'civilized' and thus were heavily penetrated through unequal treaties and territorial rights; and a periphery of colonized peoples with no formal independent standing, who emerged at different stages over the subsequent century into the world of sovereign equality. In addition, the *de facto* imposition of an inferior status on the non-Western world produced a twisted version of Bull and Watson's expansion thesis. Entry into the club of civilized states by entities such as Japan implied not only adopting the rules, institutions, and norms of European international society, but also embracing imperial modes of authority of their

---

[61] Krisch 2003.   [62] Krisch 2003: 138, emphasis added.

own, whether by annexing neighbouring territories or engaging in wars for overseas territory. 'It is no surprise,' Buzan and Lawson write, 'that those states...which sought to emulate European power, underwent both a restructuring of domestic society through industrialization and state rationalizations, and a reorientation of foreign policy towards "progressive" imperialism.'[63]

ECHOES IN CONTEMPORARY INTERNATIONAL SOCIETY

The three features of international order in the age of empire that I have highlighted in this chapter—the power of local agency, the existence of multiple and hybrid political forms, and the persistence of hierarchy under formal equality—have all continued to feature, in various degrees, in the global international society that has developed since the imperial world collapsed. The diverse and variegated forms of imperial engagement with the non-Western world, and the norms and institutions they spawned, have had significant echoes in contemporary international relations, despite their relative neglect by post-war academic writings in IR, which have been more focused on analysing the nature and consequences of anarchy. Appreciation of the scale and pace of the structural transformation of international relations brought about by the process of decolonization was for too long overshadowed by the centrality of the Cold War to the discipline of IR.[64] Today, that imbalance has largely been corrected, as scholars from various perspectives have analysed the nature and impact of the global spread of the sovereign state political form against the backdrop of empire's demise. Although the Western-colonial international society of the nineteenth and early twentieth centuries was globalized after the end of the Second World War, with the extension of formal sovereign statehood to (almost) all former colonies, significant levels of hierarchy and heterogeneity persisted. To put it most simply, while sovereignty had seemingly triumphed, equality had not.[65]

De Facto Hierarchy versus *De Jure* Equality

In the early part of the twentieth century, hierarchical practices were evident in the particular ways in which self-determination—the new standard of membership in international society—was applied to the crumbling Ottoman

---

[63] Buzan and Lawson 2015b: 42.　　[64] For an example, see Bradley 2010.
[65] Phillips and Sharman 2015: 203.

and Austro-Hungarian empires after the conclusion of the First World War. The first and most obvious point was that self-determination would not, despite its promise, have universal implications; it would be limited to territories in central, eastern, and south-eastern Europe. Second, international recognition of new states in this geographic area was not only premised on the fulfilment of criteria that extended deeply into matters of domestic jurisdiction, as specified by the Minority Treaties, but also closely controlled and manipulated by the great powers.[66] As a result, although the Treaties professed the equality of all citizens within the polity, and allocated particular groups language and cultural rights, they also created hierarchies among ethnic groups and did not extend the same protection to all.[67] Third, in the decades that followed, the League of Nations frequently invoked the stipulations of the Minority Treaties in its dealings with post-imperial states to influence the domestic policies of these new entities—in some cases threatening to intervene to reverse what the League deemed to be an abrogation of their responsibilities.[68]

But the perpetuation of inequality was manifest most vividly in the mandates system of the League of Nations, under which—according to Article 22 of the League Covenant—'advanced nations' were to administer those peoples 'not yet able to stand by themselves under the strenuous conditions of the modern world'. While in theory mandated territories were conceived as a weigh-station on the road to independent statehood, those put in charge of implementing the eventual mandates *system* were committed to ensuring that colonial control was maintained, and in some cases even enhanced, in a less overt form. As Susan Pedersen persuasively argues, the framework of League oversight primarily contributed to a change in the justification that mandatory powers offered for their authority—that is, the need to assist territories to stand on their own feet—and not to a change in imperial practices themselves. In fact, many mandated territories were less well governed than they had been as colonies and in certain instances experienced even more oppressive rule.[69] Through the creation of an impartial authority to oversee the development of former colonies, the Mandates Commission thus assisted the project of imperial legitimation more than the project of sovereign independence.

More generally, interwar internationalism proved to be 'not the antithesis to empire but its civilizer'.[70] Although the League of Nations seemed to encapsulate a model of international organization based on the formal equality of sovereign states, it was inspired by those who viewed it as a means of preserving and strengthening the British Empire by linking it more permanently to the power of the United States.[71] At least up until the entry of Germany in the mid-1920s, the organization functioned mostly as a 'League

---

[66] Jackson-Preece 1998.   [67] Fink 2004.   [68] Spanu 2015.
[69] Pedersen 2015.   [70] Mazower 2012: 167.   [71] Mazower 2012: 128–37.

of Empires', consistently pushing claims to self-determination off the table and providing a forum through which imperial authority in non-European spaces could be upheld.[72] Furthermore, despite the commonly held view that the United Nations was clearly disassociated from the ideas and infrastructure that inspired the League, the architects of the latter played a crucial role in setting the text and parameters of the global institution that arose out of the ashes of the Second World War. As Mazower reminds us, 'it was Jan Smuts, the South African premier and architect of white settler nationalism, who did more than anyone to argue for, and help draft, the UN's preamble'.[73]

The Atlantic Charter itself evinced both US ideals of self-determination and anti-colonialism, and exclusivist Victorian notions about who was entitled to sovereignty and when. Indeed, the United States did not always adhere to its own anti-imperialist rhetoric, claiming for itself a right to establish a special category, the 'strategic trust', in the former Japanese mandated islands that it conquered during the war.[74] Hence, while a variety of models for international governance circulated during the war, what emerged from the negotiations and lobbying was effectively a 'warmed-up League'—with the vital addition of the United States and the Soviet Union at its core.[75] The similarity between the two institutions was not lost on activists and intellectuals in the periphery, who saw the shift in language from colony or mandate, to 'dependent territory', as purely semantic. In fact, the newer organization in some ways retreated from egalitarian advances made by the League, by granting less power to its General Assembly and institutionalizing great power roles and privileges.

It is nonetheless important to note that, as in the earlier periods of empire, twentieth-century agents of contestation and resistance managed to curtail the full advance of civilizational logics of hierarchy and exclusion. What was novel was that they did so through the very institutions that had been created by the great powers. This trend was visible already in the era of the League of Nations when the mandates system unwittingly became, in Pedersen's words, the 'site and stake of a great international argument over imperialism's claims'.[76] At the Geneva-based headquarters of the Mandates Commission, mandatory powers were exposed to press scrutiny over alleged misrule and the pressure of non-European activists for self-determination. This unforeseen side-effect of interwar internationalism imposed concrete constraints on imperial ambitions, and in some cases either prevented annexations of territory (as in the case of south-west Africa) or led to changes in status for mandated territories (as in the case of Iraq).

Two decades later, the Trusteeship Council of the United Nations faced even greater contestation, as activists in trust territories sent petitions and

---

[72] Pedersen 2015: 403, 12.   [73] Mazower 2009: 9.   [74] Pedersen 2015: 400.
[75] Mazower 2009: 15.   [76] Pedersen 2015: 5.

lobbying missions to New York and formed alliances with members of the international human rights movement. As in the case of the Mandates Commission, the institutions of the United Nations—originally infused with imperialist logics—became a focal point for colonial contestation and served as a training ground for even further acts of resistance by the non-European world.[77] But it was Jawaharlal Nehru, who at the end of the Second World War had risen to the top of India's interim government, who led the most visible successful efforts to use the existing framework of the UN to challenge colonialism. Through the Indian motion in the new General Assembly to challenge South Africa's treatment of its Indian minority, Nehru not only won a victory for racial equality but also ignited a broader campaign to exploit Western ideas and tools of diplomacy to dismantle empire.[78]

The Universalization of Sovereignty?

The United Nations thus gradually broke free from its close ties to the defence of empire, as the latter's civilizational assumptions and practices of domination were delegitimized. Henceforth the UN both embraced and gave voice to the tide of anti-colonialism, which served as a 'moral compass' for non-aligned states during the Cold War.[79] But as the twentieth century progressed, and mandate and trusteeship systems disappeared under the weight of the norm of self-determination, gradations of sovereignty remained a prominent feature of political and economic practice. 'The agronomists, engineers, and other technocrats employed...by colonial governments after 1945', write the historians Mark Thomas and Andrew Thompson, 'migrated wholesale into the development agencies and other advisory bodies that proliferated in the former colonial world from the 1960s onwards.'[80]

The recognition of new states provides one concrete example of how these traces of hierarchy have shaped the contours of contemporary international order. Although in legal terms sovereign statehood has come to be determined by the application of clear positivist criteria, in the practice of inter-state relations the latter have been coupled with standards in economic and political development.[81] As a result, the natural end-point of self-determination—the global spread of the nation-state model—did not automatically produce equality and inclusion.[82] Instead, as Maja Spanu convincingly shows, practices of hierarchy and exclusion have continued through expectations set by more established states and international institutions about what constitutes a good

---

[77] Pedersen 2015: 399–400; Terretta 2012.
[78] Mazower 2009: chapter 4; Reus-Smit 2013a: chapter 5.
[79] Thomas and Thompson 2014: 156.   [80] Thomas and Thompson 2014: 159.
[81] Anghie 2005.   [82] This is the argument of Mayall 1990.

and legitimate political order, and through the categorization of states in terms of their democratic and liberal credentials.[83]

Despite the efforts of structural IR theories to sustain the image of anarchy, hierarchy remains part of the 'ordering' of contemporary international relations. Similarly, while such theories posit the existence of states as broadly uniform and functionally alike, the reality is that the legal form of the state obscures a wide variety of political units—a variety that significantly affects the levels and nature of both conflict and cooperation 'under anarchy'. The component parts of modern-day international society have included, *inter alia*, states that were the drivers of imperialism; settler states that are closely aligned and highly interdependent with their former colonial masters; states that were the product of post-1945 decolonization and thus assumed colonial borders; and states that have retained formal independence but also experienced ongoing tutelage under, or interference by, Western powers. Given this diverse landscape, it is difficult to hold to the assumption that the foreign policies of, and relations among, today's sovereign states are determined by a uniform set of dynamics. In addition, the institutions and norms that govern and shape such relations are deeply affected by Western principles of legitimacy, political models, and modes of economic organization. Even though these all express, and attempt to operationalize, universal values—such as human rights, self-determination, or economic development—they have frequently given rise to processes and outcomes that maintain Western privilege.[84]

Another prominent illustration of how these realities of inequality and hierarchy have affected the development of law and norms is the phenomenon of intervention (dealt with at greater length elsewhere in this volume). Over the course of the twentieth century, the legitimate justifications for the use of military force have narrowed considerably in law, seemingly constraining the previous right of the great powers to intervene and strengthening the norm of non-intervention, particularly among decolonized states.[85] However, the prevalence of a legal framework that prioritizes sovereign equality and territorial integrity belies ongoing asymmetrical patterns of interference that, in turn, often contribute to crises which legitimate the use of force by third-party states under a collective security or humanitarian banner.[86] Furthermore, even if today intervention is less obviously a tool of great power efforts to transform weaker members of international society, given concerns about the legitimacy of imposition, the promotion of 'good governance' by Western states involves the co-option of key local agents, and a mix of public and private actors who *in effect* transform, without military tools.[87] What results from these endeavours,

---

[83] Spanu 2015. [84] Pitts 2013.
[85] The classic discussion is in Vincent 1974.
[86] Pitts 2013. [87] Williams 2013.

however, is rarely the wholesale adoption of the Western political form, but hybrid arrangements with varying degrees of stability.

Formal Vestiges of Heterogeneity

One prominent explanation for post-imperial inequality in IR, represented by Robert H. Jackson, is that a gap opened up after 1945 between *de jure* sovereignty and *de facto* sovereignty: new states lacked the capacity to exercise effective control, thereby fostering instability and even facilitating the violence that has continued to plague many nation-states in the developing world.[88] While not wanting to contest this phenomenon, which remains a crucial feature of contemporary international relations, equally important to appreciate is the way in which even *de jure* sovereignty has been and continues to be partial.

The first point to stress is that there are some inequalities in international society today that are *legally* instantiated, whether we consider the treaties regulating non-proliferation, or those creating entities like the World Bank or United Nations Security Council. While these positive legal instruments give some states additional powers and rights, there are others that deny some states crucial international legal powers, such as the right traditionally granted to sovereign states to revise contracts unilaterally.[89] In the absence of this right, departing colonial powers have retained, through their corporations, substantial clout over the resources and economies of postcolonial societies.

Second, rationalist scholars have rightly drawn our attention to how the 'positive consequences of subordination' have sustained hierarchical relationships and functional differentiation in contemporary international society.[90] If we assume, along with these scholars, that hierarchies require broad participation—by the superior as well as the subordinate—then we further see how they can be founded on exchanges whereby actors trade degrees of freedom or influence for a desired social or political benefit.[91] Today's international system, as in the period of empire, is marked by quasi-protectorates and shared sovereignty arrangements,[92] particularly in the realm of 'hard' security.[93] But rather than depicting these phenomena as straightforward domination by the strong over the weak, rationalists draw our attention to the potential benefits of conscious policies of subordination—not only for so-called failing states in the developing world,[94] but also for developed liberal democracies that have accepted, and indeed depend upon, key aspects of

---

[88] Jackson 1990.   [89] Simpson 2004.   [90] Lake 2009.
[91] Bially Mattern and Zarakol Forthcoming.
[92] Cooley and Spruyt 2009; McElroy and Pearce 2006.
[93] Lake 1996.   [94] Krasner 2004.

US financial and military hegemony. Thus, some argue that semi-sovereignty is a model for the future, rather than a holdover from the past.

Finally, the diversity of political form that was so prominent in earlier centuries has in fact continued, through the presence of entities with ambiguous status in international society. There is currently a substantial category of non-UN member states in the international system, which includes Taiwan, the Turkish Republic of Northern Cyprus, Palestine, Abkazia, South Ossetia, and Kosovo. These territorial units are not universally recognized as sovereign, yet in many cases have governmental structures responsible for conducting foreign policy. They have also become a more prominent feature of international society since the end of the Cold War and exert significant influence in both their regions and beyond—thus posing questions about the impact of fragmentation on international stability.[95]

While these polities share, to varying degrees, a (yet unfulfilled) desire for independence, there are other entities that appear content living under 'classic' imperial arrangements and do not see sovereign statehood 'as the desirable and natural end-point of their political development'.[96] As a result, although they are internally self-governing and have some foreign policy rights and responsibilities, they have not attempted to exercise their right to independence. Echoes of imperial order are particularly marked in these cases since, as Sharman explains, they do not appear to conform to the contractual logic of mutual and material benefit; instead, Denmark, the Netherlands, and New Zealand are largely motivated to maintain these hierarchical relationships out of a logic of appropriateness, which recalls the interwar internationalist call to improve the well-being of less developed territories.[97] These cases underscore how imperial practices continue to be intimately tied to the identities of more powerful states. They also serve as additional proof that empire, as a form of hierarchy, is not a relic of history.

CONCLUSION

This chapter has demonstrated both how European imperial engagement with the non-Western world was highly variegated in depth and form—thus producing a complex patchwork of political forms—and how this complexity and diversity affected the nature of the global sovereign order that gradually

---

[95] Bartmann 2008. I am grateful to Shpend Kursani for pointing out the relevance of this phenomenon.

[96] Sharman 2013: 190. The key examples are the Faroe Islands (under the authority of Denmark), the Dutch Antilles (under the authority of the Netherlands), and the Cook Islands (under the authority of New Zealand).

[97] Sharman 2013.

displaced Western empires. It has done so under the working assumption that the expansion of international society is better cast as the *globalization* of international society, and that empires as well as states were the drivers of this process. In conclusion, it is worth reiterating this close connection between empire and globalization, not only when imperialism was at its strongest, but also when it was at its weakest.[98] Both the rise and the fall of formal empires have had globalizing effects, many of which, although often obscured by the Cold War, have continued to resonate. These include changing conceptions of political legitimacy, new forms of transnational connection and exchange, the mass movement of peoples through regular and irregular migration, and, less discussed here, particular kinds of violence and conflict. As Thomas and Thompson argue, although decolonization is frequently examined in national contexts, whether from the perspective of the core or from the vantage point of the periphery, it must also be studied as a global process that transmitted ideas and practices—including practices of violent struggle—from one region to another, and that established global norms around the legitimacy of anti-state resistance.[99] As Bull astutely noted almost four decades ago, one of the curiosities of international society is that war, or organized violence, is one of its ordering institutions.[100] Although Bull's object of study was the 'rule-governed' phenomenon of inter-state war, motivated primarily by great power dynamics, his own era was also marked by violent struggles to change international order on the basis of claims of justice. This extreme form of resistance was a recurring feature of international order in the age of empire, given its creation and perpetuation of structures of inequality. But it has also left indelible marks on our current, globalized international society and limited the depth of consensus that underpins its governing norms and institutions.

---

[98] Thomas and Thompson 2014: 161.
[99] Thomas and Thompson 2014: 142–4, 154–5.   [100] Bull 1977.

9

Beyond 'War in the Strict Sense'

Paul Keal

International society as it is commonly understood emerged in Europe. Its gradual globalization entailed recognition of the sovereignty of established polities such as China and the Ottoman Empire. It also involved the inclusion of non-European peoples often not recognized as constituting sovereign political entities. For them, colonization and subjugation by Europeans was a first step towards inclusion in states that were eventually recognized as sovereign members of international society. War played a key role in the European domination and the subjugation of non-European peoples, and thus helped lay the foundations for the gradual development of global international society. It was, however, frequently not war in the form most commonly defined in International Relations (IR) scholarship, and in particular by Hedley Bull in *The Anarchical Society*.[1] His analysis of war was narrow and at least partially anachronistic with regard to both the present and the distant past. The role of war in the globalization of international society extended beyond being a means merely to domination and subjugation; it was also a means to what Europeans considered the higher purpose of 'civilizing' peoples represented as 'savage'. Identifying a people as savage justified denying them sovereign rights and going to war against them. As well as this, 'it established a moral purpose for war'.[2]

Central to this chapter is the thought that the part played by war in the globalization of international society has been more complex than simply that of being the means by which Europeans were able to dominate, subordinate, and 'civilize' non-Europeans. In significant cases, war as part of this process involved cross-cultural exchanges and relationships alternating between cooperation and conflict in which non-Europeans exercised agency. Europeans formed alliances with non-Europeans and vice versa. They fought for, as well as against, each other and traded with each other all at the same time as

---

[1] Bull 1977.   [2] Pejcinovic 2013: 127.

Europeans progressively encroached on the lands of non-Europeans and denied them sovereign rights to property. The relations formed and broken laid the foundations of the political and moral character of the states that emerged and determined the status of non-Europeans in international society.

The argument is in three sections. The first concerns the definition of war and argues that moving beyond what Bull called the 'strict sense' is essential to comprehending the nature of war in the earlier phases of the globalization of international society. It invokes Edward Keene's critique of Bull in which he argues that the modern world order was founded on 'two different patterns of international and legal order' reflecting a division between savage and civilized peoples.[3] From this it proceeds to discuss the idea of 'savage' war in contrast to the military practices of peoples who thought of themselves as 'civilized'; which was part of what has been called the 'master myth of civilization locked in battle with savagery'.[4] As well as this, why constituting peoples as 'savage' was important is also discussed.

The second section identifies the types of war that were part of the process of globalizing international society, and elaborates the themes identified above by considering selected examples drawn from a period ranging from the first half of the seventeenth century through to the 1930s. There are a large number of examples that could also have been included. For example, Lacy Pejcinovic lists at least twenty sites of colonial war in nineteenth-century Africa 'between native Africa[n] tribes or "states" and European international society across the entire continent'. In these conflicts identifying Africans as savages 'justified war against them'.[5] Their purpose was explained as being, at least in part, 'to bring progress to savages and barbarians'. In contrast, the frontier wars, which followed the American War of Independence, 'were understood not so much as *civilizing missions* but as *pacification* of the "savage" Indians who stood in the way of progress'.[6] Pejcinovic's discussion of savagery as a justification for war against non-Europeans includes as well both 'the creation of British India'[7] and the Opium Wars in China as examples in which imperatives of trade were primary but also appealed to notions of savagery, barbarianism, and backwardness.[8] Given the expansion of the number of states in the international system after the Second World War, wars of decolonization might also have been included, but as with the examples dealt with by Pejcinovic there is not space here to do so. My examples are drawn from America leading up to independence, Australia, New Zealand, and Fiji. They are thus wars of colonization and my reasons for choosing them and what they represent are explained in the introduction to the second section.

---

[3] Keene 2002: 5.   [4] Jennings 1976: 146.   [5] Pejcinovic 2013: 127.
[6] Pejcinovic 2013: 129.   [7] On this, see Dalrymple Forthcoming.
[8] Pejcinovic 2013: 130–8.

The third section reflects on the role of war against non-Europeans in formulating the conception of 'sovereignty' at the core of globalized international society. It notices particularly Antony Anghie's work on the non-European sources of sovereignty[9] and returns to Keene's two patterns of international and legal order in relation to how the right to wage war was constructed by Europeans.

CONCEPTUALIZING WAR

War in the 'Strict Sense'

Bull conceptualized war as one of five interconnected or constituent institutions of international order. According to him, '[w]ar is organized violence carried on by political units against each other'.[10] In his account of international society and its expansion, these political units are essentially states and war is primarily an instrument of the state. The member states of international society at the time he wrote were conceived of as rightfully having a monopoly on the legitimate use of organized violence. His definition thus followed Max Weber, for whom the state was the 'sole source of the "right" to use violence'.[11] Weber recognized physical violence had been used by the most diverse kinds of association, but was clear that it was, in the early twentieth century, states that were entitled to its legitimate use.

In *The Anarchical Society*, Bull was careful to distinguish between organized violence which 'may be carried out by any political unit (a tribe, an ancient empire, a feudal principality, a modern civil faction) and war in the strict sense of international or interstate war, organized violence waged by sovereign states'. But, like Weber, he maintained that '[w]ithin the modern states system only war in the strict sense, international war, has been legitimate; sovereign states have sought to preserve for themselves a monopoly of the legitimate use of violence'.[12] While conceding that states have continued to want to preserve a monopoly on the legitimate use of violence, conceiving of 'war' only in this 'strict' sense is no longer tenable, and with regard to the past it is simply blind to the role that forms of war not defined in this way had in the domination and subjugation of non-European peoples, and hence the evolution of global international society. When tracing this evolution from its origins, it is not possible to ignore the violence resorted to by non-state actors and states alike in conflicts that were wars but not, at the time, always recognized as such. These were conflicts that have been studied much more by historians,

---

[9] Anghie 2005.   [10] Bull 1977: 184.
[11] Weber 1994: 310–11.   [12] Bull 1977: 185.

unburdened by the notion of war in the 'strict' sense, than they have in the literature of IR, in which states are the legitimate actors.

What does going beyond war in the 'strict' sense contribute to our understanding of the place of war in the gradual development and globalization of international society? War in the 'strict' sense is war in which states have a monopoly on the legitimate use of organized violence. It is war between states and it has been a mechanism of order in international society. In moving away from this, it is helpful to refer to Keene's argument that the modern world was founded on a 'division between two different patterns of international and legal order'.[13] The division is found in order between 'the family of civilized nations' and peoples outside that family. The first, the 'civilized family', is the one that has been dominant in the study of international relations and is the Grotian conception of international society.[14] Animating it is 'the pursuit of peaceful coexistence between equal and mutually independent sovereigns, which developed within the Westphalian system and the European society of states'.[15] More specifically, in Keene's words, 'its ultimate purpose ... was to promote the toleration of cultural and political differences between civilized peoples so as to allow them to live together in peace'. In contrast, the parallel second pattern of order encompassing those outside the civilized order, stretching back to the beginning of modern history, was not based on a states-system but instead on 'colonial and imperial systems' founded on 'the division of sovereignty across territorial borders and the enforcement of individuals' rights to their persons and property'.[16] '[H]ere the central purpose ... was to promote the civilization of decadent, backward, savage or barbaric peoples.'[17] War was a means to this end, but peoples so described were denied sovereignty and hence both property rights and the right legitimately to go to war in defence of their lands.

For Europeans, categorizing peoples as barbarians and more particularly as 'savages' was, in many cases, the basis of their justification for going to war against them. At the same time naming people as savages misrepresented them, especially in comparison to supposedly 'civilized' practices of Europeans, which is forcefully argued by Francis Jennings.

The Civilization/Savagery Myth and 'Savage War'

In the first book of a triad of magisterial studies about the conquest of America and European relations with Native Americans (or 'Indians' in the terminology of the time), Jennings devoted a chapter to 'Savage War'. The opening paragraph of it bears quoting in full.

---

[13] Keene 2002: 5.   [14] See Bull 1966.   [15] Keene 2002: 5.   [16] Keene 2002: 6.
[17] Keene 2002: 7. On the distinction between barbarians and savages, see Keal 2003: 67–73.

Myth contrasts war with savage war by accepting the former as a rational, honorable, and often progressive activity while attributing to the latter the qualities of irrationality, ferocity, and unredeemed retrogression. Savagery implies unchecked and perpetual violence. Because war is defined as organized violence between politically distinct communities, some writers have questioned whether savage conflicts really qualify for the dignity of the name war. By whatever name, savage conflicts are conceived to be irrational because they supposedly lack point or objective beyond the satisfaction of sadistic appetites that civilization inhibits, and savages are ferocious through the force of these appetites.

'These images', Jennings continues, are 'by-products of the master myth of civilization locked in battle with savagery.'[18]

He proceeds by identifying and challenging a number of misconceptions that contributed to the myth of savagery. In the first place, Europeans regarded Native Americans as 'uncivilized' because there appeared to be no 'supreme power to suppress conflicts'. In other words, there was no sovereign and no civil society as Europeans understood these. Jennings's rebuttal of this is that the inter-tribal violence, which was an undeniable part of Native American society, needed to be contrasted with the internal suppression required to maintain order in European societies. His argument is that the violence in tribal societies was limited, Native American societies did not require the same kind of suppression as European societies, and that consequently the nation states of Europe were more tightly controlled. In this and other ways, 'aboriginal Native American society appears to have been far less violent than seventeenth-century European society'.[19] The wars among Native American societies, which took place at this time, were not caused by the savagery but were part of Native Americans having to adapt to European civilization.

Contrary to popular images of Native American societies, women and children were not deliberately killed in inter-tribal conflicts and violence between men was limited. Similarly torture, in contrast to European society,[20] was, with the exception of some Iroquois practices, not part of Native American society prior to the arrival of Europeans. According to Jennings torture was, for the most part, learnt from Europeans, and then used by Native Americans in retaliation for acts perpetrated by Europeans. Consequently, he suggests that 'about midway through the seventeenth century the outlook toward torture began to change in opposite directions among the two peoples'.[21] Another practice ascribed by Europeans to Native Americans was cannibalism. This was, however, abhorrent to many Native American nations and part of the myth of savagery.[22]

---

[18] Jennings 1976: 146, emphasis added.   [19] Jennings 1976: 147.
[20] See Hunt 2007.   [21] Jennings 1976: 163.   [22] Jennings 1976: 161.

Jennings makes it clear that in challenging the conception of Native Americans as savages he was not intending

to suggest that Indians of pre-contact days were gentle pacifists whom the Europeans seduced to evil warlike ways. On the contrary, all the evidence points to a genuinely endemic state of sporadic intertribal violence. Had this base not been present, Europeans could not so readily have achieved hegemony by playing off one tribe against another. But the dispersion of violence tells us nothing about its intensity.[23]

This leads him to contrast the nature of Native American and European wars and the motivation for them. He explains that the most frequently cited motive for Native Americans going to war is 'revenge' and that this is a term which 'connotes ferocity—personal, unrestrained by charity or mercy or any of the nobler impulses of humanity—in short, savagery'.[24] He objects to this and argues that inter-tribal war was driven rather by retaliation for actual or perceived wrongs, and supports the view of Marion W. Smith that it 'was bound up in motives and restraints imposed by custom and purpose'. According to her, Native American war was a means of re-establishing 'the validity of customs which had been violated'.[25] In the same vein as Jennings and Smith, Gregory Nobles states that it was 'not that Indians practiced a "humane" form of warfare—but rather that they engaged in a limited conflict that had reasonably well defined rules and goals'.[26] In that case, it was neither mindless nor a manifestation of savage society. Indeed, identifying Native Americans as savages both misrepresented them and conveniently served as a justification for dispossessing and subjugating them. More importantly in this context is Jennings's contention that 'Europeans taught Native Americans many of the traits of "savage" war'. Further, that the intrusion of Europeans into Native American society 'created new situations to which the Indians responded by cultural change on their own initiative'. In particular, they became embroiled in 'a culture in which European motives and objectives of war multiplied war's occasions and casualties'.[27] They were thus active agents in shaping their post-contact future through being drawn into wars out of which the United States emerged as a major state in a globalizing international society.

In summary, as an integral element of the politics of discourses of war, the civilization/savagery myth had a critical role in the globalization of international society. The idea of savagery coupled with naming peoples as 'savage' sanctioned conduct permissive of war. It was also the basis of excluding people so identified from the membership of the family of civilized nations mentioned earlier.

---

[23] Jennings 1976: 153.   [24] Jennings 1976: 158.
[25] Smith 1951, cited by Jennings 1976: 158.
[26] Nobles 1997: 38.   [27] Nobles 1997: 168.

WARS OF COLONIZATION

This section canvasses five chronologically and geographically separated examples intended to illuminate several important themes in the role of war in the globalization of international society. Two of these examples, drawn from America, are the Pequot war of 1637 and the Iroquois League up to the War of Independence. The remaining three are the frontier war in Australia stretching from the late 1700s to the 1930s, the Maori Wars of 1860 to 1872, and the Colo War of 1876 in Fiji. What these examples reveal about the process of colonization as a part of the globalization of international society is as follows.

First, the types of warfare involved in colonization differed from place to place, but took two principal forms: wars of extermination and wars of resistance. Wars of extermination were sometimes sparked off as a response by settlers to wars of resistance waged by indigenous inhabitants. They were about removing peoples perceived as backward or alternatively 'doomed' races standing in the way of settlement and 'progress' and engaging in criminal acts against settlers. Wars of resistance were waged by indigenous inhabitants attempting to stop their traditional lands being taken from them, and avert subordination to settlers and the authority of colonial governments. As the case of Australia demonstrates, these two types of war were two sides of the same coin, and in common with other examples, were in essence about who had legitimate sovereign rights over property. Importantly, wars of colonization played a critical role in the European formulation of 'sovereignty'.

Second, it follows from the preceding discussion of the civilization/savagery myth that European ideas about the right to conduct wars against non-Europeans were deeply informed by how they interpreted the political and 'moral' character of the peoples they were fighting. This varied and evolved over time in tandem with rules and norms about permissible conduct. In general, the more savage or backward peoples were perceived to be, the less restrictive the rules of conduct against them became.

Third, harking back to an earlier point, wars of colonization were not a simple one-way process of subordination and domination. Relations between Europeans and indigenous peoples were not only conflictual, but often entailed alliances and complex diplomatic relationships. The example of the Iroquois League demonstrates how indigenous and European rivalries were interconnected. The globalization of rivalry between Europeans in cases when it engaged indigenous inhabitants on one side or the other was significant for how the process of globalizing international society played out. As well as this there are examples, of which the Colo War in Fiji is one, in which Europeans seeking to consolidate the process of colonization 'piggy-backed' on existing inter-tribal conflicts and rivalries. Related to this was also the practice of co-opting indigenous peoples into 'native' police forces and military units. In this way indigenous peoples played a significant role in wars of colonization.

Fourth, and related to the previous point, is that the range of wars surveyed reveals the agency that non-European peoples exercised in the process of the globalization of international society.

America

War was endemic to the European colonization of America and the birth of the United States. Writing about the struggle for control of North America, Nobles comments that '[o]ne of the great ironies of American history is that Euro-Americans could not have taken control of the continent without Indian help'.[28] They were active agents who entered into alliances with Europeans in support of their own aims. Hence throughout the eighteenth century, 'Europeans and Indians interacted with each other in ever-changing patterns of diplomacy that defied simple assumptions of military or cultural superiority'.[29] Jennings identifies four kinds war of conducted in America from the time of first contact into the seventeenth century: 'European versus European, Indian versus Indian, intermixed allies versus other allies, and, rarely, European versus Indian'.[30] The colonization of America was thus not a simple story of European conquest and subjugation. It was instead one involving a protracted period of diplomacy and shifting alliances between states, between them and Native American nations, and just between Native American nations. The wars fought were over the control of trade, and more especially land, and ultimately competing notions of sovereign rights.

An early example of inter-tribal rivalry that led to alliances with Europeans was the Pequot War of 1637, which ended with a massacre on the banks of the Mystic River. It was an event described as New England being 'introduced to the horrors of European style genocide'.[31] The precursor to this incident was a web of relations between Dutch traders, English settlers, and Pequot and Narragansett Native Americans. The Dutch had commercial links with both the Narragansetts and the Pequots. Following a Pequot attack on a party of Narragansetts, the Dutch and the Narragansetts prepared for armed retaliation and the Pequots turned to the English as allies. Subsequently, as a result of one of their tributary tribes killing an English ship's captain and then a settler, a military expedition to find the killers was mounted. When they were found, they were in turn killed by Narragansetts acting in concert with the English. Next in the sequence of events was the Pequot killing a group of English settlers in response to a plea for help from Sequin Indians who had been driven off their land. In turn this resulted in settlers supported by their Narragansett and Mohegan allies perpetrating the massacre on the Mystic.

---

[28] Nobles 1997: 64. [29] Nobles 1997: 65.
[30] Jennings 1976: 168. [31] Philbrick 2006: 179.

The irony in this is that because of their encroachment on Native American lands, the English represented a common foe for both the Narragansetts and the Pequot. Indeed before the massacre, the Pequot had foreseen that the English would continue to appropriate their country and had urged the Narragansetts to join them in resisting the English. Nobles suggests that a factor in the Narragansetts not doing this was that 'skillful English diplomacy kept them apart' from the Pequots.[32]

The Pequot War demonstrates that the colonization of America was not a simple story of Europeans opposed to Native Americans. Instead, as Nobles explains, the destruction of Pequot power was surrounded by complex 'patterns of diplomacy, trade, and warfare...Indians and Europeans seldom engaged in a simple two sided relationship...neither "Indian" nor "European" has meaning as a monolithic, cohesive culture with a sense of unity and a single-minded strategy'.[33] 'European', he continues, 'meant both the Dutch and the English, two peoples who shared similar cultural roots but who also showed intense hostility toward each other in their rivalry for New World wealth.' As well as that they were divided over religion. For their part the Native Americans had even more factors dividing them, including 'culture, kinship, confederation, or diplomatic necessity'.[34] Along with the Powhatans and all other Algonquian-speaking tribes along the east coast, the Pequot 'were eventually overshadowed' by the Iroquois Five Nations or Iroquois League, which became one of Six Nations after the Tuscarora nation joined it in 1720.[35]

Until Neta Crawford's seminal 1994 article on cooperation among Iroquois Nations, discussion of the Iroquois League was absent from IR literature. Comprised of five and later six nations, the League existed from around 1450 to 1777, when the six nations quarrelled about their role in the American War of Independence and for the first time in more than 300 years fought a battle among themselves. Crawford describes the Iroquois League as 'an international organization', which during its existence reduced conflict among its members and effectively ended war between them. The Great Law of Peace binding the five nations defined the purposes of the Iroquois League as being 'to achieve general peace and keep order and unity among the five nations, which had frequently fought one another before the Iroquois League's formation'.[36] It was concerned with providing both peace among the five nations and dealing with threats from other Native nations. During frontier wars between the British and the French, 'Iroquois League members sometimes took different sides. But there was not war between member nations of the League' during the 300 years between its formation and dissolution. Drawing on the available evidence, Crawford argues that during

---

[32] Nobles 1997: 23.   [33] Nobles 1997: 23.   [34] Nobles 1997: 24.
[35] Nobles 1997: 38.   [36] Crawford 1994: 355.

the period from 'about 1535 to 1777', there was 'a complex history of Iroquois war'. Iroquois 'were often at war with Native and European neighbors' in a pattern that 'cannot be understood outside the context of economic and political relations among Native and European nations in North America'.[37]

After the arrival of Europeans, the principal reasons for Iroquois engaging in war were to capture members of other tribes in order to replace their own people lost to diseases introduced by Europeans, to gain access to the fur trade and hence firearms, and to 'protect their land from encroachment by settlers and traders. Often the several reasons ... were intertwined'. The fur trade, however, was at the centre of the so-called Beaver wars in which Dutch, English, and French colonials and Native American nations were all involved. Native Americans brought Beaver pelts and other furs to European traders 'in exchange for European goods including weapons'.[38] In the early days of the fur trade the Iroquois were shut out and went to war in the late sixteenth century 'to plunder and break the exclusive control held by other Native nations'.[39] The French were hostile to them and they consequently turned to the British and fought battles with them against the French: '[t]he Iroquois nations were a buffer between the British and the French'. Thus Crawford cites British commissioners of trade as having written in 1754 that 'the steady adherence of these Indians to the British Interests' had secured New York and 'all the other Northern Colonys ... from the fatal effects of the encroachments of [France] ... and without their friendship and assistance' British efforts to arrest the encroachment of France may have been 'ineffectual'.[40]

It was not just that Europeans involved the Iroquois in their struggles with each other. Equally the Iroquois 'involved Europeans in their diplomacy: at least twice in the 1600s the Iroquois League asked the Dutch to mediate for them with the French'.[41] But the Iroquois League, Crawford argues, 'began increasingly to function for collective security'. Growing concern over loss of their lands drove the Iroquois, in 1762, to propose 'that all Indian nations fight against the British and the French to prevent them from taking all the Native American lands'. They did not, however, succeed in convincing other tribes. Then by 1777 there was disagreement between the Six Iroquois Nations over their role in the War of Independence. Consequently, the outbreak of fighting between Iroquois nations in August 1777 resulted in the dissolution of the League.[42] As in so many other cases elsewhere, we can only speculate about what might have happened if all Native Americans had united in a common cause against European settlers.

---

[37] Crawford 1994: 362. [38] Crawford 1994: 363.
[39] Crawford 1994: 365. [40] Crawford 1994: 367, 368.
[41] Crawford 1994: 368. [42] Crawford 1994: 370–1.

Australia

In an authoritative and persuasive study of the impact of European colonization of the Aboriginal peoples of Australia, Henry Reynolds rebuts the once common belief that settlement had been peaceful and orderly.[43] Contrary to C. W. E. Bean, author of Australia's official history of the First World War, 'who declared that war "never had happened" in Australia',[44] Reynolds argues that from the 1790s through to the 1930s, there was ongoing frontier conflict between Aboriginal tribes across Australia and European settlers. The question Reynolds poses about this is whether or not it was 'a recognizable form of warfare, or ... better seen as a form of continuing civil disturbance or even an enduring crime wave'.[45] His answer is that it was a distinctive form of war, in fact guerrilla war, fought by Aboriginals in defence of their land and sovereignty as best as they could with the means available to them. In support of this, he cites the personal papers and official correspondence of prominent administrators and other sources, all of which were clear that it was a war of resistance.

Notwithstanding the fact that because of annexation, Aboriginal peoples were regarded as subjects of the Crown, by 1825, in response to their acts of resistance, the imperial government in London was treating 'the hostile tribes as foreign enemies against whom war could be waged'.[46] Governor George Arthur, who had been a career soldier and governed Tasmania from 1824 to 1836, was emphatic that the conflict between settlers and Aborigines in Tasmania was war. Reynolds cites references to war and warfare found in Arthur's correspondence over a five-year period.

In a letter dated 1835 to Thomas Buxton, a British politician, Arthur asserted that it was not possible to disguise that the British were intruders. Aboriginal peoples, he wrote, could not

> be expected to give up or retire from their hunting grounds, unless these be purchased from them, without struggle, and, if blood is once spilled, I fear the worst consequences. The work of extermination may go on for many years in detail—a war of this kind is always one of extermination.[47]

Much later, in 1890, in a report to the South Australian parliament, the government resident in the Northern Territory similarly stated that for Aboriginals,

> Entrance into their country is an act of invasion. It is a declaration of war, and they will halt at no opportunity of attacking white invaders ... the primary fact is

---

[43] Reynolds 2013.   [44] Reynolds 2013: 18.   [45] Reynolds 2013: 47.
[46] Reynolds 2013: 63.   [47] Cited by Reynolds 2013: 71.

that the aborigines regard the land as theirs, and that the intrusion of the white man is a declaration of war.[48]

Turning to Queensland, Reynolds found that 'few colonists…[thought] that hostile Aborigines were rebellious subjects. To most people on the frontier they were enemies who were engaged in war for control of territory'.[49] In support of this, he cites statements from newspapers located in different parts of Queensland published over a forty-year period; all describing the acts violence committed by both sides as 'war' or 'warfare'. The number of casualties resulting suggests that this is justified. It estimated that during the nineteenth century, in Queensland alone, as many as 1,500 settlers and an estimated 30,000 Aborigines were killed.[50]

An important 'instrument' in the repression of Aboriginal resistance in Queensland was the Native Mounted Police. The members of this force were skilled bushmen deployed against people belonging to tribes for whom they had no empathy. Among the benefits of using native police was the ability to both keep 'much of the force's activity…secret' and if evidence of atrocity became public they 'could be blamed…and…if necessary be executed in the bush'. Reynolds explains that '[t]hey were far less aware than white police that much of their activity was quite illegal and that the ubiquitous practice of "dispersing" Aboriginal camps was more a matter of warfare than a normal police action of catching, arresting and bringing to trial know offenders'.[51]

During the early colonial period in New South Wales, settlers in extensive areas around Sydney did call 'the sustained attacks by Aboriginal people a war'.[52] Grace Karskens identifies aspects of this 'kind of war' which also characterizes wars of colonization in other places including America, New Zealand, and Fiji and made them complex. These included exploiting 'tribal rivalries and difficulties'[53] on the Cumberland plain, radiating out from Sydney. Tribes were played off against each other. There were 'shifting alliances and complex negotiations'. The antagonists were often known to their attackers. Karskens explains that:

> Aborigines and settlers in early New South Wales occupied the *same* ground in the hinterlands as well as in the towns: their lives had already become entangled. United States historian Richard White calls this social space the 'middle ground', a zone of cultural exchange, negotiation and hybridisation.[54]

It was not the peaceful transition to colonial government that many later perceived it to have been. For Aborigines, it was definitely war over 'the control of their ancient homelands'.[55] Ultimately it amounted to 'the annexation and

---

[48] Cited by Reynolds 2013: 81.   [49] Reynolds 2013: 77.   [50] Reynolds 2013: 134.
[51] Reynolds 2013: 83.   [52] Karskens 2009: 449.   [53] Karskens 2009: 481.
[54] Karskens 2009: 449.   [55] Reynolds 2013: 132.

claim of sovereignty over one of the world's great land masses. [And] ... was an event of truly global significance'.[56]

Having made his case for the frontier violence in Australia actually having been a war, Reynolds advances a challenging critique of the widely and now officially accepted idea that what it means to be an Australian was defined by the involvement of Australian forces in wars overseas, and in particular alongside New Zealand forces at Gallipoli during the First World War. The people who fought in these wars, whether of European origin or the Aboriginal people who chose to fight alongside them, are honoured in numerous memorials. By contrast there are virtually no significant memorials recognizing the people who died during the drawn-out frontier war. Ultimately his point is that it is really the frontier war that defined what it means to be Australian rather than the undeniable sacrifices made in wars on distant shores. Many Australians would most vehemently reject Reynolds's argument on this point, but if he is right, it suggests that adopting a less restrictive definition of war may also lead to new insights about what it means to talk about war shaping national identity.

New Zealand Aotearoa

A common perception about Maori peoples is that in their early encounters with Europeans, they were both more war-like and sophisticated than Australian Aboriginals. They were thus better able to resist and deal with Europeans. Writing about these early encounters, Michael King comments that '[i]n most respects, other than technological development and knowledge of the wider world, Maori were more than a match for Europeans'. According to him they were 'versatile and adaptable and potentially strong allies, particularly when they managed to incorporate Europeans into their networks of mutual obligation'.[57] At the same time, he acknowledges that they were a 'martial' people who engaged in inter-tribal wars which became more intense and deadly once they began to exchange goods for muskets. The possession of firearms allowed particular *hapu*,[58] or tribes, to prevail over others in conflicts referred to as the 'musket wars', which were at their fiercest between 1822 and 1836 and with a few exceptions, affected the whole country. These conflicts continued into the mid-1840s, and

[o]ver a period of 30 years ... [were] ... responsible for the deaths of at least 20, 000 Maori, and possibly many more ... They ceased eventually in part because

[56] Reynolds 2013: 159.   [57] King 2003: 113.
[58] A *hapu* is a clan or descendant group that is part of a wider grouping known as an *Iwi* (or tribe). The *hapu* of an *Iwi* might sometimes fight against other *hapu* belonging to the same *Iwi*.

a balance of terror was achieved once all the surviving tribes were well stocked with muskets, and in part because land sales to Europeans had the effect of 'freezing' tribal *rohe*[59] and making future conquest and migration impossible.[60]

Up until February 1840, when the Treaty of Waitangi was negotiated,[61] New Zealand remained 'unequivocally' Maori.[62] At that time there were little more than 2,000 Pakeha[63] in New Zealand. By 1858, their number had risen to 56,000, alongside 59,000 Maori, and by 1881 there were 500,000 Pakeha.[64] This influx of settlers from 1840 onwards increasingly placed pressure on Maori lands involving disputes over ownership, which were, in part, related to the Treaty of Waitangi as a basis for Maori–Pakeha relations. The treaty is famous for having an English and a Maori version, which for Maori people at least, do not correspond. It created, in particular, confusion over the meaning of 'sovereignty',[65] also mutual misunderstanding about what constituted land ownership. 'For European buyers it was a signed deed. For Maori it was a variety of factors, including inherited rights, rights obtained by conquest, and rights of occupation and use.'[66] The importance of this is that the first armed clash between Maori and Europeans after Waitangi, in 1843, was provoked by a fraudulent land deal on the South Island.[67]

In March 1845, a series of armed conflicts between Maori and imperial forces, known as the 'Northern War', was triggered by a dispute over land. This coincided with a renewal of tribal rivalries, which meant some Maori fought on the imperial side. The end of this brought relative peace for thirteen years, during which there was, 'on the surface', peaceful interaction between Maori and Pakeha.[68] A further consequence was that 'Imperial troops developed a far higher regard for Maori skills in warfare than they had held previously'.[69] Increasingly, however, Maori feared losing their ancestral lands and were mindful of the need to 'preserve customary law and traditional authority'. Maori on the North Island believed that 'the power of Europeans derived from their unity under the British Crown'. Accordingly they reasoned that '[i]f Maori could achieve a similar unity under their own king...they would be able to match European confidence and cohesion, retain their land and preserve customary law and traditional authority'.[70] Thus in 1856, a king was selected and supported by a king movement or *Kingitanga*. Europeans saw these developments as both a challenge to the sovereignty of the crown and as a ploy to prevent further land sales. In contrast, the Maori argued that the two monarchs would be complementary, but regardless of this, Governor Thomas Gore Brown declared that the Maori needed to be shown who 'ought to be in charge in the country'.[71]

---

[59] Autonomous Maori land.   [60] King 2003: 139.   [61] See Orange 2001.
[62] King 2003: 114.   [63] White settlers.   [64] King 2003: 169.
[65] King 2003: 160.   [66] King 2003: 181.   [67] King 2003: 182.
[68] King 2003: 187.   [69] King 2003: 186.   [70] King 2003: 211.
[71] King 2003: 212.

A pretext for doing so with armed force presented itself in 1859 when an Ati Awa chief, Te Teira, offered to sell land at Waitara, located in the Taranaki area on the west coast of the North Island, to the colonial government. The principal chief of the area, Wirema Kingi Te Rangitake, opposed this, but Governor Gore Brown viewed this as a sovereignty issue and insisted that the purchase go ahead. In response to this Wirema Kingi's supporters peacefully occupied the land in question in March 1860. This, in turn, 'sparked the Taranaki War', which extended on and off through to February 1872.[72] Land and sovereignty over it was at the core of the conflict and Europeans believed that the New Zealand wars 'decisive[ly] demonstrat[ed] that sovereignty rested with "the Crown"—that is, with the New Zealand Government of the day—and not with the Maori'. They thought this had been settled with the Treaty of Waitangi. But as King goes on to say: 'There was little understanding among Pakeha at this time that Maori might feel that the Treaty had been dishonoured by the Crown in its seizure, for example, of confiscated territories; or in the many other dubious ways that governments or companies or individuals had used to acquire Maori lands or resources.'[73]

Fiji: The Colo War of 1876

The transition to colonial government in Fiji, like the other examples already discussed, was neither smooth nor peaceful. It involved war, which had elements in common with those other examples. There was inter-tribal warfare, alliances between Fijians and Europeans, use of 'native police', and land was a fundamental issue. In his authoritative study of resistance in early colonial Fiji, Robert Nicole relates how the battle of Kaba of 1855 'established the island of Bau and its Vunivalu[74] Ratu Seru Cakobau, had become the most powerful political forces in Fiji'.[75] Over the next twenty years leading up to the signing, in 1874, of the Deed of Cession, which established official British colonial government, there was ongoing struggle by both inland and coastal chieftains against Cakobau and attempts to spread the influence of Bau. The inland peoples of the Colo region rejected Christianity, and because Bau was the centre of Wesleyan evangelism in Fiji, Wesleyan Christianity was perceived by the Colo people 'as an instrument for extending the influence of Bau'.[76] 'Relations between interior tribes and Bau worsened in 1871 when Cakobau and his supporters among the settler and mission communities unilaterally proclaimed him "king of Fiji" and head of a new Fiji Government.' This led to hostilities, which considerably worsened in 1873 when Cakobau

---

[72] For an account of the Maori Wars, see Belich 1986.   [73] King 2003: 221.
[74] A high-ranking chief just below the level of supreme chief.   [75] Nicole 2011: 14.
[76] Nicole 2011: 16.

initiated a campaign of subjugation and sold land he did not own. Prior to this, coastal chiefs had sold 'Colo lands without the consent or knowledge of those who owned or cultivated it'. These chiefs traded guns and ammunition for the land and thus 'consolidated military capability against foes in Colo'.[77]

The Colo were not included in discussions leading up to cession and they did not see themselves as belonging to a 'pan-Fijian political entity'. Annexation happened 'without the consent of the interior districts'.[78] Settlers wanted land that had been cultivated by these people since 'time immemorial'.[79] The problem the colonial government faced after Annexation was how the Colo could best be induced to submit to government authority. Opinion was divided over whether to send in armed native constabulary to command the submission of Colo, or to try to bring them into the new order in a way that would not run the risk of a repeat of the New Zealand wars. Walter Carew, a former planter with a command of Fijian, was given the task of arranging a meeting between Colo chiefs and the governor, which was held at Nuvoso in January 1875. The outcome of this appeared to be that the Colo would submit to the authority of the colonial government, but this soon proved to be a false hope.

A series of events followed which combined to strengthen the resolve of the Colo to maintain their independence from the government and hostile coastal tribes. At the same time, European planters eager to acquire land in the interior contrived to provoke conflict in the Sigatoka River district. Tribes of the lower Sigatoka district began preparing for war, and in response to the developing situation, Governor Gordon sent, in November 1875, a detachment of sixty armed native police to Cuvu, the home of the Nadroga who were the traditional enemy of the Colo. This unsettled the tribes of the interior and Carew urged the Governor to withdraw them. Gordon refused to do this, and asserted that the native police would be 'a great civilizing and educational instrument'.[80] For the various Colo tribes, working out how they should respond brought them together. Negotiations aimed at avoiding conflict continued but failed in April 1876, when Colo tribes attacked eight Christian villages. This marked the beginning of the Colo War, which was a guerrilla war for independence that pitted coastal chiefs and colonial soldiers, commanded by British officers, against Colo peoples of the interior. After a series of battles in different locations, the Colo were defeated by the end of June. Nicole comments that 'all key battles were won through the astuteness of Fijian Chiefs'.[81] In essence, the Colo lost their War of Independence through other Fijians advising and fighting alongside colonial forces. On 14 August, Gordon wrote a dispatch informing 'the Colonial Office of the "entire suppression of the disturbances in Viti Levu and restoration of order"'. Noteworthy is that he

[77] Nicole 2011: 20.   [78] Nicole 2011: 24.   [79] Nicole 2011: 19.
[80] Nicole 2011: 28–9.   [81] Nicole 2011: 39.

'could not use any term implying warfare because war would have meant' relinquishing his command to the military and much greater cost.[82]

It was nevertheless a 'war', and its origins 'lay in the power struggles of pre-Cession days and particularly in the unresolved question of Bauan and Christian influence in the interior of Viti Levu'.[83] Importantly Nicole stresses that '[i]t did not take place simply because of colonialism or uniquely in response to it. It had a long prior history with many interweaving factors, actors, events... There were always numerous players on centre stage, all struggling to shape the outcome of the war. No single group could ever claim monopoly over power or agency at any one time.'[84] This suggests that it could have had a different outcome.

CONSTITUTING SOVEREIGNTY AND LEGITIMATE WAR

It was mentioned earlier that wars of colonization played a critical role in the European formulation of 'sovereignty'. At the outset of European expansion,[85] the conquest of Mexico sparked off debate about both the rights of Native Americans and the obligations of Europeans towards them. Did, for instance, Native Americans have sovereign rights against Europeans? When, if at all, was it permissible to initiate a war against peoples regarded by Europeans as savage, uncivilized, or backward? These questions were fundamental to the origins and subsequent development of international law and to establishing sovereign states as having a monopoly over the right to wage war.

At the heart of international society and inscribed in international law is the mutual recognition of states as sovereign and equal. Coupled with this is war in the 'strict' sense, which takes place between states. Colonial conflicts, which resulted in Europeans subjugating and dominating non-Europeans, and eventually in decolonization to independent sovereign states, were generally not between two states. They were instead, as Anghie expresses it, 'between a sovereign European state and a non-European society that was deemed by jurists to be lacking in sovereignty—or else, at best, only partially sovereign'.[86] One implication of this is that in dealing with non-Europeans, Europeans were not bound by the rules of war as they would have been if fighting against other Europeans.

War, as part of colonization, was a means to accomplishing the civilizing mission Europeans had adopted for themselves. In relation to this, Anghie

---

[82] Nicole 2011: 43.   [83] Nicole 2011: 43.   [84] Nicole 2011: 44.
[85] For an argument that globalization began in 1492, see Hall 2003.
[86] Anghie 2005: 5.

examines the work of Francisco de Vitoria for whom the 'transformation' of the 'Indian' from savagery to civilization was achieved by waging war. He explains that Vitoria's 'concept of sovereignty is developed primarily in terms of the sovereign's rights to wage war. War is the means by which the Indians and their territory are converted into Spaniards and Spanish territory, the agency by which the Indians thus achieve their full human potential'.[87] Put differently, one culture, that of Europeans in all its variations, imposed itself, if necessary with armed force, on the cultures of non-Europeans. But at the same time cross-cultural hybridity was an important element in colonial cultures.[88]

Anghie further explains that in Vitoria's theory, Native Americans were 'excluded from the sphere of sovereignty',[89] largely by the very fact of cultural difference. Thus Vitoria proposed the 'universal law of *jus gentium*' as the means to 'bridging cultural difference', which assumes the 'other' conforming to the supposedly universal European standards encapsulated in that law. According to him, 'Indians possessed universal reason' and were capable of behaving in conformity with European mores, and so were subject to *jus gentium* and the sanctions incurred by not complying with it. These included war. 'It is precisely whatever denotes the Indian to be different—his customs, practices, rituals—which justify the disciplinary measures of war, which is directed towards effacing Indian identity and replacing it with the universal identity of the Spanish'.[90] It follows from this that for the Native Americans of Vitoria's time, and for later other peoples subjected to European colonization to achieve full sovereignty, they had first to attain statehood and accept agreed principles regulating their behaviour.

What if instead of asking when Europeans were justified in waging war, the question is turned around? Sovereignty remains the cardinal issue and is at the core of Hugo Grotius's distinction between public and private war. Related to this is also the question of whether sovereignty is divisible. In his discussion of colonialism as a form of international order parallel to that of the anarchical society of states, Keene argues that full, indivisible sovereignty was most likely never a necessary condition for going to war. Grotius's opinion was that '[o]wnership of just a fragment of sovereignty' might have been sufficient grounds to legitimately initiate a war. 'Whoever possesses a part of the sovereign power must possess also the right to defend his part.'[91]

Two centuries on from Grotius even 'just a fragment of sovereignty' was precisely what was denied to Australian Aboriginals and other colonized peoples. All but a few European settlers did not consider that Aboriginals had any sovereignty. This meant that the violent acts of resistance Aboriginals mounted in defence of their lands were not regarded as acts of war, but as the

---

[87] Anghie 2005: 23.   [88] On this, see Thomas 1994.
[89] Anghie 2005: 28.   [90] Anghie 2005: 29.
[91] Hugo Grotius, *De Jure ac Pacis*, cited by Keene 2002: 48.

criminal acts of savage and uncivilized beings. Long before this, Grotius had observed that 'shameless lust for property was want to take cover under the excuse of introducing civilization into barbaric regions'.[92] At the same time, property was central to his distinction between public and private wars. In contrast to public wars, which were between the holders of sovereign powers', private wars were those 'between individuals or corporations who lacked sovereignty, but nevertheless held certain rights that they were entitled to defend by violence if judicial recourse was denied or unavailable to them'.[93] Clearly indigenous and other non-European peoples believed they had rights to property in the form of their ancestral lands. But along with sovereignty this was also denied to them.

John Locke and other political and legal theorists developed an argument from agriculture, which coupled property ownership and rights to European agricultural practices.[94] It was asserted that natives did not possess the lands they merely 'roamed' across. To be regarded as possessing rights to land they had to be engaged in European forms of agriculture. Actually this flew in the face of the empirical evidence. It has been frequently pointed out that if the Native Americans of the New England region had not shown the pilgrims of Plymouth how to grow potatoes, they would not have survived the first winter. There and in so many other places the idea that indigenous inhabitants merely roamed across lands without occupying and cultivating them in ways that confer title served to justify war against them while simultaneously denying them the right to go to war to stop the loss of their land to Europeans. With the passage of time this changed, but in the work of Vitoria and in the early debates about who had the right to legitimately initiate war and even how it was defined, we can discern the origins of crucial rules concerning war as an institution of the evolving global international society of states.

One of the striking points related to Europeans justifying the resort to war against non-Europeans by appealing to the 'civilizing mission' is that peoples described as barbarians and savages bore some of the hallmarks attributed to 'civilized' European states in their conduct of international relations. The Iroquois League, for instance, clearly engaged in *inter-nation* relations described in terms remarkably similar to those used to characterize relations between European states and between them and advanced states belonging to non-European civilizations, such as Turkey, China, and Japan. A complex pattern of practices ranged across playing off states and non-state actors against each other, shifting alliances, diplomacy, trade arrangements, and periods alternating between war and peace.

A further and more striking point is the way 'native' peoples exercised agency and hence had a role in the way in which the globalization of international

---

[92] Keene 2002: 50. [93] Keene 2002: 52. [94] See Arneil 1996.

society occurred. Alliances between 'native' peoples and European settlers or their governments facilitated and in some cases even enabled the colonization of societies that became sovereign and independent states of global international society. They were often societies transformed by cultural exchange, negotiation, and hybridization. In the way that native peoples were co-opted into the purposes of colonizing settler societies and imperial purposes, they were to a certain extent agents of their own dispossession and destruction. We can only speculate about what might have happened had native peoples not entered into alliances with European settlers and their governments and been co-opted by them, but instead had united against them. Perhaps it would have only delayed the inevitable, but at the same time it may have resulted in a more just basis for international society.

Regardless of this, wars were part of colonization, and they often resulted in divisions related to historic injustices, misrecognition of cultures, unresolved identity issues, and dispossession. These are commonly regarded as matters internal to the states that emerged from colonialism. They nevertheless have become matters that impinge on the political and moral standing of particular states constituting global international society.

ACKNOWLEDGEMENT

I wish to thank Jacinta O'Hagan for her penetrating and extremely helpful comments on an earlier version of this chapter.

10

The Role of Civilization in the Globalization of International Society

Jacinta O'Hagan

INTRODUCTION

What role has civilization played in the globalization of international society? This chapter argues that civilizational ideas, practices, and contestations were integral to the globalization of international society, although their roles have been multifaceted and varied over time.

International society is treated in this chapter as 'realms where sovereign states are bound together by webs of shared meaning'.[1] These meanings are embodied in shared institutions and codes of rules that help to govern interaction among members and differentiate them from those outside this intersubjective realm. The expansion of European international society entails 'the social incorporation of new non-European members into this rule governed international order'.[2] The emergence of a global international society was not simply a process of geographical growth nor institutional proliferation. Rather, it was a series of complex social, political, and cultural interactions that occurred at several levels and in different contexts. Civilizational analysis allows us to look at those complex processes and contested identities that relate to intersections between political and cultural interaction.[3] By examining these intersections, civilizational analysis can help us probe the complexity, contestation, and unevenness of the globalization of international society.

There is nothing particularly new in arguing that civilization is integral to the evolution of international society. Both Martin Wight and Hedley Bull saw cultural unity as vital to the foundation of international society. Bull observed that all historical international societies 'were founded on a common culture

---

[1] Reus-Smit 2013a: 16.   [2] Reus-Smit 2013a: 30.   [3] Katzenstein 2013.

or civilization or at least some element of such a civilization'.[4] He argued that a common civilization facilitates communication and understanding, which in turn assists the evolution of common rules and institutions. Culture thus provides a crucial foundation for normative and institutional consensus in international society. Similarly, Adam Watson drew links between civilizational identities and common codes of conduct, assumptions, and values that facilitate the cohesion of international society.[5]

However, while the qualities described by Wight, Bull, and Watson remain central, the role played by civilizational ideas and practices is far more complex and contested than their analysis suggests. Civilization is invoked in multiple ways—as a noun, as a condition, as a verb, as a process, and even as a purpose—by both actors and analysts of international society. In order to fully understand the role of such a variegated concept in the globalization of international society, we first need to unpack the complexity of civilization as a concept, which reveals several discourses of civilization. In this chapter I focus on two of the most prominent of these. The first relates to the concept of civilization as a site of agency. Here civilization is used in the plural to refer to loosely bounded but discrete social entities whose interaction is integral to the dynamics of international society. The second relates to the concept of civilization in the singular. Here, civilization acts as a generative force, which contributes to the development of institutional and normative frameworks that define international society and guide relations with those perceived as 'outside' of that society. I then link these to the different dimensions of the role of civilizational ideas, practices, and contests in the globalization of international society already alluded to: respectively, civilization as a locus of agency; and civilization as a force that also helps to generate the structures, institutions, and boundaries of international society.

Analyses of the role of civilizations in the expansion of international society typically focus on the eighteenth and nineteenth centuries, whereas analyses of its role in the twentieth and twenty-first centuries are less well developed. This chapter traces the role of civilization across the broader temporal sweep of the globalization of international society in a more integrated way. It discusses the globalization of international society across three periods: the expansion of European international society (the imperial era); the dismantling of European empires (the era of decolonization); and the post-Cold War era (the era of globalization). The chapter proceeds in three sections. The first discusses the multifaceted nature of civilization, and identifies the two key discourses of civilization that contribute to its variegated role in the globalization of international society. The second and third sections use these dual

---

[4] Bull 1977: 16.   [5] Watson 1992: 312.

discourses as a mechanism to explore the multidimensional role of civilization in the globalization of international society across these three periods.

THE MULTIFACETED NATURE OF CIVILIZATION AS A CONCEPT

Venturing into definitions of civilization is like venturing into a lion's den. As Peter J. Katzenstein has noted, 'definitional disagreements about the concept of civilization are formidable and legendary'.[6] These, for instance, relate to whom or what constitutes a civilization, how one draws the boundaries of civilizations, and the degree to which civilizations should be understood as material entities or social and rhetorical constructs. This presents us with an analytical dilemma. On the one hand, there is a danger that civilizational analysis can become entrapped in definitional debates; on the other, there is the risk of insufficiently reflecting on what exactly is being referred to when the concept of civilization is invoked. This can lead to a lack of analytical clarity. One way to avoid being caught in this dilemma is to reflect more fully on the 'work' that concepts and discourses of civilizations 'do' in our understanding of world politics; that is, to examine the impact of civilizational discourse in framing and shaping political practices, identities, and dynamics. As Patrick Jackson observes, whether civilizations are real or not may be beside the point; 'what is important is whether we can find value in the concept of civilizations expressed in terms of the kinds of social dynamics and relations that the concept highlights and calls attention to'.[7] The 'work' it does will be strongly influenced by the particular conception of civilization being invoked. I will now briefly examine the emergence of these different conceptions.

The word 'civilization' entered the history of ideas at the same time as the word 'progress'. The two 'were destined to maintain a most intimate relationship'.[8] The term civilization emerges in the French and English languages in the eighteenth century. Its roots are found in the French terms *civil* (concerning political and legal issues relating to order) and *civility* (concerning issues relating to courtesy and manners). The term came to encapsulate a range of meanings associated with improvements in personal life, education, and the arts, as well as the containment of levels of interpersonal violence—a key dimension of what Norbert Elias described as 'the civilizing process'.[9] Importantly, civilization was juxtaposed with the concept of barbarism. In its English

---

[6] Katzenstein 2010.
[7] Jackson 2010: 176. Jackson is drawing here on Matthew Melko.
[8] Starobinski 2009: 153.   [9] Elias 1978.

language etymology, civilization referred to both the process and condition of refinement and human improvement.[10] For instance, Adam Ferguson and John Mill use the term to refer to the progress of human society from a state of rudeness or barbarism to a refined or polished state. In Mill's work, the state of civilization is contrasted with savagery through the application of criteria relating to social and political structure, social intercourse, and economic capacities. Human society is seen to evolve through stages of development from subsistence through to complex forms, the highest of which was 'commercial' society.[11]

The concept of civilization developed, therefore, very much within the context of the European Enlightenment and European society. Its evolution was accompanied by debate as to whether it represented a particular form of human perfectibility based on the growth of reason—civilization as a universal idea—or a condition achieved by many different societies in different ways, suggesting the existence of a plurality of civilizations.[12] This pluralist conception of civilization did not mean that all civilizations were viewed as equal. However, it provided a point of comparison between civilizations in terms of cultural, economic, political, and social development and, increasingly, scientific and technological development. In particular, it provided a means to compare Western civilization with other societies. Therefore, by the late nineteenth century, we see the emergence of two, interconnected discourses of civilization, both of which play a significant role in the globalization of international society.[13]

The discourse of civilization in the singular refers to universal processes of progress and material and social improvement, but also to the cumulative outcome of those processes. This is the achievement of an ideal form of society that stands in contrast to barbarity or savagery, as expressed in Lucien Febvre's comment, '[w]e are confident that such a civilization, in which we participate, which we propagate, benefit from and popularize, bestows on us all a certain value, prestige, and dignity'.[14] Febvre's analysis usefully highlights two aspects of this conception of civilization: that it is qualitatively superior to other forms of socio-political organization, and that it is accompanied by practices which seek to propagate this way of life. Both became critical elements of the politics of civilization in the international system. 'Civilization' became the benchmark against which other societies were evaluated. In the nineteenth century, the singular conception of civilization became intimately linked to perceptions of structures and practices of governance. This came to be articulated as 'the standards of civilization', which were premised on European perceptions of appropriate standards of governance.

---

[10] See also Bowden 2009: 26–7; Febvre 1973; and Salter 2002: 18.
[11] Bowden 2009: 31–3; Phillips 2012.   [12] Mazlish 2001: 294.
[13] See, generally, Bowden 2009: 23–46.   [14] Febvre, cited in Bowden 2009: 29.

Analysing civilizations in the plural is an even more complex task. As noted earlier, debates regarding how we should define and bound civilizations are extensive. These range from conceptions of civilizations as social formations clearly bounded by properties such as blood, religion, language, and a common worldview,[15] to seeing civilizations as much looser and more porous social complexes. The latter perspective treats civilizations as loosely coupled, internally differentiated, and weakly institutionalized social orders shaped by a variety of processes and practices over time.[16] Rather than constituted by fixed properties, they are 'constellations and arrangements of fluctuating practices and historical patterns'.[17] This points to a processual analysis of civilizations, as pioneered in the work of Shmuel Eisenstadt and Norbert Elias.[18] A processual analysis presents a civilization as 'a complex arrangement of habits, principles, and historic traditions of action on which people may draw in a variety of ways'. Civilizations thus represent 'a kind of structural context for action'.[19]

One of the benefits of a processual approach to civilizational analysis is that it provides a more dynamic account of how the social and political frontiers of civilizations are produced and reproduced. An important aspect of this is the way in which civilizational identities are invoked as a means of locating individual or collective identities in broader temporal, geographic, and cultural communities. This may entail invoking shared histories, traditions, values, or qualities such as language or religion. It may entail articulating a particular worldview or moral code. These act as resources to generate perceptions of common interests, goals, and standards of behaviour that link diffuse peoples in a form of imagined community.[20] Such invocations produce and reproduce the community's boundaries. The capacity to articulate these boundary markers can be a form of power. At the same time, civilizations are diffuse social and political entities; unlike other social actors, civilizations have no 'front office'. This makes them amorphous, but also means anyone can invoke the boundary markers to claim to act in the name, for instance, of the West or Islam. This can in turn lead to contestation over which claims are 'authentic'.[21]

These two broad discourses of civilization—the singular and the plural—are deeply interrelated and often interwoven, but 'do' different 'work' in the constitution of social and political orders. The first is very much an evaluative discourse, which acts as a generative force that contributes to the development of institutional and normative frameworks of social and political orders. The

---

[15] See, for instance, Spengler 1991; Huntington 1996.
[16] See, for instance, Katzenstein 2010: 5; Jackson 2010: 182.
[17] Jackson 2010: 184.   [18] See, for instance, Eisenstadt 2000; Elias 1978.
[19] Jackson 2010: 184.   [20] O'Hagan 2002. See also Bettiza 2014; Jackson 2010: 187.
[21] Jackson 2007: 47.

second defines and describes broad social constellations within which we can locate particular actors. Interaction between actors from different social constellations forms an important part of the dynamic of these social and political orders. Although distinct, these discourses are in dialogue and inform one another. There is a degree of co-variation between them: changes in one may influence changes within the other. This in turn has ramifications for how civilizational ideas, practices, and contests contribute to the globalization of the sovereign state order. These contributions vary with respect to how they influence the dynamics of interaction, structures of relations between actors, practices of recognition, and the constitution of boundaries.

EXPLORING CIVILIZATION IN THE GLOBALIZATION OF INTERNATIONAL SOCIETY

As noted earlier, the role of civilization in the evolution and expansion of international society has long been recognized. For Bull and Watson, as for Wight, the foundations of the contemporary sovereign state order lay in the emergence of a Christian then European international society. The expansion of this society led to the creation of a global international society that was unique in its breadth and multicultural composition. The essays in *The Expansion of International Society* trace Europeans' encounters with the peoples of the Americas, Africa, and the Asia-Pacific through trade, exploration, Christian mission, and conquest. The narrative of *The Expansion* revolves around how these encounters ultimately led to the incorporation of non-European peoples into the sovereign state order. This places processes of civilizational encounter and interaction at the heart of the expansion of international society.[22]

Interaction between European and non-European societies, however, did not automatically equate to the expansion of the membership of international society. Inclusion and exclusion in international society pivoted on the politics of recognition. The 'admission' of non-European peoples into this society which, until the late nineteenth century comprised only European peoples, followed the granting of full recognition of the sovereign autonomy of those peoples through mechanisms such as inclusion in multilateral diplomatic fora and the negotiation of equalitarian treaties. The criterion for recognition was the perceived willingness and capacity of non-European peoples to meet particular standards in their structures and practices of governance articulated as 'the standards of civilization'. These included a state's willingness and

---

[22] Bull and Watson 1984c.

capacity to guarantee the basic rights and protection of foreign nationals; to fulfil its obligations under international law, including the laws of war; to maintain a domestic system of courts, legal codes, and published laws; and to foster the existence of an organized political bureaucracy and institutions of governance, including a capacity for self-defence.[23] States adjudged to have met these criteria could then be 'admitted' to the 'family of civilized states'.

The concept of 'admission' is one that has riled many commentators given the rich, complex, and extensive networks of socio-political and economic relations that preceded European expansion. It is useful, however, insofar as it speaks to the politics of recognition which had a meaningful impact on the rights afforded to different peoples under the auspices of international law. In the eighteenth and nineteenth centuries, the European standards were integrated into the evolving body of international law to distinguish civilized from uncivilized people.

The discourse of civilization thus became a powerful mechanism for adjudicating the position of non-European societies in relation to European international society. The inability of states to meet the criteria of 'civilized' governance excluded them from 'the family of civilized states' referred to above, making them vulnerable to differential treatment under international law. This led to unequal treaty systems and capitulations, which included provisions such as extra-territorial rights or concessions on the control of customs duties. The standards were 'a natural outgrowth of the European states system' and were based on European historical experiences. They therefore provided a mechanism through which 'a "superior West" decided on the readiness for self-government of other people'.[24] 'Civilization'—as a condition—came to supersede Christianity and Europe as the principal means of demarcation of the boundaries of international society.[25]

The account of international society found in *The Expansion* provides a valuable illustration of the dual discourses of civilization. The interaction between Europe and other civilizations lies at its heart and the 'standards of civilization' acts as a powerful generative force which shape and legitimate the core institutions of that society: international law and diplomacy. At the same time, it has been criticized from a number of perspectives, including its Eurocentrism.[26] This is manifest in the sense it conveys of international society diffusing outwards from its European core to other civilizations, with expansion ultimately occurring as other civilizations incorporated European

---

[23] Gong 1984b: 14–15; Bowden 2014.   [24] Gong 1984b: 36; Buzan 2014b: 582.

[25] Gong 1984b: 5.

[26] See, for instance, Kayaoglu 2010; Suzuki et al. 2014. On Eurocentrism in analysis of the states' system more broadly, see Hobson 2009. In their defence, Bull and Watson and the contributors to *The Expansion* do speak to a number of the issues raised by critics, but their analysis lacks the depth and breadth of recent accounts such as those found in Kayaoglu 2010; Suzuki et al. 2014.

institutions, practices, and norms into their governance structures. Critics have argued that this both elides the violence and domination that were often a core aspect of the expansion, and also neglects the agency of non-Western peoples. This has been described as the 'vanguardist' approach to the expansion in which 'Europe remakes the world in its own political and economic image'.[27]

This reading of the story of international society is contested by 'syncretist' approaches, which highlight the formative influence of inter-civilizational encounters.[28] European expansion occurred within the context of sophisticated patterns of commercial interaction across Asia and West Africa, in what John M. Hobson has described as an Afro-Asian global economy, the core of which was China. Europe's engagement with these networks significantly influenced the development of its own economic networks, but also exposed it to ideas, institutions, and practices that influenced the evolution of European social and political institutions, which in turn formed the foundations of the sovereign states system.[29]

It is important to be mindful of the shifting 'terms of engagement' between European and other civilizations during the course of Europe's expansion. Early interaction was often shaped by the social and cultural norms and practices of Europe's interlocutors in China, Japan, India, or the neighbouring Ottoman Empire.[30] From Dutch traders in Japan to representatives of the British East India Company and European traders in West Africa, engagement was often negotiated on terms commensurate with the preferences of local actors. European actors therefore operated within the parameters of structures and institutions premised on non-European norms and worldviews. Accommodation developed between actors from different civilizational complexes on the basis of shared interests and cross-cultural shared norms.[31] In addition, European expansion was not a coherent and orchestrated project but was driven by the activities of a range of actors—explorers, traders, commercial companies, conquistadors, and missionaries pursuing diverse public and private interests. Their activities were not necessarily coordinated with one another: there are ample examples of Europeans with conflicting interests allying with different local actors and battling each other.[32]

The 'terms of engagement' in inter-civilizational encounters, however, changed profoundly with the growth of European economic and military power and wealth in the eighteenth and nineteenth centuries.[33] With growing

---

[27] Buzan 2010: 6.   [28] Buzan 2010: 10.

[29] Hobson 2009 points, for instance, to the influence on the Renaissance and the development of European financial institutions of Chinese military technology, and Islamic science, mathematics, and medicine.

[30] See, generally, Suzuki et al. 2014.   [31] See, generally, Suzuki et al. 2014.

[32] See, for instance, Quirk and Richardson 2014; Vigneswaren 2014.

[33] Pomeranz 2000.

differentials in material and technological power between European and non-European peoples, Europeans' sense of their civilizational superiority grew. Commensurate with this was an expansion of European authority and influence through both formal and informal empire. The divergence also influenced cognitive frameworks through which non-European societies were seen. Europeans increasingly came to view Western civilization as encompassing universal values and norms which made it exceptional as well as superior. Discourses of civilization thus came not only to describe and define different societies but to position them in hierarchies of human progress. Relations that had previously been seen as fairly equal were reconstituted into hierarchies of civilization, barbarism, and savagery. In contrast to the earlier era of civilizational encounter, non-European people came to be increasingly situated in institutional and normative structures of interaction defined by European peoples.

In the course of the nineteenth century, the discourse of civilization as material and moral progress came to both explain growing power differentials between European and non-European peoples and legitimate practices commensurate with these. This shaped perceptions of what the obligations of the 'civilized' towards the 'barbarian' were, and thus what constituted rightful conduct towards such peoples. Wight sketched three distinctive approaches in traditions of Western thought to encounters with 'barbarians'.[34] At one extreme was the idea that barbarians stood outside the community of mankind. As such they could legitimately be conquered, subjugated, and even exterminated. At the other end of the spectrum was the idea that barbarians have equal rights and as such should be fully assimilated into the structures of international society. Sitting in the middle of this spectrum was the idea that barbarians stood within the community of mankind, but were capable of exercising only partial rights. The civilized had a responsibility to bring material and moral progress to the barbarian. These obligations were expressed in concepts such as 'the civilizing mission' and the 'sacred trust of civilization'.

Here the two discourses of civilization come into dialogue with one another in the globalization of international society: the discourse of civilizations as loose social formations intersects with that of civilization as a force that helps to generate particular institutional structures and hierarchies. The blending of these two discourses has had significant ramifications. It has informed conceptions of the identity and position of actors which are then linked to conceptions of authority, obligation, and legitimate action. These conceptions were fundamental to evolving patterns of political order. As Edward Keene notes, European expansion produced two distinct although interconnected

---

[34] Wight 1992b.

orders. The intra-European order was characterized by the development of the society of sovereign states. Its purpose was to facilitate tolerance and coexistence among its diverse membership. The extra-European order was characterized by the evolution of European empires and premised on the purpose of promoting the spread of civilization to those perceived as backward, savage, or barbaric peoples.[35] International law provided the legal code that governed relations between 'civilized' and 'uncivilized' peoples, 'fulfilling a morally desirable purpose by enabling the former to bring civilization to those parts of the world that did not yet enjoy its benefits'.[36]

This approach underpinned ideas of tutelage and trusteeship that provided a moral and political foundation for colonialism. Civilization made colonization 'a justifiable policy'.[37] Civilization became a 'rhetorical commonplace'[38] as illustrated in the popular nineteenth-century mantra of expansion: 'Christianity, commerce, and civilization'. That mantra was used to legitimate a range of practices. For example, during the course of the Second Opium War, the promotion of civilization was invoked both to justify the use of force by Britain against China and to condemn it.[39] Civilization as a purpose was evoked in multilateral level fora such as the 1884–5 Berlin Conference on West Africa. The Conference's General Act mandated signatories 'to watch over the preservation of the native tribes, and to care for the improvement of their moral and material well-being'.[40] The concept of the 'sacred trust' was directly iterated in the institutions of international society, even as that society moved towards decolonization. Article 22 of the League of Nations noted that there was a 'sacred trust of civilization' to the well-being and development of former colonial peoples that should be undertaken by more advanced nations on behalf of the League. This idea persisted in the establishment of the United Nations' Trusteeship Council. Keene describes this as part of a process of the 'internationalization of the principle of civilization';[41] that is, of the promotion of civilization as a purpose of the international community—and indeed international society—as a whole.

Exploring the dual discourses of civilization brings to the fore different dimensions of the role of civilizational ideas, practices, and contests in this key phase of the globalization of international society. Delving more deeply into the multifaceted encounters between civilizations viewed as loosely bounded social formations provides us with a richer understanding of the complex relationships and forms of interaction that shaped international society. It fruitfully problematizes the more linear conception of the globalization of

---

[35] Keene 2002: 98.   [36] Keene 2002: 111. See also Koskenniemi 2001.
[37] Keene 2002. The idea of civilization, he further observes, is not merely an idea that regulates the entry of new states into international society, but also that validates an entirely different set of legal rules and political institutions in its own right (Keene 2002: 113, 117).
[38] Jackson 2007.   [39] Phillips 2012.
[40] Cited in Bowden 2009: 149.   [41] Keene 2002: 133.

international society, presenting this instead as a more fragmented and uneven process, which entailed confluences and conflicts between actors, worldviews, and practices. Examining the singular discourse of civilization tells us much about the establishment of institutional and normative criteria for recognition as a sovereign state. Civilizational discourse here helps to generate both the structure and boundaries of international society. The interweaving of these two discourses deeply informed Europeans' practices and helped to define their purpose and identity, as well as shaping the identities and practices of the non-Europeans.

THE GLOBALIZATION OF INTERNATIONAL SOCIETY AND THE DISMANTLING OF EUROPEAN EMPIRES

The previous section focused on the role of civilization in the expansion of European international society. In this section, I consider the role of civilization in the transformation of that society into a global international society. Exploring the pluralist discourse reveals how this transformation was linked to shifts in the 'terms of engagement' in civilizational interaction. Exploring the discourse of civilization in the singular reveals how a reconceptualization of the legitimacy of the 'standards of civilization' radically influenced practices of recognition and conceptions of legitimate behaviour in international society. The demise of the 'standards of civilization', however, did not lead to the demise of civilizational discourses but to their reconfiguration. This reconfiguration informed the reconceptualization of sovereignty and international law, and the normative framework of international society.

The events of the first half of the twentieth century had a profound impact on conceptions of order and of the relationship between civilization and order. The slaughters of the First and Second World Wars, and the Holocaust and the use of nuclear weapons, demonstrated clearly the capacity of Western civilization for 'barbaric acts', relocating the discourse of civilization/barbarism from one that defined the boundaries between West and the non-West to one within the West itself.[42] These events undermined the idea that there is a natural hierarchy of civilizations, and denaturalized conceptions of the superiority of Western civilization and the commensurate legitimacy of European rule over others. They also contributed to a normative shift in interpretations of sovereignty, and a reconceptualization of civilization as a criterion for self-determination.

---

[42] See Salter 2002; Adas 2004.

By the mid-twentieth century, the legitimacy of the 'standard of civilization' was cast into doubt. The right to self-determination was no longer something that could be bestowed on to a people by others, based on their perceived capacity to meet the conditions of 'civilized' government. It was instead a right that should be recognized by others, regardless of levels of development. United Nations Resolution 1514 (1960) clearly stated that the 'inadequacy of political, economic, social or educational preparedness should never serve as a pretext for delaying independence'.[43] This marked the international community's rejection of the idea of civilization as a criterion for sovereignty. The idea of what constituted 'civilized behaviour' was turned on its head. Whereas in the past it had been used to legitimate the denial of sovereign statehood and equality, the concept was now used to challenge the assumptions that had underpinned colonialism, and to legitimate norms of equality and self-determination. 'Decolonization', argues Barry Buzan, 'put an end to the "standard of civilization" as a polite term of political discourse.'[44] Civilization as a standard was being excised from the legal and normative structures of international society, facilitating the globalization of that society on the basis of formal sovereign equality. At the same time, concepts of moral and political progress that were immanent in the singular discourse of civilization were not expunged from the normative framework of international society; rather, these were reiterated *in* concepts of self-determination, racial equality, and universal human rights.

The reconfiguration of the singular discourse of civilization therefore facilitated the globalization of the sovereign state order by affecting the constitution of institutional and normative frameworks. Interwoven with this was a shift in the dynamics of civilizational interaction within international society. The emergence of new states in the wake of decolonization shifted the weight of numbers in the system towards non-Western powers, marking the emergence of an increasingly culturally diverse international society. This raised important questions about the implications of growing diversity for the identity and the cultural cohesion of international society; did this growing pluralism threaten to undermine cultural cohesion, as well as the West's continued capacity to shape this society? Bull was particularly concerned by what he called the 'revolt against the West'; that is, with challenges presented to the norms and institutions of the sovereign state order from emerging Third World powers. These included demands for national self-determination, racial equality, and economic justice.[45] While calls for justice and equality do not in and of themselves appear to contradict Western liberal values, Bull was concerned that differences in interpretations of these norms could undermine

---

[43] UNGA (United Nations General Assembly) 1960.   [44] Buzan 2014b: 585.
[45] Bull was referring here principally to the emergence of the Afro-Asian Movement, the Non-Aligned Movement, and the Group of 77. See Bull 1983, 1984c.

the cohesion of international society. At the same time, as Bull observed, the 'revolt against the West' challenged not the legitimacy of the global sovereign order itself, but how that order should be constituted. The revolt was therefore taking place *within* the context of, rather than in opposition to, the structures and institutions of the existing international society. Bull remained confident that the Western-derived international society would continue to be a valuable forum for interaction and indeed unity among civilizations. He did concede, however, that to remain robust society needed to incorporate some of the norms of other civilizations. The degree to which this has or has not occurred remains a significant issue in the ongoing globalization of international society.

The dismantling of European empires marks an important point in the globalization of international society. It entailed shifting configurations of civilizational interaction and conceptions of civilization as an evaluative criterion for recognition. These processes contributed significantly to the reconfiguration of the normative and institutional structures of international society and to the constitution of its boundaries. However, the establishment of a global sovereign state order was not the endpoint of the globalization of international society. What we see instead is the ongoing production of international society in contemporary world politics. Civilizational ideas, practices, and contests continue to play a significant although variegated role in these processes.

THE GLOBALIZATION OF INTERNATIONAL SOCIETY IN THE TWENTY-FIRST CENTURY

As noted earlier, the concept of civilization lost much of its credibility in international political discourse in the postcolonial period. Civilizational discourse, however, resurged in the 1990s, stimulated in no small part by Samuel Huntington's 'clash of civilizations' thesis. Huntington's vision of a weakly socialized international system prone to inter-civilizational conflict provided one powerful lens through which the 11 September 2001 attacks on the United States and the emergence of violent Islamic groups such as Al Qaeda were viewed. It presented a conception of civilizational interaction which fundamentally challenged the plausibility of a cohesive, multicultural international society. In contrast, Robert Jackson has argued that the sovereign state order provides crucial mechanisms for the management of cultural difference and civilizational interaction.[46] Huntington's and Jackson's theses demonstrate the continued salience of civilizational discourses to

---

[46] Jackson 2000.

contemporary international society. Civilizational ideas, practices, and contests continue to play a significant role in the production and reproduction of this order. Once again, exploring the plural and singular discourses of civilization reveals different dimensions of its role. There are several sites at which these can be explored. Here I briefly discuss three: the role of civilization in the self-conception of rising powers; the re-emergence of 'standards of civilization' in political discourse; and the use of concepts of civilization and barbarism to frame responses to violent Islamic movements.

Civilization and Challenges to Western Hegemony in International Society

A key issue running through the globalization of international society debate is the degree to which international society is a truly multicultural order or a platform for the promotion of Western values and interests. As noted earlier, patterns and structures of civilizational interaction in the past were influenced by shifting differentials in power influencing the 'terms of engagement' between actors located in different civilizational constellations. An important element of the contemporary sovereign states order is the contested position of the West in that order. The material and reputational costs of the wars in Iraq and Afghanistan and the impact of the global financial crisis all contributed to a sense that Western hegemony is no longer assured and that Western civilization is declining. The growing assertiveness of 'rising powers' (China and Russia) within the international system also challenges the West's pre-eminence. An interesting element of the policy discourse of these two powers is the way in which they invoke civilizational identities and discourses in the promotion of their foreign policies and their authority in the international system. For instance, Chinese concepts such as *tianxia* and 'harmonious world' have been rejuvenated, articulating a worldview that harks back to China's imperial and Confucian identity. These highlight China's enduring and sophisticated political and cultural traditions, which are deeply rooted in its civilization.[47] Here civilizational discourse acts to enhance China's status and forms part of a strategy to reassure the international community that China is a responsible great power. The discourse of civilization has also returned to Russia under the leadership of Vladimir Putin, who has spoken forcefully about the integrity of Russia's national identity as pressured by the

---

[47] See, for instance, People's Republic of China 2011: 'Introduction' and 'Section IV: China's Path of Peaceful Development Is a Choice Necessitated by History'. See also Zhang 2013; Callahan 2008. A further illustration of this trend is the establishment of the Confucius institutes as a mechanism of China's cultural diplomacy.

forces of globalization. It is, he argues, threatened by a pernicious Euro-Atlantic civilization that promotes a Western cosmopolitan immorality. Civilizational ideas are here invoked as a way of framing Russia's identity and the challenges it faces in today's international order.[48]

In both cases, a pluralist discourse of civilizational politics features in the rhetorical policies and practices of these two great powers. This may challenge the hegemony of the West within the international system, but does it challenge the cohesion of international society? In *The Expansion*, both Russia and China were treated as somewhat on the margins of international society. Yet in their current foreign policy rhetoric—if not always their actions—both declare their commitment to protecting the key norms and institutions of international society: sovereign independence, territorial integrity, international law, and the centrality of the United Nations. In this regard, these states seek to place themselves at the heart of international society rather than contesting its legitimacy.[49] There are interesting parallels here with Bull's reading of the 'revolt against the West'. Once again there is ongoing and vigorous contestation about how the institutions and values of international society are defined and whether they should more fully represent a diversity of perspectives within a global international society. Civilizational discourse forms an important aspect of this contestation.

The Resurgence of the 'Standard of Civilization'

Another site at which to explore the continued role of civilization in the globalization of international society is the resurgence of the language of the 'standards of civilization'. Here the 'standards of civilization' is used to critique particular values, practices, and structures associated with the liberal international order's 'good governance' agenda. These are portrayed as forming the new 'standards of civilization'. The autonomy and legitimacy of states, critics argue, is increasingly linked to their internalization of standards. While states that are weak in regard to implementing these standards formally remain sovereign states, they may find their access to important resources and institutions limited or conditional and be subjected to forms of intervention.[50] This is construed as a creeping return to the tenets of empirical or conditional sovereignty of imperial international society, where sovereign autonomy was

---

[48] See, for instance, LarouchePac 2013. There is some ambiguity as to whether Putin has sought to locate Russia as a power outside the West or as the authentic representative *of* Western civilization. On civilizational debates in Russia, see Tsygankov 2008.

[49] For further discussion of China's ambiguous relationship to international society see, for instance, Zhang 2011a; Suzuki 2014.

[50] See, for instance, Stivachtis 2008 on the use of conditionality, new 'standards of civilization', and entry into the European Union.

dependent on conformity with standards and practices defined by powerful external actors and international institutions. The use of incentives and disincentives to induce reform is treated as echoing the civilizing process of the earlier era in which developing societies were similarly 'tutored' in the ways of good governance.

The idea of the 'new standards' are most frequently invoked to critique policies in three areas: economic standards, democracy, and human rights, each of which is examined in what follows. The standard of market and financial civilization refers to the use of international mechanisms and institutions to promote a liberal economic order at both the international and domestic levels. This encompasses measures to encourage trade and financial liberalization, transparency, and regulation. For instance, methods adopted by the International Monetary Fund to encourage financial reform have been likened to the civilizing process.[51]

Democracy as a new standard of civilization speaks to the argument that democratic structures are treated as a criterion of international legitimacy: 'to put it simply', argues Christopher Hobson, 'in the twenty first century it is the ballot box that is becoming the symbol of legitimate statehood'.[52] Democracy is viewed as compatible with, and indeed as sustaining, other universal 'goods' such as freedom, accountability, the rule of law, and political progress. Taken together these qualities make democracy 'the new focal point for the new standard of civilization'.[53] The concern here is that the promotion of democracy can be used to justify forms of intervention that represent a new form of the civilizing mission.

Human rights are perhaps most widely alluded to as the new standard of civilization. International standards of human rights, argues Jack Donnelly, have become part of the calculus of everyday legitimacy in the post-Cold War order.[54] The issue is complex. The promotion of self-determination as a right was a key component of decolonization. It played a significant role in the reconceptualization of sovereignty and in the discrediting of the 'classic' standards of civilization. Human rights also became integrated into the institutional and normative framework of international society through their articulation in the United Nations Charter and subsequent covenants. In recent decades, gross violations of human rights have provided a criterion for intervention by the international community. However, the selectivity of humanitarian interventions has fuelled perceptions that protection of human rights has become a new mechanism for promoting Western values and interests. It is here that the casting of human rights as a new 'standard of civilization' becomes salient, suggesting that states are once more being

---

[51] Best 2006; Gong 2002; Fidler 2001.
[52] Hobson 2008: 84. See also Clark 2009a; Stivachtis 2008; Zhang 2014b.
[53] Hobson 2008: 84.   [54] Donnelly 1998: 20.

positioned within a moral hierarchy in international society, one which again compromises the sovereignty of dissident states.[55]

The resurgence of the 'standards of civilization' reflects the continued powerful role that civilization plays in evaluating standards and practices of governance. At the same time it is interesting to note that in these debates the term 'civilization' is often summoned not to promote these standards but to contest them. Invoking the 'standards of civilization' provides a powerful rhetorical device with which to question and criticize the strategies associated with the 'good governance' agenda by associating it with the 'civilizing process' in earlier imperial times.

Drawing the Boundaries of International Society

The discourse of civilization in the singular also remains powerful in contemporary politics in generating normative and political boundaries of international society. The juxtaposition of civilization with barbarism has become pronounced in the wake of 11 September and the war on terror, and with the emergence of violent Islamic extremist groups in conflicts such as Iraq and Syria. Organizations such as Islamic State, Al Qaeda, and Boko Haram have been roundly condemned both for their level of violence and its indiscriminate nature. Their conduct has been denounced as cruel, brutal, despicable, and 'barbaric'. The way in which civilization is used here is extremely relevant. The invocation of barbarism works to shift the civilizational discourse from a clash between civilizations to one of the struggle between civilized and barbarian. The representation of acts or actors as barbaric places them outside the boundaries of civilized societies and very much on the fringes or outside of international society.

The rise of violent Islamic extremist groups challenges international society at a number of levels. Not only does their conduct contravene key norms and institutions such as international humanitarian law and international human rights law, but their concept of political community unsettles conventional conceptions of the sovereign territorial state. In these respects, these groups do not simply contest but directly challenge the political, normative, and institutional structures of contemporary international society. Framing the response to these challenges within the terms of civilizational discourse asserts the continued legitimacy of international society: it acts to define the membership of that society with reference to moral and political criteria of civilized behaviour, and to identify the interests of members of that society with a common purpose of civilized behaviour. At the same time, by locating these

[55] Donnelly 1998; Gong 2002; Zhang 2014b; Kayaoglu 2010.

actors outside the boundaries of international society, civilizational discourse has also facilitated forms of intervention, such as rendition, torture, drone strikes, and targeted assassinations that are extremely contentious. Indeed the legitimacy of such interventions has been contested in regard to whether they are themselves commensurate with standards of 'civilized' behaviour.[56]

CONCLUSION

The complex and multifaceted nature of civilization makes it challenging and yet essential to any inquiry into the globalization of international society. Analysis of international society is littered with references to and assumptions about civilization, but these often shift almost imperceptibly across different conceptions expressed in different discourses of civilization. Disentangling these discourses can enhance our understanding of the multifaceted role of civilization in the globalization of international society. This chapter has highlighted two prominent, if broad, discourses of civilization. The discourse of civilization in the plural refers to loosely bounded but discrete social entities whose interaction is integral to the dynamics of the globalization of international society. In the discourse of civilization in the singular, civilization acts as a generative force: it contributes to the generation of institutional and normative frameworks that structure interaction within international societies, and guides relations with those perceived as 'outside' it, as well as helping to define the boundaries of the society.

Examining the globalization of international society through an exploration of these dual discourses shows us how civilizational ideas, practices, and contests have contributed to the constitution of international society. These include conceptions of the identity and interests of actors, configurations of membership, the politics of recognition and non-recognition, institutions of coexistence, and conceptions of legitimate behaviour. They did so in different ways at different junctures in the evolution of international society. In the nineteenth century, civilizational ideas, practices, and contestations were particularly important in ordering relations between European and non-European peoples. Civilization came to act as a powerful rationale for adjudicating the position of non-European societies in relation to those who formed the core of European international society. However, a reconceptualization of civilization in the twentieth century—and in particular of the legitimacy of the 'standards of civilization'—influenced important changes in practices of recognition and conceptions of legitimate behaviour, significantly facilitating the

---

[56] See Bowden 2009: chapter 5.

globalization of the sovereign state order. Civilizational ideas and practices have thus acted as sites at which boundaries are contested, norms and institutions are challenged, and rights are claimed in international society. These processes have continued in the contemporary era. Civilizational interaction continues to provide a key dynamic *within* global international society, but also a key purpose *of* international society insofar as international society is seen as a mechanism for maintaining order and facilitating civilizational interaction. Furthermore, civilization as an evaluative discourse still plays a role in iterating the boundaries of international society, as well as providing a mechanism through which both the boundaries and frameworks of international society are challenged.

ACKNOWLEDGEMENT

In addition to the editors, I am grateful for the comments on earlier drafts of this chapter provided by Paul Keal, Heloise Weber, and Mary-Louise Hickey.

11

Worlding China, 1500–1800

Yongjin Zhang

INTRODUCTION

The classical English School story dates the beginning of the expansion of European international society into East Asia in the mid-nineteenth century, when European institutions and its standard of 'civilization' were imposed through coercion on China after 1839, and on Japan after 1853. In this story, East Asia becomes an integral part of the globalization of international society only after the global transformation in the nineteenth century that opened up the power gap between the West and the rest that still defines the basic structure of global order today.[1] Such an account has conveniently, but probably also intentionally, left out complex historical processes of intensive cultural, societal, and state interactions between China/East Asia and Europe in the sixteenth to nineteenth centuries, when two incompatible world orders—Chinese and European—coexisted peacefully in East Asia before European domination was firmly established after the opening of China and Japan.

This silence is curious, because in the introductory chapter of *The Expansion of International Society*, Hedley Bull and Adam Watson noted specifically that:

> in the three centuries from 1500 to 1800, as European involvement in Asian politics persisted and grew, and with it the armed rivalry of the European powers in Asia, a loose Eurasian system or quasi-system grew up in which European states sought to deal with Asian states on the basis of moral and legal equality, until in the nineteenth century this gave place to notions of European superiority.[2]

Few efforts have been made subsequently by members of English School scholarship to explore such 'European involvement' in these three centuries

---

[1] See Buzan and Lawson (2015b) for further discussion on the global transformation in the nineteenth century and its implications for the study of international relations.
[2] Bull and Watson 1984b: 5.

and its implications for rethinking the classical story about the expansion of international society. Such neglect is clearly problematic in understanding the complexities and intricate dynamics of the globalization of international society in its longue durée, particularly before 'the secular, universal, totalizing claims of modernity gradually washed over alternative visions of socio-political order'.[3]

This chapter conducts a critical investigation of the civilizational, economic, and power-political encounters between China and Europe during the period 1500–1800, before global modernity pulled China into a single world system that Europe created. Through an analytical account of how China became an integral part of the world in the collective European imagination and practical experience, it seeks to show that changing European identity and Europe's understanding of its place in the world were manifestly informed by its precarious knowledge and contingent interpretations of the civilizational and imperial Other at the opposite end of Eurasia; and that such encounters had a transformative effect on Europe's historical, cultural, and social forma-tion and the construction of European modernity, particularly in the seven-teenth and eighteenth centuries. Worlding China in 1500–1800 was, therefore, indispensable for Europe to globalize its vision of the world in the nineteenth century when the project of European modernity became hegemonic and exhibited homogenizing effect. It is a historically contingent precursor to, and a discursively necessary preparation for, the global reach of the sovereign order to East Asia. It constitutes an integral process in the globalization of international society.

In looking at the globalization of international society as a slow and protracted historical process in East Asia with its analytical focus on the period 1500–1800, this chapter seeks to go beyond the subject–object explanatory perspective in the existing account of historical encounters of Europe and East Asia. It argues for a hermeneutics based on a dialogical subject–co-subject relationship in understanding the dynamics of cross-cultural and inter-civilizational encounters in the historical social formation of global international society. It intentionally privileges several discourses of the encounters in an attempt to provide a necessary and imperative correction to the unilinear, evolutionary conception of social change of the international that appears in much of the scholarship on world history. The rest of this chapter provides what I call an episodic examination of Chinese-European encounters in three different spatial-temporal contexts in 1500–1800, and offers a 'synthetic' account of the globalization of inter-national society in East Asia.

---

[3] Zarakol 2011: 61.

IDEAS OF AND ABOUT CHINA

China had been slowly, if also precariously, incorporated into the European imagination before the early modern period. If it was known about and discussed in antiquity, China remained a legendary land with which the post-classical European contact was, at best, tenuous. The famed Silk Road and ancient networks of trade associated with it opened long-distance political and economic relations and enabled cultural exchanges between different civilizations—Chinese, Indian, Islamic, and European. But it was Marco Polo's first-hand account of his encounter with Imperial China that made the Cathay an object of intense contemplation and fascination for Europeans. In the world of 1490, Imperial China and its tributary states, 'the Sinosphere' referred to by Andrew Phillips in Chapter 3, constituted an international system of its own that had little direct contact with Europe. In contrast to the Islamic world, whose ceaseless bloody conflict with European powers was integral to European history, Imperial China was never at war with Europe until the expansion of the European sovereign order to East Asia in the mid-nineteenth century.

Direct and substantive cultural, societal, and civilizational encounters between Europe and China began to take place rather belatedly in world historical terms only in the early sixteenth century. It is not a pure historical coincidence that it was only after the 'ages of discovery' that the Portuguese traders navigated around the South China Sea and first landed on the coast of Canton (Guangdong) in 1513, followed by European missionaries. Their arrival made the diffusion and circulation of ideas between two great civilizational centres at two extreme ends of Eurasia possible and meaningful. It was through their construction and representation of China that the European conception and imagination of 'one world' to which both Europe and China belonged was gradually crystallized. China was etched into Europe's cosmographical, geographical, cultural, religious, and philosophical understanding of the world, and was assigned a distinctive place in the European imaginary geography of the globe, an assignment that was contingent on the weighty religious, philosophical, political, and economic considerations in the sixteenth, seventeenth, and eighteenth centuries in Europe. With the growth of European knowledge of the civilizational and imperial Other, China became increasingly an inescapable component in the European understanding of itself.

Ideas of and about China travelled to Europe in the sixteenth and seventeenth centuries in the first instance through Jesuits' reports, correspondences, and other writings. Their idealization of Chinese culture and society captured the intellectual and popular imagination of Europe. As early as 1579, Jean Bodin wrote that '[t]he Spanish have remarked that the Chinese, the most Oriental of peoples, are the most ingenious and the most courteous, and that those of Brasil, the most Occidental, are the most barbarous and cruel'.[4] Typical of such idealization in the glowing missionary texts was the construction of Confucius as a primal wellspring of reason in the service of virtue and public good, which inspired the European fascination with this ancient Chinese sage during the Enlightenment period.[5] A new European image of China as a homogeneous Confucian state of unrivalled moral and political excellence, a God's country, in other words, emerged from the fresh knowledge based on the Jesuits' writings and representations and other sources of information. As Sir William Temple wrote in 1690, based on his reading of Dutch diplomatic correspondence:

> The kingdom of China seems to be framed and policed with the utmost force and reach of human wisdom, reason and contrivance; and in practice to excel the very speculations of other men, and all those imaginary schemes of the European wits, the institutions of Xenophon, the republic of Plata, the Utopias, or Oceanas, of our modern writers.[6]

China became part of Europe's world and European history in this early encounter also because of a number of challenges that the 'discovery' of China presented to the prevailing views of Christianity and European cultural premises. The full awareness for the first time in Europe of a wonderful civilization with its own tradition and religion that was more ancient than that of Europe and which owed nothing to Europe had a powerful effect. For Michel de Montaigne in the sixteenth century, Chinese history made him realize 'how much wider and more various the world is than either the ancients or ourselves have discovered'.[7] The publication in 1658 of the Jesuit missionary Martino Martini's work, *The First Ten Divisions of Chinese History*, which was the first genuine history of China in a European language, led to debates over the dating of biblical events, as it was found particularly difficult to square ancient Chinese records with the biblical chronology, which dates the Noachian flood to 2349 BC in the *Annals of the Old and New Testaments* written by Anglican archbishop, James Ussher, published in London in 1650–4. In the process of these debates, 'Chinese history was integrated into European "universal history" based on Old Testament-derived chronology'.[8] Forty years later, Louis Le Comte provoked a furious debate when he made a controversial claim in *Nouveaux Memoires sur l'etat present de la Chine* (1696) that '[t]he people of China had preserved for about two thousand years the knowledge of the True God and have honoured Him in

---

[4] Blue 1999: 59.

[5] More generally, Jesuits made an indispensable contribution to the emergence of Sinology as a discipline in Europe in the eighteenth century. Nearly 1,500 books on China were published in Europe between 1600 and 1799. It was estimated that at one time in the eighteenth century, there was in Europe more information available about China than about some parts of Europe.

[6] Blue 1999: 64.   [7] Zhang 1988: 117.   [8] Mungello 1999: 65–6.

such a manner as to serve as an example and model even for Christians'.[9] The polemics led to serious theological disputes that saw weeks of debates at the theological faculty of the Sorbonne in 1700 on the Chinese rites. However, the key issue that preoccupied the faculty of the Sorbonne in these debates 'was neither the precise nuances of Chinese terms for the divine, nor the significance of their ancestral observances, but rather the challenge the Chinese represented in these Jesuit texts to the exclusive hegemony of Christian doctrine'.[10] The enduring (Chinese) Rites controversy was culminated by the intervention of Pope Clement XI in 1704 (by a decree) and in 1715 (by a bull) to ban the Chinese Rites.[11]

If the theological controversies occasioned by Europe's encounter with China in the seventeenth century mounted a powerful challenge to the uncontested supremacy of Christianity, the 'metaphysical contact' between China and Europe in the eighteenth century was dominated by philosophical debates. Partly because of the Jesuits' success in presenting Confucianism as a philosophy that was very appealing to the cultural needs of Europe in the seventeenth and eighteenth centuries, ancient Chinese religion and philosophy found their way into the Enlightenment and were used, in particular, in support of the iconoclastic challenges of the Enlightenment to the orthodox religious doctrine. Debates about China, on its universalism and particularism alike, entered into the works of such important Enlightenment thinkers as Gottfried Wilhelm von Leibniz, Voltaire, François Quesnay, and Pierre Bayle, among others. For them, the rationalism and agnosticism associated with Confucianism were instrumental in their efforts to differentiate Christian morality from dogmas of the Church. Such interpretations of Confucianism were influential in their arguments for religious tolerance, in their attempts at relativizing Christianity, and in their advocacy of reason and attack on religious fanaticism in the philosophical spirit. The French *philosophes*, in the words of Voltaire, 'discovered there [in China] a new moral and physical universe'.[12] The Libertines used China and Confucianism as an example in arguing against the political position of the Church in Europe. Confucian classics, according to Joseph Needham, 'were read with avidity by all the forerunners of the French Revolution'.[13] What could be called 'Confucian influence' was found in the thought of leading Enlightenment thinkers such as Leibnitz, Christian Wolff,

---

[9] Quoted in Porter 2001: 111.   [10] Porter 2001: 120–1.

[11] Pope John Paul II issued an apology for this on 24 October 2001 in a message read out to an international convention held in the Gregorian University in Rome on *Matteo Ricci: For a Dialogue Between China and the West*. Making indirect reference to the Rites controversy, he said: 'I feel deep sadness for those errors and limits of the past, and I regret that in many people these failings may have given the impression of a lack of respect and esteem for the Chinese people on the part of the Catholic Church, making them feel that the Church was motivated by feelings of hostility towards China'. Pope John Paul II 2001.

[12] Quoted in Blue 1999: 66.   [13] Needham 2005: 90.

and Voltaire, among others, so much so that Confucius became for some the patron saint of the eighteenth-century Enlightenment. Voltaire, who regarded China as 'le plus sage empire de l'universe', is said to have 'transformed China into a political utopia and the ideal state of an enlightened absolutism'. In so doing, he 'held up the mirror of China to provoke self-critical reflection among European monarchs'.[14] For both Voltaire and Quesnay, China was unmistakably elevated as a model for the social and political reforms they advocated in France. The great Oriental empire became 'a whip in the hands of the Reformers with which to beat the *ancien regime*'.[15]

Such Sinophilism had its nemesis. Francis Bacon had looked at China as a 'curious, ignorant, fearful, foolish nation' in spite of his admiration of the Chinese language.[16] In the eighteenth century, the Enlightenment Sinophilism was countered by profound scepticism, disparagement, and critiques expressed by such influential thinkers as Jean-Jacques Rousseau, Denis Diderot, Montesquieu, and Nicolas de Condorcet, among others. In his *De l'esprit des lois*, Montesquieu developed the concept of oriental despotism and described the Chinese state as an exemplar of corrupted tyrant. For Condorcet, China belonged to the third 'epoch' of human history with its agriculture-based economy and society and the Chinese were condemned to a 'shameful immobility' and 'eternal mediocrity'.[17] Sinophilism of the French *philosophes* was matched by Sinophobism of representatives of the *Encyclopedie*. It is perhaps this Sinophiles–Sinophobes debate and rivalry that prompted Geoffrey Hudson to conclude that China in the eighteenth century was

> a great power culturally in Paris than was Europe in Peking....Destined in the nineteenth century and after to be violently invaded, overwhelmed and radically transformed by the progressing civilization of the West, Old China reached out and cast a spell over its future conqueror, leaving indelible traces in the cultural tradition of Europe.[18]

'Indelible traces' can also be found in popular culture in Europe embodied in the craze for things Chinese, including the so-called Chinoiserie and as reflected in Chippendale furniture and still seen in William Chamber's legacies in Kew Gardens and Christopher Wren's design of the Old Royal Naval College at Greenwich, as well as in a variety of fine porcelain designs and picturesque wallpapers in Europe. As Watson noted, 'Chinese culture made a profound impression on the educated eighteenth-century Europeans, who were attracted by the exquisite rococo works of art which the Chinese exported'.[19] It was such a rage for '"things Chinese"' that launched, in Arthur Lovejoy's words, 'the gradual conscious revolt against neo-classical standards'.[20]

---

[14] Fuchs 2006: 43. See also Davis 1983; and Lach 1945.   [15] Ch'ên 1979: 39.
[16] Blue 1999: 60.   [17] Blue 1999: 91.   [18] Hudson 1965: 236.
[19] Watson 1984a: 23.   [20] Lach 1942: 221.

Contextualizing the Sinophiles–Sinophobes rivalry in European political transformation in the late seventeenth and early eighteenth centuries, Ho-Fung Hung sees this rivalry as 'enmeshed in the conflict between the absolute monarch and the feudal aristocracy'.[21] The prevalence of Sinophilism in the early stage of the Enlightenment, in his words, 'can henceforth be explained in light of the strengthening of the monarchial order at the expense of the aristocracy in ca. 1650–1750, a period during which the European interstate system consolidated in the form of absolutism'. In a rather distinctive, if not unique, fashion, therefore, China was engaged from a cultural and geographical distance in the epic transformation of the European political order and in the emergent discourses of European modernity. Worlding China through such a largely unidirectional global flow of ideas[22] was indispensable in the European discursive construction of a world constituted by inter-civilizational encounters and cross-cultural gaze. It is integral in forging an interpretive self-reflexivity by Europe, hence its cultural self-awareness and a dense and particular cultural/civilizational identity.

The same is true of the reversal of China's fortunes in the public imagination in Europe over the course of the eighteenth century, which did not reflect changing Chinese society, but confirmed a different European gaze at China from a distance in European intellectual history. This new European gaze came as a result of the remarkable transformation brought to Europe by scientific, industrial, social, and political revolutions, which had kept Europe in turmoil, and through its internal intellectual sources including Baconian empiricism, Cartesian scepticism, and, later, Galilean physics. This transformation of Europe 'provided the temptation not only to visualize civilization as a scale on which Europe had progressed much farther than other parts of the world, but also to make a crude analysis of other civilizations in accordance with European categories and compare them with earlier stages in European civilization'.[23] The unilinear conceptions of the progress towards civilizational achievements, which were to flourish in nineteenth-century Europe, began to take shape. A restless, dynamic, and 'progressive' Europe was now compared with the immobility and changelessness of the Chinese empire. For some European observers, the discrepancy in the pace of historical change in China and the West was so striking that 'centuries have produced less change in China than a generation in Europe'.[24] By the same token, China's 'troubled story of decline was offered to the world as part of the epochal tale of Europe's own successful modernity'.[25] The Confucian political tradition, which Francois Bernier believed enabled the Chinese people to exceed all other

---

[21] Hung 2003: 264.

[22] Alain Peyrefitte (1993: 28) calls such a flow of ideas 'the dialogue of the deaf' with Europe 'doing all the talking, asking questions and giving answers, while China played the mute'.

[23] Dawson 1967: 65.   [24] Porter 2001: 220.   [25] Blue and Brook 1999: 7.

peoples in 'virtue, wisdom, prudence, good faith, sincerity, charity, gentleness, honesty, civility, gravity, modesty and obedience to the Celestial order',[26] was dismissed now as a sign of stagnation and immobility of Chinese history. Chinese antiquity, once revered as a virtue, was now regarded as a vice. Johann Gottfried von Herder described the Chinese empire as 'an embalmed mummy, wrapped in silk, and painted with hieroglyphics: its internal circulation is that of a dormouse in its winter sleep'. Georg Wilhelm Friedrich Hegel was more straightforward, when he said '[w]e have before us the oldest state and yet no past, but a state which exists today as we know it to have been in ancient times. To that extent China has no history'.[27] In the Hegelian 'world-historical' development scheme, Chinese civilization marked, not surprisingly, but its lowest level. By the early nineteenth century, uncritical idealization of China of the earlier period gave way to unreserved contempt and unequivocal disdain. The seventeenth-century image of China as 'wealthy, civilized and tolerant' was replaced by a representation of China where civility dissolved readily into barbarism. In a review of John Barrow's account of the Macartney Mission to China (discussed in the next section) published in 1805, the prestigious *Edinburgh Review* endorsed the view of China approvingly as a 'semi-barbarian race' and among 'other half-civilized nations'. It asked rhetorically:

> What else do we know with certainty of the Chinese, but their abject submission to a despotism upheld by the sordid terror of the lash—but the emprisonment and mutilation of their women—but their infanticide and unnatural vices—but their utter and unconquerable ignorance of all the exacter sciences, and all the branches of natural philosophy—but the stupid formalities which incomber their social intercourses—but their cowardice, uncleanliness, and inhumanity?[28]

In the changing European imaginative grasp of the world in the period of our concern, China had appeared in many different guises in the European imagination. Like the earlier European encounters with the New World, this encounter had far-reaching effects on the expanding geographical, cultural, as well as intellectual sensibilities and horizons of the Europeans.[29] China was entangled in the formation of Europe's early modernity in myriad ways. Early cultural encounters promoted 'the dawning realization in Europe that not all truth and virtue were contained within its own cultural and religious traditions', which in turn stimulated Europeans 'self-consciously to question their own cultural premises, to weigh them in a balance against the presuppositions and accomplishments of other high cultures, and to initiate fundamental revisions in their own views of the world, man, and the future'.[30] The rivalry

---

[26] Blue 1999: 87.   [27] Dawson 1967: 66.   [28] Quoted in Peyrefitte 1993: 491.
[29] For a fascinating study of the lasting intellectual effect on Europeans produced by Europe's encounters with the New World, see Pagden 1993.
[30] Lach 1965: 835.

between Sinophilism and Sinophobism shows how China mattered in European intellectuals' search for solutions to European problems. The entanglement of their rivalry with the conflict between the absolutist state and the contentious bourgeoisie in eighteenth-century Europe, particularly during the Enlightenment, proved influential in the transformation of political order in Europe. In the wild swing of European imagination about China between 1500 and 1800, the idea of and about China became an indispensable element in the prevailing definition of Europe's collective identity.

THE WORLD THAT THE 'CHINA TRADE' CREATED

The period 1500–1800 is frequently represented as an era of increasing European domination in global political economy. Such conventional wisdom has been typically imparted in and supported by studies of the European conquest of the Americas, the Atlantic slave trade, and the European expansion into Asia and Africa, which made the global exchange of goods possible. In the words of C. R. Boxer:

> Only after the Portuguese had worked their way down the West African coast, rounded the Cape of Good Hope, crossed the Indian Ocean and established themselves in the Spice Islands of Indonesia and on the shore of the South China Sea; only after the Spaniards had attained the same goal by way of Patagonia, the Pacific Ocean and the Philippines—then and only then was a regular and lasting maritime connection established between the four great continents.[31]

However, when first the Portuguese traders, then the Dutch and the British, arrived at the ports of East Asia seeking to profit from Chinese economic prosperity and expansion, they found a century-old and well-entrenched Sinocentric tribute–trade system matrix, which was constitutive of 'a separate Chinese-based Asian world-economy'.[32] Although the relationship between trade and tribute was never clearly understood by the Europeans, they quickly realized that a flourishing network existed of commercial trade relationships that was parallel to and in symbiosis with the China-centred tribute system. This was a world that the China trade had already created: elaborate and thriving trading networks in maritime Asia that the tribute trade had forged and multinational private traders had sustained through trading port cities in the Indian Ocean and the Pacific, which had already connected East Asia with the European market. Malay was widely used as a *lingua franca* in port cities and trading centres for commercial exchange in maritime Asia.

[31] Boxer 1969: 17.   [32] Frank 1998: 113. See also Hamashita 2008; and Kang 2010.

Chinese 'cash' was readily accepted as a medium of exchange. Even after Malacca, a traditional Chinese tributary state, was captured by the Portuguese in the early sixteenth century, it continued to follow long-established commercial practices and served as a great entrepôt for regional trade. In Malacca, foreign merchants continued to live in communities of their own under conditions resembling what would be called extraterritoriality in the nineteenth century. The interposition of the Portuguese in the trade between India and Southeast Asia inflicted great losses upon the Gujarati-Muslim merchants who had previously dominated this commerce only by taking advantage of the existing trade networks.

Whereas in the sixteenth century both the Portuguese and the Spanish 'had to participate in an intra-Asian trade network that already existed in order to obtain the goods they wanted', in the seventeenth century it was the British and the Dutch who 'had to come to terms with the existing Asian tribute trade system, adapt to it, and learn to utilize it'.[33] The Dutch 'became enthusiastic participants in the "China trade" almost as soon as they arrived in Asian waters in the early seventeenth century'.[34] The Dutch East India Company and the British East India Company effectively inserted themselves readily into the pre-existing networks of intra-Asian trade. In so doing, European traders largely 'followed the same trade routes, used the same ports and exchanged the same genre of products. They first began to use the China trade to procure products for Europe, but what proved more lasting and lucrative was the regional trade (or the country trade) involving Asian markets and trades.'[35] European participation contributed to significant expansion of the tributary trade in the region. In playing the role of intermediaries in the regional trade, however, the profit-seeking Europeans were confronted with and had to work within highly regulated and heavily guarded, yet relatively open, existing trade regimes. Often they had to go 'native', that is, to subject and adapt themselves to the local laws, rules, arrangements, and traditions in order to exploit to its own advantage opportunities provided by the complex and thriving trading networks in the region operated by non-European trade diasporas, Gujaratis, Arabs, Jews, Persians, and Chinese. In some cases, European traders entered, willingly or not, into a 'controlled relationship' in which they found

> their freedom of action limited both geographically and socially. It was the Chinese and the Japanese who decided where the two cultures meet, who should take part and which outside influence should be admitted. Subject to drastic controls, trade was tolerated and even welcomed; but the host made it plain that they did not need foreign trade and wanted to decide the terms of encounter.[36]

---

[33] Hamashita 2008: 13. [34] Atwell 1998: 396. See also Wills 1984.
[35] Nor-Afidah Abd Rahman, quoted in Zhang 2014a: 66. [36] Bitterli 1989: 133–4.

Nowhere was such a 'controlled relationship' more compellingly demonstrated than in the construction of Macao as a Portuguese enclave in the
late sixteenth and seventeenth centuries. The subjection of the European
company-state to such 'drastic controls' and local institutional arrangements
for trade in East Asia can best be illustrated by the British East India Company's dealings with the Canton system in most of the eighteenth and early
nineteenth centuries.[37] It was the Canton system that led to complaints that
the treatment of British merchants in Canton was 'scarcely compatible with
the regulations of Civilized Society',[38] and to the conception of late eighteenth-
century China as an uncooperative and potentially dangerous trading partner
for Europe. Unsurprisingly, even after the abject failure of his China mission
in the 1790s, Lord Macartney maintained that it remained a principal British
goal to 'be able to mould the China trade (as we seem to have done the trade
everywhere else) to the shape that best suit us'.[39]

The global significance of the China trade in the early modern period is
found in another instance. One particular commodity that the China trade
dealt with was the global flow of silver (and gold to a lesser extent). Imperial
China was reputed to be the 'ultimate sink' of the world's silver in the
sixteenth, seventeenth, and eighteenth centuries. 'China's dominance as an
importer of silver', Dennis O. Flynn and Arturo Giáaldez claim, 'was arguably
at least as pivotal during the birth of world trade as is the industrial world's
dominance as importers of oil in today's global marketplace'.[40] It is estimated
that China received from Europe, Japan, and Spanish America 'up to some
60,000 tons of silver . . . or perhaps half the world's tallied production of about
120,000 tons after 1600 or 137,000 tons since 1545'.[41] According to William
Atwell, Spanish-American silver flowed into China through three different
routes.[42] For the purpose of our discussion, the most important was the direct
trans-Pacific silver trade between Spanish-America and Asia carried out by the
'Manila Galleons', which is said to have shipped 10,000 tons or more of silver
to Manila and then on to China.[43] This contributed to the formation of a truly
global trading system in the early modern period, as it linked 'substantial,
direct, and continuous trade between America and Asia for the first time in
history'.[44] Adam Smith, noting the market demand of silver in East Indies, in
particular China and India, remarked that:

[37] Zhang 2014a: 65–8. See also Greenberg 1970: 41–74.   [38] Porter 2001: 207.
[39] Macartney 1962: 210.   [40] Flynn and Giráldez 1995: 206.
[41] Frank 1998: 148–9.   [42] Atwell 1998: 388–96.   [43] Frank 1998: 148.
[44] Flynn and Giráldez 1995: 201. For the impact of the Spanish-American silver flow to China
on European history in the early modern period, Flynn and Giráldez (1995: 210) further
commented: 'Revenues from overseas mines provided the fiscal foundations for the Spanish
empire . . . . Thus, the silver-industry profits that financed the Spanish empire were huge because
China had become the world's dominant silver customer. This implies that ultimately China was
responsible for a power shift within early modern Europe'.

The silver of the new continent seems in this manner to be one of the principal commodities by which the commerce between the two extremities of the old one is carried on, and by means of it, in great measure, that those distant parts of the world are connected with one another.[45]

It is worth noting that the silver bullion flow as the European financial capital advanced into Asia did not open up the Asian financial market on its own. Its entry into Asia was conditioned on several special local circumstances, which included the following:

1. In the trade between Asia and Europe, Europe suffered a trade deficit, the settlement of which was resolved through payments of silver and bills of exchange;

2. The silver provided for such trade also served as a means for trade within Asia and was used for settling intra-regional Asian business transactions as well; and,

3. Because silver cost more in Asia than in Europe, European countries took advantage of this price difference to sell their silver supplies in Asia in exchange for gold.[46]

The conventional explanation for such silver bullion flow into China/Asia was a reflection of Europe's balance of trade deficit with China, that is, the need for China's perennial export surplus (until the mid-nineteenth century) to be settled primarily through payment in silver by European traders. This was indeed the case. It was certainly true that China enjoyed industrial superiority relative to its neighbours and could claim world economic pre-eminence in production and export at the time. China was unrivalled in porcelain ceramics and had few rivals in silk production thanks to its high-productivity/low-cost competitiveness. It had a virtual monopoly on the tea trade. It was also true that the success of China's export to Europe lay in the fact that the Chinese manufacturers learned quickly to adapt their merchandise to European specifications and demand, including design. Adaptation to Spanish tastes in design allowed Chinese silks to dominate the world silk market by the turn of the seventeenth century. The porcelain makers of Jingdezhen turned to producing porcelains in Japanese and European styles as imperial orders declined after 1620.[47] Given the enduring trade patterns favourable to China's exporters, it is interesting but perhaps ultimately futile to speculate what would the Europeans have used to pay, without silver, for their purchase of tea, silk, and porcelain from China. Would the Europeans have been excluded from world trade for lack of any other means of payment?

---

[45] Quoted in Frank 1998: 131.   [46] Hamashita 2008: 48.
[47] Brook 1998: 698.

A more compelling causal explanation for China's extraordinary demand of silver is found in a number of domestic reforms carried out by Ming China (1368–1644) in the fifteenth and the sixteenth centuries. Two are worth mentioning here. One was that the Ming government progressively abandoned the paper money system that had largely collapsed towards the end of the Yuan dynasty (1271–1368).[48] Paper money was eventually replaced by silver, although it took more than a century for the Ming to silverize its monetary and fiscal systems. Had the Chinese experiment with paper money in the Tang–Song period proved to be successful for Ming China, there would not have been the 'silverization' of the world's largest economy at the time.

The other reform was Ming China's persistent experiment with simplifying tax assessment and collection and its reform of the tax structure to introduce nationwide 'the so-called "Single-Whip Method" of taxation whereby most land taxes, labor service obligations, and extra levies were commuted to payments in silver'.[49] By the time the 'single whip method' was widely implemented in the 1570s, when the Ming experienced a sharp increase in agricultural specialization and commercialization, rapid growth in silk, cotton, and porcelain industries, and a significant expansion of inter-regional trade, Ming China's fiscal and monetary systems had been substantially converted from a paper money system to silver. The power of the Chinese economy to take in the world supply of silver can be seen in one estimate: the annual tax quota for the central government of Ming China in the mid-seventeenth century amounted to 2,100 tons a year.[50] While the claim that 'the entire world economic order was—literally—Sino-centric'[51] in this period remains contestable, it is indisputable that it was a historically contingent economic transformation of China, that is, the 'silverization' of the Chinese economy, that stimulated China's insatiable demand for silver, and at the same time made bullion settlements for multilateral trade imbalances between China and Europe central to the creation of trade that was truly global for the first time in world history. By the same token, what ultimately proved to be transformative of world trade in the early modern period was not so much the economic pre-eminence of China, but particular domestic reforms in Imperial Ming China in the fifteenth and sixteenth centuries.

Contrary to conventional wisdom, in the world that the China trade created, it was China, not Europe, that was the driving force in the early modern period in the formation and transformation of regional and global political economy, which was integral to the historical social and political-economic processes in the globalization of international society.

---

[48] Paper money was first experimented, with limited success, in the Tang dynasty (619–960). It was institutionalized as official currency in the Song dynasty (960–1276).
[49] Atwell 1998: 404–5.   [50] Hamashita 2008: 49.   [51] Frank 1998: 117.

AN EMERGENT GEOGRAPHY OF POWER

Power-political encounter was conspicuously absent in the period under discussion of otherwise angst-ridden European interactions with the powerful and largely inscrutable oriental Empire. The Spanish arrived in the South China Sea and the Portuguese landed in Canton in the early sixteenth century, when the subjugation of the Americas was in full swing. Perhaps not surprisingly, no sooner had the Europeans arrived than there were calls for the use of military forces against the Chinese empire. Cristavao Vieira and Vasco Calvo, two members of the first Portuguese embassy to Beijing imprisoned by the Chinese in Canton in the 1520s, urged the Portuguese king to undertake a military expedition against China in their letters sent from the prison, which eventually reached Europe.[52] Francisco de Sande, the Spanish governor of the Philippine islands, officially proposed in 1576 a military attack on China. In his first official report dated 4 June 1596, the Spanish governor claimed that 'with two or three thousand men one can take whatever province he please. . . for the people would revolt immediately [against their tyrannical rulers]'.[53] The idea met with little enthusiasm in Europe.[54]

In the eighteenth century, George Anson, the Commodore of HMS *Centurion*, who sailed his warship into the Canton harbour against Chinese will in 1743, was the first British person to preach gunboat diplomacy against China, almost exactly one century before the First Opium War.[55] Anson seems rather fanciful, for even at the end of the eighteenth century, 'China remained a formidable adversary in the minds of British strategists'.[56] It is generally accepted that 'the forceful means of opening China's doors to foreign trade that would eventually prevail in the nineteenth century received little serious consideration prior to the Amherst embassy of 1816'.[57]

The European remapping of the geography of power in the eighteenth century took place against the backdrop of the institutional ascendancy of nation-states and constitutional republican states as the only legitimate institutional foundation of the new political order in Europe and at a time when power was increasingly territorialized. This political and institutional transformation of Europe is captured well by Shmuel Eisenstadt and Wolfgang Schluchter, when they remark that early modernity in Europe refers to the period from the sixteenth to the eighteenth centuries when territorial states

[52] Lach 1965: 734.   [53] Lach 1965: 746.

[54] In his reply to the Spanish governor dated 29 April 1577, Philip II wrote: '[a]s regards the conquest of China which you think should be undertaken forthwith, it has seemed to us here this matter should be dropped; and, on the contrary, good friendship should be sought with the Chinese. You should not act or collaborate with the piratical enemies of the said Chinese, nor give them any excuse to have just cause of complaint against our people'. Lach 1965: 746.

[55] Spence 1998: 51–8; Peyrefitte 1993: 489.   [56] Porter 2001: 206.

[57] Porter 2001: 203.

became major vehicles for resource mobilization and for the construction of collective identities. In this period, ideas of political order as a nation-state of compatriots, or alternatively as a constitutional republican state of citizens, emerged and superseded old ideas of political order. On the institutional level, it was a period of gradual replacement of an older political order—of stratum-based empires or city-states—first by national monarchies and later by nation-states and constitutional republican states.[58] The expansion of modernity beyond Europe, they further noted, 'spawned a tendency, rather new in the history of mankind, towards universal structural, institutional, and cultural frameworks'.[59]

This remapping also took place amidst social, scientific, and industrial revolutions at home in Europe. The rise and growth of rational capitalist economy unleashed an optimistic and triumphant sentiment in the public sphere of Europe and reinforced the conception of Europe as a 'progressive' continent informed by the Enlightenment idea of progress. More importantly, perhaps, this notion of Europe as a 'progressive' continent was developed in such a manner as to set Europeans apart from, and superior to, all others. European superiority was reinforced by the great expansion of European productive and scientific forces after the Industrial Revolution in the eighteenth century, a century of great economic expansion, scientific and technical development, and increased concentration of political power in Europe. The 'Moderns' in eighteenth-century France 'considered both the splendour and morals of their own times greater than those of the Ancients'.[60] Such sentiment was shared by John Entick in England when he explicitly claimed in 1774 that:

> The *Romans* could not boast of the Liberty, Rights and Privileges and that Security of Property and Person, which an *English* subject enjoys under the Protection of the Laws...the BRITISH EMPIRE, in its present State, excels both the ancient and the modern States, in Riches and Magnificence; in Dignity and Power; in Strength by Sea and Land; in Discoveries and Conquests; in Trade, Commerce and Navigation.[61]

The European remapping of the geography of power at the turn of the nineteenth century, therefore, took place in two broad contexts. One was the combined dynamics produced by industrialization, rational statement, and ideologies of progress in Europe that led to a clear shift in the mode of power, which generated a new material basis for and a new normative understanding of how power was constituted, organized, and exercised.[62] The other was the emergence of 'a culture spouting universalizing claims about enlightenment,

---

[58] Eisenstadt and Schluchter 1998: 1.   [59] Eisenstadt and Schluchter 1998: 3.
[60] Martin Bernal as quoted in Hung 2003: 263.   [61] Quoted in Armitage 2004: 103–4.
[62] Buzan and Lawson 2015b: 1.

progress, rationality, and self-interest' and 'a worldview with a marked emphasis on progress, rationality, and science; a worldview which inevitably generate[d] a universal social hierarchy predicated upon comparisons and measurements'.[63] Evaluated against 'progressive' Europe as 'an ideal type to measure deviances, to identify differences encountered in other civilizations',[64] China became a symbol of stagnation. In the words of Le Gentil, 'The permanence of their [Chinese] institutions is no evidence of their superiority, for it prevents all progress'.[65] In the view of Adam Ferguson, in the successive stages of historical progress and social formation, China had not passed from one to another because it continued to reproduce its ancient constitutions into contemporary times. Hegel took a racial turn. Chinese civilization was stuck at the lowest level of 'world-historical' development not only because of its geographical conditions but also because of the racial characteristics of its people.[66] European remapping of the geography of power was linked in this way to the emerging discourse of race wherein the image of China changed conspicuously from white to yellow.[67]

Lord Macartney, as discussed below, articulated a particular vision of Imperial Britain's position vis-à-vis Imperial China in this new geography of power after an enriching but traumatic personal experience of 'an encounter between two imperial formations each with universalistic pretensions and complex metaphysical systems to buttress their claims' during his embassy to China in 1792–4.[68] More than anything else, James Thomson's lyrics 'Rule, Britannia' published half a century earlier already encapsulated the dominant conception of the British empire in the eighteenth century as Protestant, commercial, maritime, and free.[69] Great Britain was constructing a burgeoning empire of free trade worldwide. In the words of Joseph Addison, '[t]rade, without enlarging the *British* territories, has given us a kind of Additional empire'.[70]

In this emergent geography of power, China as the civilizational Other occupied an entirely different place in the European conception of the world of the coming European domination. It was decidedly orientalized as a static, retarded, and despotic empire standing in the way of progressive commercial exchange of the emerging capitalist global economy. Lord Macartney, an exemplary representative of the British imperialist expansionist ambitions at the time, wrote at the end of his embassy to China in January 1794 that on closer inspection:

The Empire of China is an old, crazy, First rate man-of-war, which a fortunate succession of able and vigilant officers has contrived to keep afloat for these one

---

[63] Zarakol 2011: 38–9.   [64] Eisenstadt and Schluchter 1998: 7.
[65] Peyrefitte 1993: 489.   [66] Blue 1999: 91–2.   [67] Keevak 2011.
[68] Hevia 1995: 25.   [69] Armitage 2004: 94. See also Bell 2005.
[70] Quoted in Armitage 2004: 93.

hundred and fifty years past, and to overawe their neighbours merely by her bulk and appearance, but whenever an insufficient man happens to have the command upon deck, adieu to the discipline and safety of the ship.[71]

In contrast, 'Great Britain, from the weight of her riches and the genius and spirit of her people is become the first political, marine and commercial power on the globe'.[72]

Fantasizing the possibility of war between the British empire and the Chinese empire after his unsuccessful and frustrating attempt to open China for the British trade, he asked:

Can they [the Court of Pekin] be ignorant that a couple of British frigates would be an overmatch for the whole naval force of the empire, that in half a summer they could totally destroy all the navigation of their coasts and reduce the inhabitants of the maritime provinces, who subsist chiefly on fish, to absolute famine?[73]

He was self-assured that:

If indeed, the Chinese were provoked to interdict us their commerce, or do us any material injury, we certainly have the means easy enough of revenging ourselves, for a few frigates could in a few weeks destroy all their coastal navigation and intercourse from the island of Hainan to the Gulf of Pei-Chili.[74]

Such comments eerily resonate with the thought of Robinson Crusoe, the most famous fictional traveller in eighteenth-century Great Britain, when Daniel Defoe put the following into his mouth in 1719:

What is their [Chinese] trade to the universal commerce of England, Holland, France, and Spain? What are their cities to ours for wealth, strength, gaiety of apparel, rich furniture, and an infinite variety? What are their ports, supplied with a few junks and barks, to our navigation, our merchant fleets, and our large and powerful navies? Our city of London has more trade than all their mighty empire. One English, or Dutch, or French man-of-war of eighty guns would fight and destroy all the shipping of China.[75]

The Chinese empire was also vulnerable along its peripheries. Should a war break out between China and Great Britain, Lord Macartney contemplated that Great Britain

might probably be able from Bengal to excite the most serious disturbances on their Tibet frontier by means of their neighbours there, who appear to require only a little encouragement and assistance to begin. The Koreans, if they once saw ships in the Yellow Sea acting as enemies to China might be induced to attempt the recovery of their independence. The thread of connexion between this Empire

---

[71] Macartney 1962: 212.   [72] Macartney 1962: 213.
[73] Macartney 1962: 170.   [74] Macartney 1962: 210–11.
[75] Quoted in Zhang 1988: 122.

and Formosa is so slender that it must soon break of itself, but a breath of foreign interference would instantly snap it asunder.[76]

Great Britain was stopped from the use of military force in regard to China, Macartney reasoned, because of 'our present interest, our reason, and our humanity'. The break-up of China, which was not a very improbable event, 'would occasion a complete subversion of commerce, not only of Asia, but a very sensible change in other quarters of the world' and would make the Chinese market 'the cause of much rivalry and disorder'.[77] British India would 'suffer most severely' as Chinese trade was infinitely valuable as a market of cotton and opium.[78] Also important to Macartney's consideration was the imperialist rivalry from Russia. Should there be a war between Imperial Britain and Imperial China, he asked,

> Would Russia remain inactive? Would she neglect the opportunity of recovering Albazin and re-establishing her power upon the Amur? Would the ambition of the Great Catherine, that has stretched beyond Onalaska to the Eastward, over-look the provinces and partitions within grasp at her door?[79]

Through these comments, Lord Macartney etched Imperial China on the emerging imperialist geography of power unmistakably as an object of imperialist intervention and rivalry. They were prophetic words of the future power-political conflict between the two most powerful empires in the mid-nineteenth century, when the globalization of European sovereign order took a violent turn in East Asia. They also foretold of the Anglo-Russian rivalry in China in the late nineteenth century and more generally, the imperialist rivalry in China at the turn of the twentieth century.

CONCLUSION

By the end of the eighteenth century, China was fully incorporated into the cultural, intellectual, economic, imperialist, and colonial imagination of Europe. The early modern constructions of China in Europe, in David Porter's words,

> reveal a consistent predisposition to interpret and evaluate the emblems of Chinese culture on the basis of their conformity with a particular set of repre-sentational ideals. The persistence of these interpretive paradigms largely accounts for the seemingly paradoxical transmutations of the tropes underlying

---

[76] Macartney 1962: 211.   [77] Macartney 1962: 213.
[78] Macartney 1962: 212.   [79] Macartney 1962: 213.

early assertions of Chinese cultural legitimacy into catalysts of mounting scepticism and, finally, undisguised imperialist disdain.[80]

The appropriation of what 'China' was and meant proved integral in globalizing the European vision of the world. China fell progressively under the same 'civilizing' and rapacious gaze of Europe in the nineteenth century as many other non-European parts of the world, increasingly 'stigmatized as being inferior, backward, barbaric, effeminate, childish, despotic, and in need of enlightenment'.[81] The convergence of three discourses—Sinophobism, imperialism, and capitalist modernity—continued to reinforce each other in the nineteenth century to provide theoretical, political, and moral justifications for the use of force against China and to construct China as the very object of imperialist intervention and rivalry. The violent conflict between China and Europe in the mid-nineteenth century was but a logical consequence of these discourses. The ground was now discursively prepared for the global reach of sovereign order to China in the mid-nineteenth century, setting in motion what the classical English School story calls the expansion of European international society to East Asia.

In this chapter, I have chosen to traverse three spaces of Chinese–European encounter where China was pivotal to the intensive inter-civilizational and inter-continental exchanges. They demonstrate how China as an imperial entity, or the largest economy in the world, or a superior (inferior) civilization, was discursively involved in the construction of the collective identity of Europe in the early modern period. The discussion of ideas of and about China—in the theological controversies in the sixteenth and the seventeenth centuries as well as in the philosophical debates during the Enlightenment between the Sinophiles and the Sinophobes—is an attempt to trace the genealogies of Europe's historical knowledge about China. It intends to show how very influential the forged knowledge of China was in shaping modern social and political thought in Europe. It is equally importantly to show that the omnipresent fascination with China in Europe provoked enduring interpretive self-reflexivity, which produced a myriad of forms of European self-knowledge in the production of the rationalist subjectivity of Europe. Western civilization and European social formation did not stand above outside influence or interactions with other cultures. The story of the expansion of Europe to Asia cannot be told and treated in isolation from these global processes. Such interactive reading of inter-civilizational encounters prior to the nineteenth century points to the need to understand these rich and complex global processes through which international society became globalized which are largely missing in the existing English School account. The ultimate irony of this worlding China story in the early modern period is that

---

[80] Porter 2001: 241.   [81] Zarakol 2011: 54.

while China was not an organic participant in the modernization processes taking place in Europe, it featured prominently in Europe's increasingly globalized prospects as 'the most superlative objective of European expansionist fantasies'[82] and was ultimately integrated into Europe's global vision of imperialism. At the same time, China was completely and blissfully unaware of the shifting place that it was allocated in the European imagination of the world as the historical processes constituting early modernity unfolded. Nor did Europe become an integral part of the Chinese world materially, culturally, or intellectually, posing an existential dilemma to the Chinese world order and challenging the ontological security of the Chinese state until after the mid-nineteenth century, when the classical English School expansion story begins.

[82] Hevia 1995: 26.

Part IV

Institutional Contours

12

Universal Sovereignty

Barry Buzan

The story to be told in this chapter is about how sovereignty became a primary institution defining the global political order of international society. The understanding of sovereignty used here is the claim that a given collectivity of people have the right to self-government, and cannot be bound by outside rules or laws to which they have not given explicit consent. By itself, sovereignty does not specify how the relevant collectivity of people is to be legitimately determined, and various possibilities for this are in play: dynastic rights, ethno-nationalism, religion, territoriality, and popular sovereignty (civic nationalism). Since this book is about international society, the main view of sovereignty will be 'juridical' sovereignty (as given by international society through the act of recognition) as opposed to 'empirical' sovereignty (the assertion of the claim by a government on its own behalf).[1] The claim to sovereignty is about political autonomy, and therefore implies a right of non-intervention. This, however, is much more difficult to determine in practice than in principle, because quite what constitutes 'intervention' is both highly contestable and difficult to pin down. Is any interaction, such as for example trade or tourism, a form of intervention? Is intervention necessarily coercive or can it also result from consensual exchanges?

Although sovereignty developed in Europe between the fifteenth and eighteenth centuries, the main focus here is from the nineteenth century when it became universalized. Christian Reus-Smit identifies five waves of expansion of what was initially a European international society, each contingent on the disintegration of empires: 1648 (Holy Roman Empire), 1808–25 (Spanish Empire in the Americas), 1919 (Austro-Hungarian and Ottoman Empires), 1945 (beginning the general decolonization by Britain, France, the US, and other lesser imperial states), and 1991 (the Soviet Union).[2]

---

[1] Jackson 1990.   [2] Reus-Smit 2011.

The story of sovereignty becoming the main principle of governance within international society cannot be told by itself, but has to be accompanied, at a minimum, by the stories of two other primary institutions: territoriality and nationalism. Sovereignty of course also interacted strongly with other institutions such as diplomacy and international law, but these two are crucial to defining what universalized sovereignty means and how it has been practised.[3] Territoriality is the principle that political life should be organized on the basis of bounded spaces. It co-evolved with sovereignty and defined the packaging of it and the importance of borders. In principle, sovereignty as a mode of governance could function without territoriality,[4] but the choice made was to package sovereignty in a territorial way, and this combination defined what became the Westphalian state. Transfers of territory are now only legitimate by consent, and after the major round of decolonization following the end of the Second World War, the political map of the world has taken on an increasingly fixed character. The rise of nationalism as part of the revolutions of modernity during the nineteenth century profoundly redefined the foundations of sovereignty, replacing dynastic right with popular sovereignty. The modern sovereign state that became the template for global international society was not the Westphalian, absolutist one. It was the nineteenth-century nation-state that added the legitimizing, and delegitimizing, power of nationalism into the mix of sovereignty and territoriality, simultaneously both reinforcing and challenging them. The essence of the modern state is thus defined by sovereignty (defining the nature of the political claim), territoriality (defining the scope of the claim), and nationalism (defining the legitimacy of the claim). In principle this package could produce a coherent entity. In practice there are often tensions, for example where territoriality and nationalism do not line up in relation to the claim of sovereignty.[5]

---

[3] The methodology underlying this chapter is the English School's historical approach to analysing the rise, evolution, and sometimes decline, of primary institutions. See Buzan 2004, 2014a; Holsti 2004. *Primary institutions* are the deep, evolved, and quite durable practices that define rightful membership of, and conduct within, international society and are constitutive of both states and international society. They are distinct from *secondary institutions* that are purposefully designed and constructed by states and usually take organizational form. Translating this usage into that in Reus-Smit (1999) is not entirely straightforward. He quite clearly locates sovereignty as part of *constitutional structures*, and secondary institutions equate pretty clearly with his *issue-specific regimes*. But he does not discuss either nationalism or territoriality, which might count either as part of constitutional structures (as I would see it, although he does not include them there), or *fundamental institutions*, which is the category closest to most primary institutions.

[4] See Chapter 6.

[5] Bull and Watson 1984c is organized mainly in spatial, and up to a point cultural, terms, and contains no sustained discussion of sovereignty, or indeed territoriality or nationalism. There are passing mentions of all three, sovereignty and nationalism mainly in relation to the anti-colonial struggle, territoriality in relation to African traditions. The absence of a discussion about sovereignty is perhaps explained in Bull 1977 where he kicks it upstairs as a way of defining a type of international society. Bull therefore does not discuss sovereignty, or territoriality, as

Another element in this package is hierarchy.[6] Hierarchy is not an institution in its own right, but a consequence of other institutions, most notably dynasticism and great power rights. While sovereignty points towards legal and political equality, in practice, both the European and the global international societies have always blended the core principle of sovereign equality with significant elements of legitimate hierarchy.

The next section looks briefly at the early making and spread of modern sovereignty as background to what follows. I then track the universalization of sovereignty in two main phases: as divided sovereignty in a colonial international society from the nineteenth century up to 1945; and from 1945 with decolonization increasingly as universal sovereignty equality. The third section surveys the institutional and behavioural characteristics of this modern sovereignty package.

THE ORIGINS AND EARLY SPREAD OF SOVEREIGNTY: FIFTEENTH TO EIGHTEENTH CENTURIES

The story of how sovereignty and its associated society of states developed out of the medieval order is thoroughly told in the English School literature and elsewhere, and does not need repeating here.[7] Alongside sovereignty, territoriality and property rights emerged strongly during the transition from the many cross-cutting rights of the medieval order to the state-centric Westphalian one.[8] Together they constituted the anarchic Westphalian states-system, anarchy being the systemic consequence of sovereign, territorial states claiming the exclusive right of self-government for themselves.[9]

But until the fifteenth century, Europe was something of a backwater in Eurasian affairs, more a receiver than a transmitter of ideas in the great Eurasian networks. This began to change with the expansion of Europe from the late fifteenth century onwards, but only slowly and unevenly. Europeans had a relatively easy time taking over the Americas in the sixteenth and seventeenth centuries, because Eurasian diseases killed off most of the indigenous peoples. But Europeans did not become dominant in the Indian Ocean until the middle of the eighteenth century, and not in Africa or North East Asia until the middle of the nineteenth century. Other than in the

---

institutions of international society; see Buzan 2014a: 97–9. There was no coherent discussion of nationalism in the English School until Mayall 1990.

  [6] See Ian Clark's chapter in this volume.
  [7] Bull 1977: 27–40; Wight 1977: 110–73; Watson 1992: 138–262; Keohane 1995; Krasner 1999; Sørensen 1999; Jackson 2000: 156–67; Onuf 2002; Holsti 2004: 118–28.
  [8] Ruggie 1993b: 161–4; Watson 1992: 138–97.   [9] James 1999: 468.

Americas, Europe's contact with the rest of the world took place on a great variety of terms, including inferiority.[10] The result was the development from the sixteenth century of a kind of thin, multi-civilizational, global international society. Europeans had some advantage in sea power, but little or none in production or trade.

There was no smooth, steady European domination of the world from the late fifteenth century in which sovereignty expanded along with Europe's growing contact with the rest of the world. Only by the nineteenth century did Europe achieve massive advantages over the rest of the world in terms of power, trade, and knowledge. This uneven process meant that the early spread of sovereignty occurred in quite different forms in different places and at different times. In Europe itself, sovereignty evolved without any foreign imposition, but nonetheless in interplay with Europe's unfolding encounter with the rest of the world. In the Americas and later in Australia, and up to a point southern Africa, European settlers violently pushed aside indigenous populations and set up colonial states that eventually gained independence. These were largely peopled by Europeans and took a broadly European political form. Much of Africa, the Middle East, and South, Central, and South East Asia were later forcefully colonized by European powers, and had European political form imposed on them as a condition of their decolonization during the twentieth century. A handful of the more robust Eurasian powers (the Ottoman Empire, Japan, and China) managed to avoid colonization, but instead went through a process of coercive encounter with expanding European international society, and the pursuit of self-reform in order to meet the European 'standard of civilization' and avoid being taken over. In the late nineteenth century, Japan emerged from the process of encounter/reform, and the US from the process of repopulation/decolonization, to become modern, violent, colonizing powers themselves. As European power increased relative to the rest of the world, others thus had European political forms and practices imposed on them by the transplant of population, by colonization/decolonization, and/or by encounter/reform. But given that the sovereignty package was itself evolving throughout this period, what was imposed varied significantly according to when and where it was imposed.

The unevenness of this process poses problems for any attempt at a clear periodization of how sovereignty became universalized, but a rough differentiation into three phases is perhaps defensible. The first phase runs up to the nineteenth century and is defined by a dynastic form of sovereignty and relative European weakness almost everywhere except the Americas. In this phase, the evolving European practice of sovereignty and territoriality was transmitted to the Americas and Australia directly by settler colonies

---

[10] On Europeans in the Eurasian circuits, see Chapters 3 and 5. For detailed accounts of these early encounters between Europeans and the rest of the world, see Chapter 11; Suzuki et al. 2014.

forcefully displacing the indigenous inhabitants. It also made an impact on Russia, and more slowly the Ottoman Empire, through a process of encounter and reform. In relations with the rest of the world, however, Europeans did not attempt to impose their own practices, and broadly went along with the local dynastic customs, which while having many cultural variants, were not dissimilar to the dynastic structure still prevalent in Europe. The second phase runs from the nineteenth century up to 1945, and is defined by a massive increase in the relative strength of the core European/Western states in relation to the rest of the world; a shift from dynastic to popular sovereignty (that is, nationalism) in the core; and the imposition of divided sovereignty on to the periphery. The third phase runs from 1945 and is defined by the slow relative decline of Western power; the spread of popular sovereignty to the periphery; and the waning of divided sovereignty. These latter two encompass the main universalization process, and are the subject of the next section.

THE EVOLUTION AND UNIVERSALIZATION OF SOVEREIGNTY

From the nineteenth century, both the evolution and the universalization of sovereignty shifted into high gear, and this process divides into two broad phases, pre- and post-1945.

The Nineteenth Century to 1945

The key thing to understand about this phase is that it was driven by the multiple revolutions of modernity whose flowering between 1840 and 1905 transformed the world.[11] Perhaps the simplest way to capture the essence of this global transformation is that it put into place uneven and combined development of an unprecedented scale and intensity. Because the revolutions of modernity redefined so many core aspects of society, politics, technology, economy, law, and power, they massively and quickly increased the power of the few leading-edge states/societies that acquired them over those who did not. This made the world acutely uneven: in a few decades, a handful of states (Britain, the US, Germany, France, Japan, and up to a point Russia) redefined what 'development' meant and opened a massive power gap between themselves and everyone else. At the same time, this core of states was able to use the hugely increased capacity for transportation and communication opened

---

[11] For a full account, see Buzan and Lawson 2015b.

up by steamships, railways, and the telegraph to create a world in which development (and 'underdevelopment') were vastly more combined than ever before. These new technologies knitted the world together through ever more penetrative webs of trade, finance, migration, and military power projection. Economies became tightly interdependent on a much larger scale, and in much deeper ways, than ever before. For better or for worse, often both together, everything from food and energy to development and finance began to work globally, with local circuits being increasingly penetrated by and subordinated to global ones. The making of this highly uneven and combined world not surprisingly took imperial form. The small core that mastered the revolutions of modernity early used that advantage to impose themselves on a large periphery variously understood as 'traditional', 'backward', 'underdeveloped', 'uncivilized', or 'premodern'. The power gap was not just military, but economic, organizational, medical, and ideological. The terms on which world development became intensely combined were set by the way in which development had happened so unevenly.

The breadth and depth of the revolutions of modernity in the core, transformed the meaning and practice of sovereignty there in several profound ways. It was not the traditional package of dynastic territorial sovereignty that the newly empowered core projected on to the rest of the world, but a modern form—popular sovereignty—that replaced the political legitimacy of dynasticism with that of nationalism.

The distinctive modern package of sovereignty, territoriality, nationalism, and great power rights was not fully formed until the late nineteenth century. Holsti shows how borders became firmer and more precisely defined over time, both as a result of improved survey techniques, and because the administrative, political, and military needs of the emerging modern, rational, bureaucratic states demanded it.[12] The existing marriage of sovereignty and territoriality was consecrated and deeply intensified when the absolutist state became the nation-state. Nationalism sacralized territory by making it part of the heritage of the people in a way that was not present in the politics of dynastic territoriality.[13] By tightening the link between states, populations, and particular territories, nationalism raised the prominence of territoriality as the packaging of both sovereignty and nationalism. In relations between states, this generated new problems of identity, irredentism, and secessionism,[14] exemplified by the problem of Alsace-Lorraine between Germany and France from 1870 to 1945. Sovereign equality also built on the emergent institution of nationalism by linking the idea that people were equal and the sovereign equality of their states.[15] During the nineteenth century nationalism redefined the basis of legitimacy for sovereignty by shifting its foundations from

---

[12] Holsti 2004: 73–111.   [13] Mayall 2000: 84; Holsti 2004: 83–8.
[14] Mayall 1990: 57–63.   [15] Bain 2003: 173–92.

dynasticism, where the sovereign virtually was the state, to popular sovereignty where the state was in a sense owned by, and responsible to, its people. The people moved from being the subjects of a dynastic state to being the citizens of a national state.

While nationalism reinforced sovereignty and territoriality in some respects, it challenged them in others. In an ideal-type model, the package of sovereignty, territoriality, and nationalism could work smoothly if all nations were neatly contained within coherent territories. This, of course, is seldom the case in reality, meaning that sovereignty and nationalism can become competing principles for claims to territory. That was the case in German claims to the Sudetenland during the 1930s, Kosovar claims for independence from Serbia after the breakup of Yugoslavia in the 1990s, and to Russian claims to rights over ethnic Russians in its near-abroad generally, and specifically to the annexation of Crimea in 2014. The large disparity between the number of ethnic nations and the number of states generates major problems of secessionism and irredentism. The interpretation of nationalism in an ethnic way was instrumental in breaking up empires during the twentieth century. But while nationalism and popular sovereignty eventually undermined empires, for the bulk of this phase the enormous power gap, reinforced by attitudes of scientific racism,[16] meant that the polities in Europe remained as empires, most with an emergent nation-state as their core. While people in the core were becoming citizens, many of those in the periphery were becoming subjects of these newly empowered empires. The dramatic unevenness in power and development between core and periphery during this phase, meant that the initial universalization of sovereignty took place mainly as the forceful imposition of divided sovereignty in a colonial international society. This division of sovereignty took two forms. First was an explicitly imperial one in which core states had full sovereignty and periphery states did not, although there were many curious mixtures along the way such as the halfway house status of the white dominions within the British Empire.[17] Second was a more subtle form of hierarchy in which great powers had more rights and responsibilities than others, notwithstanding the general principle of sovereign equality.

Thus while popular sovereignty was taking root in the core states, divided sovereignty remained largely the rule in relations between core and periphery. The enormous increase in the power of the Western states (and a bit later Japan) over the rest of the world caused a rapid breakdown of the thin inter-civilizational international society that had developed for Africa and Eurasia. Rather than treating with the peoples and polities of Africa and Eurasia on pragmatic and relatively egalitarian terms, Western countries were now able to

---

[16] See Chapter 19.   [17] Darwin 2012.

dominate, and to occupy if they wanted, almost anywhere. From the middle of the nineteenth century onwards, China, Japan, and the Ottoman Empire were broken open, and most of Africa, and after the First World War the Middle East, were colonized. Where the Europeans did not control directly, their influence was overwhelmingly strong: 'informal' rather than formal empire. Many peoples and polities were drawn directly into the European sphere as colonies, and those that were not were subject to the 'standard of civilization', under which those in the periphery had to assimilate themselves to the institutions and practices of the core if they wanted to get recognition and avoid being colonized or subjected to unequal treaties.[18] The corrosive effect of nationalism on empire worked more quickly on the multinational continental empires in or close to Europe (especially Austria-Hungary and the Ottoman Empire, and up to a point Russia), which broke up after the First World War. Because of the enduring power gap, it took much longer to work its way through in the overseas empires, which mostly lasted until after the Second World War.

What developed during this phase was thus a Western-colonial international society on a global scale. Whether the process was repopulation (reinforced by the massive white migrations during the nineteenth century which repeopled three continents), colonization, or encounter/reform, pretty much the whole world was drawn into a Europe-centred international society and coercively subjected to its 'standard of civilization'. In this society, sovereignty was highly divided, with those in the core treating each other in terms of sovereign equality (modified by the 'legalized hegemony' of the great powers), with everyone else being arrayed along a spectrum of divided sovereignty from outright colonies through semi-autonomous protectorates and dominions, to those nominally independent, but subjected to unequal extraterritorial treaties. Divided sovereignty involved conditionality on such issues as law, property rights, human rights, and good governance. Colonized peoples were notionally under tutelage on such things. Non-colonized peoples such as in China, Japan, and the Ottoman Empire were not given full recognition until they could meet the standard. The terms of the 'standard of civilization', then as now, were a moving target, evolving in line with the leading-edge practices of modernity and projected out into the periphery.

A handful of non-Western countries made it into international society during this phase, most notably Japan, China, Turkey, Egypt, and up to a point India. In addition, the mandate system for handling the colonies of the defeated states after the First World War pointed towards independence as the eventual outcome for colonies. But the system of imperial-divided sovereignty nevertheless largely stayed in place until the breakdown of imperialism/

---

[18] Bowden 2009; Buzan 2014b: 576.

colonialism as an institution of international society after the Second World War. As William Bain argues, this was a system in which a 'superior' West decided on the readiness for self-government of less developed peoples: 'self-determination implied granting powers of self-government and autonomy in proportion to the capacity of a people to make good use of them'.[19] This phase thus generated a powerful core–periphery structure within which the West had the whip-hand over the rest, and could impose its own ever-evolving standards on them. Nationalism and popular sovereignty were not only transforming the states of the core, but also corroding the empires in the periphery. So it was not the 1648 absolutist sovereign state that Europe began to impose on the world during the nineteenth century, but the rational, national, modern state. Empires paradoxically remained strong because of the power gap, while also weakening fast because of the corrosive effects of nationalism, popular sovereignty, and the decline of dynasticism.

As noted earlier, sovereignty, and popular sovereignty in particular, contains a logic that points towards legal and political equality. In practice, however, the idea of sovereign equality has never prevailed in unqualified form. It has always been accompanied by an apparently contradictory element of legitimate hierarchy. What changed during the nineteenth century, and radically, was the basis on which the claim to hierarchic rights was made. Even after the emergence of sovereignty post-1648, the political order of international society was largely determined by dynastic principles that were essentially hierarchic. This was as true of European feudalism as it was of the ancient and classical civilizations of the Mediterranean, the Middle East, and Asia. An aristocratic hierarchy ran from emperors down through kings, princes, dukes, and barons, to knights and others at the bottom end of the status totem pole. Occasional republics such as Venice or the Netherlands were irritants, but could generally be incorporated in some way.

In a powerful argument building on the consolidation of territoriality and sovereignty, Reus-Smit makes the case that this dynastic form of hierarchy remained legitimate alongside the idea of sovereign equality introduced at Westphalia. In his view, the moral purpose of the state set up by Westphalia was fundamentally still premodern. It was intended to preserve the divinely ordained hierarchical social order of aristocratic dynasticism, while at the same time undercutting the political authority of the papacy. This generated the absolutist territorial state, dynastic diplomacy, reliance on natural law, and a status hierarchy of governments based on dynastic standing rather than sovereign equality. This system was sovereign, but not equal, because dynasticism interposed a hierarchy of aristocratic ranking on it. It predominated from 1648 to 1815, and was thereafter undermined as the revolutions of

---

[19] Bain 2003: 92.

modernity during the nineteenth century steadily unpicked the legitimacy of dynasticism.[20]

From 1815 onwards, a new form of legitimized hierarchy based on the claim of great power status came into play alongside sovereign equality. The idea that great powers have special rights and responsibilities is in a sense implicit in all of the big war-settling congresses from 1648 onwards, and Hedley Bull provides a statement of its mechanics.[21] Like the balance of power, the logic and legitimacy of great power interests grew as the dynastic principle weakened. Holsti argues that this practice becomes much more evident and formalized from the Treaty of Vienna (1815) and the Congress of Europe.[22] Gerry Simpson argues that after 1815 a quite strong form of 'legalized hegemony' developed, in which great powers saw themselves as having, and were recognized by others to have, managerial responsibility for international order.[23] That practice continued through the League of Nations after 1919 and the United Nations Security Council after 1945, both of which embodied a hybrid structure with sovereign equality recognized in a general assembly of all members, and the legalized hegemony of the great powers in a smaller council.

Thus while the decline of dynasticism facilitated the move towards a norm of sovereign equality that picked up speed during the nineteenth century, it did so alongside an institutional privileging of great powers, a hierarchy that was both *de facto* and *de jure*. Despite these developments, throughout the nineteenth century sovereign equality was available only to a minority. Until the middle of the twentieth century a Western-colonial international society prevailed in which sovereignty and sovereign equality were the privilege of the mainly Western states of the core. Under colonialism, the sovereignty of much of the periphery was folded into that of a handful of metropolitan powers.

To sum up, the sovereignty that Europe imposed on the rest of the planet during the nineteenth century was quite different from the form that emerged during the seventeenth century. While its core principle of a claim to an absolute right of self-government remained intact, it was modified by three distinctive characteristics. First, it was popular sovereignty, not dynastic. Nationalism transformed the legitimacy basis of sovereignty by transferring it from the ruler to the people. Second, again under the influence of nationalism, sovereignty was deeply infused and combined with territoriality. The ideal-type modern state was a nation-state in a tightly defined territorial package, and the poor fit of this model with the global reality has destabilized the institutional package. Third, and yet again under the influence of nationalism, the principle of sovereignty was deeply committed to the legal and political equality of sovereign states, but at the same time also acknowledged as

[20] Reus-Smit 1999: 87ff.   [21] Bull 1977: 200–29.
[22] Holsti 1991: 114–37; see also Wight 1977: 42, 136–41.
[23] Simpson 2004. See also Watson 1992: 138–262.

legitimate the 'legalized hegemony' of the great powers. What we have, then, is an evolutionary story about sovereignty that has its roots in the fifteenth century but does not develop into its modern form until late in the nineteenth century. During the nineteenth century, an expanding Europe was increasingly imposing on to the rest of the world its own evolving institutions and practices of sovereignty as the defining universal principle for international society.

1945 Onwards

Universal sovereign equality only kicked in after 1945, when the institution of imperialism/colonialism waned and large-scale decolonization began. The Second World War, with its catalogue of barbaric behaviour by Westerners to each other, delegitimized the 'standard of civilization'. It opened the way to a second phase of the universalization of sovereignty beginning with mass decolonization on the basis of a transcendental right of self-determination that trumped all arguments about unreadiness for self-government in the modern world.[24] As the remaining empires unravelled between the 1940s and the 1970s, divided sovereignty faded, and sovereign equality became more or less universal. As Alan James argued, sovereign equality had 'taken on a new vitality'.[25] This universalized sovereign equality was embedded in the United Nations system, where it continued to be accompanied by the significant derogation of 'legalized hegemony' to the great powers institutionalized in both the League of Nations and the UN. The process of decolonization thus completed the universalization of sovereignty that began with the independence revolutions of the settler states in the Americas in the late eighteenth and early nineteenth centuries, and continued with the encounter/reform process by which those not colonized sought sovereign recognition and membership of international society by meeting the 'standard of civilization'. Post-Second World War decolonization can thus be seen as the mechanism by which the modern package of sovereignty was imposed on those parts of the world (mainly Africa, the Middle East, and South and South East Asia) that had not already been drawn into the European political process in earlier phases by repopulation and encounter/reform. What seems like the last round of decolonization occurred after the end of the Cold War when the breakup of the Soviet Union and Yugoslavia produced new sets of independent sovereign states.

It is beyond the scope of this chapter to explain the causes of this universalizing process in detail, but it is worth making two observations. First is that

---

[24] Bain 2003: 134–5.   [25] James 1992: 391.

the distribution of power is a significant factor in the universalizing of sovereignty. And this is not just about the distribution of power, but also about the mode of power. The initial European success in taking over the Americas was facilitated by the large power gap between late agrarian European civilization and the indigenous civilizations in the Americas, which while sophisticated in some ways, were without iron-age technology. Rough technological and biological parity with the civilizations of Asia—in Jared Diamond's pithy phrase 'guns, germs, and steel'[26]—explains the inability of the Europeans to impose ideas on those civilizations during their long encounter from the sixteenth to the eighteenth centuries. During the nineteenth century, the revolutions of modernity opened up a mode of power difference between industrializing Europeans and the remaining late agrarian classical civilizations in Asia. This created such a huge imbalance in the distribution of power as to enable the Europeans to subordinate and impose upon all comers, forcing them into the European political and economic sphere. It is interesting that while this power gap goes a long way to explain the massive expansion of European empires in Africa and Asia during the nineteenth century, it does not fully explain why the Europeans let go of their empires as quickly as they did. Even as late as 1945, much of the periphery was still unable to harness the revolutions of modernity to more than a modest extent. Violent resistance to colonialism certainly raised the economic and moral cost of colonialism to the metropolitan powers, but even after 1945 the power gap between core and periphery remained big. Yet the Western powers gave up their empires and opened the doors of international society on the basis of sovereign equality for all.

To understand why the West let the processes of encounter/reform and decolonization give sovereign status and full membership in international society to the periphery as early as it did, one needs also to take into account the evolving ideational landscape within the core. Throughout the nineteenth and twentieth centuries, there was a long working out within the core of the ideological features of the revolutions of modernity, particularly the four ideologies of progress: liberalism, nationalism, socialism, and 'scientific' racism. The interplay of these ideologies within the core generated ideational outcomes, most notably popular sovereignty, nationalism, and liberal (and socialist) ideas about human rights, that steadily undermined the legitimacy of empire and 'scientific' racism. This worked simultaneously in both core and periphery. In the core, the consolidation of ideas about national self-determination and human rights made metropolitan citizens feel increasingly uneasy about the inequalities and oppressions of empire. In the periphery, political elites were increasingly able to mobilize the ideologies of modernity, particularly the right to national self-determination and popular sovereignty, to legitimize their claims for equal rights and

---

[26] Diamond 1997.

independence. The transfer of sovereign equality to former subjects of empire was thus a mutual process: partly given by the metropolitan cores; partly demanded, and in part taken, by the elites and peoples of the periphery. The universalization of sovereignty was thus in one sense imposed by the core as a condition of independence. But it was also embraced by the periphery as a means of regaining equal status, both racially and politically. In the middle of the twentieth century, the Western-colonial international society of the nineteenth and twentieth centuries gave way to a Western-global international society in which sovereign equality was universalized, while a mainly economic core–periphery structure favouring the West remained in place. Interestingly, while the 'legalized hegemony' of the great powers still favoured the West, the great power principle trumped an exclusively Western interest: both the Soviet Union and China were members of the privileged great power club in the United Nations Security Council.

While this general sketch of the evolution and universalization of sovereignty since 1945 is broadly accurate, the story is not quite so simple and straightforward. There are two twists in the tale to be noted: a slow but increasingly widespread closure of the power gap; and a subtle but definite re-emergence of practices similar to the 'standard of civilization'.

The closing power gap means that the Western-global international society is becoming more of a de-centred global one.[27] Fareed Zakaria labels this 'the rise of the rest', a process startlingly begun by Japan as early as the late nineteenth century, paused until the rise of the Asian Tigers in the 1970s and 1980s, and by the first decade of the twenty-first century becoming more generalized with the rise of China, India, Brazil, Turkey, and others.[28] The power gap opened up by the revolutions of modernity during the nineteenth century, and elevating the West to the position of global core, is now beginning to close as more and more peoples and societies find ways of coming to terms with modernity and acquiring its mode of power. In most places this seems to have the effect of consolidating and embedding the modern package of sovereignty, territoriality, and nationalism. As the rise of the rest progresses, it should also make the club of great powers less Western and more globally representative. On this basis it might be argued that the modern package of popular sovereignty (including both equality and hierarchy), territoriality, and nationalism, rather like football, has become quite deeply internalized among most states and peoples.

Yet at the same time, significant shadows of the old West-centric core–periphery structure remain, and since the end of the Cold War a re-emergence of a new *de facto* 'standard of civilization' has become obvious. While the Cold War was in process it overrode other political considerations.

---

[27] Buzan 2011.   [28] Zakaria 2009.

It also worked alongside the fading of initial post-1945 hopes that the periphery would quite quickly acquire 'development', also known as the basic political, economic, and social elements of modernity. In many countries development proved to be slower and more difficult than anticipated, in some ways justifying the now politically unacceptable thinking of the first half of the twentieth century about degrees of readiness/capacity for self-government under the increasingly relentless and penetrating conditions of the modern international system/society. Some postcolonial states 'failed' (for example, Somalia, Haiti, Zaire, and Afghanistan), while many others remained weak as states (for example, Pakistan, Nigeria, Ivory Coast, Sri Lanka, and Burma/Myanmar). Sovereign equality remained universal in a juridical sense in that even failed states were still recognized by international society and kept their seats in the United Nations General Assembly. But empirical sovereignty in the sense of actually being able to exercise self-government either at all, or to a decent international standard, was much more problematic. When the end of the Cold War took superpower competition out of the Third World, these issues not only acquired greater political prominence, but also exposed the operation of a new, still largely Western-driven, 'standard of civilization', albeit now using the more polite language of 'conditionality' and 'good governance'.[29]

The substance of the 'standard of civilization' thus very much remains as a practical qualification to the legal status of sovereign equality. Since all are now inside international society generally, the 'standard of civilization' game is played mainly between inner (still mainly Western) and outer circles, about who is allowed to join which clubs or organizations. As the struggles of Balkan states to join the European Union show, this game is not just between West and non-West. International society has become both more layered and more regionally differentiated, at the same time as becoming universal in terms of sovereign equality. It still contains status hierarchies mainly defined in terms of Western standards of modernity, and as in the colonial era, these standards continue to change as the frontiers of modernity—technological, behavioural, and moral—evolve. Like the classical 'standard of civilization', the new one works to differentiate the more 'civilized' from the less, and on that basis to gatekeep on access to the private goods of international society's inner circles.

The contemporary practices of conditionality and discrimination that constitute the new 'standard of civilization' can be seen in various issues. Several English School writers have noted that the 'standard of civilization' has morphed into the more polite terminology of human rights and conditionality.[30] The reason why human rights has become a new 'standard of civilization' is that

---

[29] For a detailed account of this new standard, see Buzan 2014b: 576; Stivachtis 2008: 72; Fidler 2000; Zarakol 2011: 38–56.

[30] See Chapters 16 and 17. Also Gong 1984b: 90–3, 2002; Donnelly 1998; Jackson 2000: 287–93; Keene 2002: 122–3, 147–8; Stivachtis 2008: 71; Bowden 2009.

it can easily be used as a criterion not only for conditionality regarding membership, but also for suspending the right of non-intervention that states enjoy as a corollary of sovereignty. Such usage circumvents the decolonization deal of sovereign equality for all, by declaring some states, or at least their governments (either or both), of not being fit for membership, or not fit for recognition and the right of non-intervention. Like human rights, and quite closely associated with it, democracy has also achieved some legitimacy within international society, and this is reflected in the practices and policies of a lot of intergovernmental organizations (IGOs).[31] James Mayall argues that even though democracy is far from universal, democratic values such as human rights, representative government, and the rule of law have become influential, perhaps even the standard of legitimacy, in international society.[32] Among its promoters there is consequently a tendency to revive 'standard of civilization' thinking by equating democracy with 'civilization' and non-democracy with 'barbarity'.[33]

Other criteria also back a new 'standard of civilization'. Capitalism is one, with the hegemony of the Washington consensus, and the somewhat imperious manner in which it was promoted up to 2008, easily seen in these terms.[34] Whether or not environmental stewardship will become a new 'standard of civilization' criterion is as yet unclear, although the potential is obviously there, and the topic has begun to attract some English School writing.[35] There is still disagreement about whether or not the problem exists, although this could change in the face of a suitably grave and obvious crisis such as sea-level rise. Under those conditions it is not difficult to imagine a new 'standard of civilization' discourse emerging in which those who were taking serious measures to address the problem would begin to see those who were still contributing to it as 'barbarians'. Somewhat differently positioned, but nonetheless part of the contemporary 'standard of civilization', is the issue of development. The colonial 'standard of civilization' left as its legacy to the postcolonial world the discourse of aid and development.[36] The colonial obligation of the metropolitan powers to bring their subjects up to a European 'standard of civilization' morphed into an obligation on the part of the rich world to assist in the development of the 'Third World' or 'less developed countries'.[37] Bain sees a substantial ghost of trusteeship haunting contemporary international society in its attempts to deal with failed and failing states, and in its deployment of conditionality, human rights, and good governance as entry criteria into various international clubs.[38]

---

[31] Stivachtis 2006: 102; Clark 2009a: 563–9.   [32] Mayall 2000: 64–8, 86.
[33] Stivachtis 2006:111.
[34] Fidler 2000; Gong 2002: 77; Bowden and Seabrooke 2006; Bowden 2009.
[35] Bull 1977: 293–5; Reus-Smit 1996: 96; Jackson 2000: 170–8; Hurrell 2007: 216–36; Linklater 2011; Falkner 2012: 503.
[36] Holsti 2004: 250; Bowden 2009.   [37] Bain 2003: 1–26.   [38] Bain 2003: 155–63.

Thus, while on the one hand the closing power gap is reinforcing the universalization of sovereign equality, on the other the new 'standard of civilization' is restricting and qualifying its practice. As Ian Clark warns, setting standards along these lines tends to narrow the range of rightful membership by stiffening the criteria for entry, whether to various clubs or to international society as a whole.[39] That was the point of the classical 'standard of civilization' and remains the point of contemporary proposals ranging from conditionality to a 'League of Democracies'.[40] So while the phrase 'standard of civilization' fell out of fashion after 1945, much of the practice in terms of both status hierarchies based on Western criteria of development and modernity, and membership gatekeeping largely by Western states, carries on.

THE INSTITUTIONAL CHARACTERISTICS OF THE CURRENT UNIVERSAL SOVEREIGN ORDER

The account in this chapter has sketched out when, why, and how sovereignty became effectively universalized as the political framing for a global-scale international society. It remains in this section to highlight some of the main institutional consequences of this development. As I have shown, the spread of sovereignty was uneven not only in space and time, but also in the form and meaning that sovereignty took. Sovereignty was itself evolving as it spread, although eventually a relatively uniform modern package of sovereignty, territoriality, and nationalism has become the global norm. But while this package is conceptually uniform, in practice it remains uneven. The 'legalized hegemony' exception for great powers remains in play, as does the operation of a new 'standard of civilization'. These derogations do not make sovereign equality meaningless, hypocritical, or inconsequential. But they do mean that the practical political operation of universal sovereign equality is quite far from pure, and significantly mediated by hierarchical factors. What we have, therefore, is a very particular kind of universal sovereign order, highly modified by its linkage to territoriality, nationalism, and hierarchy, that has evolved quite radically over the past five centuries. In its current package, universal sovereignty does not generate a clear, logically derived set of institutional consequences.

In this section I look at three aspects of how the contemporary package of sovereignty shapes political behaviour, through its implications for membership

---

[39] Clark 2005: 26–8.   [40] Clark 2005: 109–29, 173–89.

of international society; its interplay with other primary institutions; and its impact on secondary institutions.

Implications for Membership

Recognition of sovereign equality by other states is the key to membership in international society. As sovereignty evolved, it changed the norms and principles by which states accorded each other recognition.[41] As Gerrit W. Gong argues, this recognition has embodied widening conceptions of identity defining who was, and who was not welcome as a member of international society.[42] Up to the nineteenth century, sovereignty was a European practice linked to the narrow civilizational identity of 'Christendom'. With the expansion of international society in the late eighteenth and early nineteenth centuries to bring in the Americas and other European offshoots during the decolonization of settler states in the Americas, this identity widened to 'European culture'. During the later nineteenth century, when non-Western powers such as Japan and the Ottoman Empire began to qualify for entry, it widened again to the 'standard of civilization', which at least in principle opened a path to universal membership. In practice, all of these identities were exclusionary, creating an inside/outside structure. But after 1945, when decolonization became general, and sovereign recognition more or less universal, this exclusionary practice collapsed. Sovereignty became a universal right of peoples, albeit with ongoing contestation about how to determine which 'people' qualified for this right.

While the principle of universal sovereignty, and therefore membership, remains a key foundation of contemporary international society, in practice there has been pressure on it from two distinct, but often closely connected, directions. First, as argued earlier, has been the emergence of a new 'standard of civilization' based on mainly West-centric criteria such as human rights, democracy, and capitalism. These criteria, most strongly human rights, have driven a logic that makes recognition of sovereignty, and especially the right to non-intervention, conditional on meeting specified standards of behaviour.[43] Second has been the emergence of so-called 'weak' or 'failed' states that seem unable in practice to sustain stable or effective self-government under the highly penetrative conditions of a globalized political economy. As argued earlier, the criteria of 'degree of readiness for self-government' was fully recognized within the discourse of colonial administration up to 1945, with colonized societies being ranged along a spectrum from nearly ready in cases

---

[41] Fabry 2010.
[42] Gong 1984b: 4–6; see also Watson 1984b; Clark 2005: 35–50, 48.
[43] See Chapters 16 and 17.

like Egypt and India, to a very long way off for some small tribal societies. These classifications were not without a substantial tinge of both racism and metropolitan self-interest, but neither were they wholly wrong. Societies were very differently placed in terms of their capacity for self-government under modern conditions, often within dysfunctional colonial boundaries. Either way, this criterion was largely overridden in the rush to decolonization after 1945. It was simply assumed that a transitional period of aid by the more developed countries to the less developed ones would somehow bring everyone up to speed. In some places this did not work, leaving international society with embarrassing holes in its fabric where juridical sovereignty is recognized, but empirical sovereignty is lacking: what Robert H. Jackson labelled 'quasi-states'.[44] Such states in varying degrees become wards of international society, requiring heavy penetration by foreign governments, non-state actors, and IGOs to sustain the basic functions of government. Given the force of universal sovereignty as a principle, such derogations in the practice of self-government have to be constructed as temporary and transitional even though they may in fact be quite long term. There is thus a tension between the *de jure* principle of universal sovereignty, for which the only criteria is being a nation of some sort, and the practice of it, where judgements about either the 'standard of civilization' or the capacity for self-government equate to a *de facto* diminution of sovereign rights, and a kind of second-class membership.

Interplay with Other Primary Institutions

I have argued that the contemporary practice of universal sovereignty cannot be understood apart from its interplay with territoriality and nationalism. It is this package that not only gives universal sovereignty the particular form that it takes, but also shapes some of the other primary institutions of international society. For example, the rise of the modern form of sovereignty helped to drive parallel changes in the institutions of diplomacy and international law. As modern, rational states consolidated themselves around popular sovereignty, they moved at the same time away from dynastic diplomacy towards professionalized multilateral diplomacy, and away from natural law towards positive international law.[45] Both of these in turn connected strongly to the rise of secondary institutions, on which more below.

After 1945 the collapse of colonialism and racism (human inequality) as institutions of international society, and their replacement by universalized sovereign and human equality, also played a major role in the decline of war, another key institution of international society. Decolonization delegitimized

---

[44] Jackson 1990.   [45] See Chapter 14.

territorial transfers by conquest. At the same time, the incentives for such transfers were being eroded by the rise of the market as an institution of international society, which can be understood as a struggle about territoriality. Economic nationalists have wanted to impose territoriality on to the economic sector, while economic liberals have wanted to open borders to flows of goods, ideas, capital, and up to a point labour (that is, people). The rise of the global market has in many ways, and in most places, shot territorial borders full of large and permanent holes. Here the link to sovereignty is that much of this opening up of borders has been done by the sovereign consent of the states concerned. The rise of the market as a primary institution has thus radically changed the practice of territoriality, or from another perspective, compromised its core principle in relation to the economic sector. The contemporary form of this debate is about globalization, and whether the deterritorializing tendencies of the global economy are challenging the state as the core political player in international society. The rise of the market has certainly changed the practice of territoriality in significant ways, but it has neither displaced the close link between sovereignty and territoriality as the basic framing for world politics, nor weakened the emotional link between people and territory constructed by nationalism.

One other primary institution closely linked to sovereignty is great power management. Right from the beginning, sovereign equality has been mediated by significant elements of hierarchy, initially in the form of dynastic rankings, but increasingly from the eighteenth century in the form of the 'legalized hegemony' of the great powers.[46] This legalized hegemony both defined the special roles and privileges of the great powers in international society, and created a standing tension with the principle that sovereignty should be equal, and that it should carry a right of non-intervention. The existence of a privileged club of great powers created a standing incentive for rising powers to claim right of admission. This was Japan's obsession from the 1870s until it achieved such recognition in 1903, and also China's, which it achieved in 1943. It is now the obsession of India, Brazil, and Indonesia, and in the opposite form of trying not to be ejected from the club, of Britain, France, Germany, Japan, and Russia.

Impact on Secondary Institutions

The main impact of universal sovereignty on secondary institutions, mainly IGOs and regimes, also comes from the interplay between sovereign equality on the one hand, and the 'legalized hegemony' of the great powers on the

---

[46] See Chapter 13.

other. Although both modern popular sovereignty and secondary institutions arose around the same time during the late nineteenth century, it is difficult to argue that modern sovereignty somehow generated the formation of secondary institutions. Correlation, in this case, is not causation. The roots of secondary institutions seem instead to have fed on the vast increases in physical interaction capacity discussed earlier, plus the move towards rational states and the global expansion of the market, all of which together created demands for increased coordination and standardization.[47] These demands, along with the shift to positive international law, resulted in the emergence of IGOs as permanent features of inter-state society. The link between physical and social interaction capacity is made clear by the functions of most early IGOs: the International Telecommunications Union (1865), the Universal Postal Union (1874), the International Bureau of Weights and Measures (1875), and the International Conference for Promoting Technical Unification on the Railways (1882), as well as various river management commissions. From the 1860s onwards, IGOs multiplied rapidly. By 1913, there were forty-five, a modest start, but establishing the foundations for the more ambitious developments that followed the First World War. But while modern sovereignty did not cause IGOs, it did shape their form, especially the two-chamber structure in which some form of general assembly acknowledges the principle of universal sovereign equality, while some form of council acknowledges the 'legalized hegemony' of the great powers and their responsibilities for the management of international society.

CONCLUSIONS

Universal sovereignty, and particularly sovereign equality, is a relatively recent arrival as the main framing for international society. Older forms of it were radically different from what we have now, and there is little reason to think that this dynamism is at an end. The current package of universal sovereign equality, territoriality, and nationalism might well be quite durable in a general sense. But it is under pressure not only from contestations about the new 'standard of civilization', and from failed states, but also from the enduring tension with the hierarchical privileges of the great powers. Those privileges have proved durable for several centuries, and for most of that time they privileged Western powers in relation to the rest. Japan was for a century the only exception to Western dominance of the great power club, and in many ways did its best to become part of the West. But with 'the rise of the rest',

---

[47] Hobsbawm 1975: 82–7.

including China, India, and others, the great power club will have to become less Western. How these processes play out will be among the drivers of how the meaning of universal sovereignty, and the practices associated with it, will evolve.

The complexity of this story, and the quite dramatic evolutions that it contains, might suggest that the concept of sovereignty is incoherent and that the story should be broken up into distinct components rather than told in terms of changes along a central axis. I would resist that view, and like Holsti see it as a single story.[48] It seems to me that the essence of sovereignty remains intact throughout in two important ways. First, the definition with which I opened this chapter (that a given collectivity of people have the right to self-government, and cannot be bound by outside rules or laws to which they have not given explicit consent) can be applied to the whole story. And second, so too can the link with territoriality, which remains an essential constant for how sovereignty is packaged. These two powerful continuities make the case for thinking of this as a single evolutionary story.

---

[48] Holsti 2004: 112–42.

13

Hierarchy, Hegemony, and the Norms of International Society

Ian Clark

By common consent, it was at the height of post-1945 decolonization that international society took its greatest strides towards universality of membership. This chapter explores two interconnected features of that transition, identified by Hedley Bull in these paradoxical terms: 'The idea of the special rights and duties of great powers, moreover, embodies a principle of hierarchy that is at loggerheads with the principle of the equal sovereignty of states.'[1] Accordingly, the first issue concerns how the ostensibly more diverse international society of this period managed to integrate those practices of hierarchy that had formerly been such a prominent feature of the pre-existing European society of states. The second addresses the puzzle of how it reconciled this set of practices with the simultaneously more explicit reaffirmation of the principle of sovereign equality that accompanied the dismantling of empires. The core suggestion will be that the answer to the first question sheds considerable light on the second: global international society did not simply inherit a preformed normative infrastructure in support of hierarchy, but rather did so along with a degree of renegotiation of the very concept of 'responsibility' that had been its necessary underpinning. In this way, the chapter illustrates this volume's general theme of the dynamic, normative development at the heart of international society's globalization.

What follows explores three instances of hierarchy and hegemony in the evolving international society of the second half of the twentieth century, drawn in turn from the onset, middle, and end of the Cold War. Of the many hierarchies that potentially might be considered, the focus here will be explicitly upon those relating to great power management. The first considers its universal and formal constitutional instantiation in the United Nations

---

[1] Bull 1980: 438.

(UN) Security Council in 1944–5. The second looks at the informal conventions of great power or superpower management, such as arose during the Cold War around nuclear testing and proliferation, arms control, and conduct in crises. Finally, it reviews the apparent potential for some US-centred hegemony in the Cold War's aftermath, as demonstrated in the 'return to the Security Council', and the debates of the period about that institution's reform.

The concept through which the principle of hierarchy has been legitimated in international society has recurrently been that of 'responsibility': this has been mostly presented as the counterpart of special rights, and hence it is those gradations in responsibility, and the reasons for its relative assignment, that provide such normative support as exists for hierarchy.[2] The problem we face here is whether we can trace a single lineage directly from European principles and practices of the nineteenth century, through to the globalized international society of the second half of the twentieth century, or whether any such procedure elides the very issue of central interest to this chapter. If—as will indeed be shown—there were to be principles and practices of hierarchy aplenty in post-1945 international society, how dynamic was the very notion of responsibility upon which these rested?

Formal consent to the principle of hierarchy embedded in the UN Charter had been given already, albeit not without considerable resistance, during the negotiations of 1944–5. This, of course, preceded the profound changes in membership that were then to take place across the ensuing two decades. Accordingly, it will be shown that while formally hierarchy was adopted at this point, the focus of resistance thereafter shifted instead to those informal practices of great power management pursued outside, given the Cold War stalemate in the Security Council. Since the Security Council's prescribed role in management of collective security became mostly inoperative, the real nub of resistance transferred to the day-to-day obstacles to autonomy encountered elsewhere by a range of regional actors.

The core of these conventions was the prescriptive capacity of the superpowers to manage the newly liberated Third World, and hence the attempt to impose a continuation of hierarchy by other means. If the two superpowers had been hitherto the most vocal ideological champions of decolonization in principle, they now presented also the most tangible obstacle to its full attainment in practice. It was the negotiation of this particular hierarchy that represented the most interesting facet of the Cold War period, and the greatest threat to the normative unity of the international society project at that time. Moreover, it is in the contrast between the types of argument advanced in 1944–5 with regard to formal hierarchy, as against those deployed

---

[2] Bukovansky et al. 2012.

in the 1960s and 1970s in the context of informal hierarchy, and then again in the 1990s with regard to any informal hegemony, that we can see how the notion of responsibility had itself become the subject of profound renegotiation. The three episodes, for this reason, offer highly revealing snapshots of the normative changes that were underway.

THE EXPANSION OF INTERNATIONAL SOCIETY THESIS AND THE EQUALITY/ HIERARCHY PUZZLE

The place to begin is with that assessment of the newly expanded international society of the 1970s provided in the original Bull and Watson volume.[3] What does it convey of this period, written as it was in the Cold War's very midst, but dominated also by the recent phase of decolonization? On one reading, its pervasive themes come across as those of disorder, diversity, disunity, and cultural plurality. Nonetheless, some dissenting voices were already present, most notably in the contribution by Ronald Dore.[4] He thought that the prospects for diffusion of a common culture remained tolerably bright, especially if simultaneously accompanied by a weakening of the previous concentration of world power in the Western world.[5] Moreover, the editors too were finally to distance themselves from any overarching pessimism, when they insisted that it was wrong to think 'international society of the present time is in a state of disintegration'.[6] The reason for their demurral was above all that the norms of international society had come to be 'embraced by the non-European majority of states and peoples'.[7] So while there was evidently some degree of 'pulling apart', international society still remained central to the order-transition then underway. However, what is less clear is whether the norms embraced by the 'non-European majority' were simply the same as those accepted hitherto.

The following discussion is predicated on some initial assumptions, especially about the importance of legitimacy to arrangements of hierarchy, and with respect to hegemony as one particular instance of it. There has been a widespread revival of interest in the notion of hierarchy in International Relations.[8] As against the hitherto prevailing theoretical objection that hierarchy and anarchy are mutually exclusive (since absence of hierarchy is a *defining* quality of international life), the dominant analytical tendency is now to accept that 'hierarchy... in anarchy is not only theoretically possible but

---

[3] Bull and Watson 1984c.   [4] Dore 1984.   [5] Dore 1984: 423.
[6] Bull and Watson 1984a: 433.   [7] Bull and Watson 1984a: 435.
[8] Clark 2011b; Dunne 2003: 303; Lake 2007: 47; Hobson and Sharman 2005: 63.

is... historically common'.[9] Moreover, this display of hierarchy has not been an exclusively European tendency: Barry Buzan and Richard Little had identified it as a recurrent feature of the past 5,000 years.[10] What this literature now confirms, however, is that hierarchy can be fully grounded in societal legitimacy: it is not to be understood simply as a display of coercive power.[11]

Any such suggestions become even more puzzling, however, given the palpable heightening of tension between sovereign equality and hierarchy at that symbolic post-1945 moment. After all, decolonization lent renewed rhetorical prominence to a foundational myth of equality.[12] How then, if the new states so wholeheartedly embraced the 'sovereign state',[13] were they convinced to accept also those very hierarchical arrangements that threatened to render hollow the victory so recently won? The argument here is that, while hierarchy remained a constant presence, it was informed by a fluid notion of 'responsibility'.

Inis L. Claude recounts the received wisdom succinctly when he observed that 'the idea of international responsibility is generally associated, primarily if not exclusively, with great powers... [we] base our thinking about international relations on the expectation and the demand that great powers will carry responsibilities appropriate to their status'.[14] Even so, there remains a need to probe more closely into the precise nature of this responsibility, and the manner of its association with great power.[15] Historically, it will be shown how one such concept of responsibility, enshrined in the formal UN Charter provisions, came into conflict with alternative readings of responsibility, and was subsequently to be contested in informal principles about superpower management, particularly of regional disputes. Finally, it was the inability of the United States to satisfy this changed criterion of responsibility that thwarted any project for development of an effective post-1990 hegemony.

CONTESTING AND LEGITIMIZING HIERARCHY IN 1945

As a first case, we can explore the universal practices that were adopted formally with reference to the Security Council in the UN Charter. This provides the clearest evidence of the acceptance of hierarchy, even if far from uncontested at the time. The reasoning can be traced, for example, in the arguments about the adoption of the veto power for the permanent

---

[9] Donnelly 2006: 141.   [10] Buzan and Little 2000: 7.
[11] Cronin and Hurd 2008: 25.   [12] Buzan 2010: 5.   [13] Mayall 1990: 111.
[14] Claude 1986: 724.   [15] Clark 2014: 315.

members.[16] This is particularly revealing for what it tells us about the notion of responsibility.

Not only was the Security Council given a unique role in matters of international security, but also there was further differentiation in status with respect to the permanent and non-permanent members. This required a conscious compromise between the 'embedded hierarchy of the Great Powers', and the 'sovereign equality of states'.[17] As is well known, such a legitimated hierarchy was not readily acceded to on all fronts during the negotiations of 1944–5: this practice was already succumbing, as expressed in one recent argument, to the historical ratchet effect that locked in greater inclusiveness in these deliberations.[18] Nonetheless, many of the states that opposed it were faced with a highly constrained choice between 'an organization with Great Power privilege, or no organization at all'.[19] Hierarchy was the price exacted for making the UN possible as a functioning institution, and for this reason is widely regarded as having been coerced, rather than as expressing any genuinely consensual arrangement.

At the time, and in response to strenuous objections, two main lines of reassurance were developed. The first was that, relative to the former League of Nations Council, there was in fact no *extra* entitlement accorded to the great powers, since voting in that Council had required unanimity in any case, and hence all members of it enjoyed a veto *de facto*. This, it was commonly suggested, had been the heart of the League's problem, as it virtually ensured inaction. Accordingly, the P5 (China, France, Russia, the UK, and the US) veto was sold as a relaxation, not a tightening of what amounted to international consensus.[20] The other key point was that any special rights given to the great powers came with commensurate responsibilities. 'The Council appears Janus-faced', noted one analyst, since 'it remains a tool of the Great Powers, but it is also an instrument for constraining them.'[21] That is to say that, for those states opposed to the inequality incarnated in the Security Council, there was nonetheless a quid pro quo in the entanglement that it simultaneously created for those great powers that would otherwise have been left unfettered to act as they saw fit: 'in particular for smaller and weaker states, a legitimate Security Council imposes constraints on the ability of great powers to act unilaterally'.[22] If this is accepted, the membership and voting entitlements in the Security Council must be viewed as part of a two-way bargain, not as any straightforwardly one-sided imposition.

It is not immediately obvious that those non-European states, which were to become increasingly influential after 1945, construed the essential elements of this bargain in any radically different light. This point can be made with reference to two examples, China and India. China's delegation had been

---

[16] Clark 2005; Hurd 2007; Cronin and Hurd 2008; Morris 2013: 511.
[17] Loke 2013: 221.   [18] Pouliot and Thérien 2015: 211.   [19] Krisch 2008: 136.
[20] Clark 2005: 146.   [21] Krisch 2008: 152.   [22] Welsh and Zaum 2013: 70.

instructed by Chiang Kai-shek that the planned Security Council had to be 'as strong and powerful as possible', and its leading representative at Dumbarton Oaks, Wellington Koo, expressed the view that 'in matter of form the small nations should be given an equal status in the World Organization, but in the interest of effective action, importance should be attached to the Council'.[23] As India's post-independence position gradually emerged, it too saw the core issue in virtually the same way, as Gopal Krishna had noted in his contribution to *The Expansion*:

> in the constitution and powers of the Security Council the existing hierarchy of power was legitimized . . . India recognized the inevitability of this compromise in the given international situation and held that it was in the general interest to preserve and strengthen the structure that actually existed, although eventually it should be made more egalitarian.[24]

Importantly, as is now abundantly clear, what the 'Big Three' had been prepared to offer changed during the course of the period 1941–4, and this itself evidenced the process of accommodation that was to occur. What has been demonstrated conclusively is exactly this shift away from an enforced hierarchy—'peace by dictation' in Franklin D. Roosevelt's language—and towards one that was negotiated, and understood very much as a compromise between conflicting demands. This episode reveals 'the demonstrative willingness of the great powers to compromise and to curb their behaviour for the sake of the collective good'.[25] In short, as the great powers themselves were aware, the envisaged hierarchy changed from one imposed by coercion, to one negotiated in a bargain. Moreover, with respect to the globalization of international society then underway, there was to be no consistent difference with regard to the desirability of adopting this hierarchy, regardless of European or non-European background.

LEGITIMIZING AND CONTESTING HIERARCHY IN THE COLD WAR

The second case considers those understandings that were equally universal in their potential operational scope, but less formally set down, and nowhere agreed to in any kind of constitutional document. They reflected the fact that, given the Cold War stalemate within the Security Council, superpower management of international security had to be conducted outside that forum. Instead of taking the form of constitutional provisions, these attempts were based on a set of prudential precepts, developed from historical practice

---

[23] Loke 2013: 219.   [24] Krishna 1984: 279.   [25] Morris 2013: 528.

during the early decades of the Cold War confrontation. These came to be widely considered as enshrined in a number of principles or conventions of crisis management.[26] It needs to be emphasized immediately that these did not represent exercises in outright collaboration between the two superpowers, but instead were part of a more complex relationship of mixed motives, what Raymond Garthoff once described as the inevitable 'pattern of competition and coexistence' between the Cold War superpowers.[27] Any collaborative 'management' took place within a context of continuing competition as well. Moreover, it largely expressed the shared interests of the superpowers, rather than any constraining bargain consented to by the small and weak. While the superpowers tried to claim that they acted on behalf of a broad, collective, social purpose in ensuring that crises did not spiral out of control and into nuclear confrontation, at stake was also the subservience of client interests to the demands of that superpower competition.

The ambit of these conventions ranged widely, from the conduct of bilateral nuclear crises between the two superpowers,[28] to wider issues of nuclear deterrence and arms control. They directly implicated issues of alliance management and operations within the respective spheres of influence of both superpowers,[29] as well as relationships that were developed outside in the 'grey zones'. All the major crises of the period, from Berlin in the late 1950s, to Cuba in 1962, and to the Middle East in 1967 and 1973, went far beyond bilateral relations alone, and concerned also the behaviour of client states, such as the two Germanys, Cuba, Egypt, Israel, and various states in Africa, among others.

Given the ambivalence of the motives driving superpower actions, assessments of the practical effects of their policies have unsurprisingly been equally mixed.[30] There were indeed some positive evaluations, including that accorded by Bull:

> Yet between 1963 and 1974—from the Partial Test-Ban Treaty to the Vladivostok Accords—the superpowers nevertheless managed to create a structure of cooperation which, rudimentary although it was, was widely recognized throughout international society as a whole to embody hopes, if not for the building of peace in any positive sense then at least for the avoidance of general nuclear war.[31]

As Claude had been quick to point out, great powers were responsible not only *to* international society for their own behaviours, but additionally became responsible *for* the behaviour of those other states with which they maintained a close relationship.[32] US documents released through the National Security Archive reveal that Henry Kissinger, then secretary of state, was minded to

---

[26] Williams 1976.   [27] Garthoff 1985: 1.

[28] Specifically on the role of nuclear weapons in crisis management, see Lynn-Jones et al. 1990; Gottfried and Blair 1988.

[29] Keal 1983.   [30] George 1991.   [31] Bull 1980: 442.   [32] Claude 1986: 725.

conduct air strikes against Cuba in 1976 on account of its intervention in Angola,[33] and this manifestly risked destabilizing the wider Soviet–American relationship, on account of Moscow's seeming failure to restrain its ally.

On the deficit side of the ledger, as Bull equally admitted, 'there was concern, in some cases legitimate concern, that bargains were being struck at the expense of others'.[34] With respect to the latter, it was most notably China that developed a thesis of 'superpower hegemonism' precisely to reflect this oppositional view. Equally, it had been suggested at the time that India's primary objective was to 'preserve and further India's autonomy in a world dominated by the Atlantic and Soviet power blocs'.[35] Indeed, this was largely the rationale underlying the activities of the nonaligned movement as a whole.[36] Unlike in 1945, when the fundamental driver for acceptance of a great power hierarchy had been shared widely, if not quite universally, by the 1970s the note of contestation was much more audible. So what exactly was it that had changed in the meantime to unsettle this point of continuity in international society's normative framework?

On the face of it, nuclear weapons had strengthened the superpower hand against regional clients, as they reinforced 'great power egotism'; the result, in one opinion, was that 'states other than dominant states have *less* influence on crisis situations nowadays than they had in earlier systems'.[37] Accordingly, one of the options available to those Third World clients to get their priorities across globally was exactly to threaten a wider crisis between the two super-powers, as a means of applying pressure towards some satisfaction of their particular interests. In this specific sense, it is very clear that the revolt against the West was much broader in conception, and was in many respects a revolt against superpower tutelage, or 'hegemony' as China then preferred to char-acterize it. After all, as the Soviet imbroglio in Afghanistan was to remind us, 'nationalist forces have been as resistant to domination by Moscow as they were to Western colonialism'.[38] This broader resistance became the conduit for China's appeal to the Third World, and it was precisely in these terms that Beijing's rallying cry was issued: what conceivable progress could there be for 'liberated' former colonies if their interests were immediately subordinated, not simply to neocolonial economic arrangements, but to the implied hier-archy that made regional aspirations subservient to superpower-defined global security? These arguments struck home with particular force in the nuclear domain, and it is revealing that it was to be India that did most to voice this generic concern, on the grounds that arrangements like the Nuclear Non-Proliferation Treaty (NPT) were inherently 'discriminatory'.[39]

---

[33] BBC News 2014.   [34] Bull 1980: 444.   [35] Krishna 1984: 272.
[36] Watson 2007: 48.   [37] Bell 1971: 45.
[38] Bowker and Williams 1988: 266; also Bull 1984c: 226.
[39] See, for example, Nye 1988; Krishna 1984: 284.

For these reasons, there was self-evidently a growing tension between global norms of security (which possibly pressed in favour of these crisis management principles between the two superpowers), and the regional interests of smaller states (which suggested the need to destabilize that very relationship to advance their own ends). Accordingly, crisis management was about two separate, but interconnected, elements: managing the relationship between the two principal powers, but also managing the wider international society that could otherwise disturb that relationship. The response to nuclear proliferation was only the most visible and dramatic symptom of the incompatibility of interests that this was likely to provoke.

By the end, explanations of the demise of these conventions became heavily intertwined with the supposed reasons for the collapse of the superpower détente. The failure was accounted for in terms of 'bad faith' within the superpower peer group itself. This seemingly left out the extent to which the conventions collapsed, not simply under the weight of superpower misbehaviour (although this can hardly be discounted as one element), but because of the challenge mounted to them on the part of those other regional actors that did not wish to be constrained and controlled in this manner.

Third World states appealed to sovereign equality as a way of eroding the dominance of the superpowers when they chose to act together. So what were the tensions between the superpowers and the Third World essentially about? Did they directly concern a challenge to hierarchy, and to the idea that the superpowers should have exceptional rights not only within the formal structures of the UN, but also informally in managing security relations outside that forum? Or were the tensions instead about an underlying process of adjustment in the norm of responsibility, rather than about the practice of hierarchy as such?

CONTESTING HEGEMONY AFTER 1990

For the most part, hegemony is conceived of as referring to a situation of one leading state, unlike generic hierarchies that might involve multiple centres of power. However, contrary to widespread usage, hegemony is here distinguished from 'primacy' or 'predominance', exactly insofar as it too rests on authority relations in a context of a legitimated hierarchy.[40] This perspective draws upon an extensive understanding of the concept of hegemony as a legitimated relationship, already widespread in the social sciences literature.[41]

---

[40] Clark 2011a.
[41] Brilmayer 1994: 5; see also Brooks and Wohlforth 2008: 207; Keohane 1984: 39.

If hegemony is defined strictly as a legitimate exercise of authority by a leading state, then its only conceivable application in the post-1945 period is to the role played by the United States within its own alliance and security 'sphere of influence'. This is already a highly restricted concept at best, and could scarcely be claimed to have extended globally, given the Cold War context in which it was set. This regional application can be most clearly demonstrated in Western Europe, considered as 'an empire by invitation', and in the case of East Asia, where this theme has again been prevalent.[42] While there has latterly been scepticism about the US's continuing role in East Asia, not least because of perceptions of the greater prominence of China, it is striking that the theme of hegemony is far from eclipsed.[43]

Nonetheless, the prospect for any truly globalized hegemony emerged, in principle, only after 1990. One way of exploring the contestation around it, and its associated ideas of responsibility, is through the debate during this period about Security Council reform. What first gave rise to this was the ambivalent reaction to the conditions presented by the end of the Cold War. This promoted, initially, an unprecedented phase of Security Council activism, such as to place that body centre stage. Enthusiasm for restructuring the Security Council was, to this extent, an acknowledgement of its newly found prominence, and of the wish of various parties to influence its emerging agenda. At the same time, on the part of others, the objective was not so much to underwrite this new activism, but rather to establish safeguards against its abuse.[44]

The renegotiation of responsibility manifested itself specifically in the proposals for changing the composition of the P5, and on this issue there was no consensus among the existing permanent members. The two aligned most closely were Britain and France. For both, it was preferable that the issue of Security Council reform be addressed via expansion, rather than by any attempt to review the existing status of those two countries in the context of a single European seat. On that general basis, both Britain and France were supportive of the maximalist expansion proposals, whereby the Council would include permanent seats for all G4 claimants (Brazil, Germany, India, and Japan), as well as African representation. They had also supported an intermediate position in the meantime.[45] This softer approach reflected the reality that any immediate adoption of a G4 + Africa solution was simply off the cards. It also reflected the awkwardness that had developed in European Union (EU)–US relations over this issue in the lead up to the 2005 UN summit.[46]

---

[42] Mastanduno 2002: 181.   [43] Goh 2013: 4.
[44] Krisch 2008: 150–1; Luck 2006: 118, 2008: 81.
[45] UK Cabinet Office 2008: 48.   [46] Bolton 2007: 204, 209.

China was broadly aligned with the United States, but for reasons that only partially overlapped with concerns found in Washington. The focus of much of its policy remained Japan, and to a lesser degree India. According to then US ambassador to the UN, John Bolton, the Chinese ambassador had in effect told him that China could never live with a permanent Japanese seat.[47] Apparently, 'frustrating Japan's ambition' had been 'a top foreign policy priority' for Beijing.[48] Certainly, China collaborated to help block the G4 move ahead of the UN summit in 2005. China's UN ambassador, Wang Guangya, quite candidly suggested so to the world's press at the time.[49] It is possible that what motivated this stand is that China enjoys its status as the sole Asian permanent member, and does not wish to share this with any other state.[50]

There were also, however, wider considerations at play. China had stead-fastly adhered to the view that it would welcome Security Council expansion, provided only that it 'takes due account of the principle of equitable geo-graphical distribution and accommodates the interests of developing coun-tries'.[51] The former principle might be used to preclude both India and Japan (since Asia is already represented by China), but the latter, even if available against Japan, might work in India's favour. While opposing two of the G4 (India and Japan), China had possibly seen some advantage in admission of Brazil or Germany, as leverage against the United States.[52] At any rate, it pushed for the test of responsibility to be applied in ways that explicitly took account of both geography and stage of development.

While also resisting the G4 collectively, the US had traditionally supported the cause of Japan. During the time of the Bill Clinton administration, it was commonly understood that Washington's preferred candidates for permanent seats included both Japan and Germany. In the aftermath of the Iraq war, US support for Germany all but dissipated. In his memoir, Bolton had stated that 'a third EU seat for Germany is utterly unrealistic'.[53] Clearly, given what was regarded as its obstructive position over Iraq, Germany was no longer deemed appropriately responsible by Washington.

Much of this was clearly self-serving posturing on all sides, but was there anything more fundamental at stake? The period captures exactly the reality that the conditionality of Security Council authority is mirrored by the conditionality of the power of the leading Security Council members, as Ian Hurd suggests. In this way, Security Council action is already predicated upon what might be viewed as a balance of legitimation that issues in a complex social distribution of power: 'the power states get from associating themselves with the legitimacy of the Council and the power the Council gets from controlling the terms of that association'.[54]

---

[47] Bolton 2007: 252.   [48] Luck 2006: 120.   [49] Bolton 2007: 252.
[50] Malik 2005: 26.   [51] Quoted in Malik 2005: 20.   [52] Malik 2005: 25.
[53] Bolton 2007: 251.   [54] Hurd 2007: 133.

During the second post-Cold War decade, the problem had become that there was no precedent for the apparent contradiction 'that the remaining superpower will continue to participate ... in an institution whose purpose has become to limit its power'.[55] Fundamental to the institution of hegemony, as expressed through the Security Council, was to be precisely the attainment of a delicate balance between the harnessing and the limiting of the putative hegemon's power, rather than any exclusive pursuit of either. The manifest failure of the United States in the early 2000s to respect this delicate balance, as the two positions moved further apart, in effect brought this phase to an end.

RESPONSIBILITY IN A GLOBALIZED INTERNATIONAL SOCIETY

Bull had identified the idea of responsibility early on as the key attribute of the great powers: 'To speak of great powers ... is already to presuppose the existence of an international society in which these states are "great responsibles"'.[56] Surprisingly, given the editors' prominent concern with this thematic, it plays very little role in their account of *The Expansion*, an anomaly already noted by Edward Keene.[57]

So did ideas about this underpinning norm of responsibility actually shift between 1945 and the 1960s, and once more into the 1990s, and how did this reflect the evolution of international society in the interim? That a hierarchy had been formally established within the UN in 1945 is indubitable. Gerry Simpson refers to this specifically as the creation of a 'legalised hegemony', that embodies the previously highlighted tension between legal equality, on the one hand, and the 'special responsibility' of the great powers, on the other.[58] The debates surrounding these provisions rested on various assumptions about what gave rise to these responsibilities. One definition construes responsibility as 'the ability and willingness to provide global public goods'.[59] Certainly, in 1945, there was little agreement about any such straightforward test, and a number of discrete conceptions of responsibility were then in play. In effect, there was some conflation: that the responsibilities of the great powers derived from their part in the victory in the recent war; from the sacrifices that they had made in effecting this outcome; and, finally, also from their capacity to manage the future international order in conformity with the Charter design. To ensure that they would remain committed to the United Nations, this principle was acknowledged by the conferral of the veto.

---

[55] Weiss 2003: 153. [56] Bull 1971: 143. [57] Keene 2014: 656–7.
[58] Simpson 2004: 167. [59] Narlikar 2011: 1608.

Of the various attributions of responsibility, a direct correlation with material capability is the most common: this makes the logical connection between 'power', and the ability to manage international affairs. It is this conception that had become paramount within Europe during the second half of the eighteenth century. If we accept Keene's account, a hierarchy predicated on material capability came, during this period, to displace the 'status and precedence' understandings of hierarchy that had operated up to this point.[60] It was precisely this linkage between capability and responsibility that was considered so central in the provisions specifically pertaining to the Security Council, although arguably at the time, China and France did not pass any such a test.[61] In short, 'power and responsibility should be joined together'.[62] For those smaller and weaker states that harboured misgivings about the role of the P5, the clinching consideration overall was that this offered the possibility of some net addition to their security, given even more unattractive alternatives. The recent war had demonstrated the extent to which the small were, in any case, beholden to the strong for their security, and there was accordingly some marginal benefit in placing this relationship within an institutionalized framework. In terms of the lineage of a norm of responsibility, one interesting observation about the Chinese position in 1944 is that its then leadership 'spoke of responsibilities without rights or privileges',[63] although this appears not entirely consistent with China's overall support for the 'privileges' to be institutionalized in the Security Council.

Did these ideas about responsibility undergo any substantive change when they came increasingly to be applied, not formally within the Security Council, but rather informally outside in terms of the *de facto* management of international security affairs? Addressing this wider issue, Bull memorably criticized the superpowers for failing to play their role as 'great responsibles': 'Great powers cannot expect to be conceded special rights if they do not perform special duties. What we have been witnessing since the mid-1970s is the abandonment by the superpowers of their postures as responsible managers.'[64] Viewed in these terms, the problem was not the special rights of the great powers as such (and the hierarchy this legitimated), but rather their failure to deliver the necessary *quid pro quo* in return. The bargain, to this extent, had become too one-sided.

But was the problem that they had simply ceased to play a fixed and predetermined role as required by this norm, or was it instead that the norm itself was being pulled and reshaped in different directions? How had the norm of responsibility come to be viewed during the early part of the Cold War? In practice, a divergence had become more visible. Within the formal Security Council forum, the P5 continued to dominate, albeit that there were

[60] Keene 2013: 1077.   [61] Morris 2013: 520.
[62] Goodrich and Hambro 1949: 199.   [63] Loke 2013: 217.   [64] Bull 1980: 446.

serious limitations on their scope for action. Outside this framework, the composition of the great power club varied by issue area, such as in the NPT, but was for the most part narrowly selective with the two superpowers at its core. To this extent, there was some adjustment to the nature of the problem as it now appeared, and as highlighted by Bull: 'The question the lesser states have to ask themselves is not whether they would prefer a world order in which no states had special privileges and responsibilities, but whether they would prefer that these privileges and responsibilities were exercised by a different or a wider group of states'.[65] Hierarchy remained tolerable, provided only that its principle of selection could be more effectively justified.

What then lay at the root of this problem? Was there something different about great power behaviour outside the Security Council, beyond the fact that it took place without any constitutional sanction? The tentative suggestion here is that the objections were principally twofold. First, within the Security Council, the very fact that there was an arrangement that, *de facto*, constrained great power behaviour served as some kind of palliative. Despite continuing misgivings, the P5 role was tolerable to the degree that there were some compensating checks upon it. In any case, the stalemate within the Security Council alleviated concerns by making it seem less likely to be a source of dangerous initiatives. Second, the focus of principal concern shifted elsewhere to those special rights that the great powers were seemingly arrogating to themselves in domains beyond the Security Council's reach. Here, the goal became indeed to ensure that authority was exercised by a 'different or a wider group of states'.

The push within the ambit of the United Nations, both to increase the non-permanent membership of the Security Council (achieved in 1964), and also to rebalance the General Assembly as against the Security Council, was reflected beyond it in the widespread resistance to those informal hierarchies that seemed to be proliferating in the management of international security more generally. This was deemed 'irresponsible', both in the sense that it lacked any constitutional mandate, and also because of a perceived intensifying disjunction in how these managers represented the wide international social constituency. The former criteria that were paramount in 1945—such as the role in the Second World War, or general military capabilities—were no longer considered fully adequate as tests for great power responsibility. To this extent, responsibility came increasingly to be defined in terms of sharing and representing certain characteristics—above all status as economically 'developing' states. China alone, and only after 1971, could make any plausible claim to meet this test, as one of those enjoying special status in the Security Council

---

[65] Bull 1971: 154.

hierarchy. The emergence of the G77 (Group of 77) in 1964, as well as the specific agenda of the early 1970s demanding a New International Economic Order, suggested that these new tests of responsibility now must be applied. If hitherto 'power' had to be joined to responsibility, henceforth responsibility must reflect also the needs and interests of those who otherwise lacked it: the disempowered must be given a voice. In this way, it can be said that responsibility as the norm that underpinned hierarchy was coming to be deployed in ways that would unsettle and challenge those hierarchies that continued to be a feature of international society. As that society expanded horizontally to encompass a much larger group of states with radically different social and economic needs, contested conceptions of responsibility lay at the heart of the normative renewal that it was undergoing.

This normative adaptation was again reflected in the debate about the Security Council after 1990. One summary concerning the Iraq stand-off in the UN describes the two mutually exclusive perceptions at the time as 'the UNSC's [UN Security Council's] inability to constrain the hegemon', on the one hand, and that 'the hegemon should be afforded the exceptional exemption from the rules governing the use of force', on the other.[66] As a portrayal of the debate at the time, this captures its essentials succinctly. The problem was that, in casting the issue in those terms, the debate had missed one vital point: either prescription, pursued in isolation and to the extreme, was self-defeating. Any resolution of this inherent dilemma, by its very nature, required a reconciliation of both sets of demands, not the triumph of one over the other. Otherwise, as argued earlier, both Security Council and putative hegemon would become disempowered.

It should have come as no surprise then to realize that the very lengthy, and often acrimonious, exchanges about reform of the Security Council did not consist of objective proposals devised outside those particular frameworks of understanding, but were instead consciously developed to advance them. American power lay at the heart of what had been increasingly presented as a stark choice between these two conditions. On Iraq, as Britain's former UN ambassador had suggested, 'the question that exercised the majority of UN members was more how to restrain one member state from action without specific authorization than how to uphold the authority of the UN itself'.[67] Effectiveness, it was implied, should not be traded off against legitimacy of this kind. This remained an ongoing feature of the bargaining over Security Council reform, such that there finally emerged a widely shared preference for a more hamstrung Security Council, rather than one that was too cosy for Washington. In one such verdict, 'faced with the choice between having a more effective UN that furthered American interests and continuing with an

---

[66] Morris and Wheeler 2007: 217.   [67] Greenstock 2008: 257.

ineffective UN, many countries chose an ineffective UN'.[68] In so doing, the possibility of any US hegemony through the Security Council was ultimately negated.

Prescriptions for reform were all, explicitly or implicitly, strategies for dealing with the core dilemma created by the unusual post-Cold War distribution of power that favoured the United States and its closest partners. This highlighted the wider malaise concerning the Security Council 'as the forum for legitimising American dominance over the rest of the world'.[69] This was not an objection to a US-centred hierarchy as such, as American power remained demonstrably indispensable to Security Council action, but the new criteria of responsibility demanded a more inclusive representation of diversity than any single hegemony could possibly now deliver.

CONCLUSION

What is much less clear is whether or not any of the emerging tensions within the globalized international society were prompted by the relative absence of a common culture, as opposed simply to greater diversity of social, economic, and political circumstances. It is certainly the case that international society by the 1970s was formed by a much more heterogeneous group of states than at any time hitherto. It was this that drove the demand for international organizational structures that more accurately reflected this diversity, and catered for the special needs and problems that followed in their wake. Hence, we are told, the early meetings of the non-aligned in Belgrade and Cairo in the early 1960s affirmed 'the need for peaceful coexistence and the responsibilities of the great powers for global peace', but at the same time there was an equally overt shift of attention towards such issues as the 'fateful disparity' in living standards across the globe.[70] This structural disparity became increasingly visible only as a direct consequence of the creation of the new states as members of international society.

There has been throughout a broad acceptance of the requirement for special rights and responsibilities for certain categories of states, and the resulting hierarchy has been broadly tolerated. However, as regards its informal practices of management, as well as again within the context of US primacy, there was a much more intense dispute about the composition and membership of those states that should be charged with these responsibilities: the issue that was contested above all was who should be represented, rather than what duties were to be performed. In other words, while hierarchy in

---

[68] Stedman 2007: 942.   [69] Thakur 2006: 292.   [70] Lyon 1984: 231, 232.

itself was not opposed in principle, what became very much more open to contestation were the precise principles on which the contours of the hierarchy were to be drawn, and just how inclusive it would be as a result. This issue was placed in yet starker relief with the demise of the Cold War: the seeming shift towards a unipolar order exerted even greater pressure on the bargain about responsibility embedded in the United Nations Charter, and the special rights of the great powers if there was now only one of them.

14

The Globalization of International Law

Gerry Simpson

From the perspective of most international lawyers, the global sovereign order *is* the international legal order. So, to speak of 'the expansion of an international society of sovereign states' is to both smoothly invoke a mainstream (or idealized) international legal project and, at the same time, disarticulate some of that project's recurrent pathologies, or angst.[1] Indeed, the two principal ways in which international lawyers describe the effects of this expansion or, preferably, globalization, of international society divide along fairly sharp and recognizable theoretical (and, perhaps, temperamental) lines, with one group emphasizing enlightenment, inclusion, voluntarism and renewal, and the other describing an often bleak history of legitimation, empire, violence, exclusion and exploitation.[2]

Meanwhile, descriptions of *the way* this expansion occurred tend to be organized around two schools of thought with one thinking of expansion as a linear, progressive extension of European rule outwards into the peripheries, and the other offering a radical revision of this account that seeks to problematize either the idea of seamless expansion or excessively unitary accounts of the very nature of international society itself.[3]

---

[1] Some of this angst surrounds the centrality or otherwise of law itself as a social and political practice 'holding it all together', with many international lawyers happy to concede international law's virtuous marginality (for example, most of the field), and others keen to represent it as a constitutive (and sometimes malign) set of practices and institutions (for example, Kennedy 2005).

[2] From the former perspective, see Tesón 1992: 53; Slaughter 2004. From the latter, see Anghie 2005; Chimni 1993; Miéville 2005. See Miéville's (2005: 319) idea that 'a world structured around international law cannot but be one of imperial violence'. This split goes back to, but does not quite map on to, Hugo Grotius and Thomas Hobbes, of course (it would be odd to describe Anghie as Hobbesian). And on 'temperament', see Wight 1987: 221, 227.

[3] See, for example, Lauren Benton's work on the way in which sovereignty was received, reforged, and returned in the colonial encounter. Benton and Straumann 2010: 1; Benton 2010; Keene 2014: 651. These characterizations map on to one another to a certain extent. The Enlightenment trajectory will tend to be narrated as a progressive, linear account of expansion while fragmentary histories will be more inclined to take exploitation seriously.

The classic English School approach to this expansion is usually understood as one in which linearity and enlightenment are the dominant moods punctuated only occasionally by asides and qualifiers that barely disturb the central narrative direction or *telos*. Rereading the original *The Expansion of International Society* volume, however, one discerns a little more nuance and complexity than one might expect for the time. In Ian Brownlie's essay on international law, for example, there is some resistance to what he calls the 'Europocentric' version of the expansion of international society, and a concern to read the relations between the Europeans and others as evidence of mutuality and cooperation as well as expansion and imposition.[4] Brownlie, taking issue with the expansion thesis, notes that treaty-making between the European metropoles and an array of entities outside the European-North American region was surprisingly common in the nineteenth century.[5]

On the other hand, Brownlie's vision of law and encounter undoubtedly requires a certain amount of unpacking. His refusal of the label 'Europocentric' helps him see some of the ways in which this was not exclusively an inter-European order or simply an expanding European society, but this same refusal leads him to reject the whole idea that conquest and absorption might have been specifically European and, often extremely callous, imperial projects. As he put it, in a revealing aside: '*it happened* that a certain group of states were to become politically dominant in the world as whole'.[6] For Brownlie, the 'Europeanness' of the project was incidental, perhaps even accidental. But perhaps some of this is to be expected. After all, Eurocentrism—a tired topic to be sure—can have two quite distinct meanings. An international society whose animating ideas were derived from European modernity did first emerge in Europe between the fifteenth and nineteenth centuries *and* histories of the encounter have been overwhelmingly filtered through European epistemologies or 'under Western eyes' (we might call this a 'double-Eurocentrism').[7]

Brownlie's chapter title, meanwhile, suggests that international law is incidental, too, in the nineteenth century; there is an expansion followed by 'consequences' for international law. It is certainly the case, that, notwithstanding Martti Koskenniemi's recent revival of the Victorian men of 1871, the nineteenth century has not been international law's favourite century.[8] Indeed, it has been read in some subfields (for example, the *ius ad bellum*) as

---

[4] Brownlie 1984.   [5] A point taken up and expanded in Keene 2014.
[6] Brownlie 1984: 358, emphasis in original.
[7] There is disagreement on just how Eurocentric it is (even among scholars sympathetic to anti-colonial movements). Christopher Weeramantry (1997: 309, 317) has described international law as a 'monocultural construct'. But others have recognized the influence of non-Western traditions on the early development of international law: Alexandrowicz 1967; Chatterjee 1958. For a general discussion see, from the public international law side, Chimni 2012; and from the international relations side, Hobson 2012. The reference is to Conrad 2007.
[8] Koskenniemi 2001.

devoid of law. International legal histories are all about Westphalia and Hobbes/Hugo Grotius followed by Christian Wolff, Emer de Vattel, and Samuel von Pufendorf. Then silence, then the League of Nations. There might be the odd reference to the Universal Postal Union or the International Meteorological Organization but only as quirky, technical precursors to the serious action of multilateral renewal post-Versailles.[9] And then there are nineteenth-century 'positivists' such as Jeremy Bentham and John Austin: each denying the existence or validity of international law, so called.[10]

In this chapter I want to argue for, instead, the constitutive force of law throughout this period of globalization. In doing so, I also complicate the law story by describing both the discontinuous, heterogeneous, and geographically diffuse nature of the encounter between European law and other laws, *and* the civilizational and imperial tropes that underpinned it. In particular, and following the injunction of the editors, I want to posit a methodological shift from thinking of this process as expansion of international law to thinking of it as the globalization of global law. Of course this is an unhappy and inelegant phrase but it captures two important qualities in the story. First, the term 'globalization' suggests a less unilinear, more centrifugal process of law-making: not so much an expansion of legal forms outwards but more of a hybridization of parallel legal orders.[11] Second, *global* law implies a more thoroughgoing saturation of law through, between, and beyond the sovereign state, a sort of heteropolar, or heterojurisdictional, legal order in which law is both a public international law between states as well an assemblage of deformalized, private, interstitial norms reproduced in a number of different legal sites.[12] This legal order, although mutable and diverse, develops through a history of expansion, retraction, collaboration, and dissolution that leaves in place many of the structural hierarchies native to the international political order while at the same time creating spaces in which new hierarchies, as well as new practices of refusal and resistance, are instated.

More specifically, I argue that international law's relationship to international society continues to be defined by the ways in which it has organized relations *between* a cultural and political elite of states and the peripheries (the problems of empire, domination, exploitation, and outlawry, or entry, admission, and assimilation) in a system apparently committed to the ideals of equal sovereignty ('recessive sovereignties'); *among* sovereign states given the existence of great powers (the problems of hegemony or balance of power in a normative order committed to formal equality) ('hegemonic sovereignties'); and *between* the autonomy and independence of the sovereign state (what

---

[9] For discussion see Kennedy 1997: 106–7. See, too, Craven 2012.

[10] Bentham 1823: 256; Austin 1832: 47, 207.

[11] Although I would not want to suggest that this hybridization occurs on equal terms.

[12] The term 'heteropolar' is James Der Derian's Forthcoming 2016.

I have called 'liberal pluralism'), and, at different times, the imperatives of international regulation, world order, centrally mandated 'institutional reform' (usually a soft term for privatization), and humanitarianism (often effecting a form of 'liberal anti-pluralism') ('globalized sovereignties').[13] But I want to show, too, that amid all this, the forms of law produced are both recognizably imperial and unrecognizably fragmented and decentred, and our image of law as a relatively unified field of rules and principles designed to give shape to a public, global, humanitarian good (the last universalist ethics) is in need of significant revision and critique.[14]

ANTI-LINEARITY

Not many scholars want to be associated with a 'standard account' of anything. And so, even Hedley Bull and Adam Watson, long regarded as having themselves produced a 'standard account of the expansion of international society', refer to, and reject, an earlier 'standard account' of this development.[15] This earlier orthodoxy describes the progression of European international relations as one in which the European state system emerges and consolidates over six centuries becoming in the process prototypical. The system is marked by the presence of a repertoire of diplomatic and legal norms combined with an adherence to (or belief in) the balance of power as the institutional basis for what becomes an international society. This social order then spreads outwards into the extra-European world.[16]

Bull expresses mild discomfort with this approach in *Expansion*. He points to a pre-nineteenth-century diplomatic assumption that the international order was already a global system in which agreements were reached in, for example, the East Indies, on the basis of a rough equality and in which the 'influence of Asian international practices on the evolution of European ones' was keenly felt.[17] But the emphasis remains firmly on expansion and these extra-European influences are noted as qualifiers. He goes on immediately afterwards to say: '*Yet* it cannot be denied that the role of the Europeans in shaping an international society of worldwide dimension has been a special

---

[13] Simpson 2001.

[14] Another way to put this is to say that the chapter will consider the relationship between sovereign equality and formal and informal modes of hierarchy, between liberal pluralism and liberal empire, and between the claims of justice and order in international legal institutions.

[15] Bull 1984b: 123.

[16] For an orthodox account, see any number of texts written by international lawyers in the second half of the nineteenth century, for example Walker 1893. For a description, see Little 2013.

[17] Bull 1984b: 123.

one. It was *in fact* the European powers... [that came to dominate] ... It was *in fact* their conception of an international society of juridically equal sovereign states that came to be accepted'.[18] And, so, side gestures apart, the two standard accounts look rather similar.

Legal norms are central to these conceptions of international society in at least three respects: they provide the diplomatic glue for the establishment of relations between this circle of European states, they underpin the creation of a sovereign order by requiring that sovereignty be experienced and acquired through processes of legal recognition, and, finally, legal theory—organized around a split between natural lawyers and positivists—provides an important terrain on which debates about the very nature of this order are played out.[19]

And so, as I say, Bull's account has become a second standard account against which alternative accounts are posited both explicitly (Edward Keene and Yasuaki Onuma) and implicitly (Lauren Benton, Matthew Craven, and Michael Hardt and Antonio Negri).[20] The main thrust of these revisions has been to complicate and decentre the story, as well as law's role in it. As a general point, the expansion thesis has been criticized for underplaying the violence of encounter and the resistance experienced and offered during it. But Benton wants to show how the expansion of sovereignty to the peripheries was a far more fragmentary and geographically determined affair than that suggested by the cliché of map-drawing Europeans (for example, Hardt and Negri implicate American republican federalism in the drive to empire) at Berlin disregarding topography and carving up, or scrambling for, Africa.[21] Meanwhile, for Keene, 'expansion' is the wrong master concept and ought to be replaced by something he wants to call 'stratification'. According to Keene, the expansion thesis, positing an international society in which membership is patrolled using a standard of civilization, has 'deep roots in international law'.[22] It ought to be rejected, he argues, in favour of a sociologically nuanced approach in which agents in global society occupy positions on a more thickly imagined hierarchy according to their strength, prestige, and authority. The obsession with entry to an already constituted society would be abandoned in favour of something more richly variegated. For Onuma, in the end, what is

---

[18] Bull 1984b: 123–4, emphases added. The reference to 'facts' may betray a certain nervousness on the part of Bull (in the same way the chief executive of a bank might say 'The fact is, we protect the interests of our customers'). These 'facts' are not, after all, entirely unchallengeable. If we accept Bull's date for the emergence of a world society of sovereign states as 1945 (or between 1945 and 1960), then it might be possible to argue that this was indeed a conception of universal sovereign statehood through self-determination that came to dominate, but that this conception was a creature, not of a European nineteenth century but of Wilsonian idealism, Bolshevik tactical and anti-imperial nationalism, and Third World resistance.

[19] Boyle 1985. For a richly developed account of the natural law of the state, see Brett 2011.

[20] See Benton 2010; Craven 2012; Hardt and Negri 2000: 166–82.

[21] For example, Pakenham 1991.   [22] Keene 2014: 652.

co-produced through this encounter is an inter-civilizational international law rather than a European law fanning outwards.[23]

There is no doubt, of course, that on the one hand, public international law *is* a specifically Western form of doing business (its primary language is English, its major urban centres are European and North American, its historical antecedents are found in Western legal and political theory, and its practitioners are in many cases trained in the elite Western universities of the North).[24] On the other hand, these material and cultural aspects of the system can blind us to both the hybridity found in the society and to the existence of alternative modes of organizing international social life.[25] So that, for example, a focus on China's 'entry' to international society in the nineteenth century is mimicked today by an overattention to China's compliance with, or receptiveness to, international law and regimes (China's entry to and then 'fit' with the World Trade Organization or Chinese willingness to be less obstructive about the imposition of international criminal law in Africa) and an elision of the cultural radicalism of a particular tendency in Chinese diplomacy that emphasizes the social and familial essence of social interactions.[26]

In any event, for all the continuities mapped in this chapter between the nineteenth century and what came after, there is at least one respect in which there was a rupture in the story of law's globalization. Because at this point we have a contraction of the society, organized around or facilitated by legal categories and norms. Until the nineteenth century, there was, as we have seen according to Bull and Watson, the emergence of a 'loose Eurasian system or quasi-system' within which the European states 'sought to deal with Asian states on the basis of moral and legal equality' (this sense of equality was not always reciprocated by the Chinese or Ottomans).[27] Something in the nineteenth century, though, provoked a reversal in what might have been understood as a trajectory of cosmopolitan inclusiveness or, at least, tolerance. Perhaps it had something to do with European technological supremacy (in war-making, in transportation), an intensity of uneven development between Europe and the rest, or double-entry bookkeeping or ideational superiority but there was what R. J. Vincent called a 'racializing' of the world.[28]

---

[23] Onuma 2010.

[24] See, for example, Brierly (1963: 1): 'the special character [of international law] has been determined by that of the modern European states-system'.

[25] See Carty 2009.

[26] I suppose there is a further irony here in the fact that one Chinese approach uses some of the same language as the international lawyers of the nineteenth century with the emphasis on family and cultural affinity. See Cao 2007; Metzger 2005.

[27] Bull and Watson 1984b: 5. This, of course, is not a distinctively international society insight and a version of it goes back to Francisco de Vitoria, at least. See Scott 1934.

[28] Vincent 1984. The technological, political, and ideational motors of this change are explored in Buzan and Lawson 2013.

This racializing of the world was not, though, a unidirectional process. The encounter of North and South in the nineteenth century was an encounter of laws.[29] And this encounter of legal forms has enormous influence on the way international law develops not because ideas and institutions flowed back and forth in some free and equal exchange ideas but because international society's conception of itself was transformed by the encounter with other international societies and political life forms.[30] In one of the strongest forms of this argument, Antony Anghie famously argued that empire made international law and that it was very difficult to identify an international legal technique uncontaminated (or not rendered necessary) by the colonial experience, while Benton remarks that international law came not from Europe but from empire.[31] This is very different, then, from the idea of an already completed international society migrating outwards, encountering difference, and determining how to adjust legal forms in response to this encounter.[32]

The idea of a *sovereignty* stabilized in Europe then slowly migrating South and East needs to be complicated also. As I argue in the next section, as far as sovereignty is concerned, international law textbooks tend to offer a history that is both one of rigid bifurcations (civilized/uncivilized and so on) and a series of endless variations on the theme of sovereignty. The strict divisions are there, but to read John Westlake or James Lorimer is to appreciate the intensely stratified and unstable (in Lorimer's case to the point of a pathology) nature of nineteenth-century sovereignties.[33] Relations between Europe and the rest of the world were organized around a very protean collection of organizational forms (colonial protectorates, 'company' colonies, semi-sovereigns and so on) even if international lawyers might choose to look back on the nineteenth century as the

---

[29] Pahuja Forthcoming.   [30] Said 1978.

[31] Anghie 2005; Benton 2010: 222–78.

[32] Suzuki et al. 2014. This is partly an epistemological problem, too, about the experiences of the colonizer and the colonized. How do we know, or guess, how those who gave and those who received international society experienced the act?

[33] Simpson Forthcoming. As I argue there, Lorimer's *Institutes* are, in effect, a book-length apology or justification for a series of taxonomies of statehood. His tripartite distinction—civilized states, barbarians (the Ottomans), and savages (everywhere else)—is familiar enough (repeated, for example, in Rawls 1999) and dissected in Michel Foucault ('The savage is basically a savage who lives in a state of savagery together with other savages... [t]he barbarian, in contrast, is someone who can be understood, characterized, and defined only in relation to a civilization, and by the fact that he lives outside it. And the barbarian's relationship with that speck of civilization, and which he wants—is one of hostility and permanent warfare'). See Foucault 2003: 195. Lorimer's big idea was that uncivilized states (China, Japan, even the United States hovered around the margins of civilization) lacked a reciprocating will and so could not enter into full relations with the civilized core. Institutionally and in practice, the effects (or source) of this were found in the capitulations created under the unequal treaties between European powers and the uncivilized margins (textualizing the idea that European citizens in China required protection from barbarian local law) and in the unequal sovereignty of Siam, the Ottomans, Japan, and China (states that in most other respects seemed wholly sovereign). But Lorimer's taxonomies are extraordinarily ornate. This is no simple project of demarcation.

time of sovereignty, to be opposed to a modern international law of institution-alism and experiment.[34]

Ultimately, then, this diversity of legal forms combined with a tenacious commitment to hierarchy better explains, and is more continuous with, the post-*Expansion* story of international law's development in relation to sover-eignty. So, instead of recounting the growing stabilization of political com-munity around the sovereign form, I want to next say a little more about a pluralism of forms found in the nineteenth century, continuing into the twentieth century, and re-emerging, in contemporary international society, in newly refurbished doctrines and logics of unequal sovereignty.

RECESSIVE SOVEREIGNTIES

At the conference to establish an international criminal court in 1998 and amid the striking calls for a moral universalism (crimes against humanity) and the egalitarianism of the plenary decision-making (every state was represented at these), there was a series of meetings of a semi-formal (these were named 'formal informals') but highly influential coalition called the 'like-minded group'. This relationship between states in general and a like-minded group is at least one major feature of the globalization of international society outwards from its core. This transition from a 'polycentric global order' before 1800 to an international system in which core–periphery relations were central was mirrored in a series of international legal developments that both solidified and complicated this relationship.

The nineteenth century has been read both as an era of unstable sovereigns against which the twentieth-century project seemed to be about stabilizing sovereignty by establishing a legal order of sovereign equals, and, at the same time, a period in which the inter-sovereign order expanded and intensified. So, the nineteenth century was at once both all about sovereign equality (indeed, for some international lawyers, the Westphalian idea of sovereign equality is a creation of the nineteenth century) and at the same time about creating elaborate taxonomies of sovereign *hierarchy* configured around a strange brew of culture and race. International society as a bargain between formal universalism and cultural particularity begins here. Indeed, the nineteenth century might be understood as two centuries: a mid to late nineteenth century in which sovereignty is fragmented or dispersed, and a very late nineteenth century where it becomes more absolute and unified (all the better

---

[34] Kennedy 1997: 99. Bull seems to know this. In fact, it is clear that Bull *knew* quite a lot. *The Expansion* thesis is full of such knowledge but it is either hinted at and overqualified, or insufficiently theorized.

for progressive lawyers in the twentieth century to both universalize as 'decolonization' and then work against as 'liberal institutionalism'). International law, by the end of the century at least, then combines a standard of civilization (applied, and then later dis-applied, to Asian civilizations), a project of imperial governance (Africa), and a drive to first disaggregate sovereignty in the peripheries and then export a unified version of it back to the late-colonies.[35]

The law story is familiar in some respects. Many international law scholars of the nineteenth century (for example, Oppenheim, Westlake, and others) asserted that states were not necessarily 'members of the family of nations'. The family of nations was open only to states possessing certain abstract and often deeply cultural qualities recognizable only to other family members. Recognition then operates as a way of controlling membership of the core. This was Gerrit Gong's 'standard of civilization'. So, to quote Henry Wheaton, writing at an earlier point across the Atlantic: '[t]he public law ... has always been, and still is, limited to the civilized and Christian people of Europe or to those of European origin'.[36] But this norm operated as elusive cultural marker rather than achievable legal standard.[37] States that failed to reach the standard—Westlake had said that they lacked 'good breeding'—became more susceptible to intervention, discipline, and general loss of status.[38] Lorimer's central distinction (if not his endless classifications) was a fairly standard nineteenth-century view. Georg Hegel, too, understood that any equality between states (what he calls 'autonomy') was merely a formality.[39]

In any event—and to go back to an earlier point—uncivilized states sat beyond international law subject to it but not subjects of it. Relations in these cases were a matter of something other than, or alongside, law. James Crawford, in a footnote, compares two editions of *Oppenheim*. As he puts it, the

---

[35] Kingsbury 2002: 401, 412–13 (describing a greater sensitivity to colonial experience on the part of Lassa Oppenheim's nineteenth-century predecessors).

[36] Wheaton 1863: 16–17. Wheaton was translated into Chinese in 1864 and was regarded by the Chinese and Japanese as an authoritative source of international law doctrine and standards. See Gong 1984b: 18, 26.

[37] Michel de Montaigne 2003 saw the meaning of these cultural markers best, three hundred years before Oppenheim, in his essay '1.31: On the Cannibals'. For a discussion of the way some Russians and Eastern Europeans think international law is a language that only native speakers (in Western Europe) can ever really master, for all the talk of a juridical *lingua franca*, see Dolidze 2015.

[38] Westlake 1914: 6. See Joseph Conrad 2012 for an elaboration on these themes of stratification. Marlow describes Africans as 'savages' then 'natives', then 'enemies', then 'criminals', Joseph Conrad 2012: 24, 60, 65. 'What would be the next definition I would hear?' he exclaims at one point, Joseph Conrad 2012: 84. One gets the same feeling reading the international law of the period. See Simpson 2015, Forthcoming.

[39] Hegel 1822. For a discussion of the way in which sovereignty was both territorial (and thus excluded nomadic peoples and pirates) and social (and thus excluded incompletely socialized territorial states and civilizations), see Anghie 1999: 25. See, too, Branch 2012.

twentieth-century edition edited by Hersch Lauterpacht: 'omitted the sentence
[found in a previous edition] "It is discretion, and not International Law,
according to which the members of the Family of Nations deal with such States
as still remain outside that family"'.[40] Omitting this sentence has been the
distinctively twentieth-century project of modernizing international law in
order to formalize sovereignty while undertaking a deformalization of
inequality.

By the beginning of the twentieth century, the abstractions of 'Christianity',
'civilization', 'family membership', and 'savagery' became the substance of
'effectiveness', 'territory', and 'statehood'.[41] International society had already
been opened up to hitherto undercivilized peoples (the Japanese, Koreans,
Thais, and Chinese), and this was followed by a radical expansion in the
membership of the family of nations. The move from the abstractions of
culture and recognition to the materiality of effectiveness and the moral
certitudes around decolonization promised emancipation, and it would be
odd not to register that in some respects international law *was* formally
deracialized. After all, Japan became a 'great power' at Versailles, and China
(or a version of China) became one in 1945. But familiar hierarchies were
quickly restaged. Colonial peoples were catalogued in A, B, and C mandates—
an arrangement that recalled Pufendorf and Lorimer, especially the latter's
idea of 'nonage'—new European states were subject to the regulatory effects of
minority treaties (a form of administration not deemed necessary in the case
of the core European states with their minorities), and the post-war-era
explosion of new sovereigns was managed through a system of what Robert
H. Jackson called 'negative sovereignty'.[42] These new states were not quite
fully members of society. These were 'quasi-sovereigns' (a term used by
Jackson and, later, Benton) or conditional sovereigns. They fell short of the
standard set by the archetypal European sovereign.

Bull has described the way in which sovereignty was stabilized in 1945 when
it became the dominant form of organized political community on the planet.
The United Nations (UN) organization was indeed to be based on the
'sovereign equality' of states (these numbered around fifty) and the revival
of sovereignty in places like Poland was a key demand of the UN system. But
the UN system was also an expression of imperial prerogative.[43] Much of the
world was governed through either European empire or, in the case of the
territories of defeated imperial powers, through a UN-mandated form of
trusteeship. Sovereignty, we might say, was at a low ebb. The apparently

[40] Crawford 1979: 13, fn. 46.
[41] Walker (1893: 7) notes that by the end of the nineteenth century, the equality of states was a
'fact' but there was still at this stage an 'international circle' of states which would 'scrutinize the
credentials' of aspirant members of the society.
[42] Jackson 1990.   [43] Mazower 2009.

transformative shift in international sensibility did not take place until 1960 (or the mid-1950s), when a combination of indigenous resistance, imperial fatigue, and institutional innovation produced a form of anti-colonial international law based around the right of self-determination and the processes of decolonization.[44] The experimentalism (or condescension) of the nineteenth century (as well as the twentieth century hold-overs in 1919 (the mandates) and 1945 (trusteeship)) were abandoned in favour of a powerful and authoritative rejection of empire. On 14 December 1960, colonialism was declared to be 'an evil' in the United Nations General Assembly Declaration on the Granting of Independence to Colonial Countries and Peoples (Resolution 1514). Empire gave way to sovereignty. This was a high point of Third World optimism and resistance, and it continued as these new states challenged the existing international order, not by resisting a newly fetishized sovereignty (that would have seemed strange since this had just recently been acquired after decades of (often armed) struggle and was useful for liberationist reasons, or as a matter of rent-seeking or to secure the immunity of kleptocrats), but by grouping themselves as nodes of resistance (the Non-Aligned Movement, the Bandung Conference, and, later, the agitations around the New International Economic Order).

Meanwhile, international law was being remade or rethought by generations of lawyers from the South with the intention of rereading the historical record, and critiquing (then rehabilitating) international law. So, writing at the same time as Bull and Watson, people like Mohammed Bedjaoui, R. P. Anand, and Christopher Weeramantry (influenced by Frantz Fanon and Chinua Achebe) sought to inscribe into international law a view from the South and, at the same time, uncover the roots of international order in the residues and spectres of empire.[45] They and their successors argue that international law continues to be grounded in the sorts of exclusions, distinction, and racially inflected stratifications that were the mark of the nineteenth-century globalization of international society. Of course, the language has been altered to accommodate a powerful resistance to imperial practices and racial discrimination but as I have argued elsewhere:

> each generation of enlightened empire-builders looks back on the vulgar imperialism of the previous one. *Terra nullius* becomes colony, colony becomes trust territory, trust territory becomes territorial administration. Discredited rhetorics of separation and exclusion (the nineteenth-century distinction between civilised and uncivilised peoples; earlier distinctions between Christians and infidels) are refurbished, de-racialised or secularised (their counterparts are found in

---

[44] For a subtle discussion of self-determination, see Drew 2001.

[45] A later generation has built on this work: the less obvious suspects are, in law, Gathii 2009; and in social theory Prashad 2007; Chakrabarty 2008.

the distinctions between democratic and undemocratic sovereigns or between developed and underdeveloped states) but, in the end, the spectres of empire are always present in new programmes, logics and orientations.[46]

So, the abstractions of good governance, and earned sovereignty, are again disciplining peripheral states.[47] The contemporary version of the standard of civilization has bled into other areas of international norm development from the responsibility to protect (after all, Tony Blair called outlaws 'irresponsible states') to the idea of a failed, and therefore permeable state, to the concept of crimes against humanity, with the claims of humanity used as a way of wedging open the sovereignty of malefactors in Africa but not in North America.[48] As I have shown, these hierarchies have a long history and surprising durability in international law and society. Pufendorf distinguished between those entirely outside the system (towards whom 'it will be necessary for other men to show them no more mercy than they do birds of prey'), and the marginal cases who are 'so partial as to be just in the Observation of compacts with [only] some particular Allies...their Credit, it is evident, must very much sink, but it would be too severe to deny them every degree of esteem', and John Rawls continued as late as 1999 with the same sorts of divisions dividing states into liberal, decent, and outlaw.[49]

In this way, there is the continued consolidation of a tenacious division between states that were put on earth by God and others that are here quite by chance.[50] But this distinction reflects an even deeper and more salient division in world politics: that between the poor and rich states.[51] International lawyers still speak of sovereign equality but in the face of both sharp material differences and the formal mechanics of privilege that I discuss in the next section, this was to risk absurdity. An international law founded on 'sovereign equality' and an international legal practice of making distinctions both among sovereigns and between sovereigns and those lacking sovereignty altogether, might be understood, then, as a way of both reinforcing *and* not talking about a persistent state of affairs.

---

[46] Simpson 2012: 34–5. In fact, this was not always particularly well disguised. Civilization is still present as an organizing principle of international law as late as Hyde 1945, where it is said that in order to be a state, 'the inhabitants of the territory must have attained a degree of civilisation', quoted in Crawford 1979: 73.

[47] For a historical survey, see Bowden 2009.

[48] See, for example, Krever 2014.

[49] Tuck 1999: 161–2, quoting Pufendorf, *The Law of Nature and Nations*, 802, viii.4.5; Rawls 1999.

[50] I am paraphrasing Mikhail Gorbachev.

[51] See Prashad 2014. I am not suggesting that this distinction maps exactly on to the division of rich and poor human beings, although there is substantial overlap.

HEGEMONIC SOVEREIGNTIES

Other chapters in this volume discuss the ways in which the globalization of international society reinforced or maintained a hierarchy between an elite of hegemonic powers and the rest of international society.[52] I want to touch here on two particular aspects of this pattern. One is the way in which this hegemony is first institutionalized (at Vienna in 1815) and then legalized (at San Francisco, 135 years later). Since I have already covered some of this ground, I just want to provide a gloss tracking this development in the intervening period, through the lens of international society.[53] The other feature of this hierarchy is the way in which hegemony was subject to both *fracture and defection* (the official legalized hegemonies of any period are challenged by looser confederations of great power action) and *stratification* (the great powers arrange themselves in ways that implicate a fresh relationship between equality and hierarchy).

In 1814, the Great European powers established a post-Napoleonic pact affirming that 'relations from whence a system of real and permanent Balance of Power in Europe is to be derived, shall be regulated at the Congress upon the principles determined upon by the Allied Powers themselves'.[54] This was an arrangement to be 'regulated' (implying sustainability, repetition, and management) through a 'Congress' (a precursor to the congressional methods used a century later at Versailles and then subsequently at San Francisco) in which 'principles' (as opposed to calculations of interest, or utility) were to be the guiding concepts. This system—the Concert—was, of course, highly imperfect but it introduced the idea of collective, principled management of European relations. This system then 'globalizes' at Berlin, Versailles, and San Francisco. Indeed, this has been described as a move from the European concert to 'a World concert'.[55]

In Berlin, the European powers (and King Leopold's private company) met to develop some new principles according to which the Congo Basin and some coastal areas might be divided among the European powers. This was, of course, a highly specific and geographically particular form of globalization, but it is a formal extension of collective quasi-institutional action into extra-European settings.[56] Of course, the Hague Conferences of 1899 and 1907, the Meiji victory at Port Arthur in 1904 (at which point Japan showed itself to be 'conversant' with international law), and the prominence of the Japanese at Versailles (calling for the constitutionalization of a racial equality provision, dissenting during discussions about the arraignment of the Kaiser on charges

---

[52] See, too, Clark 1989, 2011a; Mitzen 2013.
[53] Simpson 2004, where I call this 'legalized hegemony'.
[54] The Langres Protocol, 29 January 1814.   [55] Wheaton 1916: 261.
[56] Craven 2015.

of having engaged in a war of aggression) confirmed the status of some of the great Asian civilizations and others.

Versailles, then, continued the policy of legalized hegemony but deepened the institutionalism found at Vienna (the League was a permanent machinery of public legality) and broadened the extension of supervision into Africa and the Pacific (with the establishment of mandates to be governed by the great powers with (limited) League oversight).

This combination of imperial and neo-imperial ruleship (Berlin, the mandates), with increasingly centralized and constitutionalized hegemony (the League Council, the Security Council) and the broadening of great power jurisdiction, becomes a mark of the contemporary international legal order (with its roots in the nineteenth century). The contemporary Security Council's ever-expanding sense of its own authority to act and its disregard for sovereign rights is a familiar amalgam of quasi-imperial rule and legalized hegemony. The results are found in the multiplicity of arrangements imposed by the hegemons on various agents in the global order—the establishment of UN protectorates in East Timor and Kosovo; the judicial determination of guilt and innocence in the Balkans and Africa; the imposition of sanctions on overassertive would-be regional hegemons (Iran, North Korea); and the elaboration of doctrines of intervention (the remnants of the responsibility to protect) and surveillance (the Sanctions Committee).[57] The globalization of legalized hegemony has hardly been a predictable affair but although its roots are recognizable enough, the account given here of a certain sort of authorized hegemony is both accurate and a little too seamless. In particular, it risks underplaying two complicating aspects of this dominance: defection and stratification.

The stability of legalized hegemony has been challenged at virtually every step by the threat and experience of extra-curricular action.[58] In 1815, the ink was barely dry on the Treaty of Paris before the coalition of Eastern powers was defecting from the system and establishing hierarchy within hierarchy. This coalition was inspired by a group of religious values, a fear of the spread of constitutionalism in Europe, and a set of shared cultural referents. After several botched attempts to impose a particular order on European states, and following resistance from the other great powers, the Holy Alliance petered out rather unhappily. And yet, this defection proved paradigmatic in international society. Legalized hegemony can be understood, then, as an unstable combination of formal arrangements in which rights are allocated through text and law, and extra-formal efforts to posit alternative—sometimes provisional—multilateralisms. This pattern was repeated in Berlin (in fact prior to Berlin when the Belgians and British attempt a pre-emptive allocation

---

[57] See Wilde 2008; Farrall 2007; *Prosecutor v Germain Katanga* [2014], ICC-01/04-01/07.
[58] I write about this at greater length in Simpson 2016.

of imperial assets), in Geneva (with the defection of the soon-to-be axis powers from the League system of security), in New York, where the Security apparatus established under Chapter VII of the UN Charter was abandoned in favour of the creation of security zones and accompanying multilateral security organizations (NATO, the Warsaw Pact), and where legal doctrine (the prohibition on the use of force found in Article 2(4)) was displaced by political demand (the assertion of spheres of interest on the part of the two superpowers), and, finally, in Iraq, where a coalition of the willing claimed a legal authority to preserve international peace and security beyond that given in the UN Charter.

This continual splitting of elites is linked, also, to the way in which hegemony is stratified in international law. As Keene notes: 'the "family of civilised nations" should be understood as a status group. Its members were in very different positions [to each other] in terms of the international distribution of other kinds of power'.[59] Formal legal authority has operated to obscure these differences or remove them from the constitutional frame: sovereign equality has worked best to neutralize the differences among the great powers rather than between the great powers and the rest. So, the five powers at Vienna were not, obviously, all equally great. The creation of a quasi-executive of these four (then five with the addition of France) tended to underplay the difference in power and status enjoyed by these states (say, the difference in military power between Prussia and Austria, or the clear economic or naval superiority of Great Britain) and overstate the differences between the great powers and other aspirant powers (Spain, for example). This was repeated in Berlin, where some of the colonial powers were more colonial than others and then, of course, at San Francisco in 1945 where legalized hegemony established an equality (of voting power, veto-wielding authority) that hardly reflects the different capabilities of the powers (the United States, the supreme economic and military power on the planet, the Soviet Union a long way ahead of the others, France and the UK defeated in one case and bankrupt in the other, and China, represented by a small island outpost).[60]

GLOBALIZED SOVEREIGNTIES

We can see from the foregoing that the globalization of law through sovereignty was an equivocal affair. Sovereignty or, better, sovereign equality was undercut by the persistence of cultural and economic markers, by civilizational residues, and by great power prerogative. And of course sovereignty (the

---

[59] Keene 2014: 664.   [60] I discuss this in Simpson 2004: chapter 3.

favoured aspiration of anti-colonial movements) was itself a primary effect of empire; empire had left behind its maps, its political form, its clients, and its racial categorizations (soon to acquire a horrible potency in Sri Lanka and in Rwanda).[61] The distribution of sovereignty, too, inscribed some extraordinarily resilient hierarchies into global society. To put it bluntly, some nations acquired sovereignty through decolonization and many others did not. As James Crawford has remarked, international law is supposed to tell us 'how it is that various peoples (the Lithuanians, the Thais...) have a state of their own; whereas others (the Kurds, the Tibetans...) do not'.[62]

The existence of a body like the Unrepresented Nations and Peoples Organization in The Hague, most of whose members seek to move from one category into the other, suggests that sovereignty continues to enchant non-state peoples. Their puzzlement at their inability to do so reflects the difficulty in pointing to explicit legal rules regulating this transition outside the colonial context. This sovereignty, though, apart from being subject to internal hierarchization (great powers, refurbished standards of civilization), has also been threatened by processes of integration and fragmentation. The relationship between globalization and sovereignty is frequently misunderstood, of course. There is a sense in which globalization was both an effect of sovereignty and has reproduced a universal application of sovereignty.[63] International organizations like the international criminal court are not opposable to sovereignty but reliant on it.[64] It is clear, though, that sovereignty remains one form of social organization among many: no longer occupying the position of priority it had in, say, 1945. Indeed, almost as soon as the United Nations organization based itself on the 'sovereign equality' of states, that very sovereign equality came under challenge from several different directions. The Soviets and Americans created zones of heavily mediated sovereignty in their respective spheres of operation, international economic organizations adopted increasingly intrusive mechanisms compromising recently acquired political sovereignty (from credit conditions in the 1950s through to structural adjustment in the 1980s), and whole new legal forms came into being that forced a radical rethinking of the very meaning of sovereignty (the European Union was the most prominent example of this).[65] Alongside this, the monopoly of violence held by the sovereign state—a central engine in the creation of an international society of sovereigns—is giving way again to a world of religious caliphates, subnational strongholds, warlordism, and private violence.[66]

What we have now is a global society of states and other entities, and something deeper still and both anticipated and unanticipated by Bull and

---

[61] For a radical call to redraw these maps, see wa Mutua 1995.
[62] James Crawford 2012: 117.   [63] Rosenberg 1994.
[64] Cryer 2006.   [65] For example, Walker 2006.
[66] For a prehistory, see Thomson 1996; and later, see Colás and Mabee 2011.

Watson: a world society—a society in which political and economic decisions made in one place can have very profound effects in another (a world system, if you like), but also a society in the sense that the world is held together by an intense and powerful network of private and public laws.[67] This is what Thomas Franck called international law's post-ontological moment.[68] This is not to suggest that the question of enforcement no longer remains a problem for the international legal order. But it has become, in a way, the wrong question to ask.

The global legal order, then, by the 1970s was organized around a society of sovereign states and international institutions grounded in democratic (representation), naturalistic (right), and positivist (consent) forms of justification. In one sense this order was a product of persistent imperial geographies. The Europeans left sovereignty behind, or sovereignty was globalized. In one sense colonial hierarchies were abolished during a three-decades-long process of decolonization. But inequality was reorganized around institutional and private interventions, and through the displacement of empire as control by development as promise.[69] States were organized around deracialized categories of political economy. This was a way of maintaining sovereignty as a formal category of organization (and eradicating unacceptable forms of empire and racial differentiation) while at the same time introducing new forms of highly intrusive governance and economic conditionalities.

Where is the historical role of 'law' in this story? There are two ways of approaching this history and these practices. One would think of international law as perpetually deferential (but benign). This international law—imagined as a scholarly endeavour or a marginal institutional one—tries to gain a foothold in the inhospitable world of power politics. So, this might be a history of broken laws, great power hypocrisy, or quixotic institutional architecture. But here, global law is nearly always off the hook: playing handmaiden, utopian, or gentle civilizer.

The other story would emphasize law's constitutive role in global political life and in the construction of international society. So, here both the institution of sovereignty and the institutional arrangements that seek to organize or mediate sovereignty are effects of international law. And this is an important historical story. International law, a primary mode of organizing the world since 1500 and a constitutive language and practice of empire, has continued in its private and public forms to structure and direct the current (mis) allocation of goods, economic resources, ecological remnants, and life chances on the planet. But, as Sundhya Pahuja has pointed out:

> More recently, over the last sixty or so years, international law has also become the most prominent secular language through which competing aspirations about

[67] David Kennedy's work is vital here. See Kennedy 2013. But see, too, Cutler 2003.
[68] Franck 1998.   [69] Pahuja 2011.

a better world are articulated and put into practice at a global level. In the present day, internationalised ethical engagements and the calls for global justice that accompany them almost invariably use the idioms of 'development' or 'human rights'.[70]

This—we might call it a politics of justice—has been a preoccupation of the international legal order throughout the globalization of international society. This promise of justice—endlessly and necessarily deferred—has provided an ethics of, and justification for, international law since the rise of the field as a self-conscious set of practices in the middle of the second millennium. This promise has been partly configured around a sense of obligation towards the victims, opponents, or outliers of that international order. Although this justice discourse tended to be confined to the great early texts of international law (Francisco Suárez, Grotius) and only rarely inhabited the practice of colonial or intra-European politics, it has been increasingly institutionalized as international law has globalized. But in the nineteenth century, expectations about inter-state force, the embryonic humanitarianism of wartime conduct, and some general norms of good behaviour within Europe tended not to be readily exportable across Carl Schmitt's 'amity line'.[71]

So, at least one dominant thread in the narrative of law's globalization has been the modernization of the law through universalizing norms, doctrines, and institutions of justice. Sovereignty gives way to human rights, domestic jurisdiction is cracked open by the idea of crimes against humanity, empire is transmuted into decolonization, backwardness becomes development, civilization is pluralized, immunity becomes prosecution. This is, of course, an optimistic way of recounting history but it is not entirely inaccurate. Both at the level of discursive formation (talking about human rights) and material innovation (the machinery of international criminal courts), change has certainly occurred, and these changes have opened space for forms of progressive (legal) politics (the civil rights movement, the struggle against authoritarian government).

But the globalization of law and the attendant justice projects also seem infused with familiar hierarchies so that the ascendance of liberal legalism and humanitarianism has often reproduced the very distinctions it was thought to have dissolved.[72] Meanwhile, the diversification of legal forms, the relentless everydayness of global legal order, and the totalizing presence of private and public laws certainly depart from more conventional modes of inter-sovereign law-ordering and produce a 'dynamic realm of institutional change', but they

---

[70] Pahuja Forthcoming.   [71] See Schmitt 2006.
[72] See Lang 2011; Rittich 2002; Drew Forthcoming. For more optimistic (although not over-illusioned) views, see Teitel 2011; Alter 2014.

have hardly eliminated the hierarchies and immiserations authorized by those earlier legal orders.[73]

CONCLUSION

At every turn, then, global law is a negotiation among the competing claims of hegemony, sovereignty, and institutionalism within an international society at once both universalist in tone, ambition, and sometimes institutional design, and exclusionary and anti-pluralist in some of its most deeply ingrained practices. And, as I indicated at the beginning, there are two ways in which the story of this negotiation and the story of global law has been told. In one version (upbeat, blasé), international society is held together and (almost) fully governed by a network of rules and norms of international law. The aim is to bring everyone in (to the World Trade Organization, to the human rights system, to the International Criminal Court) in order to establish a truly global international legal order. The (underdeveloped, benighted) outsiders are aberrant. They lack—but this is remediable, and there is the endlessly and fatally deferred promise of remedy—democracy, or capitalism, or food, or law.

In the other version, outsiders are constitutive. Their existence is necessary to society's self-realization. A procession of figures has filled this role: pirates, outlaws, war criminals, terrorists, refugees, starving or bombed civilians, rebels, or the world's proletarian and slum classes. The standard account of international society posed a problem that *The Expansion* thesis purported to solve. The problem was an existing international society expanding outwards and slowly developing a law of encounter or assimilation. The counter-thesis has problematized the nature of this encounter (no longer pacific or linear) and the unity of a pre-existing international society. In particular, European global law is understood to have been constituted by this encounter. In this version, international society's potency is derived, partly, from its interventions—juridical, financial, humanitarian, military, and cultural—in relation to these marginal figures. It is these interventions that help hold international society together.

---

[73] On the global legal order, see Teubner 1997; Teubner and Korth 2012. On 'legal pluralism', see Gover 2010; de Sousa Santos 2002 also discussing the way in which some of the distinctions between the civilized inside and uncivilized outside continue to operate in these new intensely globalized systems.

15

The Impact of Economic Structures on Institutions and States

Mark Beeson and Stephen Bell

In *The Expansion of International Society,* one of Hedley Bull and Adam Watson's signature contributions to English School theory was to understand an increasingly 'globalized' international society as an expanding set of collective international regimes and institutions underpinned by shared norms and common understandings among a growing 'society' of states.[1] Bull and Watson's focus was mainly on the expansionary dynamics of international society with only a limited focus on international institutions. We argue that such institutions can have important consequences for international society. Christian Reus-Smit distinguishes between 'constitutional norms' such as sovereignty, 'fundamental institutions' including the rule of law and the balance of power, and 'issue-specific' institutions that are established to shape or regulate more specific forms of behaviour among states, such as trade or financial flows.[2] Bull and Watson gave some attention to the first two categories, but not much to issue-specific institutions. Reflecting a more general lacuna in International Relations (IR) at the time, they also had little to say about the economy and how this interacted with international institutions. In this chapter we depart from Bull and Watson's approach in two ways: we focus first on 'issue-specific' institutions and second on their interaction with the economy.

The absence of political economy in Bull and Watson's work is more surprising than it might seem. Even by the early 1980s, there was already a growing literature that was calling for the discipline of IR to take the economy more seriously.[3] One would have also thought that Robert Keohane's and Joseph Nye's ground breaking analysis of political and economic 'interdependence' in an increasingly 'globalized' era would have put political economy at the

---

[1] Bull and Watson 1984c.   [2] Reus-Smit 1999.   [3] Strange 1970.

forefront of any analysis of the international system.[4] And yet, apart from Patrick O'Brien's analysis of the expansion of European capitalism during the colonial era, there is remarkably little consideration of economic forces or of the highly influential organizations that were developed to try and manage them in the period since the Second World War. Now, by contrast, some consideration of political economy in IR texts has become commonplace if not obligatory.

And yet, with the noteworthy exception of Barry Buzan, the English School has been slow to incorporate 'economic' issues into the study of international politics. As a result, there are still significant gaps in the English School understanding of the international system—especially its material base. Consequently, we take up Buzan's largely neglected call to explore interactions between English School theory and the international economy.[5] We argue that the failure to recognize the 'structural' power and impact of economic forces and their recursive, frequently unpredictable impact on politics, policymaking, and institutions more broadly represents a major lacuna in English School and broader IR scholarship. As we suggest, the role of economic forces is a key component in shaping the interaction between constitutive, fundamental, and 'issue-specific' institutions. We also argue that structural impacts on the latter institutions can rebound on more fundamental institutions and constitutional norms. If this is so, it challenges or even reverses the long-held view that it is deeper-level institutions that structure issue-specific institutions.

This chapter focuses on these gaps—on 'issue-specific' institutions and their impact on, and interaction with, the economy. In particular, we argue that such interactions can produce unforeseen structural ramifications that can rebound on institutions and their evolution. Institutions are essentially the rules and norms created by agents—in this case, primarily international organizations (IOs). Structures, by contrast, are treated here as essentially material, such as the structure of an economy or the material forces that economies generate, such as inflation or financial crises. We suggest that many of the IOs that are intended to manage economic activity are particularly prone to generating unforeseen effects as they—sometimes inadvertently—change the structural context in which such activities occur. Akin to Karl Marx's famous 'gravedigger thesis', we focus on how international economic institutions, interacting with the economy, may create the seeds of their own destruction. The focus here is mainly on the institutional architecture that emerged in the second half of the twentieth century aimed at regulating the international financial system. The system has expanded enormously since liberalization began in the 1970s, with the pace of change accelerating. In 1997, for example, global financial transactions stood at fourteen times global gross

---

[4] Keohane and Nye 1977.   [5] Buzan 2005.

domestic product (GDP), but by 2012 this figure had risen to seventy times world GDP.[6] The growth and spread of financial activity, or 'financialization',[7] not coincidently, has resulted in increasingly frequent and severe financial and economic crises. These systems have been actively shaped by states, yet their impact on regulatory, issue-specific institutions and states have been under-researched in IR literature. Buzan acknowledges this as a 'lost opportunity for the English School', suggesting that its 'understanding of what international society is about has remained narrowly cast'.[8]

We develop this argument by examining the rise and decline of the Bretton Woods-managed exchange rate regime that dominated post-Second World War international political economy. We then explore two further cases: the international financial crisis of 2008 and the subsequent Euro crisis. In the case of the post-Second World War-managed exchange rate system, we argue that this institution produced structural effects and subsequent economic crises, with states then acting to modify or abandon the original institutions as the unforeseen consequences of their original actions unfolded. State leaders subsequently developed a more market-based neoliberal order that became prominent among the Anglo-American economies until it too developed major problems. While this is consistent with English School theory in that new common understandings and norms held by actors helped forge new institutions, it is important to recognize that states confront great challenges in dealing with the structural ramifications of the large-scale economic forces that have been unleashed by so-called 'financialization' and the recent financial crises they have helped trigger.[9] These dynamics have been apparent in all the cases we consider. In similar and in different ways, these crises have and are posing major challenges to state sovereignty, international cooperation, the efficacy of institutions, and the societal order underpinning international arrangements. The focus of this chapter is, therefore, on the interaction between institutions and wider structures, and on the structural contradictions that institutional systems can often generate.

INSTITUTIONS, ECONOMIC STRUCTURES ... AND THE ENGLISH SCHOOL

Buzan is one of the few who has openly endorsed the inclusion of the 'economic sector' into the English School's purview.[10] He offers a positive assessment of the interaction between the economy and institutions, writing

---

[6] Wade 2014: 312.   [7] Van der Zwan 2014.   [8] Buzan 2005: 119.
[9] Montgomerie and Williams 2009.   [10] Buzan 2005. See also Buzan and Little 2000.

that '[t]he most obvious exemplar of solidarism in the pursuit of joint gains lies in liberal understandings of how to organise the economic sector'.[11] He sees the economy as a 'powerful structural ally' especially for solidarist theorists within the English School, with the proliferation of international economic institutions supporting a positive assessment of institution building and international collectivism.[12] Indeed, Buzan argues that 'unless states can cooperate to liberalise trade and finance, they will remain stuck with lower levels of growth and innovation, higher costs and lower efficiencies'.[13] For their part, liberal institutionalists in IR largely agree. They see institutions as assisting coordination and helping to solve collective action problems; all supporting cooperation and economic gains among states. All of these accounts emphasize the functional origins and operation of international institutions, but they do not sufficiently explore dysfunction and how developments in the economy can often play a major role in challenging such institution building.

The English School approach is significant in the IR literature because it attempts to incorporate the essentially structural and materialist elements of realism, with recognition of the importance of socially constructed institutions. Crucially, this occurs within a social context in which real agents are central and where ideas, norms, and expectations matter. It is here that English School writers and constructivists converge with their focus on interpretive agents acting within normative and institutional settings.[14] There is also a good deal of overlap here with the interpretive 'situated-agency' approach to historical institutionalism outlined by Stephen Bell (and Bell and Hui Feng) which informs much of what follows.[15] This approach starts with interpretive agents and works out to trace how agents perceive and interact dialectically with the institutions in which they are embedded as well as with wider structures; it is broadly compatible with English School theory and with more agency-based versions of constructivism.[16] All of these approaches can be used to better understand the social bases and intersubjective understandings and practices that constitute institution building and international politics.

It is important to recognize that discussions of 'institutions' are themselves contested, not least because the term is often used interchangeably with 'organizations'.[17] There is no agreed definition about the role of institutions among English School theorists, with Buzan developing a distinction between primary and secondary institutions.[18] In contrast, Reus-Smit in his depiction of the 'constitutive hierarchy of modern international institutions' posits a model of institutional development composed of 'constitutional structures' that shape meta-values and legitimate state action, 'fundamental institutions' such as

[11] Buzan 2005: 124. [12] Buzan 2005: 123. [13] Buzan 2005: 124.
[14] Dunne 1995. [15] Bell 2011; Bell and Feng 2013.
[16] Bell 2011. [17] Scott 1995. [18] Buzan 2004.

multilateralism and international law, and 'issue-specific regimes', such as the Bretton Woods system.[19] The intention here is to draw on and extend this discussion by highlighting relatively neglected impacts between constitutional norms, fundamental institutions, and 'issue-specific' institutions. We argue that the dialectical interaction between these two levels has often been underspecified and frequently conceived of as unidirectional. In other words, the expectation has been that fundamental institutions create the basic parameters within which issue-specific regimes operate. However, not only is it clear that the norms, values, and ideas embedded in different regimes are frequently contested,[20] but the actual operation of specific institutional regimes may create economic conditions that rebound upon, or interact with, fundamental institutions in unexpected ways. Indeed, we argue that specific institutions—especially at moments of economic crisis or even failure—may actually help to reconstitute fundamental institutions and constitutional norms in ways that are generally unrecognized in much of the broader theorizing. This possibility is especially visible in the economic domain, we argue, because crises and their management can be highly volatile, difficult, and necessitate rapid, event-driven ideational and institutional change.

Although we are conscious of the more pervasive, informal role of institutions as key components in the construction of social reality,[21] our principal concern in what follows is with institutions-as-organizations such as the International Monetary Fund (IMF) or the European Central Bank (ECB), and their role in overarching institutional regimes designed to address a specific problem or issue area. The particular level of analysis adopted here, therefore, is what Charles Tilly describes as the 'macro-historical', or the arena of 'big structures and large processes'.[22] However, in an attempt to ground our discussion in empirical reality, we present examples of the actual operation of specific institutional arrangements, such as the Bretton Woods system and the European Union (EU).

Across our cases, therefore, we examine the structural impact of the economy and its effects on institutions, states, and international society. One of the more challenging implications for English School conceptions of international order is that economic crises in particular may not only weaken institutions, but also weaken states, international agreements among states, and the social solidarity underpinning them. For example, despite the rudimentary social consensus underpinning reform in the wake of the 2008 financial crisis, competitive pressures between states in combination with compromised state sovereignty have weakened reform efforts and the construction of new regulatory institutions. Similarly, institutional arrangements have helped create the euro crisis that has raised profound structural challenges that have

---

[19] Reus-Smit 1999: 15.   [20] Beeson and Li 2015.
[21] Searle 1995.   [22] Tilly 1984: 61.

weakened European institutions, as well as the state solidarity and normative order that underpinned them. This has reduced the scope for international cooperation on which crisis resolution depends. Both of these latter cases raise important questions about the scale of the structural ramifications that contemporary economies are producing, and about the limits of agency and the capacities of international society when confronting large structural forces. Our case studies also raise pertinent questions about the limits of international cooperation and about solidarist conceptions within the English School; especially in relation to the economy. Arguably much can be learnt if we focus on the interaction between institutions and the economy. Such a focus will help overcome an important lacuna in English School research and perhaps help us better understand the role of states and international cooperation in dealing with financial and economic crises.

THE RISE AND DECLINE OF THE BRETTON WOODS SYSTEM

The institutions of the Bretton Woods system were established in the immediate aftermath of the Second World War to manage the international economy. Their central collective goal was to sustain the capitalist order led by the US and to avoid the policy mistakes of the interwar period at a time when the challenge posed by communism and the Soviet Union was real and credible. From an English School perspective, the significance of the Bretton Woods system was that—within the capitalist world, at least—it represented a self-conscious attempt to create an international society based on institutionalized liberal norms underpinned by a set of binding rules and agreements.[23] Significantly, the Bretton Woods system regime had consequences its architects neither envisaged nor intended, but which ultimately helped to transform some of the fundamental institutions with which it interacted.

For our purposes, the most interesting component of this new institutional architecture was the creation of a system of managed exchange rates to be regulated by the IMF. At the heart of the new agreements was what John Gerard Ruggie famously described as the 'compromise of embedded liberalism', or the retention of a good deal of national policy autonomy within the context of an increasingly integrated international economy.[24] In its heyday the closely managed system of fixed exchange rates represented a major, largely successful attempt to curb the power of financial sector actors who were seen as responsible for exacerbating the Great Depression. The principal

---

[23] Strange 1994.   [24] Ruggie 1982.

mechanism with which stability was to be maintained, and the policies of individual countries were to be coordinated, was a commitment to use monetary policy to maintain the value of domestic currencies. National currencies were loosely pegged to the US dollar, which in turn was convertible at a fixed value into gold. The job of the IMF was to help countries manage occasional balance of payments crises and help to restore currency stability. As Louis Pauly points out, the Bretton Woods system marked a major transformation and represented 'a clear breach of the formerly sacrosanct right of sovereign states to craft their economic policies without external accountability'.[25] The reason they were prepared to do this, of course, is that states judged it to be in their interests: a stable, rule-based order offered the prospect of international economic stability and badly needed economic growth and development. Whatever the 'technical' and self-interested merits of the regime, however, it is important to recognize that it represented an important, economically driven modification of the formerly inviolable idea of domestic sovereignty—one of the foundational constitutional norms of international society.

The Bretton Woods system came about largely as a consequence of American leadership and its 'hegemonic' economic and strategic position. It is no coincidence that the Bretton Woods system was anchored by the US and reflected its normative values and preferences.[26] Ian Clark addresses the fundamental problem of asymmetrical power relations by grounding them in the English School concern with values and the social construction of the international system. The key claim here from an English School perspective is that hegemony is something that is 'conferred' by other actors in the international system. Consequently, Clark argues that hegemony is best thought of as 'an institutional practice of special rights and responsibilities, conferred by international society or a constituency within it, on a state (or states) with the resources to lead'.[27] 'Rather than something unilaterally possessed by the hegemon, it is a status bestowed by others, and rests on recognition by them.'[28]

While Clark's formulation provides a persuasive English School account of the socially constructed yet hierarchical post-war international order, it is less good at dealing with hegemonic decline and unilateralism. Despite the fact that the Bretton Woods system is associated with what is considered to be the 'golden age' of post-war development,[29] the regime came to an abrupt end as a consequence of mounting structural problems and a resultant change in American policy priorities. Significantly, the willingness of the US to play the crucial role as a provider of collective international goods ended because of its own deteriorating *economic* position. Not only was the US involved in a ruinously expensive war in Vietnam, but its efforts to encourage economic reconstruction in Western Europe and Japan had proved all too successful.

---

[25] Pauly 1997: 85.　　[26] Latham 1997.　　[27] Clark 2011a: 4.
[28] Clark 2011a: 35.　　[29] Glyn et al. 1990.

Somewhat ironically, the Bretton Woods system and the economic stability and growth it helped create also helped create formidable competitors that were challenging America's economic dominance.

This deterioration in the 'structural' basis of American hegemony made the privileging of narrow national priorities or the 'unilateralist temptation' a more compelling option for the US.[30] The costs of war and growing international economic competition had induced mounting trade and domestic budgetary deficits in the US, leading Richard Nixon's administration to abandon unilaterally a highly institutionalized international order.[31] A further cause of America's problems had been mounting monetary problems, especially with the massive build-up of US dollars held in foreign banks as the US printed money to cover its external obligations. To help ensure confidence and stability the major currencies had been fixed to the dollar and the dollar fixed to gold at the rate of US$35 an ounce. The system thus had a real anchor. It became clear, however, that global economic stability could not be achieved by using a single national currency to act as a global reserve currency. The Yale University economist, Robert Triffin, pointed to this problem.[32] He argued that for the US, the system created fundamental conflicts between domestic and international economic objectives—contradictory dynamics which have still not disappeared.[33] To support international economic expansion the system required the issuance of plentiful dollars for liquidity and the build-up of foreign reserves, which implied large current account deficits for the US. More pressure was put on the system when the US issued dollars to fund the Vietnam War, instead of paying for it through taxation. The huge increase in the supply of dollars increasingly placed their value in question, added to inflationary pressures, and raised serious questions about the strength of the dollar and about the viability of the dollar's convertibility into gold; which anchored the whole system. Ultimately, the institutions of the fixed-rate regime produced broader structural effects that undermined the original institutions; essentially a dialectical interaction between structure and agency that led to a major transformation of the international order. This also ultimately provided the basis for a remarkable—largely unanticipated—growth in financial markets: the value of currencies became determined by market forces rather than the earlier managed relationship to the dollar, and new market opportunities expanded as a consequence of further liberalization.

The result was that a key part of the institutional bargain—in which other actors in international society had conferred or acquiesced to leadership by the US—began to unravel as a consequence of both the US's actions, and as a result of the reconfigured economic system that emerged as a result. The Nixon administration's decision to stop the convertibility of dollars into

---

[30] Skidmore 2011.   [31] Beeson and Broome 2010.
[32] Triffin 1960.   [33] See Kirshner 2008.

gold and to 'close the gold window' had major short- and long-term implications for other participants in what had hitherto been a highly integrated international economic order. The immediate impact was to contribute to the general economic instability and stagflation that characterized much of the turbulent 1970s.[34] The longer-term consequences have been even more profound and contained the origins of the current financial and European crisis based largely on the overextension of debt. Ultimately, the institutions of the fixed-rate regime had produced broader structural effects in the international monetary system that undermined the original institutions. The longer-term consequences of the shift from a system of managed exchange rates to the current international order in which international money markets determine the value of most of the world's currencies contains a number of important lessons. First, once structural conditions changed in the international system so too did behaviour—often in unpredictable ways. Geopolitical solidarity became less important. Institutions that had once seemed vital components of a highly regulated international order suddenly came to be seen as too constraining or costly. Second, international legitimacy may matter, but not as much as perceived 'national interests'. Hegemons can be selfish as well as benign.[35] Faced with an increasingly difficult domestic economic and political situation, the US abandoned its earlier international commitments. Third, institutional orders can change in ways their original actors may never have imagined. Not only has the role of key Bretton Woods system institutions such as the IMF completely changed, but so, too, has the international economic order that it still seeks to manage. The result is the current international financial architecture that revolves around the actions of money markets and financial institutions, and which has played such a decisive role in both the recent financial crisis and in the still evolving crisis in the EU.

THE 'GLOBAL' FINANCIAL CRISIS

From the 1970s, policymakers in the world's major financial centres worked more or less in concert, animated by shared ideas and joint policy agendas aimed at substantially changing the institutional architecture of banking and finance in a liberalizing, broadly neoliberal direction. In subsequent decades, policies of deregulation and liberalization reduced direct state controls over banking and finance and handed substantial authority to market players. This helped usher in a new age of 'financialization', marked by a major structural change that has involved a shift in the centre of gravity in contemporary

---

[34] Block 1977.   [35] Conybeare 1987.

capitalism that has made the financial sector increasingly important and powerful. Significantly, this has been driven by, and arguably benefitted, the US, the reigning hegemonic power of the era.[36] A key long-term consequence has been to encourage major changes in banking and finance and a massive expansion in financial sector activity and debt levels in the core US, UK, and European markets. In banking there has been a blurring of earlier distinctions between commercial and investment banking and the associated rise of 'trader' banks and related shadow banks that drove the derivatives trading and securitization bubble based on US sub-prime mortgages that were at the centre of the 2008 financial crisis.[37] The high-volume trading in these markets was fuelled by liberalized institutional arrangements, intense levels of market competition, as well as by high levels of bank leverage and associated dependence on short-term wholesale funding markets.[38]

The crisis that peaked in 2008 and which decimated the banking sectors of the US, the UK, and a number of European countries stemmed from the collapse of the US mortgage market in 2007. This produced balance-sheet losses especially in complex sub-prime securitized assets. Some banks in the UK also recorded losses in more traditional albeit highly leveraged lending. In October 2008, the IMF estimated that the declared losses in the sub-prime securities markets to be around US$500 billion. These losses, however, were far lower than the US$5 trillion in losses in US equity markets during the dot-com crash in the early 2000s and far lower than the assets of even a single large global bank such as JP Morgan.[39] Losses of US$500 billion nevertheless generated a full-blown financial crisis. The financial boom and subsequent crash revealed that banks were operating in a new structural context of 'systemic risk'.[40] Banks are always structurally exposed because they borrow long and lend short, exposing them to a maturity mismatch—which is why the state has traditionally provided lender of last resort support in a liquidity crisis. By 2008, however, international banks were exposed to elevated forms of structural risk due largely to their huge leverage and associated dependence on short-term wholesale funding markets. In a context of complex asset and debt structures and opaque balance sheets, uncertainty, market panic, and the subsequent freezing of global credit markets rapidly ensued. The structural context of systemic risk proved to be a situation in which relatively small perturbations could set off major chain reactions and cascading failures that brought down the entire financial systems in the core markets.

As with the Bretton Woods-managed exchange rate system, institutional arrangements eventually generated structural effects and crises. These in turn have challenged and helped to reshape the original institutional arrangements.

---

[36] Konings 2007.   [37] Krippner 2011; Dore 2008; Bell and Hindmoor 2015.
[38] Financial Crisis Inquiry Commission 2011; Bell and Hindmoor 2015.
[39] See Admati and Hellwig 2013: 60.   [40] Haldane and May 2011.

In this latter case, however, states have had major difficulties in adequately reforming the original crisis-prone institutions. Banking reforms have been introduced on a scale that would have been unthinkable prior to the crisis and that promise substantially more state intervention in banking and financial affairs. Primarily, these have included strengthening the international Basel accords and raising the levels of bank capital, new forms of system-wide 'macro-prudential' financial regulation, and 'structural' reforms aimed at shielding retail or commercial banking from riskier investment or trader banking activities.[41]

The problem with the reforms, however, is that they have not addressed a key source of the original structural problems, especially the scale of the financial sector and intense competitive pressures within it that drive risk-taking. As the IMF concludes:

> Overall, banking systems are generally more concentrated and are as reliant on wholesale funding today as they were before the crisis. Although some countries, notably the United States, have reduced their dependence on short-term funding, the bulk of the evidence suggests that the structure of the system has not changed in healthier directions and could reflect the lack of deep restructuring that should have occurred... financial systems are not safer than before the crisis... Of particular concern are the larger size of financial institutions, the greater concentration and domestic interconnectedness of financial systems, and the continued importance of non-banks in overall-intermediation. The potential future use of structured and some new derivative products could add to complexity and a mispricing of risk.[42]

In other words, financial and banking systems remain too large, too complex, and riddled with systemic risk. Risk-taking incentives and systemic risk, as key structural characteristics of the system, remain key threats. The new reforms try to shield the major banks from such threats but at best they are limited institutional responses to entrenched structural phenomena. Competitive pressures remain intense and in the context of weak lending markets, trading remains a key source of profit. Securitization markets have been decimated but new markets and sources of risk are developing. The interconnectedness of the system and high levels of systemic risk remain.

At a technical level, the reforms will be difficult to implement. Regulatory arbitrage will see the migration of risky activities to the less-regulated shadow banking sector. Moreover, the sheer size, complexity, and rapidly evolving nature of modern finance will see regulators in an endless game of catch-up with financial innovators. As Kenneth Rogoff argues, 'as finance has become more complicated, regulators have tried to keep up by adopting ever more

---

[41] Bell and Hindmoor 2015.
[42] IMF (International Monetary Fund) 2012: 101, 103–4.

complicated rules. It's an arms race that underfunded regulatory agencies have no chance of winning.'[43] The finance sector's institutional advantages are reinforced by forms of 'regulatory capture' in which it is able to influence the policy process in ways that reflects its preferences and interests.[44]

A related problem is that governments in the major economies have not fundamentally questioned the scope and scale of their financial sectors and the structural power they possess.[45] Since the crisis many banks have become larger. In the wake of massive bank bailouts, the problems of moral hazard have also worsened. Governments and political parties depend upon tax revenues and campaign contributions from the financial sector. They also rely on the jobs created by the financial sector. Highly indebted governments are increasingly dependent on credit supplied by financial markets. Governments also worry whether tougher regulation will mean losing financial sector activity to competitor states. This has been a problem in relation to toughening up the Basel capital rules, for example. As Thomas Rixen argues, in a world of mobile capital:

> Regulation is hampered by intensive jurisdictional competition. Governments fear losing internationally mobile financial activity to competitor states. They are not able to solve collective action problems to curb or ease competition amongst each other because they are influenced, even captured, by domestic financial interest groups . . . Subject to these different pressures governments can only agree on incremental and ineffective reforms, which are symbolically potent enough to soothe popular concerns.[46]

Governments thus remain materially and ideationally aligned with a large financial sector and are still wedded to the notion of supporting 'internationally competitive' financial markets. In the UK, for example, Chancellor George Osborne insisted that bank reform must proceed in a way that 'protects London's status as a global financial centre'.[47] Expanding financial empires and financialization have thus created a power structure, materially and ideationally, that has drawn in state leaders who have come to believe in and support the growth of finance and financial innovation. As Cornelia Woll points out, the capacity of financial interests to draw in the state has been less about coercive forms of 'capture' and is more about willing support and compliance due to material incentives and ideational convergence.[48] It is not surprising then that even after the most recent and devastating financial crisis, this state–finance nexus has inhibited fundamental reform of finance.[49] Although there was a debate about the potential dangers of rising asset price inflation prior to the crisis within central banks and technocratic circles,

[43] Rogoff 2012.   [44] Baker 2010; Johnson 2009.
[45] Culpepper and Reinke 2014.   [46] Rixen 2013: 436.
[47] Osborne 2010.   [48] Woll 2014.   [49] Bell and Hindmoor 2015.

governments it seemed were happy to ride the asset price booms of the 1990s and 2000s.[50] Indeed, in analysing the US situation, Nolan McCarty, Keith T. Poole, and Howard Rosenthal argue that successive governments have been compliant in fostering 'political bubbles' which they define as 'policy biases which foster and amplify market behaviours that generate financial crises'.[51] As these scholars argue, politicians have been lured by the prosperity associated with financial sector growth and have been seduced by the same forms of irrational exuberance that has gripped financial market participants.

The financial crisis has implications for English School theory and suggests that the *structural* ramifications of state-based institutions need to be probed. These effects can be large; breeding important sources of systemic risk which, when triggered, can drive perverse forms of agent–structure interaction and severe financial crises. Indeed, bankers did not wish to sell assets in a serially falling market in the teeth of the crisis; they were forced to do so by the structural pressures they confronted. Nor did they wish to freeze each other out of credit markets. Yet they were forced to. Collective agency was expressed in asset fire sales, loan refusals, and the freezing of credit markets driven by a structural context that made such behaviour more or less the only choice available. Bankers were subject to a form of power that they and their structured logic of interaction created and exerted collectively. English School theory is good at probing the social bases of institution building within broader settings internationally. However, when the English School encounters the economy, structural impacts that can matter a great deal need to be recognized.

Moreover, English School and broader IR theory typically focuses on the activities of sovereign states, but what if state sovereignty is compromised by private economic interests? As argued, this is essentially what has happened to major states in the financial heartlands of the UK and the US. As noted, this has made it more difficult to rebuild effective regulatory institutions in the wake of crises. The case of the international financial crisis therefore illustrates how major structural economic impacts can lead to crises, with subsequent impacts on institutions and state sovereignty. Moreover, although there has been a rudimentary social consensus underpinning reform in the wake of the crisis, led especially by the Group of Twenty (G20), the continuing struggle to win competitive financial advantage among key states has hampered international cooperation. Some have also argued that key international institutions such as the Basel committee on capital standards have been compromised by private financial interests.[52] English School theory is good at probing conflict and cooperation among sovereign states and revealing shared norms and standards in the institutions and practices of the members

---

[50] Hay 2013.   [51] McCarty et al. 2014: 14.   [52] Lall 2012.

of international society. But when the English School encounters the economy, critical attention is required regarding questions about structural economic impacts, state sovereignty, and international cooperation.

THE EUROPEAN CRISIS

Before considering the economic and political crisis that at the time of writing remains unresolved in the EU, a few broader comparative points are worth making. First, it is important to recognize that the very existence of the EU is largely a consequence of specific geopolitical circumstances and the impact of American hegemony. The US was desperate to shore up capitalist allies threatened by Soviet expansionism after the Second World War. Without American influence and material assistance it is debatable whether the Common Market (as it then was) would have come into existence. Geopolitics and the overarching structures of the international system were profoundly important determinants of Europe's collective development.[53] Second, within that structured environment, agents determined the precise shape of the institutions, processes, and norms that would come to govern international cooperation within the European framework. Indeed, it is possible to argue that the entire history of the EU can be read as a process of institutional innovation and experimentation within a specific yet changing context that continues to this day.[54] The end point of such processes is unknowable and non-teleological, despite the significance that is attached to the EU as the benchmark against which other regional projects are judged.[55] Indeed, our primary case study here—European monetary cooperation—is a reminder that the EU's policymakers are not infallible experts. Importantly, popular support for such arrangements is not guaranteed, nor is 'progress' inevitable.

The euro is emblematic of the EU's long-term trajectory and goals as it has developed more complex and ambitious institutions and forms of economic and political integration. The euro also remains at the centre of the most serious economic and political crisis the EU has ever experienced, which may yet culminate in the exit of one or more of its members with potentially far-reaching consequences.[56] The key question that the euro's development and current problems highlight, therefore, is whether European policymakers have overreached themselves and failed to appreciate the possible economic and structural consequences of initiatives that were primarily about progressing and entrenching *political* goals. From an English School perspective, the EU's fate is a critical test of the possible limits of solidarism, and the integrative

---

[53] Beeson 2005. [54] Sabel and Zeitlin 2010.
[55] Manners 2002; Börzel and Risse 2012. [56] Spiegel 2015.

effects of international institution-building. If international society cannot be made to work in Europe, it is unlikely to work anywhere.

It is important to emphasize just how unexpected this drawn-out crisis was, at least as far as its principal architects were concerned. The theory of 'optimum currency areas' (OCAs) that provides the intellectual support for common currencies suggests that such agreements will confer potential economic advantages on their members, especially by reducing the transaction costs associated with cross-border trade and in facilitating greater transnational economic integration. But as Benjamin J. Cohen argues, 'it is impossible to find an example of a monetary alliance motivated exclusively, or even predominantly, by concerns highlighted in OCA theory'.[57] In other words, political motivations have always been the prime driver of monetary cooperation and this has invariably led to potential economic problems being downplayed or overlooked. This is precisely what seems to have happened in Europe's case, as political leaders pressed on with greater integration and institutional innovation designed to consolidate the European project. The point to emphasize, however, is that the monetary regime created by political decisions ultimately rebounded on its architects in unforeseen ways that still threaten the continuing existence of the EU as currently constituted.

The desire to create a common currency within the EU is long-standing and has been seen as a central mechanism with which to encourage closer economic integration and convergence. Such aspirations were given concrete expression as proposals for Economic and Monetary Union (EMU) outlined under the auspices of the Treaty of Maastricht in 1992. There is some debate between observers about what played the biggest role in dramatically accelerating the desire for greater integration at this time. On the one hand, there are those scholars who stress geopolitical change, especially the end of the Cold War and the reunification of Germany. The argument here is that greater economic integration was seen as one way of offsetting fears—particularly French ones—about the implications of a reunified, increasingly powerful Germany at the centre of Europe.[58] On the other hand, Andrew Moravcsik argues that nationally embedded economic interests in Germany also played a significant role in shaping political processes at the time.[59] Whatever the precise configuration of such fluctuating forces was at the time, the outcome is clear: Maastricht prepared the ground and established the preconditions for the eventual birth of the euro.

Nevertheless, while politicians (outside countries like the UK, at least) were increasingly persuaded of the merits of a common currency as a way of promoting greater political and institutional integration, many economists remained highly sceptical.[60] It was to address the 'technical' objections and

---

[57] Cohen 1998: 84.   [58] Ross 1995.   [59] Moravcsik 1998.
[60] Feldstein 1997; de Grauwe 2006.

doubts about monetary union that the so-called 'convergence criteria' were established. These were basic targets for inflation, interest rates, exchange rate values, and fiscal stability that all prospective members were supposed to meet. Crucially, budget deficits were not supposed to exceed 3 per cent of GDP. Tight fiscal criteria were intended to 'effectively filter out countries lacking the requisite stability culture and unable to live within their means'.[61] In reality, such criteria were not enforced consistently and proved to be easily evaded, with disastrous long-term consequences.

The inauguration of the common currency in 1999 institutionalized inherent contradictions that would ultimately threaten the existence of the euro and even the EU itself. The key structural problem stemmed from the fact that membership of the common currency was composed of very different economies with profoundly different national economic circumstances and growth models.[62] One of the key institutional innovations that was undertaken to progress the EMU goals generally and the transition to a common currency in particular was the establishment of the European Central Bank in 1998. The ECB was charged with maintaining 'price stability' and can be seen as both a manifestation of international enthusiasm about the creation of independent central banks, and as a specific response to the challenge of overseeing monetary integration on an unprecedented historical scale. Significantly, the ECB was located in Germany, a move that recognized Germany's material importance as the EU's largest economy and one designed to assuage German fears about the implications of giving up the deutschemark.

The euro was rapidly accepted and initially judged a great success. For a sophisticated manufacturing economy such as export-oriented Germany, the euro enhanced competitiveness because of its comparatively low value. Significantly, all members of the euro area were treated by 'the markets' in broadly similar ways. This meant that the less productive economies on the periphery of Europe—the likes of Portugal, Ireland, and especially Greece— were able to borrow at much lower interest rates than might have been the case otherwise. This is precisely what they did, of course, with the net effect that current account deficits blew out as imports and foreign capital were sucked into these economies. In a 'normal' situation, where the peripheral economies had their own national currencies, a process of 'adjustment' would have been forced on them through currency depreciation. Because they were members of the euro, however, external market pressures were not effective in bringing about change in economies that would normally have been judged to be 'living beyond their means'. This outcome would become a key structural problem for the eurozone.

[61] Eichengreen 2008: 220.   [62] Peter A. Hall 2012.

For English School theorists, these developments and the euro crisis that eventually followed raise some difficult issues. If Buzan is correct in suggesting that 'the market' constitutes a key institution in international society, it is an especially contradictory one.[63] Market forces can be highly destabilizing and corrosive of international order. This is dramatically illustrated in the case of the euro which was inaugurated with the hope of encouraging European solidarism, but which has instead generated wider structural forces and outcomes. Such forces would manifest themselves as growing private and sovereign debt problems in the periphery that were exacerbated by the arrival of the 2008 financial crisis and which is a striking illustration of the EU's continuing vulnerability to internal and external calamities. The crisis that erupted in the US in 2008 was rapidly transmitted to Europe where it exposed the unresolved internal contradictions and economic imbalances that were entrenched with the establishment of the euro.

If the imbalances and unsupportable debt levels that had built up in the likes of Greece, Ireland, and Portugal can be thought of as essentially economic problems, their impact was not confined to the economy. On the contrary, one of the most striking and troubling features of the European crisis has been the reanimation of nationalist forces and sentiments that had once seemed permanently vanquished. Racist stereotypes about Greek fecklessness and German authoritarianism have re-emerged as these two countries have come to epitomize the very different economic and social circumstances that distinguish different European countries.[64] They are also a vivid reminder about the importance of economic power: the crisis has clearly highlighted how Germany has become the dominant actor within Europe, despite eschewing some of the traditional prerequisites of hegemony.[65]

The crisis consequently represents the most fundamental challenge that the EU has faced, and at the time of writing it remains unclear whether it will actually survive it, at least in its current form.[66] The central issue is a familiar one: is the EU going to develop even deeper forms of political and economic integration and the new institutions this implies, or will a disintegrative momentum take hold threatening the very foundations and identity of the eurozone? One of the perennial problems confronting the EU has been a lack of accountability, something its technocratic, top-down governance arrangements have exacerbated. Consequently, the low levels of normative identification and solidarity with the EU among the general population have been further diminished by the crisis, as well as by the inability of the EU's policymakers to definitively resolve it. Moreover, although the European Parliament has actually enjoyed a modest increase in authority and influence

---

[63] Buzan 2004.   [64] Barber 2012.
[65] *Economist* 2013.   [66] Alderman 2015.

relative to institutions such as the European Commission,[67] this has done little to curb the rise of anti-European sentiment, a problem that has been exacerbated by the recent influx of asylum seekers and economic migrants into Europe.

Even before this recent humanitarian crisis, however, the scale of the EU's economic problems had become so great that they were undermining Europe's fragile solidarity in two ways. First, the technocratic, unaccountable ECB has emerged as a critical part of the crisis repose. ECB President Mario Draghi's famous promise to do 'whatever it takes' to resolve the crisis was intended to both reassure skittish financial markets and to justify buying 'unlimited' quantities of sovereign bonds and more recently engage in quantitative easing. There is currently a major, unresolved policy debate about the relative merits of stimulus or at least bailout responses compared to policies of austerity; the latter favoured by the likes of Britain and even more importantly, Germany. As Gideon Rachman points out, the ECB approach is deeply unpopular among Germans who fret that they will ultimately have to underwrite such expenditures, and yet they have no democratic recourse when it comes to actually influencing ECB policy.[68] Either way, the catastrophically high levels of youth unemployment across much of Europe are a long-term threat to social stability.[69]

The economic crisis—especially when combined with the unprecedented flows of asylum seekers—is thus exposing the superficial nature of European solidarism and the contradictory impact of some of the key institutions of international society. As Peter Hall has pointed out, the internal structures and operation of differently configured forms of capitalism within Europe are being brutally exposed by the current crisis. Significantly, key members of the EU are unwilling to take the next step and embrace even more powerful supranational institutions that move the system closer to a fiscal union. As Hall notes in relation to the European debt crisis:

> it is now clear that, for the most part, feelings of social solidarity stop at national borders. Asked to rescue those suffering in southern Europe, many northern Europeans have balked. The sense of European identity for which the EU strives has been exposed as a thin veneer laid over essentially strong national identities; and that too stands in the way of an effective trans-European response to the crisis.[70]

The very possibility of international society and the creation of effective supranational and intergovernmental institutions is being put to a searching test. Sadly, it is not clear that the EU will pass it.

---

[67] Schwarzer 2009.   [68] Rachman 2012.
[69] Chaffin 2013.   [70] Peter A. Hall 2012: 367.

CONCLUSION

The neglect of economic issues has been a long-standing and widely recognized problem in approaches such as the English School. This chapter has
suggested why this is an increasingly debilitating absence for the English
School approach, and provided illustrations of how economic forces are
especially important at a time when economic crises are a recurrent feature
and driver of international relations. Approaches which neglect the economy
risk overlooking some of the key influences on contemporary international
politics. There are, for example, powerful and persuasive arguments about the
pacifying impact of economic interdependence that are central to debates
about the so-called 'capitalist peace'.[71] But even in less stable eras, economic
forces were critical determinants of state behaviour that needed to be incorporated into any comprehensive explanation of international relations. The
quintessential case in point is the breakdown of international commerce and
economic openness which culminated in the Great Depression and the rise of
fascism in Europe.

While the case studies offered here are thankfully less dramatic than the
period between the two world wars, some of the underlying dynamics are
strikingly similar. Not only is the 2008 financial crisis invariably described as
the most serious economic crisis since the Great Depression, its impact on
Europe is a reminder of just how powerful a driver of social change economic
disruption can be. In the current European case, the economic crisis also
demonstrates how unpredictable the consequences of major institutional
change and innovation can be. However normatively and pragmatically
attractive the *idea* of Europe may still be, it is plainly difficult to sustain in
unpropitious economic circumstances. Even more so when such economic
problems are overlaid with a traumatic social crisis. There is no little irony in
this given that the institutionalization of the European project was in large
part about ensuring greater economic integration to resolve Europe's historical animosities. The point to stress, once again, is that political actions can
bring about unanticipated consequences that may transform the way policymakers act and think about new problems and possibilities. In this way,
regime performance—especially at moments of crisis—may reshape fundamental institutions and constitutional norms in ways that are generally not
recognized in much English School theory.

The nature of contemporary international economic relations may make it
difficult for even the most powerful of states to pursue either a national or a
collective interest given the existence of an array of non-state actors and rising
powers with potentially different ideas about how international economic

---

[71] Gartzke 2007.

activity ought to be organized.[72] Consequently, one of the key points to emphasize here is that interplay between economic actors and structures is potentially very different from 'traditional' international relations because the actors are frequently non-state and the incentive structures (and rewards) are invariably private. This is something the English School tradition is potentially well-placed to illuminate and explain given its focus on the interaction between norms, rules, and institutions. Indeed, the active creation of, and difference between, economic systems is one of the most important fields of comparative political economy;[73] English School scholars could add an important international framework to some of these debates. Analysts of international political economy can be just as neglectful of international relations and geopolitics as IR scholars are of the economy.

One of the most important insights that emerges from an English School-oriented reading of the international economy is that economic integration really *does* seem to have had a big impact on the conduct of international relations, and this is something English School scholars can say something important about—if they choose to take it seriously. Broadly liberal ideas have been institutionalized in ways that have amounted to a highly influential policy paradigm that has underpinned not only post-war economic development,[74] but a major restructuring of the international economy itself. Not all of these changes were expected or welcome, however, and are a reminder of the unpredictable, dialectical nature of the relationship between 'big ideas', institutional development, geopolitics, and long-term structural change in the international economy.[75] At a moment when the old economic *and* geopolitical order is clearly in a state of flux as economically ascendant rising powers jostle for influence, recognizing the interactive, unpredictable nature of institutional change and its possible consequences is vital for any plausible theory of international relations.

---

[72] Schweller 2011.   [73] Hall and Soskice 2001.
[74] Babb 2012.   [75] Beeson and Li 2015.

16

Universal Human Rights

Hun Joon Kim

Universal human rights have experienced a dramatic increase in the post-Second World War period, starting with the 1948 Universal Declaration of Human Rights (hereafter Universal Declaration). States were expected to ratify human rights conventions and many governments regarded human rights treaties as normative prescriptions constituting the legitimate identity of modern nation-states. The principle of human rights is now inscribed in the constitution of most countries even though many regard them as being Western in origin. The idea of universal human rights has also been institutionalized in the form of independent and permanent human rights commissions or newly established branches of government organizations. Over time, human rights have expanded throughout the globe and have become more effective in directing the choices that states make. A distinctive feature of today's global international society is that, in addition to upholding principles of sovereign equality and territorial integrity, we have seen an ever-increasing codification of universal human rights. Indeed, it is this conjunction of sovereignty and human rights that makes today's international society so unique.

An example of this conjoined relationship between sovereignty and human rights can be seen in the declaration by the European Community (now known as the European Union) in December 1991 on the Guidelines on the Recognition of New States in Eastern Europe and in the Soviet Union. Among five general conditions required for new states, the first is respect for the United Nations (UN) Charter, the Helsinki Final Acts, and the Charter of Paris, 'especially with regard to the rule of law, democracy, and human rights',[1] and the second is the guarantee of rights for ethnic and national groups and minorities. Both the United States and European countries have been using these principles to recognize statehood. This is a prime example of the way in which the principle of sovereignty and universal human rights has

---

[1] Murphy 2012: 36.

become co-constituted in the present international society. The current era is not the first in which consideration of individuals' rights has been wedded to statehood. The principle of national self-determination, represented in Woodrow Wilson's Fourteen Points, is another example, but this principle immediately after the First World War did not have the same geographic scope and universal application as today.

There are three important questions to understand about this unique and new phenomenon. First, how should we understand the globalized sovereign order in relation to the emergence of universal human rights? Second, what are the underlying normative foundations of universal human rights in the global order? More specifically, how have human rights become institutionalized and what social and political practices hold them together? Third, how are universal human rights manifested in this global order and what are the politics surrounding them?

Some of these questions were addressed in Hedley Bull and Adam Watson's *The Expansion of International Society*. Elements of the universal principle of human rights can be seen in Bull's chapter, 'The Revolt against the West', and in R. J. Vincent's chapter, 'Racial Equality'. The revolt against Western dominance comprised five themes, one of which was the struggle for racial equality. This struggle was mainly understood as the struggle of 'non-white states and peoples against white supremacism', but the focus was on the struggle of non-white *states* rather than non-white peoples.[2] For example, Bull understood the emergence of Haiti as a black state, the Japanese victory over Russia in 1905, and the Afro-Asian non-aligned movement at Bandung, as important moments in the struggle for racial equality. In all cases, Bull's focus was on the role of under-represented non-European *states* in the system, rather than on consideration for under-represented *peoples* within those states.

Vincent maintained a similarly statist view of racial equality when he described different phases where he emphasized the independence of Haiti, Sierra Leone, and Liberia, and also the role of Japan in promoting a new concept of racial equality in the nineteenth century. For this reason, decolonization in the 1950s and 1960s is understood as the rapid expansion of racial inequality in international society.[3] Thus, for Bull and Vincent, racial equality was mostly something to be achieved through states or by state relations. In addition to this limitation, racial equality is only one part of the many struggles for universal human rights, and it does not represent the larger picture of the globalization of universal human rights.

Universal human rights were addressed by other essays in *The Expansion*, such as in James Piscatori's 'Islam in the International Order', and in Ian

---

[2] Bull 1984c: 221.   [3] Vincent 1984.

Brownlie's 'The Expansion of International Society: The Consequences for the Law of Nations'. However, universal human rights were viewed merely as a tool of the West, in which Muslim states had difficulty in subscribing to Western norms.[4] In particular, the Universal Declaration was heavily criticized for its failure to take into account 'Islamic sensitivity'. In exploring the role of international law immediately after the Second World War, Brownlie similarly argued that legal innovation and related developments in international society in the 1950s and 1960s could be traced to the Western world. In this case, the adoption of the Universal Declaration was viewed as a landmark which set 'the development and elaboration of human rights standards as legal standards'.[5]

In sum, I find the contributors to *The Expansion* retained a strong state-centric view of universal human rights, which in part reflected the limitations of the authors who had not witnessed the full-blown development of universal human rights that we see today. However, compared to contemporary International Relations (IR) scholars, Vincent and Bull made path-breaking contributions (in *The Expansion* and elsewhere) to the academic study of universal human rights by giving the issue of human rights equal weight in comparison to other issues in world politics.[6] Moreover, some of these insights, such as their understanding of human rights as a realm of contestation between the Western world and the non-Western world, are still highly relevant. The contestation around the issue has resurfaced in world politics.

This chapter examines the nature and development of universal human rights in the context of global international society after the publication of *The Expansion*. My focus on research published after *The Expansion* shows how the oppositional understanding of human rights as a threat to sovereignty has come under increasing challenge from constructivist research on universal human rights. The chapter consists of three sections. First, I examine the definition of universal human rights and explore the relationship between human rights and the principle of sovereignty. Second, I examine the detailed process of the globalization of universal human rights, focusing not only on the institutionalization and legalization of international human rights, which can be referred to as 'standard-setting',[7] but also adding two additional processes of development—investigation and accountability. In the final section, I explore the recent challenges and contestations to the principle of human rights by tracking the development of human rights since 1945, focusing both on the institutions of human rights, and on actual practices by employing qualitative pattern-matching.[8]

---

[4] Piscatori 1984.   [5] Brownlie 1984: 366.   [6] Bull 1977; Vincent 1986.
[7] Dunne 2007: 269.   [8] George and Bennett 2005.

UNIVERSAL HUMAN RIGHTS AND
UNIVERSAL SOVEREIGNTY

Rights provide 'a rational basis for a justified demand'.[9] Rights are divided into two categories—*special rights* and *general rights*. The former arise out of 'special transactions between individuals or out of some special relationship in which they stand to each other'.[10] The latter are rights that individuals have 'simply because they constitute a particular kind of moral being'.[11] By their nature, the former are particularistic, while the latter are universalistic, within the boundaries of what the contemporaries thought of as 'moral being'. Rights can be further divided into two additional categories—*individual rights* and *collective rights*. The former are those of sole persons, while the latter belong to groups. *Human rights* can be defined as 'the rights that one has because one is human'.[12] Human rights are universal rights in the sense that we consider all human beings as holders of human rights. Human rights are located where individual rights and general rights overlap. Although in this chapter my focus is on human rights as *individual* rights, I also address human rights as *collective* rights, which are increasingly challenging the notion of human rights as universal and individual rights.

IR scholars have conducted intensive research on the globalization of universal human rights.[13] The structure of international human rights law and institutions and the actual process of historical developments have been closely examined.[14] Originally, the idea of humanitarianism developed through intense conflicts and contestations with the norm of sovereignty.[15] Distinguished from human rights laws, humanitarian law originated and is still heavily based on the treatment of protected individual persons during wartime. States and non-state actors worked to expand the definition and application not only of 'protected persons' but also of 'wartime' through a series of developments in the Hague Conventions of 1900 and 1910, and in the Geneva Conventions of 1864, 1929, and 1949.

Full-scale development of human rights, however, occurred only after the end of the Second World War when the world witnessed Nazi Germany's Holocaust. The struggle began with the process of including the human rights clause in the UN Charter, and in the subsequent development of the Universal Declaration.[16] The adoption of the UN Charter and the Universal Declaration as a new norm brought both possibilities and fear at the same time. For example, the US delegates to Dumbarton Oaks were specifically instructed

[9] Shue 1996: 13.   [10] Hart 1955: 175.
[11] Reus-Smit 2013a: 37.   [12] Donnelly 2003: 7.
[13] Vincent 1986; Dunne and Wheeler 1999; Donnelly 2003; Forsythe 2006.
[14] Moyn 2010; Iriye et al. 2012.   [15] Finnemore 1996; Barnett 2011.
[16] Morsink 1999.

not to include human rights language in the Charter, while representatives from China were actively pursuing the cause of racial equality with a view to its incorporation into the Charter. However, the institutionalization of universal human rights was further accelerated with the adoption of special treaties, such as the Genocide Convention and Refugee Convention, the International Covenant on Civil and Political Rights, the Convention against Torture and Other Cruel, Inhuman or Degrading Treatment or Punishment, and the International Covenant on Economic, Social and Cultural Rights. The current UN human rights system is a good example of how universal human rights have now been institutionalized over the last sixty years.

The UN human rights system currently consists of three major bodies: the General Assembly, the Human Rights Council, and the Security Council. Major declarations, resolutions, various human rights conventions, and diverse specialized treaties are created in the General Assembly. Treaty bodies—monitoring bodies for major human rights conventions, also located within the General Assembly—receive and review the state party's self-reports on the implementation and progress of the conventions.[17] The Human Rights Council, composed of forty-seven elected UN member states, is the most active body within the UN human rights system. The most important function of the Human Rights Council is to make major decisions on human rights situations around the globe in its ten-week regular sessions. The Security Council makes important decisions regarding serious and grave human rights violations that threaten peace and security. The Security Council has various compulsory measures that it can use, such as imposing economic sanctions, referring cases to the International Criminal Court (ICC), creating ad hoc international criminal tribunals, and authorizing the use of force as a last resort.

This perspective on the development of human rights, which emphasizes the legalization and institutionalization of human rights norms, goes hand-in-hand with one of the most important philosophical foundations of human rights. After the demise of the idea that the divine being was the sole and ultimate source of moral authority, human rights rested on three philosophical foundations—natural rights, utilitarianism, and positivism.[18] Although natural rights theory and utilitarianism still provide important moral bases for universal human rights, legal positivism, which finds its moral foundation in the consent of sovereign states to be bound by law, increasingly became important in the development of international human rights law. In a sense,

---

[17] Currently, there are ten treaty bodies: the Human Rights Committee, the Committee on Economic, Social and Cultural Rights, the Committee on the Elimination of Racial Discrimination, the Committee on the Elimination of Discrimination against Women, the Committee against Torture, the Subcommittee on Prevention of Torture, the Committee on the Rights of the Child, the Committee on Migrant Workers, the Committee on the Rights of Persons with Disabilities, and the Committee on Enforced Disappearances.

[18] Shestack 1998: 201.

this also suggests one perspective on the relationship between universal human rights and universal sovereignty since legal positivists believe that 'all authority stems from what the state and officials have prescribed'.[19] The universality of human rights is now verified by the fact that most countries around the world have ratified key international human rights conventions.

However, despite the expansion of human rights law and institutions, debates have continued as to what constitutes a moral human being and which rights among many should be prioritized. Two challenges are relevant here. First is the so-called 'three generations' of human rights argument.[20] The first generation encapsulates civil and political rights, which emerged during the revolutionary era in Europe and the United States. These include the right to life and the right to free speech and thought, and are what most scholars think of as core human rights. The second generation refers to economic and social rights, which became important for the Soviet Union during the Cold War, and for China and other developing countries after the Cold War. Vincent captured this nicely when he argued that the history of East–West relations was 'in an important sense the history of a dispute about human rights'.[21] The third generation denotes collective rights that emerged from the decolonization struggle and that continued apace through the postcolonial period in Africa. Here, importance is attached to the right to self-determination, the right to economic development, the right to peace, and the right to a sustainable environment.[22]

The second challenge relates to the cultural relativism argument, or the debate between universalism and relativism.[23] This is a fundamental challenge to the idea of the universality of human rights.[24] This debate is intense, not at the level of legalization or legislation, but at the level of implementation and enforcement. The most significant challenge to the idea of universalism in human rights came in the Bangkok declaration at the 1993 World Conference on Human Rights. Representatives at the conference proclaimed a declaration, claiming that human rights must be approached from a pluralistic perspective that respects differences in culture, region, religion, and history. This further prompted the debate over 'Asian values' in other areas such as democracy.[25] Furthermore, cultural relativism became an international issue when the African Union expressed its united position against criminal proceedings at the ICC targeting only Africa leaders.

These contestations reflect the tension between human rights and sovereignty. The relationship between universal state sovereignty and universal human rights has always been problematic. Ironically, states are both protectors and abusers of the principle of human rights and thus sovereignty, and

---

[19] Shestack 1998: 209.   [20] Bell 2000.   [21] Vincent 1986: 61.
[22] Ishay 2008.   [23] Van Ness 1999.
[24] Brown 1999; Bauer and Bell 1999; Bell et al. 2001.   [25] Sen 1997.

both internal and external dimensions have been in conflict with human rights. The relationship between the two principles was usually understood as antithetical because international human rights norms question and challenge state sovereignty. Kathryn Sikkink, however, presents a more subtle argument. Universal human rights are, she claims, contributing to 'a gradual, significant, and probably irreversible transformation of sovereignty'.[26] Since sovereignty is also a norm, or a shared set of understandings and expectations about the state, a change to sovereignty becomes possible when there are wider changes about the moral purpose of statehood.

This transformation was later captured by scholars who empirically and historically examined the relationship between human rights and universal sovereignty. Stephen Krasner, for example, revisited the firm belief about the Westphalian sovereignty model in order to show that due to other important principles, such as human rights, minority rights, and democracy, breaches of sovereignty have been an enduring characteristic of international relations.[27] Autonomy and territorial integrity have consistently been violated in four ways—through conventions, contracting, coercion, and imposition. Among these, human rights is 'the most obvious class of conventions' and is a prime example of the violation of sovereignty because human rights agreements 'cover relations between rulers and ruled'. Following Sikkink, Krasner also views the principle of sovereignty as a system, which is characterized by 'competing norms, and absence of universal authority structure, and power asymmetries'. Thus, sovereignty has always been a 'compromise' with other important principles such as human rights and it is a 'cognitive script characterized by organized hypocrisy'.[28]

Christian Reus-Smit provides an innovative account of the relationship between universal sovereignty and human rights by criticizing the conventional view that treats sovereignty and human rights as two separate, zero-sum, and mutually contradictory principles. He argues that in the twenty-first century, sovereignty has been 'justified in terms of the state's role as guarantor of certain basic human rights and freedom', and thus the protection of human rights is 'integral to the moral purpose of the modern state, to the dominant rationale that licenses the organization of power and authority into territorially defined sovereign units'.[29] In other words, the moral purpose of the state is 'the augmentation of individuals' purposes and potentialities', and justice 'must apply equally to all citizens, in all like cases'.[30] Similarly, Daniel Philpott argues that the modern notion of sovereignty is based on 'the moral ideas...about rights to worship, self-determination, racial equality, and human rights'.[31]

---

[26] Sikkink 1993: 411.   [27] Krasner 1995: 115   [28] Krasner 2001: 17.
[29] Reus-Smit 2001: 519.   [30] Reus-Smit 1999: 9, 129.   [31] Philpott 2001: 6.

This understanding of sovereignty is reflected in a recent example of the use of the responsibility to protect (R2P). In 2011, Libya was convulsed by an uprising against the dictatorial rule of Muammar Qaddafi. Egregious human rights violations on the part of Qaddafi's regime not only provoked a NATO-led intervention, but also moved the ICC to indict Qaddafi, his son, and the head of security for war crimes. Yet the first blow against the regime was struck not by the United States, NATO, nor the UN, but from a much less likely source: Switzerland. On 24 February 2011, Switzerland froze US$630 million of funds controlled by Qaddafi, his sons, and others within the 'Brother Leader's' government. The Swiss government reasoned that Libyan public funds would otherwise be misappropriated by these individuals. This followed earlier action by Switzerland and other countries to freeze the assets of Zine el-Abidine Ben Ali, Hosni Mubarak, and both leaders' families and close associates after these regimes had fallen. Once more the justification was that these funds probably represented the proceeds of corruption. In Libya, Tunisia, and Egypt, there has been a strong international drive to protect civilians from their own governments.

THE GLOBALIZATION OF HUMAN RIGHTS

How, then, have universal human rights norms been globalized? The closest statement on the globalization of universal human rights in *The Expansion* is Bull's understanding that international legal rules were not only made by the European and Western powers, but that they were also 'in substantial measure made *for* them'.[32] However, what is lacking is an understanding of the internal dynamics of how a universal human rights system has been developed and intensified. In order to understand the rise and development of human rights as a global normative structure and process, two aspects must be considered—structure and process. The development and prevalence of universal human rights went through different phases, gaining legitimacy and widening their reach. First, they were institutionalized (codified or legalized) and second, through interaction, states gradually accepted the rules of the game and complied more or less with behaviours prescribed by the institutional setting.

In this section, I propose a new and comprehensive theoretical framework to help understand this development based on the tripartite process within the universal human rights normative system. The globalization of universal human rights is not a single and unidirectional process of institutionalization or legalization, but a combination of three complex processes, which for the

---

[32] Bull 1984c: 217, emphasis in original.

most part appears and interacts simultaneously. These processes are standard-setting, accountability, and investigation. Universal human rights are fundamentally a standard of behaviour and action and thus, at their very core, contain a *should statement*. This intrinsic 'sense of ought-ness' or 'logic of appropriateness' of universal human rights is often made explicit in their codification, legalization, or institutionalization, which can all be categorized as standard-setting processes. However, when the ought-ness of universal human rights ideas meet the messy, unordered, and incomplete reality, then two other processes—accountability and investigation—come into play.

Scholars of human rights have so far focused on the process of standard-setting, and have recently begun to discuss the issues of compliance, enforcement, and effectiveness, which is an accountability process.[33] An investigation process is a mode that intermediates between standard-setting and accountability, but one that has until now been overlooked. Determining whether behaviour has met expectations demands information gathering, evaluation, judgement, or, more generally, investigation. The process of comparing actions with standards to determine the appropriate response to norm violators feeds back into norm development by elaborating and entrenching the norm in question. Investigation forms a bridge between standard-setting and accountability and is the necessary intermediate stage between these two. In the remainder of the chapter, I explore the development of accountability and investigation in the realm of universal human rights.

Accountability

Human rights are a highly legalized issue area, but until recently there were few tools or sanctions to enforce the law. Where accountability existed, it tended to be reputational accountability, depending upon moral stigmatization of state violators, which is known as a naming and shaming strategy.[34] In the few cases where stronger enforcement mechanisms existed, especially in regional human rights courts in Europe and the Americas, the focus was on state legal accountability. That is, regional human rights courts, such as the European Court of Human Rights, find that states (not individuals) are in violation of their obligations and require them to provide some kind of remedy, usually in the way of changed policy.

There were, however, other measures used to change state behaviour and enforce human rights standards. The Nuremberg and Tokyo trials, and other Second World War successor trials, were one of the earliest measures used to hold individuals accountable for serious war crimes and crimes against

---

[33] Simmons 2009; Sikkink 2011; Risse et al. 2013; Hafner-Burton 2013.
[34] Keck and Sikkink 1998.

humanity. However, only leaders who ordered such crimes and then were unconditionally defeated could be held individually responsible for their crimes by the victors or by domestic or foreign courts. Another example was the nineteenth-century slave tribunals, such as the Courts of Mixed Commissions for the Abolition of the Slave Trade, which held both individuals and the state (in case the nationality of the convicted ship was identified) accountable.[35] In addition, states or a group of states used various measures to enforce human rights standards to the target countries. For example, US human rights foreign policy uses diplomacy, foreign aid, and development assistance as conciliatory measures to induce human rights-consistent behaviours. In other cases, states used public condemnation, economic sanctions, arms embargos, freezing of assets, severing relations, or military intervention.[36]

The international human rights regime is still mainly characterized by state accountability with weak enforcement mechanisms. But for a small set of core human rights and war crimes, states and international institutions are increasingly using individual criminal accountability. The legal literature uses the term 'individual criminal responsibility' for core international crimes subject to the jurisdiction of the ICC. Steven Ratner and Jason Abrams also use the term 'individual accountability for human rights abuses' to refer to the broader phenomena of holding individual state officials responsible for human rights violations.[37] In this model, specific state officials are prosecuted, and if found guilty, go to prison.

This change has emerged gradually over the last twenty years in international and domestic judicial processes. It reflects not only an increase in the legalization of international human rights, but also a specific form of legalization focused on individual accountability. This trend has been described by Sikkink as 'the justice cascade', and by Chandra Lekha Sriram as 'a revolution in accountability'.[38] This new form of development does not apply to the whole range of human rights, just to a core set of human rights violations (torture, summary execution, disappearances, and political imprisonment), genocide, war crimes, and crimes against humanity. Thus, the legalization discussed here enforces many of the non-derogable rights in the International Covenant on Civil and Political Rights, the Genocide Convention, the Committee against Torture, those parts of the Geneva Conventions prohibiting war crimes, and the Rome Statute of the ICC. Derogation is the suspension of a state's obligations to respect certain human rights during a time of national emergency and crises. Non-derogability or *jus cogens* refers to the right that states should not derogate under any circumstances.

This new focus on individual criminal accountability is reflected in the Statute of the ICC, in the ad hoc tribunals for the former Yugoslavia and

---

[35] Martinez 2012.   [36] Sikkink 2004; Brysk 2009.
[37] Ratner and Abrams 2001: 3.   [38] Sikkink 2011; Sriram 2003: 310.

Rwanda, and in the foreign universal jurisdiction cases such as that against former Chilean President Augusto Pinochet.[39] But the change has not been limited to these high-profile international tribunals and foreign cases. It is a more profound shift that also includes changes in domestic institutions. The great bulk of enforcement of core human rights norms now occur in domestic courts using a combination of national criminal law, international criminal law, and international human rights law. Even when they primarily use domestic criminal law, human rights prosecutions differ from ordinary criminal trials because they involve state officials, who historically had immunity from prosecution.[40]

Investigation

Investigation is another process by which universal human rights are expanded, but also elaborated, extended, and entrenched. The process of evaluating real behaviour against the ideal standard, and the concomitant process of revising the human rights norm in the face of new problems, contributes to both vertical intensification and horizontal expansion of human rights. Investigation is the process by which formerly unexplained phenomena are conceptualized, categorized, and understood differently to suggest a new framework, which may eventually result in new codified rules. Investigation detects but also creates problems, which then need to be addressed by further investigation. These changes accumulate as they are transferred across time, actors, and space, being further modified in the process into more generic models and practices. Thus globalization is an incremental, uneven, agglomeration of unintended and uncoordinated improvisations.

Holding those transgressing human rights norms accountable for their violations logically depends on a prior step of investigation or evaluation, which may be a formal legal process, or a much more informal matter. Holding a guilty party to account can only be done once that party has been identified as having transgressed a human rights norm. Simply sanctioning random individuals does not qualify as accountability. Investigation is the process of collecting evidence of relevant behaviour, matching that evidence against the provisions of the existing and developing human rights standards, and arriving at a judgement as to whether that behaviour is compliant or not. Yet investigating conduct in light of a particular norm may incrementally shift the norm itself: the need for judgements in novel circumstances can give rise to extensions, amendments, or elaborations of existing shared standards of appropriateness in the area of human rights.

---

[39] Roht-Arriaza 2005; Roht-Arriaza and Mariezcurrena 2006.
[40] Ratner and Abrams 2001.

With the globalization of human rights, investigation is ever-increasing and clear evidence of this can be found in the increasing use of truth commissions. A truth commission is an official government body temporarily set up to investigate a past history of human rights violations and to submit an official report.[41] Famous examples include the National Commission on the Disappearance of Persons in Argentina (1983) and the Truth and Reconciliation Commission in South Africa (1995). Truth commissions usually have a mandate of six months to two years and the mandate is set in advance with the possibility of an extension. The commissions are headed by one or several commissioners and are composed of staff members. Truth commissions can be established by a president, congress, or peace accords. Some truth commissions are empowered with certain rights and privileges such as subpoena, search and seizure, or witness protection, and all are endowed with resources and independent legal status.[42] Between 1982 and 2014, fifty-two countries established truth commissions to investigate past history of state violence and human rights violations. The number of the commissions itself increases if countries like Uruguay and South Korea, which have established more than one commission, are additionally considered. Uruguay established truth commissions in 1985 and 2002, and the Korean government established around a dozen commissions. Scholars have also identified a number of countries who are considering establishing a truth commission (for example, Kenya, Mexico, Poland, Bosnia and Herzegovina). The sheer number of truth commissions and countries considering their adoption reveals the increasing importance of investigation in the area of human rights.[43]

These developments in the investigation of human rights are not only limited to the truth commission cases. Human rights reporting is recognized as an effective tool for promoting human rights by finding new and unknown facts and disseminating information of gross and systemic human rights violations.[44] Human rights reports are an important source of information both for the target government to assess its own situation and for other states and non-governmental organizations (NGOs) to set the directions of future policies. The reports can go in both directions, reporting human rights abuses and improvements. In the case of human rights violations, gathering sufficient information is critical for putting the norm-violating state on the international agenda.[45] Although many NGOs and research centres occasionally publish press releases and short reports on individual cases, the most comprehensive and systematic reports have so far been published either by governments, mostly the US Department of State, or by international human rights NGOs, such as Human Rights Watch and Amnesty International.[46]

---

[41] Hayner 2002. [42] Dancy et al. 2010: 45. [43] Hirsch 2014: 810.
[44] Sikkink 2004; Meernik et al. 2012: 233. [45] Risse et al. 1999.
[46] Cohen 1996: 517.

Increasingly, bodies under the United Nations are establishing commissions of inquiry for the purpose of conducting international and impartial inquiries, which result in reports that reaffirm the existing standards and evaluate the current situations against these standards. So far, the United Nations has created six such commissions to investigate serious human rights violations in Sudan (for Darfur) (2004), Palestine (2009), Libya (2011), Syria (2011), North Korea (2013), and the Central African Republic (2013). The Human Rights Council also has an investigation process, called special procedures, which is a regular mechanism designed to address either specific country's human rights situations or thematic issues such as freedom of religion or human trafficking. It is an official investigation either by individual experts (special rapporteurs), or by a working group.

Currently, there are forty-one thematic mandates and fourteen country mandates in process. Since 2006, the Human Rights Council instituted the Universal Periodic Review (UPR) process which all UN member states are obliged to go through. Despite limitations, the new process is a significant development from the previous treaty monitoring process since the Human Rights Council reviews the comprehensive self-report made by the government and issues recommendations. For example, in 2009, North Korea submitted a report to the UPR. In response, the Human Rights Council issued a report with 167 recommendations, of which North Korea accepted none. However, in a more recent second round of the UPR process in 2013, North Korea made a conciliatory gesture of agreeing to consider 185 out of 268 recommendations made by the Human Rights Council.

The investigation of human rights by a neutral and independent body became an interesting trend worldwide. It started with the truth commissions that were set up to investigate the past wrongs of authoritarian governments, but which are now widely used to investigate any past crimes in many countries including the United States, Australia, and Germany. For example, in the United States, the citizens of Greensboro set up a grassroots body to investigate murders by the Ku Klux Klan in the 1960s. In Australia, a commission was established to investigate aboriginal issues, and other independent commissions of inquiry have also examined corruption, and sexual abuse offences perpetrated by Catholic priests and school teachers. In Germany, with the rise of the accountability norms, there has been an increase of lawsuits against ageing Nazi officials who had not previously been held accountable in court. With new cases and new testimonies, new technologies have been developed that can simulate what a prison guard could or could not have seen from their post.

This pattern represents what Louis Bickford refers to as unofficial truth projects.[47] These projects either take place at the sub-state level or are carried out by civil society organizations, both of which make them unlike the official

---

[47] Bickford 2007: 994.

truth-telling initiatives discussed in this chapter. Examples of unofficial truth projects include not only Brazil's Nunca Mais and Uruguay's Servicio Paz y Justicia, but also Guatemala's Recovery of Historical Memory Project, Zimbabwe's Breaking the Silence, Northern Ireland's Ardoyne Commemoration Project, and the Greensboro, North Carolina Truth and Reconciliation Commission. The presence of unofficial truth projects demonstrates a growing demand for investigation. In the cases of Aceh, Timor Leste, and the Solomon Islands, new local and customary measures were developed in the aftermath of conflicts to investigate past atrocities.[48] In sum, investigations are occurring at official and unofficial levels and within the official level across different levels—state, sub-national, regional, and international.

However, to date scholars have subsumed investigation as a component or subordinate process of either human rights norm creation or accountability. Previous perspectives tended to miss connections between different processes in the development of universal human rights. Some scholars began to pay more attention to the globalization of accountability or investigation.[49] Also, with the creation and operation of the ICC, scholars are focusing on the rise of a new norm of accountability, which was codified and practiced in the ICC.[50] These scholars, however, focused too much on the novelty of new forms of accountability (for example, human rights prosecutions or the ICC) and of investigation (for example, truth commissions) and missed the comprehensive picture where standard-setting, investigation, and accountability are simultaneously expanding and intensifying. Scholars claim that accountability and investigation are new norms and should be conceptually separate from existing human rights norms. In contrast, the processes of standard-setting, holding violators accountable, and investigation are different processes of the globalization of the same universal human rights. These three processes, and the interactions among them, are the engine that propels the implementation, elaboration, and diffusion of universal human rights. While this chapter focuses on human rights, the same modes apply to other issues such as anti-corruption, protection of the environment, R2P, or corporate social responsibility.[51]

A NEW REVOLT AGAINST UNIVERSAL HUMAN RIGHTS?

In *The Anarchical Society*, Bull argued that the doctrine of human rights and duties could be 'subversive of the whole principle and mankind should be

---

[48] Jeffery and Kim 2014.
[49] Sikkink 2011; Hirsch 2014: 810; Freeman 2006; Wiebelhaus-Brahm 2009.
[50] Simmons and Danner 2010: 225. [51] Kim and Sharman 2014: 417.

organized as a society of sovereign states'.[52] Bull had in mind the conflict between two principles prioritizing either citizens of the state or the body sovereign over its citizens, which could eventually put international society primarily governed by the principle of sovereignty 'in jeopardy'.[53] Bull, however, explicitly clarified that he was not arguing that the attempt to establish human rights and duties in international law was unfortunate or undesirable. He argued that 'in our own times the international discussion of human rights and duties in international law is more a symptom of disorder than of order'.[54]

Bull's observation relates to the tension and confrontation among states, which emerged in the form of the three generation discussion of human rights and debates around universalism and cultural relativism. However, two new challenges to the development of universal human rights norms can be added— first, resurfaced cultural relativism and issues of power in applying universal human rights in reality, and second, the effectiveness of human rights norms. These challenges are well summarized by Samuel Moyn, who argues that 'the moral world of Westerners shifted, opening a new space for the sort of utopianism' in the 1970s and further suggests that 'without transformative impact of event in the 1970s, human rights would not have become today's utopia'.[55] Here, both the Western-centred understanding of universal human rights, and the future of human rights, which is chasing after utopia, are explicitly stated.

Cultural Relativism and Power

Stephen Hopgood claims that universal human rights are 'at the verge of the imminent decay'.[56] There are different forecasts about the future of human rights because scholars have different ideas about how human rights were able to survive—given the institutional weaknesses of the regime—and even thrive over the past sixty years. For example, Tim Dunne finds two reasons: first, most liberal states domestically built their constitutions upon the principle of human rights protection, and second, strong 'human rights culture' emerged in world society.[57] In contrast, Hopgood sees the survival of universal rights as dependent upon the power of the states in Europe and North America; it therefore follows that their relative decline will bring about a corresponding reversal for human rights.[58] Hopgood argues that in the realm of human rights, 'great power politics' will return:

> The rise of China and its power to pursue an independent foreign policy in relation to international norms complements the role of the United States and Russia, all with a strong discourse of national distinctiveness. In terms of R2P,

---

[52] Bull 1977: 146.   [53] Bull 1977: 146.   [54] Bull 1977: 147.
[55] Moyn 2010: 1, 7.   [56] Hopgood 2013: ix.   [57] Dunne 2007.
[58] Hopgood 2014: 67.

India, Brazil, Russia, and China have all strongly condemned the 'neocolonial' nature of the claims made by R2P advocates. Both Brazil and India have made the point that domestic commitment to rights and democracy is very different from accepting the authority of the Global Human Rights Regime to dictate domestic priorities.[59]

The current contestation around cultural relativism and generations of rights can be illustrated by the Chinese government's response to US reports that are critical of China's human rights record. The Chinese government in turn has released annual human rights records critical of American human rights. An April 2016 Chinese report, for example, argues that 'since the US government refuses to hold up a mirror to look at itself, it has to be done with other people's help'.[60] In this debate, the fault line is not only between civil and political rights emphasized by the United States and economic rights stressed by the Chinese government, but also between how the human rights standards should be implemented in each country with different cultural traditions.

In parallel, recent scholarship has discovered that universal human rights are not as Western as previously assumed. These studies show that international human rights laws and institutions were not imposed on the 'South' by the United States and other Western European countries. For example, prominent scholars of the negotiation process of the Universal Declaration discovered that Latin American delegations played an important role at the San Francisco meeting where the UN Charter was first drafted.[61] At the Dumbarton Oaks meeting, the US delegation was instructed to avoid any detailed discussion of human rights, since it would undermine national sovereignty. Surprisingly, Latin American countries and China pressed for the inclusion of human rights language into the UN Charter. These new findings provide one solution to the issue of cultural relativism by suggesting that human rights, which are generally understood and criticized for being a Western construct imposed by Western great powers, are a global construct with inputs from both Western and non-Western states.

The Effectiveness of Human Rights Norms

The other criticism of universal human rights relates to whether various human rights laws and institutions have been and will be as effective in achieving their goals as they purport to be. This is also related to the future of universal human rights since many argue that modern human rights are at a critical juncture.[62] Beth Simmons, for example, argues that human rights,

---

[59] Hopgood 2013: 13.   [60] *Xinhua* 2016.   [61] Sikkink 2014: 389.
[62] Simmons 2014: 183; Moyn 2012: 123.

despite tremendous contributions so far, still have 'multifarious (some would say, proliferating) goals' to achieve.[63] She further predicts that despite the internal and external challenges, human rights will further adapt and expand, rather than 'collapse or disintegrate'. On the contrary, sceptics argue that human rights were ineffective overall in transforming the world, and that human rights will become ineffective due to their confusing ends and means.[64] For some, the post-11 September 2001 tendency on the part of governments to use security threats to suppress the rights of individuals is another problem that risks provoking a 'legitimacy crisis for the human rights regime'.[65]

Despite criticisms, however, the effectiveness of human rights has also been proven in various ways. For example, some have provided a very powerful argument that universal human rights have contributed to change or have transformed the sovereign state system. By exploring the process and impact of signing the 1975 Helsinki Accords, Daniel Thomas showed the possible impact that the principle of universal human rights could have on systemic change in the international order.[66] For most Eastern bloc countries, signing the Helsinki Accords opened up the floodgate of liberalization and democratization, by allowing both domestic mobilization and transnational groups to work together. Interestingly, the end of the Cold War, in turn, became a time of re-empowerment of the human rights regime by an increase in the number of democratic countries, by allowing the 1993 World Conference on Human Rights, and by building a consensus on the use of force against grave and systemic human rights violations.[67]

Reus-Smit has argued that there was an intertwined relationship between the two developments, stating that the struggle for individual rights has had a significant impact on the international system's globalization.[58] The sovereign state, as a single legitimate political organization, prevails in the world, so there has been a similar, although much contested, prevalence of universal human rights. Human rights norms provided 'moral resource for the delegitimation of colonialism and the subsequent proliferation of new sovereign states'.[69] This interpretation, however, is very different from existing narratives of the rise and development of human rights, which usually start with the adoption of the Universal Declaration, with some precursors.[70] Moreover, it differs from the interpretation of historians of human rights, and is in direct contrast to the claim of Moyn who explicitly argues that post-1945 decolonization did not represent a human rights movement.[71]

There is also a criticism against specific mechanisms devised to protect and promote human rights. Human rights prosecutions, which have dramatically

---

[63] Simmons 2014: 184.   [64] Kennedy 2005; Hopgood 2013.
[65] Dunne 2007: 269.   [66] Thomas 2001.   [67] Dunne 2007: 269.
[68] Reus-Smit 2011: 207.   [69] Reus-Smit 2001: 519.
[70] Schmitz and Sikkink 2013.   [71] Moyn 2010.

increased over the last twenty years, provide a good example. Some scholars have argued that demand for human rights may cause more harm and that human rights trials that are held after conflict resolution are detrimental to nascent peace.[72] Jack Goldsmith and Krasner contend that 'a universal jurisdiction prosecution may cause more harm than the original crime it purports to address'.[73] They argue that states that reject amnesty and insist on criminal prosecution can prolong conflict, resulting in more deaths. Jack Snyder and Leslie Vinjamuri also argue that human rights trials themselves can increase the likelihood of future atrocities, exacerbate conflict, and undermine efforts to create democracy. They claim that 'the prosecution of perpetrators according to universal standards—risks causing more atrocities than it would prevent'.[74]

Nevertheless, looking at this individual accountability model as one of the enforcement mechanisms of human rights is significant. Holding former or incumbent leaders individually accountable marks an important change, challenging the very nature of sovereignty and sovereign immunity. Previously, dictators were free to abuse and steal from their own populations with no fear of international legal consequences. Currently they can be arrested and indicted for human rights offences committed at home in third countries, and even have their overseas wealth seized. Before 1990, only a handful of former heads of state had been indicted for such crimes, but since that time, sixty-seven heads of state from forty-three countries have been indicted and the number is increasing.[75] The move towards holding state leaders accountable for human rights transgressions has occurred rapidly and was unforeseen and unexpected by many prominent scholars and policymakers.[76] In collaboration with Sikkink, I have found some empirical evidence that suggests that human rights prosecution actually deters the future violations of human rights.[77]

CONCLUSION

The perennial problem of universal human rights has involved two issues: first, despite human rights being a highly institutionalized and legalized area in world politics, it is also marked by weak enforcement mechanisms; and second, the principle of universal human rights has always been in conflict with the basic organizing principle of world politics, that is, universal state sovereignty. These arguments were a concern for the contributors to *The Expansion*. A weakness of universal human rights norms compared to other current and emerging issues at that time, such as racial equality and the rise of

[72] Goldsmith and Posner 2005.   [73] Goldsmith and Krasner 2003: 47.
[74] Snyder and Vinjamuri 2003/4: 5.   [75] Lutz and Reiger 2009.
[76] Hoffmann 1983: 19; Kissinger 2001.   [77] Kim and Sikkink 2013: 69.

the Third World, led to an omission of independent inquiry on the issue of human rights principle in *The Expansion*. Moreover, when human rights issues were considered elsewhere in *The Expansion*, even Bull and Vincent, who regarded the topic as an important issue in world politics, were either excessively sceptical about the power of human rights, or saw them as being subversive of the order established by sovereign states.

In this chapter, I have argued that both issues are not as perennial as they seem. First, recent historical and empirical scholarship has shown that universal state sovereignty and universal human rights are not as dichotomous and incompatible as had been previously thought. State sovereignty has been a porous concept where its practice and beliefs were always limited and curtailed by the principle of human rights.[78] The international community nevertheless witnessed conspicuous failures in the international human rights regime, with mass killings, genocide, and war crimes committed during conflicts in the former Yugoslavia, Rwanda, and West Africa. However, faced with these failures, the international community redefined the role of statehood in terms of a responsibility to protecting civilians within and beyond borders, while also devising new mechanisms of accountability such as the International Criminal Tribunal for the former Yugoslavia, the International Criminal Tribunal for Rwanda, and the ICC, to prevent future abuses. Recent examples of the enhanced role and expectation of states to protect the rights of individuals clearly suggest that the principle of sovereignty is transforming into a direction of incorporating universal human rights.

Second, the problem of weak enforcement has recently been strongly challenged by two other processes of globalization—investigation and accountability. Scholars have started to look into this vertical intensification of human rights standards. Certainly, in order to understand the global structure of universal human rights in the current globalized sovereign system, it is essential to understand the horizontal expansion of human rights standards across countries (geographical expansion) and also across diverse focus-areas within human rights (such as women, children, or sexual minorities). By grasping this aspect, we can understand the politics around the emergence and expansion of universal human rights as an international normative structure. Nevertheless, understanding this aspect is not enough since there is another dimension of vertical intensification where the human rights regime, once created, moves forward via enforcement of standards and investigations, and by holding responsible actors accountable.

---

[78] Glanville 2014.

Part V

Contestation

17

Sovereignty as Responsibility

Sarah Teitt

In *The Expansion of International Society*, Hedley Bull wrote of a 'revolt against Western dominance' in the post-1945 order witnessed most prominently in newly independent Asian and African states leading efforts to defend a narrow conception of sovereignty defined by unconditional rights to non-intervention and non-interference.[1] Viewing sovereignty as a necessary safeguard in a system of unequal power with a history of colonial domination and exploitation, throughout the 1960s Third World states linked their anti-colonial advocacy to emerging norms on self-determination and racial equality to demand unreserved and immediate recognition, and to fortify the sovereign right to non-interference.[2] As Robert H. Jackson argued, on these terms decolonization became a sort of 'international legal transaction' rather than a process of social learning and democratic institution building.[3] The unconditioned right to self-determination instituted a 'negative sovereignty' system that entitled newly independent states to equal external recognition and exclusive internal jurisdiction irrespective of a state's democratic constitution or ability to provide for and safeguard its citizenry.[4]

According to Jackson, the legal and normative principles that paved the way for rapid decolonization within the United Nations (UN) system created an international legal 'superstructure' that constituted a system of 'international civility' but allowed for zones of 'internal incivility'.[5] States were obliged to adhere to basic rules of peaceful conduct in their external relations but were entitled to attack or abuse their own populations with impunity.[6] The result being, the same normative forces that eradicated the formal hierarchy of colonial empire were also implicated in giving free license to authoritarian violators of human rights.[7] It was on this premise that Jack Donnelly argued

---

[1] Bull 1984c: 224.
[2] See UNGA (United Nations General Assembly) 1960, 1965, 1970, 1981.
[3] Jackson 1990: 2.   [4] Jackson 1990.   [5] Jackson 1990: 161.
[6] Jackson 1990.   [7] Jackson 1990.

that, contrary to noble aspirations for the realization of higher standards of human rights and human dignity, the right to self-determination 'was interpreted to require accepting the lowest common denominator of sovereign equality' such that 'considerations of justice were thus banished from decisions on membership in international society'.[8] Jackson's and Donnelly's observations echoed the 'revolt against the West' concerns raised by Bull—the expanding membership of the UN presented a challenge to the Western liberal project, witnessed in the rise of pluralist activism to limit the scope of legitimate justice claims in international society in a manner that privileged the international duties owed to autocratic state governments over their citizens.

This chapter examines normative developments from the 1970s that effectively pushed back on the most radical pluralist defences of sovereign rights, and over time reinterpreted sovereignty to imply human protection responsibilities that are borne by all states, and are subject to remedial action by the international community. Today, this notion of sovereignty is most readily associated with the responsibility to protect (R2P) norm and its antecedent concept of 'sovereignty as responsibility' developed by Francis Deng and his Brookings Institution colleagues in the 1990s. These concepts drew on international human rights and humanitarian law and UN humanitarian practice to posit that sovereignty implies responsibilities not only rights, and that a primary responsibility of states is the protection of their populations from widespread human rights violations. Deepening support for these norms among members of the Global North and Global South over the past decade has recast the parameters of legitimate statehood and responsible domestic governance such that it is now increasingly taboo to defend sovereignty as an unmitigated state right that should be free from international scrutiny of large-scale internal human rights abuses. As UN Secretary-General Ban Ki-moon noted in 2015, there now exists a 'consensus that spans all regions' that:

> arguments about specific national circumstances do not supersede universal obligations to safeguard populations from genocide, war crimes, ethnic cleansing, and crimes against humanity. There is no longer any question that the protection of populations from atrocity crimes is both a national and an international responsibility.[9]

This chapter charts the evolution of the international human rights and humanitarian protection regimes as enabling conditions for the development of the sovereignty as responsibility discourse. Drawing lessons from Chinese diplomacy and interpretation of international law, the first half of the chapter argues that the 'compromising' of sovereignty by human rights was not simply a Western-driven, liberal response to the worst excesses of the post-1945

---

[8] Donnelly 1998: 13.   [9] United Nations Secretary-General 2015: 4, para. 7.

'negative' sovereignty game. Rather, in the initial decades of the UN, post-colonial states played a significant role in introducing the moral language and arguments which defined sovereignty according to human protection responsibilities. The second half of the chapter examines three key normative developments in the 1990s—the democratic entitlement, the right to humanitarian assistance, and the protection of civilians in armed conflict—which linked states' international legitimacy to the will and well-being of their people, and established a field of practice that affirmed the collective international responsibility to provide humanitarian relief and protection within states. The chapter then explains how these developments provided the justificatory language and enabling principles for the emergence of the R2P norm complex. While compromises to sovereign equality have created new points of contestation in international society, the chapter concludes by arguing that this does not take the form of a radically pluralist revolt against the liberal agenda, but represents a more moderate form of resistance that seeks to inject prudential constraints and procedural justice in a system of overlapping international and domestic responsibilities.

This chapter focuses on China because China is often assumed to be a leading force behind the non-liberal 'revolt' that concerned Bull, and because a more nuanced understanding of China's interpretation of sovereignty offers a number of correctives to Bull and Adam Watson's expansion story. In Gerrit Gong's chapter in Bull and Watson's volume, China's entry into international society is described as a process of socialization into the Western 'standard of civilization' wherein China adapted and reformed domestic institutions to fit Western prescriptions.[10] Yongjin Zhang has challenged Gong's nineteenth-century optic of China's transformation into a modern state embracing the constitutional norm of sovereignty on the basis that it assumed a mono-directional flow of ideas that overlooked China's strategic agency and struggle for recognition. Zhang argued that China did not earn the benefits of full membership in the modern state system by 'meticulously fulfilling' the European standard of civilization, but by 'assertive diplomacy delivering an assault on the Western domination in China and an appeal to the protection of the rules and principles of international law'.[11] Zhang's insights help explain how China became one of the world's most enthusiastic champions of sovereignty from the early twentieth century. Like Zhang, this chapter highlights how the modern sovereignty regime did not 'expand' from the Western metropole to the non-Western periphery, but was globalized through a two-way process of adaptation and accommodation on behalf of both Western and non-Western states. However, the key point of departure here is a more nuanced interpretation of sovereignty in Chinese foreign policy. Behind China's strong rhetorical

---

[10] Gong 1984a.   [11] Zhang 1991: 15.

defence of sovereign rights, Chinese foreign policy actors have long understood sovereignty to derive from and be limited by the state's obligation to protect populations. In this sense, the first half of the chapter provides a deeper appreciation of non-Western agency in the 'compromising' of sovereignty, and substantiates the argument in the second half of the chapter that contemporary political contestation pivots less on the protection obligations which legitimate sovereignty, than the appropriate means and channels collectively to enact such duties and the fair distribution of associated costs.

SOVEREIGNTY AND INDIVIDUAL HUMAN RIGHTS

One of the key premises of the sovereignty as responsibility norm is that the globalization of the post-1945 sovereignty and human rights regimes occurred through complementary rather than competing processes. As Christian Reus-Smit has argued, conventional understandings of the oppositional relationship between sovereignty and human rights mistakenly ignore how the 'normative revolution' that ushered decolonization was made possible by developing countries grafting the right to self-determination on to existing individual human rights norms.[12] Rather than championing categorical conceptions of sovereignty divorced from human rights obligations, anti-colonial advocates characterized self-determination as a primary condition for upholding the suite of individual human rights negotiated under the Universal Declaration of Human Rights and the two International Covenants.[13] Thus, rather than simply reify sovereign rights, advocates of decolonization defended a higher moral purpose of self-determination as foundational to protecting individual human rights.[14]

The People's Republic of China's (PRC's) contestation of the apartheid regime in South Africa in the 1970s illustrates the paradoxical place of individual rights in anti-colonial advocacy. The nature of China's human rights diplomacy is somewhat surprising, as—after assuming the China seat in the UN in 1971—Beijing's defence of juridical sovereignty was so notable that Samuel Kim argued that '[s]ome wayward stranger from another planet, doing a content analysis of the annual UN debate on the state of the world, could easily take sovereignty as quintessentially a Chinese idea'.[15] Yet, China's anti-apartheid diplomacy leveraged civil and political human rights to discredit the *de jure* South African state authority—a platform often assumed to be antithetical to Chinese sovereignty-bound foreign policy, and primarily the purview of Western human rights diplomacy. For example, in 1974 China

---

[12] Reus-Smit 2001: 534.   [13] Reus-Smit 2001: 537.
[14] Reus-Smit 2001.   [15] Kim 1994: 428.

called on the UN Security Council (UNSC) to adopt a resolution that strongly condemned the 'atrocities committed by the South African authorities' and imposed a mandatory arms embargo and economic sanctions against South Africa.[16] In 1976, Beijing denounced the apartheid government's violent crackdown of student protests in Soweto, and reprimanded white South African authorities for the 'bloody suppression of the Azanian people'.[17] Later, in debates leading to the October 1977 unanimous adoption of UNSC Resolutions 417 and 418 respectively condemning the South African government's violent repression of black South Africans and imposing a mandatory arms embargo on the country, Chinese Ambassador Chen Chu deplored the brutal treatment of South African black leader Steve Biko in detention, denounced the Bantu education policy, admonished the 'racist regime' for 'large-scale brutal repression', and specifically condemned closing down newspapers, banning the activities of anti-apartheid organizations, and arresting large numbers of leaders of mass protests.[18]

China's anti-apartheid diplomacy of the 1970s reflects the broader tensions in developing countries' pluralist defence of sovereignty versus their contestation of the intra-state reach of the international human rights regime. On the one hand, expanding membership of the UN witnessed the Afro-Asian bloc pushing for resolutions which reified state rights and entrenched the perception that the UN's human rights agenda ended at the sovereign frontier. While on the other, newly independent states rallied support for anti-apartheid resolutions which expanded the UN's mandate to scrutinize widespread violations of individual human rights. For example, on the heels of the General Assembly's 1965 Declaration on the Inadmissibility of Intervention in the Domestic Affairs of States and the Protection of Their Independence and Sovereignty, in June 1967, the Economic and Social Council (ECOSOC) authorized Resolution 1235, which called on the UN Human Rights Commission to document patterns of human rights violations associated with the apartheid regime in South Africa and with racial discrimination in Southern Rhodesia, and to report to ECOSOC with recommendations for addressing these abuses.[19] Then in 1970, under Resolution 1503, ECOSOC mandated the UN Sub-Commission on the Prevention of Discrimination and Protection of Minorities to develop an individual complaint mechanism for reporting 'a consistent pattern of gross and reliably attested violations of human rights and fundamental freedoms'.[20] Although the moral momentum behind these resolutions was aimed at discrediting the apartheid regime, from the early 1980s states began to argue in the General Assembly that Resolutions 1235 and 1503

---

[16] *Peking Review* 1974.   [17] *Peking Review* 1976.
[18] UNSC (United Nations Security Council) 1977: 4.
[19] United Nations Economic and Social Council 1967.
[20] United Nations Economic and Social Council 1970.

affirmed an international mandate to scrutinize and address widespread human rights abuses within the UN Charter-based system more generally.[21] The point being, although many postcolonial states contested interference in internal affairs on the basis of human rights, their anti-apartheid diplomacy nevertheless implicitly invoked a higher purpose for self-determination that rested in the protection of individual rights. As Reus-Smit argues, rather than competing commitments, sovereignty and individual human rights evolved as interwoven entitlements.[22]

INTERNATIONAL HUMAN RIGHTS AND THE LIMITS OF DOMESTIC JURISDICTION

It was not only the role of human rights as a justificatory basis for overturning colonial administrations that wove the protection of human rights into the defining fabric of sovereignty. So too were claims that by accepting and ratifying the UN Charter and acceding to human rights conventions, states accepted human rights obligations and affirmed a legitimate oversight role of the international community.[23]

In the initial decades of the UN, states routinely attempted to narrowly interpret the Charter-based sovereign right to non-interference to rebuke international scrutiny of their human rights record, and argued that accession to the UN did not imply any domestic human rights obligations. However, with the growing body of international human rights conventions, by the end of the 1960s states found it increasingly difficult to argue that UN membership granted sovereign entitlements without corresponding protection responsibilities.[24] The 1948 Convention on the Prevention and Punishment of the Crime of Genocide outlawed genocide as a crime under international law, and committed signatories to undertake to prevent and to punish genocidal acts, wherever they may occur. The 1965 International Convention on the Elimination of All Forms of Racial Discrimination obliges signatories to refrain from discriminating on the basis of race, not to sponsor or defend racism, and to prohibit racial discrimination within their jurisdiction. The Convention further requires parties to criminalize incitement of racial hatred (Article 4), and includes an individual complaints mechanism. Implicit in the conventions against racism and genocide was the understanding that 'states collectively have the authority to determine minimum standards of conduct from which

---

[21] Beurganthal 1997: 710.   [22] Reus-Smit 2001.
[23] Vincent 1986: 152. See Articles 1(3), 55(c), and 56 for the major human rights provisions of the UN Charter.
[24] Beurganthal 1997.

none may long deviate without eventually endangering their membership in the club'.[25] Freedom from external interference, in other words, was linked to the observance of basic standards of human rights. The international mandate to scrutinize human rights abuses was further solidified through the adoption of the International Covenants on Civil and Political Rights, and on Economic, Social and Cultural Rights, which—in Thomas Buerganthal's words—effectively 'internationalized and removed from the protective domain a subject that previously was essentially within their domestic jurisdiction'.[26]

Here again, Chinese interpretations of international human rights law in the early 1980s are illustrative of sovereignty as a qualified rather than absolute right. The first official Chinese legal textbook, edited by the esteemed legal scholars Wang Tieya and Wei Min, was published in China in 1981 following Deng Xiaoping's reforms. Reading law through a Marxist–Leninist–Maoist theoretical prism, the book rejected arguments 'setting the principle of state sovereignty against the principle of human rights' on the basis that such arguments derived from the faulty Western view that individuals are the subject of international law.[27] Mirroring Beijing's official line of thought since the founding of the PRC, the book underscored the Marxist rationale that: (1) the collective is the subject of human rights, and (2) under international law the state is the embodiment of the collective. On this basis, the text posited that '[t]he principle of human rights must be subordinate to the principle of state sovereignty and cannot be superior to the principle of state sovereignty'.[28] This rationale garrisoned human rights infringements as a domestic issue shielded from international intervention by the right to non-interference.

Yet, despite the pre-eminent place of sovereignty in this text, Wang and Wei articulated a *general rather than absolute* prohibition against international intervention to rescue suffering populations based on commitments states had made in the field of human rights. Acknowledging that some acts are so egregious that states had voluntarily agreed to codify them as international crimes with corollary international obligations, the textbook determined that certain abuses could be exempt from the rule of non-interference. The book listed racial discrimination, engaging in genocide, participating in slave trade, violent abduction of hostages, participating in international terrorism, and taking 'extremely inhuman means to create, expel, and persecute refugees in a large scale way' as human rights abuses that are so serious that they become a legitimate concern of the international community.[29] It maintained that 'necessary measures taken by all states and international organizations to suppress these behaviors are consistent with generally recognized principles of international law and should not be considered as intervening in the

---

[25] Franck 1992: 78.   [26] Beurganthal 1997: 706.   [27] Cited in Chiu 1989: 17.
[28] Cited in Chiu 1989: 17.   [29] Chiu 1989.

internal affairs of a state'.[30] On this basis, leading Chinese scholars of the post-Mao era set forth a positivist interpretation of international law that allowed for the international community to take measures to stop large-scale human rights abuses if states had entered into treaties or had in some manner voluntarily subjected themselves to international law prohibiting these particular actions, or if such actions threatened international peace and security.

Importantly, it was not inconsonant with this position to insist that sovereignty trumped human rights, assert that human rights are a domestic affair shielded from international meddling, and in turn present a legal argument that unseated non-interference as the defining attribute of sovereignty in certain situations of gross abuse. The textbook is significant in light of the considerable prestige Wang and Wei enjoyed as legal scholars in China in the Deng Xiaoping Reform and Opening era, and also due to the general reluctance of Chinese scholars to veer too radically from official policy at this juncture. In other words, although not an authoritative Chinese foreign policy text, Wang and Wei's analysis offers insight into some of the earliest attempts in post-Mao China to reconcile sovereign entitlements with international human rights and humanitarian law, and points to a nascent global understanding in the late 1970s that human rights treaties had bound states to common standards of responsible state conduct which could be collectively upheld through international organizations.

The key point being, even among actors who defended what Donnelly lamented as a 'radical legal positivist' interpretation of sovereignty, the evolution of international human rights law presented an ethical rationale and legal premise that international intervention was consistent with generally accepted principles of non-interference and should not be considered to weaken or undermine sovereignty.[31] Implicit in the acknowledgement that human rights treaties conferred a collective international authority to hold states accountable for failing to stop conscious-shocking violence was the corollary prescription that states bear obligations to protect populations from such abuse. That is, the permissibility of external intervention to halt serious human rights violations effectively defined their prevention as a sovereign duty. Although China's post-Tiananmen Square crackdown foreign policy witnessed the resurgence of more categorical interpretations of sovereignty, Beijing's adamantly pluralist human rights diplomacy of the 1990s should not discount earlier debates within China that interpreted the international requirement to respect sovereignty to be limited by a state's obligation to protect its populations.

That the codification of international human rights standards defined sovereign responsibilities and placed limits on domestic jurisdiction was reflected in the 1993 Vienna Declaration on Human Rights, which declared

---

[30] Cited in Chiu 1989: 17.   [31] Donnelly 1998: 13.

that 'the promotion and protection of all human rights is a legitimate concern of the international community',[32] and underscored that 'human rights and fundamental freedoms are the birthright of all human beings; their protection is the first responsibility of Governments'.[33] Despite attempts by Asian states to press for a particularist interpretation of human rights at the World Conference, the Vienna Declaration affirmed the universality of human rights, and paved the way for creating the post of the United Nations High Commissioner for Human Rights at the end of 1993. This both reflected and marked a milestone in evolving standards of legitimacy which allowed for international scrutiny of human rights violations and placed limits on the actions states could take and still claim responsible membership and good standing in international society.

SELF-DETERMINATION AS POPULAR SOVEREIGNTY

While the late 1970s ushered a shift in 'outward' accountability where states were increasingly answerable to the international community in the field of human rights, by the late 1980s shifting standards of international legitimacy required states to demonstrate 'inward' accountability to domestic populations. Starting in 1989, the UN General Assembly and the UN Commission on Human Rights endorsed open, multiparty, secret ballot elections under universal and equal suffrage as crucial to the enjoyment of a range of other human rights and a requirement of peace.[34] Soon thereafter, the UN sent a monitoring mission to oversee elections in Nicaragua in 1990, marking the first mission of its kind in a sovereign state. Democratic elections further evolved as a basic human right in the early 1990s, as the Southern Cone trading bloc MERCOSUR, the Organization of American States (OAS), the Organization for Security and Co-operation in Europe, the African Union, the European Union, the Economic Community of West African States, the Andean Community, and the Commonwealth of Nations adopted regional instruments with provisions that proscribed coups d'état and endorsed people's right to participate in elections. These developments pointed to the emergence of the 'democratic entitlement'—an inchoate human right to democracy witnessed in the codification of the moral aspiration of Article 21(3) of the Universal Declaration of Human Rights that 'the will of the people shall be the basis of the authority of the government'.[35] The right to democracy implied that

---

[32] United Nations Human Rights Office of the High Commissioner 1993: part 1, para. 4.
[33] United Nations Human Rights Office of the High Commissioner 1993: part 1, para. 1.
[34] See UNGA (United Nations General Assembly) 1990, 1991a.
[35] See Franck 1992.

individuals should have the right to take part in the government of their country in a consultative process free from coercion, and also that each government has a duty to subject itself to the popular will, thereby allowing itself to be voted out of office.[36]

An emerging norm that tied international legitimacy with democratic elections was witnessed in the widespread opprobrium and isolation of leaders who gained power through force rather than the ballot box. For example, on 11 October 1991, in response to the military coup in Haiti, the General Assembly unanimously approved a landmark resolution which demanded the 'immediate restoration of the legitimate Government of President Jean-Bertrand Aristide, together with the full application of the National Constitution and hence the full observance of human rights in Haiti'.[37] This resolution followed by a week the decision of the OAS to collectively suspend their economic ties with Haiti until Aristide was restored to power in accordance with the constitutional rule of law. International authority to hold states accountable to democratic processes gained further ground with the UN Security Council's decision to authorize the use of force to reinstate Aristide to power in Haiti in 1994, and then to apply the same measures to return democratically elected Ahmad Tejan Kabbah to power after a military coup in Sierra Leone in 1998. As the Haiti case in particular did not represent a clear threat to international peace and security, the Security Council's invocation of its Chapter VII powers suggested that the UNSC's Charter-based mandate to preserve international peace and security had been expansively interpreted to permit collective intervention to restore democracy within states.

The correspondence between deepening norms around democratic power transitions and enhanced international authority to hold states accountable to these principles was also witnessed in the actions of the African Union, which leveraged international and regional commitments to democracy and rule of law in order to develop a 'zero tolerance' policy for military coups. In line with this policy, the African Union has resolved to take action against every member state that has experienced an unconstitutional change of government since 2003, including: Guinea-Bissau, Sao Tome and Principe in 2003; Togo in 2005; Mauritania in 2005 and 2008; Guinea in 2008; Madagascar in 2009; Niger in 2010; Mali and Guinea-Bissau in 2012; and the Central African Republic and Egypt in 2013. Through such practice, norms on self-determination evolved to permit international and regional organizations to take action to oversee, and in some cases enforce, the human rights associated with democratic governance.

From the 1990s, legal agreements and the practice of intervention pointed to converging expectations that the international legitimacy of governments

---

[36] Fox and Roth 2001: 336.
[37] UNGA (United Nations General Assembly) 1991c.

required state authorities to submit themselves to the will of their people. The obligation of states to uphold this right implied that states are democratically accountable internally to domestic populations, and externally to the international community, which rendered it less plausible for state leaders to argue that the requirement of the right to self-determination was respect for the exclusive domestic jurisdiction of states.[38] In other words, the incremental consolidation of regional and global norms underscoring the democratic entitlement from the early 1990s shifted the international meaning of sovereignty away from its narrow association with the right to non-interference, to encompass broader notions of popular sovereignty which linked good standing in the community of states with a state's accountability to its people. This was foundational to sovereignty as responsibility, which Deng argued emerged from the collective expectation that 'it is the will of the people, democratically invested in the leaders they elect freely or otherwise accept as their representatives, that entitles authorities to value and uphold the sovereignty of a nation'.[39]

HUMANITARIAN DUTIES TO CIVILIANS IN CONFLICT AND DISASTER

Alongside evolving norms holding states accountable to domestic and international audiences in the field of human rights, the late 1980s and early 1990s marked the emergence of the entitlement to humanitarian assistance and the corresponding 'collective obligation of States to bring relief and redress in human rights emergencies'.[40] Proponents articulated the rights of victims of natural disasters and complex emergencies to receive humanitarian assistance based on fundamental survival rights to life, food, shelter, sanitation, and health, and on the laws of war enshrined in the Geneva Conventions of 1949 and the Additional Protocols of 1977.[41] In 1991, the General Assembly adopted a comprehensive resolution on humanitarian relief, which included provisions for the prevention and early warning of large-scale crises, and called on impacted states to facilitate the work of the UN within their borders, and for neighbouring states to take measures to assist the delivery of

---

[38] Franck 1992: 47.   [39] Deng 1995: 263.

[40] United Nations Secretary-General 1991: 5.

[41] Article 30 of the Fourth Convention of 1949 recognizes the rights of protected persons to appeal to protecting powers, the International Committee of the Red Cross or the National Red Cross Society. The 1977 Additional Protocols to the Geneva Conventions require that relief actions 'shall be undertaken' when civilian populations are in need, which implicitly recognizes the right of civilian populations to receive humanitarian assistance. See Protocol I 1977: Article 70; Protocol II 1977: Article 18(2).

cross-border aid.[42] Interpreted as a clear affirmation of the UN's mandate to deliver emergency relief, the resolution prompted the secretary-general to establish a UN Department of Humanitarian Affairs to mobilize and coordinate the UN's response to complex emergencies and natural disasters.

While the General Assembly stressed that international emergency relief operations should abide by the principles of respect for sovereignty, impartiality, and neutrality, the deliberate targeting of displaced persons in Iraq, Bosnia, and Somalia in the early 1990s laid glaringly bare the weaknesses of these principles in addressing the security needs of internally displaced persons (IDPs), which in 1995 had mushroomed to upwards of 20 to 25 million from the approximately 1.2 million worldwide IDPs in 1982.[43] Many UN relief officials found it neither morally conscionable nor practically feasible to provide protection to refugees who had crossed international borders, but stand idly by when it came to the suffering of nearby displaced populations trapped in their home country. Yet relief actors could invoke the 1951 Refugee Convention to advocate for the rights of refugees, but lacked an equivalent international framework or mandate for upholding the rights of the internally displaced.

The IDP crisis erupted as Boutros Boutros-Ghali assumed the UN secretary-general post in early 1992, and promptly set out to cast the end of the Cold War as an opportunity to marshal the UN's capacity and will to respond to violent conflict that had taken an inordinate toll on civilian populations. One of Boutros-Ghali's first initiatives in his new office was to encourage the Security Council to hold its first ever high-level summit. At the summit held in January 1992, Boutros-Ghali called on the UNSC to uphold both the statist and globalist pillars of the UN Charter. The secretary-general contended that state sovereignty had taken on a 'new meaning' in the context of the end of the Cold War:

> Added to its dimension of right is the dimension of responsibility, both internal and external...Violation of state sovereignty is, and will remain, an offence against global order. But its misuse may also undermine human rights and jeopardize a peaceful global life. Civil wars are no longer civil, and the carnage they inflict will not let the world remain indifferent.[44]

In his first year in office, Boutros-Ghali, at the request of the UN Commission on Human Rights, issued the first secretary-general report on improving the protection of IDPs, and thereafter appointed the first special representative on IDPs, Francis Deng. It was in this role that Deng formally introduced the concept of sovereignty as responsibility to build support for an international

---

[42] UNGA (United Nations General Assembly) 1991b.
[43] Cohen and Deng 1998: 3.
[44] UNSC (United Nations Security Council) 1992: 9.

standard for IDP protection. Deng drew on provisions in international human rights and humanitarian law to develop the sovereignty as responsibility concept, which holds that the primary responsibility to protect IDPs lies with state governments, but if authorities are unable to provide assistance and protection, they could either work with outsiders to deliver protection, or obstruct external efforts and sacrifice their legitimate standing in international society.[45] Sovereignty as responsibility formed the normative rationale for the development of the Guiding Principles on Internal Displacement, which stressed that humanitarian action taken pursuant to a government's request should not be interpreted as interference in internal affairs, but as a positive affirmation of the state enacting its sovereign responsibilities.[46] The secretary-general presented the Guiding Principles to the UN Commission on Human Rights in 1998, endorsing the notion that sovereignty implied the responsibility to protect populations and the responsibility to accept international assistance where domestic capacity was lacking.

Although the Guiding Principles do not explicitly condone the delivery of aid to IDPs without the consent of the host government, Deng and Roberta Cohen—the key authors of the Guiding Principles—maintained that legitimate coercion was implied in their normative rationale: '[the] obligation imposed on states by humanitarian and human rights law to refrain from refusing reasonable offers of international assistance makes it difficult to dispute the existence of a duty to accept such offers'.[47] This duty to accept assistance or face rebuke was affirmed in the secretary-general's warning to Sudan to cease obstructing humanitarian assistance in 1995:

> Any attempt to diminish the capacity of the international community to respond to conditions of suffering and hardship among the civilian population in Sudan can only give rise to the most adamant expression of concern as a violation of recognized humanitarian principles, most importantly, the right of civilian populations to receive humanitarian assistance in times of war.[48]

That is to say, efforts to curtail the IDP crisis in the early 1990s established a justificatory discourse that opened states that refused assistance to IDPs subject to international condemnation for violating basic human rights. By the end of 1990s, the secretary-general's reform agenda had resulted in the reorganization of the Department of Humanitarian Affairs into the United Nations Office for the Coordination of Humanitarian Affairs (OCHA), with the expanded mandate to cover humanitarian response, policy development, and humanitarian advocacy. The latter gave OCHA the 'unique mandate to speak out on behalf of the people worst affected by humanitarian situations',

---

[45] Deng 1995.   [46] United Nations Economic and Social Council 1998.
[47] Cohen and Deng 1998: 7.
[48] United Nations Secretary-General 1996: para. 93.

and thereby affirmed the internationalization of the right to humanitarian assistance.[49]

INTERNATIONAL INTERVENTION
TO PROTECT CIVILIANS

While Deng's advocacy on sovereignty as responsibility focused primarily on the delivery of non-military humanitarian relief to affected IDP populations, the surge in UN peacekeeping in the early 1990s created precedents which, by the end of that decade, expanded the scope for international military deployments to provide physical protection to civilians under imminent threat of attack. The UNSC authorization of peacekeeping operations in El Salvador, Mozambique, and Cambodia in the early 1990s carved out a role for the UN to oversee large and complex multilateral interventions to help monitor and implement comprehensive peace agreements. The UN's presence was dramatic not just in scale but also in intrusiveness: many of the conflicts were intra-state in nature, and peacekeepers were mandated with an array of post-conflict, state-building tasks, including democratic institution building and overseeing elections. Established in 1992, the UN Department of Peacekeeping Operations was tasked with supporting the increasing demand of coordinating UN inter-ventions in post-Cold War conflicts.

The surge in UN peacekeeping affirmed an international monitoring and state-building role, and also led to the incremental expansion of the UNSC's mandate to respond to the deliberate targeting of populations as part of its responsibility to safeguard international peace and security. In response to the destabilizing impact of Kurdish refugees fleeing from Iraq in 1991, the UNSC for the first time deemed that refugee flows posed a threat to regional peace and security. By directly attributing the refugee crisis to Baghdad's repression, the UNSC implicitly characterized systematic discrimination and violent attacks against large civilian populations as a legitimate concern of the inter-national community.[50] Although the UNSC did not expressly authorize the safe havens and no-fly zones imposed by the US, the UK, and France to protect Kurds in northern Iraq in 1991, supporters of military action to protect Kurdish populations argued that by demanding that Iraq improve its human rights situation, UNSC Resolution 688 'provided the legitimating arguments that could plausibly be stretched to cover these actions'.[51] The following year, the UNSC mandated multilateral intervention in Somalia to deliver relief to

---

[49] United Nations Office for the Coordination of Humanitarian Affairs No date.
[50] UNSC (United Nations Security Council) 1991.   [51] Wheeler 2000: 166.

victims of famine and armed conflict. The fact that a centralized state authority had largely ceased to function in Mogadishu rendered sovereignty concerns
less salient; however, the intervention was noteworthy for once again affirming
that humanitarian distress constituted a legitimate reason for the UNSC to
intervene.

The UNSC's acknowledgement that the humanitarian impact of the crises
in Iraq and Somalia posed a threat to international peace and security, along
with emerging norms of human security in the mid-1990s, heightened expectations for the Security Council to provide relief and protection to suffering
populations. In this context, the UNSC's tepid response to genocidal violence
in Bosnia and Rwanda opened UNSC members to criticism that they had
failed their protection duties. At the end of 1999, the UN issued the reports of
the independent inquiry into the international community's failure to prevent
the massacre of 8,000 Bosnian Muslims after the fall of the UN-declared safe
area of Srebrenica in 1995, and of the independent inquiry into its failure to
halt the systematic slaughter of over 800,000 Tutsis and moderate Hutus in
Rwanda in 1994. Issued within one month of each other, and just months after
NATO's unilateral intervention to prevent ethnic cleansing in Kosovo, each
independent inquiry asserted that the international community bore a significant share of responsibility for the tragic course of events in Bosnia and
Rwanda for failing to take decisive action to protect victims and deter attacks
early in the conflicts.[52] Although this blame was shared across the UN
Secretariat and Member States, the reports emphasized that the Security
Council in particular had mistakenly stuck to a policy of impartiality and
hesitation when decisive intervention on behalf of targeted civilians against
merciless attacks was needed. In other words, criticism of the UNSC's feckless
response to Rwanda and Srebrenica pointed to normative expectations for the
Permanent 5 (P5) to side with the victims of conflict, and take measures to
protect them from attacks by their own government forces.

Similarly, the UNSC's decisions to establish the International Criminal Tribunal
for the former Yugoslavia in 1993 and the International Criminal Tribunal
for Rwanda in 1994 marked for the first time since the Nuremburg and Tokyo
War Crimes Tribunals that the international community resolved to hold
state leaders individually responsible for massive violations of human rights.
These precedents, in turn, provided the jurisprudence that paved the way for
the establishment of the International Criminal Court under the Rome Statute
of 1998. The Statute outlawed genocide, war crimes, crimes against humanity,
and aggression as international crimes, which more firmly set the 'normative
boundaries' of the international community 'by defining those actions that put
an agent outside of those boundaries'.[53]

---

[52] United Nations Secretary-General 1999; UNSC (United Nations Security Council) 1999.
[53] Welsh 2013b: 387.

Collective expectations for the UNSC to hold state perpetrators accountable and coercively intervene to protect civilians gained further ground in the ruling that NATO's decision to intervene in Kosovo without UNSC authorization was 'illegal' but 'legitimate'.[54] Given Russia and China's veto power and their seemingly staunch commitment to defending sovereignty regardless of a regime's brutality, one of the upshots of this ruling was the perception that the UNSC was an outmoded and inadequate security institution in the age of globalized human rights. Such perceptions of the UNSC's inability to prevent mass atrocities prompted arguments for finding alternative institutions of legitimate authority that could decide on the use of force, such as coalitions of liberal democracies.[55] These arguments, in turn, fuelled anxieties that vesting authority outside the UNSC threatened the 'equalitarian regime' of the Charter-based international order, and risked introducing 'destabilizing grievances' that might lead to deeper systemic contestation and broader conflict.[56] The risks associated with establishing institutions of executive authority outside the UNSC weighed heavily on UN Secretary-General Kofi Annan, who argued at the end of 1999 that the starkest moral challenge of the day was not a choice between destructive unilateral action and morally reprehensible inaction, but for the UNSC to 'find common ground in upholding the principles of the Charter, and acting in defence of our common humanity'.[57]

It was partly this concern over maintaining the UNSC's relevance and authority that provided the impetus for the UNSC's deeper engagement in protecting civilians in armed conflict from late 1999. The UNSC's ability to find common ground came first through the introduction of the Protection of Civilians in Armed Conflict, Children and Armed Conflict, and Women, Peace and Security thematic agendas in the Security Council. Introduced amid criticism that the UNSC was not fit for humanitarian purpose, these agendas led to the UNSC's unanimous endorsement of a number of ground-breaking thematic (as opposed to country-specific) resolutions affirming that the protection of populations fell within its mandate. One of the clearest examples of this affirmation was the April 2000 Resolution 1296, which noted:

> the deliberate targeting of civilian populations or other protected persons and the committing of systematic, flagrant and widespread violations of international humanitarian and human rights law in situations of armed conflict may constitute a threat to international peace and security.[58]

---

[54] Independent International Commission on Kosovo 2000.
[55] Buchanan and Keohane 2004. For their later work on this, see Buchanan and Keohane 2011.
[56] Reus-Smit 2005: 88.   [57] Annan 1999.
[58] UNSC (United Nations Security Council) 2000b.

The resolution represented a significant milestone in establishing Security Council jurisdiction over internal conflicts, as it determined that the humanitarian impact of conflict, rather than its transborder effects, qualifies as a threat to international peace and security. A few months later, in August 2000, the UNSC passed Resolution 1314 on Children and Armed Conflict, which reaffirmed the language of Resolution 1296, with the emphasis that 'flagrant and widespread' violations against children in situation of armed conflict may constitute a threat to international peace and security.[59] In October of that year, the Security Council held its first debate on Women, Peace and Security, and endorsed Resolution 1325, which recognized the gendered impact of armed conflict and women's equal participation in peace and security matters as an issue of international peace and security.[60] These resolutions followed the UNSC's unprecedented decision at the end of 1999 to mandate peacekeeping missions to protect civilians under imminent threat of attack in Sierra Leone and in Timor Leste. Although these missions deployed with the formal consent of the state concerned, the pressure applied to state authorities and regional bodies pointed to deepening collective expectations for the UNSC to authorize measures to ensure unfettered humanitarian relief and enforce civilian protection.

THE RESPONSIBILITY TO PROTECT

Drawing on precedent human rights and humanitarian relief norms, institutions, and practices, in 2001 the International Commission on Intervention and State Sovereignty (ICISS) introduced the concept of responsibility to protect as a basis for legitimating international intervention to protect imperilled population from attacks by their own government.[61] Mirroring the logic of Deng's sovereignty as responsibility concept, ICISS argued that international human rights and humanitarian law enshrined not only sovereign rights but also responsibilities, and underscored that a primary state responsibility is to protect its populations from serious suffering and harm. If a state is unable or unwilling to protect its population, R2P held that the international community can legitimately take action, including force as a last resort, to provide protection. According to Anne-Marie Slaughter, who served as the Director of Policy Planning under US Secretary of State Hillary Clinton, R2P represented one of the most important shifts in the definition of sovereignty in modern history, as it alerted states to the expectation that rather than enjoy an absolute right

---

[59] UNSC (United Nations Security Council) 2000a.
[60] UNSC (United Nations Security Council) 2000c.
[61] International Commission on Intervention and State Sovereignty 2001.

to non-intervention, a state's right to be free from external intervention was conditioned on state authorities not inflicting serious and systematic human rights abuses on their own citizens.[62]

The largest-ever gathering of heads of state and government unanimously endorsed a modified version of R2P at the 2005 World Summit.[63] In 2009, UN Secretary-General Ban issued a report that defined the 2005 World Summit endorsement of R2P according to three mutually reinforcing pillars: (1) each state's responsibility to protect its populations from genocide, war crimes, ethnic cleansing, and crimes against humanity; (2) the international community's responsibility to assist states in preventing these atrocity crimes; and (3) the international community's responsibility to take timely and decisive action, through peaceful, diplomatic, and humanitarian means, and if necessary through other more forceful means, where a state manifestly fails to protect its population.[64] Support for R2P deepened in the General Assembly and Security Council from 2009. By the end of 2015, the UNSC had passed over forty resolutions reminding states authorities of their protection responsibilities under R2P, and had authorized a number of measures to hold state leaders to account and enforce civilian protection, including the 2011 intervention to protect Libyan populations under threat of massacre by the Muammar Gaddafi regime.[65] According to the UN secretary-general's special advisor on R2P, Jennifer Welsh, such practice evidences how R2P has now become 'part of the world's diplomatic language' that shapes normative interpretations of existing rules of sovereignty and intervention, and has served to 'emphasize what is appropriate and shine a spotlight on what is deemed inappropriate' state conduct.[66] Importantly, although R2P has not altered existing law or introduced new law, it has, paraphrasing Thomas Franck, 'connected the dots of practice by lines of enunciated principle' to collectively legitimate a new international human protection regime.[67]

CONCLUSION: NEW SITES OF RESISTANCE AND CONTESTATION

Over the past four decades, the evolution of international norms and practices in the field of human rights and humanitarian protection have contributed to the collective understanding that states and the international community bear responsibilities to protect populations from serious human rights violations.

---

[62] Slaughter 2006: 2964.   [63] United Nations 2005: paras 138–40.
[64] United Nations Secretary-General 2009.
[65] For a list of these resolutions, see Global Centre for the Responsibility to Protect 2016.
[66] Welsh 2013b: 378, 387.   [67] Franck 1992: 56.

Although this trend defies the supposed 'radical' pluralism Bull described as spurring the 'revolt against the West', the consensus that underpins sovereignty as responsibility is relatively thin, and demonstrates the limits of solidarist norms in international society. That is, although there is widespread support for the general premise that sovereignty is not a license for tyranny, states continue to contest the appropriateness of external coercion as a means to protect populations.

Some of the most ardent contestation of the international authority to intervene to protect populations surfaced in the aftermath of NATO's intervention in Libya in 2011, amid widespread criticism that Western powers had illegitimately expanded the UNSC civilian protection mandate under Resolution 1973 to carry out a policy of regime change. Criticism of the intervention, most notably from BRICS (Brazil, Russia, India, China, and South Africa) leaders, evoked profound anxieties that sovereignty as responsibility norms were a veil for 'old-style' humanitarian intervention, and allowed for 'an unspecified and unaccountable' agent of the so-called international community to abuse principles for their own interest, impose external conceptions of justice on weak states, and threaten pluralism and diversity in international society.[68] The blowback from the Libyan intervention deepened resistance to P3 (France, the US, and the UK)-led efforts to compel Damascus to cease indiscriminate attacks on Syrian civilians, as China and Russia resisted and vetoed a number of comparatively mild resolutions intended to apply pressure on the Bashar al-Assad regime from 2012. The inability of the permanent members of the UNSC to find common ground is partly to blame for the escalation of the Syrian crisis, and—with nearly half of the pre-war Syrian population dead or displaced by the end of 2015—sceptics of the normative purchase of the evolving human protection regime could easily argue that beneath the veneer of consensus on R2P, international society remains deeply divided on liberal protection norms.

Contrary to concerns that Libya opened new 'legitimacy faultlines in international society' which mirrored Bull's 'revolt against the West', Jason Ralph and Adrian Gallagher argue that 'the challenge to the liberal agenda of the P3 is not radical'.[69] That is, the crux of contestation is not a return of sovereign equality that is devoid of domestic obligations or international accountability, but a call for: (1) prudential restraints on the use of major power force; (2) meeting the requirements of procedural justice in which states are reciprocally bound by rules and feel their input in decision-making processes; and (3) a fair distribution of costs.[70] Regarding the first point, Brazil and China continue to endorse force as a necessary rescue measure of last resort, but have advocated for greater monitoring and review mechanisms to ensure UNSC oversight

---

[68] Welsh 2013b: 394. [69] Ralph and Gallagher 2015: 554.
[70] Ralph and Gallagher 2015.

over R2P interventions conducted by major powers, regional arrangements, or coalitions.[71] As for greater decision-making input and reciprocity, India has linked its support for human protection norms with Security Council reform, while at the same time many developing countries contest the selective application of international accountability norms and mechanisms. For example, African leaders have taken issue with the perception that African states are the only targets for International Criminal Court jurisdiction, and members of the General Assembly routinely contest the double standards inherent in the US blocking measures to hold Israel to account for human rights violations in Gaza. Finally, many countries in the developing world are dissatisfied that Western countries are lead advocates of the evolving human protection regime, but are unwilling to sacrifice troops and treasure to deliver results to vulnerable populations. In light of the decline in Western troop contributions to UN peacekeeping missions, India and other major troop contributors press for greater input in deciding peacekeeping mandates, and a fairer distribution of the cost of providing protection in which Western states match policy prescriptions with appropriate resourcing. Part of the anxieties of troop-contributing nations is that the human protection regime is implicitly stratified between norm-maker, on the one hand, and norm implementer, on the other. In many cases, P3 countries push for peacekeeping mandates to protect civilians, while troops and practitioners from the developing world assume much of the physical risk in conducting these missions, and are thereby implicitly seen to be more expendable than their counterparts in the West.

While this contestation points to the tensions and constraints of solidarist norms of human protection, it is not, for the most part, centred on a radically pluralist rejection of an international mandate to help protect beleaguered populations. That is, even amid contestation of the appropriate remedial role of the international community in ensuring civilian protection, virtually no state expresses at liberty its right to attack its own population or denies an international mandate to take action in times of dire humanitarian crisis. In this regard, the past decade of normative consolidation of R2P, building on the decades of human rights institutionalization and humanitarian relief practice that preceded it, has helped enunciate 'a floor of decent conduct' to underpin sovereign equality, and mapped out procedures for collective action to confront impunity.[72]

---

[71] On Brazil's 'Responsibility while Protecting' initiative and China's 'Responsible Protection' concept, see Stuenkel and Tourinho 2014; Ruan 2012.

[72] This notion of a 'floor of decency/morality' comes from Vincent 1986: 126.

18

The 'Revolt against the West' Revisited

Ian Hall

Both the concept of the 'revolt against the West' and the way in which it was treated by the majority of the contributors to *The Expansion of International Society* were—and remain—controversial. The phrase pre-dated the publication of the book by almost three decades: it emerged in Britain in the late 1950s and is prominent in works like Hugh Seton-Watson's *Neither War nor Peace: The Struggle for Power in the Postwar World* and Geoffrey Barraclough's *An Introduction to Contemporary History*, which used 'The Revolt against the West' as the title of its chapter on decolonization and its aftermath.[1] Both Seton-Watson and Barraclough considered the end of empire—not the Cold War—as both the defining development of post-war international relations and the most serious challenge to international order. They were not alone: many European observers came to believe that decolonization posed threats to continued European leadership and even to the continuance of 'civilized' international relations. Others, of course, took a different view: some radical observers welcomed the revolt and supported its aims and methods.[2] But from the late 1950s at least until the late 1970s, the revolt was an object of deep concern for many European scholars and practitioners of international relations.

The concept of the 'revolt against the West' had thus acquired certain connotations well before Hedley Bull picked it up for the title of his *Expansion* essay. It was loaded, in particular, with a sense of dismay and disapproval at anti-colonialism, decolonization, and the emergence of a demanding, unsettled, and unruly 'Third World'. Although Bull was in many ways unusually sympathetic to some of its demands, as he showed in the closing pages of *The Anarchical Society* (1977) and (more clearly) in his Hagey Lectures (1984),

---

[1] Seton-Watson 1960; Barraclough 1964.
[2] See, for example, Worsley 1964, who coined that term. Peter Worsley was a sociologist and a member of the British 'New Left'.

choosing the phrase for his title aligned him with liberal and conservative critics of the postcolonial world and set him against radical enthusiasts for the revolt in that world and in the West.[3] This ideological stance coloured Bull's chapter and indeed the *Expansion* as a whole, which treated the revolt against the West as perhaps the greatest threat to the continuance of international society to have emerged since the end of the Second World War.

At the moment the *Expansion* was published, however, this belief in the corrosive quality of the revolt on international relations was starting to wane, in parallel with the influence of the postcolonial 'Third World'. The book appeared at a pivotal moment—the mid-1980s—after which the power of the postcolonial world rapidly declined, partly as a result of the growing evidence that the development models adopted by their elites after independence were failing, and partly as a consequence of the end of the Cold War, which removed both an anti-Western ally, the Soviet Union, and an ideological alternative to democratic politics and liberal development strategies. The year after *The Expansion* (1984) was published, Ethiopia's famine reached its peak, the product of shocking economic mismanagement by a Soviet-sponsored government as well as drought, and Mikhail Gorbachev rose to power in Moscow—events that began to shift the power balance back towards the West and its political and economic policies, and away from the often Soviet-inspired 'Third World'.[4] By the end of the decade, democratization and liberal economics, underpinned by the so-called Washington Consensus, were in the ascendant, and the revolt against the West diminished. Only two elements of the revolt, as we shall see, persisted: a struggle with Western values, exemplified most clearly in the continued rise of militant Islamism, and a struggle over global economic governance.

THE *EXPANSION* AND THE REVOLT

As Bull pointed out in his eponymous chapter, the phrase 'Revolt against the West' was a catch-all term, referring to five interconnected but conceptually distinct sets of events that occurred, sometimes simultaneously and sometimes in sequence, over the course of about a hundred years. In each of the five elements of the revolt, the West was the target of non-Western peoples seeking change to their modes of government, the norms and rules of international society, or the distribution of wealth within it. The revolt began in the latter half of the nineteenth century, with what Bull called the 'struggle for equal sovereignty' on the parts of China, Japan, and the Ottoman Empire, as these

---

[3] See Bull 1977: especially 290–305, as well as Bull 1983.
[4] On the Ethiopian experience of socialism, see Westad 2007: chapter 7.

states pressed to be treated as the peers of European states in international society.[5] Then came the 'anti-colonial revolution', which lasted from the First World War until the 1980s, but which peaked in the 1960s, in which colonial peoples challenged European imperial rulers and gained independent states of their own. Three other 'struggles' played themselves out during and after that revolution, which Bull termed the struggles for racial equality, economic justice, and cultural liberation.[6]

The various contributors to *The Expansion*, as well as the editors, explained and evaluated the causes and consequences of the revolt in different ways, but the majority expressed views that accorded with those of the early English School and British liberals and internationalists more generally.[7] While all recognized that a shift in material power had occurred during the first half of the twentieth century, as well as important changes like the diffusion of Western military technology and techniques to non-Western peoples,[8] the causes of decolonization and the anti-Western behaviour of postcolonial states were located by British scholars of the post-war period in ideational, psychological, and, often, what they called 'emotional' factors. Elitist internationalist liberals like Gilbert Murray blamed the spread of democracy for stoking the passions of the 'unenlightened masses', leading to rampant nationalism in Europe and in the colonies.[9] Conservatives like C. E. Carrington, Abe Bailey Professor of Commonwealth Relations at Chatham House from 1954 to 1962, agreed, railing against the popularity of nationalism, which he called 'a political concept with no logical basis',[10] and the Americans, for their 'ill-informed' criticisms of European empires and for helping to spread the doctrine of 'self-determination'.[11] Other internationalists, like the former colonial administrator and drafter of constitutions Margery Perham, were more sympathetic, acknowledging the need to restore a 'lost sense of autonomy and dignity' to colonial peoples, but lamenting the power of nationalism in the colonial and postcolonial worlds, which was waxing just as the 'rest of the world is seeking to sublimate' it.[12]

At the same time, some British scholars blamed decolonization on a failure of nerve and weakened moral character among the imperialists themselves. Seton-Watson, in his study of the Cold War, attacked the British government for its 'cowardice and treachery' in setting aside its 'obligations towards colonial people [*sic*]', insisting that good government was 'more important than self-government', and that anti-colonial nationalists had not yet shown

---

[5] These campaigns are dealt with in detail in *The Expansion*, in Naff 1984; Gong 1984a; Suganami 1984. For reassessments of these accounts, see also Suzuki 2009; Zhang 1991.
[6] Bull 1984c: 220–3.
[7] For their views, see especially Hall 2011; and more generally Hall 2012.
[8] See Howard 1984: 41–2 for a very brief discussion.
[9] Murray 1951: 22.   [10] Carrington 1955: 138.
[11] Carrington 1962.   [12] Perham 1962: 43.

their capacity to deliver it.[13] Instead, he lamented, we have seen an 'abdication' of responsibility by 'European nations, and especially by European élites, which, demoralized by the two great blood-baths in which Europe has twice done its best to commit suicide, have lost all confidence in themselves'. Decolonization represented nothing less than a symptom of the 'tragic decay of a civilization' that will lead to a 'reversion to barbarism'. This was the essence of what Seton-Watson understood by the 'revolt against the West'.[14]

The early English School shared many of these views, explaining decolonization and the wider revolt in similar terms. By the mid-1950s, Bull's erstwhile mentor Martin Wight, who only a few years earlier had argued for a deeper commitment on the part of the British to the betterment of subject peoples by paternalistic imperialism, began to paint the newly decolonized states of India and Indonesia as the new 'have-not' powers, alluding to E. H. Carr's characterization of the Axis Powers.[15] The 'have-nots' of the 1930s wanted a redistribution of colonies; the 'have-nots' of the 1950s, Wight argued, wanted the redistribution of esteem and wealth. These demands were a function, he went on, not so much of new ideas, but of a similarly emotional 'state of mind' to that which prevailed among the Axis Powers in the 1930s, 'in which resentment, a sense of inferiority, and self-pity are prime ingredients', leading to demands for the 'rectification' of past injustices.[16] These demands were conventionally expressed in liberal terms, in the language of self-determination, but so fervent and violent was anti-colonial nationalism, the result was not 'freedom and fulfilment' but perpetual war, periodic insurrection, 'repudiation of agreements', and the 'dissolution of moral ties' in international society.[17]

In the main, the contributors to *The Expansion* were just as unsympathetic to those who had revolted, critical of the arguments they advanced to justify their causes, and just as condemnatory about the consequences of the revolt. Even Bull, who had spent considerable time and effort in the 1970s in India and elsewhere in the developing world, trying to understand the underlying arguments that motivated the revolt, evinced deep concern about its supposed deleterious impact on international society.[18] He showed some consideration for non-Western demands for equal rights, self-determination, and some measure of economic justice, but recognized that a gulf had emerged between the West and non-West on, as he put it, 'a wide range of normative issues', noted that this had generated disillusionment in the West about the United Nations (UN), and worried that both developments might undermine the core institutions of international society.[19] Similarly, in their chapters, both Peter

---

[13] Seton-Watson 1960: 269.   [14] Seton-Watson 1960: 461–2.
[15] See Lewis et al. 1951; Carr 1939.   [16] Wight 1956: 249–50.
[17] Wight 1960: 307–8.
[18] On Bull's various travels and attitudes, see especially Ayson 2012.
[19] Bull 1984c: 227.

Lyon and R. J. Vincent showed some sympathy for aspects of the revolt—for the concept and practice of non-alignment, in Lyon's case, and for the demand for racial quality, in Vincent's—but criticized the excesses in which they believed developing states and their elites had indulged.[20] Only Ali Mazrui stood up for the revolutionaries in his chapter, but even he was critical of the consequences of their actions, denouncing what he called the 'prison-houses' of the sovereign state and global capitalism, which were constructed by the West during decolonization to reincarcerate Africans.[21]

Like the earlier British writers on the revolt, Bull and most of the other contributors to *The Expansion* argued that the main drivers of change were ideational. The European imperial order in Africa and Asia fell apart, he argued, because of a 'psychological awakening' among non-Western peoples, who looked to the state as a means of liberation, because of a 'weakening' in the will of the West and doubts over the profitability of empire, because of the impact of the Russian revolution on proletarians everywhere, and because of a 'new legal and moral climate of international relations' brought about in the 1950s and early 1960s by the Non-Aligned Movement and then the Group of 77. He recognized, like Michael Howard, that the 'existence' of what Bull called 'a more general equilibrium of power' in world politics was an important underlying condition, but emphasized ideational change as the main driver of the revolt.[22]

Others also emphasized ideational change over material. Vincent argued the struggle for racial equality, and indeed anti-white racism, were the unintended consequences of European actions in Africa and Asia, which had generated worldwide 'colour-consciousness' where there was none before.[23] Wight and Bull's erstwhile colleague at the London School of Economics, Elie Kedourie, went far further, blaming all modern ills on the spread of pernicious ideas of national self-determination and class struggle, which fed and reinforced a disastrous ideological style of politics.[24] 'The new international disorder', as he called it, was the result of the West's error in making national self-determination 'the sole and overriding aim of all political action', for this was a 'recipe for perpetual war'.[25] Combined with the 'doctrine of class struggle' that emerged from the Russian revolution, the concept of self-determination had undermined the two foundations on which European international society had been built: the balance of power carefully contrived by statesmen and the 'consciousness of a common civilization, common political attitudes, and...common language of international politics' they had shared.[26] Kedourie attacked the product of this doctrine, decolonization, which had generated the 'imitation states' of the Third World, 'formally

---

[20] See Lyon 1984; Vincent 1984.   [21] Mazrui 1984: 289.   [22] Bull 1984c: 224–7.
[23] Vincent 1984: 241.   [24] Kedourie 1984: 349, 351.   [25] Kedourie 1984: 349.
[26] Kedourie 1984: 347.

sovereign' but with rulers who 'labour under strong feelings of insecurity...
generated by their lack of legitimacy', and who embrace 'an ideological style of
politics'—often Soviet-inspired—in response.[27]

Paler versions of these arguments cropped up elsewhere in the book,
normally expressed in tones that were more condescending than condemnatory. Like Kedourie, Adam Watson noted the legitimacy gap that he thought
yawned in postcolonial states between Westernized elites and 'the great
unwesternized majority of their own people'.[28] Adda Bozeman, for her part,
also cast doubt on whether non-Western peoples could ever properly adopt
and utilize Western forms of government and economic management. Non-
Western cultures, she argued, including both Hinduism and Confucianism,
had certain virtues, but were not 'hospitable to innovation', and because of
such inherent weaknesses, non-Western peoples would continue to struggle to
fully realize political institutions invented in the West, including the sovereign
state. Post-colonial Westernizers in non-Western states were thus doomed to
fail, she argued, as the underlying culture of their societies proved resistant to
Western concepts and practices: 'Ideas are not transferable in their authenti-
city, however adept and dedicated the translators'.[29] Thus the sovereign state,
democracy, diplomacy, and all those other European inventions passed to
non-Western peoples during international society's expansion would not take
root, and disorder would replace them, domestically and internationally.
Bozeman ended on a sad note: 'occidental diplomacy must henceforth be
prepared to function again, as it did before the nineteenth century, in a world
that has no common culture and no overarching political order, and that is no
longer prepared to abide by western standards of international conduct'.[30]

These themes—and others—were picked up once more in the editors'
conclusion, which meditated on the impact of the revolt on international
society as a whole. Bull and Watson argued that the revolt had:

> brought about a new legal and moral climate in world affairs in which colonial
> rule, and by extension rule by settler minorities, came to be regarded as illegit-
> imate. They found a new target in neo-colonialism.... They upheld the equality
> of races, especially in relation to the white supremacist governments of southern
> Africa. They formulated demands for economic justice as between rich and poor
> nations, culminating in their proposal in 1974 for a New International Economic
> Order. They found a new field of endeavour in the idea of cultural liberation...
> They propagated a Third World ideology or world view, derived partly from
> Leninism, that...had a deep impact on the way in which world affairs were
> perceived not only in Third World and Soviet bloc countries but in the Western
> countries also.[31]

---

[27] Kedourie 1984: 351.   [28] Watson 1984a: 32.   [29] Bozeman 1984: 392.
[30] Bozeman 1984: 406.   [31] Bull and Watson 1984a: 428–9.

As a consequence of all of this, they argued, states are now 'less united by a sense of a common interest in a framework of rules and institutions governing their relations'.[32] In part, this was because some of these states were only states 'by courtesy', and the presence of 'pseudo-states or quasi-states within the international society of today...makes for a weakening of cohesion'.[33] Some areas of the world are now, to all intents and purposes, ungoverned and in an 'endemic war or state of war'; some states, where they do exist, repudiate the basic rules of international society.[34] And all the while, the 'cultural heterogeneity of the global international society...is evidently a factor making against consensus about its underlying rules and institutions'—a factor made worse when Westernized elites signed up to agreements frowned upon by their non-Westernized populations.[35]

Bull and Watson concluded with two observations. They noted that the 'fact that...international society...has outgrown its original cultural base is...a basic source of weakness'.[36] But then they noted that all was not lost. International society was not disintegrating; rather, its capacity to absorb new states indicated an underlying strength. Moreover, Bull and Watson argued that, even in 'revolt', most 'Third World' states were not repudiating international society altogether, but rather were aiming 'to improve their own positions within that society', still deeply attached to the basic concepts of sovereignty, equality, non-intervention, and so on.[37] And above it all, in the rarefied domain of international diplomacy there was a cultural unity of sorts in a common adherence to a 'cosmopolitan culture of modernity'.[38]

In sum, the majority of the contributors to *The Expansion* portrayed the revolt against the West as brought about by ideational change and as perhaps the most significant threat to international society, in its inherited European form, to have emerged since the end of the Second World War. The revolt was caused by the spread of liberal and nationalist ideas from the West to the non-West, generating what Bull called a 'psychological or spiritual awakening'.[39] At the same time, doubts grew in the West about the justifications hitherto offered for the maintenance of empire, the Russian revolution spread more ideas antithetical to imperialism, and as decolonization progressed, new ideas emerged from the emerging Global South that challenged the international economic order, asserted racial equality, and advanced claims about the value of non-Western cultural concepts and practices. And these ideas implicitly or explicitly challenged the ideas and shared values that shaped the core institutions of international society, and allowed them to function smoothly.

---

[32] Bull and Watson 1984a: 430.   [33] Bull and Watson 1984a: 430.
[34] Bull and Watson 1984a: 431–2.   [35] Bull and Watson 1984a: 432.
[36] Bull and Watson 1984a: 433.   [37] Bull and Watson 1984a: 434.
[38] Bull and Watson 1984a: 435.   [39] Bull 1984c: 224.

BEYOND THE REVOLT

Many criticisms have been made of *The Expansion* and its account of the development of international society. Clearly, the book is unabashedly and unapologetically Eurocentric. For all the talk of revolts and crises in international society, moreover, the book still points to the enduring nature of its core institutions, and, by implication, to the superior sagacity of the Europeans who constructed them. Although 'African, Asian, and Latin American states' have brought about a 'massive revision of international rules and conventions', the editors observed, in the final analysis they had nonetheless 'accepted' the 'rules and institutions of European international society . . . as the basis of their international relations'.[40] The editors recognized, of course, that Europe's 'ascendancy' in the world had by the time of writing 'vanished', but that the 'international political structure' Europe had bequeathed to contemporary international society remained.[41]

Perhaps for that reason the book neglected to discuss in detail that 'massive revision' of rules and conventions, the normative agendas at play in that process, and the agents and their means of change. True, Lyon provided a description—but not an explanation or evaluation—of the emergence of the Third World views on security, economic development, trade, and cooperation, Vincent contributed an intellectual history of the idea of racial equality, and Gopal Krishna outlined India's retreat from its activism under its first prime minister, Jawaharlal Nehru. But only Ian Brownlie's chapter on international law and Michael Palliser's on diplomacy came close to explaining exactly how and why the institutions of international society had changed during and after decolonization.[42]

The view that decolonization and the postcolonial states it produced had little impact on international society, apart from threatening the cultural values that supposedly underpinned it, persisted into the second phase of English School writing, which began in the early 1990s. James Mayall assessed the causes of decolonization but not its consequences; Robert H. Jackson examined some of the consequences, but focused on the effects on postcolonial states, not international society, except insofar as that society was forced to act as their custodians.[43]

Meanwhile, Vincent's work on non-intervention and on human rights, along with Andrew Linklater's work on critical theory and political community, helped to stimulate a whole new area of English School concern with individual rights, which emerged in parallel with the humanitarian crises and Western interventions that captured much of the attention of the discipline of

---

[40] Bull and Watson 1984b: 1–2.   [41] Bull and Watson 1984b: 2.
[42] Krishna 1984; Brownlie 1984: especially 366–7; Palliser 1984.
[43] Mayall 1990; Jackson 1990.

International Relations scholarship in Britain throughout the 1990s.[44] Yet despite this new interest in rights, norms, and legitimacy, and a growing concern for the relationship between international society and what they termed 'world society', the new English School did not return, in the main, to re-evaluate the revolt against the West or its impact on international society.[45] Instead, the consensus view remained that, to use Ian Clark's words:

> the so-called 'revolt' against the West...resulted in the paradoxical reaffirmation of the Western state form as the ticket for admission into international society....
> While decolonization reflected the delegitimation of the former practices of colonialism, it also endorsed other traditional principles, especially those pertaining to sovereignty and non-intervention.[46]

In other words, for those writing in the 1990s and afterwards, the revolt had been all sound and fury, signifying very little.

This view has only recently been challenged, most notably by Christian Reus-Smit, who argues that the English School's explanation of the revolt is inchoate and flawed, that it downplays the 'political struggles' that 'drove each wave' of the expansion of international society and the changes to the normative order that accompanied them.[47] Reus-Smit highlights the English School's ongoing struggle to explain, rather than merely describe, how international society has developed over time, struggles which some think can be resolved by appealing to the concept of 'world society' as a putative source of new norms and values that come to shape the institutions of international society.[48]

Recent work in the English School tradition has also suggested that today's global international society—and, by implication, the global international society that has existed since the entry of non-European states—may not display the kind of homogeneity of attitudes about its core institutions (war, the balance of power, great powers, law, and diplomacy) that the first and second phases of the English School believed. Instead, works like Barry Buzan and Yongjin Zhang's volume on East Asian international society, and Buzan and Ana Gonzalez-Perez's edited book on the Middle East, suggest that regional international societies exist with differing ideas about how those institutions should be organized and should operate.[49] The next section draws upon these arguments to evaluate the legacies of the revolt and to analyse the persistence of the struggles for what Bull called 'cultural liberation' and 'economic justice'.

---

[44] See, especially, Vincent 1974, 1986; Linklater 1982; Wheeler 1992, 2000.
[45] See, for example, Buzan 2004.
[46] Clark 2005: 161. See also the otherwise excellent Clark 2007, which also elides any substantive discussion of decolonization and its aftermath.
[47] Reus-Smit 2013a.   [48] See, especially, Clark 2007; Buzan 2004.
[49] Buzan and Zhang 2014; Buzan and Gonzalez-Perez 2009.

REVOLT, RESISTANCE, AND REVISIONISM

Thirty years on from *The Expansion of International Society*, it is clear that at least three of the five partially overlapping phases of the revolt against the West are now finished, and the postcolonial world, in the main, 'won'. What Bull called the 'struggle for equal sovereignty'—essentially, the struggle for unqualified recognition of the sovereignty of non-Western states—ended, in formal terms, with the UN Charter, although in practice the qualification of recognition by standards imposed by the West lingered into the 1970s. The anti-colonial revolution is also over, at least in terms of revolution against European rulers leading to the establishment of formally independent sovereign states, although quasi-colonial rule arguably lingers in some parts of the world. And the struggle for formal racial equality between states and within them ended with the winding-up of white minority rule in South Africa in the early 1990s—even if, as Audie Klotz argues, the struggle to address the deeper-seated legacies of racism continues.[50]

In each of these areas, despite what Bull called a 'rearguard action' fought by the West, the revolt had met with a 'measure of success'.[51] The postcolonial world had, he observed, 'overturned the old structure of international law and organization that once served to sanctify their subject status'.[52] Admittedly, they had done this by turning Western tools against the West. Both Gerrit Gong and Hidemi Suganami observed that China and Japan successfully used Western concepts of international law to assert and establish their claims to sovereign equality.[53] And Bull made much of the ways in which the United Nations and other international institutions, the products of Western liberal internationalism, were used and in some cases subverted by non-Western states pursuing different agendas. These practices, he rightly noted, had done much to generate disillusionment about the UN and internationalism more broadly in Western states.[54]

Bull does not seem to have appreciated, however, the extent to which these victories for the Third World masked an underlying balance of power that continued to favour the West, and Western political and economic models, nor did he anticipate the reassertion of Western leadership over the normative agenda of international relations that began in the 1980s, and dominated the 1990s. Under these latter pressures, towards the end of the 1980s and into the 1990s, the revolt was diminished, but changed in focus, to re-emerge in different forms after 2001. This change occurred in a context in which

---

[50] On the extraordinary success of anti-apartheid activists in changing United States policy on South Africa, see especially Klotz 1995b. See also Chapter 19 by Klotz in this volume.
[51] Bull 1984c: 228.   [52] Bull 1984c: 227.
[53] Gong 1984a: 181, 183; Suganami 1984: 195. See also Bull 1984b: 121.
[54] Bull 1984c: 227–8.

Western political and economic policies, and Western values, were near-unassailable. The discrediting of authoritarianism and controlled economies as a means of achieving growth and development, and the collapse of the Soviet Union, robbed those inclined towards such policies in the postcolonial world of the ideational and financial resources that it could use to resist the West. Many were swept away by the 'third wave' of democratization and the liberal 'Washington Consensus', which insisted upon the control of public debt, deregulation, privatization, tax system reform, trade liberalization, and the encouragement of foreign direct investment as a means of achieving growth and development.[55] And then, in the 1990s, came a renewed emphasis on human rights and a new willingness on the part of Western states to actively intervene, either with political and economic sanctions, or with military force, to uphold them.[56]

These developments changed the nature of the revolt. So too did two further developments. The first was the extraordinary economic growth experienced in the 1990s and afterwards in significant parts of what was once the Third World, most obviously in China, but also in South Korea and Taiwan, parts of South East and South Asia, the Gulf region, and parts of Africa, Latin America, and the Pacific. As wealth grew in these non-Western regions, sometimes as a result of the application of Western political and economic models and sometimes by the use of modified models designed to take advantage of the liberal global economy but maintain local elite control, like the East Asian 'developmental state', power began to shift away from the European Atlantic world. And at the same time, what Buzan and George Lawson have called the 'interaction capacity' of human societies increased dramatically, with the acceleration of the process of connecting individuals and groups across the world which began in the nineteenth century, but which sped up during the 1990s and afterwards with the proliferation of microprocessors and the advent of the Internet.[57]

Together, these developments have created a new context in which negotiation and contestation between the West and the non-Western world takes place, generating new topics to contest and new means by which to contest them. And although the struggles for equal sovereignty, statehood, and racial equality were over, what Bull called 'cultural liberation' and 'economic justice' remained at issue, generating what might be considered a new phase in the revolt.

The first struggle is manifest in ongoing arguments about the values that should underpin international society and that should be promoted or tolerated by that society, and those that should be condemned. It is played out in debates about democracy promotion, human rights, and humanitarian intervention, in particular, or in violent struggles between the West and

---

[55] On the third wave, see Huntington 1991; on the Washington Consensus, see Gore 2000.
[56] See Barnett 2005; Wheeler 2000.   [57] Buzan and Lawson 2015b.

non-Western groups espousing values radically at odds with the West, like those that adhere to militant Islamism. And the second struggle has been transformed from contestation between different economic models—essentially between market liberalism and state control—into contestation about who regulates the global market.

The struggle for 'cultural liberation'—which might be better termed a struggle over values or against Western values—has played out, and continues to play out, in a number of different ways. The contributors to *The Expansion* concerned themselves with two manifestations of the phenomenon: what might be called 'traditionalist' resistance to Westernizing elites, which both Bozeman and Watson discuss in their chapters, and the rise of new nationalist and religious movements, discussed in Bull's piece on the revolt, which notes (in passing) the emergence of Islamic fundamentalism, Hindu and Sikh neo-traditionalism, and other groups presenting alternatives to European values, and especially in James Piscatori's chapter on 'Islamic reassertion'.[58] Some of these movements have persisted after 1985; some have grown stronger; and others have emerged. They are manifest in the so-called 'Asian values' debate of the 1990s, as well as in various nationalist ideologies, like neo-Confucianism in China or *Hindutva* (literally, Hindu-ness) in India.[59]

The most significant challenge to Western values persists, however, in the forms of political and militant Islamism. In *The Expansion*, Piscatori identified four drivers of 'Islamic reassertion'—and arguably all four are still relevant thirty years later. Backed by the US, Israel continues to keep its Arab enemies, including Palestinian militants in the Occupied Territories and outside them, in check, and this continues to depress 'morale' in the Muslim world as a whole, and among Arabs in particular. Modernization continues to create acute tensions, socially—most obviously when it comes to gender issues—and economically. The 'universal crisis of modernity', as Piscatori called it, might be less keenly felt in some parts of the West, especially Europe, which has essentially abandoned religion, but continues to have some influence in the Muslim world, where religion proves a secure identity. Finally, the politics of many Muslim societies, especially in the Arab world, where authoritarianism has been repeatedly challenged, but not fully shaken, continues to generate tensions that favour the rise of radical Islamism as an alternative mode of political organization.[60]

Since 1985, more drivers have emerged. First, the 'resource curse' suffered by the Gulf Arab states has had contradictory effects, but ones that aid anti-Western feeling and the capacity to act upon it. Oil has generated wealth, inequality, and rapid, dislocating social change: an opening up to Western culture and consumerism, and fast-improving levels of education for a young workforce with few job prospects. Gulf Arabs with an anti-Western agenda,

---

[58] Bull 1984c: 224.   [59] See, respectively, Barr 2000; Gries 2004; Jaffrelot 1999.
[60] Piscatori 1984: 309.

and sufficient contacts within social and economic elites, now have the means and the knowledge to act to try to realize it, as we saw so clearly with Osama bin Laden. Second, the Iranian revolution provided hope to budding Islamist rebels that one day, with the proper work, secular authoritarianism could be replaced with theocratic rule. Third, the Afghan war against the Soviets provided yet another source of hope to such rebels, convincing many that religious fervour and dogged persistence could bring about the defeat of superpowers. Fourth, Western actions and especially military interventions in the Middle East and elsewhere in the Muslim world (in Iraq, the Balkans, Afghanistan, and so on) have given rise to a narrative of Western aggression against Islam carefully nurtured by Islamists, tied into longer narratives of European colonial aggression and humiliation.[61] The emergence of the Internet and the proliferation of computers have allowed these narratives to circulate faster and to reach more people than they could in the mid-1980s.

In its most extreme and militant forms, like that of *Daesh* or Islamic State, as Andrew Phillips argues, Islamism offers not just an alternative to Western values, and the political and economic policies which spring from them, but also a threat to international order, in that it holds out the hope of replacing international society with a unified Islamic *Umma* under a Caliph.[62]

Other anti-Western nationalist movements, and states sceptical about Western values in international relations, are more accommodated to international society and to its primary institutions. Manjari Chatterjee Miller has argued—persuasively—that contemporary Chinese and Indian foreign policy continues to be influenced by memories—real and retrospectively constructed —of historic wrongs committed by Western states against their peoples.[63] On her account, the campaign to right the wrongs of empire did not stop with the attainment of national self-determination and territorial sovereignty, but continues in the form of the pursuit of material power and especially of higher status markers appropriate to their perceived level of dignity.

Importantly, however, these struggles do not involve challenges to the form or content of what Reus-Smit calls the constitutional and fundamental institutions of international society.[64] Indeed, Chinese and Indian radicalism about these institutions has markedly declined, to be replaced with conservatism. In the 1950s and 1960s, both preached non-alignment and peaceful coexistence, condemning war and great power politics as obsolete Western practices, international law as skewed to Western interests, and favouring open and public diplomacy as opposed to the more traditional forms.[65] Today, however,

---

[61] The literature on these drivers is huge and growing, but see Gerges 2009.
[62] Phillips 2014b.   [63] Miller 2013.   [64] Reus-Smit 1999: 13–15.
[65] See the 'Five Principles of Peaceful Coexistence' enshrined in the so-called *Panchsheel* agreement between the two, properly called the 'Agreement (with Exchange of Notes) on Trade and Intercourse between Tibet Region of China and India', concluded on 29 April 1954.

China and India are conservative powers, at least with regard to the primary institutions, advocating strict interpretations especially of sovereignty and non-intervention, practising balance of power politics, viewing war as an instrument of state policy, and convinced of the necessity of great power management, with great powers accorded 'special responsibilities', especially concerning international security. These beliefs underpin China's push for a state-centric and hierarchical 'new model of great power relations', as Xi Jinping terms it, as well as India's desire for a permanent seat on the UN Security Council, and both states wish for their regional spheres of influence to be recognized by the West.

Rather than seeking the reform of international society, these postcolonial states—and others in Africa, Asia, and Latin America, but in stark contrast to non-state movements like militant Islamism—now 'revolt against the West' by resisting Western attempts to institutionalize new international norms and practices that accord with Western values. They are sceptical especially of democracy promotion and humanitarian intervention. Throughout the post-Cold War period, China has, on the whole, remained silent on these topics, protesting—sometimes obliquely and sometimes directly—only when its interests are perceived to be threatened.[66] India has been more openly critical, displaying reluctance, despite its own democratic tradition, to proselytize, questioning even the UN Security Council-sanctioned action to expel Iraqi forces from Kuwait in 1991, and displaying deep concerns about the succession of interventions that followed, and the attempt to institutionalize the 'responsibility to protect'.[67]

Alongside these debates about values runs another debate about global economic governance that follows from the struggle for economic justice Bull described. That earlier struggle pitted the 'Third World against global liberalism', as Stephen D. Krasner put it in his classic study of this topic. It had two aspects: an attempt to give developing states a greater say in international institutions and an attempt to extend the sovereignty of developing states over their own resources.[68] These claims were framed in terms of recompense for European exploitation of peoples and resources in their colonial possessions. They were to be realized by the creation of new institutions within the UN system, dominated now by postcolonial states, such as the United Nations Conference on Trade and Development, and by the assertion of sovereign power over economic assets within the borders of developing world states.

This struggle was transformed in the years immediately following the appearance of *The Expansion* and Krasner's *Structural Conflict*. First, the West used international institutions, particularly the International Monetary Fund (IMF), as a tool for reasserting a liberal economic agenda in the

---

[66] Snetkov and Lanteigne 2015.   [67] See, inter alia, Mohan 2007; Hall 2013.
[68] Krasner 1985: 6–7.

developing world. Second, as we have seen, the collapse of the Soviet Union discredited state control as a model of economic development. Third, China, and to a much lesser extent India, reformed their economies to better align them with global markets, and to take advantage of global capital and knowledge resources, and they were integrated into that economy by the leading Western powers, especially the United States.

In this context, the struggle for economic justice was transformed from one in which the West was asked for capital and know-how on the grounds that these were owed the postcolonial world, as reparations for past wrongs, into one in which postcolonial states were asking simply for an equal or appropriate say in the regulation of the global economy. True, issues of past wrongs continue to surface in some discussions about the global economy—most notably in debates about historic responsibilities for carbon emissions and the allocation of responsibilities for addressing climate change. But in the main, for postcolonial states, the struggle for economic justice now concerns the distribution of offices and voting rights in international financial and trade institutions like the IMF, the World Bank, and the World Trade Organization. To those ends, postcolonial states have taken advantage of their inclusion in forums like the G20 (Group of Twenty) to press for a greater say, or, to maintain pressure, created their own parallel institutions, such as the BRICS (Brazil, Russia, India, China, and South Africa) Summit and attendant bank, or the Chinese-sponsored Asian Infrastructure Investment Bank.

Of course, the struggle for economic justice has also continued in other settings, most notably in the rapidly evolving space of global civil society, and there developing world concerns continue to be framed in terms of economic justice for past and present exploitation that would be familiar to Bull. But as global civil society has acquired more of a voice in global forums, postcolonial states have arguably retreated from the push for economic justice framed in terms of reparations for historic wrongs or the distribution of global wealth.

CONCLUSION

The revolt against the West is largely over, replaced by resistance in some areas to Western values, and by revisionism, especially with regard to global economic governance. But this is not to say that international society has continued unchanged since *The Expansion* appeared, nor to say that core problems in English School thinking about the non-Western world and its relationship with that society are resolved. The debate about the revolt in that book, and within the English School before and afterwards, raised vexed issues for English School theories about what sustains international society and how it evolves.

There are two accounts of the origins of international society within the English School. The first sees it as a product of European contrivance, its institutions built over 400 years in line with changing ideas nevertheless particular to Europe's cultural inheritance, which is given to the rest of the world, whereupon its institutions and underlying ideas are accepted, rejected, modified, or undermined. This is the story Wight told and the story that is elaborated upon in *The Expansion*. In *The Anarchical Society*, Bull famously told a different tale, arguing that international society could have come into being in the absence of European ideas and European contrivance. Instead, it could have emerged simply as political actors recognize common interests and contrive to make and uphold rules and institutions to promote and defend them.[69] Bull tried to paper over the gap between his functionalist explanation and Wight's Eurocentric account by suggesting that if a 'common culture or civilisation' underpinned a society of states, 'they may make for easier communication and closer awareness and understanding between one state and another, and thus facilitate the definition of common rules and the evolution of common institutions'. And he added that they may also 'reinforce the sense of common interests that impels states to accept common rules and institutions with a sense of common values'.[70] But the gap is still clear and the consequences for thinking about the expansion and the globalization of international society are significant.

If Bull was right, then the contributors to *The Expansion* had no reason to be so anxious and angry about the revolt against the West, for once the non-West realized that it could gain more than it might lose by upholding the norms, rules, and institutions of international society, they would do so. Bull argued in *The Anarchical Society* that 'at no stage' in modern international relations 'can it be said that the conception of the common interests of states, of common rules accepted and common institutions worked by them, has ceased to exert an influence'.[71] If that was right, the revolt must be seen as epiphenomenal, or at least as a transitory weakening of ties that cannot be unbound.

But to view the revolt in that light is unhelpful, because it reinforces the idea that international society is unchanging, when it is constantly changing. Wight's approach, in this light, is preferable: he argued that the institutions of international society—understood as bundles of ideas, norms, rules, and practices—change over time as they are reinterpreted by agents, and new institutions arise alongside them. Using that approach focuses attention on the debates about institutions, on the differences of view between states and non-state actors about how they should function, who should run them, and by what rules. His late essay on 'International Legitimacy' in *Systems of States*

---

[69] Bull 1977: 3–73.   [70] Bull 1977: 15.   [71] Bull 1977: 40.

illustrates that well, tracing the rise and fall of different ideas of legitimacy and how they shaped political practice.[72]

We lack a similar holistic account of how, over the past century and a half, the various political debates that Bull grouped under the heading of the revolt against the West arose, played out, and in turn shaped the institutions of international society. We lack, for example, an adequate understanding of the ways in which anti-colonial movements and postcolonial states used, modified, and affirmed the diplomatic system—and we lack this partly because of narratives like those presented in *The Expansion*, which suggest an unchanging-ness in international society where there was clearly contestation and change.

[72] Wight 1977.

19

Racial Inequality

Audie Klotz

In his contribution to *The Expansion of International Society*, R. J. Vincent wrote an insightful commentary on racial equality that, three decades later, remains a surprisingly fresh perspective on overlooked issues in International Relations (IR) scholarship.[1] Categorical inferiorities were, he noted, commonplace during the peak phase of European expansion. From this baseline, Vincent argued that equality had expanded over the past two centuries. Boldly, his first sentence proclaimed that, '[o]ne of the marks of the transition from a European to a global international order has been the passing, at least in terms of the number of white states compared to non-white, of white predominance in international society'.[2]

Adopting standard war-based periodization, Vincent delineated three phases in this macro-historical trend against racism: abolition of slavery starting in the early 1800s, Japan's counter-hegemonic role in the interwar period, and African decolonization after the Second World War. But rather than simply trumpeting the post-1945 era of decolonization as the marker of a truly global order based on state sovereignty, he emphasized multifaceted struggles to remove prejudice as a fundamental feature in the ongoing evolution of international society.[3] While optimistic due to substantial progress towards the elimination of prejudice, his conclusion nevertheless noted myriad inequalities, presciently foreshadowing abiding contestation in contemporary global politics.

Vincent thus pre-empted many criticisms of the international society approach that inform this book project, such as problematizing sovereignty, concentrating on global processes, and avoiding narrow Eurocentric histories.[4]

---

[1] Vincent 1984. On the dearth of attention to race in the discipline, see Vitalis 2000: 332–7.
[2] Vincent 1984: 239. For a similar assessment based on international law, see Lyons 1989: 77.
[3] Vincent 1984: 252–3.   [4] See Chapters 1, 2, and 22.

Yet using recognition of 'white' and 'non-white' states as a key indicator, while consistent with the IR literature, hides as much as it reveals. Because racism does not always explicitly manifest itself when most deeply entrenched, it can remain endemic around the world despite formal changes in international society.[5] Still, racism in 2014 *is* different from racism in 1914, or 1814.

Since prejudices are rooted in a variety of intellectual and cultural notions, not necessarily syncretic or predominant, I follow John Cell, who argued that understanding racism's mutability necessitates the exploration of counterfactual explanations (although he does not use that exact term). Racism, he argues, cannot be the sole or sufficient cause of discrimination, which has ranged in form from extermination and slavery to deportation and segregation.[6] Similarly, the end of white minority rule, whether measured by the adoption of universal franchise or other metrics, does not signal the demise of racism, because prejudice morphs.

Complicating my analytical task, Vincent's analysis was vague about causes. Aside from claiming that race informed civilizational standards, rather than the reverse, he mentions specific historical causes—collective shock from European fratricide in the First World War and Nazi atrocities in the Second World War—which underscore conventional Eurocentric war-based periodization.[7] Like many IR scholars, he implied a progressive role for British and American hegemony, yet he also rooted earlier racism in British expansion.[8] These contradictory claims glossed over significant evidence of racial *inequality* throughout the historical periods covered, not least the United States after 1945. Furthermore, Vincent omitted potential processes such as gradual democratization that might explain trends towards formal racial equality and perhaps help us to avoid reducing the metric of racism to white minority rule.

Hence, while sympathetic to Vincent's analysis, I employ a broader notion of human equality in my exploration of racism across the past two centuries. Crucially, gender and racial hierarchies were—and remain—intricately linked. If racism is indeed antithetical to liberalism, then the gradual triumph of liberal individualism should simultaneously improve gender equality, but the evidence turns out to be mixed. With an eye towards what can be gleaned about the globalization of international society, I reassess Vincent's three themes: abolition, migration, and decolonization. Finding many reasons to resist a teleological storyline, I stress abiding tensions between liberal egalitarianism and racial hierarchy.

---

[5] For stunning illustrations of these deep prejudices, see Nederveen Pieterse 1992.
[6] Cell 1982: 4. [7] Vincent 1984: 239, 240, 252.
[8] For an explicit version of this argument, see Lauren 1988: 290-1.

BEFORE HEGEMONY: ABOLITION

The discourses and policies that get labelled racist have certainly evolved over the past two centuries, along with the ideological bases of prejudice. Despite relying heavily on British thinkers, Vincent did acknowledge such a diversity of foundations for prejudice by pointing to the destabilizing significance of French revolutionary ideals, especially as instigation for insurrection in Haiti.[9] Yet his discussion also understated the complexities of abolitionism, which he portrayed as rooted in egalitarianism.[10] My more sceptical (yet still Anglo-centric) historical examination of nascent liberal hegemony underscores that, rather than providing evidence of anti-racism, abolition actually ushered in the intensified racism of Victorian high imperialism.[11] Ironically, Queen Victoria's reign also solidified exclusion of women from the political sphere.[12]

In contrast to Vincent's focus on Haiti, the standard tale of abolition in the IR literature begins in 1807 with British legislation outlawing the slave trade. These analyses have replicated the classic division between liberals, who tend to trumpet humanitarian motives, versus realists or Marxists, who insist on material advantages.[13] As Joel Quirk convincingly summarizes the historical evidence, any such mono-causal argument falls short in explaining such a profound policy reversal, which advocates justified in terms of both morality and interests.[14] Nor did British maritime hegemony translate into abolition of either the slave trade or slavery, as is often asserted. Its ships conducted the bulk of the trade, but self-enforcement made only a minor dent, and other European countries followed reluctantly, doing little more than formally declaring their moral objections at the Congress of Vienna in 1814-15.[15]

What did change was escalating public rejection of slavery, salient despite very limited franchise for men and none for women. Reforms in 1832 only expanded male franchise modestly, leaving the aristocracy firmly in control. Hence the prevalence of extra-parliamentary methods of expressing opinion, such as petitions, in the second protracted phase of abolition, which ran roughly from the British outlawing slavery within its own imperial territories in 1834, though civil war in the United States, to Brazilian abolition in 1888.[16] In particular, British responses to the Confederacy captured the tensions

---

[9] Vincent 1984: 242-4.   [10] Vincent 1984: 243.   [11] Quirk 2011: 57-8, 70-2.
[12] Towns 2010b: 55-6, 64-5, 70-9, 82-3, 90, 93.
[13] For example, Ray 1989: 407-15; Kaufmann and Pape 1999.
[14] Quirk 2011: 28, 32-4, 39-49; also Midgley 1986: 40, 93. While similarly stressing that British politicians focused on national moral redemption, Kaufmann and Pape 1999: 643-62 make a narrower analytical claim based on domestic coalitions that unduly downplays transnational influences (c.f., Midgley 1986: 123-42).
[15] Quirk 2011: 26-7, 30, 59-60, 198-9; Kaufmann and Pape 1999: 634, 655, 658-9; Lauren 1988: 24-31.
[16] Midgley 1986: 35, 154-5; Kaufmann and Pape 1999: 659-61; Quirk 2011: 50-3, 60-4, 73-5.

between anti-slavery sentiment and strategic calculus: mixed motives and diverse material interests led to ambivalent neutrality.[17]

Then, rather than emancipation marking a clear step on the path towards racial equality, as Vincent implied, the second half of the nineteenth century entrenched prejudice. Notably, British self-perceptions of moral superiority reinforced notions that civilized Europeans rightly dominated less civilized others. Such views, which Neta C. Crawford aptly labelled 'aggressive humanitarianism', underpinned competition for colonial realms.[18] Similar sentiments drove American expansion.[19] This 'new religion of whiteness' led W. E. B. Du Bois to predict that 'the problem of the color line' would predominate in the twentieth century.[20]

Marilyn Lake and Henry Reynolds described this 'imagined community of white men' as transnational in 'inspiration and identifications', even though their goals were primarily national.[21] In essence, these men created what Vincent called 'white states', those with white populations and, by implication, white ruling elites.[22] The 1890s were crucial years in the emergence of segregation as a specific institutional form of white dominance. Contrary to any story of a progressive trend against racism, the United States and the British Dominions, with London's support, actively promoted segregation as a response to socio-economic pressures associated with urbanization. One of the most striking policies that developed within this white Anglosphere is the literacy test, first as a tool to counter emancipation, the focus in this section, then as a technology of immigration control, addressed in the next section.[23]

In both circumstances, self-avowed advocates of democracy embraced racist policies primarily targeting Africans and Asians, although their prejudices also extended to select Europeans, such as Catholics and Jews. This regressive trend began when former slaves became US citizens in 1865. Dramatic changes for blacks initiated during the period of so-called Reconstruction included (the possibility of) land ownership, widespread establishment of (less than equal) public education, and franchise (for men).[24] These new rights were not uniformly embraced, even beyond the former Confederacy. On both sides of the Atlantic and throughout the British Empire, extremely influential

---

[17] Steele 2005: 530-7.

[18] Crawford 2002: 203. See also Vitalis 2000: 341; Quirk 2011: 58, 66-70. Vincent 1984: 240, 248-50 admitted almost as much.

[19] Lauren 1988: 41; Vitalis 2000: 341, 345-6; Crawford 2002: 236.

[20] Quoted in Lake and Reynolds 2008: 2. See also Huttenback 1976: 14-21.

[21] Lake and Reynolds 2008: 4.

[22] Vincent 1984: 239. South Africa complicates his focus on population.

[23] This section elaborates on US dimensions of the literacy test's diffusion across the Anglosphere, analysed in Klotz 2013.

[24] Foner 1988; King and Smith 2005: 77, 81, 87.

liberals, as well as some abolitionists, argued that democracy required racial homogeneity.[25]

Modifying educational requirements for franchise used elsewhere, the literacy test originated as a clever attempt to eliminate the black vote despite constitutional protections, notably the fourteenth and fifteenth Amendments. Adopted first by Mississippi in 1890, the malleable requirement of a signature and basic knowledge of the constitution served two purposes. By excluding some poorer whites as well as blacks, the measure could arguably be defended as non-discriminatory, hence not abrogating the fifteenth Amendment. In addition, by allowing a low-level bureaucrat, such as a registrar, to administer the test provided discretion in the application of the test, thereby ensuring leniency for whites and stringency for blacks.[26]

Fuelled by perceptions that Reconstruction had failed, the Supreme Court's infamous acceptance of separate-but-equal in its *Plessy v. Ferguson* ruling of 1896 removed a key constitutional barrier, thereby launching the so-called Jim Crow era.[27] With northern acceptance, most southern states followed Mississippi's lead on the literacy test: South Carolina in 1895, Louisiana in 1900, Alabama in 1901, and Georgia in 1908.[28] That many white elites sought to exclude both blacks and illiterate whites should come as no surprise, given the widespread acceptance of education and property qualifications in Britain and across its Dominions. Even the Cape Colony (later one of four provinces in a unified South Africa) took up the literacy test as a weapon of disenfranchisement to supplement property qualifications that already excluded almost all non-white voters.[29]

Still, new segregationist laws did not automatically pass, since some legislators had been elected under the old Reconstruction rules. Consequently, two trends emerged by the late 1890s: party politics focused on competition for white populist voters and violent intimidation of would-be black voters. One long-lasting result was the consolidation of Democratic Party predominance in the region; another was the salience of the Ku Klux Klan.[30] Much like the differences between industrial Johannesburg and mercantile Cape Town in South Africa, emerging cities in the so-called New South served as the epicentres of segregation, not least because of the absence of longstanding patriarchal hierarchies, which prevailed in established cities of the so-called

---

[25] Lauren 1988: 33–7; Lake and Reynolds 2008 49–74.

[26] Cell 1982: 184–5; Lake and Reynolds 2008: 62–3, 66–7.

[27] Cell 1982: 86; Lauren 1988: 49; King and Smith 2005: 81, 87; Lake and Reynolds 2008: 64–5, 68–9; Jung 2015: 77–9.

[28] Cell 1982: 25; Lake and Reynolds 2008: 63.

[29] Huttenback 1976: 206; Lake and Reynolds 2008: 63, 71–2. In contrast, Vincent (1984: 249, 252) repeats the standard British imperial line of the Cape being liberal, whereas intolerant Afrikaners were to blame for segregation.

[30] Cell 1982: 88–9, 120–1, 170; King and Smith 2005: 81.

Old South.[31] As Cell succinctly summarized, segregation 'was born and grew to maturity in the vigorous environment of a new society that was attempting to modernize'.[32]

Remarkably, Cell's discussion of US disenfranchisement in the 1890s made no mention of the lack of female suffrage. Even Eric Foner's magisterial *Reconstruction* merely notes in passing that the Freedmen's Bureau summarily designated men as heads of household, in effect allocating to them a profound range of legal, economic, and social powers.[33] Indeed, their studies replicate the normalization of gender discrimination, which was explicitly affirmed during the 1870s. The fourteenth Amendment specifically distinguished rights based on gender, by declaring full citizenship to all 'persons' in Section 1, but limiting franchise to men only in Section 2, an exclusion unanimously upheld by the Supreme Court in *Minor v. Happersett*.[34] Furthermore, in its *Bradwell v. State* ruling, the Supreme Court upheld an Illinois statute that barred women from practising law.[35]

Women had played a major role in mobilization against slavery, but their own rights would have to wait. Why? Elsewhere, the relationship between racial and gender exclusions provides some insights into the absence of support for universal franchise in the late 1800s. The 1890s were a time not only of rising segregation in the American South; burgeoning transnational migration flows created comparable political tensions in white-dominated societies that had not experienced slavery on a grand scale. Notably, Australia recognized the strategic value of granting franchise to white women in 1902 as a way to dilute the significance of any non-whites who did manage to qualify.[36] In contrast, such electoral manipulation was not necessary in the United States, because its 1790 naturalization law already limited access to Europeans, a provision modified only to accommodate former slaves.[37] Thus in practice, legislation defined the inherently fluid boundaries of race in ways that become more visible with the addition of gender questions.

These parallels between the United States and the British Dominions also underscore that slavery as well as its legacies should be viewed as an integral part of a global migration system.[38] Wholesale disenfranchisement and the prevalence of lynching, alongside harsh socio-economic aspects of segregation, created fertile ground for massive internal migration of blacks to the

---

[31] Cell 1982: 134-5.   [32] Cell 1982: 169.   [33] Foner 1988: 87.

[34] Fourteenth Amendment, <http://www.law.cornell.edu/constitution/amendmentxiv>; *Minor v. Happersett*, <https://www.law.cornell.edu/supremecourt/text/88/162>.

[35] *Bradwell v. The State*, <http://www.law.cornell.edu/supremecourt/text/83/130>.

[36] Huttenback 1976: 290-1, 313, 321-2; Lake and Reynolds 2008: 155-8; Klotz 2013: 242.

[37] King and Smith 2005: 89; Lake and Reynolds 2008: 266-7; FitzGerald and Cook-Martín 2014: 86-8; Jung 2015: 70-2.

[38] African-Americans have largely been omitted in the US immigration literature, with a few exceptions such as King 2000; Fox 2012; FitzGerald and Cook-Martín 2014; Jung 2015.

industrial north—conditions so dire that Isabel Wilkerson pointedly applied the term refugees.[39] And this increased internal mobility for blacks, previously denied in the antebellum period, made feasible some of the most racist immigration legislation in US history. The quota acts of 1921 and 1924 aimed to filter out certain undesirable Europeans and Afro-Caribbean blacks, while also banning Asians.[40]

Such contrasts and ironies make Vincent's core theme of racism's steady decline difficult to swallow. So, what affects its ebb and flow? Answering that question means delving deeper into both advocacy of and opposition to racism. Vincent acknowledges as much when he proceeded to discuss Japan's efforts to promote equality, albeit at the same time that it perpetuated a hierarchy among Asians, which he overlooks.[41] His emphasis on Japan as more than just a rising military threat in the Pacific offered a refreshing counterpoint to typical Eurocentrism in IR theories of the 1980s, even if his narrative oversimplifies.

COUNTERING HEGEMONY: MIGRATION

To probe Vincent's implicit claim about the role of hegemons in driving change, I elaborate in this section on how overlapping strands of Anglo-Asian debate produced hierarchies relevant for understanding racism on a global scale. Extending the story of Jim Crow literacy tests, I trace the use of language restrictions on immigration as a racist tool, following the same timeframe as Vincent's analysis of Japan. This global history of immigration policy places Asia as the crucial terrain for analysis of racism from the late nineteenth into the early twentieth centuries, a time of intense debate over the future of the British Empire. Perhaps because the United States refused to join the League of Nations, Americancentric IR scholarship understates the significance of this period.

Although Britain had outlawed slavery within its realms by 1834, critics claimed that the working conditions for contract labour, its main substitute, were not much better, and other consequences, such as failed efforts at repatriation once contracts expired, had unintended ripple effects. Particularly noteworthy, merchants who followed indentured servants to the colony of Natal (later one of four provinces in a unified South Africa) could claim rights

---

[39] Wilkerson 2010: 179. This so-called 'Great Migration' and its connection to global migration patterns get surprisingly little mention (for example, Cell 1982: 113).

[40] Lauren 1988: 110–11; King 2000: 85–228; King and Smith 2005: 88–9; Fitzgerald and Cook-Martín 2014: 98, 101–4, 108.

[41] Vincent 1984: 244–7.

as imperial subjects, rights denied to contract labourers.[42] As in concurrent post-bellum US debates, a wide array of putative democrats believed that even well-educated Indians, most famous among them the London-trained lawyer Mohandas Gandhi, did not possess requisite characteristics of civilization for political participation. For example, Natal disqualified Indians from voting in 1896 with a generic restriction on anyone from a country without parliamentary institutions, even though property qualifications alone already ensured that a minimal number of Indians qualified to vote. In 1897, furthermore, Natal refused a trading license to anyone who did not keep records in English and implemented a literacy test for potential immigrants.[43]

Simultaneously, mutually reinforcing situations developed in Australia and California, thanks to discoveries of gold. Chinese migrated to pre-federation Australian shores on a large scale starting in the 1850s, where they encountered escalating animosities. Unlike British Indians, their limited rights relied mainly on bilateral treaties. Crucially, the Treaty of Nanking, which had opened China to British trade in the 1840s, guaranteed freedom of movement for Chinese within the British Empire. Consequently, British pressure to comply with that treaty led Victoria and New South Wales to repeal discriminatory measures in the mid-1860s, with modest effect. Fuelling Chinese concerns, Australian efforts at exclusion persisted, including a special conference convened in 1888.[44]

At the same time, Chinese had been equally unwelcome migrants to California. Indeed, the Australians keenly watched the fate of US initiatives, which eventually resulted in the Chinese Exclusion Act of 1882 and additional bans with the annexation of Hawaii in 1898, among other restrictive measures. In the United States, the rights of Chinese depended on the Burlingame Treaty of 1868, which Californians adamantly opposed. In contrast to Australia, however, constitutional limitations and other institutional constraints favoured federal jurisdiction, often to the general frustration of Californians.[45]

Despite these setbacks, neither Australian xenophobes nor those in California relented. Sharing strategies, they experimented with an array of creative measures aimed at severely limiting inflows of Asians in the first place, as well as restricting the exercise of any rights by those who did arrive. For example, California copied the head tax from Queensland in the 1870s.[46] And in 1901, with explicit encouragement from London, a federated Australia immediately

---

[42] Metcalf 2007; Klotz 2013: 61-9.
[43] Huttenback 1976: 52-8, 139-45, 196-206; Bhana and Pachai 1984: 84-6 (on franchise), 45 (on licenses), and 57 (on immigration); Lauren 1988: 52; Lake and Reynolds 2008: 118-21, 129-31; Klotz 2013: 69-72.
[44] Huttenback 1976: 61-125, 240-61; Lake and Reynolds 2008: 20-1, 24-6, 34-41; Klotz 2013: 72-4.
[45] Lake and Reynolds 2008: 20, 26, 28, 35, 139-43; Fitzgerald and Cook-Martín 2014: 91-6.
[46] Huttenback 1976: 315; Lake and Reynolds 2008: 28-9.

adopted the Natal model of a literacy test for potential immigrants, itself developed to circumvent a repeat of the failure in 1896 of an attempt at explicitly racist exclusion by New South Wales. Federated Australia also delegated greater jurisdiction to examining officials in the selection of language, along the lines of Mississippi's flexible Jim Crow procedures.[47]

For Australia and the United States, British Indians were less significant as the intended target than Chinese and Japanese migrants. More effectively than China, Japan opposed exclusionary policies, especially Australia's literacy test. In 1894, Japan had negotiated a commercial treaty with Britain (and a comparable one with the United States) which guaranteed rights of mobility within the empire, but only if the Dominions signed within two years. Except for Queensland, the Australian colonies refused, instead extending anti-Chinese measures to the Japanese as well. In turn, Japan objected to being classified together with China, viewed as less civilized. Federated Australia's literacy test then exacerbated that insult by allowing the use of European languages other than English but not Japanese. Adopted after considerable diplomatic pressure, an amendment to allow for literacy in any language made little difference in practice, due to the discretion provided to an examining officer.[48]

Widely admired as an ally, Japan expected equitable treatment, which placed London in a quandary. Adverse reactions to Japan's defeat of Russia in 1905 seemed to trump any potential amelioration of tensions over immigration. For instance, xenophobic sentiments flared in California, which had been percolating since Japanese migrants (not covered by the Chinese Exclusion Act) started to arrive in noticeable numbers a decade earlier. Friendly diplomatic relations still prevailed, however, producing the Gentleman's Agreement of 1907, which included a commitment by Japan to reduce emigration in exchange for better treatment of those already in California. The year before, Britain and Japan had reached a similar agreement for British Columbia, as a condition of Canada finally signing the 1894 trade agreement. Neither compromise quelled local opposition. Protestors up and down the west coast of North America, sometimes violent, made little distinction between Asian targets.[49]

At stake in the run-up to the First World War was more than recognition of great power status, Vincent's focus. Alliances frayed as a direct result of Japan's humiliation over discriminatory migration policies, a factor that he surprisingly omits.[50] Even its effective measures to reduce emigration did not diminish insatiable racist sentiments in Australia and North America. For

---

[47] Huttenback 1976: 154-69, 279-81, 306-9; Lauren 1988: 53; Lake and Reynolds 2008: 35, 125-31, 137; Klotz 2013: 74-9.

[48] Huttenback 1976: 281-4, 302-10, 314; Lake and Reynolds 2008: 143-50, 162, 170.

[49] Huttenback 1976: 126-38, 168-94, 261-78; Lauren 1988: 54; Lake and Reynolds 2008: 170-7, 179-80, 263, 278; Klotz 2013: 80-2; Fitzgerald and Cook-Martín 2014: 96-8.

[50] Vincent (1984: 245, 247) does later mention controversies over Asian migration but not linked to Japan's status. He also overstates South Africa as a major destination for Chinese.

instance, Australia talked of an independent navy, while the United States military paid more attention to the Pacific.[51] Diplomatic solutions no longer sufficed. In California, anti-Asian sentiments produced a lightly veiled Alien Land Law in 1913 that barred foreigners who were ineligible for citizenship (in other words, Asians) from owning land. Consequently, Japan's calls for racial equality escalated, which in turn fuelled claims by Australia among others of its threatening aggressiveness.[52]

Having nonetheless remained on the British side during the war, Japan earned a seat at the negotiating table in 1919. Taking up US President Woodrow Wilson's universalistic rhetoric at Versailles, its representatives proposed language for the League of Nations Covenant that would have protected foreigners from discrimination based on race or nationality within the signatories' territories. Opponents feared that such a racial equality clause would have eviscerated a slew of their restrictive immigration policies. In particular, Australia refused to budge, even on modified versions, but alone it would not have had sufficient leverage. Blocking Japan, Britain took cover under Australia's (and the other Dominions') objections, while the United States, in turn, could blame Britain. Notably, Wilson (as chair of the final session) accepted majority decisions on other issues, whereas he insisted on unanimity in the debate about a racial equality clause.[53]

Despite its apparent inconsistencies, Wilson's position should not come as a surprise. A segregationist at heart, he had increased discriminatory measures within the White House and Washington's bureaucracies. Plus he was vulnerable electorally, dependent especially on California, where anti-Asian sentiment ran highest.[54] Hence he had little reason, personally or politically, to undermine Australia at Versailles. His views also fit with the rising tide of scientific racism in immigration policy; by 1924, Japanese migration to the United States would be banned outright. Yet domestic considerations alone did not always prevail; US immigration and naturalization policies at the time remained rife with anomalies. For instance, Japanese, Assyrians, and British Indians were sometimes treated as white, whereas Filipinos and Mexicans, not considered white, did qualify for various rights.[55] Opposition to US imperial expansion by southern racists partially explains one anomaly: they settled for limiting any rights of those annexed, specifically Filipinos and Puerto Ricans.[56]

[51] Lauren 1988: 55; Lake and Reynolds 2008: 193, 204.
[52] Lauren 1988: 56-7, 66-7, 79-80; Lake and Reynolds 2008: 265-6, 271, 275-6.
[53] Lauren 1988: 80-95; Lake and Reynolds 2008: 278-9, 282, 289-302, 308. Vincent (1984: 245) did briefly acknowledge the White Australia policy and Wilson's procedural role.
[54] Lauren 1988: 83-4; Vitalis 2000: 338; King and Smith 2005: 85-7; Lake and Reynolds 2008: 292-3, 301-2, 320-1; Klotz 2013: 238.
[55] Lake and Reynolds 2008: 320-4; FitzGerald and Cook-Martín 2014: 88-9, 102-6, 109-10; Jung 2015: 77.
[56] Lauren 1988: 62-3; King and Smith 2005: 81, 87.

Only after 1919 and defeat of the racial equality clause did immigration become generally accepted as an issue of domestic jurisdiction, but the international salience of migration does not end with Japan's diplomatic defeat. Interconnections between immigration and strategic concerns explain significant shifts away from formal racism after 1945. Notably, both the United States and Canada initially loosened restrictions because nationalist China was a key ally during the Second World War—in stark contrast to their internment camps for citizens of Japanese descent. Gradually, burgeoning domestic and international rights-based mobilization led to the elimination of explicitly discriminatory immigration policies by the 1960s; even Australia reformed by the 1970s.[57]

Yet the interwar period—apogee of prejudice—also corresponds to the major expansion of voting rights for women, as well as the elimination of property qualifications for men.[58] These contrasting trajectories underscore the unsettled status of individual rights in international society. As for Vincent's analysis specifically, this history calls into question his key term, 'white state', because self-avowed democratic leaders and their policies in the Dominions and the United States were blatantly racist, regardless of minority or majority rule. It also challenges the characterization commonplace among IR scholars, and reiterated by Vincent, of the United States as the liberal, anti-colonial hegemon in the post-1945 era.[59]

AFTER HEGEMONY: DECOLONIZATION

The dramatic creation of new states in Africa during the 1950s and 1960s understandably garners major attention from international society scholars, since they use state recognition as the primary indicator of membership in an international society. Yet Vincent's corresponding claim of racism's decline during decolonization is problematic for many of the same reasons that the rise of racism after abolition challenged the standard liberal teleology.[60] The United States and the Dominions all continued to pursue overtly racist policies into the 1960s, even though South Africa was the only one governed by a white minority electorate. But my purpose here is not to suggest an alternative metric.[61] Instead, I push against Vincent's state-centric focus by linking

---

[57] Taylor 1991: 4–6; Lake and Reynolds 2008: 342, 352–3; Klotz 2013: 258, 266; Fitzgerald and Cook-Martín 2014: 90, 110–11, 114–15.

[58] Towns 2010b: 94–5.   [59] Vincent 1984: 252.   [60] Vincent 1984: 247–53.

[61] As Kwame Anthony Appiah (1992: 45) observed, 'there is nothing in the world that can do all we ask race to do for us'.

transnational anti-racist activism from before the Second World War to the post-1945 human rights story.

To untangle the distinctive role of global race politics from the conventional liberal human rights narrative, I return once again to the 1890s, with the pre-history of anti-apartheid activism. As already noted in the diffusion story of the literacy test, discrimination against Asians in South Africa and elsewhere often avoided blatantly racist restrictions. British commitments in the Proclamation of 1857, enshrined at the time of India's formal incorporation into the empire, created more stringent constraints than bilateral treaties with China and Japan. Hence the Colonial Office enthusiastically embraced Natal's literacy test in 1897, which was also adopted with a few modifications by the Union of South Africa in 1910. During these two decades, Gandhi led Indians both locally and transnationally in vociferous protests against laws that limited their rights as British subjects, with mixed results.[62]

As segregation in South Africa escalated during the 1920s, so did India's international activism. After becoming a member of the League of Nations, alongside the British Dominions, India joined Japan and China in voicing concerns about racism, as well as colonialism, which carried over to debates about participating in the Second World War. However, on the specific issue of South Africa, India had agreed to pursue its concerns at intra-imperial conferences, rather than trying to ramp up international pressure.[63] This longer narrative underscores India's persistent significance, a point that Vincent (among others) only briefly mentioned.[64]

Increasingly frustrated with South African intransigence and British ambivalence, India made greater use of international arenas after the Second World War. Along with China, it revived Japan's earlier fight for racial equality, including a proposal for a clause in the United Nations Charter that ultimately garnered only vague aspirational rhetoric. Still, racial discrimination was recognized in Article 55c as one obstacle to human rights and fundamental freedoms.[65] Seizing upon these new proclamations, as well as the 1948 Universal Declaration of Human Rights, transnational allies ranging from anti-colonial nationalists to African-Americans all pushed for implementation. Repeating what had happened in the aftermath of the First World War, military service by colonial subjects to defend democracy reinvigorated their demands for greater rights after the Second World War, as did

---

[62] Huttenback 1971, 1976: 145-54, 208-40; Lake and Reynolds 2008: 214-24, 228-35; Klotz 2013: 59-72, 83-108.

[63] Von Eschen 1997: 28-32; Klotz 2013: 264.

[64] Vincent 1984: 250; Lake and Reynolds 2008: 326-7.

[65] Lauren 1988: 86, 92, 104-5, 138, 148-58; Lyons 1989: 76-7; Lake and Reynolds 2008: 342. Again Vincent (1984: 252) glosses over the diplomatic struggles to get reluctant 'white states' to accept such provisions, leading him to an overly sanguine view of their aversion to racism.

African-Americans, who still faced the prospect of being lynched or engulfed in race riots.[66]

Spanning these wide-ranging concerns and constituencies, India succeeded in getting South Africa on the agenda at the first session of the United Nations (UN) General Assembly, despite the extraordinary international stature of its prime minister, Jan Smuts, who predictably invoked domestic jurisdiction.[67] At this point, the UN merely monitored the dispute between India and South Africa, encouraging negotiations. Soon after the National Party came to power in 1948, officially adopting apartheid, the General Assembly created an ad hoc commission, and by focusing especially on the potential of South Africa's new segregationist Group Areas Act to fuel race conflict, set the stage for treating discrimination against Indians and Africans as an international issue beyond the bounds of domestic jurisdiction.[68]

Concurrently, opponents of segregation in the United States used the precedent of South Africa on the UN agenda to call for similar scrutiny, albeit with less success. As the Cold War took hold in the early 1950s, the US government sidelined many transnational activists by tarring them as communists, even though the electoral dominance of racist 'Dixiecrat' politicians already muted their influence.[69] Yet, because of sensitivity to international pressures, the Harry S. Truman administration did make significant reforms, including desegregation of the military and federal bureaucracies, and subsequent administrations did too.[70] Although they did not include this US example, Margaret Keck and Kathryn Sikkink dubbed such a pincer-process the 'boomerang effect'.[71] Similar boomerang pressures had a more limited (although not trivial) effect on South Africa in the 1950s and 1960s.[72]

Anti-communism remained a powerful brake on commitments to racial equality, until a substantial number of African countries gained independence, and hence UN membership.[73] Spurred by headline-grabbing violence against protestors in the South African township of Sharpeville, international discourse on the potential implications of apartheid escalated. The Security Council immediately took up the issue at a special session in 1960, amid

[66] Lauren 1988: 71-3, 83-4, 96, 99, 138-40, 163-4; von Eschen 1997: 22-43, 110-11; Lake and Reynolds 2008: 306-8; Wilkerson 2010: 145.
[67] United Nations 1946-7: 144-5; Lauren 1988: 159-60, 167-71; Klotz 1995a: 41-3; von Eschen 1997: 83-7; Lake and Reynolds 2008: 343-7.
[68] United Nations 1952: 297-306; Klotz 1995a: 43-4.
[69] Lauren 1988: 172-4, 226, 233; Klotz 1995a 95-7; von Eschen 1997: 84, 96-121, 134-43; King and Smith 2005: 87.
[70] Lauren 1988: 187-95, 228-9; Lyons 1989: 88-9; von Eschen 1997: 113-14; King and Smith 2005: 82-3; FitzGerald and Cook-Martín 2014: 112-13.
[71] Keck and Sikkink 1998: 12-13.
[72] Black 1999: 83-8.
[73] Lauren 1988: 216-20, 226-7; Lyons 1989: 77; Klotz 1995a: 75-6; von Eschen 1997: 86-7, 167-89; Lake and Reynolds 2008: 349-50; FitzGerald and Cook-Martín 2014: 119.

escalating calls from the General Assembly for collective action, notably sanctions.[74] Making an unprecedented concession to human rights over domestic jurisdiction in 1963, the Security Council declared apartheid a threat to international peace and security and established a voluntary arms embargo.[75] Similar violence against protestors in Soweto produced, among many other consequences, the upgrade of the Security Council arms embargo to mandatory in 1977.[76]

While the rest of the anti-apartheid story has become common knowledge in the human rights literature—even if analysts and activists will never reach consensus on key factors—two points merit more attention here. First, South Africa played a special role because human rights activists subsequently undermined other countries' invocation of domestic jurisdiction based on the apartheid precedent. Second, the two putative liberal hegemons, Britain and the United States, initially opposed most major anti-apartheid initiatives. I will briefly address each point by starting with an observation and then a question. The 1963 Security Council decision on sanctions was a milestone, yet the liberal human rights agenda did not gain significant traction until the 1970s. Why?

Apartheid got on international agendas as unique, garnering support from an astoundingly diverse range of critics, from anti-torture moderates to anti-colonial radicals.[77] Thus South Africa did not necessarily or inherently set a precedent. Replicating such a broad coalition was impossible, but activists learned to employ 'sufficient similarity' rather than 'strict equivalence', to borrow Quirk's distinction in the slavery debate.[78] Routinely referred to as the first contemporary human rights case, Chile illustrates this sufficiency strategy, but not surprisingly, similar efforts did not always succeed.[79] On the one hand, white minority rule in Rhodesia, readily recognized as only slightly less draconian than apartheid, did become the target of sanctions and other pressures, ultimately leading to Zimbabwean independence in 1980.[80] On the other hand, comparisons between Israel and South Africa polarized UN members in the 1970s, and still do today.[81]

Perhaps the most significant parallel between abolitionism and anti-apartheid activism derives from recalling that the use of petitions reflected the absence of a direct political voice for the majority—in the 1800s, women were denied the franchise and only a fraction of men could vote, due to

---

[74] United Nations 1960: 142-54, 1961: 108-17; Lauren 1988: 256-8; Klotz 1995a: 44-5; Black 1999: 83-4.
[75] United Nations 1963: 13-24; Klotz 1995a 45-8; Black 1999: 86.
[76] United Nations 1977: 137-47; Lauren 1988: 260-1; Klotz 1995a: 50-1; Black 1999: 88-90.
[77] Klotz 1995a: 53-4; Black 1999: 79-82.   [78] Quirk 2011: 9-10.
[79] Keck and Sikkink 1998: 22, 80-2, 88-90, 101, 206.
[80] Lauren 1988: 245-8, 251; Klotz 1995a: 76-8; Black 1999: 81.
[81] Lauren 1988: 237-9, 250-2; Lyons 1989: 86, 93-5.

class-based or racial exclusions. And the transnational anti-apartheid movement coalesced, in part, because blacks were denied the right to vote in South Africa. At the risk of extrapolating too far, we should acknowledge contemporary international parallels in what even Vincent acknowledged looked to critics like a global caste system.[82] For instance, the UN system allows for only partial representation; many current calls for reforms to the Security Council and the International Criminal Court point to structural inequities that provide disproportionate decision-making power to the Global North and especially Europe. Similarly, the pattern of signatories to the UN convention on rights for migrant workers starkly reflects the global economic division between wealthy and poor.

While such structural inequalities should not be reduced to racism alone, the long legacies of both liberal imperialism and discriminatory citizenship also should not be ignored. Yet as the biologically based markers of scientific racism have morphed into cultural manifestations of prejudice, any assessment of a fundamental trend towards greater equality—Vincent's core claim—becomes ever more difficult. The evolution of US foreign policy towards (South) Africa in the past half-century illustrates these complexities, which manifest significant parallels in its immigration policy as well. For instance, the confluence of transformative US civil rights legislation in 1964 and 1965 alongside major immigration reform in 1965, as well as its adoption of the UN International Convention on the Elimination of All Forms of Racial Discrimination in 1966, is not coincidental, although too often each sphere is viewed in isolation from the others.[83]

As I have previously documented, transnational mobilization against apartheid—especially the US lagging behind even moderate allies such as Canada and Australia—challenges key presumptions about liberal hegemony.[84] Penny von Eschen's analysis of race and US foreign policy towards Africa during the early years of the Cold War confirms this assessment by offering an explanation: the suppression of transnational activists left the liberal wing of the African-American community to take up the mantle, a shift reinforced within the domestic civil rights movement.[85] Simultaneously, pressures for removal of blatantly racist national origin quotas in immigration, spurred in part by alliances with Japan, nationalist China, and South Korea, filtered through similar anti-communist parameters.[86]

---

[82] Vincent 1984: 253.

[83] King and Smith 2005: 89. Lyons (1989: 86-7, 109-10) argued that the separation of race and religion was a key factor in US support for the convention, which it signed in 1966, because it unlinked its domestic civil rights agenda from controversy over Zionism. Still, ratification waited until 1994.

[84] Klotz 1995a: 56-71, 100-11; also Black 1999: 94-6, 106-7.

[85] Von Eschen 1997: 1-3, 143-6, 153-61; also FitzGerald and Cook-Martín 2014: 113.

[86] FitzGerald and Cook-Martín 2014: 116-18.

One additional consequence was a surprising degree of insulation between these two strands of activism, replicated in a division between scholarly literatures.[87] Ironically, the label African-American, intentionally or not, signals a shift in recent decades away from race as the predominant frame to multiculturalism, not unlike the previous shift by liberal-leaning black activists towards identifying as loyal Americans rather than members of an African diaspora, which von Eschen noted during the Cold War.[88] Thus the language of post-racial politics obscures deeply embedded legacies of racism, including aspects such as *de facto* segregation due to economic inequalities in housing and education, as well as disproportionate incarceration rates for black men, all of which tend to be less salient for generating rights-based international pressures.[89] A similar process of depoliticization manifests in South Africa, where implementation of universal suffrage alone could not possibly eliminate all the structural inequalities produced over centuries, especially when the wider global context reinforced moderate reforms.[90]

CONCLUSION

Throughout this chapter, I have used Vincent as a focal point for engaging with general issues that this volume as a whole seeks to address. In such a short piece, I have not done justice to the vast historical literatures on each of the themes with which I have engaged. Instead, I have aimed to provide references that include some who wrote around the same time as Vincent, in order to demonstrate that my supplements to his narrative were no secret. And I have purposely selected ideologically similar—that is, liberal—historiographies, in order to engage Vincent and the international society school on its own terms.[91] Consequently, I have not acknowledged a wider swathe of literatures on race, including critical race studies and postcolonial theory, as is needed for a deeper understanding of these issues.

Yet even this narrower, liberal institutional perspective adds significantly to our understanding of global race politics. By applying the process-oriented approach that Tim Dunne and Christian Reus-Smit advocate, I find that Eurocentrism is a surprisingly small part of the problems in teleological history. Even including contestation, as both my chapter and Vincent's do, only adds adaptation to assuage excessive determinism without providing a clear framework for better macro-historiography. Therefore, as the next step,

---

[87] FitzGerald and Cook-Martín 2014: 119-20, 123.
[88] King and Smith 2005: 84, 89; von Eschen 1997: 145, 188-9.
[89] King and Smith 2005: 83; Jung 2015: 14-16.
[90] Black 1999: 79, 103.   [91] Lustick 1996.

I recommend extending the 'racial institutional orders' framework that Desmond King and Rogers Smith developed for grasping tensions between racism and liberalism within the United States.[92]

Specifically, King and Smith delineated two contending traditions, one white supremacist, another transformational egalitarian. At its analytical heart are complex coalitions, which remain stable only so long as overarching goals remain sufficiently broad to encompass diverse interests. Thus the forces that aligned to challenge slavery encompassed avowed white supremacists as well as radicals advocating human equality. Conversely, crucial shifts occur when key coalition partners defect. For instance, President Truman reweighed ideological and instrumental factors when he opted to ally with anti-segregationists.

King and Smith also emphasized that even after explicit racism subsides, 'unseen impacts' remain salient. In their subfield of American political development, key institutions include federal bureaucracies and Congress. For example, the electoral system over-represented the slave-holding South before the Civil War, and still does.[93] Similarly, the National Party in South Africa won the critical 1948 election without a majority of (white) votes because the system overweighted rural constituencies.[94] At the same time, though, each country also had a court system, admittedly much weaker in South Africa, which provided an avenue for egalitarians to fight for rights. While King and Smith concentrated on the domestic sphere, Robert Vitalis extended the notion of institutionalized racial order to US foreign policy by documenting the export of its segregationist practices.[95]

This racial orders framework readily applies to the past two centuries of liberal hegemony, as I have described in this chapter, because its institutional foundation meshes well with many assumptions that underpin the international society approach. But, to scale up internationally, the obvious next question is *which* institutions? Providing some guidance, Lake and Reynolds provocatively referred to a transnational network of white men, which serves as an analogue to contemporary emphases on transnationalism, nongovernmental organizations, and social networks. Their portrait and its contemporary extension fit the definition of institutional order outlined by King and Smith: a coalition of institutions and actors based on shared 'goals, rules, roles and boundaries' that manifest in formal statutes, administrative procedures, and political agendas.[96]

The origins and diffusion of the literacy test as a means of preserving white supremacy without explicitly racist exclusions illustrates well how these formal

---

[92] King and Smith 2005: 75-6.   [93] King and Smith 2005: 80, 84-8.
[94] Klotz 2013: 125-6, 135-6, 182.
[95] Vitalis (2000: 336, 341, 347, 356) applied Smith's earlier work.
[96] King and Smith 2005: 78-9.

rules and informal practices can gel within an international institutional order. Yet so much of the institutional infrastructure in the late 1890s was based on the British Empire, with no clear contemporary corollary. So instead of trying to portray the United Nations as the inherited epicentre or to pin down some sort of institutional regime complex, I recommend a different reading of Lake and Reynolds, one that focuses on people—but not solely the intellectuals and politicians who figure in their networks.

Anglosphere history of the global colour line revolved around racists seeking to manage human mobility: from slavery through Asian exclusions to the internal Great Migration. As current calls for military interdictions of migrants on the Mediterranean and along Canada's western coast, incarceration of undocumented immigrants alongside criminals in the US, and internment of asylum seekers by Australia and South Africa illustrate, demographics remain the epicentre of contemporary global race politics.

20

Gender, Power, and International Society

Ann E. Towns

The Expansion of International Society—like subsequent English School work—is silent on questions of gender in the society of states. This silence conceals as much as it reveals, as the practice of writing gender dynamics out of history is indicative of inattentiveness to gender in the theoretical and empirical commitments of the English School endeavour. To date, Barry Buzan and George Lawson have been most forthcoming about this silence in an unusually frank disclosure of how gender was written out of their monumental new book *The Global Transformation*. In this disclosure, Buzan, in disagreement with Lawson, first questions the relevance of gender to their long nineteenth-century international relations story. He then also points out that gender scholarship has tended to shy away from the grand narratives typical of English School works. What is the big gender story of the nineteenth century, he asks?[1]

The aim of this chapter is to provide one of multiple possible big gender stories, about the centrality of gender in the development and globalization of state polities between the eighteenth and twentieth centuries. Drawing on my previous work but also pulling together a wealth of secondary sources on the gendered organization of polities around the world, I show that how polities sorted men and women out of or into office was very much part of the dynamic of world politics. In the seventeenth and eighteenth centuries, the world was filled with an assortment of polities which rested on diverse gender arrangements—some included female rule, whereas others were male dominated. However, by the late nineteenth and early twentieth centuries, state institutions and political office across the world became populated almost exclusively by men. Formal international relations, needless to say, thus became placed in the hands of men. Transnational processes—including European colonialism and the international diffusion of European scientific

---

[1] Buzan and Lawson 2015a: 80-1, 2015b.

and other ideas about proper relations of men and women to the state—were pivotal for the global standardization of gender arrangements that excluded women from political power. The expansion of the ideas and practices of European-dominated international society thus helped spread and standardize male rule, displacing gender arrangements that empowered women politically in Africa, Native America, and Asia. This standardization then set the stage for the massive transnational women's movements that characterized the twentieth century, movements involving every continent and which have successfully struggled to change the norms of international society and to bring women (back) into political power, now as voters, public officials, and civil servants of states.

The chapter focuses on the globalization of gender arrangements of political office, the formal positions of political rule. It is important to note that gender is not unidimensional, instead consisting of social, cultural, material, and political spheres that intersect in complex ways. It is thus difficult to speak meaningfully of some general status of women or men in any given society.[2] 'The big gender story' in international society likely would look very different were one to centre on the gender organization of the economy, reproduction, marriage, and so on. So to be clear, this is a story about the globalization of the gender organization of political rule and political office, a story which primarily involves elite men and women. I hope others will provide additional stories.

The remainder of the chapter is organized into four sections. The first demonstrates the diverse ways in which gender was organized in polities around the world in the eighteenth and nineteenth centuries. The chapter then discusses how this diversity gave way to more uniform exclusion of women, as the barring of female political power became an informal standard of civilization in international society, embedded in relations of European colonialism. The third section proceeds to the global struggles for political inclusion of the twentieth century—inclusion as voters, political officials, and civil servants of states—with a focus on the waves of transnational suffrage activism that engulfed many parts of the world. The final and concluding section discusses the chapter in light of some of the main themes of the book.

A HETEROGENEOUS HISTORY OF DIVERSE GENDER ARRANGEMENTS

Prior to the late nineteenth century, there was a great deal of diversity in the gender arrangements of polities around the world. Glossing over important

---

[2] See, for example, Crummey 1981; Hanretta 1998.

complexities both in terms of how gender was practised and how gender figured into the organization of political power, let me nonetheless try to provide a brief, partial, and simplified survey of the centuries immediately preceding the late nineteenth century to substantiate this claim. As Christian Reus-Smit and Tim Dunne note in Chapter 1, before the state became the dominant political organization, the world consisted of a multitude of polities. These polities in turn rested on a variety of gender arrangements, arrangements which sometimes entailed exclusively male rule and other times also included female political leadership. Strict matriarchal polities, in which title holders were exclusively female and political power exercised solely by women, seem to have been very rare or non-existent, however.[3] The range thus seems to have been one from patriarchal, male-dominated forms of political organization to gender-mixed or gender-balanced polities.

In the nineteenth century, political authority and office was practised by women in a range of polities across the world. In the monarchies of West Africa, what Kamene Okonjo has called dual-sex political systems, were often in place.[4] In such systems, female titles or 'stools' paralleled male ones. For instance, among the Akan—a large population of present-day Ghana and Ivory Coast—every office in the political hierarchy from top to bottom had female and male counterparts.[5] Tarikhu Farrar writes that

> In precolonial Akan society, women did not normally come under the authority of men. All issues pertaining primarily or exclusively to women (and there were many—political, economic and cultural) were addressed within the context of this female political hierarchy. Furthermore, issues involving both females and males—issues like adultery, rape, marital conflict, and so forth—were also handled by female stool-holders.[6]

The male king's council dealt with long-distance trade, diplomacy, and warfare, holding authority over the entire population in these spheres. The queen mother—the most senior woman in the royal matrilineage—represented the female half of Akan society in the king's council. What is more, queen mothers could and occasionally did occupy the male royal stool, particularly when no suitable male heir could be found.[7] Igbo societies, in the south-east of present-day Nigeria, were also organized into dual-sex political systems.[8] Among some Igbo communities, flexible gender classifications were practiced. This separated sex from gender, so that some biological women were classified as male and could operate as male daughters or female husbands.[9] This in turn meant that in addition to the female councils, male women participated in the male political councils.

---

[3] See, for example, Farrar 1997. [4] Okonjo 1976.
[5] See, for example, Arhin 1983. [6] Farrar 1997: 588.   [7] Farrar 1997: 579.
[8] Okonjo 1976; Amadiume 1987. [9] Amadiume 1987.

Many eighteenth- and nineteenth-century Native American societies also understood gender as flexible and varying, including a third gender and the option of men assuming women's roles and vice versa.[10] And the scholarship on the political status of native women during this period shows that they held power and status roughly equivalent to those of men in most Native American societies, often with separate-but-equal institutions.[11] In some native societies, such as several Plateau groups, women did serve as chiefs on the same terms as men.[12] In general, however, it was uncommon that women held the position of chief.[13] For instance, among the Iroquois, women were not allowed to serve on the Council of Elders, the highest ruling body. Women nonetheless held important political positions, for instance by holding the power to raise and depose male chiefs.[14] Women also had veto power in the declaration of war, as well as occasional power over the conduct of war and the establishment of treaties.[15]

Many South East Asian societies of the eighteenth and nineteenth centuries likewise saw women in political office. Austronesian societies—which include present-day Indonesia, Malaysia, the Philippines, Polynesia, and more—'have been more inclined than perhaps any other major population group to place high-born women on the throne'.[16] Focusing on an earlier period, Mary John Mananzan documents the egalitarian status of women in pre-colonial Philippine society, then tracing the institutionalization of male rule that resulted from Spanish colonization in the sixteenth century.[17] Interestingly, in contrast with the Akan, women in South East Asia also had an important role in trade and diplomacy. Anthony Reid describes the use of female envoys and mediators around South East Asia.[18] In Java and some other parts of the island world, there was even a preference for using women as envoys, particularly during peace negotiations.[19]

A range of other polities were more male dominated while nonetheless in various ways leaving some room for women to hold office and exercise political power. For instance, the nineteenth- and early twentieth-century Mende and Sherbro polities of present-day Sierra Leone were male dominated while leaving considerable room for female rule. Carol Hoffer shows that in 1914, of the eighty-four Mende and Sherbro chiefdoms, 12 per cent were headed by women.[20] Nineteenth-century Kikuyu, in present-day Kenya, also centred political decision-making around men. Some Kikuyu areas nonetheless deployed women's councils, but these were 'limited in the sense that women's decisions were considered binding on women, while men's decisions bound the whole group, both men and women'.[21] The list of polities that made

---

[10] For example, Williams 1986.   [11] Shoemaker 1995; Klein and Ackerman 1995.
[12] Ackerman 1995: 90.   [13] Shoemaker 1995; Klein and Ackerman 1995.
[14] Brown 1970: 154.   [15] Brown 1970.   [16] Reid 1988: 640.
[17] Mananzan 1990.   [18] Reid 1988: 635-7.   [19] Reid 1988: 636.
[20] Hoffer 1972: 152.   [21] Clark 1980: 360.

some or significant, although not equal, room for women in political office could be made longer, including the Bemba of present-day Zambia.[22]

Yet other eighteenth- and nineteenth-century political systems were almost entirely male dominated, with very little or no ability for women to occupy political positions. These include larger polities such as imperial China, Korea, Qajar Persia, the Ottoman Empire, and a number of others. In imperial China, informed by neo-Confucian notions of a basic inequality between men and women, political rule and civil service office became firmly rooted as male. With the spread and entrenchment of neo-Confucianism in Korea between the fourteenth and seventeenth centuries, women were shut out of political office there as well.[23] Previously, in the Korean kingdom Unified Silla (668–935 AD), no fewer than three women had occupied the throne. At that time, although the throne was generally inherited through a male line of succession, whether a candidate for the throne belonged to the right sacred bone rank was of more importance than sex/gender. If the male line of a bone branch had come to an end, women were able to ascend the throne.[24] In some cases, even in the more constricted systems, royal or elite women could nonetheless occasionally occupy the throne. In imperial China and Korea, for instance, if the king or emperor died and the male candidate for the throne was too young, the position was usually occupied by an empress dowager. Over a dozen empress dowagers have governed imperial China over the centuries.

European states were also generally restrictive in terms of women holding political office during the centuries preceding the nineteenth, more so than during the Middle Ages. However, there were no standardized expectations or practices with respect to gender and political rule in the European absolutist state. In many parts of Europe, women thus could and did reign as queens in an era when the power of the state was vested in the sovereign. They also occasionally held other political office or had other forms of institutionalized political power. Many European monarchies relied on male-preference succession rules which nonetheless allowed female members of a royal family to inherit the throne, generally in the absence of living brothers or surviving legitimate descendants of deceased brothers. Monarchies governed by such rules include the kingdoms of England and Scotland, Spain prior to 1713, Monaco, Russia after 1797 (before 1797, succession rules in Russia were less formalized and a number of women held the throne), the eighteenth-century Habsburg empire, and a number of others. Queen regents were indeed not uncommon among these kingdoms. What is more, English high-born women could inherit state office with their property, English abbesses were called to the first English parliaments, and Queen Ann decreed that unmarried women could vote for the English parliament.[25]

---

[22] Brown 1970: 154.　　　[23] Kim 1976.
[24] Kim 1976: 26.　　　[25] Styrkársdóttir 1998: 48.

Among other European monarchies, most notably those governed by Salic law, women could not inherit the throne. In France, female rule had been prohibited with reference to Salic law since the fifteenth century.[26] The new monarchy of Belgium introduced Salic law in 1830 and Denmark did so in 1853, thus putting an end to the possibility of female succession to the Danish throne. The nineteenth-century kingdoms of Bulgaria, Romania, Serbia, and Montenegro also used Salic law, barring women from rule. Spain adopted Salic law in 1713 but repudiated it again in 1830 as a foreign, French import.[27] Somewhat earlier, eighteenth-century Sweden became influenced by French ideas of the state as a male body politic, introducing a prohibition of female succession in the constitution of 1720.[28] Until then, there had been female monarchs such as Queen Kristina (regent 1632-54), and women had served as state officials. As an example, two of the royal postmasters were women in the seventeenth century, presiding over the entire national postal service.[29] In these cases, women could occasionally rule as queen dowagers, but they could not serve as queen regents.

To sum up, then, there was a great deal of diversity in how gender was organized into the various polities of the eighteenth and early nineteenth centuries. The political organizations of many larger empires—China, Qajar Persia, the Ottoman Empire—seem to have been almost entirely male dominated. European states were also restrictive, but a number of states, including imperial states, provided some room for female rule and/or women holding political office, including the British Empire and Russia. Yet other polities, primarily in western Africa, South East Asia/Austronesia, and Native America, had gender arrangements that accorded roughly equal political power to men and women. And many political systems provided some, if far from equal, room for female rule. Prior to the nineteenth century, in short, political office and formal political authority were not standardized across the world as an all-male arena.

THE EXCLUSION OF WOMEN AS A STANDARD OF CIVILIZATION

The diversity of gender arrangements was to give way to standardized male domination of political power across polities in the mid to late nineteenth century. Starting in the late eighteenth and accelerating during the second half of the nineteenth century, explicit and full-scale bans on the participation of

[26] Taylor 2006.   [27] Nenner 1995.
[28] Weibull 1997: 58-69.   [29] Ohlander 2000: 118.

women in politics or public office were formalized into law across Europe. The English House of Commons forbade women from attending its debates in 1778. A little over fifty years later, in 1832, women were then expressly prohibited from voting in the House of Commons, as suffrage law replaced the language of 'person' with 'male person'.[30] Women's political organizations were likewise prohibited in France in 1793, and new laws forbade women from belonging to or creating political associations in 1848.[31] In Prussia, women were no longer allowed to attend political meetings and they were stripped of all political rights in 1851. Similar legal changes explicitly barring women from participation in politics or public office of European states were made in the Netherlands (1887), Germany (1900), Austria (1907), Italy (1912), and Portugal (1913).[32]

These changes took place as European colonialism intensified. During the second half of the nineteenth century and into the early twentieth, European powers (but also the US and Japan) pursued colonial territories on an unprecedented scale, primarily in Africa and Asia. The impact on the political organization of colonized areas was severe, including a fundamental restructuring of political authority as male. The colonial administrative systems of warrant chiefs, court clerks, court messengers, and so on were populated exclusively by men, displacing prior forms of institutionalized female political authority. Even in systems of indirect colonial rule, only the authority of male chiefs was recognized and female chiefs were bypassed and disempowered.[33] There was a systematic male bias in the colonial education programmes as well, steering girls away from leadership and public office. As Ifi Amadiume contends, 'while boys were prepared for government, trade, industry, church and educational services, girls were prepared for domestic services and taught cooking, cleaning, childcare and sewing'.[34] As a result of European colonialism, in short, matrilineal kinship systems and female political authority were severely challenged and declined significantly across Africa, South East Asia, and Native America.[35] Indeed, as one scholar contends, 'on a global scale matriliny declined in the face of the modern nation-state, and it was especially assaulted by European colonialism'.[36]

The loss of political authority caused distress and sometimes overt resistance among the women affected. For instance, in Igboland, in what is now south-eastern Nigeria, the erosion of women's power led to riots in 1929—the 1929 Women's War.[37] In the aftermath of the riots, Igbo women demanded

---

[30] Reuterskiöld 1911: 70.   [31] Reuterskiöld 1911: 79.
[32] Bock 2002: 133.   [33] Amadiume 1987; Awe 1977; Oyewùmí 1997.
[34] Amadiume 1987: 135.
[35] See, for example, Awe 1977; Coquery-Vidrovitch 1997; Hale 1996; Hoffer 1972: 152; Okonjo 1976; Amadiume 1987; Oyewùmí 1997; Parpart 1988; Sacks 1982; Shoemaker 1995; Klein and Ackerman 1995; van Allen 1976.
[36] Fluehr-Lobban 1998: 5.   [37] Amadiume 1987: 135.

that 'all white men should go to their own country'.[38] Short of that, they asked that women be allowed to serve on the Native Courts and a woman be appointed a district officer. These demands 'were in line with the power of women in traditional Igbo society but were regarded by the British as irrational and ridiculous'.[39] Governance reforms created in 1933 therefore ignored the women's traditional political role.

By the late nineteenth and early twentieth centuries, then, the prior world of diverse forms of organizing gender and power had turned more uniformly into male-dominated polities. Some parts of the world were already permeated by male rule—again, for example, China, the Ottoman Empire, and Persia. (There is naturally a history to the development of male rule in these empires as well, a history with important international dimensions, but that falls outside of the scope of this chapter.) In the late nineteenth century, the polities that still had institutionalized female political authority saw that authority rapidly displaced, as European ideas about male political authority were transported through colonialism.

As I have shown previously, these changes were expressly supported by international norms connecting the advancement of civilization with the exclusion of women from politics.[40] The discursive foundation of these norms was complex, involving new understandings in Europe of men and women as different in essence, the shift from absolutism to the constitutional state and its reliance on a public–private divide, and the tying of women to the private, non-political sphere. In Europe, the importance of removing women from political rule and the incipient public sphere for the advancement of society was supported by the new social sciences, which provided ample evidence that female political authority was a 'savage' practice. Scholarship in the emerging fields of anthropology and geography pointed to the elevated political status of women among societies in Africa, Asia, and Native America.[41] For some political actors, such as many socialists, the power of women in 'primitive' societies was interpreted as evidence of the detrimental effects of capitalist advancement on women. August Bebel of the German Social Democratic Party developed this point in his highly influential *Woman and Socialism* in 1879, arguing that:

> In present day bourgeois society woman holds the second place. Man leads; she follows. The present relation is diametrically opposed to that which prevailed during the matriarchal period. The evolution of primitive communism to the rule of private property has primarily brought about this transformation.[42]

[38] Van Allen 1976: 74.   [39] Van Allen 1976: 74.
[40] Towns 2009, 2010b, 2014.   [41] Campbell 1892; Man 1883; Pike 1892.
[42] Bebel 1910 [1879]: 96.

Five years later, in the 1884 *Origin of the Family, Private Property, and the State*—another landmark socialist text on the woman question—Friedrich Engels similarly argued that '[a]mong all savages and all barbarians of the lower and middle stages, and to a certain extent the upper stage also, the position of women is not only free, but honorable'.[43]

For many other political actors, however, evidence of the political power of women in Africa, Asia, and Native America was used to fuel arguments that women had no place in politics in 'civilized society'. Such evidence was used to disclaim the calls for women's suffrage, calls which arose in response to the prohibitions on female political participation in the emerging democracies. For instance, in 1884, noted US historian and anti-women's suffrage activist Francis Parkman argued that:

> [T]he social power of women has grown with the growth of civilization, but their political power has diminished. In former times and under low social conditions, women have occasionally had a degree of power in public affairs unknown in the foremost nations of the modern world. The most savage tribes on [the North American] continent, the Six Nations of New York, listened in solemn assembly, to the counsels of its matrons, with a deference that has no parallel among its civilized successors. The people of ancient Lycia, at a time when they were semi-barbarians, gave such power to their women that they were reported to live under a gynecocracy, or female government. The word gynecocracy, by the way, belongs to antiquity. It has no application in modern life; and, in the past, its applications were found, not in the higher developments of ancient society, but in the lower. Four hundred years before Christ, the question of giving political power to women was agitated among the most civilized of the ancient peoples, the Athenians, and they would not follow the example of their barbarian neighbors.[44]

In an argument against women's suffrage in an 1897 debate in the British House of Commons, Conservative member C. W. Radcliffe Cooke likewise contended that in civilized society, women do not and should not hold political power. 'When other civilized nations begin to grant the franchise to women, it might be time for the most civilized nation in the world to see whether it would be well to follow their example', he claimed.[45] A major Swedish government report on the idea of women's political suffrage around the world also concluded that suffrage was not a standard of behaviour applicable to the 'old civilized world'.[46]

In sum, then, by the early twentieth century, the practice of excluding women from politics had become institutionalized globally. Nineteenth-century European colonialism and its violent subjugation of African, Asian, and Native American polities was central to this development. Discourses connecting the civilizational advancement of a society with exclusively male-populated

---

[43] Engels 1972 [1884]: 82. [44] Parkman 1884: 10-11.
[45] As quoted in Dalziel 1994: 42-3. [46] Reuterskiöld 1911: 76.

politics had furthermore become pervasive, not only in Europe but in many other parts of the world.[47] Barring women from political power had become a standard of civilization, not formalized in international law but nonetheless influential as a set of informal expectations of appropriate behaviour setting aside civilized from 'Other' societies. The gendered character of political power was very much part of the hierarchical international order that international society rested upon. And it was in this context of international hierarchy that transnational movements for women's political empowerment emerged and operated.

TWENTIETH AND TWENTY-FIRST-CENTURY GLOBAL INCLUSION TRENDS AND TRANSNATIONAL STRUGGLES

The contemporary world looks quite different from a century ago. For one, the polities of the world are now organized as states which, despite their variations, also share many institutional features. What is more, the past century saw some remarkable changes, on a global scale, in terms of how men, women, and political power are institutionalized into the state. A minority of states now bar women from political power or public office as such. Virtually every state now provides suffrage rights to women on the same terms as men, so that women can participate in elections as voters to the same extent as men. Almost every state has lifted prior bans on women holding elected or other public office as well as on women's participation in political organizations. Women may thus serve as heads of the executive, and an increasing number are being elected president or prime minister.[48] As of January 2014, twenty-four women—roughly 13 per cent—served as heads of state or government, not counting monarchs.[49] What is more, positive measures actively to recruit and incorporate women into public office have emerged in a large number of countries. In well over fifty states, sex quotas have been adopted for the national legislature, with the aim of reaching 25–50 per cent female representatives. Such quota laws have primarily been adopted in Latin America, Africa, and Asia—exceptionally few European or North American states have bothered with quota legislation.[50] Although there is great variation in the world, ranging from Rwanda's 64 per cent female legislators to the four states that have none (Micronesia, Palau, Qatar, and Vanuatu), forty states now have 30 per cent female legislators or more and ninety states have 20 per cent female

---

[47] Towns 2010b, 2014: 595.   [48] Jalalzai 2008.
[49] Inter-Parliamentary Union 2014.   [50] See, for example, Towns 2012.

legislators or more.[51] Governments in many states are likewise actively including women in the cabinet, sometimes with informal parity goals or at least the goal of one-third female ministers.[52] Again, there is considerable variation. As of January 2014, 57 per cent of the ministers in Nicaragua and Sweden were female, whereas eight states had no women at all in the cabinet.[53] Thirty-five states had 30 per cent or more female ministers, and sixty-nine states had 20 per cent or more female cabinet members.[54]

Clearly, this is quite a change from the formal and legal exclusion of women from the states of international society a century ago. And it is a change that has come about through a great deal of mobilization and sustained activism. Social movements across the world have agitated for women's access to political power. In many cases, these movements were transnational in nature, connecting actors across borders to bring about policy and institutional changes in particular states. In many other cases, the primary actors were domestic organizations which nonetheless drew on models, arguments, and repertoires of action from abroad. In some cases, activists have furthermore worked in concert with international or regional organizations to open space for women's political participation domestically. The globalization of female-inclusive state models of organizing political power indeed underscores a point made in Chapter 1, that states are embedded in wider systems of actors and interactions. It also highlights the role of struggle and contestation in globalization, struggle which takes place in an international order that continues to be hierarchical. In the rest of this section, I use the worldwide fight for women's suffrage to illustrate these arguments about the role of struggle, the embeddedness of states, and the hierarchical nature of international society. This case also highlights that the struggles for female inclusion in state institutions were global in scope and not well conceived of simply as Westernization.

The Globalization of Women's Suffrage

The movement for women's suffrage emerged in the context of the spreading bans on women's political participation among what was then called 'civilized states' and into a highly stratified international society.[55] The norm that

---

[51] Inter-Parliamentary Union 2014.

[52] Escobar-Lemmon and Taylor-Robinson 2005; Krook and O'Brien 2012.

[53] Bosnia Herzegovina, Brunei, Lebanon, Pakistan, San Marino, Saudi Arabia, Solomon Islands, and Vanuatu.

[54] Escobar-Lemmon and Taylor-Robinson 2005; Krook and O'Brien 2012.

[55] This section draws heavily—sometimes almost verbatim—on Ann E. Towns, *Women and States: Norms and Hierarchies in International Society* (adapted), 9780521768856, (2010) © Cambridge University Press 2010, reproduced with permission. (Towns 2010b: chapter 4.)

civilized states keep women out of politics and political power was thus always contested, never fully accepted, and had to be bolstered and justified continuously. In Europe, calls for the inclusion of women in politics were made not long after women's political activities were prohibited. The first domestic women's suffrage associations also formed at this time, across Europe and some of its former colonies.

By the late nineteenth century, the first efforts to connect the various domestic suffrage organizations emerged. Transnational suffrage activism then developed across the world in four overlapping but nonetheless distinctive waves, waves which were differentiated by their geographical scope, membership, and suffrage argument: waves in civilized society (1900s–20s), the socialist world (1900s–20s), the Americas (1920s–40s), and Afro-Asia (1930s–60s).[56] Each wave, and the fact that there were waves of this kind, was shaped by the stratified character of international society. Each of these waves of activism and suffrage adoption is discussed in turn.

The first wave of transnational suffrage activism developed within the society of so-called 'civilized states', from the turn of the twentieth century until the 1920s. Colonialism and the international relations of inequality it entailed fundamentally influenced this activism, and its activities were primarily by and for the 'civilized' world. A number of transnational women's organizations advocated for women's right to vote, but few were as important as the well-known International Woman Suffrage Alliance (IWSA), founded in Berlin in 1904 'to secure the enfranchisement of the women of all nations'.[57] The IWSA will thus be used to illustrate the contours of the first wave of women's suffrage activism. The organization was large, tying together national chapters in over thirty states by 1920.[58] Representatives of the national sections would meet at international congresses to discuss strategies, setbacks, and successes. Until the 1930s, the nationality of the IWSA officers, the association's official languages (English and French), and the congress locations were exclusively European. The country sections point to a slightly larger membership circle by 1920, including Argentina, Australia, white South Africa, and Uruguay, as well as China and Russia on the outskirts of civilized society.[59] As a clear indicator of the geographical focus of the organization, despite its aim to enfranchise women of *all* nations, the organization moved to work on other issues once most of Europe and the Anglo-European settler states had adopted women's suffrage legislation by the early 1920s.[60] The existing suffrage organizations of Latin America and Asia that had still not achieved their goal were thus left to struggle without the support of the IWSA. The IWSA was a child of the society of civilized states, in short.

---

[56] Towns 2010b: 81-121.   [57] Rupp 1997: 122.   [58] Rupp 1997: 16-18.
[59] Rupp 1997: 16-19.   [60] Rupp 1997: 23.

The IWSA did go to great lengths to reach out to non-European women beyond Europe and North America, particularly in areas with colonial relations to Britain. IWSA president Carrie Chapman Catt undertook a quite remarkable suffrage tour with Dutch activist Aletta Jacobs in 1911–12, travelling by boat to Egypt, Israel, Palestine, South Africa, Sri Lanka, India, Indonesia, the Philippines, Hong Kong, China, and Japan.[61] The tour was not very successful in terms of establishing new suffrage organizations, however.[62] Upon their return, trying to digest the disappointing results, Catt and Jacobs came to the conclusion that in order to take hold, women's suffrage activism required that a society had reached a certain level of civilization.[63] Much like the discourse which undergirded the ban on women from politics and political power, they thus also connected suffrage with civilization. Indeed, as we saw earlier, those who favoured a ban on women's political power, including opponents to women's suffrage, regularly argued that 'the propaganda of woman suffrage is part and parcel of the world-wide movement for the overthrow of the present order of civilized society'.[64] European and North American suffragists countered by presenting themselves as vanguard agents of civilization, contending that extending the vote to women would help further a society's advancement. Particularly during times of war, they argued that female political influence was needed to counter the destructive—'savage'—instinct in men which brought societies to destruction.[65]

The mobilization for women's right to vote brought a wave of suffrage legislation to the targeted states. Women first gained the vote in new states on the outskirts of 'civilized society'—New Zealand (1893), Australia (1902), Finland (1906), and Norway (1907)—rather than in core European states such as Great Britain or France. By 1919, another twenty European states had adopted suffrage laws. An additional cluster of states enfranchised women after the Second World War. For a few European states—for example, Switzerland (1971) and Lichtenstein (1984)—it would take many additional decades to accept women as voters. It was thus not until the 1980s that all European and Anglo-European settler states had adopted women's suffrage laws.

A second wave of transnational suffrage mobilization developed among socialist activists, simultaneously but largely parallel to the suffragism of the society of civilized states, roughly from 1907 and also until the 1920s.[66] This was a distinct wave in two respects. First, socialist women organized independently, and the centre of their organization was located more towards the east of Europe. Second, these women had a distinctive diagnosis of the problem that the women's vote was meant to solve. What many suffragists

---

[61] Bosch 1999.   [62] Bosch 1999: 17.   [63] Bosch 1999:17.
[64] Illinois Association Opposed to the Extension of Suffrage to Women 1900: 2.
[65] Towns 2010b: 93.   [66] Towns 2010b: 93.

referred to as 'Western civilization' was to them 'bourgeois capitalism' and the primary source of the subordination of women. The suffragist claim that women's voting rights were an indicator of civilized progress and a standard of civilization thus posed a challenge for socialist women who favoured the vote.

There had been multiple, failed attempts to organize women separately within the socialist international infrastructure since the 1860s. At the 1907 Congress of the Second Socialist International in Stuttgart, a permanent International Women's Bureau was created along with a women's journal which was to reach 125,000 people by 1914.[67] All socialist parties were furthermore required to fight for universal male *and* female suffrage, a resolution which was quite a feat. These were accomplishments of the relentless work of Clara Zetkin of the German Social Democratic Party and other European women. Indeed, the geographical scope of this circle of socialist women was to remain limited to Europe and North America until the 1920s, much like the IWSA. The working language was German (rather than the French and English of the IWSA), and German and Russian women were most active in the Women's International, in contrast with the Anglo-European core of the IWSA. Like the IWSA, despite interactions with women in Asia and Latin America, the Women's International never became a force in bringing suffrage activism to areas outside of Europe.

Cooperation with 'bourgeois' suffragism was prohibited in the Women's International. Alexandra Kollontai of the Russian Bolsheviks explained that 'different aims and understandings of how political rights are to be used create an unbridgeable gulf between bourgeois and proletarian women'.[68] There were nonetheless some shared ideas within the two suffrage movements. Importantly, socialist approaches to the so-called woman question also saw history as a set of progressive stages from primitive to advanced. As discussed earlier, a number of socialist thinkers had upheld 'the primitive stage' as a form of primitive communism in which women thrived. With the development of capitalism and the spread of Christianity—seen as two cornerstones of Western civilization—women became increasingly oppressed and subordinated to men. August Bebel, Karl Marx, Engels, Zetkin, and a number of others argued that capitalism produced institutions necessary for its maintenance that subjugated women even more than men. Most importantly, women emerged as property, prostitutes, housewives, and particularly exploited workers under capitalism and the bourgeois state. As Zetkin contended in a 1920 instructive text for the Communist International, capitalism used 'the backward character of old-style housekeeping...to keep women intellectually and politically

---

[67] Towns 2010b: 96.   [68] Kollontai 1909: 72.

backward by blocking them from participating in society'.[69] In this context, Zetkin and others came to the conviction that women should have

> universal suffrage, not as a reward for the political maturity, but as an effective means of educating and organizing the masses... it is our duty through intensive work of enlightenment and organization so to raise the standard of political intelligence and maturity in our proletarian women that it will soon be impossible for the reaction to count on the women's vote.[70]

Through suffrage and political education, women could become a resource for socialist advancement.

The Stuttgart resolution had determined that universal suffrage be placed on all socialist party platforms in 1907. The socialist suffrage efforts came to fruition after the First World War, as a host of new states emerged under socialist rule. Communist workers' and peasants' governments enfranchised women in the newly created states of Belarus (1919), Latvia (1918), and Lithuania (1918). The Bolsheviks adopted a new Russian constitution that endorsed universal suffrage in 1918. Ukraine adopted universal suffrage in 1919. In a number of other new states, women's suffrage came with their formal incorporation into Soviet Russia: Armenia and Azerbaijan in 1921, and Kazakhstan and Tajikistan in 1924. Mongolia, which had a constitution closely modelled on the Soviet Union, also recognized universal suffrage in 1924.[71]

In the 1920s, the geographical scope of the Women's International was extended to incorporate some socialist parties of pre-capitalist and colonial areas outside of Europe and the US. However, just as the Women's International was beginning to reach outward, it dwindled. Its last conference was held in 1926, and its institutional means to promote the enfranchisement of women around the world was dismantled. This took place at the same time as the IWSA abandoned suffrage as a main goal. From the mid-1920s onwards, in short, European suffrage mobilization was no longer an important force for the extension of the right to vote for women. But by then, the baton had been passed on.

A third wave of transnational suffragism developed in Latin America between the 1920s and 1940s.[72] Domestic voices and organizations in favour of women's suffrage had emerged by the turn of the twentieth century in the Americas. For example, the Argentine socialist party supported universal suffrage already in 1900, much earlier than most European parties.[73] The first transnational gathering to discuss suffrage took place in 1910, at the First International Feminine Congress in Argentina. A decade later, in the early 1920s, domestic and transnational suffrage mobilization really took off, as a result of the travelling, networking, active borrowing, and selective importing of ideas and strategies by Latin American women from Europeans and North Americans. The geographical

---

[69] Zetkin 1991.   [70] Zetkin 1906: 18.   [71] Towns 2010b: 101–2.
[72] Towns 2010b: 104–5.   [73] Lavrin 1995: 259–60.

scope of this wave was also bounded, limited to the Americas with few if any attempts to bring suffrage to women outside the continent. In contrast with European suffragists, who had created non-governmental institutional frameworks to advocate for suffrage, the Latin American activists made the governmental Pan-American institutional infrastructure a mobilizing arena. The new Inter-American Commission of Women was created in Havana in 1928 'to take up the consideration of the civil and political equality of women in the continent'.[74] By the time of the great breakthrough in adoption of women's suffrage legislation in Latin America, after the outbreak of the Second World War, the Pan-American Union had been supportive of women's suffrage for two decades. No fewer than four intergovernmental declarations and resolutions advocating adoption of women's suffrage had been produced by the Pan-American Conferences between 1933 and 1945. These conferences also generated the world's first treaty on women's political rights in 1948.[75]

Women's suffrage did not enter the Pan-American arena without effort. It took considerable strategic work and organizing by a network of activists from a range of countries to bring reluctant and sometimes resistant state representatives to support women's right to vote.[76] Domestic mobilization was, in turn, strengthened by the Pan-American Union resolutions and conferences, as domestic suffrage organizations could make use of the international events and proclamations to further legitimize their cause. Thus in 1929, Ecuador became the first state of South America to grant women suffrage. By 1961, thirty-two years after Ecuador, all the states of Latin America had enfranchised women.[77]

If the geographical scope and timing of mobilization and legislation point to a Pan-American wave of suffragism, the arguments and justifications for enfranchising women also situated 'the Americas' as a distinctive region with respect to 'civilization'. Latin American suffragists represented suffrage and the political empowerment of women more broadly as European and 'civilized'.[78] The political empowerment of women in Native America, pre-colonial Africa, or Asia rarely if ever entered the discussions, and the then-contemporary suffrage struggles that had developed in Asia (with the exception of Japan) did not seem to register at all. Instead, as Peruvian suffragist María Jesús Alvarado Rivera proclaimed, women's political mobilization was a phenomenon of civilized states: 'in the whole civilized world, in secular Europe as well as in young America and the transformed Japan, the feminist movement is developing with an incomparable force'.[79]

Latin America was prevalently represented as 'less advanced' on the scale of social evolution, however. As suffrage was identified as typical of more advanced societies, there was deep scepticism—even among some suffragists— about the wisdom of enfranchising women in a 'less advanced' cultural and

---

[74] Scott 1931: 408.   [75] Towns 2010a.   [76] Towns 2010a.
[77] Towns 2010a.   [78] Towns 2010b: 107-15.   [79] Alvarado Rivera 1910.

social environment. Suffrage opponents regularly argued that in contrast with the core states of civilized society, Latin American countries were 'not ready' for women to vote.[80] Women's lack of education and literacy was central: with lower levels of formal schooling than men, it was argued, Latin American women had less culture and consciousness and thus could not be entrusted with the vote. As the National Women's Council of Peru stated in 1938, 'woman's absolute and unconditional civil and political equality signifies an exceedingly radical change for the Latin American society, since its women are perhaps not properly prepared'.[81] In such a context, many suffragists came to argue that granting *some* women the vote would be proper, namely Spanish-speaking women with a formal education. Suffrage activists in countries with substantial indigenous populations such as Bolivia, Colombia, Guatemala, and Peru thus attempted to distinguish women who were presumably ready to vote from the illiterate (read: indigenous) and unworthy. This appeal for limited suffrage rights, to the 1933 Seventh International Conference of American States by a Bolivian suffragist, is a typical illustration of this line of argument:

> Bolivia's legislation still does not treat women's rights as in other States or nations of more advanced civilization...[Although cultured women should be granted suffrage], there are not sufficient reasons why the semi-literate and wretched masses, under the unconditional servitude of the sordid *caudillismo*, and with unspeakable passions, should suppress the cultured elements of either sex, in a country that—sincerely or sarcastically—calls itself democratic.[82]

Once the vote was extended to women in Latin America, literacy requirements were often put in place which excluded large parts of the population from voting. Such restrictions furthermore tended to exclude women to a much larger degree than men, since women's literacy rates were far lower. In some cases—for example, El Salvador (1939), Panama (1941), and Guatemala (1945), literacy requirements were placed exclusively on women, while not on the male electorate.

In the fourth wave of transnational suffrage activism in Africa and Asia between the 1930s and 1960s, women's suffrage often first developed as a concern within the vast European colonial dominions. Women were sometimes enfranchised in the context of limited self-government, within the auspices of an imperial European state. For instance, France quickly extended the vote to women in five African colonies upon granting French women suffrage in 1944. The British were more reluctant, waiting until the mid-1950s before enfranchising women in an African colony (Ghana). National independence was necessary for suffrage in many other cases.[83] Perhaps most

---

[80] Towns 2010b: 108.   [81] *El Comercio* 1938 (my translation).

[82] Merino Carvallo 1937: 111 (my translation).

[83] For example, Jamaica (1944), Gabon (1956), Malaysia (1957), Mauritania (1961), Algeria (1961), Uganda (1962), the Congo (1963), and Bahrain (1971/3).

noteworthy, women were never enfranchised anywhere under Portuguese rule until independence. In yet other cases, suffrage was not extended to women until several years after independence.[84]

The research on women's suffrage in postcolonial states is still limited. However, existing studies suggest that mobilization was often necessary, despite the fact that a large number of states in the world had accepted women's suffrage by the mid-1940s. Mobilization sometime between the 1930s to 1960s preceded the adoption of suffrage legislation in a number of colonized, decolonized, and/or newly created states, such as in Bahamas, the Dutch East Indies, Egypt, India, Nigeria, Sudan, and India.[85] Often, suffrage activism was transnationally connected. For instance, women's suffrage was on the agenda of the 1958 Asian-African Conference on Women in Colombo and the 1961 Afro-Asian Women's Conference in Cairo, both offspring of the Non-Aligned and Afro-Asian Solidarity Movements.

The enfranchisement of women was not yet a standard held out for all states of international society, as the predominant discourse was one about civilized states and the women's vote. In a context of national independence struggles, this hardly facilitated the efforts of Asian and African suffrage activists. Instead, the new insistence by Europeans that political equality was a European and 'civilized' invention helped prod forward arguments for the rejection of suffrage among independence fighters, as the opposition to suffrage became a manner of rejecting the West. Afro-Asian suffragists countered by crafting arguments about the political power of women in pre-colonial polities of Africa and Asia. They drew on intellectuals such as Ziya Gökalp of Turkey, who had proclaimed that 'old Turks were both democratic and feminist'.[86] And they often distanced themselves quite clearly from European suffragists, making clear—as did Indian delegate Shareefeh Hamid Ali at the 1935 International Alliance for Suffrage and Equal Citizenship congress in Istanbul—that they did not 'admire European civilization'.[87] Despite what Europeans may claim, they insisted, the political empowerment of women was not a European invention.

CONCLUSIONS

Gender is a central element in international society. A gender lens seems crucial for pointing out the obvious fact that those in charge of nineteenth-century states and international affairs were virtually all male. This was not always so, however, as this chapter has demonstrated. There were furthermore

---

[84] For example, Cambodia, Morocco, the Central African Republic, Egypt, Sudan, Jordan, Yemen, and Iraq.

[85] Towns 2010b: 116–17.   [86] Arat 2000: 109.   [87] Rupp 1997: 79–80.

clear and pivotal international dimensions in the global standardization of male rule in the nineteenth century, including transnational practices and relations of European colonialism and transnationally circulating scientific and political ideas about proper relations between women and politics. The worldwide changes towards inclusion of women as state office holders, voters, and civil servants are also fundamentally international, resting on transnational activism, international hierarchy, and internationally circulating ideas and repertoires of action.

Several of this volume's central themes emerged in the analysis. First, the chapter illustrates the claim that states are embedded in a wider system of actors and interactions—webs of scientists, political thinkers, social movement activists, and international organizations shaped the form and behaviour of states. The hierarchies of international society are furthermore front and centre in the globalization of the exclusion of women from political rule as well as in the subsequent transnational efforts to include women in the state polity. The political status of women was one means by which states were positioned in the ranking order of international society, and the political status of women could therefore also be used to contest and attempt to change international hierarchy or a particular state's position therein. Finally, the chapter has made clear that the political empowerment of women is not well conceived of as a Western or liberal phenomenon, for at least three reasons. First, women exercised political power in a wide variety of polities around the world in the eighteenth and nineteenth centuries, a period during which political space for European women was severely curtailed. Second, the exclusion of women from political power became universalized through nineteenth-century European colonialism and European scientific and political ideas. And third, the struggles for political empowerment have taken place in every part of the world. In Africa and Asia in particular, these struggles have not necessarily upheld Europe or the West as a model. Instead, pre-colonial gender arrangements were often identified as inspiration. In telling this big gender story, the chapter thus also helps unsettle the common sense account that universalizes male political domination and locates the political empowerment of women to contemporary Europe.

21

Communication

Lene Hansen

As Tim Dunne and Christian Reus-Smit note in Part I, this book treats the globalization of international society as an ongoing process. The world may, in short, have changed between 1984 and 2017 in ways that warrant an empirical and theoretical updating of the framework originally presented in *The Expansion of International Society*. Hedley Bull, Adam Watson, and their contributors lived in a world that knew no twenty-four-hour news networks providing extensive real-time coverage broadcast to (almost) global audiences. The graphic, interactive universe of the Internet with homepages, Facebook, and YouTube did not yet exist, and there were no mobile phone technologies that allowed the uploading and circulation of photos, video, and text messages. As a consequence those living in authoritarian states have gained unprecedented avenues for bringing human rights abuses, violence, and resistance to the attention of the outside world, and 'accidental' images like the Abu Ghraib prison photos produced for an insider crowd might go viral harming states' international reputation. Yet, the story of the transformations in communication technologies since 1984 is not only one of states finding their sovereignty undermined or of 'world society' coming together across borders. Governments and international institutions have taken to new media technologies to propagate their positions on foreign policy events, for example through the use of Twitter. States such as China, Pakistan, and Thailand block access to parts of the Internet deemed politically threatening or at odds with cultural norms.[1] 'Bloggers' posting critiques online have been imprisoned and punished by flogging.

The communications technologies introduced since 1984 not only call for an empirical updating of the analyses presented in *The Expansion of International Society*; they also raise crucial theoretical questions. Is it, for example, still valid to define international society as 'a group of states' leaving other options, like Bull and Watson did, in the bracket of '(or, more generally, a

---

[1] Deibert 2013: 39.

group of independent political communities)'?[2] Is the understanding of 'political community' itself in flux? Are the rules and institutions that govern inter-state (and inter-group) relations the same in the era of instant online communication as they were when *The Expansion of International Society* was published? This chapter explores these questions, situating them within a wider historical and theoretical engagement with the role that communication has played in the formation and expansion of international society. Put differently, the speed with which new technologies have been introduced since 1984 may give the impression that communication has become significant for international society only in the past thirty years. Such an impression is supported by a first glance at *The Expansion of International Society*: there is no chapter devoted to communication, the book's index offers only five entries thereto organized by the subentries 'advances in', 'and diplomacy', and 'result of revolution in', and there is no explicit definition of what communication is. But first glances might be deceptive. As will be argued in this chapter, a close reading of *The Expansion of International Society* reveals that communication *did* in fact play a role in the book's conceptual framework as well as in its historical analysis of the formation of international society in Europe and its expansion to the rest of the world. Communication has, in short, been crucial to international society since its inception.

How should we define communication? The word 'communication' appears explicitly in *The Expansion of International Society* in two ways: as referring to communication technology and as diplomatic communication. Yet, if we adopt a conception of communication to include references to words we would associate with the broader phenomena of communication, for example to 'dialogue', we see a deeper engagement with communication in *The Expansion of International Society*. Drawing on a wider body of social theory and theories about communication, this chapter presents a theorization of communication that includes four conceptualizations, each of which can be found in *The Expansion of International Society*. The first conceptualization concerns communication as a social, political, and normative engagement with the world, for example by dialogue rather than brute force. The second conceptualization points to the specific form that communication takes, for instance written, spoken, or bodily. The third conceptualization of communication is as something that institutions practice, for example the institution of diplomacy, and the fourth conceptualization of communication is as technology. The advantages of theorizing communication as comprising these four conceptualizations rather than delimiting it to technology and diplomacy are three. First, it provides a lens through which to identify and structure the explicit and implicit references to communication in *The Expansion of International*

---

[2] Bull and Watson 1984b: 1.

Society. Second, it allows us to theorize communication not merely as a set of material technologies that impact the world in a deterministic and non-social manner, but to see how communication technologies are connected to agency and processes. Third, by foregrounding theoretical concepts rather than current technologies, the long history of communication's impact on international society can be studied, and the chances that the framework might be useful for scholars working on communication and international society beyond 2017 are heightened.

The chapter falls into four parts. The first part positions communication as a factor impacting international society and lays out the methodology through which *The Expansion of International Society* has been analysed. The second part provides an account of communication as consisting of the four conceptualizations laid out above. These conceptualizations can be identified in *The Expansion of International Society*, although only as fragments. This section therefore offers a 'reconstructive reading' that traces the significance of these fragments for the formation and evolution of international society. A full account of the impact of communication for the expansion of international society is beyond the scope of the chapter, but the third section provides one indication of how such historical analysis might be conducted, taking the printing press as a case in point. The fourth section turns to developments since 1984 where new avenues for communication below and across state boundaries have been created.

COMMUNICATION AS A DRIVER OF INTERNATIONAL SOCIETY

To briefly recapitulate, the main ambition of Bull and Watson was to provide a historical account of the political processes that began in Europe after 1500 as a hegemonial system gradually gave way to a non-hegemonial one.[3] What should be traced and explained was the formation of a particular form of inter-state relations, namely that of international society, and its changes over time as it moved from Europe towards spanning the globe. The formation and development of international society was intertwined with the formation of like units, more specifically states, and an acceptance by these states of 'international norms based upon equality and reciprocity'. At least in some cases to enter international society required 'cultural change within the countries concerned'.[4] In what was a very detailed historical account of world history from 1500 onwards, some of the key developments were, according

---

[3] Bull and Watson 1984b: 6. [4] Bull 1984b: 121.

to Bull, the 'progressive development' of relations between European states in the nineteenth century,[5] the emergence of an 'actual international society worldview' around the First World War, and the challenge to international society brought about by decolonization and the 'revolt against the West' that began after the Second World War.[6] Communication impacts this process in three ways. First, it is a *precondition* for the formation of states of a sufficient size and for these states to have enough contact with each other that an international society can begin to exist. In the terminology of Barry Buzan, the interaction capacity—that is, the 'absolute quality of technological and societal capabilities across the system'[7]—has to move beyond a certain threshold. Second, communication acts—for the most part—as a *driver* of the expansion of international society by supporting the creation of states outside of Europe and for these states to be socialized into the rules and institutions that form international society. Third, communication might also be a *threat* to international society—at least in its traditional form—as it is explicitly mentioned by Bull as one of the factors spurring the revolt against the West.[8]

There is little explicit consideration in *The Expansion of International Society* as to what international society would look like were the revolt ultimately successful.[9] Logically, one option would be a contraction of international society from having a universal reach to covering only parts of the globe. Or, rather than international society being rolled back to cover, for example, Europe and the Americas, it might undergo a deeper transformation in some of its key components. Based on the original definition of international society, provided below, such transformation can take three different forms:

> By an international society we mean a group of *states* (or, more generally, *a group of independent political communities*) which not merely form a system, in the sense that the behaviour of each is a necessary factor in the calculations of the others, but also have established by *dialogue and consent* common *rules and institutions* for the conduct of their relations, and recognize their common interest in maintaining these arrangements.[10]

First, change can take place in the 'rules and institutions' that tie international society together. Second, what qualifies as 'dialogue and consent' might be transformed. Third, the entities that make up international society might change. Bull and Watson left the option open that international society could exist between other forms of 'independent political communities' than states. If one sticks strictly to *The Expansion of International Society* it is hard however to imagine what such non-state entities would be: empires are

---

[5] See also Kedourie 1984: 347–8.   [6] Bull 1984b: 120–5, 1984c: 217.
[7] Buzan et al. 1993: 79.   [8] Bull 1984c: 222.   [9] Buzan 2014a: 69.
[10] Bull and Watson 1984b: 1, emphasis added.

constituted as hierarchically organized and tribes are seen as too small and discontinuous to be able to achieve the interaction capacity required to enter international society. A more radical form of change than that envisioned by Bull and Watson is thus to open international society up for being comprised by other entities than 'independent political communities'. A justification for such conceptual expansion that remains close to the framework of *The Expansion of International Society* is that we cannot understand 'international society classic'—the rules and regulations that states have established by dialogue and consent—without taking other entities into concern. We will return to the question of how international society might have changed since 1984 in section four. For now, we should note that it is possible, perhaps even likely, that the three types of change—in rules and institutions, in dialogue and consent, and in the entities themselves—are interlinked if and when encountered empirically. In other words, communication may not 'only' be a factor in the creation of an international society in Europe and exported to the rest of the world; it may also challenge the way in which we theorize international society itself.

FROM FRAGMENTS TO FRAMEWORK: A RECONSTRUCTIVE READING

The Expansion of International Society did not, as noted earlier, provide an explicit definition of communication. Drawing on writings in the fields of communication, media studies, sociology, and philosophy, I suggest that 'communication' itself is neither self-explanatory nor should it be reduced to technology. Rather it should be theorized as composed of four more specific conceptualizations: as a mode of engaging with the world, as a specific form through which meaning is conveyed, as something that institutions practice, and as technology. Analytically and methodologically, this theorization of communication has been reached through a two-step procedure. In the first step, *The Expansion of International Society* was read for references to communication including both explicit usages of the word 'communication' and implicit references, for example to 'dialogue', 'writing', or specific communications technologies. These references come to considerably more than the five noted in the book's index and they are important for the way in which international society is theorized and historicized, yet they are also only fragments. The second step was therefore to (re)construct these fragments such that they provide a more coherent, structured account of the role that communication plays for the formation and expansion of international society. There are differences between chapters in the extent to which they address communication as well as more substantial differences in how they represent the processes, actors, and dynamics of world politics. Yet the strategy has been to downplay the discussion of such differences in favour of reconstructing 'a' framework for understanding communication and international society.[11] Taken together the two steps amount to a 'double reading'—the reading of *The Expansion of International Society* and the reading of general communications literature are brought together.

The framework is a 'theory' in the sense that it 'organises a field systematically, structures questions, and establishes a coherent and rigorous set of interrelated concepts and categories'.[12] As Buzan and Ole Wæver explain, this understanding of theory is widely shared by Europeans—and reflected in *The Expansion of International Society*—and does not demand that causal, testable hypotheses are generated, not to mention tested.[13] Epistemologically, the four conceptions of communication have the status of lenses, that is, they allow for different aspects of a phenomenon to come into view. The technology of the telephone, for example, facilitates immediate, oral dialogue thus providing the institution of diplomacy with opportunities as well as challenges. The four conceptions are not, in other words, variables that can be separated from one another and whose significance can be tested. In principle, there is no rule as to which conception should be addressed first or the order in which the four conceptions are applied analytically. Scholars may adopt the chronology they find most useful for the temporal perspective adopted or the particular way in which the analysis of communication connects with one's work in general. In this chapter, technology is used as the conception which organizes the analysis. More specifically, three technologies—the printing press, the Internet, and embedded cameras—are employed to first, exemplify how historical analysis of international society and communication pre-1984 can be conducted; and second, to structure the account of changes in communications past 1984. This however is only one way in which to apply the theoretical framework; an international political theorist might, for example, begin the analysis with the question of 'dialogue', a student of diplomacy with communication as an institution of practice.

---

[11] This strategy was chosen because the pursuit of internal differences within *The Expansion of International Society* would have taken space away from the analysis of contemporary international society.

[12] Buzan and Wæver 2003: 83.

[13] One might add that the field of International Relations (IR) has been pretty thin so far in terms of works that explicitly link communication and world politics. As a consequence there are not many, if any, rival theories against which the reconstructed framework could be tested. Although close to twenty years old, Deibert 1997 may still provide the most thorough account of how communication and international politics can be brought together.

Communication as a Mode of Engagement with Others

The first conceptualization of communication that *The Expansion of International Society* evokes is that of communication as a *mode of engagement with others*. This concerns deep-seated philosophical beliefs about what constitutes possible and appropriate ways for individuals and institutions to 'speak'—literally and metaphorically—to one another. It also raises ontological questions about what is language—is it a neutral medium for the expression of opinions, or always, as Michel Foucault for example argued, established through and displaying relations of power.[14] Given that this conceptualization of communication is the most abstract and explicitly normative of the four dimensions of communication, it is quite fitting that it plays a central role in the very definition of international society itself: international society must be 'established by dialogue and consent' rather than by violence and repression.[15]

To 'dialogue' is essentially to communicate. It requires at least two parties between which there is an exchange; if only one party spoke, it would be a monologue. Communication as dialogue echoes the Latin roots of the word *communico* which means to do something together or to share. For communication, or dialogue, to constitute 'sharing' requires that one not only states one's position, but that one also seeks to make oneself comprehensible to others. To consider the comprehensibility of one's communication thus involves putting oneself in the place of the other asking (at least implicitly) 'how would she/he understand what I'm about to say?' Probably the most well-known political theorist on communication and politics is Jürgen Habermas, who defined communicative rationality as 'the central experience of the unconstrained, unifying, consensus-bringing force of argumentative speech, in which different participants overcome their merely subjective views'.[16] Yet one does not need to embrace Habermas's theorization of communicative action to hold that communication as 'dialogue' is significant for the formation and expansion of international society. Nor would it be accurate to portray Bull and Watson as implicit Habermasians. What it suggests is 'only' that we consider how states—and other potentially relevant entities—engage one another.

In spite of 'dialogue's' central position in the definition of international society, there is no further discussion in *The Expansion of International Society* of how it should be understood or operationalized. As critiques of *The Expansion of International Society*, including Dunne and Reus-Smit in Part I, have pointed out, one of the book's major shortcomings is that it neglects the violence and domination enacted as European states brought the rest of the

---

[14] Foucault 1980.   [15] Bull and Watson 1984b: 1.
[16] Habermas 1984: 10. For works linking Habermas to IR, see Ashley 1981; Risse 2000.

world into international society. Thus there is a tension between the 'dialogue' claimed to define international society and the process through which the latter was universalized. This tension is exacerbated by the lack of further theoretical engagement with the ontological and normative status of 'dialogue' or with the methodology that may capture it empirically. Nor do any of the book's historical chapters provide an explicit account of how 'dialogue' was achieved or not. Perhaps the clearest implicit way that 'dialogue' appears is through the recurring concern that decolonization threatens the rules and institutions said to form international society; in other words, that non-Western newcomers to international society adopt a different and far more confrontational understanding of 'dialogue' than that of its long-term members. The absence of a deeper theoretical and historical-empirical engagement with 'dialogue' may not merely be an oversight, but may be linked to the rationalist position adopted by Bull and Watson.[17] As Dunne and Reus-Smit explain, the incorporation of non-European states into international society was presented by Bull and Watson as a rational decision not only for the Europeans but for the non-European states as well. Effectively, the rational nature of this 'decision' may therefore have eliminated the need for a deeper analysis of how 'dialogue' was established and evolved historically as international society expanded. Or, to put it in the context of Bull and Watson's definition, the (seeming) 'consent' of the incoming states overrides the need to more critically scrutinize how 'dialogue' is achieved.[18]

The significance of the first fragment of communication in *The Expansion of International Society* is thus not that the book provides us with an unproblematic account of the role of dialogue in international society. It is rather that by being critical of the undertheorized, yet important status that dialogue and consent play for Bull and Watson, we become aware of how important are assumptions about such communicative modes of engagement. Ontological and normative assumptions about how states, individuals, and institutions engage one another vary depending on which philosophical position one draws upon, as illustrated by the differences between Foucault and Habermas. Yet both Foucault and Habermas developed their ontological positions with reference to historical and geographical contexts. As our concern is with the expansion and changes in international society across time and place, it seems reasonable to include contextual conditions in our consideration of the modes of engagement that can take place. Concretely, for example, our ontological and normative assumptions about what is 'dialogue' may for example be

---

[17] See Chapters 1 and 2.

[18] A deconstructivist, Jacques Derrida-inspired reading might add that the 'and' between 'dialogue' and 'consent' is rather an 'and/or' and thus that there is a substitutability and therefore instability in the relationship between the two terms that continues throughout *The Expansion of International Society*.

revised as newspapers, town halls, and face-to-face communication are re-placed by digitally mediated encounters online.

Communication as a Form of Meaning Conveyance

The second conceptualization of communication that can be seen in fragments in *The Expansion of International Society* is of communication as referring to the *form through which meaning is conveyed*. As Ronald J. Deibert argues, '[t]he ability to communicate complex symbols and ideas is generally considered to be one of the distinguishing characteristics of the human species'.[19] Yet there are a number of different forms through which such communication can take place. One way to distinguish forms of communication is according to the sign system that is adopted. Communication can for example be verbal, visual, or bodily. This conceptualization can be identified in *The Expansion of International Society* as writing is constituted as superior to oral communi-cation. 'Written records' are a feature of 'elaborate civilizations', whereas 'less developed culture' is 'usually pre-literate'.[20] Literacy is not only a sign of culture and civilization, but it also allows for 'more complex social organization', more specifically for larger and more continuous political communities to be formed.[21] Bull and Watson do not explain in further detail how written communication supports the establishment of independent political commu-nities (states) and the formation of an international society between them. It seems logical, however, that writing allowed for a wider and more reliable distribution of communication than oral forms could provide. Oral commu-nication required physical co-presence between speaker and receiver or a physical transmission of the message that often took time and involved the risk of the message being distorted or intercepted along the way. As argued in more detail in the next section, the arrival of the printing press in the fifteenth century further added to the speed with which authorities could reach their subjects.

Another way to distinguish the form through which meaning is conveyed is according to the kind of knowledge that is invoked, or, to adopt Foucault's terminology, which epistemic regime is institutionalized.[22] Contrast for example the difference in how warfare is conveyed through numbers and statistics or through the recital of a poem. Some communities see dreams as having predictive power, others deem then 'only' a product of the psyche.[23] From the perspective of the globalization of international society, a crucial question is the

---

[19] Deibert 1997: 1.
[20] Bull and Watson 1984b: 2. A more dichotomous and hierarchical construction of writing/ Europe/modern and speech/Africa/primitive is found in Bozeman 1984: 403.
[21] Bull 1984a: 102–3.   [22] Foucault 1970.   [23] Der Derian 2001.

extent to which epistemic regimes can be said to be shared, how they have
developed historically, and which hierarchies and marginalization have been
enforced to produce certain forms of knowledge as superior over others.

Communication as Institutional Practice

The third conceptualization of communication as invoked by *The Expansion
of International Society* is through its connection to diplomacy as *an institution of practice*.[24] To take Emanuel Adler and Vincent Pouliot's definition,
practices are 'socially meaningful patterns of action which, in being performed
more or less competently, simultaneously embody, act out, and possibly reify
background knowledge and discourse in and on the material world'.[25] Adding
'institutions' to 'practices', 'institutions of practice' are the material structures
and artefacts as well as the norms, principles, and conventions upon which
practices are drawing and reproducing. Diplomacy has concrete material
manifestations, for example, in the form of buildings that are classified as
embassies, and with that classification comes a set of normative codes, principles, and conventions that guide how states engage with one another. Some
scholars of diplomacy argue that not only is there a link between communication and diplomacy, the definition of diplomacy *is* as an institution of
communicative practice. According to James Der Derian, diplomacy is
'a system of communication, negotiation and information' that provides a
mediation of the estrangement that states inevitably confront when facing one
another.[26]

   Diplomacy takes a prominent place in several of the chapters of *The Expansion
of International Society* and it is frequently mentioned as an institution through
which states communicate. Watson defines diplomatic dialogue as the superior
institution managing European international society in the eighteenth century.[27]
Bull adopts a similar view, identifying diplomatic representation, international
law, and multilateral conferences (themselves a form of diplomacy) as crucial to
international society becoming a worldwide phenomenon around the time of
the First World War.[28] The view that diplomatic communication formed an
important part of the 'package' of norms with which members of international

---

[24] For a discussion of the English School and the practice turn in IR, see Little 2011; Navari
2011.
[25] Adler and Pouliot 2011: 6.   [26] Der Derian 1987: 6–7.
[27] Watson 1984a: 25. Watson's explicit coupling of 'dialogue' and 'diplomacy' raises the
question as to whether the first and the third conception of communication should be seen as
one rather than two conceptions; see also Watson 1982. Yet while for Watson the two were
connected, the first conception as laid out here is broader and thus not confined to the institution
of diplomacy.
[28] Bull 1984b: 120–1. See also Wight 1977: 22–33.

society needed to comply is echoed by Thomas Naff's account of the integration of the Ottoman Empire into the European state system in the eighteenth century and in Gerrit W. Gong's analysis of the demands made by the Western powers on China after the Boxer rebellion in 1900.[29] The chapter by Michael Palliser points to a number of challenges to traditional diplomatic practice caused by new communication technologies: television has made publics concerned about 'far away events' pressuring governments to act, 'classic techniques of discreet and secret diplomacy' have become difficult to uphold, and the speed of diplomatic communication has been vastly increased by technologies such as the telegraph and the telephone as have the demands for quick responses.[30] Palliser also notes that heads of states have been able to meet more frequently and as such meetings are 'eminently newsworthy'; the public's expectations of what such meetings can achieve are easily exaggerated.[31] Palliser suggested that traditional norms of diplomatic communication were put under pressure with potentially wider implications for international society. Yet neither he nor any of the other contributors to *The Expansion of International Society* explicitly considered that the actors of diplomacy might change.

Communication as Technology

The fourth conceptualization of communication that can be identified within *The Expansion of International Society* is that of communication as technology. The impact of technology on the institution of diplomacy was noted earlier, and 'communication' is used as shorthand for 'communication technology', for example in Bull's account of the factors that led to the 'progressive development' of international society in Europe during the nineteenth century.[32] Communications technologies also play a role in Bull's account of 'the revolt against the West' as the struggle for economic justice is precipitated not only by the gap in living standards between most Western states on the one hand and most Third World states on the other, but also by the fact that the 'consciousness of the gap was growing as a result of the revolution in communications'.[33] Adopting Bull's distinction between a society of states and world society, Ronald Dore holds that there is 'no reason to doubt that the increasing density of communication...is leading to an increasing similarity of these urban middle-class cultures—an increasing fleshing out of a skeletal "world culture", and its diffusion to larger numbers of people'.[34] Dore also argues, however, that this is seen as a Western culture and that the dominance

---

[29] Naff 1984: 153; Gong 1984a: 177.   [30] Palliser 1984: 371.
[31] Palliser 1984: 378–9.   [32] Bull 1984b: 125.
[33] Bull 1984c: 222.   [34] Dore 1984: 417–19.

of the West hinders the creation of a universal, world society. Specific communication technologies are mentioned very briefly by Ali Mazrui who notes that the radio was crucial to the mobilization of Africans against the colonial order during the Second World War, and by Patrick O'Brien who lists printing as one of the innovations to reach Europe from China between the twelfth and fifteenth centuries.[35]

Extrapolating from the fragments in *The Expansion of International Society*, communication technologies may seem like the most obvious 'drivers' of international society. The printing press, the telegraph, radio, and television are tangible, material objects whose discovery and spread can be more easily identified than the ontological assumptions held about the 'dialogue' between states. Yet, technology is created and appropriated through social use and political decisions and thus does not determine the other three conceptions of communication or the formation and trajectory of international society. Particularly significant about communication technology as a driver of international society is its ability to connect states and other entities and to relay news and information from political leaders to their publics. What should be considered when analysing technology is also the circulation rate, that is, the speed and range with which communication can take place; the extent to which communication can remain secure or private if need be; and the ability of states (and other authorities) to control the flow of information.

The four conceptions, their fragmented form in *The Expansion of International Society*, and their general theoretical status can be seen in Table 21.1.

Table 21.1 Conceptions of communication

Conceptions of communication	Fragment in *The Expansion*	General theoretical status
Mode of engagement	• 'Dialogue' in the definition of international society	• Ontological and normative assumptions • Contextual conditions
Meaning conveyance	• Written communication superior to oral	• Sign system • Epistemic regime
Institution of practice	• Diplomacy	• Actors • Norms of engagement
Technology	• Telegraph • Telephone • Radio • Television	• Connecting states/entities • Distributing news/information • Speed, reach, control/privacy

[35] Mazrui 1984: 297–8; O'Brien 1984: 51.

COMMUNICATION FROM 1500 TO 1984: THE PRINTING PRESS

To identify and address all the 'communication holes' in the historical analysis presented in *The Expansion of International Society* would fill a small book, and there are several ways in which that analysis might be structured. To illustrate what such an analysis might look like, let me briefly provide the example of the printing press. It is difficult to rank communication technologies according to their significance for international society. As Buzan and George Lawson have argued, the introduction of the telegraph and the radio during the nineteenth century were revolutionary technologies in that they radically increased the speed and range of communication.[36] Taking an even longer view of international society from 1500 onwards, the mechanical printing press might well be the most important technology to have been invented. As noted earlier, this is a use of the theoretical framework that starts from 'technology' as a conception of communication. To illustrate how the four conceptions enter the analysis, I note them in brackets the first time that they appear.

Printing was listed very briefly by O'Brien as one of the technologies that reached Europe from China between the twelfth and fifteenth centuries (communication as technology).[37] In Europe, Johannes Gutenberg is credited with the invention of the mechanical printing press around 1450 and this technology spread throughout Europe from the fifteenth century onwards. The first book published by Gutenberg was the bible, and the printing press also facilitated the large-scale production of letters of indulgence used by the Catholic church to pardon sinners. The sale of such indulgences for profit, and thus the commercial use of religion to benefit the church, stood at the centre of Martin Luther's attack on Catholicism in his *Ninety-five Theses* in 1517. Following the Reformation, which caused the split between Catholicism and Protestantism, the Thirty Years War and the Eighty Years War were concluded by the Peace of Westphalia in 1648. Westphalia is credited with initiating the move towards sovereign territorial states, which was crucial for the formation of international society chronicled in *The Expansion of International Society*. In short, the introduction of the printing press in Europe around 1450 can be connected to the genesis of the political communities making up international society 200 years later.

The printing press also played a crucial role in the spread of nationalism in the nineteenth century, particularly through the media of the newspaper (communication as meaning conveyance). Bull and Watson's preference for written communication has already been mentioned, and the significance of

---

[36] Buzan and Lawson 2015b: 75–7. [37] O'Brien 1984: 51.

writing and reading for building modern states is stressed by Benedict Anderson who famously described the nation as an 'imagined community' where 'the members of even the smallest nation will never know most of their fellow-members, meet them, or even hear of them, yet in the minds of each lives the image of their communion'.[38] Reading formed a crucial glue through which such community-building took place. The consumption of the daily newspaper was, held Anderson, a 'mass ceremony' where 'each communicant is well aware that the ceremony he performs is being replicated simultaneously by thousands (or millions) of others of whose existence he is confident, yet of whose identity he has not the slightest notion'.[39] In other words, the significance of the newspaper can be seen as twofold: in terms of content as a vehicle for disseminating the discourse of nationalism, and in terms of practice as a medium that allowed a national community to be formed. The newspaper can also be seen as a vehicle for a particular form of national 'dialogue' as newspaper editors and writers would engage with each other and with readers (communications as a mode of engagement). Such engagement might be heated, but it would nevertheless be conducted through verbal rather than physical combat.

The printing press also had implications for the formation of international society through the changes it brought to the production of treaties and other legally binding texts (communication as practiced by the institution of diplomacy). By the beginning of the fifteenth century, and thus before the introduction of the printing press in Europe, treaties were written by hand, usually in as many copies as there were signatories.[40] Treaties could then be copied by hand, but this was a time-consuming process and susceptible to human errors. Those holding the original treaty could be worried that it might be stolen or lost and that a copy might be insufficient to make the treaty be respected. By the time that the two treaties of Osnabrück and Münster that together made up the Treaty of Westphalia were signed, the printing press had been institutionalized. A year after the treaty was concluded, it was translated from Latin into German and published by Philipp Jacob Fischer in Frankfurt am Main. This increased the speed and range with which the treaty could be circulated. The mechanical reproduction of the treaty also meant that there was only one version being circulated and that each copy therefore could be trusted.[41] The institution of diplomacy was thus impacted in significant ways by the printing press as there was easier access to agreed-upon texts and thus less need for solving disputes over the wording of treaties.

---

[38] Anderson 1991: 6.   [39] Anderson 1991: 35.

[40] I am grateful to Markus von Hedemann, editor in chief of *Diplomatarium Danicum*, for information about the circulation of medieval texts.

[41] See also Benjamin 1999 [1933].

COMMUNICATION, INTERNATIONAL SOCIETY, AND THE DIGITAL REVOLUTION

Here I provide a brief analysis of how communication has changed since 1984 and what the implications might be for international society. As before, I start from the introduction of new technologies—the Internet and cameras embedded in other devices, most importantly mobile phones—then address the other conceptions in turn. Given the choice of technology as the structuring lens, it should be reiterated that technology is not a deterministic force that changes international society irrespectively of human agency. Diplomats and heads of states do, for example, impact the social status of technologies like Twitter and Facebook by using them to send messages during war and negotiations.[42] We should also recall that 1984 is an arbitrary date insofar as it corresponds with the publication of *The Expansion of International Society* rather than because of a change in international society or in communication technology. That said, the three decades since 1984 have seen major events like the end of the Cold War and 11 September 2001, and a range of new communications technologies have been introduced. It seems therefore a good time to ask whether international society itself has undergone fundamental transformations in its rules and institutions, the form that its dialogue takes, and if entities other than states should be seen as members.

Technology: Digital and Interactive

Looking at the changes in communication that have occurred since 1984, the most profound have undoubtedly been those that arose from the way in which computers and digital technologies have moved from the realm of the military and highly specialized computer scientists to becoming objects we encounter and carry with us everywhere.[43] At the core of this development stands the Internet and its transformation from a text-based medium to the graphic and easily searchable format of the World Wide Web. Comparing the technologies of the twentieth and twenty-first centuries to those of the nineteenth century, Buzan and Lawson argue that only the Internet 'has increased the reach, depth and impact of the communications revolution in ways that could be seen as transformative'.[44] To account properly for the revolution in communication technology since 1984 requires therefore that we defamiliarize ourselves with many of the technologies with which we are now deeply accustomed.

---

[42] Heemsbergen and Lindgren 2014.
[43] For an account of the relations between computer science and American national security discourse during the Cold War, see Edwards 1996.
[44] Buzan and Lawson 2015b: 83.

When computers first became available to Western consumers in the late 1980s, their function was largely that of an advanced typewriter. The main advantage of the computer over the typewriter was that the former allowed for text to be endlessly edited, stored, and reused without having to be re-entered. At that stage, computers were not linked to networks and text was transferred via floppy disks. Computers and their users have become globally connected because of the Internet.

The Internet began as ARPANET, a packet-switching technology developed by the US military in the 1970s to protect information in the advent of nuclear war. Packet switching implies that a message is broken down into smaller sequences that are then sent through the routing system of the Internet and assembled at the other end. In the event of a war that could 'take out' parts of the Internet, the broken-down messages would be sent on alternative routes, thus ensuring that communication was still possible. By the late 1980s and early 1990s, ARPANET became known as the Internet and was made available to universities and research communities. Yet, as Deibert notes, 'the truly revolutionary development...has been the emergence of the World-Wide Web, which permits the integration of hypertextual links and multimedia in a single platform'.[45] The World Wide Web version of the Internet now comes with browsers like Explorer and search engines like Google that allow us to type a request for a homepage either directly into the browser or into a search field. This combination of hardware and software has facilitated an expanding list of activities that previously took place 'in real life' such as paying bills, filing taxes, or buying plane tickets, to move online. One consequence of the move of such activities from offline to online is that time becomes suspended: the Internet never sleeps, and once something is uploaded it is immediately available for others to see, listen to, and share. Television and radio are increasingly accessible for streaming, and movies are now purchased online through companies like Netflix rather than being rented or bought. Contrast the media environment of nineteenth-century newspaper-reading national publics with around-the-clock cable television channels like CNN and Al Jazeera, available across major parts of the globe. The possibilities for social networking have been equally radically transformed: email enables virtually instant communication and social networking services like Facebook provide endless options for encounters and community building. Digital communication technologies do not simply convey messages to a receiving audience, as was the case with television and radio, but are something with which we interact. Traditional communication studies models that separated sharply between producers and consumers have thus had to be revised to allow for terms such as 'user-generated content', 'citizen journalism', and 'blogger'. The

---

[45] Deibert 1997: 133.

interconnectivity between communications technologies has also risen dramatically. Telephones have moved from being land based to being 'mobile' and are no longer objects used by people just to speak to one another but also to send text messages and answer emails. The incorporation of cameras and recording functions allows photos and videos to be shot and instantly uploaded to the Internet.

As with other technologies, digital ones have possibilities as well as vulnerabilities. The extensiveness and interconnectivity of communications technologies have led to concern over critical infrastructure, that is, the risk that system failure, accidents, or attacks cause the Internet to cease operating or, on a smaller scale, that homepages and digital functions are 'brought down', for example by denial of service attacks where a website is bombarded with so many requests for access that it 'goes down'.[46] One of the most prominent instances of such cyberwarfare took place in Estonia in 2007 where websites of the two largest banks, government agencies, and news media crashed. Claiming that the attacks originated in Russia, Estonia tried to convince its NATO allies that this was an act of cyberwar.[47] Another set of risks arises not from when and if the Internet breaks down, but from the amount of data that private and public institutions are able—or requested—to compile and the possibilities that this provides governments for tracking and prosecuting their citizens.[48]

In sum, the developments in communication technologies particularly since the late 1980s have, in combination with the end of the Cold War and the lowering of the costs of computer purchase and use, connected institutions and individuals within and across borders to an unprecedented extent. While there is certainly a substantial amount of 'old' inter-state international society in place, this suggests that a range of entities not envisioned by Bull and Watson are now worthy of being considered in an analysis of international society. Individuals can connect and form communities in ways that may in some cases be seen as a burgeoning world society; the commercial actors who develop the software which gives the Internet its constantly evolving interactive form might be so influential that they should be considered a part of international society proper.

Mode of Engagement: From Real to Virtual Identity

The revolution in communication technology that the Internet is said to have brought about is 'a revolution' precisely because it triggers new questions, possibilities, and challenges in the other three conceptions of communication

---

[46] Dunn Cavelty and Kristensen 2008.   [47] Hansen and Nissenbaum 2009.
[48] Deibert 2013.

as well. At the level of communication as a mode of engagement, the digital environment has raised some of the most classic questions concerning politics, democracy, and participation. One optimistic position has argued that the Internet creates progressive new avenues for political involvement and activism, for example through online communities between people who are living in remote locations or within repressive regimes. A more negative reading holds that virtual politics easily becomes populist and susceptible to fleeting fashions, and that 'dialogue' online often deteriorates into verbal and visual abuse.[49] The difference between these positions is frequently reflected in more concrete debates over events of significance for international society, most explicitly perhaps over how to interpret instances where a cause 'goes viral' and spreads at a rapid pace. Take for example the expression 'je suis Charlie' coined immediately after the fatal shootings of twelve cartoonists and staff at the French satirical magazine, *Charlie Hebdo*, in Paris in January 2015. Within a few days the hashtag #jesuischarlie had been tweeted more than five million times. On the one hand, this might be seen as a worldwide expression of solidarity and support and thus an indication of the capacity of world society to unite. A more tempered or pessimistic reading on the other hand might be that retweeting a popular message—which takes a few seconds—comes closer to jumping a fashion trend than a genuine political act. The speed and ease with which communication can take place in the digital environment can be seen a boosting as well as undermining political 'dialogue'.

Another important aspect at the heart of the ontological and normative debates over the digital environment is the significance bestowed upon physical presence—that is, whether human beings act differently and more responsibly when face-to-face. Or, if not face-to-face, whether it is important to be able to establish with certainty the identity of the other. Is identity connected to the human body and a coherent self, or can one have multiple identities, being one person in 'real life' and another when online?[50] To ask 'what is a person?' is to enter into the most classical realm of philosophy, theology, and psychology. It is also a question that has played itself out in discussions of 'bloggers' who have received status as human rights activists and 'critical world society voices'.[51] In June 2011, for example, global media followed the case of American-Syrian Amina Arraf whose blog 'A Gay Girl in Damascus' provided information about human rights abuses committed by the Syrian government. When Amina's cousin posted a message on the blog that Amina had been apprehended by Syrian government security agents, the US State

---

[49] For an early, but still instructive account of these debates, see Poster 2001.

[50] Sherry Turkle (1995) provides a classic study of identity construction in the early, text-based days of the Internet.

[51] One well-known blogger is the 2014 Nobel Peace Prize laureate, Malala Yousafzai, who, at the age of eleven, began writing a blog under a pseudonym.

Department began an investigation into her disappearance. Soon, however, the hunt for Amina led to the discovery that the person running the blog was not a lesbian living in Damascus, but a forty-year-old heterosexual American, Tom MacMaster, who was pursuing a master's degree at the University of Edinburgh. All webpages have Internet Protocol (IP) addresses and Amina's was based in Scotland, but proxy servers can be used to blur the physical position of a site and is a strategy often used by critical bloggers. When 'Amina' MacMaster was asked why his IP address was not within Syria, he explained the Scottish location on those grounds. While the incident sparked a debate about the veracity of online sources, MacMaster insisted that '[w]hile the narrative voice may have been fictional, the facts on this blog are true and not misleading as to the situation on the ground...I do not believe that I have harmed anyone—I feel that I have created an important voice for issues I feel strongly about'.[52] Many would see 'Amina', as the *Washington Post* put it, as a 'hoax',[53] but one might also understand 'Amina-MacMaster' as a digital destabilization of old, modern conventions about authorship and authentic identity as residing within one, physical, and clearly demarcated body only.

Meaning Conveyance: Visual Sign Systems

Probably the most striking shift at the level of how meaning is conveyed from 1984 to 2017 has been the rise of visual communication. Television is of course a technology that predates 1984, but the arrival of twenty-four-hour cable news channels with real-time coverage only became a widely available feature after the Cold War. CNN's coverage of the bombardment of Baghdad during the Gulf War of 1991 gave birth to 'the CNN effect', that is, the notion that news media can generate foreign policy interventions, particularly in the case of humanitarian atrocities.[54] Moving into the 1990s and 2000s, the invention of the World Wide Web combined with embedded camera and video recording to allow for images to be produced, uploaded, and circulated almost instantaneously. The attacks of 11 September 2001 would arguably have been a very different phenomenon had they not been captured by countless numbers of photographs and video from Ground Zero in the minutes and hours after the planes hit the World Trade Center in New York.

Although research on the CNN effect has questioned the ability of news media to act as an independent driver of humanitarian interventions, governments and international institutions are now confronting a media environment

---

[52] Bell and Flock 2011.   [53] Bell and Flock 2011.
[54] Livingston and Eachus 1995; Robinson 2002.

where images are hard to control. During the wars in Afghanistan and Iraq in the 2000s, the US military adopted a practice of journalists becoming 'embedded' with the troops. Such attempts to control the flow of news, not least images, were challenged by 'accidental images' such as those from the Abu Ghraib prison. Originally produced by American servicemen and women working at the prison for circulation and consumption by a closed circle of insiders, they found their way into the global media. In spite of American President George W. Bush's attempt to portray the 'Abu Ghraib' scandal as the product of a few bad apples, the photos of the hooded prisoner on a box and of the female prison guard Lynndie England holding a prisoner on a leash became global icons.[55]

Images enter into international society in complicated ways. They might draw attention to human rights abuses, either through activists posting them online, or inadvertently as was the case at Abu Ghraib. Images are generally seen as providing a better kind of documentation than textual reports and, equally importantly, as generating an emotional response within those watching.[56] Such emotional responses might then in turn be seen as a way to mobilize world and international society against regimes that violate human rights. Crucial here is the ability of images to circulate beyond linguistic borders and thus to be meaningful 'utterances' outside of what might have been their context of production.

Yet, there are also ways in which the rise of visual communication might support traditional, state-based international society. Visual-aesthetic representations have been crucial to mobilizing not only popular opposition to repressive regimes, but support for the latter as well.[57] Fascist Italy and Nazi Germany are among the historical cases of such image-conscious regimes; a recent example was the visual staging of the funeral of North Korean 'Dear Leader' Kim Jong-il in December 2011. Another note of caution relates to the speed and range with which images are uploaded, circulated, but also, potentially, forgotten. David D. Perlmutter has argued, for example, that we now live in the age of 'hypericons' which 'pass by fleetingly, gain attention, and then are replaced quickly by new icons'.[58] It is certainly possible to find images that seem to comply with Perlmutter's diagnosis. Take the example of the 2009 video and still images of the dying Iranian activist Neda Agha Soltan who was described as a web 2.0 icon of unrest, yet which today might not be remembered by many.[59] Nevertheless, some images—like the hooded man from Abu Ghraib and the 2014 pre-beheading shot of American photojournalist James Wright Foley—still manage to insert themselves more permanently in our collective visual memory.

---

[55] Hansen 2015.   [56] Bleiker et al. 2013; Hutchison 2014.
[57] Benjamin 1999 [1933].   [58] Perlmutter 2005: 119.   [59] Mortensen 2011.

Institutions of Practice: Citizen, Corporate, and Twitter Diplomacy

The discussion has already touched upon several developments that challenge the traditional institution of diplomacy as consisting of states and reliant upon confidential communication. In terms of who may count as diplomatic actors, the coinage of terms like 'citizen diplomacy' and 'celebrity diplomacy' underscore that there is considerable support for a broader understanding of who practices diplomacy.[60] Digital communication has been crucial for such actors to appear. The fact that private companies are essential to the way digital communication works makes them worthy of being considered as new actors in international society: think, for example, of the extent to which telecommunications companies are involved in monitoring potential terrorist activity or how governments use online platforms to conduct public diplomacy. Digital corporations have perhaps become so important to international society that they should be considered as new institutions of practice in ways that intersect with the traditional institution practising communication in international society, namely diplomacy.

Turning to the latter, the digital environment has provided states with new avenues through which to conduct public diplomacy, and state representatives are increasingly using Twitter to comment on international affairs, on occasion even during ongoing negotiations. Tools like Twitter allow politicians and diplomats to adopt a personal, emphatic, and humorous style, thus making them appear as subjects worthy of their positions of authority, yet at the same time attractively 'like us other humans'.[61] Such strategies may backfire, however, as in the infamous case of Deputy Assistant Secretary of State Colleen Graffey, with responsibility for US public diplomacy in Europe, who in 2008 tweeted about purchasing a bathing suit in the midst of a Middle Eastern crisis.[62] Another challenge to traditional international society stems from the transition of diplomatic communication to digital formats shown most pointedly in the case of the WikiLeaks diplomatic cable releases. The cables had been sent from US embassies around the world to Washington between 1966 and 2010, and the release of these cables began in November 2010 as a small number appeared in a selection of newspapers including *The New York Times*, *The Guardian*, and *Der Spiegel*. By September 2011, WikiLeaks had made more than 250,000 cables available. As Mark Page and J. E. Spence explain, trust and confidentiality is crucial to the institution of diplomacy, not least when compromises need to be found and agreements brokered. The threat that the WikiLeaks release posed was thus that it 'violates that trust and decreases the other party's confidence in the individual official and home

---

[60] Richey 2015.   [61] Hansen 2005.   [62] Cull 2011: 5.

Table 21.2 Communication and international society post-1984

Conceptions of communication	Post-1984 developments	General theoretical status
Mode of engagement	• Virtual • Instant • Dispersed/networked	• Ontological and normative assumptions • Contextual conditions
Meaning conveyance	• Digital • Visuality	• Sign system • Epistemic regime
Institution of practice	• Citizen diplomacy/ activism • Digital corporations	• Actors • Norms of engagement
Technology	• Computers • Internet • Software • Mobile phones	• Connecting states/entities • Distributing news/information • Speed, reach, control/privacy

government generally, to keep things secret'.[63] In other words, the danger of WikiLeaks was not only that specific pieces of classified information were being released, but that it had also been possible for an individual, Bradley/ Chelsea Manning, to gain access to, copy, and easily forward that amount of material to WikiLeaks. As Nicholas J. Cull has argued, 'all it took to challenge the diplomatic order of the day was a single individual with a well-placed accomplice and a little technical know-how'.[64] As of 2017, the consequences of the diplomatic cable release are still hard to assess, yet the revelations about the widespread surveillance programs made public by Edward Snowden in 2013 underlines a general tension between the ability to store (big) data and the ability to ensure them.

The developments since 1984 and their connection to conceptions of communication can be seen in Table 21.2.

CONCLUSION

This chapter has sought to position 'communication' as a theme that was downplayed in *The Expansion of International Society*, yet which is worthy of closer theoretical and historical-empirical scrutiny. Arguing that 'communication' should be theorized as made up not only of communications technologies, I have suggested that when modes of engagement, forms of meaning conveyance, and institutions of practice are included, we get a better grasp of

---

[63] Page and Spence 2011: 238.   [64] Cull 2011: 1–2.

the ways in which international society has evolved and changed. Pointing briefly to the printing press and then in more detail to the changes caused by digital technologies post-1984, I have indicated how such a theoretical framework might be put to use. The information presented here is only a glimpse of what can be said about communication and international society. More research could be carried out on specific technologies, particular moments in time and place, and on the past twenty years. Similarly, a deepening of the conceptualizations of communications particularly in the context of a globalizing international society is in order. If we do not want to always be trailing the latest 'revolutionary' communications technology, we need strong concepts and thorough historical contextualization.

ACKNOWLEDGEMENT

Research for this chapter was supported by the Danish Council for Independent Research—Social Sciences, Grant Number DFF—1327-00056B.

Part VI

Conclusion

22

Conclusion

Tim Dunne and Christian Reus-Smit

At the time that *The Expansion of International Society* was being written and edited, the academic study of International Relations (IR) was entering a new and hostile phase. No more did the landscape look as it did in the 1960s when the first collection of British Committee essays was published.[1] Back then, only two approaches competed for 'our attention', as Hedley Bull put it; they were the stylized 'classical' and 'scientific' approaches.[2] By the 1980s, new paradigms had been added reflecting global power shifts, although material changes in the balance of power seemed to be of less significance than the theoretical and normative battle that commenced after the publication of Kenneth Waltz's *Theory of International Politics*.[3] In the nearly four decades or so that followed Waltz's intervention, IR has continued to fragment to the point where proponents of different grand theories (the 'isms') have tended to seek security in their separate 'camps' rather than engage productively with each other.[4]

The Expansion has been largely ignored in the *sturm und drang* of the paradigm wars that have featured so prominently. Proponents of neorealism and neoliberalism did not consider the book as being IR, regarding it instead as a collection of essays on diplomatic or international history.[5] Neither did critical theorists find anything in the book to support their emancipatory project—how could they given that *The Expansion* neither offers a theoretical account of change[6] nor a conception of history which has a cosmopolitan end-state. Or, putting it another way, no Marx and no Hegel.

---

[1] Butterfield and Wight 1966.   [2] Bull 1966: 361.
[3] Waltz 1979.   [4] Sylvester 2013.
[5] See Waltz's comments in an interview with Fred Halliday and Justin Rosenberg (1998: 385): 'I respect Hedley Bull very much, and Martin Wight very much. But they did theory in a sense that is not recognised as theory by philosophers of science'.
[6] See Chapters 1 and 2 in this volume.

The new edition of *The Expansion*[7] is likely to encounter a different reception in light of the 'historical turn' in IR, and the 'international turns' in history and political theory. IR is reconnecting with world history as it seeks to comprehend the transformation from the current configuration of world order to one where powerful non-Western states are either demanding more influence in the institutions that were built to 'rule the world' after 1945, or are building new ones, such as the Asian Infrastructure Investment Bank. The capability of international society to adapt to new configurations of private and public power is an important question that will not detain us right now; instead, the point to underscore is that the scale of the theoretical challenge of understanding future possible world orders is driving many mainstream IR scholars back to reconsider the conditions that led to the emergence of a hegemonic Atlantic-led order.[8]

The turn to history is also visible among those seeking to advance what Amitav Acharya and others call 'global international relations'. At the outset, it is important to note that his intention is not to replace IR so much as to reimagine it. More substantively, by global IR Acharya means an account of 'how we got this way' that rejects ethnocentrism in favour of an account of universality that is sensitive to diversity and contingency. This means looking past 'the American and Western dominance of the field' in order to reflect cultural diversity and recognize 'the contributions of "non-Western" peoples and societies'.[9] And it means redefining standard accounts of agency in which decisions are taken by 'sovereigns' or by 'the Great Powers' as though this seamlessly leads to a political outcome. Agency exists in multiple modalities, including forms of resistance, actions that are principled, actions that follow standard operating procedures, and practices that reflect localized constructions of world order.

A second move in global IR requires going beyond the silences and exclusions of familiar metanarratives about the triumph of 'the West' to utilize ideas and theories from the non-Western world. This takes us beyond critique. It also takes us beyond the kind of epistemic fragmentation that emerges through deconstructions of universalism. As Andrew Hurrell argues, ideas and concepts from the Global South must do more than stress the unique and the separate and package them as alternative schools of thought. Whether divided by regions, experiences, or 'schools' and traditions of thought, the task for 'pluralistic universalism' (as Acharya calls it) is to reconnect with the global by demonstrating how the contestation between diverse narratives has played out.[10] This means showing the relevance and application of 'differently situated accounts, narratives, and stories about the global and its associated and related concepts and ideas'.[11]

---

[7] Bull and Watson Forthcoming.   [8] Ikenberry 2011; Kupchan 2012.
[9] Acharya 2016: 4.   [10] Acharya 2014: 649–50.   [11] Hurrell 2016: 151.

What does *The Globalization of International Society* contribute to these two broad agendas of the emergent global IR?

BREAKING THE 'NORM OF NOT NOTICING'

It is fair to say that many of the authors in the original *The Expansion* failed to look past the relationship between the forms of knowledge they were articulating and the dominance of the European nation-state structure. The upshot is that *The Expansion* became, in many respects, the kind of ethnocentric account of the history of international society that global IR must both challenge and overcome.[12] This narrative assumes that Europe 'rose' to dominance some time between 1492 and 1648 primarily because of the establishment of anti-hegemonic institutions and practices; that a continuous process of socializing 'the rest' into European norms and institutions prevailed thereafter; and that this expansion culminated in a universal international society where all peoples were accorded sovereignty on the basis of formal legal equality. Bull and Adam Watson present this triumphalist story as being 'the historical record'[13] rather than a reflection of their subject positions in elite Western universities. The historical record of IR has in fact been shaped by a 'norm of not noticing'.[14] Not noticing genocide, famine, dispossession, institutionalized racism. Not noticing that these were not consequences of modernization; they were frequently political choices and policy preferences which enabled and sustained empires.

From the outset, the editors and contributors to *The Globalization of International Society* have maintained an ambivalent attitude towards the 1984 book and the Bull–Watson framework around which it is structured. At a time when the related field of history put nationalism in the foreground 'while keeping internationalism beyond view',[15] where political theory was preoccupied with the state as an actor as opposed to 'its powers or its rights as an international actor',[16] and where mainstream IR had taken flight from the humanities in search of behavioural social science,[17] *The Expansion* was continuing the world historic perspective that Martin Wight had adopted in the mid-1960s.[18] One way of capturing this ambivalence is by appropriating a phrase from a leading postcolonial theorist—*The Expansion* is an 'indispensable' yet 'inadequate' part of the global IR conversation.[19]

---

[12] For a bold critique of English School and constructivist 'silence and bias', see Suzuki et al. 2014: 5–8.
[13] Bull and Watson 1984b: 2.   [14] Vitalis 2000.   [15] Sluga 2013: 9.
[16] Armitage 2013: 3.   [17] Hoffmann 1977.   [18] Later published as Wight 1977.
[19] Chakrabarty 2008: 6.

Empirically, many contributors to *The Globalization of International Society* challenge, implicitly and explicitly, the history that is told in *The Expansion*. From both Andrew Phillips and Hendrik Spruyt, we have learned about globalization processes linking civilizations prior to the 'breakout' of European powers.[20] From Heather Rae and Yongjin Zhang we discover how the connected histories of regions—Aztec, Chinese, Ottoman—shaped European identity before and during Europe's 'take off'.[21] Paul Keal and Jennifer M. Welsh reveal the interdependence between sovereignty and empire, and how war was an instrument for maintaining patterns of domination and subordination often justified, as Jacinta O'Hagan reminds us, by civilizational discourses.[22] Barry Buzan shows that one of the most important phases in the many expansions of international society took place from the middle of the nineteenth century to the middle of the twentieth century, a period in which 'Western-colonial international society' became global in scale.[23] Ian Clark adds a significant twist to this argument when he shows how the formal hierarchies and privileges assumed by European powers persisted after 1945 despite the emergence of the principle of sovereign equality that had been the undoing of empires.[24]

Normatively, contributors to this volume openly challenge the interplay of coercion and consent that underpins the standard account of the emergence of universal international society. The assumption that the great powers accorded to themselves special privileges after 1945 and that these were accepted by the rest of international society, is brought into question on a daily basis in various global institutions. Stratification is also evident, as Gerry Simpson notes, in the scripts that are used by international actors to justify interventions against terrorists or perpetrators of genocide and other mass-atrocity crimes.[25] These hierarchies and divisions have been reinstated rather than eradicated as international society has globalized. Mark Beeson and Stephen Bell concur with Simpson in regarding international society as an assemblage of rules and institutions that are incapable of reconciling countervailing forces, such as delivering on commitments to generate a more just world order without having the capability or will to control the succession of economic crises brought about by private actors in pursuit of short-term material gains.[26]

A further sociological limitation in the 1984 book is the lack of specificity as to how normative diffusion was negotiated. Hun Joon Kim's analysis of human rights is indicative of the difference that a richer sociological account

---

[20] Chapters 3 and 5.   [21] Chapters 4 and 11.

[22] Chapters 9, 8, and 10. In an earlier contribution to the debate about the role of the 'standard of civilization' in regulating entry into international society, Zhang (1991: 15) argued that China did not earn the benefits of full membership by 'meticulously fulfilling' the European standard. Rather, it was through 'assertive diplomacy delivering an assault on the Western domination in China and an appeal to the protection of the rules and principles of international law'.

[23] Chapter 12.   [24] See Chapter 13.   [25] Chapter 14.   [26] Chapter 15.

can make. He shows how two normative processes of globalization—investigation and accountability—are to an extent closing the gap between the ambition of universal human rights and their weak institutionalization.[27] The dark side of norm diffusion is evident in Audie Klotz's chapter, where forms of racial exclusion—such as literacy tests for immigrants—were widely in use by many states in the Global North. These exclusions did not in any straightforward manner decline after decolonization. Instead, the United States and the Dominions 'all continued to purse overly racist policies into the 1960s'. Throughout her discussion on 'racial inequality', Klotz participates in an imaginary dialogue with R. J. Vincent who wrote the original chapter on 'racial equality' in *The Expansion*.[28] In a telling passage, Klotz notes that her contribution drew on literature that was published when Vincent would have been writing his chapter. Racist policies and practices were 'no secret', at the time.[29]

SCALING UP TO STRENGTHEN GLOBAL ORDER

What about the different and more challenging registers in which new and diverse forms of knowledge and methods are required to generate ideas and programmes that will strengthen global order? Here we focus on three possibilities that are discussed in the book (there are others we could have chosen).

The study of regions has been prominent in recent contributions to global IR. In the context of *The Expansion* the region of most interest to Bull and Watson was the non-Western world which overtly began to stir at the 1955 Afro-Asian Conference at Bandung. Ian Hall's essay is a retrospective evaluation of Bull's chapter in *The Expansion* on 'the revolt against the West'. As Hall reminds us, Bull sought to understand the contestation though a reflexive engagement with the major 'Third World' powers. To do this, Bull 'spent considerable time and effort in the 1970s in India and elsewhere in the developing world, trying to understand the underlying arguments that motivated the revolt'.[30] Bull was, in a sense, pursuing what David Armitage has referred to as 'both "upward" and "downward" hermeneutics'.[31] The upshot of Bull's engagement with India and the Global South in general is that he recognized that the demands of the Global South needed to be heard, and he argued that the institutions of international society had to accommodate their just demands. At the same time, as we saw in Chapter 1, Bull and his colleagues defended a conservative position on the impact of the relationship between culture and order, viewing diversity as a source of instability.

---

[27] Chapter 16.   [28] Vincent 1984.   [29] Chapter 19.
[30] Chapter 18.   [31] Armitage 2013: 8.

How might 'the revolt' be re-evaluated using a global IR lens? By scaling up from the regional to the global it is apparent that both practitioners and academics confused the revolt against the West with a revolt against the norms of international society. Bandung is illustrative of this confusion.[32] The leaders of the twenty-nine countries that gathered in Indonesia were certainly united by anti-colonialism and anti-racism, and were suspicious of white, Western governments; but their vision of peaceful coexistence was entirely consistent with a pluralist conception of international society. In this regard, the Ten Bandung Principles showed that the rising Global South were aligning themselves with a particular reading of the United Nations (UN) Charter in which norms of sovereignty, self-determination, and human rights were thought to be reconcilable.[33]

Norm revisionism has been more ubiquitous in Western capitals during recent decades than it has been in the Global South, none more so than in relation to the argument that both non-intervention and the non-use of force can be overridden in the name of maintaining international peace and security. Mark Mazower situates arguments for intervention in the context of European imperialism:

> New and much more conditional attitudes towards sovereignty, already evident throughout the human rights revolution of the 1970s, were now taken up within the United Nations system itself, and it became the instrument of a new civilizing mission that, much like the old one from which it sprang, relied heavily on the language of international law and the appeal to universal moral values for its legitimation.[34]

Mazower, and also Simpson, are endorsing a view that the institutions of international society, led by former imperial powers, can never have 'clean hands' given their blood-stained past.[35] And Keal's haunting conclusion adds grist to the mill with the thought that past injustices continue to 'impinge on the political and moral standing of particular states constituting global international society'.[36]

There are two possible counterarguments on which global IR can draw to reopen a space for moral agency, both gesturing towards the kind of 'pluralistic universalism' as intimated by Acharya. As Sarah Teitt shows in her analysis of sovereignty and responsibility, the global conversation about human rights protection is both real and consequential. This conversation

---

[32] Devetak et al. Forthcoming.
[33] This reading of self-determination as a foundation for human rights protection, in the context of decolonization claims, is found in Reus-Smit 2001: 534.
[34] Mazower 2012: 379.
[35] Chapter 14. For an account of the horrors committed by the great powers during the Cold War, see Bellamy 2012.
[36] Chapter 9.

continues today despite becoming discordant during the Syrian conflict where there has been a chronic failure to protect. Yet rather than abandon the 2005 World Summit commitment on the part of UN member states to take 'timely and decisive action' to prevent (or roll back) atrocity crimes, the UN Secretary-General Ban Ki-moon has instead sought to reframe the responsible protection agenda as a 'friend' of sovereignty rather than its enemy. Such a move could easily be dismissed as a diplomatic manoeuvre, but that would understate how a Korean-born global diplomat would see the grafting and localizing of human rights norms on to state sovereignty as being consistent with pluralistic universalism. As Teitt puts it, in ways that reinforce the global scale of the conversation about human protection, '[d]eepening support for these norms among members of the Global North and Global South over the past decade has recast the parameters of legitimate statehood and responsible domestic governance such that it is now increasingly taboo to defend sovereignty as an unmitigated state right that should be free from international scrutiny of large-scale internal human rights abuses'.[37]

Critics of interventionist rhetoric and strategies are unlikely to be persuaded that 'responsible protection' has become a genuinely shared moral purpose in international society today. One reason for these doubts lies in the limited capacity of the institutions of international society to pursue strategies that can serve the world common good rather than benefit a small proportion of it. The intervention debate highlights the danger of an overly polarized conversation about the moral worth of international institutions. Again there is much to gain from turning to world historians to find a way forward. As Richard Devetak and Emily Tannock argue, a preferred method is not to replace Eurocentrism with Occidentalism.[38] Better to avoid altogether, as Christopher Bayly suggests, 'constructing a meta-narrative of vice and virtue'.[39] Taking up this position does not mean conceding the fact–value distinction. It is possible to condemn perpetrators of particular atrocities without playing the role of a 'hanging judge' in relation to European empires or even international society today.[40]

'We are as we are because we got this way'.[41] If Ken Booth is right, then the most significant contribution of this book concerns the multiple and diverse ways in which international society has become globalized. We have not sought to replace one ethnocentric account with another; instead, we offer an array of insights that bring the background to the foreground—the hybridity, the diversity, and the multiple conceptions of agency. The practices and possibilities of indigenous communities are a case in point. As Ann E. Towns

---

[37] Chapter 17.   [38] Chapter 7.
[39] Bayly 2006: 388. Andrew Phillips (2016) refers to a 'syncretist' approach that can mediate the vice–virtue trap.
[40] Skinner 2000: 99–100.   [41] Quoted in Booth 2007: 119.

reminds us, in many African indigenous communities prior to European colonization, women maintained 'separate-but-equal' forms of institutional power.[42] The League of Iroquois, as Neta C. Crawford maintains, constructed a normative order with elaborated procedures for resolving conflicts among its members—which valued consent above all else. These insights are powerful because they subvert some of the taken-for-granted assumptions about the history of representative institutions and security regimes, and they are powerful in relation to present possibilities. Crawford puts this point better than we can, which is why we close *The Globalization of International Society* with her words: 'If the historical narrative is amended, our sense of what is possible in the present and future might also be altered. The real world could be otherwise. In fact, it already is.'[43]

---

[42] Chapter 20.   [43] Chapter 6.

References

Abulafia, David. 2008. *The Discovery of Mankind: Atlantic Encounters in the Age of Columbus*. New Haven, CT: Yale University Press.

Abu-Lughod, Janet L. 1989. *Before European Hegemony: The World System AD 1250–1350*. New York: Oxford University Press.

Acharya, Amitav. 2004. 'How Ideas Spread: Whose Norms Matter? Norm Localization and Institutional Change in Asian Regionalism'. *International Organization* 58 (2): pp. 239–75.

Acharya, Amitav. 2009. *Whose Ideas Matter? Agency and Power in Asian Regionalism*. Ithaca, NY: Cornell University Press.

Acharya, Amitav. 2014. 'Global International Relations (IR) and Regional Worlds: A New Agenda for International Studies'. *International Studies Quarterly* 58 (4): pp. 647–59.

Acharya, Amitav. 2016. 'Advancing Global IR: Challenges, Contentions, and Contributions'. *International Studies Review* 18 (1): pp. 4–15.

Ackerman, Lillian A. 1995. 'Complementary but Equal: Gender Status in the Plateau'. In *Women and Power in Native North America*, edited by Laura E. Klein and Lillian A. Ackerman, pp. 75–100. Norman, OK: University of Oklahoma Press.

Adas, Michael. 2004. 'Contested Hegemony: The Great War and the Afro-Asian Assault on the Civilizing Mission Ideology'. *Journal of World History* 15 (1): pp. 31–63.

Adler, Emanuel, and Vincent Pouliot. 2011. 'International Practices: Introduction and Framework'. In *International Practices*, edited by Emanuel Adler and Vincent Pouliot, pp. 3–35. Cambridge: Cambridge University Press.

Admati, Anat, and Martin Hellwig. 2013. *The Bankers' New Clothes: What's Wrong with Banking and What to Do About It*. Princeton, NJ: Princeton University Press.

Akasoy, Anna. 2013. 'Mehmed II as a Patron of Greek Philosophy: Latin and Byzantine Perspectives'. In *The Renaissance and the Ottoman World*, edited by Anna Contadini and Claire Norton, pp. 245–56. Farnham, Surrey: Ashgate.

Alderman, Liz. 2015. 'Greece's Relationship with Eurozone is Tested by Election'. *New York Times*, 5 January.

Alexander, Jeffrey C. 2004. 'Cultural Pragmatics: Social Performance between Ritual and Strategy'. *Sociological Theory* 22 (4): pp. 527–73.

Alexandrowicz, Charles. 1967. *An Introduction to the History of the Law of Nations in the East Indies*. Oxford: Clarendon Press.

Alter, Karen J. 2014. *The New Terrain of International Law: Courts, Politics, Rights*. Princeton, NJ: Princeton University Press.

Alvarado Rivera, Maria Jesús. 1910. 'El Feminismo'. Paper presented at the First International Feminine Congress, Buenos Aires, Stencil, Biblioteca Nacional del Perú.

Amadiume, Ifi. 1987. *Male Daughters, Female Husbands: Gender and Sex in an African Society*. London: Zed Books.

Andaya, Leonard Y. 1993. 'Cultural State Formation in Eastern Indonesia'. In *South East Asia in the Early Modern Era: Trade, Power, and Belief*, edited by Anthony Reid, pp. 23–41. Ithaca, NY: Cornell University Press.

Anderson, Benedict. 1991. *Imagined Communities: Reflections on the Origin and Spread of Nationalism*, rev. edn. London: Verso.

Anderson, Fred. 2000. *Crucible of War: The Seven Years' War and the Fate of Empire in British North America, 1754–1766*. New York: Alfred A. Knopf.

Anderson, M. S. 1988. *War and Society in Europe of the Old Regime, 1618–1789*. London: Fontana Press.

Anghie, Antony. 1999. 'Finding the Peripheries: Sovereignty and Colonialism in Nineteenth-Century International Law'. *Harvard International Law Journal* 40 (1): pp. 1–80.

Anghie, Antony. 2005. *Imperialism, Sovereignty and the Making of International Law*. Cambridge: Cambridge University Press.

Annan, Kofi. 1999. 'Two Concepts of Sovereignty'. *The Economist*, 16 September.

Appiah, Kwame Anthony. 1992. *In My Father's House: Africa in the Philosophy of Culture*. Oxford: Oxford University Press.

Arat, Yesim. 2000. 'From Emancipation to Liberation: The Changing Role of Women in Turkey's Public Realm'. *Journal of International Affairs* 54 (1): pp. 107–23.

Arhin, Kwame. 1983. 'The Political and Military Roles of Akan Women'. In *Female and Male in West Africa*, edited by Christine Oppong, pp. 91–8. London: George Allen & Unwin.

Arjomand, Saïd Amir. 2001. 'Perso-Indian Statecraft, Greek Political Science and the Muslim Idea of Government'. *International Sociology* 16 (3): pp. 455–73.

Arjomand, Saïd Amir. 2008. 'The Salience of Political Ethic in the Spread of Persianate Islam'. *Journal of Persianate Studies* 1 (1): pp. 5–29.

Armitage, David. 2000. *The Ideological Origins of the British Empire*. Cambridge: Cambridge University Press.

Armitage, David. 2004. 'The British Conception of Empire in the Eighteenth Century'. In *Greater Britain, 1516–1776: Essays in Atlantic History*, David Armitage, pp. 90–107. Aldershot: Ashgate.

Armitage, David. 2007. *The Declaration of Independence: A Global History*. Cambridge, MA: Harvard University Press.

Armitage, David. 2013. *Foundations of Modern International Thought*. Cambridge: Cambridge University Press.

Armitage, David, and Sanjay Subrahmanyam, eds. 2010. *The Age of Revolutions in Global Context, c. 1760–1840*. New York: Palgrave Macmillan.

Armstrong, Karen. 2000. *The Battle for God: Fundamentalism in Judaism, Christianity and Islam*. London: Harper Collins.

Armstrong, Karen. 2014. *Fields of Blood: Religion and the History of Violence*. London: The Bodley Head.

Arnason, Johann P. 2004. 'Parallels and Divergences: Perspectives on the Early Second Millennium'. *Medieval Encounters* 10 (1): pp. 13–40.

Arneil, Barbara. 1996. *John Locke and America: The Defence of English Colonialism*. Oxford: Clarendon Press.

Ashley, Richard K. 1981. 'Political Realism and Human Interests'. *International Studies Quarterly* 25 (2): pp. 204–36.

Atwell, William. 1998. 'Ming China and the Emerging World Economy, c. 1470–1650'. In *The Cambridge History of China*, vol. 8, The Ming Dynasty, 1368–1644, Part 2, edited by Dennis C. Twitchett and Frederick W. Mote, pp. 376–416. Cambridge: Cambridge University Press.

Atwood, Christopher P. 2013. 'Partners in Profit: Empires, Merchants, and Local Governments in the Mongol Empire and Qing Mongolia'. Conference Paper, SSRC Inter-Asian Connections IV: Istanbul. Koç University, 2–5 October.

Austin, John. 1832. *The Province of Jurisprudence Determined*. London: J. Murray.

Awe, Bolanle. 1977. 'The Iyalode in the Traditional Yoruba Political System'. In *Sexual Stratification: A Cross-Cultural View*, edited by Alice Schlegel, pp. 144–95. New York: Columbia University Press.

Aydin, Cemil. 2013. 'Transformation of Inter-Asian Regional Connections from Early Modern to Modern Period'. Conference Paper, SSRC Inter-Asian Connections IV: Istanbul. Koç University, 2–5 October.

Ayson, Robert. 2012. *Hedley Bull and the Accommodation of Power*. Basingstoke: Palgrave Macmillan.

Babb, Sarah. 2012. 'The Washington Consensus as Transnational Policy Paradigm: Its Origins, Trajectory and Likely Successor'. *Review of International Political Economy* 20 (2): pp. 268–97.

Badie, Bertrand, and Pierre Birnbaum. 1983. *The Sociology of the State*, trans. Arthur Goldhammer. Chicago, IL: University of Chicago Press.

Bain, William. 2003. *Between Anarchy and Society: Trusteeship and the Obligations of Power*. Oxford: Oxford University Press.

Bain, William. 2013. 'Vitoria: The Law of War, Saving the Innocent, and the Image of God'. In *Just and Unjust Intervention: European Thinkers from Vitoria to Mill*, edited by Stefano Recchia and Jennifer M. Welsh, pp. 70–95. Cambridge: Cambridge University Press.

Baker, Andrew. 2010. 'Restraining Regulatory Capture? Anglo-America, Crisis Politics and Trajectories of Change in Global Financial Governance'. *International Affairs* 86 (3): pp. 647–63.

Bang, Peter Fibiger. 2011. 'Lord of All the World: The State, Heterogeneous Power and Hegemony in the Roman and Mughal Empires'. In *Tributary Empires in Global History*, edited by Peter Fibiger Bang and C. A. Bayly, pp. 171–92. London: Palgrave Macmillan.

Barber, Tony. 2012. 'Greeks Direct Cries of Pain at Germany'. *Financial Times*, 14 February.

Barbour, Richmond. 1998. 'Power and Distant Display: Early English "Ambassadors" in Moghul India'. *Huntington Library Quarterly* 61 (3–4): pp. 343–68.

Barkey, Karen. 2005. 'Islam and Toleration: Studying the Ottoman Imperial Model'. *International Journal of Politics, Culture, and Society* 19 (1/2): pp. 5–19.

Barkey, Karen. 2008. *Empire of Difference: The Ottomans in Comparative Perspective*. Cambridge: Cambridge University Press.

Barkey, Karen. 2014a. 'Empire and Toleration: A Comparative Sociology of Toleration within Empire'. In *Boundaries of Toleration*, edited by Alfred Stepan and Charles Taylor, pp. 203–32. New York: Columbia University Press.

Barkey, Karen. 2014b. 'Political Legitimacy and Islam in the Ottoman Empire: Lessons Learned'. *Philosophy and Social Criticism* 40 (4–5): pp. 469–77.

Barnett, Michael. 2005. 'Humanitarianism Transformed'. *Perspectives on Politics* 3 (4): pp. 723–40.

Barnett, Michael. 2011. *Empire of Humanity: A History of Humanitarianism*. Ithaca, NY: Cornell University Press.

Barr, Michael D. 2000. 'Lee Kuan Yew and the "Asian Values" Debate'. *Asian Studies Review* 24 (3): pp. 309–34.

Barraclough, Geoffrey. 1964. *An Introduction to Contemporary History*. London: C. A. Watt.

Barrett, Ward. 1990. 'World Bullion Flows, 1450–1800'. In *The Rise of Merchant Empires: Long-Distance Trade in the Early Modern World 1350–1750*, edited by James D. Tracy, pp. 224–54. New York: Cambridge University Press.

Bartlett, Robert. 1994. *The Making of Europe: Conquest, Colonization, and Cultural Change, 950–1350*. Princeton, NJ: Princeton University Press.

Bartmann, Barry. 2008. 'Between *De Jure* and *De Facto* Statehood: Revisiting the Status Issue for Taiwan'. *Island Studies Journal* 3 (1): pp. 113–28.

Bauer, Joanne R., and Daniel A. Bell, eds. 1999. *The East Asian Challenge for Human Rights*. Cambridge: Cambridge University Press.

Baugh, Daniel. 2011. *The Global Seven Years War, 1754–1763: Britain and France in a Great Power Contest*. New York: Pearson.

Baugh, Daniel A. 1998. 'Withdrawing from Europe: Anglo-French Maritime Geopolitics, 1750–1800'. *International History Review* 20 (1): pp. 1–32.

Bayly, C. A. 2004. *The Birth of the Modern World, 1780–1914: Global Connections and Comparisons*. Malden, MA: Wiley-Blackwell.

Bayly, Christopher A. 2006. 'Moral Judgment: Empire, Nation and History'. *European Review* 14 (3): pp. 385–91.

BBC News. 2014. 'Henry Kissinger "Considered Cuba Air Strikes" in 1976'. 1 October, <http://www.bbc.co.uk/news/29441281>.

Bebel, August. 1910 [1879]. *Woman and Socialism*. New York: Socialist Literature.

Bedford, David, and Thom Workman. 1997. 'The Great Law of Peace: Alternative Inter-National Practices and the Iroquoian Confederacy'. *Alternatives: Global, Local, Political* 22 (1): pp. 87–111.

Beeson, Mark. 2005. 'Rethinking Regionalism: Europe and East Asia in Comparative Historical Perspective'. *Journal of European Public Policy* 12 (6): pp. 969–85.

Beeson, Mark, and André Broome. 2010. 'Hegemonic Instability and East Asia: Contradictions, Crises and US Power'. *Globalizations* 7 (4): pp. 507–23.

Beeson, Mark, and Fujian Li. 2015. 'What Consensus? Geopolitics and Policy Paradigms in China and the United States'. *International Affairs* 91 (1): pp. 93–109.

Beier, J. Marshall. 2005. *International Relations in Uncommon Places: Indigeneity, Cosmology, and the Limits of International Theory*. New York: Palgrave Macmillan.

Beier, J. Marshall. 2009a. 'Forgetting, Remembering, and Finding Indigenous Peoples in International Relations'. In *Indigenous Diplomacies*, edited by J. Marshall Beier, pp. 11–27. New York: Palgrave Macmillan.

Beier, J. Marshall. 2009b. 'Introduction: *Indigenous* Diplomacies as Indigenous *Diplomacies*'. In *Indigenous Diplomacies*, edited by J. Marshall Beier, pp. 1–10. New York: Palgrave Macmillan.

Belich, James. 1986. *The New Zealand Wars and the Victorian Interpretation of Racial Conflict*. Auckland: Auckland University Press.

Belich, James. 2009. *Replenishing the Earth: The Settler Revolution and the Rise of the Anglo-World, 1783–1939*. Oxford: Oxford University Press.

Bell, Coral. 1971. *The Conventions of Crisis: A Study in Diplomatic Management*. Oxford: Oxford University Press.

Bell, Daniel A. 2000. *East Meets West: Human Rights and Democracy in East Asia*. Princeton, NJ: Princeton University Press.

Bell, Duncan S. A. 2005. 'Dissolving Distance: Technology, Space, and Empire in British Political Thought, 1770–1900'. *Journal of Modern History* 77 (3): pp. 523–62.

Bell, Lynda S., Andrew J. Nathan, and Ilan Peleg, eds. 2001. *Negotiating Culture and Human Rights*. New York: Columbia University Press.

Bell, Melissa, and Elizabeth Flock. 2011. '"A Gay Girl in Damascus" Comes Clean'. *Washington Post*, 12 June.

Bell, Stephen. 2011. 'Do We Really Need a New "Constructivist Institutionalism" to Explain Institutional Change?' *British Journal of Political Science* 41 (4): pp. 883–906.

Bell, Stephen, and Hui Feng. 2013. *The Rise of the People's Bank of China: The Politics of Institutional Change*. Cambridge, MA: Harvard University Press.

Bell, Stephen, and Andrew Hindmoor. 2015. *Masters of the Universe, Slaves of the Market*. Cambridge, MA: Harvard University Press.

Bellamy, Alex J. 2012. *Massacres and Morality: Mass Atrocities in an Age of Civilian Immunity*. Oxford: Oxford University Press.

Bellenoit, Hayden. 2013. 'Paper, Revenue Administration and *Munshi-Gari* in 18th Century India'. Conference Paper, SSRC Inter-Asian Connections IV: Istanbul. Koç University, 2–5 October.

Bendix, Reinhard. 1978. *Kings or People: Power and the Mandate to Rule*. Berkeley, CA: University of California Press.

Benjamin, Walter. 1999 [1933]. 'The Work of Art in the Age of Mechanical Reproduction'. In *Illuminations: Essays and Reflections*, ed. Hannah Arendt, pp. 217–51. London: Pimlico.

Bentham, Jeremy. 1823. *An Introduction to the Principles of Morals and Legislation*, vol. 2. London: W. Pickering and R. Wilson.

Bentley, Jerry H. 1993. *Old World Encounters: Cross-Cultural Contacts and Exchanges in Pre-Modern Times*. New York: Oxford University Press.

Bentley, Jerry H. 1998. 'Hemispheric Integration, 500–1500 CE'. *Journal of World History* 9 (2): pp. 237–54.

Bentley, Jerry H. 1999. 'Sea and Ocean Basins as Frameworks of Historical Analysis'. *Geographical Review* 89 (2): pp. 215–24.

Benton, Lauren. 2002. *Law and Colonial Cultures: Legal Regimes in World History, 1400–1900*. Cambridge: Cambridge University Press.

Benton, Lauren. 2008. 'From International Law to Imperial Constitutions: The Problem of Quasi-Sovereignty, 1870–1900'. *Law and History Review* 26 (3): pp. 595–619.

Benton, Lauren. 2010. *A Search for Sovereignty: Law and Geography in European Empires, 1400–1900*. Cambridge: Cambridge University Press.

Benton, Lauren, and Richard J. Ross. 2013. 'Empires and Legal Pluralism: Jurisdiction, Sovereignty, and Political Imagination in the Early Modern World'. In *Legal Pluralism and Empires, 1500–1800*, edited by Lauren Benton and Richard J. Ross, pp. 1–20. New York: New York University Press.

Benton, Lauren, and Benjamin Straumann. 2010. 'Acquiring Empire through Law: From Roman Doctrine to Early Modern European Practice'. *Law and History Review* 28 (1): pp. 1–38.

Berg, Maxine, ed. 2013. *Writing the History of the Global: Challenges for the 21st Century*. Oxford: Oxford University Press for the British Academy.

Berman, Harold J. 1983. *Law and Revolution: The Formation of the Western Legal Tradition*. Cambridge, MA: Harvard University Press.

Bernard, Jacques. 1972. 'Trade and Finance in the Middle Ages 900–1500'. In *The Fontana Economic History of Europe*, vol. 1, The Middle Ages, edited by Carlo M. Cipolla, pp. 274–338. Glasgow: Collins/Fontana.

Berrey, Ellen. 2015. *The Enigma of Diversity: The Language of Race and the Limits of Racial Justice*. Chicago, IL: University of Chicago Press.

Best, Jaqueline. 2006. 'Civilizing Through Transparency: The International Monetary Fund'. In *Global Standards of Market Civilization*, edited by Brett Bowden and Leonard Seabrooke, pp. 134–45. Abingdon, Oxon: Routledge.

Bettiza, Gregorio. 2014. 'Civilizational Analysis in International Relations: Mapping the Field and Advancing a "Civilizational Politics" Line of Research'. *International Studies Review* 16 (1): pp. 1–28.

Beurganthal, Thomas. 1997. 'The Normative and Institutional Evolution of International Human Rights'. *Human Rights Quarterly* 19 (4): pp. 703–23.

Bhana, Surendra, and Bridglal Pachai, eds. 1984. *A Documentary History of Indian South Africans*. Cape Town: David Philip.

Bially Mattern, Janice, and Ayşe Zarakol. Forthcoming. 'Hierarchies in World Politics'. *International Organization*.

Bickford, Louis. 2007. 'Unofficial Truth Projects'. *Human Rights Quarterly* 29 (4): pp. 994–1035.

Bitterli, Urs. 1989. *Cultures in Conflict: Encounters between European and Non-European Cultures, 1492–1800*. Cambridge: Polity Press.

Black, David. 1999. 'The Long and Winding Road: International Norms and Domestic Political Change in South Africa'. In *The Power of Human Rights: International Norms and Domestic Change*, edited by Thomas Risse, Stephen C. Ropp, and Kathryn Sikkink, pp. 78–108. Cambridge: Cambridge University Press.

Black, Jeremy. 1992. *Pitt the Elder*. Cambridge: Cambridge University Press.

Black, Jeremy. 2007. *European Warfare in a Global Context, 1660–1815*. Abingdon, Oxon: Routledge.

Blanning, T. C. W. 2002. *The Culture of Power and the Power of Culture: Old Regime Europe 1660–1789*. Oxford: Oxford University Press.

Blanning, Tim. 2007. *The Pursuit of Glory: Europe 1648–1815*. London: Penguin Books.

Bleiker, Roland, David Campbell, Emma Hutchison, and Xzarina Nicholson. 2013. 'The Visual Dehumanisation of Refugees'. *Australian Journal of Political Science* 48 (4): pp. 398–416.

Block, Fred L. 1977. *The Origins of International Economic Disorder: A Study of United States International Monetary Policy from World War II to the Present*. Berkeley, CA: University of California Press.

Blockmans, Wim. 1988. 'Princes Conquérants et Bourgeois Calculateurs'. In *La Ville, la Bourgeoisie et la Genèse de L'État Moderne*, edited by Neithard Bulst and Jean-Philippe Genet, pp. 169–81. Paris: CNRS.

Blockmans, Wim. 1989. 'Voracious States and Obstructing Cities: An Aspect of State Formation in Preindustrial Europe'. *Theory and Society* 18 (5): pp. 733–55.

Blue, Gregory. 1999. 'China and Western Social Thought in the Modern Period'. In *China and Historical Capitalism: Genealogies of Sinological Knowledge*, edited by Timothy Brook and Gregory Blue, pp. 57–109. Cambridge: Cambridge University Press.

Blue, Gregory, and Timothy Brook. 1999. 'Introduction'. In *China and Historical Capitalism: Genealogies of Sinological Knowledge*, edited by Timothy Brook and Gregory Blue, pp. 1–9. Cambridge: Cambridge University Press.

Bock, Gisela. 2002. *Women in European History*. Oxford: Blackwell.

Bolton, John R. 2007. *Surrender is Not an Option: Defending America at the United Nations and Abroad*. New York: Threshold Editions.

Boone, Elizabeth H. 1989. 'Incarnations of the Aztec Supernatural: The Image of Huitzilopochtli in Mexico and Europe'. *Transactions of the American Philosophical Society* 79 (2): pp. 1–107.

Boone, Elizabeth Hill. 1994. 'Aztec Pictorial Histories: Records without Words'. In *Writing Without Words: Alternative Literacies in Mesoamerica and the Andes*, edited by Elizabeth Hill Boone and Walter D. Mignolo, pp. 50–76. Durham, NC: Duke University Press.

Booth, Ken. 2007. *Theory of World Security*. Cambridge: Cambridge University Press.

Börzel, Tanja A., and Thomas Risse. 2012. 'From Europeanisation to Diffusion: Introduction'. *West European Politics* 35 (1): pp. 1–19.

Bosch, Mineke. 1999. 'Colonial Dimensions of Dutch Women's Suffrage: Aletta Jacobs's Travel Letters from Africa and Asia, 1911–1912'. *Journal of Women's History* 11 (2): pp. 8–34.

Bossenga, Gail. 2010. 'Financial Origins of the French Revolution'. In *From Deficit to Deluge: The Origins of the French Revolution*, edited by Thomas E. Kaiser and Dale K. Van Kley, pp. 37–66. Stanford, CA: Stanford University Press.

Botero, Giovanni. 1630 [1591]. *Relations of the Most Famous Kingdomes and Common-wealths Thorowout the World*, trans. Robert Johnson. London.

Bowden, Brett. 2005. 'The Colonial Origins of International Law: European Expansion and the Classical Standard of Civilization'. *Journal of the History of International Law* 7 (1): pp. 1–23.

Bowden, Brett. 2009. *The Empire of Civilization: The Evolution of an Imperial Idea*. Chicago, IL: University of Chicago Press.

Bowden, Brett. 2014. 'To Rethink Standards of Civilisation, Start with the End'. *Millennium: Journal of International Studies* 42 (3): pp. 614–31.

Bowden, Brett, and Leonard Seabrooke, eds. 2006. *Global Standards of Market Civilization*. Abingdon, Oxon: Routledge.

Bowker, Mike, and Phil Williams. 1988. *Superpower Détente: A Reappraisal*. London: Sage.

Boxer, C. R. 1969. *The Portuguese Seaborne Empire, 1415–1825*. London: Hutchinson.

Boyle, James. 1985. 'Ideals and Things: International Legal Scholarship and the Prison-House of Language'. *Harvard International Law Journal* 26: pp. 327–59.

Bozeman, Adda. 1984. 'The International Order in a Multicultural World'. In *The Expansion of International Society*, edited by Hedley Bull and Adam Watson, pp. 387–406. Oxford: Clarendon Press.

Bradley, Mark Philip. 2010. 'Decolonization, the Global South, and the Cold War, 1919–1962'. In *The Cambridge History of the Cold War*, vol. 1, Origins, edited by Mervyn P. Leffler and Odd Arne Westad, pp. 464–85. Cambridge: Cambridge University Press.

Branch, Jordan. 2012. '"Colonial Reflection" and Territoriality: The Peripheral Origins of Sovereign Statehood'. *European Journal of International Relations* 18 (2): pp. 277–97.

Brett, Anabelle S. 2011. *Changes of State: Nature and the Limits of the City in Early Modern Natural Law*. Princeton, NJ: Princeton University Press.

Brierly, James. 1963. *The Law of Nations: An Introduction to the International Law of Peace*, ed. Humphrey Waldock, 6th ed. Oxford: Clarendon Press.

Brilmayer, Lea. 1994. *American Hegemony: Political Morality in a One-Superpower World*. New Haven, CT: Yale University Press.

Brook, Timothy. 1998. 'Communications and Commerce'. In *The Cambridge History of China*, vol. 8, The Ming Dynasty, 1368–1644, Part 2, edited by Dennis C. Twitchett and Frederick W. Mote, pp. 579–707. Cambridge: Cambridge University Press.

Brooks, Stephen G., and William C. Wohlforth. 2008. *World Out of Balance: International Relations and the Challenge of American Primacy*. Princeton, NJ: Princeton University Press.

Brotton, Jerry. 2012. *A History of the World in Twelve Maps*. London: Penguin Books.

Brown, Chris. 1999. 'Universal Human Rights: A Critic'. In *Human Rights in Global Politics*, edited by Tim Dunne and Nicholas J. Wheeler, pp. 103–27. Cambridge: Cambridge University Press.

Brown, Judith K. 1970. 'Economic Organization and the Position of Women among the Iroquois'. *Ethnohistory* 17 (3/4): pp. 151–67.

Brownlie, Ian. 1984. 'The Expansion of International Society: The Consequences for the Law of Nations'. In *The Expansion of International Society*, edited by Hedley Bull and Adam Watson, pp. 357–69. Oxford: Clarendon Press.

Brubaker, Rogers, and Frederick Cooper. 2000. 'Beyond "Identity"'. *Theory and Society* 29 (1): pp. 1–47.

Brysk, Alison. 2009. *Global Good Samaritans: Human Rights as Foreign Policy*. Oxford: Oxford University Press.

Buchanan, Allen, and Robert O. Keohane. 2004. 'The Preventive Use of Force: A Cosmopolitan Institutional Proposal'. *Ethics and International Affairs* 18 (1): pp. 1–22.

Buchanan, Allen, and Robert O. Keohane. 2011. 'Precommitment Regimes for Intervention: Supplementing the Security Council'. *Ethics and International Affairs* 25 (1): pp. 41–63.

Bukovansky, Mlada, Ian Clark, Robyn Eckersley, Richard Price, Christian Reus-Smit, and Nicholas J. Wheeler. 2012. *Special Responsibilities: Global Problems and American Power*. Cambridge: Cambridge University Press.

Bull, Hedley. 1966. 'The Grotian Conception of International Society'. In *Diplomatic Investigations: Essays in the Theory of International Politics*, edited by Herbert Butterfield and Martin Wight, pp. 51–73. London: George Allen and Unwin.

Bull, Hedley. 1971. 'World Order and the Super Powers'. In *Super Powers and World Order*, edited by Carsten Holbraad, pp. 140–54. Canberra: ANU Press.

Bull, Hedley. 1977. *The Anarchical Society: A Study of Order in World Politics*. London: Macmillan.

Bull, Hedley. 1980. 'The Great Irresponsibles? The United States, the Soviet Union, and World Order'. *International Journal* 35 (3): pp. 437–47.

Bull, Hedley. 1983. 'Justice in International Relations'. 1983–4 Hagey Lectures Waterloo, ON: University of Waterloo, 12–13 October.

Bull, Hedley. 1984a. 'European States and African Political Communities'. In *The Expansion of International Society*, edited by Hedley Bull and Adam Watson, pp. 99–114. Oxford: Clarendon Press.

Bull, Hedley. 1984b. 'The Emergence of a Universal International Society'. In *The Expansion of International Society*, edited by Hedley Bull and Adam Watson, pp. 117–26. Oxford: Clarendon Press.

Bull, Hedley. 1984c. 'The Revolt against the West'. In *The Expansion of International Society*, edited by Hedley Bull and Adam Watson, pp. 217–28. Oxford: Clarendon Press.

Bull, Hedley, and Adam Watson. 1984a. 'Conclusion'. In *The Expansion of International Society*, edited by Hedley Bull and Adam Watson, pp. 425–35. Oxford: Clarendon Press.

Bull, Hedley, and Adam Watson. 1984b. 'Introduction'. In *The Expansion of International Society*, edited by Hedley Bull and Adam Watson, pp. 1–9. Oxford: Clarendon Press.

Bull, Hedley, and Adam Watson, eds. 1984c. *The Expansion of International Society*. Oxford: Clarendon Press.

Bull, Hedley, and Adam Watson, eds. Forthcoming. *The Expansion of International Society*. Oxford: Oxford University Press.

Burbank, Jane, and Frederick Cooper. 2010. *Empires in World History: Power and the Politics of Difference*. Princeton, NJ: Princeton University Press.

Burbank, Jane, and Frederick Cooper. 2013. 'Rules of Law, Politics of Empire'. In *Legal Pluralism and Empires, 1500–1850*, edited by Lauren Benton and Richard J. Ross, pp. 279–93. New York: New York University Press.

Burkhardt, Johannes. 2012. 'Religious War or Imperial War? Views of the Seven Years' War from Germany and Rome'. In *The Seven Years' War: Global Views*, edited by Mark H. Danley and Patrick J. Speelman, pp. 107–33. Leiden: Brill.

Butterfield, Herbert. 1973. *The Whig Interpretation of History*. Harmondsworth: Penguin Books.

Butterfield, Herbert, and Martin Wight, eds. 1966. *Diplomatic Investigations: Essays in the Theory of International Politics*. London: George Allen and Unwin.

Buzan, Barry. 1993. 'From International System to International Society: Structural Realism and Regime Theory Meet the English School'. *International Organization* 47 (3): pp. 327–52.

Buzan, Barry. 2004. *From International Society to World Society? English School Theory and the Social Structure of Globalisation*. Cambridge: Cambridge University Press.

Buzan, Barry. 2005. 'International Political Economy and Globalization'. In *International Society and its Critics*, edited by Alex J. Bellamy, pp. 115–33. Oxford: Oxford University Press.

Buzan, Barry. 2010. 'Culture and International Society'. *International Affairs* 86 (1): pp. 1–25.

Buzan, Barry. 2011. 'A World Order Without Superpowers: Decentred Globalism'. *International Relations* 25 (1): pp. 3–23.

Buzan, Barry. 2014a. *An Introduction to the English School of International Relations: The Societal Approach*. Cambridge: Polity Press.

Buzan, Barry. 2014b. 'The "Standard of Civilisation" as an English School Concept'. *Millennium: Journal of International Studies* 42 (3): pp. 576–94.

Buzan, Barry, and Ana Gonzalez-Perez, eds. 2009. *International Society and the Middle East: English School Theory at the Regional Level*. Basingstoke: Palgrave Macmillan.

Buzan, Barry, and George Lawson. 2013. 'The Global Transformation: The Nineteenth Century and the Making of Modern International Relations'. *International Studies Quarterly* 57 (3): pp. 620–34.

Buzan, Barry, and George Lawson. 2015a. '"On Co-Authorship and Prediction"'. *International Politics Reviews* 3 (October): pp. 79–83.

Buzan, Barry, and George Lawson. 2015b. *The Global Transformation: History, Modernity and the Making of International Relations*. Cambridge: Cambridge University Press.

Buzan, Barry, and Richard Little. 2000. *International Systems in World History: Remaking the Study of International Relations*. Oxford: Oxford University Press.

Buzan, Barry, and Richard Little. 2014. 'The Historical Expansion of International Society'. In *Guide to the English School in International Studies*, edited by Cornelia Navari and Daniel Green, pp. 59–75. Chichester, West Sussex: Wiley-Blackwell.

Buzan, Barry, and Ole Wæver. 2003. *Regions and Powers: The Structure of International Security*. Cambridge: Cambridge University Press.

Buzan, Barry, and Yongjin Zhang, eds. 2014. *Contesting International Society in East Asia*. Cambridge: Cambridge University Press.

Buzan, Barry, Charles Jones, and Richard Little. 1993. *The Logic of Anarchy: Neorealism to Structural Realism*. New York: Columbia University Press.

Callahan, William A. 2008. 'Chinese Visions of World Order: Post-hegemonic or a New Hegemony?' *International Studies Review* 10 (4): pp. 749–61.

Cama, Timothy, and Megan R. Wilson. 2015. 'Tribes Say No to Keystone'. *The Hill*, 14 April, <http://thehill.com/policy/energy-environment/238691-tribes-say-no-to-keystone>.

Cameron, Euan. 2012. *The European Reformation*, 2nd ed. Oxford: Oxford University Press.

Campbell, Charles W. 1892. 'A Journey through North Korea to the Ch'ang-pai Shan'. *Proceedings of the Royal Geographical Society and Monthly Record of Geography* 14 (3): pp. 141–61.

Campbell, David. 1992. *Writing Security: United States Foreign Policy and the Politics of Identity*. Minneapolis, MN: University of Minnesota Press.

Cao, Qing. 2007. 'Confucian Vision of a New World Order? Culturalist Discourse, Foreign Policy and the Press in Contemporary China'. *International Communication Gazette* 69 (5): pp. 431–50.

Carr, E. H. 1939. *The Twenty Years' Crisis, 1919–1939: An Introduction to the Study of International Relations*. London: Macmillan.

Carrasco, David. 2011. *The Aztecs: A Very Short Introduction*. New York: Oxford University Press.

Carrington, C. E. 1955. 'A New Theory of the Commonwealth'. *International Affairs* 31 (2): pp. 137–48.

Carrington, C. E. 1962. *The Liquidation of the British Empire*. Toronto: Clarke.

Carty, Anthony. 2009. 'Book Review: How International Law Works: A Rational Choice Theory'. *Melbourne Journal of International Law* 10 (2): pp. 691–701.

Casale, Giancarlo. 2010. *The Ottoman Age of Exploration*. Oxford: Oxford University Press.

Cell, John W. 1982. *The Highest Stage of White Supremacy: The Origins of Segregation in South Africa and the American South*. Cambridge: Cambridge University Press.

Chaffin, Joshua. 2013. 'Europe United by Hostility'. *Financial Times*, 15 October.

Chakrabarty, Dipesh. 2008. *Provincializing Europe: Postcolonial Thought and Historical Difference*, new ed. Princeton, NJ: Princeton University Press.

Chann, Naindeep. 2013. 'Searching for the *Sahib-Qiran*: Claims, Contestations, and Connections in the Early Modern Islamicate Empires'. Conference Paper, SSRC Inter-Asian Connections IV: Istanbul. Koç University, 2–5 October.

Chase-Dunn, Christopher, and Richard Rubinson. 1979. 'Toward a Structural Perspective on the World-System'. *Politics & Society* 7 (4): pp. 453–76.

Chatterjee, Hiralal. 1958. *International Law and Inter-State Relations in Ancient India*. Calcutta: Mukhopadhyay.

Chauduri, K. N. 1991. 'Reflections on the Organizing Principle of Premodern Trade'. In *The Political Economy of Merchant Empires: State Power and World Trade, 1350–1750*, edited by James D. Tracy, pp. 421–42. New York: Cambridge University Press.

Ch'ên, Jerome. 1979. *China and the West: Society and Culture, 1815–1937*. London: HarperCollins.

Chen, Sanping. 2002. 'Son of Heaven and Son of God: Interactions among Ancient Asiatic Cultures Regarding Sacral Kingship and Theophoric Names'. *Journal of the Royal Asiatic Society Third Series* 12 (3): pp. 289–325.

Chia Ning. 2012. '*Lifanyuan* and the Management of Population Diversity in Early Qing (1636–1795)'. Working Paper No. 139. Halle: Max Planck Institute for Social Anthropology.

Chimni, B. S. 1993. *International Law and World Order: A Critique of Contemporary Approaches*. New Delhi: Sage.

Chimni, B. S. 2012. 'Legitimating the International Rule of Law'. In *The Cambridge Companion to International Law*, edited by James Crawford and Martti Koskenniemi, pp. 290–308. Cambridge: Cambridge University Press.

Chiu, Hungdah. 1989. 'Chinese Attitude toward International Law of Human Rights in the Post-Mao Era'. Occasional Papers in Contemporary Asian Studies 5. Baltimore, MD: School of Law, University of Maryland.

Churchill, Winston S. 1957. *A History of the English-Speaking Peoples*, vol. 3, The Age of Revolution. New York: Dodd, Mead and Company.

Cipolla, Carlo. 1965. *Guns, Sails, and Empires: Technological Innovation and the Early Phases of European Expansion, 1400–1700*. Manhattan, KS: Sunflower University Press.

Clark, Carolyn M. 1980. 'Land and Food, Women and Power, in Nineteenth Century Kikuyu'. *Africa: Journal of the International African Institute* 50 (4): pp. 357–70.

Clark, Christopher. 2007. *Iron Kingdom: The Rise and Downfall of Prussia, 1600–1947*. London: Penguin Books.

Clark, Ian. 1989. *The Hierarchy of States: Reform and Resistance in the International Order*. Cambridge: Cambridge University Press.

Clark, Ian. 2005. *Legitimacy in International Society*. Oxford: Oxford University Press.

Clark, Ian. 2007. *International Legitimacy and World Society*. Oxford: Oxford University Press.

Clark, Ian. 2009a. 'Democracy in International Society: Promotion or Exclusion?' *Millennium: Journal of International Studies* 37 (3): pp. 563–81.

Clark, Ian. 2009b. 'How Hierarchical Can International Society Be?' *International Relations* 23 (3): pp. 464–80.

Clark, Ian. 2011a. *Hegemony in International Society*. Oxford: Oxford University Press.

Clark, Ian. 2011b. 'How Hierarchical Can International Society Be?' In *Realism and World Politics*, edited by Ken Booth, pp. 271–87. Abingdon, Oxon: Routledge.

Clark, Ian. 2014. 'International Society and China: The Power of Norms and the Norms of Power'. *Chinese Journal of International Politics* 7 (3): pp. 315–40.

Claude, Inis L. 1986. 'The Common Defense and Great-Power Responsibilities'. *Political Science Quarterly* 101 (5): pp. 719–32.

Clendinnen, Inge. 1991a. *Aztecs*. Cambridge: Cambridge University Press.

Clendinnen, Inge. 1991b. '"Fierce and Unnatural Cruelty": Cortés and the Conquest of Mexico'. *Representations* 33 (SI): pp. 65–100.

Cohen, Benjamin J. 1998. *The Geography of Money*. Ithaca, NY: Cornell University Press.

Cohen, Jean. 2012. *Globalization and Sovereignty: Rethinking Legality, Legitimacy, and Constitutionalism*. Cambridge: Cambridge University Press.

Cohen, Roberta, and Francis M. Deng. 1998. *Masses in Flight: The Global Crisis of Internal Displacement*. Washington, DC: Brookings Institution Press.

Cohen, Stanley. 1996. 'Government Responses to Human Rights Reports: Claims, Denials, and Counterclaims'. *Human Rights Quarterly* 18 (3): pp. 517–43.

Colás, Alejandro, and Bryan Mabee, eds. 2011. *Mercenaries, Pirates, Bandits and Empires: Private Violence in Historical Context*. London: Hurst.

Connolly, William E. 1991. *Identity/Difference: Democratic Negotiations of Political Paradox*. Minneapolis, MN: University of Minnesota Press.

Conrad, Geoffrey W., and Arthur A. Demarest. 1984. *Religion and Empire: The Dynamics of Aztec and Inca Expansionism*. Cambridge: Cambridge University Press.

Conrad, Joseph. 2007. *Under Western Eyes*. London: Penguin Books.

Conrad, Joseph. 2012. *Heart of Darkness*. London: Penguin Books.

Conrad, Sebastian. 2012. 'Enlightenment in Global History: A Historiographical Critique'. *American Historical Review* 117 (4): pp. 999–1027.

El Comercio. 1938. 'Consejo Nacional de Mujeres del Perú', 17 July.

Conybeare, John A. C. 1987. *Trade Wars: The Theory and Practice of International Commercial Rivalry*. New York: Columbia University Press.

Cooley, Alexander, and Hendrik Spruyt. 2009. *Contracting States: Sovereign Transfers in International Relations*. Princeton, NJ: Princeton University Press.

Coquery-Vidrovitch, Catherine. 1997. *African Women: A Modern History*. Boulder, CO: Westview Press.

Craven, Matthew. 2012. 'The Invention of a Tradition: Westlake, the Berlin Conference and the Historicisation of International Law'. In *Constructing International*

Law: The Birth of a Discipline, edited by Milos Vec and Luigi Nuzzo, pp. 363–403. Frankfurt am Main: Klosterman.

Craven, Matthew. 2015. 'Between Law and History: The Berlin Conference of 1884–1885 and the Logic of Free Trade'. *London Review of International Law* 3 (1): pp. 31–59.

Crawford, James. 1979. *The Creation of States in International Law*. Oxford: Oxford University Press.

Crawford, James. 2012. 'Sovereignty as a Legal Value'. In *The Cambridge Companion to International Law*, edited by James Crawford and Martti Koskenniemi, pp. 117–33. Cambridge: Cambridge University Press.

Crawford, Neta C. 1994. 'A Security Regime among Democracies: Cooperation among Iroquois Nations'. *International Organization* 48 (3): pp. 345–85.

Crawford, Neta C. 2002. *Argument and Change in World Politics: Ethics, Decolonization, and Humanitarian Intervention*. Cambridge: Cambridge University Press.

Crawford, Neta C. 2011. 'Human Nature and World Politics: Rethinking "Man"'. In *Realism and World Politics*, edited by Ken Booth, pp. 158–76. Abingdon, Oxon: Routledge.

Crawford, Neta C. 2012. 'Human Nature and World Politics: *Ecce* Hayward Alker's *Homo Politicus* as *Homo Humanitatis*'. In *Alker and IR: Global Studies in an Interconnected World*, edited by Renée Marlin-Bennett, pp. 13–27. New York: Routledge.

Crawford, Neta C. 2013. 'How Fighting "Indians" Shaped US Warfare from the Colonial Era to the Present'. Paper presented to the International Studies Association, annual meeting, San Francisco, 31 March.

Crawford, Neta C. 2014. 'Rethinking "International Relations Theory" as if North and South American "Indians" Mattered'. Paper presented to the International Studies Association, annual meeting, 26–9 March.

Cronin, Bruce, and Ian Hurd. 2008. 'Introduction'. In *The UN Security Council and the Politics of International Authority*, edited by Bruce Cronin and Ian Hurd, pp. 3–22. London: Routledge.

Crossley, Pamela Kyle. 1999. *A Translucent Mirror: History and Identity in Qing Imperial Ideology*. Berkeley, CA: University of California Press.

Crummey, Donald. 1981. 'Women and Landed Property in Gondarine Ethiopia'. *International Journal of African Historical Studies* 14 (3): pp. 444–65.

Cryer, Robert. 2006. 'International Criminal Law vs State Sovereignty: Another Round?' *European Journal of International Law* 16 (5): pp. 979–1000.

Cull, Nicholas J. 2011. 'WikiLeaks, Public Diplomacy 2.0 and the State of Digital Public Diplomacy'. *Place Branding and Public Diplomacy* 7 (1): pp. 1–8.

Culpepper, Pepper D., and Raphael Reinke. 2014. 'Structural Power and Bank Bailouts in the United Kingdom and the United States'. *Politics & Society* 42 (4): pp. 427–54.

Curtin, Philip D. 1984. *Cross-Cultural Trade in World History*. New York: Cambridge University Press.

Cutler, A. Claire. 2003. *Private Power and Global Authority: Transnational Merchant Law in the Global Political Economy*. Cambridge: Cambridge University Press.

Dale, Stephen. 2010. 'India under Mughal Rule'. In *The New Cambridge History of Islam*, vol. 3, The Eastern Islamic World, Eleventh to Eighteenth Centuries, edited by David O. Morgan and Anthony Reid, pp. 266–314. New York: Cambridge University Press.

Dale, Stephen F. 2009. *The Muslim Empires of the Ottomans, Safavids, and Mughals.* New York: Cambridge University Press.

Dalrymple, William. Forthcoming. *The Anarchy: How a Corporation Replaced the Mughal Empire, 1756–1803.* London: Bloomsbury and Knopf.

Dalziel, Raewyn. 1994. 'Presenting the Enfranchisement of New Zealand Women Abroad'. In *Suffrage and Beyond: International Feminist Perspectives,* edited by Caroline Daley and Melanie Nolan, pp. 42–64. New York: New York University Press.

Dancy, Geoff, Hunjoon Kim, and Eric Wiebelhaus-Brahm. 2010. 'The Turn to Truth: Trends in Truth Commission Experimentation'. *Journal of Human Rights* 9 (1): pp. 45–64.

Danley, Mark H. 2012. 'The "Problem" of the Seven Years' War'. In *The Seven Years' War: Global Views,* edited by Mark H. Danley and Patrick J. Speelman, pp. xxiii–lvii. Leiden: Brill.

Darwin, John. 2008a. *After Tamerlane: The Global History of Empire since 1405.* New York: Bloomsbury.

Darwin, John. 2008b. *After Tamerlane: The Rise and Fall of Global Empires, 1400–2000.* London: Penguin Books.

Darwin, John. 2012. *Unfinished Empire: The Global Expansion of Britain.* London: Penguin.

Davis, Walter W. 1983. 'China, the Confucian Ideal, and the European Age of Enlightenment'. *Journal of the History of Ideas* 44 (4): pp. 523–48.

Dawson, Raymond. 1967. *The Chinese Chameleon: An Analysis of European Conceptions of Chinese Civilization.* London: Oxford University Press.

De Grauwe, Paul. 2006. 'What Have we Learnt about Monetary Integration since the Maastricht Treaty?' *JCMS: Journal of Common Market Studies* 44 (4): pp. 711–30.

De Montaigne, Michel. 2003. *The Complete Essays,* ed. and trans. M. A. Screech. London: Penguin.

De Rojas, José Luis. 2012. *Tenochtitlan: Capital of the Aztec Empire.* Gainesville, FL: University Press of Florida.

De Sousa Santos, Boaventura. 2002. *Toward a New Legal Common Sense: Law, Globalization, and Emancipation,* 2nd ed. London: Butterworths.

Deibert, Ronald J. 1997. *Parchment, Printing, and Hypermedia: Communication in World Order Transformation.* New York: Columbia University Press.

Deibert, Ronald J. 2013. *Black Code: Surveillance, Privacy, and the Dark Side of the Internet,* expanded ed. Toronto: McClelland & Stewart.

Deng, Francis M. 1995. 'Frontiers of Sovereignty: A Framework of Protection, Assistance and Development for the Internally Displaced'. *Leiden Journal of International Law* 8 (2): pp. 249–86.

Der Derian, James. 1987. *On Diplomacy: A Genealogy of Western Estrangement.* Oxford: Blackwell.

Der Derian, James. 2001. 'Global Events, National Security, and Virtual Theory'. *Millennium: Journal of International Studies* 30 (3): pp. 669–90.

Der Derian, James. Forthcoming 2016. *Critical International Relations: An Introduction: From the Barbarian to the Cyborg.* London: Routledge.

Deudney, Daniel H. 2007. *Bounding Power: Republican Security Theory from the Polis to the Global Village*. Princeton, NJ: Princeton University Press.

de Vattel, Emer. 2008. *The Law of Nations: Or, Principles of the Law of Nature, Applied to the Conduct and Affairs of Nations and Sovereigns, with Three Early Essays on the Origin and Nature of Natural Law and on Luxury*, ed. Béla Kapossy and Richard Whatmore. Indianapolis, IN: Liberty Fund.

Devetak, Richard. 2013. '"The Fear of Universal Monarchy": Balance of Power as an Ordering Practice of Liberty'. In *Liberal World Orders*, edited by Tim Dunne and Trine Flockhart, pp. 121–37. Oxford: Oxford University Press.

Devetak, Richard, Tim Dunne, and Ririn Tri Nurhayati. Forthcoming 2016. 'Bandung 60 Years On: Revolt and Resilience in International Society'. *Australian Journal of International Affairs* 1–16.

Diamond, Jared. 1997. *Guns, Germs, and Steel: The Fates of Human Societies*. New York: W. W. Norton & Company.

Dolidze, Anna. 2015. 'How Well Does Russia Speak the Language of International Law?' Open Democracy, 6 February, <https://www.opendemocracy.net/od-russia/anna-dolidze/how-well-does-russia-speak-language-of-international-law>.

Donelan, Michael. 1984. 'Spain and the Indies'. In *The Expansion of International Society*, edited by Hedley Bull and Adam Watson, pp. 75–85. Oxford: Clarendon Press.

Donnelly, Jack. 1998. 'Human Rights: A New Standard of Civilization?' *International Affairs* 74 (1): pp. 1–23.

Donnelly, Jack. 2003. *Universal Human Rights in Theory and Practice*. Ithaca, NY: Cornell University Press.

Donnelly, Jack. 2006. 'Sovereign Inequalities and Hierarchy in Anarchy: American Power and International Society'. *European Journal of International Relations* 12 (2): pp. 139–70.

Dore, Ronald. 1984. 'Unity and Diversity in Contemporary World Culture'. In *The Expansion of International Society*, edited by Hedley Bull and Adam Watson, pp. 407–24. Oxford: Clarendon Press.

Dore, Ronald. 2008. 'Financialization of the Global Economy'. *Industrial and Corporate Change* 17 (6): pp. 1097–112.

Doyle, Michael W. 1986. *Empires*. Ithaca, NY: Cornell University Press.

Drew, Catriona. 2001. 'The East Timor Story: International Law on Trial'. *European Journal of International Law* 12 (4): pp. 651–84.

Drew, Catriona. Forthcoming 2017. *Population Transfer in International Law: The Untold Story of Self-Determination*. Cambridge: Cambridge University Press.

Dull, Jonathan R. 2005. *The French Navy and the Seven Years' War*. Lincoln, NE: University of Nebraska Press.

Dunn Cavelty Myriam, and Kristian Søby Kristensen, eds. 2008. *Security 'the Homeland': Critical Infrastructure, Risk and InSecurity*. London: Routledge.

Dunne, Tim. 2003. 'Society and Hierarchy in International Relations'. *International Relations* 17 (3): pp. 303–20.

Dunne, Tim. 2007. '"The Rules of the Game are Changing": Fundamental Human Rights in Crisis after 9/11'. *International Politics* 44 (2/3): pp. 269–86.

Dunne, Tim, and Richard Little. 2014. 'The International System–International Society Distinction'. In *Guide to the English School in International Studies*, edited by

Cornelia Navari and Daniel Green, pp. 91–107. Chichester, West Sussex: Wiley-Blackwell.

Dunne, Tim, and Nicholas J. Wheeler, eds. 1999. *Human Rights in Global Politics*. Cambridge: Cambridge University Press.

Dunne, Timothy. 1995. 'The Social Construction of International Society'. *European Journal of International Relations* 1 (3): pp. 367–89.

Dunne, Timothy. 1998. *Inventing International Society: A History of the English School*. New York: St. Martin's Press in association with St. Antony's College, Oxford.

Economist. 2013. 'Europe's Reluctant Hegemon'. 15 June.

Edwards, Paul N. 1996. *The Closed World: Computers and the Politics of Discourse in Cold War America*. Cambridge, MA: MIT Press.

Eichengreen, Barry J. 2008. *Globalizing Capital: A History of the International Monetary System*, 2nd ed. Princeton, NJ: Princeton University Press.

Eisenstadt, S. N. 2000. 'The Civilizational Dimension in Sociological Analysis'. *Thesis Eleven* 62 (1): pp. 1–21.

Eisenstadt, Shmuel N., and Wolfgang Schluchter. 1998. 'Introduction: Paths to Early Modernities: A Comparative View'. *Daedalus* 127 (3): pp. 1–18.

Eliade, Mircea. 1959. *The Sacred and the Profane: The Nature of Religion*. New York: Harcourt Brace Jovanovich.

Elias, Norbert. 1978. *The Civilizing Process: The History of Manners*, trans. Edmund Jephcott. Oxford: Basil Blackwell.

Elliott, J. H. 1992a. 'A Europe of Composite Monarchies'. *Past & Present* 137: pp. 48–71.

Elliott, J. H. 1992b. *The Old World and the New: 1492–1650*. Cambridge: Cambridge University Press.

Elliott, J. H. 2015. 'Mexicans, Spaniards, Incas and Their Art'. *New York Review of Books*, 9 July: pp. 58–60.

Engels, Friedrich. 1972 [1884]. *The Origin of the Family, Private Property, and the State, in the Light of the Researches of Lewis H. Morgan*. New York: International Publishers.

Epp, Roger. 2010. 'The British Committee on the Theory of International Politics and Central Figures in the English School'. In *The International Studies Encyclopedia*, edited by Robert A. Denemark. London: Blackwell Publishing.

Epp, Roger. 2014. 'The British Committee on the Theory of International Politics and its Central Figures'. In *Guide to the English School in International Studies*, edited by Cornelia Navari and Daniel Green, pp. 25–36. Chichester, West Sussex: Wiley-Blackwell.

Escobar-Lemmon, Maria, and Michelle M. Taylor-Robinson. 2005. 'Women Ministers in Latin American Government: When, Where, and Why?' *American Journal of Political Science* 49 (4): pp. 829–44.

Fabry, Mikulas. 2010. *Recognizing States: International Society and the Establishment of New States Since 1776*. Oxford: Oxford University Press.

Fairbank, J. K. 1942. 'Tributary Trade and China's Relations with the West'. *Far Eastern Quarterly* 1 (2): pp. 129–49.

Fairbank, John King, and Merle Goldman. 2006. *China: A New History*, 2nd ed. Cambridge, MA: Belknap Press.

Falkner, Robert. 2012. 'Global Environmentalism and the Greening of International Society'. *International Affairs* 88 (3): pp. 503–22.

Farrall, Jeremy. 2007. *United Nations Sanctions and the Rule of Law*. Cambridge: Cambridge University Press.

Farrar, Tarikhu. 1997. 'The Queenmother, Matriarchy, and the Question of Female Political Authority in Precolonial West African Monarchy'. *Journal of Black Studies* 27 (5): pp. 579–97.

Febvre, Lucien. 1973. '*Civilisation*: Evolution of a Word and a Group of Ideas'. In *A New Kind of History: From the Writings of Febvre*, ed. Peter Burke, trans. K. Folca, pp. 219–57. London: Routledge & Kegan Paul.

Feldstein, Martin. 1997. 'EMU and International Conflict'. *Foreign Affairs* 76 (6): pp. 60–73.

Ferguson, Yale H., and Richard W. Mansbach. 1996. 'Political Space and Westphalian States in a World of "Polities": Beyond Inside/Outside'. *Global Governance* 2 (2): pp. 261–87.

Fernández-Armesto, Felipe. 2013. *1492: The Year Our World Began*. London: Bloomsbury.

Fidler, David P. 2000. 'A Kinder, Gentler System of Capitulations? International Law, Structural Adjustment Policies, and the Standard of Liberal, Globalized Civilization'. *Texas International Law Journal* 35 (3): pp. 387–413.

Fidler, David P. 2001. 'The Return of the Standard of Civilization'. *Chicago Journal of International Law* 2 (1): pp. 137–57.

Financial Crisis Inquiry Commission. 2011. *The Financial Crisis Inquiry Report. Final Report of the National Commission on the Causes of the Financial and Economic Crisis in the United States*. New York: FCIS, <http://www.gpo.gov/fdsys/pkg/GPO-FCIC/pdf/GPO-FCIC.pdf>.

Fink, Carole. 2004. *Defending the Rights of Others: The Great Powers, the Jews, and International Minority Protection, 1878–1938*. New York: Cambridge University Press.

Finkel, Caroline. 2005a. *Osman's Dream: The Story of the Ottoman Empire, 1300–1923*. New York: Basic Books.

Finkel, Caroline. 2005b. '"The Treacherous Cleverness of Hindsight": Myths of Ottoman Decay'. In *Re-Orienting the Renaissance: Cultural Exchanges with the East*, edited by Gerald MacLean, pp. 148–74. Houndmills: Palgrave Macmillan.

Finlay, Robert. 1991. 'The Treasure-Ships of Zheng He: Chinese Maritime Imperialism in the Age of Discovery'. *Terrae Incognitae* 23 (1): pp. 1–12.

Finnemore, Martha. 1996. *National Interests in International Society*. Ithaca, NY: Cornell University Press.

FitzGerald, David, and David Cook-Martín. 2014. *Culling the Masses: The Democratic Origins of Racist Immigration Policy in the Americas*. Cambridge, MA: Harvard University Press.

Fitzmaurice, Andrew. 2007. 'The Commercial Ideology of Colonization in Jacobean England: Robert Johnson, Giovanni Botero, and the Pursuit of Greatness'. *William and Mary Quarterly* 64 (4): pp. 791–820.

Fitzmaurice, Andrew. 2014. *Sovereignty, Property and Empire, 1500–2000*. Cambridge: Cambridge University Press.

Fluehr-Lobban, Carolyn. 1998. 'Nubian Queens in the Nile Valley and Afro-Asiatic Cultural History'. Paper presented at the Ninth International Conference for Nubian Studies, Museum of Fine Arts, Boston, 20–6 August, pp. 1–9.

Flynn, Dennis O., and Arturo Giráldez. 1995. 'Born with a "Silver Spoon": The Origin of World Trade in 1571'. *Journal of World History* 6 (2): pp. 201–21.

Foltz, Richard. 2010. *Religions of the Silk Road: Premodern Patterns of Globalization*, 2nd ed. New York: Palgrave Macmillan.

Foner, Eric. 1988. *Reconstruction: America's Unfinished Revolution, 1863–1877*. New York: Harper & Row.

Forsythe, David P. 2006. *Human Rights in International Relations*, 2nd ed. Cambridge: Cambridge University Press.

Foucault, Michel. 1970. *The Order of Things: An Archaeology of the Human Sciences*. New York: Vintage Books.

Foucault, Michel. 1977. 'Nietzsche, Genealogy, History'. In *Language, Counter-Memory, Practice: Selected Essays and Interviews*, Michel Foucault, ed. Donald F. Bouchard, pp. 139–64. Ithaca, NY: Cornell University Press.

Foucault, Michel. 1980. *Power/Knowledge: Selected Interviews & Other Writings 1972–1977*, ed. Colin Gordon. New York: Pantheon Books.

Foucault, Michel. 2003. *'Society Must be Defended': Lectures at the Collège de France 1975–1976*, ed. Arnold Davidson, trans. Graham Burchell. London: Verso.

Fox, Cybelle. 2012. *Three Worlds of Relief: Race, Immigration, and the American Welfare State from the Progressive Era to the New Deal*. Princeton, NJ: Princeton University Press.

Fox, Gregory H., and Brad R. Roth. 2001. 'Democracy and International Law'. *Review of International Studies* 27 (3): pp. 327–52.

Franck, Thomas M. 1992. 'The Emerging Right to Democratic Governance'. *American Journal of International Law* 86 (1): pp. 46–91.

Franck, Thomas M. 1998. *Fairness in International Law and Institutions*. Oxford: Clarendon Press.

Frank, Andre Gunder. 1998. *ReOrient: Global Economy in the Asian Age*. Berkeley, CA: University of California Press.

Freeman, Mark. 2006. *Truth Commissions and Procedural Fairness*. Cambridge: Cambridge University Press.

Fuchs, Thomas. 2006. 'The European China: Receptions from Leibniz to Kant'. *Journal of Chinese Philosophy* 33 (1): pp. 35–49.

Gann, L. H., and Peter Duignan. 1967. *Burden of Empire: An Appraisal of Western Colonialism in Africa South of the Sahara*. New York: Praeger.

Garthoff, Raymond L. 1985. *Détente and Confrontation: American-Soviet Relations from Nixon to Reagan*. Washington, DC: Brookings Institution.

Gartzke, Erik. 2007. 'The Capitalist Peace'. *American Journal of Political Science* 51 (1): pp. 166–91.

Gathii, James Thuo. 2009. *War, Commerce, and International Law*. Oxford: Oxford University Press.

Geertz, Clifford. 1973. *The Interpretation of Cultures: Selected Essays*. New York: Basic Books.

Gellner, Ernest. 1995. *Anthropology and Politics: Revolutions in the Sacred Grove.* Oxford: Blackwell.

George, Alexander L., ed. 1991. *Avoiding War: Problems of Crisis Management.* Boulder, CO: Westview Press.

George, Alexander L., and Andrew Bennett. 2005. *Case Studies and Theory Development in the Social Sciences.* Cambridge, MA: MIT Press.

George, Jim. 1994. *Discourses of Global Politics: A Critical ReIntroduction to International Relations.* Boulder, CO: Lynne Rienner.

Gerges, Fawaz A. 2009. *The Far Enemy: Why Jihad went Global,* 2nd ed. Cambridge: Cambridge University Press.

Glanville, Luke. 2014. *Sovereignty and the Responsibility to Protect: A New History.* Chicago, IL: University of Chicago Press.

Global Centre for the Responsibility to Protect. 2016. 'UN Security Council Resolutions Referencing R2P'. 7 January, <http://www.globalr2p.org/resources/335>.

Glyn, Andrew, Alan Hughes, Alain Lipietz, and Ajit Singh. 1990. 'The Rise and Fall of the Golden Age'. In *The Golden Age of Capitalism: Reinterpreting the Postwar Experience,* edited by Stephen A. Marlin and Juliet B. Schor, pp. 39–125. Oxford: Oxford University Press.

Goffman, Daniel. 2002. *The Ottoman Empire and Early Modern Europe.* Cambridge: Cambridge University Press.

Goh, Evelyn. 2013. *The Struggle for Order: Hegemony, Hierarchy, and Transition in Post-Cold War East Asia.* Oxford: Oxford University Press.

Goldsmith, Jack, and Stephen D. Krasner. 2003. 'The Limits of Idealism'. *Daedalus* 132 (1): pp. 47–63.

Goldsmith, Jack L., and Eric A. Posner. 2005. *The Limits of International Law.* Oxford: Oxford University Press.

Gommans, Jos. 1998a. 'The Eurasian Frontier after the First Millennium AD: Reflections along the Fringe of Time and Space'. *Medieval History Journal* 1 (1): pp. 125–43.

Gommans, Jos. 1998b. 'The Silent Frontier of South Asia, c. AD 1100–1800'. *Journal of World History* 9 (1): pp. 1–23.

Gommans, Jos. 2007. 'Warhorse and Post-Nomadic Empire in Asia, c. 1000–1800'. *Journal of Global History* 2 (1): pp. 1–21.

Gong, Gerrit W. 1984a. 'China's Entry into International Society'. In *The Expansion of International Society,* edited by Hedley Bull and Adam Watson, pp. 171–83. Oxford: Clarendon Press.

Gong, Gerrit W. 1984b. *The Standard of 'Civilization' in International Society.* Oxford: Clarendon Press.

Gong, Gerrit W. 2002. 'Standards of Civilization Today'. In *Globalization and Civilizations,* edited by Mehdi Mozaffari, pp. 77–96. London: Routledge.

Goodrich, Leland M., and Edvard Hambro. 1949. *Charter of the United Nations: Commentary and Documents.* London: Stevens & Sons.

Goodwin, Godfrey. 2006. *The Janissaries.* London: Saqi Books.

Gore, Charles. 2000. 'The Rise and Fall of the Washington Consensus as a Paradigm for Developing Countries'. *World Development* 28 (5): pp. 789–804.

Gottfried, Kurt, and Bruce G. Blair, eds. 1988. *Crisis Stability and Nuclear War*. New York: Oxford University Press.

Gover, Kirsty. 2010. *Tribal Constitutionalism: States, Tribes, and the Governance of Membership*. Oxford: Oxford University Press.

Grafton, Anthony, with April Shelford and Nancy Siraisi. 1992. *New Worlds, Ancient Texts: The Power of Tradition and the Shock of Discovery*. Cambridge, MA: Belknap Press of Harvard University Press.

Greenberg, Michael. 1970. *British Trade and the Opening of China, 1840–42*. Cambridge: Cambridge University Press.

Greenblatt, Stephen. 2011. *The Swerve: How the World Became Modern*. New York: W. W. Norton.

Greengrass, Mark. 2014. *Christendom Destroyed: Europe 1517–1648*. London: Penguin Books.

Greenstock, Jeremy. 2008. 'The Security Council in the Post-Cold War World'. In *The United Nations Security Council and War: The Evolution of Thought and Practice since 1945*, edited by Vaughan Lowe, Adam Roberts, Jennifer Welsh, and Dominik Zaum, pp. 248–62. Oxford: Oxford University Press.

Greif, Avner. 1992. 'Institutions and International Trade: Lessons from the Commercial Revolution'. *American Economic Review* 82 (2): pp. 128–33.

Gries, Peter Hays. 2004. *China's New Nationalism: Pride, Politics, and Diplomacy*. Berkeley, CA: University of California Press.

Habermas, Jürgen. 1984. *The Theory of Communicative Action*, vol. 1, Reason and the Rationalization of Society. Boston, MA: Beacon Press.

Hafner-Burton, Emilie M. 2013. *Making Human Rights a Reality*. Princeton, NJ: Princeton University Press.

Hager Jr, Robert P., and David A. Lake. 2000. 'Balancing Empires: Competitive Decolonization in International Politics'. *Security Studies* 9 (3): pp. 108–48.

Haldane, Andrew G., and Robert M. May. 2011. 'Systemic Risk in Banking Ecosystems'. *Nature* 469 (20): pp. 351–5.

Hale, Sondra. 1996. *Gender Politics in Sudan: Islamism, Socialism, and the State*. Boulder, CO: Westview Press.

Halikowski-Smith, Stefan. 2006. '"The Friendship of Kings was in the Ambassadors": Portuguese Diplomatic Embassies in Asia and Africa during the Sixteenth and Seventeenth Centuries'. *Portuguese Studies* 22 (1): pp. 101–34.

Hall, Anthony J. 2003. *The American Empire and the Fourth World: The Bowl with One Spoon*, vol. 1. Montreal: McGill-Queen's University Press.

Hall, Ian. 2011. 'The Revolt against the West: Decolonisation and its Repercussions in British International Thought, 1945–75'. *International History Review* 33 (1): pp. 43–64.

Hall, Ian. 2012. *Dilemmas of Decline: British Intellectuals and World Politics, 1945–1975*. Berkeley, CA: University of California Press.

Hall, Ian. 2013. 'Tilting at Windmills? The Indian Debate over the Responsibility to Protect after UNSC 1973'. *Global Responsibility to Protect* 5 (1): pp. 84–108.

Hall, Peter A. 2012. 'The Economics and Politics of the Euro Crisis'. *German Politics* 21 (4): pp. 355–71.

Hall, Peter A., and David Soskice, eds. 2001. *Varieties of Capitalism: The Institutional Foundations of Comparative Advantage*. Oxford: Oxford University Press.

Halliday, Fred, and Justin Rosenberg. 1998. 'Interview with Ken Waltz: Conducted by Fred Halliday and Justin Rosenberg'. *Review of International Studies* 24 (3): pp. 371–86.

Halliday, Paul D. 2013. 'Laws' Histories: Pluralisms, Pluralities, Diversity'. In *Legal Pluralism and Empires, 1500–1850*, edited by Lauren Benton and Richard J. Ross, pp. 261–77. New York: New York University Press.

Hamashita, Takeshi. 2008. *China, East Asia and the Global Economy: Regional and Historical Perspectives*. London: Routledge.

Hannerz, Ulf. 1992. *Cultural Complexity: Studies in the Social Organization of Meaning*. New York: Columbia University Press.

Hannerz, Ulf. 2010. 'Diversity is Our Business'. *American Anthropologist* 112 (4): pp. 539–51.

Hanretta, Sean. 1998. 'Women, Marginality and the Zulu State: Women's Institutions and Power in the Early Nineteenth Century'. *Journal of African History* 39 (3): pp. 389–415.

Hansen, Lene. 2005. 'The Politics of Digital Autobiography: Understanding www.johnkerry.com'. In *Interface://Culture—The World Wide Web as Political Resource and Aesthetic Form*, edited by Klaus Bruhn Jensen, pp. 151–75. Copenhagen: Samfundslitteratur Press.

Hansen, Lene. 2015. 'How Images Make World Politics: International Icons and the Case of Abu Ghraib'. *Review of International Studies* 41 (2): pp. 263–88.

Hansen, Lene, and Helen Nissenbaum. 2009. 'Digital Disaster, Cyber Security, and the Copenhagen School'. *International Studies Quarterly* 53 (4): pp. 1155–75.

Hao Shiyuan. 2012. 'Ethnicities and Ethnic Relations'. In *Chinese Society: Change and Transformation*, edited by Li Peilin, pp. 86–107. Abingdon, Oxon: Routledge.

Hardt, Michael, and Antonio Negri. 2000. *Empire*. Cambridge, MA: Harvard University Press.

Hart, H. L. A. 1955. 'Are There Any Natural Rights?' *Philosophical Review* 64 (2): pp. 175–91.

Hawken, Paul. 2007. *Blessed Unrest: How the Largest Movement in the World Came into Being and Why No One Saw it Coming*. New York: Viking.

Hay, Colin. 2013. *The Failure of Anglo-Liberal Capitalism*. Basingstoke: Palgrave Macmillan.

Hayner, Priscilla B. 2002. *Unspeakable Truths: Transitional Justice and the Challenge of Truth Commissions*. New York: Routledge.

Heemsbergen, Luke Justin, and Simon Lindgren. 2014. 'The Power of Precision Air Strikes and Social Media Feeds in the 2012 Israel-Hamas Conflict: "Targeting Transparency"'. *Australian Journal of International Affairs* 68 (5): pp. 569–91.

Hegel, Georg. 1822. *Elements of the Philosophy of Right*. London: Penguin.

Hegel, Georg. 1956. *The Philosophy of History*. New York: Dover.

Heine-Geldern, Robert. 1942. 'Conceptions of State and Kingship in South East Asia'. *Far Eastern Quarterly* 2 (1): pp. 15–30.

Held, David. 2013. 'The Diffusion of Authority'. In *International Organization and Global Governance*, edited by Thomas G. Weiss and Rorden Wilkinson, pp. 60–72. London: Routledge.

Held, David, Anthony McGrew, David Goldblatt, and Jonathan Perraton. 1999. *Global Transformations: Politics, Economics and Culture*. Cambridge: Polity Press.

Hevia, James L. 1995. *Cherishing Men from Afar: Qing Guest Ritual and the Macartney Embassy of 1793*. Durham, NC: Duke University Press.

Hinsley, F. H. 1986. *Sovereignty*, 2nd ed. Cambridge: Cambridge University Press.

Hirsch, Michal Ben-Josef. 2014. 'Ideational Change and the Emergence of the International Norm of Truth and Reconciliation Commissions'. *European Journal of International Relations* 20 (3): pp. 810–33.

Hobsbawm, Eric. 1975. *The Age of Capital, 1848–1875*. London: Abacus.

Hobsbawn, E. J. 1990. *Nations and Nationalism since 1780: Programme, Myth, Reality*. New York: Cambridge University Press.

Hobson, Christopher. 2008. '"Democracy as Civilisation"'. *Global Society* 22 (1): pp. 75–95.

Hobson, Christopher. 2015. *The Rise of Democracy: Revolution, War and Transformations in International Politics since 1776*. Edinburgh: Edinburgh University Press.

Hobson, John M. 2004. *The Eastern Origins of Western Civilisation*. Cambridge: Cambridge University Press.

Hobson, John M. 2007. 'Reconstructing International Relations through World History: Oriental Globalization and the Global-Dialogic Conception of Inter-Civilizational Relations'. *International Politics* 44 (4): pp. 414–30.

Hobson, John M. 2009. 'Provincializing Westphalia: The Eastern Origins of Sovereignty'. *International Politics* 46 (6): pp. 671–90.

Hobson, John M. 2012. *The Eurocentric Conception of World Politics: Western International Theory, 1760–2010*. Cambridge: Cambridge University Press.

Hobson, John M., and J. C. Sharman. 2005. 'The Enduring Place of Hierarchy in World Politics: Tracing the Social Logics of Hierarchy and Political Change'. *European Journal of International Relations* 11 (1): pp. 63–98.

Hodgson, Marshall G. S. 1963. 'The Interrelations of Societies in History'. *Comparative Studies in Society and History* 5 (2): pp. 227–50.

Hodgson, Marshall G. S. 1993. *Rethinking World History: Essays on Europe, Islam, and World History*. Cambridge: Cambridge University Press.

Hodgson, Marshall G. S. 2009. *The Venture of Islam*, vol. 1, The Classical Age of Islam. Chicago, IL: University of Chicago Press.

Hoffer, Carol P. 1972. 'Mende and Sherbro Women in High Office'. *Canadian Journal of African Studies* 6 (2): pp. 151–64.

Hoffmann, Stanley. 1977. 'An American Social Science: International Relations'. *Daedalus* 106 (3): pp. 41–60.

Hoffmann, Stanley. 1983. 'Reaching for the Most Difficult: Human Rights as a Foreign Policy Goal'. *Daedalus* 112 (4): pp. 19–49.

Holsti, Kalevi J. 1991. *Peace and War: Armed Conflicts and International Order 1648–1989*. Cambridge: Cambridge University Press.

Holsti, Kalevi J. 2004. *Taming the Sovereigns: Institutional Change in International Politics*. Cambridge: Cambridge University Press.

Hont, Istvan. 2005. *Jealousy of Trade: International Competition and the Nation-State in Historical Perspective*. Cambridge, MA: Belknap Press of Harvard University Press.

Hopgood, Stephen. 2013. *The Endtimes of Human Rights*. Ithaca, NY: Cornell University Press.

Hopgood, Stephen. 2014. 'Challenges to the Global Human Rights Regime: Are Human Rights Still an Effective Language for Social Change?' *SUR—International Journal on Human Rights* 11 (20): pp. 67–75.

Hopkins, A. G., ed. 2002. *Globalization in World History*. New York: Random House.

Howard, Michael. 1984. 'The Military Factor in European Expansion'. In *The Expansion of International Society*, edited by Hedley Bull and Adam Watson, pp. 33–42. Oxford: Clarendon Press.

Hudson, Geoffrey F. 1965. *Europe and China: A Survey of Their Relations from the Earliest Times to 1800*. London: Edward Arnold.

Hui, Victoria Tin-bor. 2005. *War and State Formation in Ancient China and Early Modern Europe*. Cambridge: Cambridge University Press.

Hung, Ho-Fung. 2003. 'Orientalist Knowledge and Social Theories: China and the European Conceptions of East–West Differences from 1600 to 1900'. *Sociological Theory* 21 (3): pp. 254–80.

Hunt, Lynn. 2007. *Inventing Human Rights: A History*. New York: W. W. Norton.

Hunter, Ian. 2012. '"A *Jus gentium* for America": The Rules of War and the Rule of Law in the Revolutionary United States'. *Journal of the History of International Law* 14 (2): pp. 173–206.

Huntington, Samuel P. 1991. *The Third Wave: Democratization in the Late Twentieth Century*. Norman, OK: University of Oklahoma Press.

Huntington, Samuel P. 1996. *The Clash of Civilizations and the Remaking of World Order*. New York: Simon & Schuster.

Hurd, Ian. 2007. *After Anarchy: Legitimacy and Power in the United Nations Security Council*. Princeton, NJ: Princeton University Press.

Hurrell, Andrew. 2007. *On Global Order: Power, Values, and the Constitution of International Society*. Oxford: Oxford University Press.

Hurrell, Andrew. 2016. 'Beyond Critique: How to Study Global IR?' *International Studies Review* 18 (1): pp. 149–51.

Hutchison, Emma. 2014. 'A Global Politics of Pity? Disaster Imagery and the Emotional Construction of Solidarity after the 2004 Asian Tsunami'. *International Political Sociology* 8 (1): pp. 1–19.

Huttenback, Robert A. 1971. *Gandhi in South Africa: British Imperialism and the Indian Question, 1860–1914*. Ithaca, NY: Cornell University Press.

Huttenback, Robert A. 1976. *Racism and Empire: White Settlers and Colored Immigrants in the British Self-Governing Colonies 1830–1910*. Ithaca, NY: Cornell University Press.

Hyde, Charles. 1945. *International Law, Chiefly as Interpreted and Applied by the United States*, 2nd rev. ed. Boston, MA: Little, Brown.

Ikenberry, G. John. 2011. *Liberal Leviathan: The Origins, Crisis, and Transformation of the American World Order*. Princeton, NJ: Princeton University Press.

Illinois Association Opposed to the Extension of Suffrage to Women. 1900. 'Address to the Voters of the Middle West'. Chicago, IL: Illinois Association Opposed to the Extension of Suffrage to Women.

Imber, Colin. 2012. 'Government, Administration and Law'. In *The Cambridge History of Turkey*, vol. 2, The Ottoman Empire as a World Power, 1453–1603, edited by Suraiya N. Faroqhi and Kate Fleet, pp. 205–40. Cambridge: Cambridge University Press.

IMF (International Monetary Fund). 2012. *Global Financial Stability Report: The Quest for Lasting Stability*. Washington, DC: IMF, <http://www.imf.org/external/pubs/ft/gfsr/2012/01/>.

'In Congress, July 4, 1776. A Declaration By the Representatives of the United States of America, in General Congress Assembled'. 2007. In *The Declaration of Independence: A Global History*, David Armitage, pp. 165–71. Cambridge, MA: Harvard University Press.

Independent International Commission on Kosovo. 2000. *The Kosovo Report: Conflict, International Response, Lessons Learned*. Oxford: Oxford University Press.

Inglis, David. 2010. 'Civilizations or Globalizations? Intellectual Rapprochements and Historical World-Visions'. *European Journal of Social Theory* 13 (1): pp. 135–52.

International Commission on Intervention and State Sovereignty. 2001. *The Responsibility to Protect*. Ottowa: International Development Research Centre.

Inter-Parliamentary Union. 2014. 'Women in Politics: 2014'. http://ipu.org/pdf/publications/wmnmap14_en.pdf.

Ion, Dora. 2012. *Kant and International Relations Theory: Cosmopolitan Community-Building*. New York: Routledge.

Iriye, Akira, Petra Goedde, and William I. Hitchcock, eds. 2012. *The Human Rights Revolution: An International History*. Oxford: Oxford University Press.

Ishay, Micheline R. 2008. *The History of Human Rights: From Ancient Times to the Globalization Era*. Berkeley, CA: University of California Press.

Jackson, Patrick Thaddeus. 2007. 'Civilizations as Actors: A Transactional Account'. In *Civilizational Identity: The Production and Reproduction of 'Civilizations' in International Relations*, edited by Martin Hall and Patrick Thaddeus Jackson, pp. 33–49. Basingtoke: Palgrave Macmillan.

Jackson, Patrick Thaddeus. 2010. 'How to Think about Civilizations'. In *Civilizations in World Politics: Plural and Pluralist Perspectives*, edited by Peter J. Katzenstein, pp. 176–200. Abingdon, Oxon: Routledge.

Jackson, Robert H. 1990. *Quasi-States: Sovereignty, International Relations and the Third World*. Cambridge: Cambridge University Press.

Jackson, Robert H. 2000. *The Global Covenant: Human Conduct in a World of States*. Oxford: Oxford University Press.

Jackson-Preece, Jennifer. 1998. *National Minorities and the European Nation-States System*. Oxford: Oxford University Press.

Jaffrelot, Christophe. 1999. *The Hindu Nationalist Movement and Indian Politics, 1925 to the 1990s*. New Delhi: Penguin.

Jalalzai, Farida. 2008. 'Women Rule: Shattering the Executive Glass Ceiling'. *Politics & Gender* 4 (2): pp. 205–31.

James, Alan. 1992. 'The Equality of States: Contemporary Manifestations of an Ancient Doctrine'. *Review of International Studies* 18 (4): pp. 377–91.

James, Alan. 1999. 'The Practice of Sovereign Statehood in Contemporary International Society'. *Political Studies* 47 (3): pp. 457–73.

Jardine, Lisa, and Jerry Brotton. 2000. *Global Interests: Renaissance Art between East and West*. London: Reaktion Books.

Jefferson, Thomas. 1803. 'Letter from Thomas Jefferson to Congress'. 18 January, <http://www.nebraskastudies.org/transcript/Letter_Jefferson_%20percent20to_congrs.htm>.

Jeffery, Renée, and Hun Joon Kim, eds. 2014. *Transitional Justice in the Asia-Pacific*. Cambridge: Cambridge University Press.

Jennings, Francis. 1976. *The Invasion of America: Indians, Colonialism, and the Cant of Conquest*. New York: W. W. Norton.

Jiang, Yonglin. 2011. *The Mandate of Heaven and the Great Ming Code*. Seattle, WA: University of Washington Press.

Johnson, Simon. 2009. 'The Quiet Coup'. *The Atlantic Monthly*, May.

Jones, Dorothy V. 1982. *License for Empire: Colonialism by Treaty in Early America*. Chicago, IL: University of Chicago Press.

Jung, Moon-Kie. 2015. *Beneath the Surface of White Supremacy: Denaturalizing US Racisms Past and Present*. Stanford, CA: Stanford University Press.

Kang, David C. 2010. *East Asia before the West: Five Centuries of Trade and Tribute*. New York: Columbia University Press.

Kant, Immanuel. 2007. *The Critique of Judgment*. Indianapolis, IN: Hackett Publishing Co.

Karskens, Grace. 2009. *The Colony: A History of Early Sydney*. Sydney: Allen & Unwin.

Katzenstein, Peter J. 2010. 'A World of Plural and Pluralist Civilizations: Multiple Actors, Traditions, and Practices'. In *Civilizations in World Politics: Plural and Pluralist Perspectives*, edited by Peter J. Katzenstein, pp. 1–40. Abingdon, Oxon: Routledge.

Katzenstein, Peter J. 2013. 'Preface'. In *Sinicization and the Rise of China: Civilizational Processes Beyond East and West*, edited by Peter J. Katzenstein, pp. xi–xv. Abingdon, Oxon: Routledge.

Kaufmann, Chaim D., and Robert A. Pape. 1999. 'Explaining Costly International Moral Action: Britain's Sixty-Year Campaign against the Atlantic Slave Trade'. *International Organization* 53 (4): pp. 631–68.

Kayaoglu, Turan. 2010. 'Westphalian Eurocentrism in International Relations Theory'. *International Studies Review* 12 (2): pp. 193–217.

Keal, Paul. 1983. *Unspoken Rules and Superpower Dominance*. New York: St. Martin's Press.

Keal, Paul. 2003. *European Conquest and the Rights of Indigenous Peoples: The Moral Backwardness of International Society*. Cambridge: Cambridge University Press.

Keck, Margaret E., and Kathryn Sikkink. 1998. *Activists beyond Borders: Advocacy Networks in International Politics*. Ithaca, NY: Cornell University Press.

Kedourie, Elie. 1984. 'A New International Disorder'. In *The Expansion of International Society*, edited by Hedley Bull and Adam Watson, pp. 347–55. Oxford: Clarendon Press.

Keene, Edward. 2002. *Beyond the Anarchical Society: Grotius, Colonialism and Order in World Politics*. Cambridge: Cambridge University Press.

Keene, Edward. 2013. 'International Hierarchy and the Origins of the Modern Practice of Intervention'. *Review of International Studies* 39 (5): pp. 1077–90.

Keene, Edward. 2014. 'The Standard of "Civilisation", the Expansion Thesis and the 19th-Century International Social Space'. *Millennium: Journal of International Studies* 42 (3): pp. 651–73.

Keevak, Michael. 2011. *Becoming Yellow: A Short History of Racial Thinking*. Princeton, NJ: Princeton University Press.

Kennedy, David. 1997. 'International Law and the Nineteenth Century: History of an Illusion'. *Quinnipiac Law Review* 17 (1): pp. 99–138.

Kennedy, David. 2005. *The Dark Sides of Virtue: Reassessing International Humanitarianism*. Princeton, NJ: Princeton University Press.

Kennedy, David. 2013. 'Law and the Political Economy of the World'. *Leiden Journal of International Law* 26 (1): pp. 7–48.

Keohane, Robert O. 1984. *After Hegemony: Cooperation and Discord in the World Political Economy*. Princeton, NJ: Princeton University Press.

Keohane, Robert O. 1995. 'Hobbes' Dilemma and Institutional Change in World Politics: Sovereignty in International Society'. In *Whose World Order? Uneven Globalization and the End of the Cold War*, edited by Hans-Henrik Holm and Georg Sørensen, pp. 165–86. Boulder, CO: Westview Press.

Keohane, Robert O., and Joseph S. Nye. 1977. *Power and Interdependence: World Politics in Transition*. Boston, MA: Little, Brown & Co.

Khan, Iqtidar Alam. 2009. 'Tracing Sources of Principles of Mughal Governance: A Critique of Recent Historiography'. *Social Scientist* 37 (5–6): pp. 45–54.

Kim, Hun Joon, and J. C. Sharman. 2014. 'Accounts and Accountability: Corruption, Human Rights, and Individual Accountability Norms'. *International Organization* 68 (2): pp. 417–48.

Kim, Hun Joon, and Kathryn Sikkink. 2013. 'How Do Human Rights Prosecutions Improve Human Rights after Transition?' *Interdisciplinary Journal of Human Rights Law* 7 (1): pp. 69–90.

Kim, Key-Hiuk. 1980. *The Last Phase of the East Asian World Order: Korea, Japan, and the Chinese Empire, 1860–1882*. Berkeley, CA: University of California Press.

Kim, Samuel S. 1994. 'Sovereignty in the Chinese Image of World Order'. In *Essays in Honour of Wang Tieya*, edited by Ronald St. John Macdonald, pp. 425–46. Dordrecht: Martinus Nijhoff Publishers.

Kim, Yung-Chung, ed. 1976. *Women of Korea: A History From Ancient Times to 1945*. Seoul: Ewah Womans University Press.

King, Desmond. 2000. *Making Americans: Immigration, Race, and the Origins of the Diverse Democracy*. Cambridge, MA: Harvard University Press.

King, Desmond S., and Rogers M. Smith. 2005. 'Racial Orders in American Political Development'. *American Political Science Review* 99 (1): pp. 75–92.

King, Michael. 2003. *The Penguin History of New Zealand*. Auckland: Penguin.

Kingsbury, Benedict. 2002. 'Legal Positivism as Normative Politics: International Society, Balance of Power and Lassa Oppenheim's Positive International Law'. *European Journal of International Law* 13 (2): pp. 401–36.

Kirshner, Jonathan. 2008. 'Globalization, American Power, and International Security'. *Political Science Quarterly* 123 (3): pp. 363–89.

Kissinger, Henry. 2001. 'The Pitfalls of Universal Jurisdiction'. *Foreign Affairs* 80 (4): pp. 86–96.

Klein, Laura F., and Lillian A. Ackerman, eds. 1995. *Women and Power in Native North America*. Norman, OK: University of Oklahoma Press.

Klotz, Audie. 1995a. *Norms in International Relations: The Struggle against Apartheid*. Ithaca, NY: Cornell University Press.

Klotz, Audie. 1995b. 'Norms Reconstituting Interests: Global Racial Equality and US Sanctions against South Africa'. *International Organization* 49 (3): pp. 451–78.

Klotz, Audie. 2013. *Migration and National Identity in South Africa, 1860–2010*. New York: Cambridge University Press.

Kollontai, Alexandra. 1909. 'The Struggle for Political Rights'. In *Alexandra Kollontai, Selected Writings*, edited by Alix Holt, pp. 58–74. London: Allison & Busby.

Konings, Martijn. 2007. 'The Institutional Foundations of US Structural Power in International Finance: From the Re-Emergence of Global Finance to the Monetarist Turn'. *Review of International Political Economy* 15 (1): pp. 35–61.

Koskenniemi, Martti. 2001. *The Gentle Civilizer of Nations: The Rise and Fall of International Law 1870–1960*. Cambridge: Cambridge University Press.

Krasner, Stephen D. 1985. *Structural Conflict: The Third World against Global Liberalism*. Berkeley, CA: University of California Press.

Krasner, Stephen D. 1995–6. 'Compromising Westphalia'. *International Security* 20 (3): pp. 115–51.

Krasner, Stephen D. 1999. *Sovereignty: Organized Hypocrisy*. Princeton, NJ: Princeton University Press.

Krasner, Stephen D. 2001. 'Rethinking the Sovereign State Model'. *Review of International Studies* 27 (5): pp. 17–42.

Krasner, Stephen D. 2004. 'Sharing Sovereignty: New Institutions for Collapsed and Failing States'. *International Security* 29 (2): pp. 85–120.

Krever, Tor. 2014. 'Dispensing Global Justice'. *New Left Review* 85 (January–February): pp. 67–97.

Krippner, Greta R. 2011. *Capitalizing on Crisis: The Political Origins of the Rise of Finance*. Cambridge, MA: Harvard University Press.

Krisch, Nico. 2003. 'More Equal Than the Rest? Hierarchy, Equality and US Predominance in International Law'. In *United States Hegemony and the Foundations of International Law*, edited by Michael Byers and Georg Nolte, pp. 135–75. Cambridge: Cambridge University Press.

Krisch, Nico. 2008. 'The Security Council and the Great Powers'. In *The United Nations Security Council and War: The Evolution of Thought and Practice since 1945*, edited by Vaughan Lowe, Adam Roberts, Jennifer Welsh, and Dominik Zaum, pp. 133–53. Oxford: Oxford University Press.

Krishna, Gopal. 1984. 'India and the International Order–Retreat from Idealism'. In *The Expansion of International Society*, edited by Hedley Bull and Adam Watson, pp. 269–87. Oxford: Clarendon Press.

Krook, Mona Lena, and Diana Z. O'Brien. 2012. 'All the President's Men? The Appointment of Female Cabinet Ministers Worldwide'. *Journal of Politics* 74 (3): pp. 840–55.

Krstić, Tijana. 2011. *Contested Conversions to Islam: Narratives of Religious Change in the Early Modern Ottoman Empire*. Stanford, CA: Stanford University Press.

Kula, Witold. 1986. *Measures and Men*. Princeton, NJ: Princeton University Press.

Kupchan, Charles A. 2012. *No One's World: The West, the Rising Rest, and the Coming Global Turn*. Oxford: Oxford University Press.

Lach, Donald F. 1942. 'China and the Era of the Enlightenment'. *Journal of Modern History* 14 (2): pp. 209–23.

Lach, Donald F. 1945. 'Leibniz and China'. *Journal of the History of Ideas* 6 (4): pp. 436–55.

Lach, Donald F. 1965. *Asia in the Making of Europe*, vol. I, Book Two, The Century of Discovery. Chicago, IL: University of Chicago Press.

Lake, David A. 1996. 'Anarchy, Hierarchy, and the Variety of International Relations'. *International Organization* 50 (1): pp. 1–33.

Lake, David A. 2007. 'Escape from the State of Nature: Authority and Hierarchy in World Politics'. *International Security* 32 (1): pp. 47–79.

Lake, David A. 2009. *Hierarchy in International Relations*. Ithaca, NY: Cornell University Press.

Lake, Marilyn, and Henry Reynolds. 2008. *Drawing the Global Colour Line: White Men's Countries and the Question of Racial Equality*. Cambridge: Cambridge University Press.

Lall, Ranjit. 2012. 'From Failure to Failure: The Politics of International Banking Regulation'. *Review of International Political Economy* 19 (4): pp. 609–38.

Lam, Truong Buu. 1968. 'Intervention versus Tribute in Sino-Vietnamese Relations, 1788–1790'. In *The Chinese World Order: Traditional China's Foreign Relations*, edited by John King Fairbank, pp. 165–79. Cambridge, MA: Harvard University Press.

L'Amour, Louis. 1980. *Lonely on the Mountain: A Novel*. New York: Bantam Books.

Landa, Janet T. 1981. 'A Theory of the Ethnically Homogeneous Middleman Group: An Institutional Alternative to Contract Law'. *Journal of Legal Studies* 10 (2): pp. 349–62.

Lang, Andrew. 2011. *World Trade Law after Neoliberalism: Re-imagining the Global Economic Order*. Oxford: Oxford University Press.

LarouchePac. 2013. 'Vladimir Putin Delivers Speech on National Identity and Western Civilization'. 23 September, <http://archive.larouchepac.com/node/28244>.

Latham, Robert. 1997. *The Liberal Moment: Modernity, Security, and the Making of Postwar International Order*. New York: Columbia University Press.

Latour, Bruno. 2005. *Reassembling the Social: An Introduction to Actor-Network Theory*. Oxford: Oxford University Press.

Lauren, Paul Gordon. 1988. *Power and Prejudice: The Politics and Diplomacy of Racial Discrimination*. Boulder, CO: Westview.

Lavrin, Asunción. 1995. *Women, Feminism, and Social Change in Argentina, Chile, and Uruguay, 1890–1940*. Lincoln, NE: University of Nebraska Press.

Lawrence, Bruce B. 2010. 'Islam in Afro-Eurasia: A Bridge Civilization'. In *Civilizations in World Politics: Plural and Pluralist Perspectives*, edited by Peter J. Katzenstein, pp. 157–75. Abingdon, Oxon: Routledge.

Lebow, Richard Ned. 2012. *The Politics and Ethics of Identity: In Search of Ourselves*. Cambridge: Cambridge University Press.

Lesaffer, Randall. 2003. 'Charles V, *Monarchia Universalis* and the Law of Nations 1515–1530'. *Tijdschrift voor Rechtsgeschiedenis* 71 (1–2): pp. 79–123.

Lesaffer, Randall. 2012. 'Peace Treaties and the Formation of International Law'. In *The Oxford Handbook of the History of International Law*, edited by Bardo Fassbender and Anne Peters, pp. 71–94. Oxford: Oxford University Press.

Lewis, Archibald R., and Timothy J. Runyan. 1985. *European Naval and Maritime History, 300–1500*. Bloomington, IN: Indiana University Press.

Lewis, W. Arthur, Michael Scott, Martin Wight, and Colin Legum. 1951. *Attitude to Africa*. Harmondsworth: Penguin.

Lieberman, Victor B. 1987. 'Reinterpreting Burmese History'. *Comparative Studies in Society and History* 29 (1): pp. 162–94.

Linklater, Andrew. 1982. *Men and Citizens in the Theory of International Relations*. London: Macmillan.

Linklater, Andrew. 2011. *The Problem of Harm in World Politics: Theoretical Investigations*. Cambridge: Cambridge University Press.

Little, Richard. 2005. 'The English School and World History'. In *International Society and its Critics*, edited by Alex J. Bellamy, pp. 45–63. Oxford: Oxford University Press.

Little, Richard. 2011. 'Britain's Response to the Spanish Civil War: Investigating the Implications of Foregrounding Practice for English School Thinking'. In *International Practices*, edited by Emanuel Adler and Vincent Pouliot, pp. 174–99. Cambridge: Cambridge University Press.

Little, Richard. 2013. 'Reassessing the Expansion of the International Society'. *E-International Relations* May, <http://www.e-ir.info/2013/05/02/reassessing-the-expansion-of-the-international-society/>.

Liu, Xinru. 2001. 'The Silk Road: Overland Trade and Cultural Interactions in Eurasia'. In *Agricultural and Pastoral Societies in Ancient and Classical History*, edited by Michael Adas, pp. 151–79. Philadelphia, PA: Temple University Press.

Livingston, Steven, and Todd Eachus. 1995. 'Humanitarian Crises and US Foreign Policy: Somalia and the CNN Effect Reconsidered'. *Political Communication* 12 (4): pp. 413–29.

Loke, Beverley. 2013. 'Conceptualising the Role and Responsibility of Great Power: China's Participation in Negotiations toward a Post-Second World War Order'. *Diplomacy & Statecraft* 24 (2): pp. 209–26.

López Austin, Alfredo. 2004. 'Myth, Belief, Narration, Image: Reflections on Mesoamerican Mythology'. *Journal of the Southwest* 46 (4): pp. 601–20.

Luck, Edward C. 2006. *UN Security Council: Practice and Promise*. London: Routledge.

Luck, Edward C. 2008. 'A Council for All Seasons: The Creation of the Security Council and its Relevance Today'. In *The United Nations Security Council and War: The Evolution of Thought and Practice since 1945*, edited by Vaughan Lowe, Adam Roberts, Jennifer Welsh, and Dominik Zaum, pp. 61–85. Oxford: Oxford University Press.

Luh, Jürgen. 2012. 'Frederick the Great and the First "World" War'. In *The Seven Years' War: Global Views*, edited by Mark H. Danley and Patrick J. Speelman, pp. 1–21. Leiden: Brill.

Lustick, Ian S. 1996. 'History, Historiography, and Political Science: Multiple Historical Records and the Problem of Selection Bias'. *American Political Science Review* 90 (3): pp. 605–18.

Lutz, Ellen L., and Caitlin Reiger, eds. 2009. *Prosecuting Heads of State*. Cambridge: Cambridge University Press.

Lynn-Jones, Sean M., Steven E. Miller, and Stephen Van Evera, eds. 1990. *Nuclear Diplomacy and Crisis Management: An International Security Reader*. Cambridge, MA: MIT Press.

Lyon, Peter. 1984. 'The Emergence of the Third World'. In *The Expansion of International Society*, edited by Hedley Bull and Adam Watson, pp. 229–37. Oxford: Clarendon Press.

Lyons, Gene M. 1989. 'In Search of Racial Equality: The Elimination of Racial Discrimination'. In *Global Issues in the United Nations' Framework*, edited by Paul Taylor and A. J. R. Groom, pp. 75–115. New York: St. Martins.

Macartney, George. 1962. *An Embassy to China: Lord Macartney's Journal 1793–1794*, ed. J. L. Cranmer-Byng. London: Longmans.

MacDonald, David. 2014. 'Situating Indigenous Conceptions of Power and Governance in IR'. Paper presented to the International Studies Association, annual meeting, March.

MacLean, Gerald. 2005. 'Introduction: Re-Orienting the Renaissance'. In *Re-Orienting the Renaissance: Cultural Exchanges with the East*, edited by Gerald MacLean, pp. 1–28. Houndmills: Palgrave Macmillan.

Malcolm, Noel. 2015. *Agents of Empire: Knights, Corsairs, Jesuits, and Spies in the Sixteenth-Century Mediterranean World*. London: Penguin Books.

Malik, J. Mohan. 2005. 'Security Council Reform: China Signals its Veto'. *World Policy Journal* 22 (1): pp. 19–29.

Malik, Kennan. 2015. 'The Failure of Multiculturalism: Community versus Society in Europe'. *Foreign Affairs* 94 (2): pp. 21–32.

Man, E. H. 1883. *The Andamanese Islanders*. London: Bibling & Sons Ltd.

Mananzan, Mary John. 1990. 'The Filipino Women: Before and After the Spanish Conquest of the Philippines'. In *Essays on Women*, edited by Mary John Mananzan, pp. 6–35. Manila: Institute of Women's Studies, St. Scholastica's College.

Mancke, Elizabeth. 2009. 'Empire and State'. In *The British Atlantic World, 1500–1800*, edited by David Armitage and Michael Braddick, pp. 193–213, 2nd ed. New York: Palgrave Macmillan.

Manners, Ian. 2002. 'Normative Power Europe: A Contradiction in Terms?' *JCMS: Journal of Common Market Studies* 40 (2): pp. 235–58.

Martell, Luke. 2007. 'The Third Wave in Globalization Theory'. *International Studies Review* 9 (2): pp. 173–96.

Martinez, Jenny S. 2012. *The Slave Trade and the Origins of International Human Rights Law*. Oxford: Oxford University Press.

Mastanduno, Michael. 2002. 'Incomplete Hegemony and Security Order in the Asia-Pacific'. In *America Unrivaled: The Future of the Balance of Power*, edited by G. John Ikenberry, pp. 181–210. Ithaca, NY: Cornell University Press.

Matsuda, Matt K. 2012. *Pacific Worlds: A History of Seas, Peoples, and Cultures*. Cambridge: Cambridge University Press.

Mayall, James. 1990. *Nationalism and International Society*. Cambridge: Cambridge University Press.

Mayall, James. 2000. *World Politics: Progress and its Limits*. Cambridge: Polity Press.

Mazlish, Bruce. 2001. 'Civilization in a Historical and Global Perspective'. *International Sociology* 16 (3): pp. 293–300.

Mazower, Mark. 2009. *No Enchanted Palace: The End of Empire and the Ideological Origins of the United Nations*. Princeton, NJ: Princeton University Press.

Mazower, Mark. 2012. *Governing the World: The History of an Idea*. London: Allen Lane.

Mazrui, Ali. 1984. 'Africa Entrapped: Between the Protestant Ethic and the Legacy of Westphalia'. In *The Expansion of International Society*, edited by Hedley Bull and Adam Watson, pp. 289–308. Oxford: Clarendon Press.

McCarty, Nolan, Keith T. Poole, and Howard Rosenthal. 2014. *Political Bubbles: Financial Crises and the Failure of American Democracy*. Princeton, NJ: Princeton University Press.

McElroy, Jerome L., and Kara B. Pearce. 2006. 'The Advantages of Political Affiliation: Dependent and Independent Small-Island Profiles'. *Round Table* 95 (386): pp. 529–39.

McNeill, William H. 1974. *Venice: The Hinge of Europe, 1081–1797*. Chicago, IL: University of Chicago Press.

McNeill, William H. 1976. *Plagues and Peoples*. New York: Anchor.

McNeill, William H. 2009. *The Rise of the West: A History of the Human Community*. Chicago, IL: University of Chicago Press.

Meernik, James, Rosa Aloisi, Marsha Sowell, and Angela Nichols. 2012. 'The Impact of Human Rights Organizations on Naming and Shaming Campaigns'. *Journal of Conflict Resolution* 56 (2): pp. 233–56.

Mehta, Uday Singh. 1999. *Liberalism and Empire: A Study in Nineteenth-Century British Liberal Thought*. Chicago, IL: University of Chicago Press.

Merino Carvallo, Nelly. 1937. 'Mi Opinión Sobre Derechos Femeninos'. In *La Condición Juridical o Situación Legal de la Mujer en Bolivia*, edited by José Macedonio Urquidi, pp. 111–12. Cochabamba: La Aurora.

Mertes, Tom, ed. 2004. *A Movement of Movements: Is Another World Really Possible?* London: Verso.

Metcalf, Thomas R. 2007. *Imperial Connections: India in the Indian Ocean Arena, 1860–1920*. Berkeley, CA: University of California Press.

Metzger, Thomas. 2005. *A Cloud Across the Pacific: Essays on the Clash between Chinese and Western Political Theories Today*. Hong Kong: Chinese University Press.

Meyer, John W., John Boli, George M. Thomas, and Francisco O. Ramirez. 1997. 'World Society and the Nation-State'. *American Journal of Sociology* 103 (1): pp. 144–81.

Midgley, Clare. 1986. *Women against Slavery: The British Campaign 1780–1870*. London: Macmillan.

Miéville, China. 2005. *Between Equal Rights: A Marxist Theory of International Law*. Leiden: Brill.

Miller, Manjari Chatterjee. 2013. *Wronged by Empire: Post-Imperial Ideology and Foreign Policy in India and China*. Stanford, CA: Stanford University Press.

Mitzen, Jennifer. 2013. *Power in Concert: The Nineteenth-Century Origins of Global Governance*. Chicago, IL: University of Chicago Press.

Moctezuma, Eduardo Matos. 1991. 'The Templo Mayor of Tenochtitlan'. In *Mesoamerican Architecture as a Cultural Symbol*, edited by Jeff Karl Kowalski, pp. 198–291. New York: Oxford University Press.

Mohan, C. Raja. 2007. 'Balancing Interests and Values: India's Struggle with Democracy Promotion'. *Washington Quarterly* 30 (3): pp. 99–115.

Mokyr, Joel. 2014. 'China, Europe and the Onset of Modern Economic Growth'. Presentation at the Buffett Institute, Northwestern University, Evanston, IL, 21 November.

Montgomerie, Johnna, and Karel Williams. 2009. 'Financialised Capitalism: After the Crisis and Beyond Neoliberalism'. *Competition and Change* 13 (2): 99–107.

Moore, R. I. 1997. 'The Birth of Europe as a Eurasian Phenomenon'. *Modern Asian Studies* 31 (3): pp. 583–601.

Moravcsik, Andrew. 1998. *The Choice for Europe: Social Purpose and State Power from Messina to Maastricht*. Ithaca, NY: Cornell University Press.

Morris, Justin. 2013. 'From "Peace by Dictation" to International Organisation: Great Power Responsibility and the Creation of the United Nations'. *International History Review* 35 (3): pp. 511–33.

Morris, Justin, and Nicholas J. Wheeler. 2007. 'The Security Council's Crisis of Legitimacy and the Use of Force'. *International Politics* 44 (2/3): pp. 214–31.

Morsink, Johannes. 1999. *The Universal Declaration of Human Rights: Origins, Drafting, and Intent*. Philadelphia, PA: University of Pennsylvania Press.

Mortensen, Mette. 2011. 'When Citizen Photojournalism Sets the News Agenda: Neda Agha Soltan as a Web 2.0 Icon of Post-Election Unrest in Iran'. *Global Media and Communication* 7 (1): pp. 4–16.

Moyn, Samuel. 2010. *The Last Utopia: Human Rights in History*. Cambridge, MA: Harvard University Press.

Moyn, Samuel. 2012. 'Substance, Scale, and Salience: The Recent Historiography of Human Rights'. *Annual Review of Law and Social Science* 8: pp. 123–40.

Mungello, David E. 1999. *The Great Encounter of China and the West, 1500–1800*. Lanham, MD: Rowman & Littlefield.

Murphy, Sean D. 2012. *Principles of International Law*, 2nd ed. St. Paul, MN: West.

Murray, Gilbert. 1951. *Advance under Fire*. London: Victor Gollancz.

Muthu, Sankar. 2003. *Enlightenment against Empire*. Princeton, NJ: Princeton University Press.

Naff, Thomas. 1984. 'The Ottoman Empire and the European States System'. In *The Expansion of International Society*, edited by Hedley Bull and Adam Watson, pp. 143–69. Oxford: Clarendon Press.

Narlikar, Amrita. 2011. 'Is India a Responsible Great Power?' *Third World Quarterly* 32 (9): pp. 1607–21.

Navari, Cornelia, ed. 2009. *Theorising International Society: English School Methods*. Basingstoke: Palgrave Macmillan.

Navari, Cornelia. 2011. 'The Concept of Practice in the English School'. *European Journal of International Relations* 17 (4): pp. 611–30.

Nederveen Pieterse, Jan. 1992. *White on Black: Images of Africa and Blacks in Western Popular Culture*. New Haven, CT: Yale University Press.

Needham, Joseph. 2005. *Within the Four Seas: The Dialogue of East and West.* Abingdon, Oxon: Routledge.

Nenner, Howard. 1995. *The Right to be King: The Succession to the Crown of England 1603–1714.* Chapel Hill, NC: University of North Carolina Press.

Neumann, Iver B. 1996. 'Self and Other in International Relations'. *European Journal of International Relations* 2 (2): pp. 139–74.

Neumann, Iver B. 2011. 'Entry into International Society Reconceptualised: The Case of Russia'. *Review of International Studies* 37 (2): pp. 463–84.

Neumann, Iver B., and Jennifer M. Welsh. 1991. 'The Other in European Self-Definition: An Addendum to the Literature on International Society'. *Review of International Studies* 17 (4): pp. 327–48.

Nexon, Daniel H. 2009. *The Struggle for Power in Early Modern Europe: Religious Conflict, Dynastic Empires, and International Change.* Princeton, NJ: Princeton University Press.

Nicole, Robert. 2011. *Disturbing History: Resistance in Early Colonial Fiji.* Honolulu, HI: University of Hawai'i Press.

Nobles, Gregory H. 1997. *American Frontiers: Cultural Encounters and Continental Conquest.* Harmondsworth: Penguin.

North, Douglass C. 1981. *Structure and Change in Economic History.* New York: W. W. Norton.

North, Douglass C., and Barry R. Weingast. 1989. 'Constitutions and Commitment: The Evolution of Institutions Governing Public Choice in Seventeenth-Century England'. *Journal of Economic History* 49 (4): pp. 803–32.

Norton, Claire. 2013. 'Blurring the Boundaries: Intellectual and Cultural Interactions between the Eastern and Western; Christian and Muslim Worlds'. In *The Renaissance and the Ottoman World*, edited by Anna Contadini and Claire Norton, pp. 3–21. Farnham, Surrey: Ashgate.

Nye, Joseph S. 1988. 'US-Soviet Cooperation in a Nonproliferation Regime'. In *US-Soviet Security Cooperation: Achievements, Failures, Lessons*, edited by Alexander L. George, Philip J. Farley, and Alexander Dallin, pp. 336–52. New York: Oxford University Press.

O'Brien, Patrick. 1984. 'Europe in the World Economy'. In *The Expansion of International Society*, edited by Hedley Bull and Adam Watson, pp. 43–60. Oxford: Clarendon Press.

O'Hagan, Jacinta. 2002. *Conceptualizing the West in International Relations: From Spengler to Said.* Houndmills, Basingstoke: Palgrave.

Ohlander, Ann-Sofie. 2000. *Staten var en man: om kvinnor och män i statens tjänst i historien.* Stockholm: utvecklingsrådet för den statliga sektorn.

Okonjo, Kamene. 1976. 'The Dual-Sex Political System in Operation: Igbo Women and Community Politics in Midwestern Nigeria'. In *Women in Africa: Studies in Social and Economic Change*, edited by Nancy J. Hafkin and Edna G. Bay, pp. 45–58. Palo Alto, CA: Stanford University Press.

Oliver, Robert T. 1959. 'The Confucian Rhetorical Tradition in Korea during the Yi Dynasty 1392–1910'. *Quarterly Journal of Speech* 45 (4): pp. 363–73.

Onuf, Nicholas. 2002. 'Institutions, Intentions and International Relations'. *Review of International Studies* 28 (2): pp. 211–28.

Onuma, Yasuaki. 2000. 'When was the Law of International Society Born? An Inquiry of the History of International Law from an Intercivilizational Perspective'. *Journal of the History of International Law* 2 (1): pp. 1–66.

Onuma, Yasuaki. 2010. *A Transcivilizational Perspective on International Law*. Leiden: Brill.

Orange, Claudia. 2001. *The Story of a Treaty*. Wellington: Bridget Williams Books.

Osborne, George. 2010. 'Chancellor George Osborne's Mansion House Speech'. London, 16 June, <http://www.telegraph.co.uk/finance/economics/8578168/Chancellor-George-Osbornes-Mansion-House-speech-in-full.html>.

O'Shea, John M., Ashley K. Lemke, Elizabeth P. Sonnenburg, Robert G. Reynolds, and Brian D. Abbott. 2014. 'A 9,000-Year-Old Caribou Hunting Structure Beneath Lake Huron'. *Proceedings of the National Academy of Sciences of the United States of America* 111 (19): pp. 6911–15.

Oyewùmí, Oyèrónké. 1997. *The Invention of Women: Making an African Sense of Western Gender Discourses*. Minneapolis, MI: University of Minnesota Press.

Pagden, Anthony. 1993. *European Encounters with the New World: From Renaissance to Romanticism*. New Haven, CT: Yale University Press.

Pagden, Anthony. 1995. *Lords of All the World: Ideologies of Empire in Spain, Britain and France, c.1500–c.1800*. New Haven, CT: Yale University Press.

Pagden, Anthony. 2009. *Worlds at War: The 2,500-Year Struggle between East and West*. New York: Random House.

Pagden, Anthony. 2011. 'The Challenge of the New'. In *The Oxford Handbook of the Atlantic World: 1450–1850*, edited by Nicholas Canny and Philip Morgan, pp. 449–62. Oxford: Oxford University Press.

Pagden, Anthony. 2012. 'Conquest and the Just War: The "School of Salamanca" and the "Affair of the Indies"'. In *Empire and Modern Political Thought*, edited by Sankar Muthu, pp. 30–60. Cambridge: Cambridge University Press.

Page, Mark, and J. E. Spence. 2011. 'Open Secrets Questionably Arrived At: The Impact of WikiLeaks on Diplomacy'. *Defence Studies* 11 (2): pp. 234–43.

Pahuja, Sundhya. 2011. *Decolonising International Law: Development, Economic Growth and the Politics of Universality*. Cambridge: Cambridge University Press.

Pahuja, Sundhya. Forthcoming. 'Changing the World: The Ethical Impulse and International Law'. In *Who's Afraid of International Law?* edited by Raimond Gaita and Gerry Simpson. Melbourne: Monash University Publishing.

Pakenham, Thomas. 1991. *The Scramble for Africa: White Man's Conquest of the Dark Continent from 1876 to 1912*. London: Abacus.

Palliser, Michael. 1984. 'Diplomacy Today'. In *The Expansion of International Society*, edited by Hedley Bull and Adam Watson, pp. 371–85. Oxford: Clarendon Press.

Parkman, Francis. 1884. 'Some of the Reasons against Woman Suffrage'. Albany, NY: Women's Anti-Suffrage Association of the Third Judicial District of the State of New York.

Parpart, Jane L. 1988. 'Women and the State in Africa'. In *The Precarious Balance: State and Society in Africa*, edited by Donald Rothchild and Naomi Chazan, pp. 208–30. Boulder, CO: Westview Press.

Parry, J. H. 1981. *The Discovery of the Sea*. Berkeley, CA: University of California Press.

Patten, Alan. 2014. *Equal Recognition: The Moral Foundations of Minority Rights.* Princeton, NJ: Princeton University Press.

Pauly, Louis W. 1997. *Who Elected the Bankers? Surveillance and Control in the World Economy.* Ithaca, NY: Cornell University Press.

Pedersen, Susan. 2015. *The Guardians: The League of Nations and the Crisis of Empire.* Oxford: Oxford University Press.

Pejcinovic, Lacy. 2013. *War in International Society.* Abingdon, Oxon: Routledge.

Peking Review. 1974. 'United Nations: Expulsion of South African Racist Regime Demanded'. 17, 8 November.

Peking Review. 1976. 'Statement by Chinese Foreign Ministry Spokesman: Condemning South African Authorities for Suppression of Azanian People'. 27, 2 July.

People's Republic of China. 2011. 'Full Text: China's Peaceful Development'. Information Office of the State Council, Beijing, September, <http://www.gov.cn/english/official/2011-09/06/content_1941354_5.htm>.

Perham, Margery. 1962. *The Colonial Reckoning: The End of Imperial Rule in Africa in the Light of British Experience.* London: Collins.

Perlmutter, David D. 2005. 'Photojournalism and Foreign Affairs'. *Orbis* 49 (1): pp. 109–22.

Peyrefitte, Alain. 1993. *The Collision of Two Civilisations: The British Expedition to China, 1792-4.* London: Harvill.

Philbrick, Nathaniel. 2006. *Mayflower: A Voyage to War.* Hammersmith: Harper Press.

Phillips, Andrew. 2011. *War, Religion and Empire: The Transformation of International Orders.* Cambridge: Cambridge University Press.

Phillips, Andrew. 2012. 'Saving Civilization from Empire: Belligerency, Pacifism and the Two Faces of Civilization during the Second Opium War'. *European Journal of International Relations* 18 (1): pp. 5–27.

Phillips, Andrew. 2014a. 'Civilising Missions and the Rise of International Hierarchies in Early Modern Asia'. *Millennium: Journal of International Studies* 42 (3): pp. 697–717.

Phillips, Andrew. 2014b. 'The Islamic State's Challenge to International Order'. *Australian Journal of International Affairs* 68 (5): pp. 495–8.

Phillips, Andrew. 2016. 'Global IR Meets Global History: Sovereignty, Modernity, and the International System's Expansion in the Indian Ocean Region'. *International Studies Review* 18 (1): pp. 62–77.

Phillips, Andrew, and J. C. Sharman. 2015. *International Order in Diversity: War, Trade and Rule in the Indian Ocean.* Cambridge: Cambridge University Press.

Philpott, Daniel. 2001. *Revolutions in Sovereignty: How Ideas Shaped Modern International Relations.* Princeton, NJ: Princeton University Press.

Pike, Warburton. 1892. *Journeys to the Barren Grounds of Northern Canada through the Subarctic Forests.* London: Macmillan.

Pirenne, Henri. 1956. *Economic and Social History of Medieval Europe.* New York: Harcourt Brace Jovanovich.

Piscatori, James. 1984. 'Islam in the International Order'. In *The Expansion of International Society,* edited by Hedley Bull and Adam Watson, pp. 309–21. Oxford: Clarendon Press.

Pitts, Jennifer. 2005. *A Turn to Empire: The Rise of Imperial Liberalism in Britain and France*. Princeton, NJ: Princeton University Press.

Pitts, Jennifer. 2013. 'Intervention and Sovereign Equality: Legacies of Vattel'. In *Just and Unjust Interventions: European Thinkers from Vitoria to Mill*, edited by Stefano Recchia and Jennifer M. Welsh, pp. 132–53. Cambridge: Cambridge University Press.

Pomeranz, Kenneth. 2000. *The Great Divergence: China, Europe, and the Making of the Modern World Economy*. Princeton, NJ: Princeton University Press.

Pope John Paul II. 2001. 'In Quest of Dialogue with China'. *Fidelio* 10 (3), <http://www.schillerinstitute.org/fid_97–01/013_invite_dialogue_JPII.html>.

Porter, David. 2001. *Ideographia: The Chinese Cipher in Early Modern Europe*. Stanford, CA: Stanford University Press.

Poster, Mark. 2001. *What's the Matter with the Internet?* Minneapolis, MN: University of Minnesota Press.

Pouliot, Vincent, and Jean-Philippe Thérien. 2015. 'The Politics of Inclusion: Changing Patterns in the Governance of International Security'. *Review of International Studies* 41 (2): pp. 211–37.

Prange, Sebastian R. 2008. 'Scholars and the Sea: A Historiography of the Indian Ocean'. *History Compass* 6 (5): pp. 1382–93.

Prashad, Vijay. 2007. *The Darker Nations: A People's History of the Third World*. New York: The New Press.

Prashad, Vijay. 2014. *The Poorer Nations: A Possible History of the Global South*. London: Verso.

Protocol I. 1977. Protocol Additional to the Geneva Conventions of 12 August 1949, and Relating to the Protection of Victims of International Armed Conflicts Protocol I, 8 June.

Protocol II. 1977. Protocol Additional to the Geneva Conventions of 12 August 1949, and Relating to the Protection of Victims of Non-International Armed Conflicts Protocol II, 8 June.

Purdue, Peter C. 2005. *China Marches West: The Qing Conquest of Central Eurasia*. Cambridge, MA: Belknap Press of Harvard University Press.

Purdue, Peter C. 2009. 'China and Other Colonial Empires'. *Journal of American-East Asian Relations* 16 (1–2): pp. 85–103.

Purvis, Thomas L. 2003. 'The Seven Years' War and its Political Legacy'. In *A Companion to the American Revolution*, edited by Jack P. Greene and J. R. Pole, pp. 112–17. Oxford: Blackwell.

Quirk, Joel. 2011. *The Anti-Slavery Project: From the Slave Trade to Human Trafficking*. Philadelphia, PA: University of Pennsylvania Press.

Quirk, Joel, and David Richardson. 2014. 'Europeans, Africans and the Atlantic World, 1450–1850'. In *International Orders in the Early Modern World: Before the Rise of the West*, edited by Shogo Suzuki, Yongjin Zhang, and Joel Quirk, pp. 138–58. Abingdon, Oxon: Routledge.

Raby, Julian. 1982. 'A Sultan of Paradox: Mehmed the Conqueror as a Patron of the Arts'. *Oxford Art Journal* 5 (1): pp. 3–8.

Rachman, Gideon. 2012. 'Democracy Loses in Struggle to Save Euro'. *Financial Times*, 10 September.

Rae, Heather. 2002. *State Identities and the Homogenisation of Peoples*. Cambridge: Cambridge University Press.

Ralph, Jason, and Adrian Gallagher. 2015. 'Legitimacy Faultlines in International Society: The Responsibility to Protect and Prosecute after Libya'. *Review of International Studies* 41 (3): pp. 553–73.

Ratner, Steven R., and Jason S. Abrams. 2001. *Accountability for Human Rights Atrocities in International Law: Beyond the Nuremberg Legacy*. Oxford: Oxford University Press.

Rawls, John. 1999. *The Law of Peoples: With 'The Idea of Public Reason Revisited'*. Cambridge, MA: Harvard University Press.

Ray, James Lee. 1989. 'The Abolition of Slavery and the End of International War'. *International Organization* 43 (3): pp. 405–39.

Reid, Anthony. 1988. 'Female Roles in Pre-Colonial South East Asia'. *Modern Asian Studies* 22 (3): pp. 629–45.

Reid, Anthony. 1993. 'Introduction: A Time and a Place'. In *South East Asia in the Early Modern Era: Trade, Power, and Belief*, edited by Anthony Reid, pp. 1–19. Ithaca, NY: Cornell University Press.

Reid, Anthony. 2010. 'Islam in South-East Asia and the Indian Ocean Littoral, 1500–1800: Expansion, Polarisation, Synthesis'. In *The New Cambridge History of Islam*, vol. 3, The Eastern Islamic World, Eleventh to Eighteenth Centuries, edited by David O. Morgan and Anthony Reid, pp. 427–69. New York: Cambridge University Press.

Reus-Smit, Christian. 1996. 'The Normative Structure of International Society'. In *Earthly Goods: Environmental Change and Social Justice*, edited by Fen Osler Hampson and Judith Reppy, pp. 96–121. Ithaca, NY: Cornell University Press.

Reus-Smit, Christian. 1999. *The Moral Purpose of the State: Culture, Social Identity, and Institutional Rationality in International Relations*. Princeton, NJ: Princeton University Press.

Reus-Smit, Christian. 2001. 'Human Rights and the Social Construction of Sovereignty'. *Review of International Studies* 27 (4): pp. 519–38.

Reus-Smit, Christian. 2005. 'Liberal Hierarchy and the Licence to Use Force'. *Review of International Studies* 31 (S1): pp. 71–92.

Reus-Smit, Christian. 2011. 'Struggles for Individual Rights and the Expansion of the International System'. *International Organization* 65 (2): pp. 207–42.

Reus-Smit, Christian. 2013a. *Individual Rights and the Making of the International System*. Cambridge: Cambridge University Press.

Reus-Smit, Christian. 2013b. 'The Liberal International Order Reconsidered'. In *After Liberalism? The Future of Liberalism in International Relations*, edited by Rebekka Friedman, Kevork Oskanian, and Ramon Pacheco Pardo, pp. 167–86. London: Palgrave Macmillan.

Reuterskiöld, Carl Axel. 1911. *Politisk rösträtt för kvinnor: utredning anbefalld genom nådigt beslut den 30 april 1909. 1. Om utvecklingen och tillämpningen i utlandet af idéen om kvinnans politiska rösträtt*. Uppsala: Almqvist and Wiksell.

Reynolds, Henry. 2013. *Forgotten War*. Sydney: NewSouth Publishing.

Richey, Lisa Ann. 2015. *Celebrity Humanitarianism and North–South Relations: Politics, Place and Power*. New York: Routledge.

Risse, Thomas. 2000. '"Let's Argue!": Communicative Action in World Politics'. *International Organization* 54 (1): pp. 1–39.

Risse, Thomas, Stephen C. Ropp, and Kathryn Sikkink, eds. 1999. *The Power of Human Rights: International Norms and Domestic Change*. Cambridge: Cambridge University Press.

Risse, Thomas, Stephen C. Ropp, and Kathryn Sikkink, eds. 2013. *The Persistent Power of Human Rights: From Commitment to Compliance*. Cambridge: Cambridge University Press.

Rittich, Kerry. 2002. *Recharacterizing Restructuring: Law, Distribution and Gender in Market Reform*. The Hague: Kluwer.

Rixen, Thomas. 2013. 'Why Reregulation After the Crisis Is Feeble: Shadow Banking, Offshore Financial Centers, and Jurisdictional Competition'. *Regulation and Governance* 7 (4): pp. 435–59.

Robinson, Piers. 2002. *The CNN Effect: The Myth of News, Foreign Policy and Intervention*. New York: Routledge.

Rockwell, Stephen J. 2010. *Indian Affairs and the Administrative State in the Nineteenth Century*. Cambridge: Cambridge University Press.

Rogoff, Kenneth. 2012. 'Financial Regulation Isn't Fixed, It's Just More Complicated'. *The Guardian*, 10 September.

Roht-Arriaza, Naomi. 2005. *The Pinochet Effect: Transnational Justice in the Age of Human Rights*. Philadelphia, PA: University of Pennsylvania Press.

Roht-Arriaza, Naomi, and Javier Mariezcurrena, eds. 2006. *Transitional Justice in the Twenty-First Century: Beyond Truth versus Justice*. Cambridge: Cambridge University Press.

Rosenberg, Justin. 1994. *The Empire of Civil Society: A Critique of the Realist Theory of International Relations*. London: Verso.

Ross, George. 1995. *Jacques Delors and European Integration*. Cambridge: Cambridge University Press.

Rousseau, David, and Karl Mueller. 1995. 'Peaceful Democrats or Pragmatic Realists? Revisiting the Iroquois League'. Paper presented to the American Political Science Association, annual meeting, Chicago, 3 September.

Rousseau, Jean-Jacques. 1974. *The Essential Rousseau: The Social Contract, Discourse on the Origin of Inequality, Discourse on the Arts and Sciences, The Creed of a Savoyard Priest*, trans. Lowell Bair. New York: Mentor.

Roy, Tirthankar. 2012. *India in the World Economy: From Antiquity to the Present*. New York: Cambridge University Press.

Ruan, Zongze. 2012. 'Responsible Protection: Building a Safer World'. *China International Studies* 34 (May/June).

Ruggie, John Gerard. 1982. 'International Regimes, Transactions, and Change: Embedded Liberalism in the Postwar Economic Order'. *International Organization* 36 (2): pp. 379–415.

Ruggie, John Gerard. 1983. 'Continuity and Transformation in the World Polity: Toward a Neorealist Synthesis'. *World Politics* 35 (2): pp. 261–85.

Ruggie, John Gerard. 1993a. 'Multilateralism: The Anatomy of an Institution'. In *Multilateralism Matters: The Theory and Praxis of an Institutional Form*, edited by John Gerard Ruggie, pp. 3–48. New York: Columbia University Press.

Ruggie, John Gerard. 1993b. 'Territoriality and Beyond: Problematizing Modernity in International Relations'. *International Organization* 47 (1): pp. 139–74.

Rupp, Leila J. 1997. *Worlds of Women: The Making of an International Women's Movement.* Princeton, NJ: Princeton University Press.

Ryan, Michael T. 1981. 'Assimilating New Worlds in the Sixteenth and Seventeenth Centuries'. *Comparative Studies in Society and History* 23 (4): pp. 519–38.

Sabel, Charles F., and Jonathan Zeitlin, eds. 2010. *Experimentalist Governance in the European Union: Towards a New Architecture.* Oxford: Oxford University Press.

Sacks, Karen. 1982. 'An Overview of Women and Power in Africa'. In *Perspectives on Power: Women in Africa, Asia and Latin America,* edited by Jean F. O'Barr, pp. 1–120. Durham, NC: Center for International Studies, Duke University.

Sahin, Emrah. 2012. 'Ottoman Institutions, Millet System: 1250 to 1920: Middle East'. In *Cultural Sociology of the Middle East, Asia, & Africa: An Encyclopedia,* vol. 1, edited by Andrea L. Stanton, pp. 181–3. Thousand Oaks, CA: Sage.

Said, Edward W. 1978. *Orientalism.* New York: Vintage Books.

Salisbury, Neal. 1996. 'The Indians' Old World: Native Americans and the Coming of Europeans'. *William and Mary Quarterly* 53 (3): pp. 435–58.

Salter, Mark B. 2002. *Barbarians and Civilization in International Relations.* London: Pluto Press.

Saunders, David. 1997. *Anti-Lawyers: Religion and the Critics of Law and State.* London: Routledge.

Scammel, G. V. 1981. *The World Encompassed: The First European Maritime Empires c. 800–1650.* Berkeley, CA: University of California Press.

Schilling, Heinz. 2008. *Early Modern European Civilization and its Political and Cultural Dynamism.* Lebanon, NH: University Press of New England.

Schmitt, Carl. 2006. *The Nomos of the Earth in the International Law of the Jus Publicum Europaeum,* trans. G. L. Ulmen. New York: Telos Press.

Schmitz, Hans Peter, and Kathryn Sikkink. 2013. 'International Human Rights'. In *Handbook of International Relations,* edited by Walter Carlsnaes, Thomas Risse, and Beth A. Simmons, pp. 827–51, 2nd ed. London: Sage.

Schumann, Matt, and Karl Schweizer. 2008. *The Seven Years War: A Transatlantic History.* London: Routledge.

Schwarzer, Daniela. 2009. 'The Euro Area Crises, Shifting Power Relations and Institutional Change in the European Union'. *Global Policy* 3 (December): pp. 28–41.

Schweller, Randall. 2011. 'Emerging Powers in an Age of Disorder'. *Global Governance: A Review of Multilateralism and International Organizations* 17 (3): pp. 285–97.

Scott, H. M. 2001. *The Emergence of the Eastern Powers, 1756–1775.* Cambridge: Cambridge University Press.

Scott, Hamish. 2011. 'The Seven Years War and Europe's Ancien Régime'. *War in History* 18 (4): pp. 419–55.

Scott, James, ed. 1931. *The International Conferences of American States, 1889–1928: A Collection of the Conventions, Recommendations, Resolutions, Reports and Motions Adopted by the First Six International Conferences of the American States.* New York: Oxford University Press.

Scott, James Brown. 1934. *The Spanish Origin of International Law: Francisco de Vitoria and his Law of Nations.* Oxford: Clarendon Press.

Scott, John. 2011. *Conceptualising the Social World: Principles of Sociological Analysis.* Cambridge: Cambridge University Press.

Scott, W. Richard. 1995. *Institutions and Organizations.* London: Sage.

Searle, John R. 1995. *The Construction of Social Reality.* New York: Free Press.

Sen, Amartya. 1997. 'Human Rights and Asian Values'. *New Republic,* 14–21 July: pp. 33–40.

Seton-Watson, Hugh. 1960. *Neither War nor Peace: The Struggle for Power in the Postwar World.* London: Methuen.

Shaffer, Lynda. 1995. *Maritime South East Asia to 1500.* Armonk, NY: M. E. Sharpe.

Sharman, J. C. 2013. 'International Hierarchies and Contemporary Imperial Governance: A Tale of Three Kingdoms'. *European Journal of International Relations* 19 (2): pp. 189–207.

Shaw, Karena. 2008. *Indigeneity and Political Theory: Sovereignty and the Limits of the Political.* New York: Routledge.

Shennan, J. H. 1995. *International Relations in Europe, 1689–1789.* London: Routledge.

Shestack, Jerome J. 1998. 'The Philosophic Foundations of Human Rights'. *Human Rights Quarterly* 20 (2): pp. 201–34.

Shilliam, Robbie, ed. 2011. *International Relations and Non-Western Thought: Imperialism, Colonialism and Investigations of Global Modernity.* Abingdon, Oxon: Routledge.

Shoemaker, Nancy. 1995. 'Introduction'. In *Negotiators of Change: Historical Perspectives on Native American Women,* edited by Nancy Shoemaker, pp. 1–25. New York: Routledge.

Shue, Henry. 1996. *Basic Rights: Subsistence, Affluence, and US Foreign Policy,* 2nd ed. Princeton, NJ: Princeton University Press.

Sikkink, Kathryn. 1993. 'Human Rights, Principled Issue-Networks, and Sovereignty in Latin America'. *International Organization* 47 (3): pp. 411–41.

Sikkink, Kathryn. 2004. *Mixed Signals: US Human Rights Policy and Latin America.* Ithaca, NY: Cornell University Press.

Sikkink, Kathryn. 2011. *The Justice Cascade: How Human Rights Prosecutions Are Changing World Politics.* New York: Norton.

Sikkink, Kathryn. 2014. 'Latin American Countries as Norm Protagonists of the Idea of International Human Rights'. *Global Governance* 20 (3): pp. 389–404.

Simmons, Beth A. 2009. *Mobilizing for Human Rights: International Law in Domestic Politics.* Cambridge: Cambridge University Press.

Simmons, Beth A. 2014. 'The Future of the Human Rights Movement'. *Ethics and International Affairs* 28 (2): pp. 183–96.

Simmons, Beth Ann, and Allison Danner. 2010. 'Credible Commitments and the International Criminal Court'. *International Organization* 64 (2): pp. 225–56.

Simms, Brendan. 2007. *Three Victories and a Defeat: The Rise and Fall of the First British Empire.* London: Penguin Books.

Simms, Brendan. 2014. *Europe: The Struggle for Supremacy, from 1453 to the Present.* London: Penguin Books.

Simpson, Gerry. 2001. 'Two Liberalisms'. *European Journal of International Law* 12 (3): pp. 537–71.

Simpson, Gerry. 2004. *Great Powers and Outlaw States: Unequal Sovereigns in the International Legal Order.* Cambridge: Cambridge University Press.

Simpson, Gerry. 2012. 'International Law in Diplomatic History'. In *The Cambridge Companion to International Law,* edited by James Crawford and Martti Koskenniemi, pp. 25–46. Cambridge: Cambridge University Press.

Simpson, Gerry. 2015. 'The Sentimental Life of International Law'. *London Review of International Law* 3 (1): pp. 3–29.

Simpson, Gerry. 2016. 'Humanity, Law, Force'. In *Strengthening the Rule of Law through the UN Security Council,* edited by Jeremy Farrall and Hilary Charlesworth, pp. 72–86. Abingdon, Oxon: Routledge.

Simpson, Gerry. Forthcoming. 'James Lorimer and the Character of Sovereigns: The *Institutes* as 21st Century Treatise'. *European Journal of International Law.*

Skidmore, David A. 2011. *The Unilateralist Temptation in American Foreign Policy.* New York: Routledge.

Skinner, Quentin. 2000. *Machiavelli: A Very Short Introduction.* Oxford: Oxford University Press.

Slaughter, Anne-Marie. 2004. *A New World Order.* Princeton, NJ: Princeton University Press.

Slaughter, Anne-Marie. 2006. 'A New UN For a New Century'. *Fordham Law Review* 74 (6): pp. 2961–70.

Sluga, Glenda. 2013. *Internationalism in the Age of Nationalism.* Philadelphia, PA: University of Pennsylvania Press.

Smith, Adam. 1993. *An Inquiry into the Nature and Causes of the Wealth of Nations,* ed. Kathryn Sutherland. Oxford: Oxford University Press.

Smith, Heather A., and Gary N. Wilson. 2009. 'Inuit Transnational Activism: Cooperation and Resistance in the Face of Global Change'. In *Indigenous Diplomacies,* edited by J. Marshall Beier, pp. 171–85. New York: Palgrave Macmillan.

Smith, Marian W. 1951. 'American Indian Warfare'. *Transactions of the New York Academy of Sciences,* 2nd series, 13 (8): pp. 348–65.

Smith, Michael E. 2013. *The Aztecs,* 3rd ed. Malden, MA: Wiley-Blackwell.

Smith, Paul Jakov. 2004. 'Eurasian Transformations of the Tenth to Thirteenth Centuries: The View from Song China, 960–1279'. *Medieval Encounters* 10 (1): pp. 279–308.

Snetkov, Aglaya, and Marc Lanteigne. 2015. '"The Loud Dissenter and its Cautious Partner": Russia, China, Global Governance and Humanitarian Intervention'. *International Relations of the Asia-Pacific* 15 (1): pp. 113–46.

Snyder, Jack, and Leslie Vinjamuri. 2003/4. 'Trials and Errors: Principle and Pragmatism in Strategies of International Justice'. *International Security* 28 (3): pp. 5–44.

Soguk, Nevzat. 2009. 'Communication/Excommunication: Transversal Indigenous Diplomacies in Global Politics'. In *Indigenous Diplomacies,* edited by J. Marshall Beier, pp. 29–46. New York: Palgrave Macmillan.

Sood, Gagan D. S. 2011. 'Circulation and Exchange in Islamicate Eurasia: A Regional Approach to the Early Modern World'. *Past & Present* 212 (1): pp. 113–62.

Sørensen, Georg. 1999. 'Sovereignty: Change and Continuity in a Fundamental Institution'. *Political Studies* 47 (3): pp. 590–604.

Spanu, Maja. 2015. 'The Idea of Self-Determination: Hierarchy and Order after Empire'. Doctoral Dissertation, European University Institute, Florence.

Spence, Jonathan D. 1998. *The Chan's Great Continent: China in Western Minds*. New York and London: Allen Lane.

Spengler, Oswald. 1991. *The Decline of the West*, ed. Arthur Helps and Helmut Werner, trans. Charles F. Atkinson. New York: Oxford University Press.

Spiegel, Peter. 2015. 'Eurozone Fears a Deal with Tsipras More Than Grexit'. *Financial Times*, 6 January.

Spruyt, Hendrik. 1994. *The Sovereign State and Its Competitors: An Analysis of Systems Change*. Princeton, NJ: Princeton University Press.

Spruyt, Hendrik. 2005. *Ending Empire: Contested Sovereignty and Territorial Partition*. Ithaca, NY: Cornell University Press.

Sriram, Chandra Lekha. 2003. 'Revolutions in Accountability: New Approaches to Past Abuses'. *American University International Law Review* 19 (2): pp. 301–429.

Starobinski, Jean. 2009. 'The Word *Civilization*'. In *Civilization: Critical Concepts in Political Science*, vol. 1, The Origins and Meaning of Civilization, edited by Brett Bowden, pp. 151–85. Abingdon, Oxon: Routledge.

Stedman, Stephen John. 2007. 'UN Transformation in an Era of Soft Balancing'. *International Affairs* 83 (5): pp. 933–44.

Steele, Brent J. 2005. 'Ontological Security and the Power of Self-Identity: British Neutrality and the American Civil War'. *Review of International Studies* 31 (3): pp. 519–40.

Steinberg, Philip E. 2001. *The Social Construction of the Ocean*. Cambridge: Cambridge University Press.

Stivachtis, Yannis A. 2006. 'Democracy, the Highest Stage of "Civilised" Statehood'. *Global Dialogue* 8 (3–4): pp. 101–12.

Stivachtis, Yannis A. 2008. 'Civilization and International Society: The Case of European Union Expansion'. *Contemporary Politics* 14 (1): pp. 71–89.

Strang, David. 1990. 'From Dependency to Sovereignty: An Event History Analysis of Decolonization 1870–1987'. *American Sociological Review* 55 (6): pp. 846–60.

Strang, David. 1991a. 'Anomaly and Commonplace in European Political Expansion: Realist and Institutionalist Accounts'. *International Organization* 45 (2): pp. 143–62.

Strang, David. 1991b. 'Global Patterns of Decolonization, 1500–1987'. *International Studies Quarterly* 35 (4): pp. 429–54.

Strange, Susan. 1970. 'International Economics and International Relations: A Case of Mutual Neglect'. *International Affairs* 46 (2): pp. 304–15.

Strange, Susan. 1994. *States and Markets*, 2nd ed. London: Pinter Publishers.

Strayer, Joseph R. 1970. *On the Medieval Origins of the Modern State*. Princeton, NJ: Princeton University Press.

Stuenkel, Oliver, and Marcos Tourinho. 2014. 'Regulating Intervention: Brazil and the Responsibility to Protect'. *Conflict, Security & Development* 14 (4): pp. 379–402.

Styrkársdóttir, Audur. 1998. *From Feminism to Class Politics: The Rise and Decline of Women's Politics in Reykjavik, 1908–1922*. Umeå: Statsvetenskapliga institutionen, Umeå Universitet.

Subrahmanyam, Sanjay. 1997. 'Connected Histories: Notes towards a Reconfiguration of Early Modern Eurasia'. *Modern Asian Studies* 31 (3): pp. 735–62.

Subrahmanyam, Sanjay. 2005. 'On World Historians in the Sixteenth Century'. *Representations* 91 (1): pp. 26–57.

Subrahmanyam, Sanjay. 2006. 'A Tale of Three Empires: Mughals, Ottomans, and Habsburgs in a Comparative Context'. *Common Knowledge* 12 (1): pp. 66–92.

Subrahmanyam, Sanjay. 2007. 'Holding the World in Balance: The Connected Histories of the Iberian Overseas Empires, 1500–1640'. *American Historical Review* 112 (5): pp. 1359–85.

Suganami, Hidemi. 1984. 'Japan's Entry into International Society'. In *The Expansion of International Society*, edited by Hedley Bull and Adam Watson, pp. 185–99. Oxford: Clarendon Press.

Suganami, Hidemi. 2014. 'The Historical Development of the English School'. In *Guide to the English School in International Studies*, edited by Cornelia Navari and Daniel Green, pp. 7–24. Chichester, West Sussex: Wiley-Blackwell.

Suzuki, Shogo. 2009. *Civilization and Empire: China and Japan's Encounter with European International Society*. Abingdon, Oxon: Routledge.

Suzuki, Shogo. 2014. 'Journey to the West: China Debates Its "Great Power" Identity'. *Millennium: Journal of International Studies* 42 (3): pp. 632–50.

Suzuki, Shogo, Yongjin Zhang, and Joel Quirk, eds. 2014. *International Orders in the Early Modern World: Before the Rise of the West*. Abingdon, Oxon: Routledge.

Swidler, Ann. 1986. 'Culture in Action: Symbols and Strategies'. *American Sociological Review* 51 (2): pp. 273–86.

Sylvester, Christine. 2013. 'Experiencing the End and Afterlives of International Relations/Theory'. *European Journal of International Relations* 19 (3): pp. 609–26.

Tambiah, Stanley J. 2013. 'The Galactic Polity in South East Asia'. *Journal of Ethnographic Theory* 3 (3): pp. 503–34.

Taylor, Craig. 2006. 'The Salic Law, French Queenship, and the Defense of Women in the Late Middle Ages'. *French Historical Studies* 29 (4): pp. 543–64.

Taylor, Charles. 1989. *Sources of the Self: The Making of the Modern Identity*. Cambridge, MA: Harvard University Press.

Taylor, K. W. 1991. 'Racism in Canadian Immigration Policy'. *Canadian Ethnic Studies* 23 (1): pp. 1–20.

Teitel, Ruti. 2011. *Humanity's Law*. Oxford: Oxford University Press.

Terretta, Meredith, 2012. '"We Had Been Fooled into Thinking that the UN Watches over the Entire World": Human Rights, UN Trust Territories, and Africa's Decolonization'. *Human Rights Quarterly* 34 (2): pp. 329–60.

Tesón, Fernando R. 1992. 'The Kantian Theory of International Law'. *Columbia Law Review* 92 (1): pp. 53–102.

Teubner, Gunther, ed. 1997. *Global Law without a State*. Dartmouth: Aldershot.

Teubner, Gunther, and Peter Korth. 2012. 'Two Kinds of Legal Pluralism: Collision of Transnational Regimes in the Double Fragmentation of World Society'. In *Regime Interaction in International Law: Facing Fragmentation*, edited by Margaret A. Young, pp. 23–54. Cambridge: Cambridge University Press.

Thakur, Ramesh. 2006. *The United Nations, Peace and Security: From Collective Security to the Responsibility to Protect*. Cambridge: Cambridge University Press.

Thomas, Daniel C. 2001. *The Helsinki Effect: International Norms, Human Rights, and the Demise of Communism*. Princeton, NJ: Princeton University Press.

Thomas, Martin, and Andrew Thompson. 2014. 'Empire and Globalisation: From "High Imperialism" to Decolonisation'. *International Historical Review* 36 (1): pp. 142–70.

Thomas, Nicholas. 1994. *Colonialism's Culture: Anthropology, Travel and Government*. Carlton, Victoria: Melbourne University Press.

Thomson, Janice E. 1996. *Mercenaries, Pirates, and Sovereigns: State-Building and Extraterritorial Violence in Early Modern Europe*. Princeton, NJ: Princeton University Press.

Tilly, Charles. 1984. *Big Structures, Large Processes, Huge Comparisons*. New York: Russell Sage Foundation.

Tilly, Charles. 1985. 'War Making and State Making as Organized Crime'. In *Bringing the State Back In*, edited by Peter Evans, Dietrich Rueschemeyer, and Theda Skocpol, pp. 169–91. Cambridge: Cambridge University Press.

Tilly, Charles. 2005. *Trust and Rule*. New York: Cambridge University Press.

Toby, Ronald P. 1991. *State and Diplomacy in Early Modern Japan: Asia in the Development of the Tokugawa Bakufu*. Stanford, CA: Stanford University Press.

Todorov, Tzvetan. 1984. *The Conquest of America: The Question of the Other*. New York: Harper & Row.

Towns, Ann. 2009. 'The Status of Women as a Standard of "Civilization"'. *European Journal of International Relations* 15 (4): pp. 681–706.

Towns, Ann. 2010a. 'The Inter-American Commission of Women and Women's Suffrage, 1920–1945'. *Journal of Latin American Studies* 42 (4): pp. 779–807.

Towns, Ann E. 2010b. *Women and States: Norms and Hierarchies in International Society*. Cambridge: Cambridge University Press.

Towns, Ann E. 2012. 'Norms and Social Hierarchies: Understanding Policy Diffusion "From Below"'. *International Organization* 66 (2): pp. 179–209.

Towns, Ann E. 2014. 'Carrying the Load of Civilisation: The Status of Women and Challenged Hierarchies'. *Millennium: Journal of International Studies* 42 (3): pp. 595–613.

Tracy, James D., ed. 1990. *The Rise of Merchant Empires: Long-Distance Trade in the Early Modern World 1350–1750*. New York: Cambridge University Press.

Tracy, James D., ed. 1991. *The Political Economy of Merchant Empires: State Power and World Trade, 1350–1750*. New York: Cambridge University Press.

Triffin, Robert. 1960. *Gold and the Dollar Crisis: The Future of Convertibility*. New Haven, CT: Yale University Press.

Tsygankov, Andrei P. 2008. 'Self and Other in International Relations Theory: Learning from Russian Civilizational Debates'. *International Studies Review* 10 (4): pp. 762–75.

Tuck, Richard. 1999. *The Rights of War and Peace: Political Thought and the International Order from Grotius to Kant*. Oxford: Oxford University Press.

Tully, James. 1995. *Strange Multiplicity: Constitutionalism in an Age of Diversity*. Cambridge: Cambridge University Press.

Turkle, Sherry. 1995. *Life on the Screen: Identity in the Age of the Internet*. New York: Simon & Schuster.

UK Cabinet Office. 2008. *The National Security Strategy of the United Kingdom: Security in an Interdependent World*, Cm 7291. Norwich: Stationery Office.

Ullman, William. 1976. 'The Medieval Papal Court as an International Tribunal'. In *The Papacy and Political Ideas in the Middle Ages*, edited by William Ullman, pp. 365–71. London: Valorium Reprints.

UNGA (United Nations General Assembly). 1960. 'Declaration on the Granting of Independence to Colonial Countries and Peoples'. Resolution 1514, A/RES/15/1514, 14 December.

UNGA (United Nations General Assembly). 1965. 'Declaration on the Inadmissibility of Intervention in the Domestic Affairs of States and the Protection of their Independence and Sovereignty'. Resolution 2131, A/RES/20/2131, 21 December.

UNGA (United Nations General Assembly). 1970. 'Declaration on Principles of International Law Concerning Friendly Relations and Co-operation among States in Accordance with the Charter of the United Nations'. Resolution 2625, A/RES/25/2625, 24 October.

UNGA (United Nations General Assembly). 1981. 'Declaration on the Inadmissibility of Intervention and Interference in the Internal Affairs of States'. Resolution 36/103, A/RES/36/103, 9 December.

UNGA (United Nations General Assembly). 1990. 'Enhancing the Effectiveness of the Principle of Periodic and Genuine Elections'. Resolution 45/150, A/RES/45/150, 18 December.

UNGA (United Nations General Assembly). 1991a. 'Enhancing the Effectiveness of the Principle of Periodic and Genuine Elections'. Resolution 46/137, A/RES/46/137, 17 December.

UNGA (United Nations General Assembly). 1991b. 'Strengthening the Coordination of Humanitarian Emergency Assistance of the United Nations'. Resolution 46/182, A/RES/46/182, 19 December.

UNGA (United Nations General Assembly). 1991c. 'The Situation of Democracy and Human Rights in Haiti'. Resolution 46/7, A/RES/46/7, 11 October.

Unger, Roberto. 1987. *Plasticity into Power: Comparative-Historical Studies of the Institutional Conditions of Economic and Military Success*. New York: Cambridge University Press.

United Nations. 1946–7. *Yearbook of the United Nations*. New York: United Nations.

United Nations. 1952. *Yearbook of the United Nations*. New York: United Nations.

United Nations. 1960. *Yearbook of the United Nations*. New York: United Nations.

United Nations. 1961. *Yearbook of the United Nations*. New York: United Nations.

United Nations. 1963. *Yearbook of the United Nations*. New York: United Nations.

United Nations. 1977. *Yearbook of the United Nations*. New York: United Nations.

United Nations. 2005. 'World Summit Outcome Document'. A/RES/60/1, 16 September.

United Nations Economic and Social Council. 1967. Resolution 1235 XLII, 6 June.

United Nations Economic and Social Council. 1970. Resolution 1503 XLVIII, 27 May.

United Nations Economic and Social Council. 1998. 'Guiding Principles on Internal Displacement'. E/CN.4/1998/53/Add.2, 11 February.

United Nations Human Rights Office of the High Commissioner. 1993. 'Vienna Declaration and Programme of Action'. Adopted by the World Conference on Human Rights, Vienna, 25 June.

United Nations Office for the Coordination of Humanitarian Affairs. No date. 'Advocacy in Action', <http://www.unocha.org/what-we-do/advocacy/overview>.

United Nations Secretary-General. 1991. 'Report of the Secretary-General on the Work of the Organization'. A/46/1, 13 September.

United Nations Secretary-General. 1996. 'Emergency Assistance to the Sudan: Report of the Secretary-General'. A/51/326, 4 September.

United Nations Secretary-General. 1999. 'Report of the Secretary-General Pursuant to General Assembly Resolution 53/55: The Fall of Srebrenica'. A/54/549, 15 November.

United Nations Secretary-General. 2009. 'Implementing the Responsibility to Protect: Report of the Secretary-General'. A/63/677, 12 January.

United Nations Secretary-General. 2015. 'A Vital and Enduring Commitment: Implementing the Responsibility to Protect: Report of the Secretary-General'. A/69/981, 13 July.

UNSC (United Nations Security Council). 1977. 'Verbatim Record on South African Apartheid'. S/PV.2037, 25 October.

UNSC (United Nations Security Council). 1991. 'The Situation in Iraq'. Resolution 688, 5 April.

UNSC (United Nations Security Council). 1992. 'Verbatim Record of the Security Council Summit'. S/PV.3046, 31 January.

UNSC (United Nations Security Council). 1999. 'Report of the Independent Inquiry into the Actions of the United Nations during the 1994 Genocide in Rwanda'. S/1999/1257, 15 December.

UNSC (United Nations Security Council). 2000a. 'Children and Armed Conflict'. Resolution 1314, S/RES/1314, 11 August.

UNSC (United Nations Security Council). 2000b. 'Protection of Civilians in Armed Conflict'. Resolution 1296, S/RES/1296, 19 April.

UNSC (United Nations Security Council). 2000c. 'Women, Peace and Security'. Resolution 1325, S/RES/1325, 31 October.

Van Allen, Judith. 1976. '"Aba Riots" or Igbo "Women's War"? Ideology, Stratification, and the Invisibility of Women'. In *Women in Africa: Studies in Social and Economic Change*, edited by Nancy J. Hafkin and Edna G. Bay, pp. 59–86. Palo Alto, CA: Stanford University Press.

Van de Harr, Edwin. 2013. 'David Hume and Adam Smith on International Ethics and Humanitarian Intervention'. In *Just and Unjust Interventions: European Thinkers from Vitoria to Mill*, edited by Stefano Recchia and Jennifer M. Welsh, pp. 154–75. Cambridge: Cambridge University Press.

Van der Zwan, Natascha. 2014. 'Making Sense of Financialization'. *Socio-Economic Review* 12 (1): pp. 99–129.

Van Fraassen, Ch. F. '1992. Maluku en de Ambonse eilanden tot het midden van de 17e eeuw.: Socio-kosmische ordening en politieke verhoudingen'. In *Sedjarah Maluku*, edited by G. J. Knaap, W. Manuhutu, and H. Smeets, pp. 33–53. Amsterdam: Van Soeren and Co.

Van Ness, Peter, ed. 1999. *Debating Human Rights: Critical Essays from the United States and Asia*. New York: Routledge.

Vigezzi, Brunello. 2014. 'The British Committee and International Society: History and Theory'. In *Guide to the English School in International Studies*, edited by Cornelia Navari and Daniel Green, pp. 37–58. Chichester, West Sussex: Wiley-Blackwell.

Vigezzi, Bruno. 2005. *The British Committee on the Theory of International Politics (1954–1985): The Rediscovery of History*, trans. Ian Harvey. Milan: Edizioni Unicopli.

Vigneswaren, Darshan. 2014. 'A Corrupt International Society: How Britain Was Duped Into Its First Indian Conquest'. In *International Orders in the Early Modern World: Before the Rise of the West*, edited by Shogo Suzuki, Yongjing Zhang, and Joel Quirk, pp. 94–117. Abingdon, Oxon: Routledge.

Vignoles, Vivian L., Seth J. Schwartz, and Koen Luyckx. 2011. 'Introduction: Towards an Integrative View of Identity'. In *Handbook of Identity Theory and Research*, vol. 1, Structures and Processes, edited by Seth J. Schwartz, Koen Luyckx, and Vivian L. Vignoles, pp. 1–26. New York: Springer.

Vincent, R. J. 1974. *Nonintervention and International Order*. Princeton, NJ: Princeton University Press.

Vincent, R. J. 1984. 'Racial Equality'. In *The Expansion of International Society*, edited by Hedley Bull and Adam Watson, pp. 239–54. Oxford: Clarendon Press.

Vincent, R. J. 1986. *Human Rights and International Relations*. Cambridge: Cambridge University Press.

Vink, Markus P. M. 2007. 'Indian Ocean Studies and the "New Thalassology"'. *Journal of Global History* 2 (1): pp. 41–62.

Vitalis, Robert. 2000. 'The Graceful and Generous Liberal Gesture: Making Racism Invisible in American International Relations'. *Millennium: Journal of International Studies* 29 (2): pp. 331–56.

Voll, John. 1994. 'Islam as a Special World-System'. *Journal of World History* 5 (2): pp. 213–26.

Von Eschen, Penny M. 1997. *Race against Empire: Black Americans and Anticolonialism, 1937–1957*. Ithaca, NY: Cornell University Press.

wa Mutua, Makau. 1995. 'Why Redraw the Map of Africa: A Moral and Legal Inquiry'. *Michigan Journal of International Law* 16 (4): 1113–76.

Wade, Robert Hunter. 2014. 'Growth, Inequality, and Poverty: Evidence, Arguments, and Economists'. In *Global Political Economy*, edited by John Ravenhill, pp. 305–43, 4th ed. Oxford: Oxford University Press.

Waldron, Arthur. 1990. *The Great Wall of China: From History to Myth*. Cambridge: Cambridge University Press.

Walker, Neil, ed. 2006. *Sovereignty in Transition: Essays in European Law*. Oxford: Hart.

Walker, Thomas. 1893. *The Science of International Law*. London: C. J. Clay and Sons.

Wallerstein, Immanuel. 1974. *The Modern World-System*, vol. 1, Capitalist Agriculture and the Origins of the European World-Economy in the Sixteenth Century. Orlando, FL: Academic Press.

Wallerstein, Immanuel. 1980. *The Modern World-System*, vol. 2, Mercantilism and the Consolidation of the European World-Economy, 1600–1750. New York: Academic Press.

Waltz, Kenneth N. 1959. *Man, the State, and War: A Theoretical Analysis*. New York: Columbia University Press.

Waltz, Kenneth N. 1979. *Theory of International Politics*. New York: Random House.

Ward, Matthew C. 2012. 'Understanding Native American Alliances'. In *The Seven Years' War: Global Views*, edited by Mark H. Danley and Patrick J. Speelman, pp. 47–71. Leiden: Brill.

Watson, Adam. 1982. *Diplomacy: The Dialogue Between States*. London: Routledge.

Watson, Adam. 1984a. 'European International Society and its Expansion'. In *The Expansion of International Society*, edited by Hedley Bull and Adam Watson, pp. 13–32. Oxford: Clarendon Press.

Watson, Adam. 1984b. 'New States in the Americas'. In *The Expansion of International Society*, edited by Hedley Bull and Adam Watson, pp. 127–41. Oxford: Clarendon Press.

Watson, Adam. 1992. *The Evolution of International Society: A Comparative Historical Analysis*. London: Routledge.

Watson, Adam. 2007. *Hegemony and History*. Abingdon, Oxon: Routledge.

Weber, Max. 1994. *Weber: Political Writings*, ed. Peter Lassman, trans. Ronald Speirs. Cambridge: Cambridge University Press.

Weeramantry, Christopher G. 1997. 'Constitutional and Institutional Developments: The Function of the International Court of Justice in the Development of International Law'. *Leiden Journal of International Law* 10 (2): pp. 309–40.

Weibull, Jörgen. 1997. *Sveriges Historia*. Stockholm: Svenska Institutet.

Weiss, Thomas G. 2003. 'The Illusion of UN Security Council Reform', *Washington Quarterly* 26 (4): pp. 147–61.

Welsh, Jennifer, and Dominik Zaum. 2013. 'Legitimation and the UN Security Council'. In *Legitimating International Organizations*, edited by Dominik Zaum, pp. 65–87. Oxford: Oxford University Press.

Welsh, Jennifer M. 2013a. 'Edmund Burke and Intervention: Empire and Neighborhood'. In *Just and Unjust Interventions: European Thinkers from Vitoria to Mill*, edited by Stefano Recchia and Jennifer M. Welsh, pp. 219–36. Cambridge: Cambridge University Press.

Welsh, Jennifer M. 2013b. 'Norm Contestation and the Responsibility to Protect'. *Global Responsibility to Protect* 5 (4): pp. 365–96.

Wendt, Alexander. 1992. 'Anarchy is what States Make of It: The Social Construction of Power Politics'. *International Organization* 46 (2): pp. 391–425.

Wendt, Alexander. 1994. 'Collective Identity Formation and the International State'. *American Political Science Review* 88 (2): pp. 384–96.

Westad, Odd Arne. 2007. *The Global Cold War: Third World Interventions and the Making of Our Times*. Cambridge: Cambridge University Press.

Westlake, John. 1914. *The Collected Papers of John Westlake on Public International Law*, ed. L. Oppenheim. Cambridge: Cambridge University Press.

Wheatley, Paul. 1967. 'City as Symbol'. Inaugural Lecture delivered at University College, London, 20 November.

Wheaton, Henry. 1863. *Elements of International Law*, ed. William Beach Lawrence, 2nd annotated ed. London: Sampson Low, Son and Company.

Wheaton, Henry. 1916. *Elements of International Law*, ed. Coleman Phillipson, 5th English ed. London: Stevens and Sons.

Wheeler, Nicholas J. 1992. 'Pluralist or Solidarist Conceptions of International Society: Bull and Vincent on Humanitarian Intervention'. *Millennium: Journal of International Studies* 21 (3): pp. 463–87.

Wheeler, Nicholas J. 2000. *Saving Strangers: Humanitarian Intervention in International Society*. Oxford: Oxford University Press.

Wiebelhaus-Brahm, Eric. 2009. *Truth Commissions and Transitional Societies: The Impact on Human Rights and Democracy.* New York: Routledge.

Wight, Martin. 1956. 'The Power Struggle within the United Nations'. *Proceedings of the Institute of World Affairs* 33rd session, 32 (December): pp. 247–59.

Wight, Martin. 1960. 'Brutus in Foreign Policy: The Memoirs of Sir Anthony Eden'. *International Affairs* 36 (3): pp. 299–309.

Wight, Martin. 1977. *Systems of States*, ed. Hedley Bull. Leicester: Leicester University Press.

Wight, Martin. 1987. 'An Anatomy of International Thought'. *Review of International Studies* 13 (3): pp. 221–7.

Wight, Martin. 1992a. *International Theory: The Three Traditions*, ed. Gabriele Wight and Brian Porter. London: Leicester University Press for the Royal Institute of International Affairs.

Wight, Martin. 1992b. 'Theory of Mankind: "Barbarians"'. In *International Theory: The Three Traditions*, ed. Gabriele Wight and Brian Porter, pp. 49–98. London: Leicester University Press for the Royal Institute of International Affairs.

Wilde, Ralph. 2008. *International Territorial Administration: How Trusteeship and the Civilizing Mission Never Went Away.* Oxford: Oxford University Press.

Wilkerson, Isabel. 2010. *The Warmth of Other Suns: The Epic Story of America's Great Migration.* New York: Vintage.

Williams, David. 2013. 'Development, Intervention, and International Order'. *Review of International Studies* 39 (5): pp. 1213–31.

Williams, Phil. 1976. *Crisis Management: Confrontation and Diplomacy in the Nuclear Age.* London: Martin Robertson.

Williams, Walter L. 1986. *The Spirit and the Flesh: Sexual Diversity in American Indian Culture.* Boston, MA: Beacon Press.

Wills, John E. 1984. *Embassies and Illusions: Dutch and Portuguese Envoys to K'ang-hsi, 1666–1687.* Cambridge, MA: Harvard University.

Woll, Cornelia. 2014. *The Power of Collective Inaction: Bank Bailouts in Comparison.* Ithaca, NY: Cornell University Press.

Wong, John. 2013. 'Traversing the Laws of the Lands: The Strategic Use of Different Legal Systems by Houqua and his China Trade Partners in the Canton System'. Conference Paper, SSRC Inter-Asian Connections IV: Istanbul. Koç University, 2–5 October.

Wood, Gordon S. 2002. *The American Revolution: A History.* London: Phoenix.

Worsley, Peter. 1964. *The Third World.* London: Weidenfeld & Nicolson.

Xinhua. 2016. 'China Doubts US Rights Report'. 15 April.

Zakaria, Fareed. 2009. *The Post-American World: And the Rise of the Rest.* London: Penguin.

Zarakol, Ayşe. 2011. *After Defeat: How the East Learned to Live with the West.* Cambridge: Cambridge University Press.

Zetkin, Clara. 1906. 'Woman Suffrage'. Speech delivered at Mannheim Socialist Women's Conference. London: Twentieth Century Press.

Zetkin, Clara. 1991. 'Theses for the Communist Women's Movement'. Resolution adopted by the Comintern Executive Committee in 1920. In *Workers of the World and Oppressed Peoples, Unite! Proceedings and Documents of the Second Congress, 1920*, vol. I, edited by John Riddel, pp. 977–98. New York: Pathfinder.

Zhang, Feng. 2009. 'Rethinking the "Tribute System": Broadening the Conceptual Horizon of Historical East Asian Politics'. *Chinese Journal of International Politics* 2 (4): pp. 545–74.

Zhang, Feng. 2013. 'The Rise of Chinese Exceptionalism in International Relations'. *European Journal of International Relations* 19 (2): pp. 305–28.

Zhang, Longxi. 1988. 'The Myth of the Other: China in the Eyes of the West'. *Critical Inquiry* 15 (1): pp. 108–31.

Zhang, Xiaoming. 2011a. 'A Rising China and Normative Changes in International Society'. *East Asia* 28 (3): pp. 235–46.

Zhang, Xiaoming. 2011b. 'China in the Conception of International Society: The English School's Engagements with China'. *Review of International Studies* 37 (2): pp. 763–86.

Zhang, Yongjin. 1991. 'China's Entry into International Society: Beyond the Standard of "Civilization"'. *Review of International Studies* 17 (1): pp. 3–16.

Zhang, Yongjin. 2014a. 'Curious and Exotic Encounters: Europeans as Supplicants in the Chinese Imperium, 1513–1793'. In *International Orders in the Early Modern World: Before the Rise of the West*, edited by Shogo Suzuki, Yongjin Zhang, and Joel Quirk, pp. 55–75. Abingdon, Oxon: Routledge.

Zhang, Yongjin. 2014b. 'The Standard of "Civilization" Redux: Towards the Expansion of International Society 3.0?' *Millennium: Journal of International Studies* 42 (3): pp. 674–96.

Index